Writing and Reading Across the Curriculum

Writing and Reading Across the Curriculum

LAURENCE BEHRENS
The American University

LEONARD J. ROSEN
Bentley College

Little, Brown and Company
Boston   Toronto

Library of Congress Catalog Card No. 81-84231

ISBN 0-316-09132-4

9 8 7 6 5 4 3 2

MU

Published simultaneously in Canada
by Little, Brown & Company (Canada) Limited

Printed in the United States of America

*To Bonnie
and Michael*

A Note to the Instructor

Most new texts probably arise from a sense of dissatisfaction or frustration over what is currently available. *Writing and Reading Across the Curriculum* is such a text and addresses what we feel is an urgent need for composition readers to be more responsive than they generally have been to the requirements of the rest of the curriculum.

With this in mind, we designed a text-reader in which the majority of selections reflect the kind of subjects — and the kinds of writing — studied by college freshmen in their other courses. These selections tend to be expository rather than reflective, informational rather than polemical, public rather than personal, articles rather than essays. Most important, the selections on each subject are closely related to one another. This allows students to view a particular academic issue from a number of different perspectives. For instance, they read how a psychologist, a legal scholar, a professional soldier, a playwright, and others approach the issue of obedience to authority, and how each of these specialists presents his characteristic assumptions and observations about the subject. Students will also be able to practice three essential college-level skills: they will learn to read and summarize an article (or story, report, essay, and so on); to read several articles on a particular topic and synthesize them according to one or more rhetorical schemes; and to read an article and write a critique of it, identifying and discussing the author's (and their own) assumptions.

We would not ban short stories, plays, poems — or for that matter, essays — from the composition classroom. We do feel, however, that freshmen taking college composition have a big enough job mastering the problems of college-level reading and writing without also having to tackle the problems of literary analysis. We include literary artists in the text because their perspectives are invaluable in balancing the perspectives of historians, scientists, and others; but by the same token, the literary perspective should itself be balanced. One of the advantages of "writing and reading across the curriculum" is that students are exposed to a variety of perspectives, so that they can develop an appreciation of the complexity and interrelatedness of human endeavor, and can begin to make the kind of hard choices that will lead them to their fields of major inquiry.

In the typical two-phase composition course, at least one phase, we believe, should be conceived and structured as a "service" course, whose main purpose is to prepare students for college level writing and whose reading materials attempt to represent the variety of college-level work. It is not easy for students to read writers like Bruno Bettelheim and Philippe Ariès with comprehension. It is not easy for them to write good syntheses of several articles on the implications of the Milgram experiment or on the relationship between politics and personality. But they will be considerably more capable of doing such tasks if they have already done tasks like them in their freshman composition course. This is the rationale of *Writing and Reading Across the Curriculum.*

THE ORGANIZATION OF THIS BOOK

In Chapter 1 we *discuss* the summary, the critique, and various kinds of synthesis. Some of the passages on which we base our examples are excerpted from readings that appear at greater length farther on in the book. We recommend that students read this chapter carefully — particularly that they read and understand the three Six-Step Processes, to which they should refer often when preparing their assignments. Highlighting or underlining theses and topic sentences, as in the models, is a good way for students to reinforce the importance of such sentences.

In Chapter 2 we *demonstrate* the techniques of summary, synthesis, and critique as they are applied to readings on a particular subject — the American presidency. This is a practice chapter.

Chapters 3 through 11 constitute the body of the book; each consists of related readings on a particular topic, followed by three sets of questions: *Review Questions* primarily to test recall of the main facts and ideas presented in the reading; *Discussion Questions* to stimulate thinking about the issues raised in the reading; and *Writing Suggestions* to elicit personal responses to the reading. At the end of each chapter, *Summary, Synthesis, and Critique Activities* allow the student to practice typical college writing assignments. *Research Topics* and *Additional Readings* encourage further investigation of the topic at hand.

Chapter 12, "Personality," provides a *rhetorical focus* to the various readings. Passages have been selected that exemplify one or more of the most common rhetorical modes or patterns of writing — description, narration, classification, comparison-contrast, and so on. This chapter is followed by a brief rhetorical table of contents — a selection of passages and paragraphs in other chapters that exemplify the chief rhetorical modes.

A WORD OF THANKS

It's a pleasure to acknowledge those colleagues and friends who first directed us to some of the readings, provided access to their personal libraries, offered suggestions and moral support, and read and commented upon drafts of the manuscript: Bill Leap, Jack Jorgens, Rudolph von Abele, Kermit Moyer, Tom Cannon, and Jane Stanhope — all of The American University. Thanks also to Elaine Maimon of Beaver College, Bob Reising of Pembroke State University, and to the many students of our composition courses who, without knowingly volunteering, field tested most of the material here and let us know when we hadn't made things clear. Finally, our special gratitude to the splendid crew at Little, Brown — Chuck Christensen, Carolyn Potts, Donna McCormick, Joan Feinberg, and Cynthia Chapin.

A Note to the Student

Your psychology professor assigns you to write a critical report on a recently published book on human motivation. You are expected to consult additional sources, such as book reviews and related material on the subject.

Your professor is making a number of critical assumptions about your capabilities. Among them:

- that you can read and comprehend college-level material
- that you can synthesize separate pieces of related material
- that you can intelligently respond to such material

In fact, these same assumptions underlie practically all college writing assignments. Your professors will expect you to demonstrate that you can read and understand not only textbooks, but also critical articles and books, primary sources, and other material related to a subject of study. For instance: in researching a paper on the Great Depression, you might read the historical survey you find in your history text, a speech by President Roosevelt reprinted in *The New York Times,* and a first-hand account of the people's suffering by someone who toured the country during the 1930s and witnessed harrowing scenes of poverty and despair. In a political science paper you might discuss the concept of "executive privilege" in light of James Madison's Federalist Paper No. 51 on the proposed Constitutional provision for division of powers among the three branches of government. In a sociology paper you might undertake a critical analysis of your assigned text, which happens to be Marxist.

The subjects are different, of course; but the skills you need to work with them are the same. You must be able to read and comprehend. You must be able to perceive relationships among several pieces of source material. And you must be able to apply your own critical judgments to these various materials.

Writing and Reading Across the Curriculum provides you with the opportunity to practice the three, essential, college-level skills we have just outlined and the forms of writing associated with them, namely:

- the *summary*
- the *synthesis*
- the *critique*

This text is divided into chapters (such as "The Age of Computers," "Politics and Language," "Death and Dying," and "Obedience to Authority"), which are comprised of the types of selections you will be asked to read in other courses. In "Obedience to Authority," for example, you will find a description of the famous Milgram experiment (which demonstrated that "ordinary" Americans can be intimidated by authority figures into inflicting unbearable pain on other people); a review of Milgram's work; an official U.S. report on the My Lai massacre in which an American soldier (who claimed that he merely followed orders) was convicted of murdering Vietnamese civilians; a psychologist's explanation of such combat behavior; and finally, a selection from Jean Anouilh's *Antigone,* which powerfully dramatizes the eternal conflict between individual conscience and state authority.

Various sets of questions following the readings will allow you to practice typical college writing assignments. Writing Suggestions asks you for personal, sometimes imaginative responses to the readings. Summary, Synthesis, Critique Assignments near the end of each chapter allow you to practice the most typical college writing assignments — assignments of the type that are covered in detail in the first two chapters of this book. For instance, you may be asked to *describe* the Milgram experiment, and the reactions to it, or to *compare and contrast* a controlled experiment to a real life or a dramatic situation. Research Topics at the end of each chapter allows you to pursue in greater detail the subjects covered in each chapter, using sources you find yourself.

Our selection of passages includes articles written by economists, sociologists, psychologists, legal experts, dramatists, historians, and specialists from other fields. Our aim is that you become familiar with the various subjects and styles of academic writing and that you come to appreciate the interrelatedness of knowledge. Psychiatrists, historians, and novelists have different ways of contributing to our understanding of death and dying. Political scientists and career counselors, as well as psychologists, can contribute to our understanding of personality. Don't assume that the novel you read in your literature course has nothing to do with an assigned article from your economics course. Human activity and human behavior are classified into separate subjects only for convenience.

We hope, therefore, that your composition course will serve as a kind of bridge to your other courses, and that as a result of this work you can become more skillful at perceiving relationships among diverse topics. Because it involves such critical and widely applicable skills, your composition course may well turn out to be one of the most valuable, and one of the most interesting, of your academic career.

Contents

7. The Age of Computers — and Beyond   251

"We are at the dawn of the era of the smart machine — an 'information age' that will change forever the way an entire nation works, plays, travels and even thinks."

A columnist discovers that the conversion to computerization in the newsroom will take some getting used to.

A "super system programmer" describes both the exhilirations and the discontents of creating advanced computer programs.

A science-fiction writer predicts that by the end of the century every student will learn from a personal, book-sized electronic tutor — which will have the information storage capacity of an entire library.

An astronomer suggests that in time a new species of intelligent life will arise out of obsolescent man — the supercomputer.

9. A Woman's Role 352

Writing and Reading Across the Curriculum

How to Write Summaries, Syntheses, and Critiques

The summary, the synthesis, and the critique are the basic modes of college writing. Though not appropriate for every college writing situation (for instance, field trip reports or creative writing projects), they are central to so many others that the effort you invest in learning to write them will pay academic dividends long after you have finished with college composition. In this chapter, we will explain what these modes are and how to employ them in a systematic way. We will also provide numerous models, based on brief reading selections, some of which appear in fuller form later in the book. But passages on almost any subject — from genetic engineering to the rock music business — can be used for summary, synthesis, and critique practice, as we will demonstrate.

SUMMARY

The best way to demonstrate your comprehension of the information and the ideas in any piece of writing — from a single paragraph to an entire book — is to compose an accurate, clearly organized, and clearly written summary of that piece. By a summary, we mean a brief restatement, in your own words, of the content of a passage. This restatement should focus on the passage's central idea. It should indicate all the main points in the passage that support this central idea and the relationships between them, including their order and their emphasis. In the case of longer pieces, it should also include a very few important illustrations or examples from the passage. And it should indicate the slant, bias, and possibly even the tone of the piece, if these are important. But the summary should not contain any of your own ideas, opinions, or conclusions.

A good summary, therefore, has these three qualities: *brevity, completeness,* and *objectivity.*

It may seem to you that being able to tell (or to retell) exactly what a passage says is a skill that ought to be taken for granted in anyone who can read at high-school level. As long as the material isn't too difficult or technical — as long as we're not asking a high-school student to read a graduate-level treatise on abnormal psychology or a historian to read an article on biophysics, there should be no problem.

Unfortunately, there is a problem. The problem is that for all kinds of reasons people don't always read closely. In fact, it's probably safe to say that they usually don't. Either they read so inattentively that they skip over words, phrases, or even whole sentences; or if they do see the words in front of them, they see them without registering their significance, without thinking about their implications. (Of course, this is not always the reader's fault. Many pieces are so badly written or carelessly presented that they invite this kind of slack reading.)

Usually, when a reader fails to pick up the meaning and the implications of a sentence or two, there's no real harm done. (An exception: you could lose credit on an exam or paper because you failed to read or to realize the significance of a crucial direction by your instructor.) Rather, it's over the longer stretches of reading — the paragraph, the section, the article, or the chapter — that inattentive or haphazard reading creates problems. Over these longer stretches, you have to try not only to catch every word, but also to perceive the shape of the argument. You have to grasp the central idea, to distinguish the main points that comprise it, to relate the parts to the whole, and to note key examples. This kind of reading, of course, takes a lot more energy and determination than casual reading. But in the long run, it's an energy-saving method because it enables you to retain the content of the material and to use that content as a basis for your own responses. In other words, it allows you to develop an accurate and coherent written commentary that goes beyond summary.

You probably won't often be asked simply to write summaries of material that you have read. But writing summaries is an excellent way of encouraging the essential habit of close, accurate, thoughtful reading. It is also an excellent way of encouraging your writing habits in general, since a good summary exhibits almost all of the qualities of any other piece of good writing: unity, clarity, coherence, accuracy, tightness, stylistic maturity, and of course grammatical correctness.

Exercise

Read the following passage. Underline the essential information. You may want to make brief notations in the margins.

It is one of the lowliest of nature's creatures, a rod-shaped beastie 1 less than a ten-thousandth of an inch long. Its normal habitat is the intestine. Its functions there are still basically unknown. Yet this tiny parcel of protoplasm has now become the center of a stormy controversy that has divided the scientific community, stirred fears — often farfetched — about tampering with nature, and raised the prospect of unprecedented federal and local controls on basic scientific research. Last week the bacterium known to scientists as *Escherichia coli* (*E. coli*, for short) even became a preoccupation at the highest levels of government.

Appearing before a Senate subcommittee on behalf of the Carter 2 Administration, HEW Secretary Joseph Califano asked Congress to impose federal restrictions on recombinant DNA research, a new form of genetic inquiry involving *E. coli*. The urgency of Califano's request underlined the remarkable fact that a longtime dream of science, genetic engineering, is at hand — and, some fear, already out of hand. In laboratories across the nation, scientists are combining segments of *E. coli's* DNA with the DNA of plants, animals and other bacteria. By this process, they may well be creating forms of life different from any that exist on earth.

That this exciting new research holds great promise but could   3
also pose some peril was stressed in the day-long testimony before Senator Edward Kennedy's health subcommittee. Califano called recombinant DNA "a scientific tool of enormous potential." He also warned about possible — though unknown — hazards and concluded: "There is no reasonable alternative to regulation under law." Massachusetts Governor Michael Dukakis, involved in the controversy over genetic-engineering projects at Harvard and M.I.T., argued for the public right to regulate the research. Said he: "Genetic manipulation to create new forms of life places biologists at a threshold similar to that which physicists reached when they first split the atom. I think it is fair to say that the genie is out of the bottle."

The issue, stated simply, is whether that genie is good or evil.   4
Proponents of this research in DNA — the master molecule of life — are convinced that it can help point the way toward a new promised land — of understanding and perhaps curing cancer and such inherited diseases as diabetes and hemophilia; of inexpensive new vaccines; of plants that draw their nitrogen directly from the air rather than from costly fertilizers; of a vastly improved knowledge of the genetics of all plants and animals, including eventually even humans.

Opponents of the new research acknowledge its likely bounty,   5
but fear that those benefits might be outweighed by unforeseeable risks. What would happen, they ask, if by accident or design, one variety of re-engineered *E. coli* proved dangerous? By escaping from the lab and multiplying, their scenario goes, it could find its way into human intestines and cause baffling diseases. Beyond any immediate danger, others say, there are vast unknowns and moral implications. Do not intervene in evolution, they warn in effect, because "it's not nice to fool Mother Nature." Caltech's biology chairman, Robert Sinsheimer, concludes: "Biologists have become, without wanting it, the custodians of great and terrible power. It is idle to pretend otherwise."[1]

You begin writing a summary by reviewing your underlinings and notes. From the first paragraph of this passage you learn of the controversy sparked by *E. coli,* an intestinal bacterium used for genetic research, and

---

[1] Excerpt from "Tinkering with Life," *Time,* April 14, 1977. Reprinted by permission from *Time, The Weekly Newsmagazine;* Copyright Time Inc. 1977.

you learn the subject of the article — the extent to which government will become involved with the regulation of scientific research. In the second paragraph you should have noted that genetic engineers are using *E. coli* to create what may be new life forms. Government officials who fear that such tampering with the DNA of a bacterium may be dangerous are seeking to control genetic research through regulations. You might, in the margin, have labeled the third paragraph "opinions of experts: pro/con." We learn that while genetic engineering research in its present stage of "infancy" (though note the date of the passage — April, 1977) is exciting and promising, it nonetheless poses hazards — a situation that Governor Dukakis likens to early atomic research. In the fourth and fifth paragraphs we find a discussion of the benefits (possible cures for cancer and new fertilizers) and the hazards (genetic "creations" which may escape from biological laboratories) of genetic engineering.

Here is an example of how the passage might look after you have finished marking it in preparation for writing a summary:

It is one of the lowliest of nature's creatures, a rod-shaped beastie less than a ten-thousandth of an inch long. Its normal habitat is the intestine. Its functions there are still basically unknown. Yet this tiny parcel of protoplasm has now become the center of a stormy controversy that has divided the scientific community, stirred fears — often farfetched — about tampering with nature, and raised the prospect of unprecedented federal and local controls on basic scientific research. Last week the bacterium known to scientists as *Escherichia coli* (*E. coli.* for short) even became a preoccupation at the highest levels of government.

controversy over E. coli research

Appearing before a Senate subcommittee on behalf of the Carter Administration, HEW Secretary Joseph Califano asked Congress to impose federal restrictions on recombinant DNA research, a new form of genetic inquiry involving *E. coli*. The urgency of Califano's request underlined the remarkable fact that a longtime dream of science, genetic engineering, is at hand — and, some fear, already out of hand. In laboratories across the nation, scientists are combining segments of *E. coli's* DNA with the DNA of plants, animals and other bacteria. By this process, they may well be creating forms of life different from any that exist on earth.

should gov't regulate creation of new life forms?

That this exciting new research holds great promise but could also pose some peril was stressed

in the day-long testimony before Senator Edward
Kennedy's health subcommittee. Califano called recombinant DNA "a scientific tool of enormous potential." He also warned about possible — though unknown — hazards and concluded: "There is no
reasonable alternative to regulation under law." Massachusetts Governor Michael Dukakis, involved in the
controversy over genetic-engineering projects at Harvard and M.I.T., argued for the public right to regulate the research. Said he, "Genetic manipulation to
create new forms of life places biologists at a threshold similar to that which physicists reached when they
first split the atom. I think it is fair to say that the
genie is out of the bottle."

opinions of experts: pro & con

The issue, stated simply, is whether that genie is   4
good or evil. Proponents of this research in DNA —
the master molecule of life — are convinced that it
can help point the way toward a new promised
land — of understanding and perhaps curing cancer
and such inherited diseases as diabetes and hemophilia; of inexpensive new vaccines; of plants that
draw their nitrogen directly from the air rather than
from costly fertilizers; of a vastly improved knowledge of the genetics of all plants and animals, including eventually even humans.

possible benefits of DNA research

Opponents of the new research acknowledge its   5
likely bounty, but fear that those benefits might be
outweighed by unforeseeable risks. What would happen, they ask, if by accident or design, one variety of
re-engineered *E. coli* proved dangerous? By escaping
from the lab and multiplying, their scenario goes, it
could find its way into human intestines and cause
baffling diseases. Beyond any immediate danger,
others say, there are vast unknowns and moral implications. Do not intervene in evolution, they warn in
effect, because "it's not nice to fool Mother Nature."
Caltech's biology chairman, Robert Sinsheimer, concludes: "Biologists have become, without wanting it,
the custodians of great and terrible power. It is idle to
pretend otherwise."

possible hazards

When writing a summary, be aware of how the information in one
paragraph is related to the information in others. For instance, in paragraph
1 we find mention of a storm of controversy — which is then explained
in paragraph 2. Paragraph 3, with its emphasis on the benefits and
hazards of genetic engineering, "sets up" the explicit examples of para-

graphs 4 and 5. Having noted the passage's organization, you can then proceed with your summary:

Scientists may be creating new forms of life by combining the DNA of a common bacterium (*E. coli*, found in the human intestine) with the DNA of plants and animals. Some officials believe that the experiments should be regulated by the government, since, at this early stage in the development of genetic engineering, no one knows how safe these creations may be. Supporters of genetic engineering research claim that continued experimentation may lead to a cure for cancer and improved agricultural techniques, and that government intervention would only be a hindrance. Opponents argue that scientists may unwittingly be creating genetic "monsters" that could escape from laboratories and create baffling diseases. The controversy is reminiscent of the one stirred by the first splitting of the atom and the advent of the atomic age: to what end will scientists use their new power?

Notice how we rearrange information in the passage to fit our purpose in the summary. We take part of a sentence in the second paragraph of the passage, ". . . scientists are combining . . . ," and make it the subject of the summary's first sentence. We think it is important to define the subject of the controversy before describing the positions of the two sides. Note also how we combine the information from the first paragraph of the excerpt (that *E. coli* is a bacterium found in the human intestine) with the first sentence of the summary. Having described the subject of the controversy, we turn to the controversy itself: the question of government interference in genetic research. Here, we mention advocates and opponents of the research and conclude with Dukakis's analogy, likening the present state of genetic engineering research to early nuclear research (information that is located in the middle of the passage).

How long should a summary be? This depends both on the length of the original passage and on the purpose of the summary. But a good rule of thumb is that a summary should be no longer than one-quarter the length of the original passage. Of course, if you were summarizing an entire chapter or even an entire book, it would have to be much shorter than that. This particular summary is about one-quarter the length of the original passage; and while it should certainly be no longer, it could very well be shorter:

A controversy exists over whether the federal government should regulate genetic engineering research. Scientists have expressed fears that the research may lead to the creation of dangerous new life forms.

The writing of summaries is the most basic of college-level skills, upon which more sophisticated types of writing depend. In mastering this skill, many students have found the following system helpful.

A Six-Step Process for Writing Summaries

1 *Read* the passage carefully.

2 *Reread.* This time divide the passage into sections or stages of thought. *Label,* on the passage itself, each section or stage of thought. *Underline* key ideas and terms.

3 *Write one-sentence summaries,* on a separate sheet of paper, of each stage of thought or, if appropriate, of each paragraph.

4 *Write a topic sentence — a one-sentence summary of the entire passage.* The topic sentence should express the central idea of the passage, as you have determined it from the above steps. You may find it useful to keep in mind the information contained in the lead sentence or paragraph of most newspaper articles — the *what, who, why, where, when,* and *how* of the matter. In the case of persuasive passages, summarize in a sentence the author's conclusion. In the case of descriptive passages, indicate the subject of the description and its key feature(s).

5 *Write the first draft of your summary* by combining the topic sentence with the information from step 3. Eliminate repetition and combine sentences for a smooth and logical flow of ideas.

6 *Revise your summary,* inserting transitional words and phrases where necessary to ensure coherence. Check for style. Avoid series of short, choppy sentences. Check for grammatical correctness, punctuation, spelling.

SYNTHESIS

A synthesis is a piece of writing that combines information and ideas from two or more sources. It follows that your ability to write syntheses depends upon your ability to infer relationships among essays, articles, and the like. This process is nothing new for you, since you infer relationships all the time — say, between something you've read in the newspaper and something you've observed for yourself, or between the teaching styles of your favorite and least favorite instructors. In fact, if you've written research papers, you've already written syntheses. In an *academic* synthesis, you make explicit the relationships that you have inferred among separate pieces of writing.

Sometimes this process can be tricky. Say that you have read three articles — A, B, and C — that you must synthesize. Just what *is* the relationship among them? Is the information in A an extended example of the generalizations in C? Would it be useful to compare A with B? Having read and considered A, B, and C, can you infer something else — D?

Description, Process, and Definition Syntheses

In this section we will discuss three possibilities: *description, process,* and *definition.* We group these together because they are the least complicated of the syntheses you will be asked to write.

Exercise

Read the following three passages, excerpted from articles in the chapter on the Great Depression, and consider how you would discuss the relationships among them.

A. OKLAHOMA CITY, Jan. 20 (AP). — A crowd of men and women, 1
shouting that they were hungry and jobless, raided a grocery store
near the City Hall today. Twenty-six of the men were arrested. Scores
loitered near the city jail following the arrests, but kept well out of
range of fire hose made ready for use in case of another disturbance.

The police tonight broke up a second meeting of about one 2
hundred unemployed men and arrested Francis Owens, alleged head
of the "Oklahoma City Unemployed Council," who was accused of
instigating the raid.

Before the grocery was entered, a delegation of unemployed, led 3
by Owens, had demanded of City Manager E. M. Fry that the authorities
furnish immediate relief. Owens rejected a request by Mr. Fry for
the names and addresses of the "Unemployed Council," said to number
2,500 men and women, both whites and Negroes.

The raiders disregarded efforts of H. A. Shaw, the store manager, 4
to quiet them.

"It is too late to bargain with us," the leaders shouted, as they 5
stripped the shelves.

The police hastily assembled emergency squads and dispersed 6
the crowd numbering 500, with tear gas. Only those who were
trapped in the wrecked store were arrested. Five women among them
were released. The windows of the store were smashed as the raiders
attempted to flee.[2]

B. During the last three months I have visited, as I have said, 1
some twenty states of this wonderfully rich and beautiful country.
Here are some of the things I heard and saw:

In the state of Washington I was told that the forest fires raging 2
in that region all summer and fall were caused by unemployed timber
workers and bankrupt farmers in an endeavor to earn a few honest
dollars as firefighters. The last thing I saw on the night I left Seattle

---

[2] "Hunger Riots," *The New York Times,* Jan. 21, 1931.

was numbers of women searching for scraps of food in the refuse piles of the principal market of that city. A number of Montana citizens told me of thousands of bushels of wheat left in the fields uncut on account of its low price that hardly paid for the harvesting. In Oregon I saw thousands of bushels of apples rotting in the orchards. Only absolute[ly] flawless apples were still salable, at from 40 to 50 cents a box containing 200 apples. At the same time, there are millions of children who, on account of the poverty of their parents, will not eat one apple this winter.

While I was in Oregon the Portland *Oregonian* bemoaned the fact   3 that thousands of ewes were killed by the sheep raisers because they did not bring enough in the market to pay the freight on them. And while Oregon sheep raisers fed mutton to the buzzards, I saw men picking for meat scraps in the garbage cans in the cities of New York and Chicago. I talked to one man in a restaurant in Chicago. He told me of his experience in raising sheep. He said that he had killed 3,000 sheep this fall and thrown them down the canyon, because it cost $1.10 to ship a sheep, and then he would get less than a dollar for it. He said he could not afford to feed the sheep, and he would not let them starve, so he just cut their throats and threw them down the canyon.[3]

C. Highway 66 is the main migrant road. 66 — the long concrete   1 path across the country, waving gently up and down on the map, from the Mississippi to Bakersfield — over the red lands and the gray lands, twisting up into the mountains, crossing the Divide and down into the bright and terrible desert, and across the desert to the mountains again, and into the rich California valleys.

66 is the path of a people in flight, refugees from dust and   2 shrinking land, from the thunder of tractors and shrinking ownership, from the desert's slow northward invasion, from the twisting winds that howl up out of Texas, from the floods that bring no richness to the land and steal what little richness is there. From all of these the people are in flight, and they come into 66 from the tributary side roads, from the wagon tracks and the rutted country roads. 66 is the mother road, the road of flight. . . .

The people in flight streamed out on 66, sometimes a single car,   3 sometimes a little caravan. All day they rolled slowly along the road, and at night they stopped near water. In the day ancient leaky radiators sent up columns of steam, loose connecting rods hammered and

---

[3] Oscar Ameringer, "The Plague of Plenty," *Unemployment Relief Hearings*, S. 174 . . . 1932.

pounded. And the men driving the trucks and the overloaded cars listened apprehensively. How far between towns? It is a terror between towns. If something breaks — well, if something breaks we camp right here while Jim walks to town and gets a part and walks back and — how much food we got?

Listen to the motor. Listen to the wheels. Listen with your ears 4 and with your hands on the steering wheel; listen with the palm of your hand on the gear-shift lever; listen with your feet on the floor boards. Listen to the pounding old jalopy with all your senses, for a change of tone, a variation of rhythm may mean — a week here? That rattle — that's tappets. Don't hurt a bit. Tappets can rattle till Jesus comes again without no harm. But that thudding as the car moves along — can't hear that — just kind of feel it. Maybe oil isn't gettin' someplace. Maybe a bearing's startin' to go. Jesus, if it's a bearing, what'll we do? Money's goin' fast.[4]

How are these passages related? There are several possibilities. The first is that each *describes* living conditions during the depression years. In this case, a summary of each of the excerpts, taken together, and connected with appropriate transitions, would yield a coherent description. A skeleton of the synthesis might appear as follows:

Thesis: The depression years were a grim time for Americans.
Summary of "Hunger Riots"
   transition (in italics in the example below)
Summary of "The Plague of Plenty"
   transition (in italics in the example below)
Summary of passage from The Grapes of Wrath

Here's a sample *description synthesis:*

The depression years were a grim time for Americans. In Okla- 1 homa City in 1931 crowds of desperately hungry men and women raided a grocery, clearing the shelves of food. The incident was allegedly instigated by Francis Owens, the leader of the "Oklahoma City Unemployed Council," a citizens' group outraged that people did not have enough food to eat. Frustrated that city officials were not listening to their grievances, members of the council risked arrest and looted the store.

Oklahoma newspaper editor Oscar Ameringer, testifying before a 2 *Congressional committee, told of others forced to desperate measures: families rummaging through trash heaps in search of food scraps and farmers destroying livestock and crops before they got to*

---

[4] John Steinbeck, *The Grapes of Wrath*, N.Y.: Viking Penguin, 1939.

market. The reason? Ranchers were losing money, their sheep not bringing enough cash at market to pay the expense of raising or even shipping them. Similarly, bushels of apples and wheat lay rotting because farmers, indignant at having to lose money to feed other people, refused to ship their goods to market.

John Steinbeck captures the mood of these years in a passage 3 *from his novel,* The Grapes of Wrath. Faced with desolate living conditions, migrant workers made their way along Highway 66, the "concrete path across the country" that led to the promise of rich valleys in California. Steinbeck calls 66 the "path of a people in flight," of a people beleaguered by "twisting winds that howl up from Texas" and by floods and desert heat. Their desperation is apparent in their total dependence on broken-down automobiles to deliver them to a better world. Steinbeck creates a pathetic scene, one that reveals, as do the hunger riots in Oklahoma and Ameringer's report, the grim world of the people who struggled through the Great Depression.

In this synthesis we did nothing more complicated than join together a series of summaries. The challenge lies in converting separate summaries into a coherent, smoothly flowing description. To do this, the thesis must be broad enough so that every part of the synthesis is "contained" by it; that is, each part of the synthesis must have some clear connection with the thesis.

Notice how the first transition (sentence 1, paragraph 2) refers *back* to the first paragraph ("others forced to desperate measures") and *forward* to the subject of the Ameringer passage, the waste of food. The second transition (sentence 1, paragraph 3) is a straightforward one: the phrase "the mood of these years" ties the first two-thirds of the synthesis to the last third, Steinbeck's description of Highway 66. In the last sentence, we restate the thesis more forcefully than at first, taking advantage of the information we've summarized.

It is entirely possible that you might have inferred a different relationship among the articles. Perhaps you felt that the individual passages demonstrated a *process,* one that is not explicitly stated in any of the excerpts, but that is nonetheless common to all. The process: how individuals will take steps to assure their survival. A process synthesis answers the question "How does A lead to B?" If A were the troop deployment at the Battle of Gettysburg, then B might be the outcome of the battle; if B were a three-tiered wedding cake, A would be the steps involved in making the cake. In a process synthesis, you need not worry about why A leads to B — why a certain troop deployment leads to a certain outcome or why cake dough rises as it does. In this type of synthesis you are concerned only that something happens in a particular order. The *causes* of that order are sometimes quite complex, something we will deal with in later sections on *arguments* and *critiques.*

So it is possible to read these passages on the depression as something other than a simple description of those years. A process synthesis would have a thesis sentence quite different from that of a *description* synthesis. Also, you would not merely be writing a summary of each of the pieces; rather, you would need to observe carefully the process apparent in each piece and relate that process to your thesis.

A skeleton of the process synthesis might appear as follows:

Thesis: In times of adversity, individuals will take various steps to assure their survival, a lesson made apparent in three articles on the Great Depression.

Discussion of A: Though citizens are hungry and complain about lack of food, city officials do not respond positively. Frustration leads citizens to loot grocery store.

transition (in italics in the example below)

Discussion of B: Farmers spend a certain amount of money to grow crops and raise livestock, an investment they must recover in order to remain in business. During the depression, farmers could not recover this investment and took the seemingly bizarre action of destroying their products while people around the country starved.

transition (in italics in the example below)

Discussion of C: Migrant farmers also take steps to assure their survival — by dreaming of a new prosperity available in the rich valleys of California.

Conclusion

Here is a sample *process synthesis:*

In times of adversity, individuals will take various steps to assure   1
their survival, a lesson made apparent in three articles on the Great
Depression. The *New York Times* account of the hunger riots in Oklahoma City in 1931 vividly shows a *primary* response to poverty and hunger — riot. In this passage we find a group of citizens who have been denied what they feel their country should guarantee them — food enough to survive.

Their response to poverty occurred in stages. First, because of   2
hunger, individual citizens complained to city officials. These officials, powerless to change the overwhelming economic facts of the depression, could not respond in a way that would satisfy the angry, hungry protesters. Convinced that a collective voice would be more persuasive than individual voices, the citizens formed the "Oklahoma City Unemployed Council" and made demands that, once again, city officials could not meet. The citizens became desperate and looted a grocery store.

The producers of food were no less desperate than the hungry 3
consumers. Many faced total ruin when they found that harvesting
their crops and shipping their livestock would not bring in enough
money to recover their investment. Some felt that they had no choice
but to slaughter their livestock and let their crops rot in the fields,
ironically and sadly in a time when so many were hungry. Since the
farmers' response was based on economic considerations and not on
hunger pains, their response can be termed *secondary.*

John Steinbeck portrays an entirely different response to adversity 4
in The Grapes of Wrath, *in which he depicts the migrant workers who
fled depressed conditions in search of better lives elsewhere —
specifically, in California.* Their response to adversity involved a
dream, not unlike the dream of immigrants from Europe at the beginning of the twentieth century. The dream usually begins with some
hardship — in this case, economic hardship. The heads of a family
decide that there is no decent future in the present situation and that
they must move to where a brighter future is possible. So the family
packs its belongings and piles into a broken-down automobile upon
which they must depend to deliver them to their new home —
California. People's desperation is shown in Steinbeck's description of
their dependence on an automobile. They "listen" to the car with their
entire bodies, dreading every new sound, hoping that if the car is to
break down, it will at least do so in a town where a mechanic can fix it.
Such desperate risks demonstrate the lengths to which people will go
to assure their survival. If one cannot support oneself and one's family
in the place where one lives, then it is necessary to move on.

The responses to adversity in each of these passages are differ-   5
ent. In the first we see an immediate and angry response to hunger. In
the second we see a response based not directly on hunger, but on
survival in the marketplace. And in the third we see a visionary response that may be deluded, but that nevertheless has the power to
inspire. In each case, adversity sets in motion a process that leads to
self-preservation.

Notice how each section of this synthesis is contained by the thesis —
that various responses to adversity lead to one conclusion: self-preservation. In the synthesis we emphasize different responses, which we term
"primary" (based on hunger), "secondary" (based on market conditions),
and "entirely different" (based on less tangible needs than hunger; that is,
the need for hope). The purpose of the italicized transitions should be easy
enough to detect: reread them and note how we are trying to join separate
sections of the synthesis. The conclusion, like that of the description
synthesis, restates in more emphatic terms the thesis and ties the component parts of the synthesis together. Notice that each paragraph treats a
process — the sense of each paragraph being that A leads to B. The

responsibility of the writer of a process synthesis is to demonstrate, by reference to the text, *how* this process takes place.

It may be that you follow these different syntheses well enough, but that you have not inferred the same relationships among the three articles. Again, this difference points to the creativity needed for writing syntheses: no two people will synthesize articles in precisely the same way.

A third way of relating the excerpts might turn on a *definition* you have inferred. Perhaps you felt that these passages provide a useful definition of despair. Fine. By this point, you should have an idea of how you might organize the excerpts in a way that will support your reading.

A skeleton outline of the definition synthesis might be organized as follows:

Thesis: Taken collectively, the three pieces about the quality of life during the Great Depression yield a useful definition of economic despair.

Discussion of A: Economic despair is evident when the unavailability of money leads to a disintegration of rules.
transition (in italics in the example below)

Discussion of B: Economic despair is evident when farmers do not have enough confidence in their financial system to continue participating in it.
transition (in italics in the example below)

Discussion of C: Economic despair leads to uprootedness and to the hope, perhaps naive, of a better life.

Conclusion

Here is a sample *definition synthesis:*

Taken collectively, the three pieces about the quality of life during   1
the Great Depression yield a useful definition of economic despair. One sign of economic despair is evident in "Hunger Riots," a news account about the recklessness that can sweep over people when the economic base of their lives dissolves. The citizens of Oklahoma City were desperate: conventional efforts to ensure their well-being proved fruitless when city officials could not meet their demands. So rather than abide by the rules that had failed them, the citizens of Oklahoma City rioted. Such despair, based on economic deprivation, robs people of their civility.

Another aspect of economic despair is apparent in Ameringer's   2
observations in "The Plague of Plenty." Farmers who let their crops go to waste or who kill off their livestock rather than take a loss at the marketplace demonstrate a loss of faith in their country's economic system. One wouldn't expect of farmers, who can provide their own meals, the same kind of despair that triggered the riot of hungry

people. Instead, the farmers' despair took the form of disgruntlement. Since they were not going to receive a fair market price for their crops, and they would actually have to take a *loss* in order to get their goods to market, they would simply opt out and refuse to participate in a broken economic system.

A third type of economic despair is artfully described by John   3
Steinbeck, in a passage from The Grapes of Wrath. Steinbeck is able to capture the sense of uprootedness, coupled with a sense of longing, of people who feel that they have nothing left to lose. On Highway 66, one finds pilgrims searching for a new land. Their belief, naive perhaps, but necessary to them, is that the place where they are going promises a better life than the place they have left. Their faith seems based more on their golden vision of California than on any firm knowledge of opportunities the state has to offer. One can feel their desperation as Steinbeck describes them "listening" with their entire bodies to their dilapidated automobiles, their only transportation to the new world. Every unexpected sound the car makes could become the obstacle that keeps them from their goal. Perhaps the car will break down and they will never get to California.

Economic deprivation brings on despair, which can take at least   4
three forms: a recklessness that deprives people of their civility, a loss of faith in the economic system upon which a nation's well-being depends, and an uprootedness and sense of longing that can drive people away from family and friends in search of better living conditions — which may or may not exist elsewhere.

We have discussed three types of synthesis: description, process, and definition. In each of these we took identical passages and "wove" them together in different ways. No one of these syntheses is more "correct" than the others, for we have cited evidence from the passages themselves to support our various theses.

Without this kind of supporting evidence, your thesis will not be convincing, and no one will have much reason to take your opinions seriously. In other words, you are "right" to the extent that you have carefully and reasonably documented your claims. Of course, the key word here is "reasonably." What counts as reasonable evidence or a reasonable thesis? There are no sure answers other than common sense. It would be ridiculous to claim that these passages, taken collectively, amount to a definition of insomnia or to a description of the Rose Bowl Parade. When you are seeking relationships among articles, look for those relationships that account for the greatest amount of information and ideas in each of the articles. And don't "bend" the articles to fit your thesis. Let your thesis develop out of the articles themselves. Alexander Pope put it nicely when he urged readers to "discover" truths, not to "devise" them.

It may be helpful, at this point, to sum up the qualities of a good synthesis:

- It should be held together by a *thesis* that is supported by evidence from the passages themselves.
- It should have an introduction, a body, and a conclusion.
- It should be written in your own words, though you may quote briefly.
- It need not include *all* of the information from the source passages, only that information needed to support the thesis. It is *selective,* unlike a summary.
- The sources of the information and ideas should be credited in the body of the synthesis.

Although the basic relationships among passages will be different for different kinds of syntheses, the process of developing the syntheses is quite similar. We recommend to you the following system.

A Six-Step Process for Writing Syntheses

1　*Read* the passages carefully.

2　*Reread.* This time label or underline each passage for main ideas, key terms, and any details you want to use in the synthesis.

3　*Determine the relationships among the passages.* Which of the following relationships seems most appropriate?
   a. the information in the passages may be seen to constitute a *description* or a *definition* of something; or it may illustrate a *process;*
   b. the information in the passages may serve as *examples* of some proposition expressed or implied in one or more of the passages; or as particular *examples* of a general situation; (example syntheses discussed below)
   c. the information and ideas in the passages may be *compared and contrasted;* (comparison-contrast synthesis discussed below)
   d. the information and ideas in the passages may be used as the basis for an *argument* you want to pursue. (argument syntheses discussed below)

4　*Write the thesis sentence.* The thesis sentence should indicate the central idea that holds together the main points of the synthesis, and it should make clear the relationship (see above) among the main points. *Note:* the thesis sentence does not have to be the first sentence; often it is *the final sentence of the first paragraph.*

5　*Write the first draft of your synthesis,* including the lead-in, if necessary, to your *thesis sentence.* If the material permits, begin each paragraph with a *topic sentence*. Insert *transitional words and phrases* to indicate the relationship of one idea to the next.

Note: the most useful organizational structure for description, process, definition, and example syntheses — the "workhorse" structure — is:

Thesis paragraph (thesis sentence may be the final sentence)
    transition
Example A (built on first passage)
    transition
Example B (built on second passage)
    transition
Example C (built on third passage)
Conclusion

Don't try to discuss every aspect of each article you synthesize. Be selective, using only what you need to support your thesis. Use your own words; quote sparingly. Inject no idea or opinion that cannot be substantiated by the information you cite.

6 *Revise* your synthesis, inserting transitional words and phrases where necessary. Make sure that the synthesis reads smoothly, logically, and clearly from beginning to end. Check for grammatical correctness, punctuation, spelling.

This system can be successfully applied to description, process, and definition syntheses, as well as (with organizational modifications) to the other types, to which we now turn.

We cannot too strongly emphasize the importance of understanding, *before* you write your synthesis, the basic relationships you will use to synthesize separate materials. Your synthesis will be successful to the extent that you are aware of these relationships and to the extent that you devise a thesis sentence that expresses the central relationship.

Example Synthesis

Another common way of synthesizing, or weaving, separate passages into a coherent essay is to cite the material in one passage as an example of what is being discussed in another. If you think back to high-school English and the comments your teacher made on your papers, one comment you'll probably remember is "too vague — be specific!" Your teacher was asking you to use examples to demonstrate your point. It's easy to neglect examples when you are gliding smoothly along from one generalization to another. But these examples are sorely missed by the reader looking for something definite to hold on to.

Examples make your essays precise. Whether you are discussing one passage or several, you must provide supporting evidence. If you were reviewing a single article or book (as in a critique, discussed below), you would focus your discussion on specific points in the author's material. If you were writing a synthesis of several pieces, you might find that one or more pieces contains specific examples of generalizations made in the others. But we can best demonstrate the general principle by showing you how an example synthesis is constructed.

Exercise

Read the following three passages on the rock music business:

A. The record business has become what Neil Bogart, president 1 of Casablanca Record and Filmworks, calls "a gambler's game." The stakes, certainly, are almost dizzying. In the last five years, a company's average up-front-investment in a rock album (i.e., the outlay before it gets to market) has risen from about $100,000 to close to $250,000, partly because of the costs of sophisticated recording techniques and partly because musicians and producers are commanding higher royalties. Royalty rates have almost doubled in ten years; today they average between 10 and 15 percent of the suggested retail price.

For superstars, they are much higher. Last year, when Warner 2 Brothers wanted to sign Paul Simon (originally of Simon and Garfunkel), who had previously been with CBS, it reportedly guaranteed him over $13 million. Earlier this year, as Paul McCartney's contract with Capitol Records was expiring, CBS, in a fit of Beatlemania, is said to have signed a three-album contract guaranteeing McCartney $8 million — $2 million per album for only the U.S. and Canadian rights, and another $2 million to secure the temporary rights to some of the Beatle's old recordings.

Just to break even, according to one executive's calculation, CBS 3 will have to sell more than two million copies of each release. And once McCartney and his group, Wings, earn back the $2 million guarantee on each record, they will receive a 22 percent royalty rate on any additional sales — or nearly $2 per $8.98 album. Obviously, only well-heeled record companies can afford the prices commanded by these new musical tycoons. As Casablanca's Bogart succinctly puts it: "The small labels can't compete financially in getting an act." Indeed, the big record companies have been waving dollars at artists on the brink of success and luring them away from the small, underfinanced labels.

With such high up-front costs, companies are straining for vol- 4 ume, and this helps to push promotion costs up a few octaves. Record companies spend lavishly "hyping" their products — planning concert tours, staging autographing sessions in record stores, arranging radio and television appearances, and plastering pictures of their stars on those mammoth billboards that line Los Angeles' Sunset

Strip. The average rock promotion budget has increased threefold, to about $150,000, in the last five years. For an album by a top-selling artist, a company can easily spend over $1 million. Says Harry Anger, a senior vice president for marketing at one of Polygram's labels, "If pitching is 70 percent of baseball, promotion is 70 percent of the record business." Even unknowns are costly. They usually don't make money at first, on either their records or concert appearances, so the record companies send them off to make them known — paying for their instruments, lighting systems, costumes, and, in one case, for the purchase of two Greyhound buses to carry all the stuff.[5]

B. Promotion often resembles a military campaign and involves 1 people who seem to be generals deploying forces over a vast battle terrain, mounting attacks, retreating, then attacking in other areas; they chart wins and losses and territory gained at New York head-quarters, evaluate intelligence (the charts and tip sheets and promo-tion reports) and send soldiers (the field promotion men) into various skirmishes or to make counterattacks. The stakes are very high. Thousands of singles are released each year; only a few hundred make it into the charts — and make money.

The goal, simply enough, is to have each record tested. The 2 promotion man can't do anything about quality — the point is to get the record heard in the marketplace. If it fails after that, the Promo-tion Department isn't to blame. Naturally artists, their managers and A&R men tend to see things differently. An artist and his manager are always kept informed of a single's progress. But sometimes — all too often — it doesn't get any play and gathers no momentum; it is impossible to spread it out.

The artist always says, "My God, it didn't get tested properly! You 3 lost it! The company never paid any attention to it!" I usually tried to make sure that we weren't excessively vulnerable to this charge. But 98 percent of the time the cries still come and you have to ignore them if you feel a thorough effort was made. Obviously some records are worked harder than others — but that's always the case where em-phasis and direction have to be given. For real creative excellence among a week's releases sticks out and demands your attention. It's inevitable that you'll devote more energy to some records than to others.[6]

---

[5] Peter Bernstein, excerpt from "The Rock Music Business: Rocking to the Big Money Beat" from *Fortune Magazine*, April 23, 1979. © 1979 Time, Inc. All rights reserved.
[6] From pages 198–199 in *Clive: Inside the Record Business* by Clive Davis with James Willwerth. Copyright © 1974 by Clive Davis and James Willwerth. Reprinted by permission of William Morrow & Company.

C. Throughout his unconventional career, Springsteen has   1
found people who felt he was born to star. From the moment he and
his abrasive new manager, Mike Appel, walked into Columbia Records in 1972 to audition for the legendary John Hammond — discov-
erer of Billie Holiday, Aretha Franklin and Bob Dylan — Springsteen
was the subject of high-pressure salesmanship. "I went into a state of
shock as soon as I walked in," says Springsteen. "Before I ever played
a note Mike starts screamin' and yellin' 'bout me. I'm shrivelin' up and
thinkin', 'Please, Mike, give me a break. Let me play a damn song.' So,
dig this, before I ever played a note the hype began."

"The kid absolutely knocked me out," Hammond recalls. "I only   2
hear somebody really good once every ten years, and not only was
Bruce the best, he was a lot better than Dylan when I first heard *him*."
Within a week, Springsteen was signed to Columbia and although he
and Appel had little previous recording experience, they insisted on
producing their own album — the uneven "Greetings From Asbury
Park, N.J." released in January 1973. At the time Bruce had no band;
he sang alone with an acoustic guitar. And because of the originality
of his lyrics — and perhaps the familiarity of their cadence — he was
compared to Dylan.

Oh, some hazard from Harvard
Was skunked on beer playin'
Backyard bombadier
Yes and Scotland Yard was trying
Hard, they sent some dude with a
Callin' card
He said, "Do what you like but don't do it here."[7]

The comparison was so tantalizingly close that Columbia pro-   3
moted the first album with ads announcing they had the new Bob
Dylan. The cover letter on the records Columbia sent to the DJ's flatly
stated the same thing. But the hard sell backfired. "The Dylan hype
from Columbia was a turnoff," said Dave Herman, the early-morning
DJ for WNEW-FM, the trend-setting pop station in New York. "I
didn't even bother to listen to it. I didn't want Columbia to think they
got me."

Without radio airplay — the single most important ingredient in   4
any hit — a record dies. Though the Springsteen campaign was a
special project of then Columbia president Clive Davis, who personally read Springsteen's lyrics on a promotional film, and even though
Bruce got good notices from important rock publications like Craw-

---

[7] From Bruce Springsteen's "Blinded by the Light": Copyright © 1972 by
Bruce Springsteen and Laurel Canyon Music Ltd. Reprinted by permission.

daddy, only a handful of the 100 or so major FM stations across the country played him. The record sold less than 50,000 copies. "He was just another media hype that failed," said Herman. "He was already a dead artist who bombed out on his first album."[8]

How are these passages related? We think that they can be organized as an *example* synthesis. The first excerpt would be the principal passage, since, of the three, it has the widest scope. From his perspective "inside the record industry," Clive Davis exemplifies Bernstein's points for discussion about record promotion. And the passage on Bruce Springsteen provides an explicit example of record industry "hype."

Here's a skeleton outline of an example synthesis:

Thesis: The very large sums of money involved in signing artists and producing records make it necessary for record company executives to vigorously promote or "hype" their products.

Discussion of Bernstein: Present (essentially) a summary, ending with an assertion of the need for extensive promotion.
  transition (in italics in the example below)

Discussion of Davis: Davis reiterates Bernstein's conclusion and compares record promotion to a military campaign. Emphasize Davis's point that promotion can't hide lack of talent.
  transition (in italics in the example below)

Discussion of Springsteen passage: Although lack of talent was not the issue with Springsteen, the promotion of his records nonetheless failed. Disc jockeys were annoyed with the hype from Columbia Records.

Conclusion

Here's a sample *example synthesis:*

According to Peter Bernstein's "Rocking to the Big Money Beat," [1] the amount of money that the recording industry invests in a rock album is "dizzying." For lesser-known artists, $250,000 is the average amount; for superstars like Paul Simon, the investment can go as high as thirteen million dollars. The costs are astronomical for two reasons: sophisticated recording techniques and high royalty rates commanded by artists and their producers. In a recent deal with Paul McCartney, Capitol Records guaranteed its popular artist eight million dollars for three albums — which means that in order to break even on any one album, Capitol will have to sell at least two million discs. Amounts of this kind prohibit small record labels from competing in the bidding to

---

[8] Maureen Orth, Janet Huck, and Peter Greensberg, excerpt from "Making of a Rock Star" in *Newsweek*, 10/27/75. Copyright 1975 by Newsweek, Inc. All rights reserved. Reprinted by permission.

sign recording artists. The sums of money involved in signing artists and producing single records make it necessary for record company executives to vigorously promote, or "hype," their products.

Harry Anger, a vice-president for marketing at Polygram, says, "If pitching is 70 percent of baseball, promotion is 70 percent of the record business." *Clive Davis, in his book* Clive: Inside the Record Business, *agrees, and compares record promotion not to baseball but to a military campaign.* Marketing people "deploy forces over a vast battle terrain"; they "retreat" from promoting records in some areas and "attack" in others. The stakes of the "battle" are very high, since thousands of records are released each year but only a few hundred make money. The odds against any particular record "making it" seem overwhelming; and recording artists, faced with an album that doesn't sell, are likely to blame the record company for poor promotion. *Yet, as the article on Bruce Springsteen illustrates, even an extravagant promotional campaign is no guarantee of a record's financial success.*

The "hype" worked for Springsteen at first — his manager, Mike Appel, "sold" him well enough to get an audition with John Hammond, the man who discovered Billie Holiday and Bob Dylan. Hammond was impressed with Springsteen ("The kid absolutely knocked me out") and signed him with Columbia Records in 1972. Then the hype began in earnest. Because of the sensuality of his lyrics, Springsteen was billed as "the new Bob Dylan," a comparison that offended disc jockeys, whose airplay of records determines an artist's financial success. The jocks didn't play cuts from Springsteen's "Greetings from Asbury Park, N.J." and the record sold fewer than 50,000 copies. Even though Springsteen eventually became a superstar, he was considered, early in his career, "just another media hype that failed."

From these sources, then, we see both the importance and the limitations of promoting a recording artist. Bernstein discusses promotion from the vantage point of an observer "outside" of the record industry; Clive Davis repeats the message from the "inside"; and the story of Bruce Springsteen provides an example of the paradoxes of record promotion: if an artist is not "hyped," albums will fail, and even if he is "hyped," he is not assured of financial success.

Let's analyze the structure of this synthesis. Notice first, *the location of the thesis statement at the end of the first paragraph.* What precedes this statement is a summary of the Bernstein excerpt that justifies the thesis. The first sentence of the second paragraph comes from the Bernstein excerpt, but the remainder of the paragraph comes from the piece by Clive Davis. We've done this because of the neat transition this arrangement provides: Bernstein quotes a record executive who compares promotion to baseball. The Davis piece begins with a comparison between the promotion of records and a military campaign. Linking the two comparisons makes for an obvioûs transition between the excerpts.

Strictly speaking, only the discussion of Bruce Springsteen provides an explicit example of industry "hype." Davis essentially reiterates Bernstein's conclusion — that hype is important to the industry. Notice the transition from paragraph two to three. We use a statement that Davis makes about the failure of some records to sell in order to lead into the failure of Springsteen's first album. Note also that the last sentence of the second paragraph, our transition sentence, begins with "Yet . . ." We are making a distinction between albums that fail because they are not promoted and albums that fail because the promotions failed.

Comparison-Contrast Synthesis

The comparison-contrast synthesis builds upon the example synthesis. You'll remember in the previous discussion that we cited aspects of Bruce Springsteen's career that exemplified remarks made by Peter Bernstein and Clive Davis. In a comparison-contrast synthesis, your responsibility is to observe two or more subjects (scientific studies, novels, states of affairs, etc.), to note their *similarities* (the comparisons) and their *differences* (the contrasts) and to document your assertions by citing examples.

When you write a comparison-contrast synthesis, it's important that you adhere to the following principles:

1. When looking for aspects of two or more things to compare and contrast, *you must look for elements of the same class.* As your fourth-grade teacher would say, you compare apples with apples, not apples with oranges. If your composition instructor asked you to compare and contrast aspects of two cities in which you have lived, you wouldn't attempt to discuss the climate in Cheyenne, Wyoming, with modern building design in Miami, Florida. Climates and buildings are not of the same class, even though they are both aspects of the cities you've been asked to discuss. What you could more reasonably discuss is (a) the climates of the two cities or (b) the design of modern buildings in the two cities or (c) the effects of the two climates on the design of modern buildings in the two cities. (We'll assume, for later discussion purposes, the third possibility.)

2. When deciding which aspects of your subjects are to be compared and contrasted, make certain that these aspects are, in fact, discussable. *You must be able to discover significant criteria for comparison and contrast.* In our example of climate and building design in Miami and Cheyenne, it would be worth neither your time nor the time of your readers to explain how the buildings in Miami, because of the city's temperate climate, have more screened-in windows than buildings in

Cheyenne. To make your comparison-contrast synthesis meaningful, your observations have to go "deeper" than the obvious. You have to discover significant, subtle similarities and differences. This is not to say you should ignore the obvious: mention it, account for it, but go on to discuss at length more important matters. Our Miami-Cheyenne synthesis might focus on the criteria of types of erosion in the two cities and efforts by architects to combat the erosion.

3. After you have discovered significant criteria for comparison and contrast, *you must cite specific examples that demonstrate the application of your criteria.* First, set up your criteria, establishing the area of discussion. Then use precise terms and examples to show how your criteria operate in the specific cases you're considering. For instance: in the first section of your climate/building-design paper, you should be quite specific in explaining what you mean by "erosion" and in differentiating between types of erosion. Specifically, you might discuss erosion due to wave action and salt spray in Miami as opposed to erosion due to rain runoff and wind in Cheyenne. You would go into enough detail in your discussion of climate so that you could convincingly demonstrate why homes in Cheyenne are built into the ground with roofs sloped to deflect the wind, as opposed to homes along the Miami coast, which are built aboveground on massive concrete foundations. Thus, you will have discussed, in specific terms, the similarities between living in Cheyenne and Miami (that aspects of climate — such as erosion — affect the design of homes) and the differences (that differences in climate lead to different, particular applications of building design).

4. Before writing your comparison-contrast synthesis, *you must decide on the structure or organization of your synthesis.* The two most often-used comparison-contrast structures are exemplified as follows.

I.   *Thesis:* Erosion affects the way buildings are designed in Miami and in Cheyenne.

   a. Discuss *all aspects of A* (erosion and its effects on building design in *Miami*).

   b. Discuss *all aspects of B* (erosion and its effects on building design in *Cheyenne*).

   c. Compare and contrast A and B.

   Note: This structure works well in a short paper, one in which the reader can remember your discussion of A while he or she reads the discussion of B. But if the paper is more than a couple of pages long, if you want to compare several different aspects of the two climates and their effects on building design, you should probably work with the following structure.

II.   *Thesis:* Erosion, amounts of precipitation, hours of daylight, and average temperature all have a bearing on the way houses are designed in Miami and in Cheyenne.

    a. Discuss *first criterion* of comparison and contrast; apply it to A and B (e.g., criterion of *erosion* and its effect on roof design and type of foundation in *Miami and Cheyenne*).

    b. Discuss *second criterion* of comparison and contrast (e.g., amount of *precipitation* and its effect on house design in *Miami and Cheyenne*).

    c. Discuss *third (and possibly fourth) criterion* and show its application.

The comparison-contrast synthesis is a useful learning device because it requires that you examine two subjects in terms of one another. In this way, both subjects receive a comparative analysis that suggests subtleties that might not otherwise have come to your attention. Perhaps (to continue with the above example) you were never conscious of how climatic conditions in Miami affected the design of your home until you moved to Cheyenne and noticed a relationship there between climate and building design. Once you have conducted your comparison and contrast analysis, the subjects of your study will remain vivid in your memory.

Exercise

Read the following two excerpts from Chapter 11, "Personality," and consider possible criteria of comparison-contrast.

A. A classical theory of human types, offered by ancient Greek [1] physicians, focussed on the emotional (temperamental) attributes of human personality and was based on a relatively primitive understanding of human biology (specifically, bodily physiology), which prevailed at that time. According to these early theorists, emotional equilibrium (indeed, general health) depended on an appropriate balance among four fluids (humours) within the body. It was held that physiological imbalance (produced by an excess of one of the humours, for example) would be reflected in bodily illness and in exaggerated personality traits. Thus, if a person had an excess of blood (one of the four humours), he was expected to have a sanguine temperament; that is, to be optimistic, enthusiastic, and excitable. The modern term hot-blooded may be a survival of this Greek theory of human personality; the notion was so influential that for many centuries physicians throughout the Western world continued the practice of bleeding people who suffered from medical and psychiatric disorders. Such people are still said to be in "bad humour."

Too much of a humour called black bile (congealed blood from the spleen) was believed to produce a melancholic temperament. The term melancholia literally means black bile, and there are literary allusions to venting one's spleen. When someone was oversupplied with yellow bile (the yellow-green gall secreted by the liver and stored in the gall bladder), he was held to become choleric; that is, to be angry, irritable, and to view his world with a jaundiced eye. Jaundice remains in modern medical language as a disease of the liver or gall bladder in which bile is present in the body to such a degree that the eyeballs and body may turn yellow. Finally, with an abundance of the humour called phlegm (as secreted in the throat), people were supposed to become stolid, apathetic, and undemonstrative; that is, to grow phlegmatic. 2

As biological science has progressed, these primitive concepts of body chemistry have been replaced by more subtle and complex biological theories of personality. Thus, the chemical factors associated with given psychological dispositions are now more likely to be understood in terms of hormones (as from the thyroid gland), nerve impulses, and so-called psychotropic drugs such as tranquillizers.[9] 3

B. 1. The tradition-directed person feels the impact of his culture as a unit, but it is nevertheless mediated through the specific, small number of individuals with whom he is in daily contact. These expect of him not so much that he be a certain type of person but that he behave in the approved way. Consequently the sanction for behavior tends to be the fear of being *shamed*. 1

2. The inner-directed person has early incorporated a psychic gyroscope which is set going by his parents and can receive signals later on from other authorities who resemble his parents. He goes through life less independent than he seems, obeying this internal piloting. Getting off course, whether in response to inner impulses or to the fluctuating voices of contemporaries, may lead to the feeling of *guilt*. 2

Since the direction to be taken in life has been learned in the privacy of the home from a small number of guides and since principles, rather than details of behavior, are internalized, the inner-directed person is capable of great stability. Especially so when it turns out that his fellows have gyroscopes too, spinning at the same speed and set in the same direction. But many inner-directed individuals can remain stable even when the reinforcement of social approval is not available — as in the upright life of the stock Englishman isolated in the tropics. 3

---

[9] From "Personalities, Theories of" in *Encyclopaedia Britannica*, 15th Edition (1974), 14:115. Copyright 1974 by Encyclopaedia Britannica.

3. Contrasted with such a type as this, the other-directed person   4
learns to respond to signals from a far wider circle than is constituted
by his parents. The family is no longer a closely knit unit to which he
belongs but merely a part of a wider social environment to which he
early becomes attentive. In these respects the other-directed person
resembles the tradition-directed person: both live in a group milieu
and lack the inner-directed person's capacity to go it alone. The
nature of this group milieu, however, differs radically in the two
cases. The other-directed person is cosmopolitan. For him the border
between the familiar and the strange — a border clearly marked in
the societies depending on tradition-direction — has broken down.
As the family continuously absorbs the strange and so reshapes itself,
so the strange becomes familiar. While the inner-directed person
could be "at home abroad" by virtue of his relative insensitivity to
others, the other-directed person is, in a sense, at home everywhere
and nowhere, capable of a rapid if sometimes superficial intimacy
with and response to everyone.[10]

Here's a skeleton outline of our synthesis:

Thesis: "The Four Humours" and "Three Types of Character Structure" reveal different approaches to personality.

Criterion 1: Each passage presents classifications of personality
   types. (*first comparison*)
   a. "Four Humours"
   b. "Three Types"
   transition (in italics in the example below)

Criterion 2: Each passage reveals a distinct approach to personality
   classification. (*first contrast*)
   a. "Four Humours" — physiological approach
   b. "Three Types" — sociological approach
   transition (in italics in the example below)

Criterion 3: Each passage shows a distinct pattern of cause and effect
   in regard to personality. (*second contrast*)
   transition (in italics in the example below)

Criterion 4: Both approaches exhibit the weakness of oversimplification. (*second comparison*)

---

[10] David Riesman, Reuel Denny, and Nathan Glazer, "Three Types of Character Structure," from *The Lonely Crowd,* New Haven, Conn.: Yale University
Press, 1950.

Here's a sample *comparison-contrast* synthesis:

"The Four Humours," a passage from *The Encyclopedia Brittanica,* 　1
by Edgar F. Borgatta, and "Three Types of Character Structure" by
David Riesman, Reuel Denny, and Nathan Glazer, reveal different
approaches to personality. Both passages present a classification, or
set of categories, for discussing personality. In reviewing the classical
theory of personality types, Borgatta presents a fourfold classification
based on bodily "humours," the four fluids which, according to classical physiologists, control one's general health and disposition. A pre-
dominance of any one of the humours was believed to result in a
psychological imbalance: a person with an excess of blood was expected to be enthusiastic or "sanguine"; an excess of black bile was
said to result in melancholy; too much yellow bile made one irritable or
"choleric"; and an excess of phlegm was thought to make one apathetic, or "phlegmatic."

David Riesman and his co-authors of *The Lonely Crowd* identify 　2
three types of character structure: the tradition-directed person, who
lives life "acceptably" according to the social expectations of the
immediate community (family, friends); the inner-directed person,
whose "psychic gyroscope," or learned set of values and principles of
behavior, allows him or her to remain stable in varied social environments; and the other-directed person, whose dependence on a large
community (larger than family and friends) sometimes results in
superficially close relationships.

While Borgatta and Riesman et al. offer classifications of human 　3
personality types, they do so in different ways. Borgatta explains that
the ancient Greeks believed that differences in personality could be
explained in *physiological* terms, by analyzing the four bodily humours.
Riesman et al., on the other hand, believe that character traits are
caused by *sociological* factors — the relationships one has with family,
friends, business associates, and even larger groups, such as city,
state, or national populace. A second difference between the two
systems of classification is the pattern of cause and effect they assume. The classical physiologists began with the *causes* of personality
differences (the four humours) and proceeded with an explanation of
their *effects* (e.g., an excess of blood makes one excitable). Riesman et
al. assume in their discussion the three basic personality types, which
one might call effects, and then deduce their causes (principles of
behavior learned in the home).

Because both authors offer classifications, their discussions reveal 　4
the weakness common to all classifications: oversimplification. Categorical terms do not always satisfactorily describe individual cases.
When one classifies types of people, one ceases to be interested in (or
at least de-emphasizes) individual differences that distinguish people

within a single personality type. In other words, categories like "inner-directed" or "phlegmatic" are useful only up to a point; the categories can tell us nothing about how Jones and Wykofsky, who are both inner-directed, differ from one another. The individual tends to "vanish" in a system of classification. However, such systems are valuable in helping us to understand personality, as long as we recognize the limits of their usefulness. It is useful to be aware, for instance, of the similarities between the inner-directed Jefferson and the inner-directed Lincoln, as long as we remain aware that their differences were far more significant.

There are other ways to organize a comparison-contrast synthesis. As you will see, they are usually not as effective as our sample.

The first alternative is the easiest possible comparison-contrast synthesis that one could write. Based on these two excerpts, it would have stated only that each author classifies types of personality — one according to bodily humours and the other according to social relationships. Such a synthesis would have taken the following form:

First Passage–Second Passage Approach: *Thesis*

Summary of "The Four Humours"

Summary of "Three Types of Character Structure"

Discussion of comparison-contrast: point out that both excerpts present classifications and that these classifications differ.

Another alternative is to compare first and to contrast second (or possibly vice versa). Thus you would begin with a consideration of the similarities and continue with a discussion of the differences. Such a synthesis would take the following form:

Similarities–Differences Approach: *Thesis*

Similarities:

(a) Both passages present classifications of personality types.

(b) Both approaches have the weakness of oversimplification.

Differences:

(a) Each passage reveals a distinct approach to personality classification.

(b) Each passage shows a distinct pattern of cause and effect in regard to personality.

Note that this outline is simply a rearrangement of our original sample outline, which was based on criteria. We believe that the *criterion* approach is preferable to the other two alternatives (the *first passage-second passage* approach or the *similarities-differences* approach) because it produces a more readable, clear, and logically developed essay, an essay developed primarily on the basis of *ideas* rather than primarily on the basis of some arbitrary structure.

Our sample synthesis is based entirely on the two excerpts, yet it is more sophisticated than a simple summary of the excerpts or an analysis that does not go beyond the obvious. Notice that we adhered to the four principles of comparison-contrast discussed earlier: (1) we discussed elements of the same class (types of personality); (2) we discovered significant criteria of comparison-contrast (physiological vs. sociological systems of classification, patterns of cause and effect, weaknesses of classifications); (3) we cited specific references in the excerpts; and (4) we wrote the synthesis according to a predetermined outline.

It's entirely possible that two students comparing and contrasting the same articles will discuss different aspects of those articles. It's not likely in any event that you could discuss *all* categories of comparison and contrast in your synthesis, as there are bound to be certain categories about which, for lack of experience, you are not aware. This is not a major problem; as you become more widely read in a field, more categories of comparison and contrast will suggest themselves to you. Regardless of your knowledge and experience, however, you will want to choose only those categories that you feel merit serious attention. For example, even though similarities and differences exist between the writing styles of the two passages on personality, you might not consider these particular similarities and differences significant enough to discuss.

Argument Synthesis

The syntheses we've discussed so far are "expository" in nature; that is, in describing, explaining processes, defining, giving examples, and comparing and contrasting, you are "exposing" or presenting information and ideas. Many of your assignments in college will be expository. Your instructors will typically test your understanding of a subject by asking you to compare and contrast, to give examples, and to explain or discuss.

Another way an instructor can gauge your mastery of a subject is by asking you to *argue* a position, based on material you have read in class. To write a convincing argument requires a degree of sophistication beyond that needed to write, say, an example synthesis. In an argument you will *use* your example synthesis to demonstrate a point you wish to make. An argument, more than any other form of writing, reflects the way you *think,* reflects the quality of your thought.

Think back to the example synthesis earlier in this unit. Our thesis was that "The very large sums of money involved in signing artists and producing records makes it necessary for record company executives to promote vigorously, or 'hype,' their products." We proceeded to develop the synthesis by discussing Bruce Springsteen's career as an example of Bernstein's and Davis's conclusions. Our synthesis is a neutral one — which is to say, we haven't injected our own opinions about record promotion into the synthesis. We could, however, construct an *argument* based on the synthesis. In order to do this, we would have to think about the implications of what we have read; we would have to develop another thesis, which is not explicitly mentioned in any of our source material.

Moreover, this thesis would have to be *debatable;* that is, it would have to be a thesis about which reasonable people could disagree. Otherwise, it would be a self-evident fact, not a basis for argument. (An example of a nondebatable thesis: "The rock music business is extremely lucrative.")

Suppose we reread the passages on rock music and decide to argue the thesis that "The high financial stakes involved in commercially successful record production and promotion place significant limits on the musician's artistic freedom." A thesis like this might use an example synthesis as a basis for discussion. Then, we would argue that many artists, faced with the pressures that Springsteen faced early in his career, would have turned away from developing their own style of music in order to write songs that would sell and make them a great deal of money. We might point out that the "hype" leads to two kinds of success in the record business — commercial and artistic. Oftentimes, artistically innovative musicians — who don't wish to compromise their art — can't make enough money at their craft to eat regularly, while pop musicians, who are less experimental and who produce what the record company promoters want them to produce, live in penthouses and drive fancy cars.

But we could also, with equal rigor, have argued the opposite: that "The high financial stakes involved in commercially successful record production assure that only the finest artistic products ever reach the marketplace." We would argue, in this case, that only the talented musicians — who are consistently innovative — attain commercial success, a statement we would support by citing the Bernstein/Davis/Springsteen example synthesis.

Incidentally, in arguing either of these theses, we would have to be very careful in defining what we meant by "artistic." In any argument, you want to define carefully your key terms so that there is no confusion about just exactly what they mean. Additionally, of course, you must carefully present your evidence, so that you can persuade your reader into thinking as you do. More realistically, your goal in an argument should be to present your reader with compelling reasons why he or she should regard your views as intelligent and responsible and worthy of serious consideration. Seldom do we ever conclusively "prove" a proposition; if we did, all argument would stop. Rather, we attempt to suggest and to persuade, as convincingly as we can. Too often, inexperienced writers conclude an argument by declaring, "Thus, as anyone can see . . ." Problems are seldom so unequivocally resolved, and arguments that end so stridently seldom need to be taken seriously.

Once you have decided on the thesis you wish to argue, your responsibility is to present evidence, as methodically as you can, that will support and make credible this thesis. One time-honored method of presenting the parts of your argument is as follows:

1. *Introduction* — in which you provide background information (perhaps a brief analysis of the problem, an anecdote, a quotation, or a question) which provides a context for the discussion to follow;

2. *Thesis statement* — in which you state the argument you wish to pursue (this statement often appears as the final sentence of the introductory paragraph);

3. *Confirmation of your position* — in which you cite evidence to support your thesis, generally in increasing order of importance, the most important evidence last;

4. *Refutation of opposing positions* — in which you consider and respond to the most damaging arguments against your thesis. You should be aware that opposing arguments will probably have *some* merit; often a refutation involves demonstrating why your argument has greater merit than opposing ones;

5. *Conclusion* — in which you review your argument and restate your thesis.

In some cases, you may wish to reverse the order of (3) and (4).

Essentially, you want to argue what you know, or are willing to know, after conducting basic research. In this text we've provided the basic research (though you may wish to research a subject further). When your instructor assigns you to write an argument on one of the subjects in the text, you will need: (1) to determine the basic issues linking the articles together; (2) to determine a particular issue that interests you; (3) to determine your position on that issue, a thesis you want to argue; (4) to develop an outline of your argument, based on the steps discussed in the previous paragraph.

A caution: an opinion, no matter how dearly held, does not constitute an argument. An argument is a logical presentation of material, based on evidence that confirms your thesis and refutes arguments against it.

And another caution: you want to cite evidence that supports your argument without creating the impression that you have chosen only part of the evidence and ignored an equally or more important other part. Your evidence must not be atypical. If you fail to consider all of the evidence, then your argument will be simplistic, deceptive, and ultimately irresponsible.

Exercise

Our sample argument is based on two brief excerpts from Chapter 7, "The Age of Computers and Beyond":

A. A revolution is under way. Most Americans are already well   1
aware of the gee-whiz gadgetry that is emerging, in rapidly accelerating bursts, from the world's high-technology laboratories. But most of
us perceive only dimly how pervasive and profound the changes of
the next twenty years will be. We are at the dawn of the era of the
smart machine — an "information age" that will change forever the
way an entire nation works, plays, travels and even thinks. Just as the
industrial revolution dramatically expanded the strength of man's
muscles and the reach of his hand, so the smart-machine revolution
will magnify the power of his brain. But unlike the industrial revolution, which depended on finite resources such as iron and oil, the new
information age will be fired by a seemingly limitless resource — the
inexhaustible supply of knowledge itself. Even computer scientists,
who best understand the galloping technology and its potential, are
struck by its implications. "It is really awesome," says L. C. Thomas of
Bell Laboratories. "Every day is just as scary as the day before."

The driving force behind the revolution is the development of   2
two fundamental and interactive technologies — computers and integrated circuits. Today, tiny silicon chips half the size of a fingernail
are etched with circuitry powerful enough to book seats on jumbo jets
(and keep the planes working smoothly in the air), cut complex
swatches of fabric with little wastage, help children learn to spell and
play chess well enough to beat all but the grandest masters. The new
technology means that bits of computing power can be distributed
wherever they might be useful — the way small electric motors have
become ubiquitous — or combined in giant mainframe computers to
provide enormous problem-solving potential. In addition, this "computational plenty" is making smart machines easier to use and more
forgiving of unskilled programing. Machines are even communicating with each other. "What's next?" asks Peter E. Hart, director of the
SRI International artificial-intelligence center. "More to the point,
what's *not* next?"[11]

B. We are now witnessing one of the swiftest and most momen-   1
tous revolutions in the entire history of technology. For more than a
century the slide rule was the essential tool of engineers, scientists,
and anyone else whose work involved extensive calculations. Then,
just a decade ago, the invention of the pocket calculator made the
slide rule obsolete almost overnight, and with it whole libraries of
logarithmic and trigonometric tables.

There has never been so stupendous an advance in so short a   2
time. Simply no comparison can be made between the two devices.

---

[11] Merrill Sheils and William Cook, "And Man Created the Chip," *Newsweek*,
June 30, 1980.

The pocket calculator is millions of times more accurate and scores of times swifter than the slide rule, and it now actually costs less. It's as if we'd jumped overnight from bullock carts to the Concorde — and Concorde were cheaper! No wonder the slide rule manufacturers have gone out of business. If you have a good slide rule, leave it in your will. It will someday be a valuable antique.

Pocket calculators are already having a profound effect on the teaching of mathematics, even at the level of elementary arithmetic. But they are about to be succeeded by devices of much greater power and sophistication — machines that may change the very nature of the educational system. 3

The great development in our near future is the portable electronic library — a library not only of books, but of films and music. It will be about the size of an average book and will probably open in the same way. One half will be the screen, with high-definition, full-color display. The other will be a keyboard, much like one of today's computer consoles, with the full alphabet, digits, basic mathematical functions, and a large number of special keys — perhaps 100 keys in all. It won't be as small as some of today's midget calculators, which have to be operated with toothpicks. 4

In theory, such a device could have enough memory to hold all the books in the world. But we may settle for something more modest, like the *Encyclopaedia Britannica,* the *Oxford English Dictionary,* and *Roget's Thesaurus.* (Incidentally, Peter Mark Roget was the inventor of the log-log slide rule.) Whole additional libraries, stored in small, plug-in memory modules, could be inserted into the portable library when necessary. All this technology has already been developed, though for other uses. Oddly enough, the most skilled practitioners of this new art are the designers of video games. 5

Reading material may be displayed as a fixed page or else "scrolled" so that it rolls upward at a comfortable reading rate. Pictures could appear as in an ordinary book, but they may eventually be displayed as three-dimensional holographic images. Text and imagery, of course, will be accompanied by sound. Today's tape recorders can reproduce an entire symphony on a cassette. The electronic library may be able to play back the complete works of Beethoven while displaying the scores on its screen. 6

And how nice to be able to summon up Lord Clark's *Civilisation* or Jacob Bronowski's *Ascent of Man* whenever or wherever you felt like it! (Yes, I know that these tapes currently cost about $2,000 apiece, unless you are lucky or wicked enough to have a pirated copy. But one day the BBC will get its money back, and thereafter the price will be peanuts.)[12] 7

---

[12] Arthur C. Clarke, "Electronic Tutors," *Omni,* June 2, 1980.

Based on these brief excerpts, we wish to argue the following thesis: "Computers are a mixed blessing for society."

Here is our skeleton outline:

Introduction: Establish that people in the United States have become extraordinarily dependent on computers to process their information for them; cite examples.

Thesis: Computers are a mixed blessing for society.

Confirmation:

    a. Computers dehumanize transactions; people dealing with machines rather than with other people.

    b. Students' competence in mathematics and writing, as measured by standardized tests, is decreasing; computers, which encourage punch-in information and which do all the hard work for us, could make this situation even worse.

Refutation: Offer a refutation of each confirmation as we make it (short cuts are to be applauded; computers do help us immensely; they do the drudgery); but we pay a price for this help.

Conclusion

Our sample *argument* synthesis:

The lives of Americans are becoming increasingly involved with machines that think for them. "We are at the dawn of the era of the smart machine," say the authors of a cover story on the subject in *Newsweek*, "that will change forever the way an entire nation works," beginning a revolution that will be to the brain what the industrial revolution was to the hand. Tiny silicon chips already process enough information to direct air travel, to instruct machines how to cut fabric — even to play chess with, and defeat, the masters. To be sure, the development of computers for household as well as industrial use will change for the better the quality of our lives: computers will help us save energy, reduce the amount of drudgery which most of us endure around tax season, make access to libraries easier. Yet there is a certain danger involved with this proliferation of technology. Computers are a mixed blessing for society.   1

Most of us have benefited from the convenience of computer technology, one example of which is the now ubiquitous "24-Hour Teller" at shopping malls around the country. It is convenient indeed at four o'clock in the morning, just before you and the family are about to drive to your favorite vacation spot, to stop off at the 24-Hour Teller and withdraw two hundred dollars for last-minute traveling expenses that you hadn't anticipated at the close of banking hours the previous day. Rather than delay your trip until 10 A.M., you can feed the machine your card, punch in your secret code, and — voilà! — two hundred   2 dollars appears. Undoubtedly, computers have made our living more convenient. But by virtue of this convenience, computers have also allowed people to interact with one another a little bit less each day. Even during regular banking hours, I often do my banking at a machine because it is quicker and more consistently accurate than human bank tellers. In addition, computerized tellers don't demand three kinds of identification and need to check my signature against bank records. Why be impatient with a person when a computer can give you a quick, correct response? I leave the bank with one check in the credit column for convenience and one check in the debit column for laziness; and, if I want to berate myself, an extra debit for an ever so tiny bit of inhumanity. Am I suggesting that we unplug all of the 24-Hour Tellers in the country? Of course not. (Like everyone else, I occasionally need extra cash at four o'clock in the morning!) I *do* suggest that we think about some of the less obvious ramifications of patronizing machines (and computerized banking is only one example) instead of people.

As Arthur C. Clarke notes, "We are witnessing one of the swiftest and most momentous revolutions in the entire history of technology." He points out that pocket calculators are already profoundly affecting the teaching of mathematics and arithmetic. And soon we'll have portable, electronic libraries of books, film, and music — libraries we can talk back to. The prospects are tantalizing, and we can look forward to the day when such technology becomes available: heretofore undreamed-of access to knowledge will be possible. And yet there is something worrisome in all this. At the moment in our history when more knowledge than ever is being made available to our students, their abilities to process that knowledge intelligently and systematically seems to be declining — at least, so suggest the results of several widely-administered standardized tests. No doubt, computer technology can help relieve the problem; but will we allow computers to take over our responsibility to think for ourselves? High school students are unable to perform basic mathematical computations; so they rely on pocket calculators to do their computations for them. Why shouldn't they? It is so easy to punch the buttons and instantaneously get the answers. I don't honestly expect our young men and women to stop using calculators. But I do expect (and insist, for that matter) that students use calculators as an *aid* to knowledge and not as a *substitute* for knowledge. I am not suggesting that we renounce our computers because there is a danger that we may lose control of our own intelligence. Rather, I am suggesting that (at the very least) we start worrying about the trend of allowing things to do for us what we would be better off doing for ourselves.

Computers are a mixed blessing. We may, as a result of relying too heavily upon these machines, allow ourselves to grow intellectually lazy and to prefer to push buttons rather than to transact business with other human beings. We should not allow this. The expanded problem-solving capacity of our computers can certainly help us live more comfortable, productive lives. The prospects are exciting. But they are also troubling.

We have already outlined the structure of this argument. Notice that our thesis is a modest one, an *arguable* one. We do not wish to argue that computer technology is "evil." That would be simplistic. We are more interested in qualifying what seems in the *Newsweek* and the Clarke excerpts an unqualified enthusiasm for computers. We share the enthusiasm, but offer certain warnings. Note also that our warnings do not take on the tone (to quote William Faulkner) of the "ding-dong of doom." We wish to argue quietly and convincingly that our observations should be given serious consideration and that our thesis is a reasonable one.

We have made sparing use of the two excerpts, actually relying on them not so much for specific information as for a general context in which we could develop our argument. In your argument you will always want to take account of available evidence: our evidence — the use of 24-Hour Tellers and pocket calculators — is based on personal experience, and we urge you to take advantage of what you know from your own experience when you are writing an argument. For example, in arguing this thesis (if you believe it) you could just as well have cited your observations that many children now prefer electronic baseball to real baseball; or you might have noticed that children much prefer the electronic organ, which is relatively easy to play well, to the piano, which is difficult and time-consuming to learn. Or you may have called attention to the problems of invasion of privacy and theft by computer that the new technology makes possible.

A caution, though: for academic purposes, an authoritative argument should be solidly grounded on academic sources. Your personal observations and experiences, if they are relevant, can be useful; but always try to refer to the latest research on your subject. To prepare a convincing argument, you will usually need to spend some time in the library.

To conclude, then: in the argument above, we would have been simplistic had we summarily rejected the obvious evidence that computers help people enormously. We acknowledged that evidence, but at the same time we turned it to our advantage. Our posture was that no one would argue against the usefulness of computers; but one might reasonably argue that if computers influence us to speak to people less and do less thinking for ourselves, then they are something less than an unqualified boon to society.

CRITIQUE

A critique is not a listing of complaints or faults, but a careful analysis of an argument to determine what is said, how well the points are made, what assumptions underlie the argument, what issues are overlooked, and what implications can be drawn from such observations. Of course, when you make your analysis, you bring your own set of assumptions, expectations, or perspectives that inform your analysis at every step. Your reader should be justified in critiquing your critique at least partially on the basis of your own assumptions, whether they are stated or not.

A critique is a personal response, an opinion, an evaluation. Yet by themselves personal responses often don't communicate much. A movie is "great." A book is "fascinating." A theory is "provocative." "I didn't like it." These are all responses, and as such, they're a valid, even essential part of your understanding of the material. But such responses won't help illuminate the material for anyone else if you haven't explained how you arrived at your conclusions.

The critique must be systematic. You respond to the material according to some set of criteria, criteria that are explicit, so that your reader can follow the process of thought by which you arrived at your conclusions. You can write a "rave" or you can write a "pan" (or anything in between), but your reader's assessment of *your* assessment will depend upon how well you choose your criteria and how well you use them.

What are the criteria for a good critique, and how should they be used?

This is a difficult question to answer. There is no easy, ready-made formula for writing a critique. A good critique requires discernment, sensitivity, imagination, a sense of proportion — qualities that can be developed only through repeated practice. If you were to analyze a group of three first-rate book reviews, you'd be unlikely to find that they had been written according to a single, prefabricated method. In fact, there's a good chance the authors would insist that they had not written according to method at all: they just wrote (they would claim) what they felt, what they *had* to write, as best they could.

We concede the danger that writing critiques by method produces mechanical, unimaginative analyses. But for inexperienced writers there are even greater dangers in writing critiques *without* a method. These problems are familiar enough to any teacher: writing that is undeveloped, padded, unsupported, irrelevant, rambling, incomplete. A good critique starts with the realization that certain ground has to be covered and that in order to cover the ground, certain questions have to be answered—or at least asked.

So while bearing in mind the fact that a critique involves your asking and coming to grips with the *particular* questions raised by a *particular* piece, you can nevertheless begin to think critically by asking yourself a number of more general questions. Among them:

■   What is the *nature* of the piece? Who wrote it, and what are his/her qualifications for writing it? Why was the piece written? What was the occasion for it? Who is the intended audience?

- What is the *significance* of the piece? What relation does it bear to other material on the same subject, or to other material by the same author?
- What are the *objectives* of the piece? What kind of material is presented to achieve those objectives? How well are the objectives achieved?
- What is the *design, plan, or method* of the piece? Is this design, plan, or method well conceived? Does it help achieve the objectives?
- What is the particular *appeal* (or lack of appeal) of the piece? What are some of its most striking or illuminating qualities? What are its most striking deficiencies? Does it have a distinctive style or tone? Is the material presented with skill, flair, elegance?
- What *assumptions* underlie the piece? Are the assumptions explicit or implicit? Are some of the assumptions particularly offensive to many people today? What biases pervade the piece? Are the assumptions and biases obvious, or do they lurk behind a stance of neutrality and objectivity?
- How do the assumptions and biases affect the *validity* of the piece? How do the assumptions of the author compare with your own assumptions? What evidence or ideas has the author failed to consider? Do your own knowledge and experience allow you to support the author's position? How would you assess the author's judgments and conclusions?

Note that this series of questions is *not* designed as an outline (we will suggest an outline for critiques later on). If you tried to answer every one of these questions, and in this particular order, your critique would probably be mechanical, overlong, and repetitious. As we've indicated, your response has to be systematic, but there's always the danger of the system overwhelming the response. Remember that the critique is ultimately a *personal* reaction, a meeting of three minds — your own, that of the author you are discussing, and that of your reader. These questions may help you to come to grips with your subject. But they are designed to stimulate thought, not to replace it. Don't hesitate to substitute *your own* questions, or to follow the promptings of your own responses.

One set of questions that may seem somewhat confusing is the set dealing with the *assumptions* of the author. An assumption is a belief, often taken for granted by the author, about human nature or about how the world works. When preparing your critique, you should determine the relationship between an author's assumptions (seldom explicit) and his or her stated beliefs and conclusions. We don't mean to imply that assumptions are necessarily insidious. Rather, we mean to emphasize the fact that assumptions, because they are often hidden, should be brought to the surface for examination.

Assumptions underlie all our behavior. A person who never locks the door when leaving home probably assumes that houses in that particular area don't get burglarized. The person may be right or wrong in this assumption. Or the assumption may have been valid in 1962 but not in 1982. The same person who laments, after the house *is* burglarized, "I can't believe it! This is such a quiet neighborhood!" assumes that houses in quiet neighborhoods don't get burglarized. Here is a more academic example. The author of a book on underdeveloped nations may include a section outlining the resources and the time that will be required to industrialize a particular country and so upgrade the general welfare. His assumption — that industrialization in that particular country will ensure or even has anything to do with what the people themselves consider their general welfare — may or may not be valid. But it certainly should be critically examined.

In fact, *all* assumptions should be critically examined, even those that seem to be in harmony with what you believe (and so seem beyond examination!). For example, an editorialist may advocate stricter campaign financing laws so that corrupt officials may eventually be rooted out of government. The editorialist's assumption is that it is better to have honest officials governing than corrupt ones. This may well be true. On the other hand, it's entirely possible that a corrupt official may govern better — more ably, more wisely — than an honest one. The point is that you need to search for the assumptions, the basic beliefs about how the world operates (or should operate) that underlie the author's arguments—not necessarily to discredit them, but to examine their validity. And in the absence of more "scientific" criteria, "validity" may simply mean how well the author's assumptions stack up against your own experience, observations, and reading. After determining the validity of these assumptions, you're in a better position to assess the overall value of the piece.

A caution, however: don't assume a direct correlation between validity and value. The overall value of an article or a book may depend only to a small degree upon the validity of the author's assumptions. For instance, a sociologist may do a fine job of gathering statistical data about the incidence of crime in urban centers along the eastern seaboard. The sociologist might also be a radical Marxist, and you may disagree with her subsequent analysis of the data. Yet you may find the data extremely valuable for your own work or for the work of others.

From your first responses to your final draft, the critique is *yours*. You are entitled to respond to and to develop a position about a piece in any way that pleases you, provided that you are willing to take responsibility for what you write and are prepared to defend it. The critique provides an occasion for you to help illuminate an author's ideas for others. But equally important, it provides an occasion for you to illuminate these ideas to yourself, and even more important, to illuminate *your own* ideas to yourself. For in the process of writing a critical assessment, you are forced to examine your own knowledge, your own beliefs, your own assumptions. In a sense, then, the critique is a way of learning more about yourself.

Exercise

When preparing a critique you should find the following six-step process[13] helpful.

A Six-Step Process for Writing Critiques

1 Introduce the subject of your critique — the piece under analysis and the author. Give some preliminary information about both. Then indicate the main point you intend to pursue in your discussion.

2 Review the background facts or issues that must be understood before the point of the article being critiqued can be appreciated. Additional biographical data? Is this one of a series of essays on this theme?

3 Review the information (including the author's key assumptions) that must be understood before the position you plan to take on the article can be appreciated. What are your assumptions? Do they differ or agree with those of the author?

4 Summarize the argument of the author. No editorialization yet. Be as objective as possible.
Note: you may choose to reverse the order of steps 3 and 4.

5 Review the author's argument in light of the position you identified in step 1 and further elaborated in step 3. Make certain that all points relate to your central thesis.

6 State your conclusions, reminding the reader of the points you have made and the reasons you have for making them. You are not making arbitrary judgments but are measuring the validity of a presentation in terms of a carefully defined set of criteria that you have provided. What emerges from your analysis?

Example Critique

We have selected an article from Chapter 3, "Morality and the Movies," for critiquing. Since this article is somewhat longer than the other

---

[13] We gratefully acknowledge the assistance of William Leap, professor of anthropology at the American University, who provided the outline upon which we based this six-step process, as well as parts of the definition of critique.

examples we have reprinted in this unit, please turn to page 125 and read "Where Do You Draw the Line?" by Victor B. Cline before proceeding with the model critique below.

[1]   In "Where Do You Draw the Line?" Victor B. Cline asserts that society must draw the line *somewhere* on media violence and pornography, and he goes on to specify just where. Cline, a professor of psychology at the University of Utah, is an expert on the effects of media violence and pornography, and so his opinions carry considerable weight. But, ultimately, his defense of censorship fails to convince.

[2]   Few citizens of democratic societies are comfortable with the theory or the practice of censorship, since it takes away freedom of choice from the citizen and places it in the hands of a censor board of dubious qualifications. In this country, the 1930 Motion Picture Production Code had the effect for almost two generations of sanitizing films (and, by extension, TV drama) to the point where the versions of life they presented were barely recognizable. Married couples never slept in the same bed. No one ever said anything stronger than "Darn!" — whatever the provocation.

[3]   The 1930 code has long since been abandoned, and we are well rid of such puritanical restrictions. But is the issue of censorship so clear? Is it the 1930 censorship code or nothing? (The 1968 code is not really a censorship system but a rating system: for X-rated films, anything goes.) Does society have the right to declare that some forms of entertainment are so vile, so antisocial, that it allows their presentation at the risk of its own integrity, if not its existence as a civilized entity?

Cline has gathered together a number of essays and position papers on the question of censorship. "Where Do You Draw the Line?" forms the preface and the conclusion to this collection. There are serious questions here; to blithely argue "no censorship!" is as irresponsible as to argue its opposite. But the questions must be argued well; they must be argued fairly, with discrimination between cases, without stacking of evidence, and to whatever extent possible, without the emotional distortions or the crusadism that has marred the censorship movement in the past.

[4]   Cline begins by alluding to the many sacrifices that individuals have made in the name of free speech, and by suggesting why free speech is so essential to democratic societies. He then turns his attention to the problems of unrestricted free speech. Those who subscribe to an "absolutist" position on freedom of speech, he observes, must believe that there should be no restrictions on media violence and pornography. But the absolutist position is problematic,

for studies have linked children's exposure to TV violence with aggressive behavior.

Cline asserts that society must draw the line of censorship somewhere, and he offers a fourfold test to determine just when material "runs counter to the welfare of the citizenry." As to the question of *who* should make this determination, Cline suggests juries, selected to represent a cross section of the community. He concedes that standards will vary from one community to another; but he argues that a jury approach is preferable to censorship rulings by individual judges, who will be unable to overcome all of their personal biases. Members of a jury, he assumes, would cancel out each other's biases.

Cline believes that censorship is necessary because media violence and pornography assault "taboos that are intrinsic to the social order." He sees his own position as a responsible middle ground between the dangers of anarchy on the one hand and totalitarianism on the other. Furthermore, he asserts that the price of avoiding these extremes involves accepting another's authority and relinquishing the "sensuality of the irresponsible." He concludes by declaring that the consequence of "sexual anarchism" is an ignoble, brutalized regression from civilization and humanity.

5   On its face, Cline's argument sounds eminently reasonable. But it is marred by selective use of evidence, by emotionalism, and by a basic distrust of the public to act in its own best "welfare." Cline begins his discussion with what appears to be a neutral position. Indeed, as the editor of an anthology containing a wide range of positions, his purpose seems to be to advocate a "middle way" between the extreme positions (extreme restrictiveness and extreme libertarianism) of the censorship debate. After a gallant salute to the historical martyrs for free speech, he stakes out a position against violence and so disarms many who might question why censors have always been more tolerant of violence than of sex. But at the same time, Cline stacks the deck. He quotes Norman Podhoretz, a self-acknowledged (indeed a model) absolutist, who nonetheless finds himself plagued by doubts about the wisdom of his absolutist position. Next, he raises the questions of "many thoughtful people" (implying that those without such questions are not thoughtful) and cites evidence that appears to damn the absolutist position — like the study that links TV violence to aggressive behavior. (He does not consider the "catharsis" theory of violence — that a child who watches a violent TV show may be *less* likely to hit people or destroy property because the TV violence has drained off violent impulses. Nor does he cite the many studies that find no link between pornography and sex crimes, and indeed that give additional credence to the "catharsis" theory.) Cline resorts to a highly emotional appeal by raising the horror of "filmed or live sexual sado-masochism in a public theater." Yet the standards he later suggests to prevent such outrages could well be used by a jury to ban far milder and less generally offensive forms of pornography.

But even if we allow Cline his right to downplay evidence that might persuade him to reconsider his procensorship position, his presentation remains fraught with difficulties. He discusses free speech as if it were composed of only one element: freedom to *speak*. But there is a second element which is equally important: freedom to *listen*. Cline suggests that "Great artistic freedom would exist [given his brand of censorship] but material that is exploitive or destructive would be limited. In no way would expression of *ideas,* regardless of worth, or nonworth, heretical or conventional, be limited." But Cline does not consider the right that citizens of a free society have to listen to (or view) whatever material they choose. He assumes that audiences, as potential viewers of media violence and pornography, should not have the right to act as their own censors.

Further, he fails to distinguish between *types* of threats when he asserts that the line of censorship "needs to be drawn for the same reason we need to control airborne pollutants, excessive noise, heroin traffic, and other social dangers — for the welfare of the citizenry." Is it reasonable to lump all these "social dangers" together? The reasoning here is not valid, for individuals have no *choice* when they are exposed to airborne pollutants or excessive noise; clearly, these dangers should be restricted through legislation. Concerning drugs, the issue is less clear. No reasonable person will defend the use of heroin as a narcotic. But if we are discussing "social dangers" on the level of pornography, then a milder narcotic like marijuana would seem more analogous. If this drug were legalized, would individuals lose all sense of restraint and become "dope fiends"? Cline would have to say yes, since he assumes throughout his article that individuals will become corrupted if given the chance to do so. This seems a dreary, hopeless view of human potential.

In his conclusion, Cline turns his argument for censorship into a crusader-like defense of Western society. While one may agree with his position that "pornography and media violence assault taboos . . . that are intrinsic to the social order," it is somewhat more difficult to believe his suggestion that these assaults come only from "nihilists and totalitarians" who are "enemies of our kind of society." Apart from the unwarranted categorizing of all of his readers into an amorphous "us," the *us* versus *them* reasoning of this argument dangerously converts the procensorship position into a defense of civilization itself. Indeed, defending "our kind of society" sounds ominously like the kind of rhetoric designed to stir people to support totalitarian regimes.

When Cline implies that such nihilists and totalitarians should be denied the right of free speech, he directly contradicts the doctrine to which he referred in the beginning of his article: that open discussion is "not only a legitimate outlet for dissent, but it also reduces the likelihood of more violent forms of social protest."

6 Cline's defense of censorship is therefore problematic on two counts: (1) he assumes that people will not act in their own best interests if given the chance of practicing self-censorship; (2) he therefore turns censorship into a defense of civilization in general. If we believe ourselves to be decent, intelligent, reasonable beings, then we should leave the decision of whether or not to censor up to the individual, who should be trusted to regulate himself and his children more equitably than any censorship board — or jury. As long as media violence and pornography are not forced upon us, we should continue to exercise our freedom to *choose,* and so safeguard the right of freedom of speech guaranteed to us by the Constitution.

It's important to remember that since critiques are *personal* responses, no two people's critiques of the same article will be identical, or even very similar. In fact, the two editors of this book differed considerably in their responses to Cline's passage. The sample critique was written by one of us; had the other written the critique, it would have been considerably less negative. The other would have said that in some cases — including cases of extreme violence — the rights of society *do* take precedence over the rights of the individual, and that society *does* have the right to draw a line. And he would have agreed with Cline's assumption that under certain circumstances, individuals will indeed be corrupted — to the ultimate misfortune of society (as the alarmingly high degree of drug abuse shows). Another critic might have focused on other issues entirely, such as why Cline never considers the *reasons* that media violence and pornography are so alluring. And yet another might have zeroed in on Cline's fourfold test for questionable material, considering the differences between this test and other methods of censorship. Regardless of your critical position, you owe your reader a careful presentation of the author's position and your own, including any pertinent background information.

The numbers preceding some of the paragraphs indicate how our sample critique conforms to the six-step process. In section 1 we indicate what we are going to discuss, and in a sentence indicate our overall thesis ("But ultimately, his defense of censorship fails to convince.") In section 2, we provide some background information about censorship of films in the United States. In section 3 we indicate some of the criteria by which Cline's discussion will be assessed; these are *our* assumptions about how the issue of censorship should be discussed. Section 4 presents a summary of Cline's article. In section 5, by far the longest section and the main body of the critique, we review Cline's argument in light of the criteria we have sketched earlier. Finally, in section 6, we sum up our conclusions. Note finally, that in following this outline, we have answered many of the questions we posed earlier about the subject of a critique: its nature, its significance, its objectives, its appeal, its assumptions, and its validity.

The Presidency: A Practice Unit for Summary, Synthesis, and Critique

The reading selections in this unit on the Presidency are typical of those in the other units of this book. First, they deal with a subject that you might study in depth in another course, such as political science or American history. Second, these selections are closely related to one another; as you read them you should be able to perceive relationships and later to express them in writing.

In the preceding unit, we introduced the techniques of summary, synthesis, and critique and demonstrated how these techniques could be applied to brief excerpts from various passages in this book. Here, we will suggest how these techniques can be applied to longer passages, all on the same general subject. In this unit we will not provide sample summaries, syntheses, or critiques. Rather, it will be for you to write after we have suggested ways of approaching the various assignments.

SUMMARY

Read the following passage by John Sears, former campaign manager for President Ronald Reagan. It was written shortly after Reagan's election but before his inauguration.

PRESIDENT REAGAN

John Sears

Ronald Reagan, son of a shoe salesman from Tampico, Illinois, is now   1
the president-elect of the United States. That's pretty good for a guy
who would have settled for being the play-by-play man for the Chicago Cubs. Today, Reagan has everyone on his side. But what kind of
a president will he be?

Every four years, men issue self-serving statements aimed at   2
convincing the public they are qualified to be president. The truth is
there is no way to become qualified to be president except by holding
the job, and as Jimmy Carter can now attest, the price of gaining this
experience may be political defeat.

We have had only three outstanding presidents in the less than   3
200 years we have held elections: George Washington, who gave the
office an identity somewhere between that of king and prime minister; Abraham Lincoln, who, in order to save the Union, took unto the
office powers that it didn't have and were forbidden to it by the
Constitution; and Franklin Roosevelt, who molded the presidency
into an effective tool for coping with America's international responsibilities. There were four other men who fought the office to a little
better than a tie (Andrew Jackson, Theodore Roosevelt, Woodrow
Wilson, and Harry Truman), but because they lacked wisdom, or
sought refuge in arrogance, or failed to maintain their touch with the
people, or served during a time when change was more difficult, they
failed to realize its full potential. All the other thirty-one men who
have held office were engulfed by it.

Ronald Reagan now becomes the oldest of the 39 men to hold   4
this unique position. Whether he becomes one of the few successes or
joins the many failures depends first on whether he possesses the
qualities that the 7 shared and the 31 lacked.

Self-Knowledge

Since the primary prerequisite for handling the presidency is to   5
ignore the immensity of it, a president must find the confidence to do
so in self-knowledge. In a strange way, a man must have already
survived some experience that tested his self-doubt in order to
achieve the inner strength necessary to cope with the presidency.

Harry Truman was a failure for the first 50 years of his life; it   6
never bothered him that he might fail as president. He'd already
failed; he wasn't afraid of it.

Franklin Roosevelt lost the use of his legs to a child's disease. This   7
patrician, this snob, crawled on his belly until he could hoist himself
up on braces. The presidency never had a chance of beating him; he
dominated it. He had it licked every time he got up on his feet.

Abraham Lincoln never had a proper education. Every time a ray   8
of happiness seemed ready to shine on him, he'd lose an election, fall
into debt, or someone close to him would die. The politicians laughed
at him. But by his essential patience and devotion, by the very manner
of his life and even his death, there was no greater human being than
Lincoln; this country bumpkin who had known such misery bent the
presidency to his own persuasion. We don't really remember *President*
Lincoln; we remember *Lincoln;* Lincoln knew who he was. The presidency wasn't big enough for him.

Reagan knows himself better than most presidents, and he has   9
kept his identity separate from politics. He doesn't really enjoy talking
about politics. He'd rather talk about Hollywood or the Screen Actors

Guild. He's proud of having been an actor, and the very fact that he may always be more proud of this accomplishment gives him a fighting chance to be a good president.

People who have been close to Reagan know that in private 10 conversation he constantly harks back to his life in the movie industry and as a union official and politician during his Hollywood years. It is his real identity, the self he has neither lost nor abandoned and from which he truly speaks as a man. Reagan knows who he is, and therefore he possesses the first prerequisite for being a good president.

acting His life in the movie industry

Empathy

Once the election is over, a president must quickly realize that he 11 owes his fidelity to *all* the people, most especially those who didn't vote for him. Empathy allows a president to be trusted. It is the mechanism for achieving consensus. Leadership is a combination of convincing people that you know what their circumstances are and that you are a fair person. Empathy is a necessary ingredient of both requirements.

Most of our better presidents learned to empathize through suf- 12 fering personal tragedy or failure. The man who has gained success too easily finds it difficult to lead. There is something about losing and coming back from it that burns character into a man's soul, breeds confidence without arrogance, and makes a man believable when he talks about problems. You can tell if a president knows what he's talking about: He's got lines in his face, his voice is controlled, his words are compassionate. Presidents always try to act as though they know what they're talking about. Only a few really do.

Reagan is a man for whom advancement in life has come easily. 13 Good looks, charm, and simply being friendly to people have taken him a long way. Although the public record is obviously not the last word, it seems that only two events in Reagan's life were the source of any anxiety: His father had a drinking problem, and his first marriage, to Jane Wyman, ended in divorce.

But these were not things that Reagan felt responsible for. While 14 they obviously took a toll on him personally, in the end he could throw them off and place the blame elsewhere; they had no lasting effect on him. They were not akin to Truman's lifetime of failure, Franklin Roosevelt's loss of the use of his legs, Jackson's muddled personal life, or Teddy Roosevelt's conquering of physical weakness and the death of his young bride.

Finding the requisite empathy for the millions of people for 15 whom life has not flowed so well will be a major problem for Reagan. In a way, the good life for which Reagan often expresses his gratitude in private and the good fortune that has catapulted him to the pinnacle of politics will be his greatest enemies in office. Unfortunately, the only way to gain empathy is to suffer true adversity. If this must be done in office, then the possibilities are good that we all will suffer.

Strength in Decision-Making

The good presidents we have had have known what they wanted   16
to do and then, by the force of their will, made it happen. The office demands decisions, and not to make them is a worse offense than being wrong. The presidency is what the people look to for example in finding the will to make difficult decisions in their own lives. When the president seems immobile, the country is.

To a large degree, Reagan sounds as if he knows where he is   17
going. Often the perception of action is even more valuable than the fact, so he starts out in decent shape. But this decision-making function deserves close examination.

If you're an actor, you get up in the middle of the night to go to   18
work. Your place of business is a set designed to look real. You get into a costume, people bring you coffee, you're made up. A crew in charge of cameras, lighting, scripts, and other details moves about. You don't question what they're doing. Someone explains today's scene. You perform. Then you do the same thing over and over again until the director is satisfied. Critics ultimately review the picture. You become used to receiving the credit or taking the blame for a product that was not wholly yours.

Presidents are writers, directors, producers, and actors rolled   19
into one. They're the whole show. They take advice, but only at their own risk. It's their own neck, nobody else's. Just as an actor can't blame a poor performance on poor direction, a president can't blame his foreign policy on the secretary of state. There's no way to hide.

Reagan is comfortable with the essential responsibility of the   20
presidency. He is prepared by the discipline of his former profession to let the critics judge his performance. But can he adjust to a situation where there are no retakes, where others will be looking for him to describe the scene? And can he also play the role that is now demanded of him?

I have been asked many times how Reagan goes about making a   21
decision. The answer is that his decisions rarely originate with him. He is an endorser. It is fair to say that on some occasions he is presented with options and selects one, but it is also true that in other instances he simply looks to someone to tell him what to do.

It is this endorsing process that accounts for the difference be-   22
tween Reagan's tough-sounding campaign stances and his more moderate record as governor of California. The stump speeches are Reagan the performer playing to a known audience and sending the

crowd away with its money's worth. As governor, there was no crowd, merely decisions to be made, only a few of which were exciting. Reagan sat with his California Cabinet more as an equal than as its leader. Once consensus was arrived at or conflict resolved, he emerged as the spokesman, as the performer.

It didn't bother him that many decisions reached during his 23 governorship were in severe conflict with his campaign oratory. While he was running for governor, one of his pledges was to hold the line on state taxes; one of his first acts as governor was to raise taxes. Reagan sees no conflict in this; it simply had to be done. His advisers had no option that would allow the pledge to be kept.

I would point out that there are indeed limits to the advice that 24 Reagan will accept. Had his director in *Bedtime for Bonzo* demanded that he play a pivotal scene in the nude, he would have refused. If nuclear war were suggested as one option to President Reagan, he'd pick something short of it. If his advisers are adequate, there is nothing to fear from President Reagan.

But he can be guided, and presidents who are too easily guided 25 run the risk of losing the confidence of the people. This was one of President Carter's problems; people didn't think he was in charge.

Indeed, this is the difference between being governor of Califor- 26 nia and being president. It's not just that the job is bigger; more, it's that you must dominate it. You don't come to terms with the presidency; you grab it by the neck and you never let go.

This is not to say that Reagan's decision-making process won't 27 work. Major contributions from his advisers won't necessarily deprive his administration of the possibility of having a direction, of being decisive, and of providing the country with leadership. Reagan's essential value has always been as the "out-front" person willing to take the credit or the blame for what has been a combined effort.

Reagan possesses other qualities that will help him be a good 28 president. He is a delegator. All of our presidents since Kennedy have tried to hold the power of the office close to them, thus wasting most of it. Reagan receives information best in conversation with his advisers and doesn't encourage the mindless transfer of knowledge by sterile memorandums. Paper cannot talk back, cannot be questioned, and cannot truly reflect the contours of any human problem.

A Reagan administration can go a long way toward restoring the 29 confidence of those who look to us to maintain order in the world, simply because Reagan is perceived as a stronger man than Carter. During the campaign, Reagan developed a personal relationship with Henry Kissinger, and even if Dr. Kissinger is not included in the first wave of Reagan-administration appointees, I expect that his advice will be sought often. On the domestic front, the country is ready for some original approaches to the economy, the energy problem, job creation, and urban deterioration. For some time, the people have been willing to move away from totally federal solutions to complex domestic problems. The Reagan election is more a message to change domestic policy than a signal to alter our foreign relations.

Don't expect President Reagan to embark on any foreign trips in   30
the first year of his administration. Ronald Reagan, being a delegator and believing that good administration calls for relying on advisers, will not rush to exercise personal diplomacy. He has never had great exposure in world politics, never enjoyed the perspective of foreigners, and knows that he must first acquire some familiarity with the foreign-policy field before putting his personal stamp on this country's foreign relations.

Most of the upper-level appointees to the new administration will   31
be drawn from the ranks of experienced participants in the Ford and Nixon years. Such men as George Shultz, Alexander Haig, John Connally, William Simon, Caspar Weinberger, Alan Greenspan, and Arthur Burns can be expected to be included in a Reagan presidency. The Republican establishment may not be as creative as some critics would like, but after the chaotic Carter years, the people should feel reassured that the government is functioning and problems are being addressed in an orderly fashion. One of Carter's biggest mistakes was in not calling more upon the Democratic establishment. He lost the press and then the people as the perception grew that he really didn't have qualified people to lend credibility to his decisions. . . .

Soon, Ronald Reagan will lose touch with what he has known of   32
the people, he will hear mainly good news, and even his friends will be reluctant to criticize him. Then he will have only his knowledge of himself to fall back on and his instincts in choosing his advisers. Soon he will grasp the size of the job he has won and wonder why he ever spent the last twelve years of his life seeking it. He will look out from the rowboat and see no land, only the emptiness of the sea, and realize he has only himself to rely on. Then we will find out whether he can row the boat, and we can measure him against the other 38 men who have tried. We all must hope that he responds. He may not notice, but we're all in the boat with him.

How would you go about preparing a summary of this passage? Let's proceed through the six-step process to see what would happen.

1   After a careful first reading, reread the passage, alert for the sections or the stages of thought by which it progresses. Here, the writer has already been of some help, since the article is clearly divided into sections, three of which are subtitled: "Self-Knowledge," "Empathy," and "Strength in Decision-Making." The first four paragraphs form the introduction; the last five paragraphs form the conclusion. (It would be possible, however, to

consider only the last paragraph as a conclusion, and the preceding four as another untitled section dealing with Reagan's "other qualities.")

2   Now label the main points of each section and indicate (perhaps by underlining) the key supporting information. Let's consider the first two sections as an example. What are the main points of the introduction? Of the thirty-eight men who have been president, only seven have succeeded; the others, who lacked the essential qualities of successful presidents, were "engulfed" by the office. Does Ronald Reagan have the qualities necessary to keep from being engulfed?

A marginal note doesn't have to be very long, of course. All you need is a brief notation such as, "Only 7 of 38 presidents succeeded. Does Reagan have qualities for success?" Although there are several other ideas in the introductory paragraphs, they are all subordinate to this one. If you want to mention particular supporting information in your summary (such as the three "outstanding" presidents), underline this information in the passage or write it in the margin.

What are the main points of the next section, on self-knowledge? In the order in which they are developed, they are the following: Successful presidents possess a self-knowledge based on experiences that have tested their self-doubt. This was true of presidents Truman, Franklin Roosevelt, and Lincoln. Reagan's experiences in the movie industry have given him a good measure of self-knowledge, as well as an identity separate from politics. Your marginal notation would be much briefer: perhaps "Self-knowledge from experience — Truman, FDR, Lincoln/ Reagan's movie past has given him identity."

3   After going through the entire passage this way, look back at your marginal notations and your underlining. Then on a separate sheet of paper write a single sentence for each section or stage of thought. Thus, your sentence for the section we have just discussed might be: "Self-knowledge comes from testing experiences, like those of Truman, FDR, and Lincoln; Reagan's past in movies has given him an identity." This is just a slightly expanded, grammatical version of your marginal note. But the step of transferring the ideas, in your own words, onto a separate sheet of paper is an important one because it frees you from over-dependence on the original passage. Otherwise, you could find yourself writing your summary with eyes darting back and forth between summary and passage; and you will tend to rely too heavily on the phrasing of the original.

4   Your next step is to write a topic sentence. It should express the central idea of the passage as a whole and indicate the relationships among the subsidiary ideas. A possible topic sentence for your summary would be: "Ronald Reagan has a good chance of succeeding as president of the United States because he has demonstrated in his earlier career several of the essential qualities of successful presidents." First, this sentence indicates the central idea of the passage. Second, it indicates that the rest of the summary will be devoted to an analysis of the "several . . . essential

qualities" of successful presidents as well as of Reagan's earlier career. (Note that in the topic sentence you could not accurately claim that Reagan has *all* of the qualities of successful presidents, because Sears is not sure that the Reagan of 1980 has a sufficient measure of empathy.)

5   Now write the remainder of this summary. Take the ideas one at a time, in the order in which they occur in the original passage. You can use the sentences you wrote during step 3 as a basis for your summary, but you will have to revise them so that they read more smoothly and so that they are clearly connected to the sentences before and after.

6   Finally, revise the summary, inserting transitional words and phrases where necessary.

DESCRIPTION SYNTHESIS

Read the following two passages:

PRESIDENTIAL TYPES
Louis Koenig

Without undue violence to history, it is possible to divide the Presidents the United States has had into three recurrent types with a view to assessing their suitability as models for the contemporary Chief Executive who is both strong and responsive to democratic constraints.   1

The most numerous type is one that might be styled a "literalist" President. Madison, Buchanan, Taft, and, to a degree, Eisenhower are of this school. The mark of the literalist President, as his title suggests, is close obedience to the letter of the Constitution. If anything, he is apt to veer too far toward the democratic end of the spectrum and permit the undue sacrifice of power and strength. Taft, who, with Buchanan, was the most literal of the Presidents, formulated the operative belief of the literalists: 2

> The true view of the Executive function is . . . that the President can exercise no power which cannot be fairly and reasonably traced to some specific grant of power or justly implied and included within such express grant as proper and necessary to its exercise. Such specific grant must be either in the Federal Constitution or in an act of Congress passed in pursuance thereof. There is no undefined residuum of power which he can exercise because it seems to him to be in the public interest.

The Taft-like President tends also to live by the Whig assumption 3
that the legislative power is popular and the executive monarchical.
He is respectful, even deferential, to Congress. "My duty," James
Buchanan was prone to say, "is to execute the laws . . . and not my
individual opinions." When Congress did nothing in the face of
gathering rebellion, Buchanan too did nothing. In a later day, President
Eisenhower is reported sometimes to have remarked privately to
his aides that he felt called upon to "restore" to Congress powers that
Franklin Roosevelt had "usurped." In public pronouncement and
personal act, Eisenhower was respectful of Congressional prerogative
and the doctrine of separation of powers. "Our very form of Government,"
he declared to the Convention of the National Young Republican
Organization in 1953, "is in peril unless each branch willingly
accepts and discharges its own clear responsibilities — and respects
the rights and responsibilities of the others."

The Taft-like President makes little use of his independent 4
powers or prerogative (his powers, for example, as Commander-in-
Chief and as implied in the executive power clause). He exerts political
pressure sparingly. Symptomatic of his approach is James Bryce's
observation that the typical nineteenth-century President's communications
to Congress were so perfunctory that "the expression of his
wishes . . . in messages has not necessarily any more effect on Congress
than an article in a prominent party newspaper."

The literalist President has little taste for innovation in social 5
policy. He is nostalgic for the past and urges it be used as a blueprint
for the future. He feels, as Taft did, that the bane of government is
"ill-digested legislation" and that "real progress in government must
be by slow stages." It is a view that Theodore Roosevelt found upheld
in society by "most able lawyers who are past middle age" and "large
numbers of well-meaning, respectable citizens."

The Presidency in the manner of Taft and Buchanan is, on its 6
face, inadequate for the necessities of the contemporary Presidency
faced with grave social and environmental problems at home and the
dynamics of foreign affairs, with opportunities of detente with old
opponents in order to provide good offices for building peace among
warring nations, for disarmament and expanded trade. The past,
which the literalist Presidency venerates, can be only a partial and
imperfect guide to the present and future. It excessively neglects the
President's independent powers, which again and again have been a
constructive force in times of crisis and change. Its neglect of politics
abdicates action to passivity and, as the experience of many nineteenth-century
Presidents proves, can thoroughly reduce the President
from leader to clerk. The best proof of the inadequacy of the
literalist model is the abandonment of its key concepts by Presidents
who once had taken them up. Cleveland at first proposed to be a

literalist President, spurning to use patronage and pressure upon Congress and declaring, "I did not come here to legislate." But when Congress blocked the bills he was driven to sponsor, his attitude changed, and he went furiously to work to win votes by promising jobs. Dwight Eisenhower, for all his professed deference to Congress and distaste for politics, in time did push his legislative program, and his campaigning in Congressional elections was on a scale comparable to Franklin Roosevelt's.

At the opposite end of the spectrum from the literalist President   7 is the "strong" President, typified by Washington, Jackson, Lincoln, Wilson, and the Roosevelts. He generally, although not exclusively, flourishes in times of crisis and change — during a war or a depression — and when political movements such as progressivism are at their crests. He interprets his powers with liberality; he is a precedent-maker and precedent-breaker to the point where the legality of his acts is questioned or disproved. His bible is the "stewardship theory" of Theodore Roosevelt, who felt that it was the President's "duty to do anything that the needs of the nation demanded unless such action was forbidden by the Constitution or by the laws." "I acted for the public welfare," Roosevelt said. "I acted for the common well-being of all our people." But the peril of the strong Presidency, as recent experience unfortunately illuminates, is its penchant for straying into illegality, its thrust beyond normal constraints, its excessive infringement of democratic values and processes. The march of its logic is toward the dictatorial, and the effort to keep it within acceptable democratic bounds imposes extra strains on the vigor and competence of surrogate institutions — Congress, the courts, the parties, interest groups, and organized opinion.

In his most fruitful moments, the strong President provides   8 leadership, in Franklin Roosevelt's words, "alert and sensitive to change," which in the Jefferson-Jackson tradition means that the government must act positively in promoting a good life, and in the Wilson tradition means that the nation cannot shun or escape its obligations of world leadership. His orientation is less to the past than to the future, which he approaches with hope and plan. He is skillful politically and is concerned more with substance than with form. When necessary, he resorts to bold action, whether economic, social, diplomatic, or military, which he does not avoid for the sake of containing the national debt. He accepts and abides a strong Congress but purposefully uses the lawmaking process. He has the gift of inspiring and rallying the people with messages that mix practicality and prophecy. In his view, the President as a person must dominate the Presidency as an institution. He, a fleeting political figure, must bend, divert, and lead the cumbrous bureaucratic executive branch according to his purpose. But he must walk a tightrope in order not to slip into behavior that violates or jeopardizes democratic processes.

Between the strong and literalist Presidents is a middle ground that many Chief Executives have occupied; it unites elements of both extremes. This middle ground need not now detain us. The magnitude of problems and opportunities at home and abroad makes clear that only one of the three available Presidential types is suitable for the future. For the United States to best cope with problems and capitalize on opportunities requires a Presidency that is continuously strong, rather than intermittently, as a major source of constructive accomplishment to deal positively with society's problems and to bring the greatest good to the greatest number of people. On the other hand, as the Watergate experience and the excesses of Presidential war-making illuminate in clearest hieroglyphics, that all may understand, the strong Presidency bears the risk of antidemocratic behavior. The risk must be managed and overcome by the enhancement of democratic safeguards capable of containing substantial Presidential power within limits compatible with a free society. Most of the Framers of the Constitution — though not all — were confident that they had mastered the problem of the strong Presidency coexisting harmoniously with human liberty. Since their time, the adequacy of their solution has sometimes come into question, especially after the Watergate tragedy. In the 1970s and beyond, a central problem of American politics and political science, if not *the* central problem, is the coupling of the strong Presidency with the institutions and processes of democracy in ways that are enduring and safe for liberty.

FOUR TYPES OF PRESIDENTIAL CHARACTER

James D. Barber

The first baseline in defining Presidential types is *activity-passivity*. How much energy does the man invest in his Presidency? Lyndon Johnson went at his day like a human cyclone, coming to rest long after the sun went down. Calvin Coolidge often slept eleven hours a night and still needed a nap in the middle of the day. In between the Presidents array themselves on the high or low side of the activity line.

The second baseline is *positive-negative affect* toward one's activ-

From the book *The Presidential Character*, 2nd Edition by James David Barber. © 1977 by James David Barber. Published by Prentice-Hall, Inc., Englewood Cliffs, N.J. 07632. Reprinted by permission of the publisher.

ity — that is, how he feels about what he does. Relatively speaking, does he seem to experience his political life as happy or sad, enjoyable or discouraging, positive or negative in its main effect. The feeling I am after here is not grim satisfaction in a job well done, not some philosophical conclusion. The idea is this: is he someone who, on the surfaces we can see, gives forth the feeling that he has *fun* in political life? Franklin Roosevelt's Secretary of War, Henry L. Stimson wrote that the Roosevelts "not only understood the *use* of power, they knew the *enjoyment* of power, too. . . . Whether a man is burdened by power or enjoys power; whether he is trapped by responsibility or made free by it; whether he is moved by other people and outer forces or moves them — that is the essence of leadership."

The positive-negative baseline, then, is a general symptom of the   3
fit between the man and his experience, a kind of register of *felt* satisfaction.

Why might we expect these two simple dimensions to outline the   4
main character types? Because they stand for two central features of anyone's orientation toward life. In nearly every study of personality, some form of the active-passive contrast is critical; the general tendency to act or be acted upon is evident in such concepts as dominance-submission, extraversion-introversion, aggression-timidity, attack-defense, fight-flight, engagement-withdrawal, approach-avoidance. In everyday life we sense quickly the general energy output of the people we deal with. Similarly we catch on fairly quickly to the affect dimension — whether the person seems to be optimistic or pessimistic, hopeful or skeptical, happy or sad. The two baselines are clear and they are also independent of one another: all of us know people who are very active but seem discouraged, others who are quite passive but seem happy, and so forth. The activity baseline refers to what one does, the affect baseline to how one feels about what he does.

Both are crude clues to character. They are leads into four basic   5
character patterns long familiar in psychological research. In summary form, these are the main configurations:

Active-positive: There is a congruence, a consistency, between   6
much activity and the enjoyment of it, indicating relatively high self-esteem and relative success in relating to the environment. The man shows an orientation toward productiveness as a value and an ability to use his styles flexibly, adaptively, suiting the dance to the music. He sees himself as developing over time toward relatively well defined personal goals — growing toward his image of himself as he might yet be. There is an emphasis on rational mastery, on using the brain to move the feet. This may get him into trouble; he may fail to take

account of the irrational in politics. Not everyone he deals with sees things his way and he may find it hard to understand why.

Active-negative: The contradiction here is between relatively in- 7 tense effort and relatively low emotional reward for that effort. The activity has a compulsive quality, as if the man were trying to make up for something or to escape from anxiety into hard work. He seems ambitious, striving upward, power-seeking. His stance toward the environment is aggressive and he has a persistent problem in managing his aggressive feelings. His self-image is vague and discontinuous. Life is a hard struggle to achieve and hold power, hampered by the condemnations of a perfectionistic conscience. Active-negative types pour energy into the political system, but it is an energy distorted from within.

Passive-positive: This is the receptive, compliant, other-directed 8 character whose life is a search for affection as a reward for being agreeable and cooperative rather than personally assertive. The contradiction is between low self-esteem (on grounds of being unlovable, unattractive) and a superficial optimism. A hopeful attitude helps dispel doubt and elicits encouragement from others. Passive-positive types help soften the harsh edges of politics. But their dependence and the fragility of their hopes and enjoyments make disappointment in politics likely.

Passive-negative: The factors are consistent — but how are we to 9 account for the man's *political* role-taking? Why is someone who does little in politics and enjoys it less there at all? The answer lies in the passive-negative's character-rooted orientation toward doing dutiful service; this compensates for low self-esteem based on a sense of uselessness. Passive-negative types are in politics because they think they ought to be. They may be well adapted to certain nonpolitical roles, but they lack the experience and flexibility to perform effectively as political leaders. Their tendency is to withdraw, to escape from the conflict and uncertainty of politics by emphasizing vague principles (especially prohibitions) and procedural arrangements. They become guardians of the right and proper way, above the sordid politicking of lesser men.

Active-positive Presidents want most to achieve results. Active- 10 negatives aim to get and keep power. Passive-positives are after love. Passive-negatives emphasize their civic virtue. The relation of activity to enjoyment in a President thus tends to outline a cluster of characteristics, to set apart the adapted from the compulsive, compliant, and withdrawn types.

The first four Presidents of the United States, conveniently, ran 11 through this gamut of character types. (Remember, we are talking about tendencies, broad directions; no individual man exactly fits a category.) George Washington — clearly the most important President in the pantheon — established the fundamental legitimacy of an American government at a time when this was a matter in considerable question. Washington's dignity, judiciousness, his aloof air of reserve and dedication to duty fit the passive-negative or withdrawing type best. Washington did not seek innovation, he sought stability. He longed to retire to Mount Vernon, but fortunately was persuaded to stay on through a second term, in which, by rising above the political conflict between Hamilton and Jefferson and inspiring confidence in his own integrity, he gave the nation time to develop the organized means for peaceful change.

John Adams followed, a dour New England Puritan, much given to work and worry, an impatient and irascible man — an active-negative President, a compulsive type. Adams was far more partisan than Washington; the survival of the system through his Presidency demonstrated that the nation could tolerate, for a time, domination by one of its nascent political parties. As President, an angry Adams brought the United States to the brink of war with France, and presided over the new nation's first experiment in political repression: the Alien and Sedition Acts, forbidding, among other things, unlawful combinations "with intent to oppose any measure or measures of the government of the United States," or "any false, scandalous, and malicious writing or writings against the United States, or the President of the United States, with intent to defame . . . or to bring them or either of them, into contempt or disrepute." 12

Then came Jefferson. He too had his troubles and failures — in the design of national defense, for example. As for his Presidential character (only one element in success or failure), Jefferson was clearly active-positive. A child of the Enlightenment, he applied his reason to organizing connections with Congress aimed at strengthening the more popular forces. A man of catholic interests and delightful humor, Jefferson combined a clear and open vision of what the country could be with a profound political sense, expressed in his famous phrase, "Every difference of opinion is not a difference of principle." 13

14

The fourth President was James Madison, "Little Jemmy," the constitutional philosopher thrown into the White House at a time of great international turmoil. Madison comes closest to the passive-positive, or compliant, type; he suffered from irresolution, tried to compromise his way out, and gave in too readily to the "warhawks" urging combat with Britain. The nation drifted into war, and Madison wound up ineptly commanding his collection of amateur generals in the streets of Washington. General Jackson's victory at New Orleans saved the Madison administration's historical reputation; but he left the Presidency with the United States close to bankruptcy and secession.

These four Presidents — like all Presidents — were persons try-   15
ing to cope with the roles they had won by using the equipment they had built over a lifetime. The President is not some shapeless organism in a flood of novelties, but a man with a memory in a system with a history. Like all of us, he draws on his past to shape his future. The pathetic hope that the White House will turn a Caligula into a Marcus Aurelius is as naive as the fear that ultimate power inevitably corrupts. The problem is to understand — and to state understandably — what in the personal past foreshadows the Presidential future.

A description synthesis based on these two passages would explain two different ways of classifying presidents into types. As in the example of the description synthesis on the depression in the previous unit, this synthesis would be organized more or less as two summaries connected by a suitable transition. We say "more or less" because, strictly speaking, you wouldn't have to write a formal summary of each piece, in the sense that you would have to cover *all* of the main points in the order that they occur. For example, you could write a synthesis of the information in these passages without covering the final page or so in Barber's piece, in which he shows how the first four presidents exemplified each of his four types. But of course you would have to summarize accurately the essential characteristics of each of the presidential types discussed by Koenig and Barber.

Follow the six-step process.

1 and **2**   After reading the passages carefully, reread them, this time labeling for main ideas and key terms. It is not necessary for this synthesis, as it is for a summary, to isolate the separate sections of which the passages are composed. What is more important is that you determine the central idea in each passage. In "Presidential Types," the central idea is that there have been three types of presidents: the "literalist" president, the strong president, and the middle-of-the-road president; of these, the strong president is the type most needed by the nation. What is the central idea of Barber's passage?

3   Next, determine the relationship between these two passages. The clearest basis of relationship is that both passages present types of presidents. Thus, the most obvious format for a description synthesis would be to first discuss Koenig's passage and then, after a suitable transition, Barber's.

4   Write your thesis sentence. One possibility: "Political scientists Louis Koenig and James Barber have each devised ways of classifying presidents into types."

The skeleton outline would look like this:

Thesis: Political scientists Louis Koenig and James Barber have each
devised ways of classifying presidents into types.
Summary of Koenig
    transition
Summary of Barber

☐5 and ☐6   Now, *write this synthesis.*

DEFINITION SYNTHESIS

Read the following passage:

EVALUATING PRESIDENTS
Clinton Rossiter

We cannot come to close grips with the modern Presidency as an   1
institution or as a force in history unless we talk in highly personal
terms about the men who have held it. Woodrow Wilson once remarked that "governments are what politicians make them, and it is
easier to write of the President than of the Presidency." . . .

Let us place ourselves, if we can, on the throne of posterity, and   2
from that serene point of vantage let us look back objectively, as we
expect our great-grandchildren to look back, at the achievements of
each of these men.

"Ranking the Presidents" has always been a Favorite Indoor   3
Sport of history-minded Americans, and I see no reason why we
should not play it with Roosevelt, Truman, and Eisenhower as happily as we play it with Jackson, Cleveland, and Harding. I am especially concerned to anticipate the opinions of our descendants about
the "greatness" of our last three Presidents. Will Roosevelt be ranked
with Lincoln or Wilson? Will Truman be compared with Johnson or
Theodore Roosevelt? Will the old soldier named Eisenhower be
placed just below the old soldier named Washington or just above the
old soldier named Grant? The answers to these questions lie in still
other questions which historians like to ask about Presidents long
dead. I have made a rough content analysis of more than one hundred serious presidential biographies, and I have found the same
standards applied again and again. . . .

In what sort of times did he live? A man cannot possibly be   4
judged a great President unless he holds office in great times. Wash-

From *The American Presidency,* Revised Edition, © 1960 by Clinton Rossiter.
Reprinted by permission of Harcourt Brace Jovanovich, Inc.

ington's eminence arose from the founding of the republic, Jackson's from the upsurge of democracy, Lincoln's from the Civil War, and Wilson's from World War I. We have no right even to consider a man for membership in this exclusive club unless he, too, presides over the nation in challenging years. This standard may work unfairly on Presidents who live under sunny skies, but that is the way that history is written.

If the times were great, how bravely and imaginatively did he   5
bear the burden of extraordinary responsibility? A successful President must do a great deal more than stand quiet watch over the lottery of history: he must be a forceful leader — of Congress, the administration, and the American people; he must make the hard decisions that have to be made, and make most of them correctly; he must work hard at being President and see that these decisions are carried out.

What was his philosophy of presidential power? To be a great   6
President a man must think like a great President; he must follow Theodore Roosevelt and choose to be a "Jackson-Lincoln," a man of strength and independence, rather than a "Buchanan," a deferential Whig. Indeed, if he is not widely and persistently accused in his own time of "subverting the Constitution," he may as well forget about being judged a truly eminent man by future generations.

What sort of technician was he? How efficiently did he organize   7
his energies, direct his lieutenants, and thus exercise his powers? Lincoln could be an indifferent administrator and yet a great President, but the rise of the modern state has made it impossible for an inefficient President to discharge even a fraction of his duties with much hope of success.

What men did he call on for help? Did he, like Washington, have   8
his Jefferson and Hamilton? Did he, like Lincoln, have his Seward and Chase? Did he have his great lieutenants, and his efficient sergeants, too? If the modern Presidency, as I have insisted, is irrevocably institutionalized, the modern President must do even better than Washington and Lincoln on this score, for he can no longer expect to accomplish much of anything unless he surrounds himself with able technicians as well as wise statesmen and shrewd politicians.

What manner of man was he beneath the trappings of office? We   9
remember a President as much for his quirks and quips as for his deeds and decisions. If he is not the sort of man around whose person legends will arise in profusion, he will surely not meet the final test of presidential greatness: to be enshrined as a folk hero in the American consciousness.

What was his influence on the Presidency? We are not likely to   10
rate a President highly if he weakens the office through cowardice or neglect. A place at the top of the ladder is reserved only for those

Presidents who have added to the office by setting precedents for other Presidents to follow.

Finally, what was his influence on history? In particular, did he inspire or represent, and find words to explain, some earth-shaking readjustment in the pattern of American society? More than one President has been granted a high place in history because he sensed the direction of American democracy in his times and bent or hastened its onward course — or even, as in the case of Theodore Roosevelt, confined himself largely to pointing out the way that his successors would have to travel.   11

You have now read enough passages on the presidency to be able to write a definition synthesis, one that attempts a definition of a successful president. Rossiter in this passage, Sears in his article on Reagan, Koenig and Barber in their descriptions of presidential types, all discuss qualities that they believe successful or great presidents must have. For Sears, as you have seen, a successful president must have self-knowledge, must have empathy, and must show strength in decision-making. For Koenig, a successful president must be a strong president. Barber appears to believe that active-positive presidents have the greatest chance of success (although we must keep in mind that he classified Washington, one of the greatest presidents, as a passive-negative type). Clinton Rossiter believes that a great president must live in challenging times, must exercise his responsibilities with bravery and imagination, must be a good administrator, and must have a powerful influence on history.

Notice that some of Rossiter's criteria for greatness tie in with the criteria of other political scientists. Thus, when he asks, "What was his philosophy of presidential power?" he answers, in effect, by saying that he must be one of Koenig's "strong" presidents. And his question about what "manner of man" the president is ties in with Barber's analysis of presidential character.

Since you have already made careful notes on these articles for your summary and description synthesis, writing a definition synthesis should not be difficult. Follow the six-step process as in the model on pages 16–17 of Chapter 1. Handle it in essentially the same way you handled the description synthesis: summarize the key points of each passage and join the summaries with appropriate transitions. *Remember to include a thesis sentence in the first paragraph.* Avoid overgeneral thesis sentences, such as "Political scientists have different ideas about the qualities that make for successful presidents." A better, more specific one for these passages might be: "Political scientists agree that a successful president must have a strong personality, but they differ about other necessary qualities." A thesis sentence like this, in fact, would allow you to avoid writing simply a series of connected summaries. The first part of the synthesis could be devoted to a consideration of the president as a strong personality, as discussed in each passage. Then, the synthesis could take up each passage in turn as it considers the other necessary qualities of success.

Your skeleton outline might look like this:

Thesis: Political scientists agree that a successful president must have a strong personality, but they differ about other necessary qualities.

Strong personality
  a. Koenig
  b. Barber
  c. Rossiter
  d. Sears

Other criteria for success
  a. Barber
  b. Rossiter
  c. Sears

Now write your synthesis.

EXAMPLE SYNTHESIS

Recall Koenig's general comments on the two main presidential types, the "literalist" and the "strong" presidents. Now read the following passages:

THE "STRONG" EXECUTIVE
Theodore Roosevelt

. . . I regard the memories of Washington and Lincoln as priceless   1
heritages for our people, just because they are the memories of strong
men, of men who cannot be accused of weakness or timidity, of men
who I believe were quite as strong for instance as Cromwell or Bis-
marck, and very much stronger than the Louis Napoleon type, who,
nevertheless, led careers marked by disinterestedness just as much as
by strength; who, like Timoleon and Hampden, in very deed, and not
as a mere matter of oratory or fine writing, put the public good, the
good of the people as a whole, as the first of all considerations.

Now, my ambition is that, in however small a way, the work I do   2

Theodore Roosevelt, "The 'Strong' Executive" from letter by President The-
odore Roosevelt to George Otto Trevelyan, June 19, 1908, from *Letters of
Theodore Roosevelt*, edited by Elting E. Morrison; Copyright 1952 by Elting E.
Morrison, © 1980 by Elting E. Morrison. Published by Harvard University
Press. Reprinted by permission of the publisher.

shall be along the Washington and Lincoln lines. While President I have *been* President, emphatically; I have used every ounce of power there was in the office and I have not cared a rap for the criticisms of those who spoke of my "usurpation of power"; for I knew that the talk was all nonsense and that there was no usurpation. I believe that the efficiency of this Government depends upon its possessing a strong central executive, and wherever I could establish a precedent for strength in the executive, as I did for instance as regards external affairs in the case of sending the fleet around the world,[1] taking Panama, settling affairs of Santo Domingo and Cuba; or as I did in internal affairs in settling the anthracite coal strike, in keeping order in Nevada this year when the Federation of Miners threatened anarchy, or as I have done in bringing the big corporations to book — why, in all these cases I have felt not merely that my action was right in itself, but that in showing the strength of, or in giving strength to, the executive, I was establishing a precedent of value. I believe in a strong executive; I believe in power; but I believe that responsibility should go with power, and that it is not well that the strong executive should be a perpetual executive. Above all and beyond all I believe as I have said before that the salvation of this country depends upon Washington and Lincoln representing the type of leader to which we are true. I hope that in my acts I have been a good President, a President who has deserved well of the Republic; but most of all, I believe that whatever value my service may have comes even more from what I *am* than from what I *do*. I may be mistaken, but it is my belief that the bulk of my countrymen, the men whom Abraham Lincoln called "the plain people" — the farmers, mechanics, small tradesmen, hard-working professional men — feel that I am in a peculiar sense their President, that I represent the democracy in somewhat the fashion that Lincoln did, that is, not in any demagogic way but with the sincere effort to stand for a government by the people and for the people.

---

[1] It was Theodore Roosevelt who played the greatest practical joke on Congress that any President has ever essayed: he desperately wanted to send the U.S. fleet around the world to "show the flag" and generate international prestige, but an economy-minded Congress refused an adequate appropriation. Undaunted, T. R. sent the fleet off and then, when the battlewagons were roughly half-way around the globe, mildly asked Congress if it would like to provide funds to bring the Navy home. Since the presumable alternative was to sell the ships for scrap iron in Bombay, the infuriated solons put up the money. The President's roars of laughter (T. R. had a laugh that could break glassware) were allegedly heard as far out of Washington as Alexandria, Virginia. (From *The Presidency: Documents in American Government*, edited by John H. Roche and Leonard W. Levy, published by Harcourt Brace Jovanovich, Inc., 1964. Reprinted by permission of the publisher.)

A RESTRICTED VIEW OF THE OFFICE
William Howard Taft

While it is important to mark out the exclusive field of jurisdiction of   1
each branch of the government, Legislative, Executive and Judicial, it
should be said that in the proper working of the government there
must be cooperation of all branches, and without a willingness of each
branch to perform its function, there will follow a hopeless obstruc-
tion to the progress of the whole government. Neither branch can
compel the other to affirmative action, and each branch can greatly
hinder the other in the attainment of the object of its activities and the
exercise of its discretion.

. . . The true view of the Executive function is, as I conceive it,   2
that the President can exercise no power which cannot be fairly and
reasonably traced to some specific grant of power or justly implied
and included within such express grant as proper and necessary to its
exercise. Such specific grant must be either in the Federal Constitution or in an act of Congress passed in pursuance thereof. There is no
undefined residuum of power which he can exercise because it seems
to him to be in the public interest, and there is nothing in the Neagle
case and its definition of a law of the United States, or in other
precedents, warranting such an inference. The grants of Executive
power are necessarily in general terms in order not to embarrass the
Executive within the field of action plainly marked for him, but his
jurisdiction must be justified and vindicated by affirmative constitutional or statutory provision, or it does not exist. There have not been
wanting, however, eminent men in high public office holding a different view and who have insisted upon the necessity for an undefined
residuum of Executive power in the public interest. They have not
been confined to the present generation.

. . . I may add that Mr. Roosevelt, by way of illustrating his   3
meaning as to the differing usefulness of Presidents, divides the
Presidents into two classes, and designates them as "Lincoln Presidents" and "Buchanan Presidents." In order more fully to illustrate
his division of Presidents on their merits, he places himself in the
Lincoln class of Presidents, and me in the Buchanan class. The
identification of Mr. Roosevelt with Mr. Lincoln might otherwise have
escaped notice, because there are many differences between the two,
presumably superficial, which would give the impartial student of
history a different impression. It suggests a story which a friend of

From William Howard Taft, *Our Chief Magistrate and His Powers* (New York:
Columbia University Press, 1925), pp. 138–140. Copyright 1916 by Columbia
University Press. Reprinted by permission of Columbia University Press.

mine told of his little daughter Mary. As he came walking home after a business day, she ran out from the house to greet him, all aglow with the importance of what she wished to tell him. She said, "Papa, I am the best scholar in the class." The father's heart throbbed with pleasure as he inquired, "Why, Mary, you surprise me. When did the teacher tell you? This afternoon?" "Oh, no," Mary's reply was, "the teacher didn't tell me — I just noticed it myself."

My judgment is that the view of Mr. Garfield and Mr. Roosevelt,   4
ascribing an undefined residuum of power to the President, is an unsafe doctrine and that it might lead under emergencies to results of an arbitrary character, doing irremediable injustice to private right. The mainspring of such a view is that the Executive is charged with responsibility for the welfare of all the people in a general way, that he is to play the part of a Universal Providence and set all things right, and that anything that in his judgment will help the people he ought to do, unless he is expressly forbidden not to do it. The wide field of action that this would give to the Executive one can hardly limit.

IT IS PREEMINENTLY A PLACE OF MORAL LEADERSHIP

Franklin D. Roosevelt

. . . The Presidency is not merely an administrative office. That's the   1
least of it. It is more than an engineering job, efficient or inefficient. It is preeminently a place of moral leadership. All our great Presidents were leaders of thought at times when certain historic ideas in the life of the nation had to be clarified. Washington personified the idea of federal union. Jefferson practically originated the party system as we know it by opposing the democratic theory to the republicanism of Hamilton. This theory was reaffirmed by Jackson. Two great principles of our government were forever put beyond question by Lincoln. Cleveland, coming into office following an era of great political corruption, typified rugged honesty. T. R. and Wilson were both moral leaders, each in his own way and for his own time, who used the Presidency as a pulpit.

Isn't that what the office is — a superb opportunity for reapply-   2
ing, applying in new conditions, the simple rules of human conduct we always go back to? I stress the modern application, because we are always moving on; the technical and economic environment changes,

Excerpted from "Roosevelt's View of the Big Job" by Ann O'Hare McCormack. © 1932–1960 by The New York Times Company. Reprinted by permission. This article first appeared in *The New York Times Magazine* on September 12, 1932.

and never so quickly as now. Without leadership alert and sensitive to change, we are bogged up or lose our way, as we have lost it in the past decade. . . .

Recall step 3 of the six-step process: what is the *relationship* among these three passages? Clearly, it is that they provide specific examples of the two main types Koenig discussed in general terms. It is true that Koenig also provides examples of the types he discusses; he even calls the literalist president a "Taft-like President." It is also true that the three statements by U.S. presidents are general, in that they all deal with the way in which the powers of the presidency *should* be used. Nonetheless, the most obvious way that these passages are related is that the three presidents, in these statements, reveal themselves to be examples of either the literalist or the strong presidents.

A synthesis of these passages might logically begin with a summary of Koenig's passage and proceed with a discussion of how the literalist president is exemplified by Taft and the strong president by Theodore Roosevelt and Franklin Roosevelt. You could provide quotations from the presidential statements, as well as summaries of them. On the other hand, the Koenig passage could be summarized and parts of the summary could be expanded and developed with the examples of these three presidents.

Here are two possible skeleton outlines:

1. *Thesis:* William Howard Taft is a good example of Koenig's "literalist" president, while Theodore Roosevelt and Franklin D. Roosevelt are examples of Koenig's "strong" president.

   Discussion of Koenig's types

       Example of Taft as literalist president

       Examples of Theodore Roosevelt and Franklin D. Roosevelt as strong presidents

2. *Thesis:* (Same as above)

   Discussion of Koenig's types

       Extended example of Taft as literalist president

       Extended examples of Theodore Roosevelt and Franklin Roosevelt as strong presidents

Notice that the second outline would lead to a synthesis that is a sequence of three summaries contained within another, overall summary.

Now write an example synthesis based on one of these two outlines.

Alternative Assignment

Read the 1930 Production Code in the Morality and the Movies unit, pages 92–102. In a written (example) synthesis, cite one movie you have seen recently as a good, bad, or middling example of what a film "should be," according to the 1930 Code. *You will review the movie in terms of only one section of the Code:* that is, in terms of crimes against the law *or* sex *or* vulgarity, and so on.

COMPARISON-CONTRAST SYNTHESIS

The passages we have already presented in this chapter could be used as source material for a comparison-contrast synthesis. For instance, a comparison-contrast synthesis could be written on Koenig's and Barber's classifications of presidential types.

Here is a sample outline of such a synthesis, organized by *article:*

Thesis: Louis Koenig uses political criteria to classify presidents, while James Barber uses psychological criteria.

Koenig's primarily political criteria
   transition
Barber's primarily psychological criteria

A sample outline for a comparison-contrast synthesis organized by *criteria* is as follows:

Thesis: Presidents have been classified according to how they use the powers of their office and according to how they feel about the necessity for social change.

A. *Use of power* (*criterion 1*)
   1. Types of presidents who use no more powers than are specified
     a. Koenig (literalist)
     b. Barber (passive-positive, passive-negative)
   2. Types of presidents who expand their specified powers
     a. Koenig (strong presidents)
     b. Barber (active-positive, active-negative)
B. *Social change* (*criterion 2*)
   1. Types of presidents who see little need for social change
     a. Koenig (literalist president)
     b. Barber (passive-positive, passive-negative)
   2. Types of presidents who believe in social change
     a. Koenig (strong presidents)
     b. Barber (active-positive)

The three brief presidential statements just presented could be compared and contrasted with one another, rather than discussed in terms of Koenig's general categories.

Write a comparison-contrast synthesis based on one of the two out-lines or on just the three presidential statements in this section.

Alternative Assignment

Read Charles Perrault's and Anne Sexton's versions of "Cinderella" in the chapter on Fairy Tales, pages 164 and 170. Write a comparison and contrast synthesis based on *a few* significant criteria.

ARGUMENT SYNTHESIS

Read the following description of President Franklin D. Roosevelt:

FRANKLIN D. ROOSEVELT: THE PATRICIAN AS OPPORTUNIST
Richard Hofstadter

Once during the early years of the Wilson administration Eleanor   1
Roosevelt and her husband, the Assistant Secretary of the Navy, were
lunching with Henry Adams. Roosevelt was speaking earnestly about
some governmental matter that concerned him, when his aged host
turned on him fiercely: "Young man, I have lived in this house many
years and seen the occupants of that White House across the square
come and go, and nothing that you minor officials or the occupants of
that house can do will affect the history of the world for long."

It was not often that Adams's superlative ironies were uninten-   2
tional. Although the influence of great men is usually exaggerated,
Roosevelt must be granted at least a marginal influence upon the
course of history. No personality has ever expressed the American
popular temper so articulately or with such exclusiveness. In the
Progressive era national reform leadership was divided among Theodore Roosevelt, Wilson, Bryan, and La Follette. In the age of the New
Deal it was monopolized by one man, whose passing left American
liberalism demoralized and all but helpless.

At the heart of the New Deal there was not a philosophy but a   3
temperament. The essence of this temperament was Roosevelt's
confidence that even when he was operating in unfamiliar territory he
could do no wrong, commit no serious mistakes. From the standpoint
of an economic technician this assurance seemed almost mad at times,

From *The American Political Tradition and the Men Who Made It,* by Richard Hofstadter. Copyright 1948 by Alfred A. Knopf, Inc. Reprinted by permission of Alfred A. Knopf, Inc.

for example when he tossed back his head, laughed, and said to a group of silver Senators: "I experimented with gold and that was a flop. Why shouldn't I experiment a little with silver?" And yet there was a kind of intuitive wisdom under the harum-scarum surface of his methods. When he came to power, the people had seen stagnation go dangerously far. They wanted experiment, activity, trial and error, anything that would convey a sense of movement and novelty. At the very beginning of his candidacy Roosevelt, without heed for tradition or formality, flew to the 1932 nominating convention and addressed it in person instead of waiting for weeks in the customary pose of ceremonious ignorance. A trivial act in itself, the device gave the public an impression of vigor and originality that was never permitted to die. Although, as we shall see, Roosevelt had been reared on a social and economic philosophy rather similar to Hoover's, he succeeded at once in communicating the fact that his temperament was antithetical. When Hoover bumbled that it was necessary only to restore confidence, the nation laughed bitterly. When Roosevelt said: "The only thing we have to fear is fear itself," essentially the same thread bare half-true idea, the nation was thrilled. Hoover had lacked motion; Roosevelt lacked direction. But his capacity for growth, or at least for change, was enormous. Flexibility was both his strength and his weakness. Where Hoover had been remote and abstract, a doctrinaire who thought in fixed principles and moved cautiously in the rarefied atmosphere of the managerial classes, Roosevelt was warm, personal, concrete, and impulsive. Hoover was often reserved with valued associates. Roosevelt could say "my old friend" in eleven languages. He had little regard for abstract principle but a sharp intuitive knowledge of popular feeling. Because he was content in large measure to follow public opinion, he was able to give it that necessary additional impulse of leadership which can translate desires into policies. Hoover had never been able to convey to the masses a clear picture of what he was trying to do; Roosevelt was often able to suggest a clear and forceful line of policy when none in fact existed.

Raymond Moley tells an instructive story of Roosevelt's relations⁴ with Hoover in the interim between Roosevelt's election and inauguration. A conference had been arranged between the two men to discuss continuity of policy on the vexing question of foreign debts. Roosevelt, ill-informed on the facts, brought Moley with him as ballast and also carried a set of little cards in his hand as reminders of the questions he wanted to put to Hoover. Hoover talked for some time, revealing a mastery of all facets of the question which profoundly impressed Professor Moley. In contrast with the state of their information was the manner of the two men. Hoover, plainly disconcerted at this meeting with the man who had beaten him in the campaign, was shy and ill at ease and kept his eyes on the pattern of the carpet in the Red Room. Roosevelt was relaxed, informal, and cordial. That he was operating in *terra incognita* did not seem to trouble him in the least.

Roosevelt's admirers, their minds fixed on the image of a wise,   5
benevolent, provident father, have portrayed him as an ardent social reformer and sometimes as a master planner. His critics, coldly examining the step-by-step emergence of his measures, studying the supremely haphazard way in which they were so often administered, finding how little he actually had to do with so many of his "achievements," have come to the opposite conclusion that his successes were purely accidental, just as a certain portion of a number of random shots is likely to hit a target. It is true, it is bound to be true, that there is a vast disproportion between Roosevelt's personal stature and the Roosevelt legend, but not everything that comes in haphazard fashion is necessarily an accident. During his presidential period the nation was confronted with a completely novel situation for which the traditional, commonly accepted philosophies afforded no guide. An era of fumbling and muddling-through was inevitable. Only a leader with an experimental temper could have made the New Deal possible.

Roosevelt was, moreover, a public instrument of the most delicate   6
receptivity. Although he lacked depth, he had great breadth. A warm-hearted, informal patrician, he hated to disappoint, liked to play the bountiful friend. He felt that if a large number of people wanted something very badly, it was important that they be given some measure of satisfaction — and he allowed neither economic dogmas nor political precedents to inhibit him. The story of the WPA cultural projects illustrates his intensely personal methods and the results they yielded. When relief was being organized in the early stages of the New Deal, someone pointed out to him that a great many competent painters were poverty-stricken and desperate. Now, Roosevelt had no taste for painting, very little interest in artists and writers as a group, and no preconceived theories about the responsibility of the State for cultural welfare; but his decision to help the artists came immediately and spontaneously. "Why not?" he said. "They are human beings. They have to live. I guess the only thing they can do is paint and surely there must be some public place where paintings are wanted." And so painters were included in the benefits of CWA. Ultimately, under the WPA, relief was extended to musicians, dancers, actors, writers, historians, even to students trying to finance themselves through college. A generation of artists and intellectuals was nursed through a trying period and became wedded to the New Deal and devoted to Roosevelt liberalism.

What impression of F.D.R. does Hofstadter attempt to provide? This is an account less of Roosevelt, the president of the U.S., than of Roosevelt, the man — a warm, generous, spontaneous, and intensely vital human being. Hofstadter does consider Roosevelt's political philosophy, but he finds this aspect of the man less impressive than his character. As he notes, "At the heart of the New Deal there was not a philosophy but a temperament. . . . Roosevelt was often able to suggest a clear and forceful line of policy when none in fact existed."

After reading this passage, you might reasonably conclude that Roosevelt's greatness was less a matter of his political philosophy or his positions on the issues than of his character. And having concluded this, you might go on to generalize the proposition. What was true for Roosevelt might well be true for other presidents. During a presidential campaign, we scrutinize with microscopic intensity the candidates' positions on the issues. But perhaps we should devote even more intense scrutiny to their characters. Positions on the issues, after all, can and do change with the circumstances; even political philosophies may shift because all presidents must compromise to get their programs enacted into law. But character is far more stable, far more resistant to change, since character is usually fully formed before the candidate even knows what a political philosophy is.

The idea that character is crucial to a president should now be a familiar one to you. This idea, after all, is central to a number of pieces that you have already read in this chapter — for example, Sears's "President Reagan," and Barber's "Four Types of Presidential Character." In addition, Roosevelt's description of the presidency as "preeminently a place of moral leadership" supports the idea of the vital importance of character.

Thus, you could use material from these pieces, as well as from Hofstadter's piece, to support your thesis. Here is a sample outline:

Thesis: A president's most important quality is not his political philosophy or his positions on the issues, but his character.

A. *Barber:* Discussion of relationship between character and presidential performance; summary of four types of presidential character.

B. *Sears:* Successful presidents need self-knowledge, empathy, and strength in decision-making.

C. *Hofstadter:* Example of Roosevelt, who demonstrated "intuitive wisdom" and "an impression of vigor and originality"; note story of how, during the depression, he helped the artists out of a sense of compassion and empathy.

D. *Roosevelt:* "The presidency is not merely an administrative office. That's the least of it. It is more than an engineering job, efficient or inefficient. It is preeminently a place of moral leadership."

Of course, there are other ways in which you could support your thesis. Your supporting material might be organized in a different way. You could decide not to use all of the pieces here; or you could decide to research additional material to support your thesis. You could develop additional ideas on this subject and provide additional supporting material from your own knowledge of American history. As you develop these ideas you may find that your original thesis is changing, becoming more refined, more specific, taking on a new shape. It's even possible that after additional research and reflection, you may begin to doubt the truth of your original thesis. Perhaps it now seems to you that political philosophy *is,* after all, the most crucial thing. If this is what you now believe, say so, and cite your supporting evidence. Don't be afraid to change your thesis as circumstances demand — any more than presidential candidates are afraid to change *their* positions on the issues! In fact, it's much better to form your thesis *after* you have done a good bit of research than before; otherwise, your argument may well have that "canned" aroma.

Now write an argument on this subject.

CRITIQUE

Read the following passage:

JOHN F. KENNEDY'S INAUGURAL ADDRESS

Vice President Johnson, Mr. Speaker, Mr. Chief Justice, President Eisenhower, Vice President Nixon, President Truman, Reverend Clergy, fellow citizens:

We observe today not a victory of party but a celebration of freedom — symbolizing an end as well as a beginning — signifying renewal as well as change. For I have sworn before you and Almighty God the same solemn oath our forebears prescribed nearly a century and three quarters ago. 1

The world is very different now. For man holds in his mortal hands the power to abolish all forms of human poverty and all forms of human life. And yet the same revolutionary beliefs for which our forebears fought are still at issue around the globe — the belief that the rights of man come not from the generosity of the state but from the hand of God. 2

We dare not forget today that we are the heirs of that first revolution. Let the word go forth from this time and place, to friend 3

John F. Kennedy, "Inaugural Address." *Public Papers of the Presidents of the United States, John F. Kennedy, 1961* (Washington, D.C.: U.S. Government Printing Office, 1962), pp. 1–3.

and foe alike, that the torch has been passed to a new generation of Americans — born in this century, tempered by war, disciplined by a hard and bitter peace, proud of our ancient heritage — and unwilling to witness or permit the slow undoing of those human rights to which this nation has always been committed, and to which we are committed today at home and around the world.

Let every nation know, whether it wishes us well or ill, that we shall pay any price, bear any burden, meet any hardship, support any friend, oppose any foe to assure the survival and the success of liberty. 4

This much we pledge — and more. 5

To those old allies whose cultural and spiritual origins we share, we pledge the loyalty of faithful friends. United, there is little we cannot do in a host of cooperative ventures. Divided, there is little we can do — for we dare not meet a powerful challenge at odds and split asunder. 6

To those new states whom we welcome to the ranks of the free, we pledge our word that one form of colonial control shall not have passed away merely to be replaced by a far more iron tyranny. We shall not always expect to find them supporting our view. But we shall always hope to find them strongly supporting their own freedom — and to remember that, in the past, those who foolishly sought power by riding the back of the tiger ended up inside. 7

To those people in the huts and villages of half the globe struggling to break the bonds of mass misery, we pledge our best efforts to help them help themselves, for whatever period is required — not because the communists may be doing it, not because we seek their votes, but because it is right. If a free society cannot help the many who are poor, it cannot save the few who are rich. 8

To our sister republics south of our border, we offer a special pledge — to convert our good words into good deeds — in a new alliance for progress — to assist free men and free governments in casting off the chains of poverty. But this peaceful revolution of hope cannot become the prey of hostile powers. Let all our neighbors know that we shall join with them to oppose aggression or subversion anywhere in the Americas. And let every other power know that this Hemisphere intends to remain the master of its own house. 9

To that world assembly of sovereign states, the United Nations, our last best hope in an age where the instruments of war have far outpaced the instruments of peace, we renew our pledge of support — to prevent it from becoming merely a forum for invective — to strengthen its shield of the new and the weak — and to enlarge the area in which its writ may run. 10

Finally, to those nations who would make themselves our adversary, we offer not a pledge but a request: that both sides begin anew the quest for peace, before the dark powers of destruction unleashed 11 by science engulf all humanity in planned or accidental self-destruction.

We dare not tempt them with weakness. For only when our arms   12
are sufficient beyond doubt can we be certain beyond doubt that they
will never be employed.

But neither can two great and powerful groups of nations take   13
comfort from our present course — both sides overburdened by the
cost of modern weapons, both rightly alarmed by the steady spread of
the deadly atom, yet both racing to alter that uncertain balance of
terror that stays the hand of mankind's final war.

So let us begin anew — remembering on both sides that civility is   14
not a sign of weakness, and sincerity is always subject to proof. Let us
never negotiate out of fear. But let us never fear to negotiate.

Let both sides explore what problems unite us instead of belabor-   15
ing those problems which divide us.

Let both sides, for the first time, formulate serious and precise   16
proposals for the inspection and control of arms — and bring the
absolute power to destroy other nations under the absolute control of
all nations.

Let both sides seek to invoke the wonders of science instead of its   17
terrors. Together let us explore the stars, conquer the deserts, eradi-
cate disease, tap the ocean depths and encourage the arts and commerce.

Let both sides unite to heed in all corners of the earth the   18
command of Isaiah — to "undo the heavy burdens . . . (and) let the
oppressed go free."

And if a beach-head of cooperation may push back the jungle of   19
suspicion, let both sides join in creating a new endeavor, not a new
balance of power, but a new world of law, where the strong are just
and the weak secure and the peace preserved.

All this will not be finished in the first one hundred days. Nor will   20
it be finished in the first one thousand days, nor in the life of this
Administration, nor even perhaps in our lifetime on this planet. But
let us begin.

In your hands, my fellow citizens, more than mine, will rest the   21
final success or failure of our course. Since this country was founded,
each generation of Americans has been summoned to give testimony
to its national loyalty. The graves of young Americans who answered
the call to service surround the globe.

Now the trumpet summons us again — not as a call to bear arms,   22
though arms we need — not as a call to battle, though embattled we
are — but a call to bear the burden of a long twilight struggle, year in
and year out, "rejoicing in hope, patient in tribulation" — a struggle
against the common enemies of man: tyranny, poverty, disease and
war itself.

Can we forge against these enemies a grand and global alliance,   23
North and South, East and West, that can assure a more fruitful life
for all mankind? Will you join in that historic effort?

In the long history of the world, only a few generations have been   24
granted the role of defending freedom in its hour of maximum
danger. I do not shrink from this responsibility — I welcome it. I do
not believe that any of us would exchange places with any other
people or any other generation. The energy, the faith, the devotion
which we bring to this endeavor will light our country and all who
serve it — and the glow from that fire can truly light the world.

And so, my fellow Americans: ask not what your country can do   25
for you — ask what you can do for your country.

My fellow citizens of the world: ask not what America will do for   26
you, but what together we can do for the freedom of man.

Finally, whether you are citizens of America or citizens of the   27
world, ask of us here the same high standards of strength and sacrifice
which we ask of you. With a good conscience our only sure reward,
with history the final judge of our deeds, let us go forth to lead the
land we love, asking His blessing and His help, but knowing that here
on earth God's work must truly be our own.

This eloquent, stirring speech is (along with F.D.R.'s "we have nothing
to fear but fear itself" speech) one of the most famous inaugural addresses of the century. It is so renowned that it seems almost beyond
commentary. And yet it is no less subject to critical comment than a
newspaper editorial. What is the nature of this speech? What is its
significance? What are its objectives? What is its design? What is its
particular appeal? What assumptions underlie it? How do its assumptions
and biases affect its validity or its value? Such questions as these (though
not necessarily all of them) must be answered if we are to come to grips
with Kennedy's message, if we are to begin to evaluate it.

As you prepare your critique, go through the separate questions and
make notes of the answers that occur to you. Underline sentences and
phrases in the passage that seem particularly significant, and tie them,
where possible, to the answers you have noted down. At this stage, don't
worry about organizing your responses; the immediate problem is to gather
information and ideas that will underlie your critique.

Here's a sampling of possible responses to the sets of questions.
Please note, however: formulating such responses requires a historical
perspective that you are not expected to have unless you have either lived
through the period in question or have done some research on it. In other
words, to write a good critique (and in particular, to write about the
significance and the *validity* of the text under consideration), you must be
able to go beyond the text itself and set it in some kind of historical or
cultural context. Either you must provide the context through your own

knowledge and experience, or you must provide it through study. Let us assume, then, for the purpose of this example, that you have made yourself knowledgeable about the various active and passive roles that American governments have played in domestic and foreign policy since the late 1950s.

Nature: Inaugural address written by incoming president (and/or his speechwriter); addressed to all Americans and to the rest of world.

Significance: Set the tone of the Kennedy administration ("the New Frontier") and of the 1960s ("a new generation of Americans"); marked the beginning of an activist government and an activist social era, in contrast to the relative passivity of the Eisenhower era; reaffirmed America's world role, especially in upholding freedom, defending against aggression, providing economic aid to underdeveloped nations, promoting social welfare.

Objectives: To inspire Americans to do all of these things; to assure America's friends of its continued support; to warn potential enemies of its resolve, but to negotiate in good faith to reduce the threat of nuclear holocaust.

Design: Begins with general comments on the state of the world and America's main goal "to assure the survival and the success of liberty"; continues with messages to various peoples and nations of the world; continues with invitation to begin work; concludes with an appeal to all Americans to join together for the country and for "the freedom of man."

Appeal: Immensely eloquent speech, filled with ringing, memorable phrases ("Ask not what your country can do for you — ask what you can do for your country"); written with great rhetorical skill (phrases like "pay any price, bear any burden, meet any hardship, support any friend, oppose any foe . . ." which demonstrate the use of repetition, balance, rhythm, even alliteration, to generate power and harmony); appeals to the noblest motives of both Americans and the other peoples of the world.

Assumptions: Assumes that American power and wealth, as well as American will, are almost unlimited; assumes that we can do anything we set our minds to ("man holds in his hands the power to abolish all forms of human poverty. . . ." "United, there is little we cannot do in a host of cooperative ventures"); assumes that America has a responsibility to assist developing nations; assumes the moral authority of the U.S. ("we pledge our best efforts . . . because it is right"); assumes America's special role in the world is to defend and to preserve freedom; assumes that citizens as well as government have a responsibility to aid in this effort.

Validity: In retrospect, Kennedy assumed U.S. could do too much, both in the world and at home; falsely assumed U.S. has almost limitless resources; Kennedy and the people around him were young, energetic, and glamorous, in contrast to what seemed the tired, plodding government of Eisenhower, and they were deceived into thinking that their youth, energy, and glamour would accomplish more than they actually could; failed to anticipate growing independence of third world nations; but the Kennedy administration did inspire a generation of Americans, did help them to realize their responsibilities to other nations (Peace Corps a Kennedy legacy); did make the decision to put a man on the moon; did give the nation a new image, both at home and abroad; did encourage positive feelings toward public service; and did launch the nation into an exciting new era of activism and humanitarian concern.

Of course, in your actual critique you may use only a fraction of the material you have jotted down in your notes. How much you use, and which of it you will use, will depend upon your thesis. You may, for example, want to criticize it only as a speech, limiting yourself to the way in which the ideas are expressed and ignoring or downplaying its social implications. In such a case your thesis might be: "John F. Kennedy's inaugural address is a highly eloquent speech, making use of a wide array of rhetorical devices." The critique following this thesis would probably be organized by the types of rhetorical devices you want to consider (for example: repetition, balance, metaphor, comparison-contrast). There might be a brief introduction on the nature of the speech and perhaps its objectives; but the critique would mostly be devoted to a discussion of the speech's appeal.

On the other hand, if you attempted to use most of the ideas jotted down, you might develop a thesis like this: "John F. Kennedy's inaugural address was immensely eloquent and inspirational, but it unfortunately was symptomatic of America's false conviction during the 1960s that its power and resources were unlimited."

The critique following this thesis would be, of course, more comprehensive than the first one; but because the emphasis appears to be somewhat negative, the analysis of the speech's eloquence and rhetorical skill would be considerably less detailed. A critique using this thesis might be organized as follows:

A. Subject of critique; *thesis;*
B. Background facts — *nature, significance, objectives, design* of address;
C. Summary of address;

D. Background to your own position — a generation away from delivery of speech; different perspective from that of contemporary audience;

E. Review of address in accordance with your criteria: *appeal* of address; *assumptions* behind it; *validity* of assumptions and overall *value* of address;

F. Conclusion.

In general, whatever you write during the latter part of your critique will be the overall impression it conveys. If, toward the end, you placed heavy emphasis on assumptions that, in retrospect, have proven wrong, you might conclude with a discussion of examples of the limits and perhaps even the abuses of American power. In this case, the overall impression of the critique would probably be negative.

But you may choose to make your critique more positive in tone. Suppose you adjusted your thesis so that it now read: "Although Kennedy's inaugural address assumed that America's power and resources were greater than they actually were, it was a highly inspirational and powerful speech that set the tone for a new generation of socially responsible Americans."

The structure of this thesis sentence, with the positive aspects last, indicates the overall structure, and therefore the tone, of the critique. In this version, there would be some difference in part D of the critique; and part E would now look like this:

E. Review of address in accordance with your criteria: *assumptions* of address; *appeal* of address, including its influence, which accounts for its *value;*

In this version, the final assumption you choose to discuss may be that public service is a virtue as well as a duty. This could lead you to a consideration of such matters as the Peace Corps and the Kennedy government inspiring a new generation of young people to select careers in public service. You would not ignore the fact that some of Kennedy's assumptions turned out to be wrong, but you would maintain that these faults are much outweighed by the great inspirational value of the address.

Now write a critique of Kennedy's speech.

Exercise in Comparative Critique

You may find it interesting to compare Kennedy's inaugural address with those of two other presidents — Franklin D. Roosevelt and the man with whom we began this unit on the presidency, Ronald Reagan. Compare and contrast these addresses in terms of their subject matter, their degrees of eloquence, and whatever other factors seem most striking. Or you may wish, instead of preparing a critique of Kennedy's address, to prepare a critique on either Roosevelt's or Reagan's, following the six-step process.

Note: we have provided the first of Roosevelt's four inaugural addresses, delivered on March 4, 1933. For background to this speech, read Watts and Davis's piece, "The Depression" in the chapter on the Great Depression.

FRANKLIN D. ROOSEVELT'S INAUGURAL ADDRESS

I am certain that my fellow Americans expect that on my induction 1
into the Presidency I will address them with a candor and a decision which the present situation of our Nation impels. This is preeminently the time to speak the truth, the whole truth, frankly and boldly. Nor need we shrink from honestly facing conditions in our country today. This great Nation will endure as it has endured, will revive and will prosper. So, first of all, let me assert my firm belief that the only thing we have to fear is fear itself — nameless, unreasoning, unjustified terror which paralyzes needed efforts to convert retreat into advance. In every dark hour of our national life a leadership of frankness and vigor has met with that understanding and support of the people themselves which is essential to victory. I am convinced that you will again give that support to leadership in these critical days.

In such a spirit on my part and on yours we face our common 2
difficulties. They concern, thank God, only material things. Values have shrunken to fantastic levels; taxes have risen; our ability to pay has fallen; government of all kinds is faced by serious curtailment of income; the means of exchange are frozen in the currents of trade; the withered leaves of industrial enterprise lie on every side; farmers find no markets for their produce; the savings of many years in thousands of families are gone.

More important, a host of unemployed citizens face the grim 3
problem of existence, and an equally great number toil with little return. Only a foolish optimist can deny the dark realities of the moment.

Yet our distress comes from no failure of substance. We are 4
stricken by no plague of locusts. Compared with the perils which our forefathers conquered because they believed and were not afraid, we have still much to be thankful for. Nature still offers her bounty and human efforts have multiplied it. Plenty is at our doorstep, but a generous use of it languishes in the very sight of the supply. Primarily this is because rulers of the exchange of mankind's goods have failed

Franklin D. Roosevelt, "Inaugural Address." *The Public Papers and Addresses of Franklin D. Roosevelt,* Vol. II (New York: Random House, 1938), pp. 11–16.

through their own stubbornness and their own incompetence, have admitted their failure, and have abdicated. Practices of the unscrupulous money changers stand indicted in the court of public opinion, rejected by the hearts and minds of men.

True they have tried, but their efforts have been cast in the 5 pattern of an outworn tradition. Faced by failure of credit they have proposed only the lending of more money. Stripped of the lure of profit by which to induce our people to follow their false leadership, they have resorted to exhortations, pleading tearfully for restored confidence. They know only the rules of a generation of self-seekers. They have no vision, and when there is no vision the people perish.

The money changers have fled from their high seats in the 6 temple of our civilization. We may now restore that temple to the ancient truths. The measure of the restoration lies in the extent to which we apply social values more noble than mere monetary profit.

Happiness lies not in the mere possession of money; it lies in the 7 joy of achievement, in the thrill of creative effort. The joy and moral stimulation of work no longer must be forgotten in the mad chase of evanescent profits. These dark days will be worth all they cost us if they teach us that our true destiny is not to be ministered unto but to minister to ourselves and to our fellow men.

Recognition of the falsity of material wealth as the standard of 8 success goes hand in hand with the abandonment of the false belief that public office and high political position are to be valued only by the standards of pride of place and personal profit; and there must be an end to a conduct in banking and in business which too often has given to a sacred trust the likeness of callous and selfish wrongdoing. Small wonder that confidence languishes, for it thrives only on honesty, on honor, on the sacredness of obligations, on faithful protection, on unselfish performance; without them it cannot live.

Restoration calls, however, not for changes in ethics alone. This 9 Nation asks for action, and action now.

Our greatest primary task is to put people to work. This is no 10 unsolvable problem if we face it wisely and courageously. It can be accomplished in part by direct recruiting by the Government itself, treating the task as we would treat the emergency of a war, but at the same time, through this employment, accomplishing greatly needed projects to stimulate and reorganize the use of our natural resources.

Hand in hand with this we must frankly recognize the over- 11 balance of population in our industrial centers and, by engaging on a national scale in a redistribution, endeavor to provide a better use of the land for those best fitted for the land. The task can be helped by definite efforts to raise the values of agricultural products and with this the power to purchase the output of our cities. It can be helped by preventing realistically the tragedy of the growing loss through foreclosure of our small homes and our farms. It can be helped by insistence that the Federal, State, and local Governments act forthwith on the demand that their cost be drastically reduced. It can be helped by the unifying of relief activities which today are often scattered, uneconomical, and unequal. It can be helped by national planning for and supervision of all forms of transportation and of communications and other utilities which have a definitely public character. There are many ways in which it can be helped, but it can never be helped merely by talking about it. We must act and act quickly.

Finally, in our progress toward a resumption of work we require   12
two safeguards against a return of the evils of the old order: there must be a strict supervision of all banking and credits and investments, so that there will be an end to speculation with other people's money; and there must be provision for an adequate but sound currency.

These are the lines of attack. I shall presently urge upon a new   13
Congress, in special session, detailed measures for their fulfillment, and I shall seek the immediate assistance of the several States.

Through this program of action we address ourselves to putting   14
our own national house in order and making income balance outgo. Our international trade relations, though vastly important, are in point of time and necessity secondary to the establishment of a sound national economy. I favor as a practical policy the putting of first things first. I shall spare no effort to restore world trade by international economic readjustment, but the emergency at home cannot wait on that accomplishment.

The basic thought that guides these specific means of national   15
recovery is not narrowly nationalistic. It is the insistence, as a first consideration, upon the interdependence of the various elements in and parts of the United States — a recognition of the old and permanently important manifestation of the American spirit of the pioneer. It is the way to recovery. It is the immediate way. It is the strongest assurance that the recovery will endure.

In the field of world policy I would dedicate this Nation to the   16
policy of the good neighbor — the neighbor who resolutely respects himself and, because he does so, respects the rights of others — the neighbor who respects his obligations and respects the sanctity of his agreements in and with a world of neighbors.

If I read the temper of our people correctly, we now realize as we   17
have never realized before our interdependence on each other; that we cannot merely take but we must give as well; that if we are to go forward, we must move as a trained and loyal army willing to sacrifice for the good of a common discipline, because without such discipline no progress is made, no leadership becomes effective. We are, I know,

ready and willing to submit our lives and property to such discipline, because it makes possible a leadership which aims at a larger good. This I propose to offer, pledging that the larger purposes will bind upon us all as a sacred obligation with a unity of duty hitherto evoked only in time of armed strife.

With this pledge taken, I assume unhesitatingly the leadership of 18 this great army of our people dedicated to a disciplined attack upon our common problems.

Action in this image and to this end is feasible under the form of 19 government which we have inherited from our ancestors. Our Constitution is so simple and practical that it is possible always to meet extraordinary needs by changes in emphasis and arrangement without loss of essential form. That is why our constitutional system has proved itself the most superbly enduring political mechanism the modern world has produced. It has met every stress of vast expansion of territory, of foreign wars, of bitter internal strife, of world relations.

It is to be hoped that the normal balance of Executive and 20 legislative authority may be wholly adequate to meet the unprecedented task before us. But it may be that an unprecedented demand and need for undelayed action may call for temporary departure from that normal balance of public procedure.

I am prepared under my constitutional duty to recommend the 21 measures that a stricken Nation in the midst of a stricken world may require. These measures, or such other measures as the Congress may build out of its experience and wisdom, I shall seek, within my constitutional authority, to bring to speedy adoption.

But in the event that the Congress shall fail to take one of these 22 two courses, and in the event that the national emergency is still critical, I shall not evade the clear course of duty that will then confront me. I shall ask the Congress for the one remaining instrument to meet the crisis — broad Executive power to wage a war against the emergency, as great as the power that would be given to me if we were in fact invaded by a foreign foe.

For the trust reposed in me I will return the courage and the 23 devotion that befit the time. I can do no less.

We face the arduous days that lie before us in the warm courage 24 of national unity; with the clear consciousness of seeking old and precious moral values; with the clean satisfaction that comes from the stern performance of duty by old and young alike. We aim at the assurance of a rounded and permanent national life.

We do not distrust the future of essential democracy. The people 25 of the United States have not failed. In their need they have registered a mandate that they want direct, vigorous action. They have asked for discipline and direction under leadership. They have made me the present instrument of their wishes. In the spirit of the gift I take it.

In this dedication of a Nation we humbly ask the blessing of God. 26 May He protect each and every one of us. May He guide me in the days to come.

RONALD REAGAN'S
INAUGURAL ADDRESS

To a few of us here today this is a solemn and most momentous 1 occasion. And, yet, in the history of our Nation it is a commonplace occurrence. The orderly transfer of authority as called for in the Constitution routinely takes place, as it has for almost two centuries, and few of us stop to think how unique we really are. In the eyes of many in the world, this every-4-year ceremony we accept as normal is nothing less than a miracle.

Mr. President, I want our fellow citizens to know how much you 2 did to carry on this tradition. By your gracious cooperation in the transition process you have shown a watching world that we are a united people pledged to maintaining a political system which guarantees individual liberty to a greater degree than any other, and I thank you and your people for all your help in maintaining the continuity which is the bulwark of our Republic.

The business of our Nation goes forward. These United States 3 are confronted with an economic affliction of great proportions. We suffer from the longest and one of the worst sustained inflations in our national history. It distorts our economic decisions, penalizes thrift, and crushes the struggling young and the fixed-income elderly alike. It threatens to shatter the lives of millions of our people.

Idle industries have cast workers into unemployment, human 4 misery, and personal indignity. Those who do work are denied a fair return for their labor by a tax system which penalizes successful achievement and keeps us from maintaining full productivity.

But great as our tax burden is, it has not kept pace with public 5 spending. For decades we have piled deficit upon deficit, mortgaging our future and our children's future for the temporary convenience of the present. To continue this long trend is to guarantee tremendous social, cultural, political, and economic upheavals.

You and I, as individuals, can, by borrowing, live beyond our 6 means, but for only a limited period of time. Why, then, should we think that collectively, as a nation, we're not bound by that same

Ronald Reagan, "Inaugural Address." *Weekly Compilation of Presidential Papers: A Quarterly Index*, 17, no. 4 (1981), pp. 1–5.

limitation? We must act today in order to preserve tomorrow. And let there be no misunderstanding — we are going to begin to act, beginning today.

The economic ills we suffer have come upon us over several 7 decades. They will not go away in days, weeks, or months, but they will go away. They will go away because we as Americans have the capacity now, as we've had in the past, to do whatever needs to be done to preserve this last and greatest bastion of freedom.

In this present crisis, government is not the solution to our 8 problem; government is the problem. From time to time we've been tempted to believe that society has become too complex to be managed by self-rule, that government by an elite group is superior to government for, by, and of the people. Well, if no one among us is capable of governing himself, then who among us has the capacity to govern someone else? All of us together — in and out of government — must bear the burden. The solutions we seek must be equitable with no one group singled out to pay a higher price.

We hear much of special interest groups. Well, our concern must 9 be for a special interest group that has been too long neglected. It knows no sectional boundaries or ethnic and racial divisions, and it crosses political party lines. It is made up of men and women who raise our food, patrol our streets, man our mines and factories, teach our children, keep our homes, and heal us when we're sick — professionals, industrialists, shopkeepers, clerks, cabbies, and truckdrivers. They are, in short, "We the people," this breed called Americans.

Well, this administration's objective will be a healthy, vigorous, 10 growing economy that provides equal opportunities for all Americans with no barriers born of bigotry or discrimination. Putting America back to work means putting all Americans back to work. Ending inflation means freeing all Americans from the terror of runaway living costs. All must share in the productive work of this "new beginning," and all must share in the bounty of a revived economy. With the idealism and fair play which are the core of our system and our strength, we can have a strong and prosperous America, at peace with itself and the world.

So, as we begin, let us take inventory. We are a nation that has a 11 government — not the other way around. And this makes us special among the nations of the Earth. Our government has no power except that granted it by the people. It is time to check and reverse the growth of government which shows signs of having grown beyond the consent of the governed.

It is my intention to curb the size and influence of the Federal 12 establishment and to demand recognition of the distinction between the powers granted to the Federal Government and those reserved to the States or to the people. All of us need to be reminded that the

Federal Government did not create the States; the States created the Federal Government.

Now, so there will be no misunderstanding, it's not my intention 13 to do away with government. It is rather to make it work — work with us, not over us; to stand by our side, not ride on our back. Government can and must provide opportunity, not smother it; foster productivity, not stifle it.

If we look to the answer as to why for so many years we achieved 14 so much, prospered as no other people on Earth, it was because here in this land we unleashed the energy and individual genius of man to a greater extent than has ever been done before. Freedom and the dignity of the individual have been more available and assured here than in any other place on Earth. The price for this freedom at times has been high. But we have never been unwilling to pay that price.

It is no coincidence that our present troubles parallel and are 15 proportionate to the intervention and intrusion in our lives that result from unnecessary and excessive growth of government. It is time for us to realize that we're too great a nation to limit ourselves to small dreams. We're not, as some would have us believe, doomed to an inevitable decline. I do not believe in a fate that will fall on us no matter what we do. I do believe in a fate that will fall on us if we do nothing. So, with all the creative energy at our command, let us begin an era of national renewal. Let us renew our determination, our courage, and our strength. And let us renew our faith and our hope.

We have every right to dream heroic dreams. Those who say that 16 we're in a time when there are no heroes, they just don't know where to look. You can see heroes every day going in and out of factory gates. Others, a handful in number, produce enough food to feed all of us and then the world beyond. You meet heroes across a counter. And they're on both sides of that counter. There are entrepreneurs with faith in themselves and faith in an idea who create new jobs, new wealth and opportunity. They're individuals and families whose taxes support the government and whose voluntary gifts support church, charity, culture, art, and education. Their patriotism is quiet but deep. Their values sustain our national life.

Now, I have used the words "they" and "their" in speaking of 17 these heroes. I could say "you" and "your," because I'm addressing the heroes of whom I speak — you, the citizens of this blessed land. Your dreams, your hopes, your goals are going to be the dreams, the hopes, and the goals of this administration, so help me God.

We shall reflect the compassion that is so much a part of your 18 makeup. How can we love our country and not love our countrymen; and loving them, reach out a hand when they fall, heal them when they're sick, and provide opportunity to make them self-sufficient so they will be equal in fact and not just in theory?

Can we solve the problems confronting us? Well, the answer is an 19 unequivocal and emphatic "yes." To paraphrase Winston Churchill, I did not take the oath I've just taken with the intention of presiding over the dissolution of the world's strongest economy.

In the days ahead I will propose removing the roadblocks that 20 have slowed our economy and reduced productivity. Steps will be taken aimed at restoring the balance between the various levels of government. Progress may be slow, measured in inches and feet, not miles, but we will progress. It is time to reawaken this industrial giant, to get government back within its means, and to lighten our punitive tax burden. And these will be our first priorities, and on these princi- ples there will be no compromise.

On the eve of our struggle for independence a man who might 21 have been one of the greatest among the Founding Fathers, Dr. Joseph Warren, president of the Massachusetts Congress, said to his fellow Americans, "Our country is in danger, but not to be despaired of. . . . On you depend the fortunes of America. You are to decide the important question upon which rests the happiness and the liberty of millions yet unborn. Act worthy of yourselves."

Well, I believe we, the Americans of today, are ready to act 22 worthy of ourselves, ready to do what must be done to ensure happi- ness and liberty for ourselves, our children, and our children's chil- dren. And as we renew ourselves here in our own land, we will be seen as having greater strength throughout the world. We will again be the exemplar of freedom and a beacon of hope for those who do not now have freedom.

To those neighbors and allies who share our freedom, we will 23 strengthen our historic ties and assure them of our support and firm commitment. We will match loyalty with loyalty. We will strive for mutually beneficial relations. We will not use our friendship to impose on their sovereignty, for our own sovereignty is not for sale.

As for the enemies of freedom, those who are potential adver- 24 saries, they will be reminded that peace is the highest aspiration of the American people. We will negotiate for it, sacrifice for it; we will not surrender for it now or ever.

Our forbearance should never be misunderstood. Our reluctance 25 for conflict should not be misjudged as a failure of will. When action is required to preserve our national security, we will act. We will main- tain sufficient strength to prevail if need be, knowing that if we do so we have the best chance of never having to use that strength.

Above all we must realize that no arsenal or no weapon in the 26 arsenals of the world is so formidable as the will and moral courage of free men and women. It is a weapon our adversaries in today's world do not have. It is a weapon that we as Americans do have. Let that be understood by those who practice terrorism and prey upon their neighbors.

I'm told that tens of thousands of prayer meetings are being held 27
on this day, and for that I'm deeply grateful. We are a nation under God, and I believe God intended for us to be free. It would be fitting and good, I think, if on each Inaugural Day in future years it should be declared a day of prayer.

This is the first time in our history that this ceremony has been 28
held, as you've been told, on this West Front of the Capitol. Standing here, one faces a magnificent vista, opening up on this city's special beauty and history. At the end of this open mall are those shrines to the giants on whose shoulders we stand.

Directly in front of me, the monument to a monumental man, 29
George Washington, father of our country. A man of humility who came to greatness reluctantly. He led America out of revolutionary victory into infant nationhood. Off to one side, the stately memorial to Thomas Jefferson. The Declaration of Independence flames with his eloquence. And then, beyond the Reflecting Pool, the dignified columns of the Lincoln Memorial. Whoever would understand in his heart the meaning of America will find it in the life of Abraham Lincoln.

Beyond those monuments to heroism is the Potomac River, and 30
on the far shore the sloping hills of Arlington National Cemetery, with its row upon row of simple white markers bearing crosses or Stars of David. They add up to only a tiny fraction of the price that has been paid for our freedom.

Each one of those markers is a monument to the kind of hero I 31
spoke of earlier. Their lives ended in places called Belleau Wood, The Argonne, Omaha Beach, Salerno, and halfway around the world on Guadalcanal, Tarawa, Pork Chop Hill, the Chosin Reservoir, and in a hundred rice paddies and jungles of a place called Vietnam.

Under one such marker lies a young man, Martin Treptow, who 32
left his job in a small town barbershop in 1917 to go to France with the famed Rainbow Division. There, on the western front, he was killed trying to carry a message between battalions under heavy artillery fire.

We're told that on his body was found a diary. On the flyleaf 33
under the heading, "My Pledge," he had written these words: "America must win this war. Therefore I will work, I will save, I will sacrifice, I will endure, I will fight cheerfully and do my utmost, as if the issue of the whole struggle depended on me alone."

The crisis we are facing today does not require of us the kind of 34
sacrifice that Martin Treptow and so many thousands of others were

called upon to make. It does require, however, our best effort and our willingness to believe in ourselves and to believe in our capacity to perform great deeds, to believe that together with God's help we can and will resolve the problems which now confront us.

And after all, why shouldn't we believe that? We are Americans.   35
God bless you, and thank you.   36

3 Morality and the Movies

When Charlie Chaplin submitted to the censors the script for his 1947 film *Monsieur Verdoux,* he was notified that unless numerous changes were made in his bitterly satirical story, it would not be approved for distribution. Chaplin was advised that "the story has about it a distasteful flavor of illicit sex, which in our judgement is not good." He was also cautioned that "there should be no showing of, or suggestions of, toilets in the bathroom."

Modern audiences justifiably laugh at such Victorian delicacy; but as the recurring public furors over sex and violence in the media suggest, the issues behind censorship are not entirely trivial. Implicit in most censorship is the idea that mass entertainment has considerable power to influence moral and social attitudes. Implicit also is the idea that people who are repeatedly exposed to films in which brutality or insensitivity are made to seem "cool" will gradually, though inevitably, become brutalized or desensitized themselves. What is the effect on children who view films in which people's heads are blown apart by remote control? (Children aren't supposed to see such R-rated films, but many do, brought along by parents who can't or don't want to hire a sitter.) And isn't there something disquieting about films in which criminals — robbers and murderers — are made sympathetic characters?

Of course, few people in a democracy are comfortable with the idea of censorship, whether imposed by state boards or by the industry itself. We assume in an open society that people have the right, as well as the wisdom, to choose for themselves what they will see, what they will allow their children to see. Many people throughout history have suffered and died for the right of free speech and the open interchange of ideas; and whenever we restrict such rights, we diminish democracy. But nagging doubts remain. Our country has one of the highest rates of violent crime in the world. Could media violence be a contributing factor? Some years ago, a Florida youth accused of murder used as his defense the claim that he had been "brainwashed" by all the violence he saw on TV. Many argue that society has no obligation to allow the unrestricted dissemination of antisocial attitudes that could result in depriving some citizens of their right to life, liberty, and the pursuit of happiness. As satirist Jonathan Swift observed in *Gulliver's Travels:* "a man may be allowed to keep poisons in his closet, but not to vend them about as cordials."

The selections in this chapter are intended to provide food for thought on this issue. First, we present the Motion Picture Production Code of 1930, which laid down general and particular restrictions on the content of

American films, restrictions that were to remain in effect for almost two generations. (The blandness and sheer unreality of many of the films of the 1930s, '40s, and '50s are a direct result of this Code.) In "The Struggle over *Double Indemnity*," Murray Schumach shows how the Code prevented the filming of a best-selling (though arguably unwholesome) novel for almost a decade. Following is an official description of the 1968 rating system, still in effect, which replaced the 1930 Production Code. The relaxation and final abandonment of the old Code made possible the production of films like *Bonnie and Clyde* and *Deep Throat*, popular films that depicted heretofore forbidden levels of violence and sex. Whether or not such levels of violence and sex are socially harmful has been the subject of much debate; our selection "Sex and Violence: Pornography Hurts" summarizes the results of two recent experiments on this subject. In "Anyone for Clean Movies?" Patricia Morrisroe explains why the G-rated movie is going the way of the dinosaurs. Finally, Victor Cline poses the basic question of censorship in a free society: "Where Do You Draw the Line?"

THE MOTION PICTURE PRODUCTION CODE (1930)

Sex and violence on the screen are not new issues. In the Roaring Twenties there was increasing pressure from civic and religious groups to ban depictions of "immorality" from the screen. State censorship boards flourished, but the pressure groups wanted a more comprehensive ban on objectionable material. Faced with the threat of federal censorship, the film producers decided to clean their own house. In 1930, the Motion Picture Producers and Distributors of America (known as the Hays Office, after its first head, Will H. Hays) established the Production Code. At first, adherence to the Code was voluntary; but in 1934 Joseph Breen, newly appointed head of the M.P.P.D.A., gave the Code teeth. Henceforth, all newly produced films had to be submitted for approval to the Production Code Administration, which had the power to award or to withhold the Code seal. Without a Code seal, it was almost impossible for a film to be shown anywhere in the United States, since exhibitors would not accept it. At about the same time, the Catholic Legion of Decency was formed to advise the faithful which films were and were not objectionable, in whole or in part.

Although in later years, unpunished violations of the Code were increasingly common, the Code remained officially in force until 1968, when it was replaced with the current rating system.

☐

Preamble

The Motion Picture Production Code was formulated and formally   1
adopted by The Association of Motion Picture Producers Inc., (California) and The Motion Picture Association of America, Inc., (New York) in March, 1930.

Motion picture producers recognize the high trust and   2
confidence which have been placed in them by the people of the world and which have made motion pictures a universal form of entertainment.

They recognize their responsibility to the public because of this   3
trust and because entertainment and art are important influences in the life of a nation.

Hence, though regarding motion pictures primarily as entertain-   4
ment without any explicit purpose of teaching or propaganda, they know that the motion picture within its own field of entertainment may be directly responsible for spiritual or moral progress, for higher types of social life, and for much correct thinking.

During the rapid transition from silent to talking pictures they   5
realized the necessity and the opportunity of subscribing to a Code to govern the production of talking pictures and of reacknowledging this responsibility.

On their part, they ask from the public and from public leaders a   6
sympathetic understanding of their purposes and problems and a spirit of cooperation that will allow them the freedom and opportunity necessary to bring the motion picture to a still higher level of wholesome entertainment for all the people.

General Principles

1. No picture shall be produced which will lower the moral   7
standards of those who see it. Hence the sympathy of the audience shall never be thrown to the side of crime, wrong-doing, evil or sin.

Reprinted by permission of the Motion Picture Association of America, Inc. Preamble and Production Code from "The Motion Picture Production Code" adopted in March 1930 by the Association of Motion Picture Producers, Inc. (California), and the Motion Picture Association of America, Inc. (New York). Footnotes are from Jack Vizzard, See No Evil, copyright © 1970 by Jack Vizzard.

2. Correct standards of life, subject only to the requirements of   8
drama and entertainment, shall be presented.

3. Law, natural or human, shall not be ridiculed, nor shall sym-   9
pathy be created for its violation.

Reasons Underlying The General Principles

I. No picture shall be produced which will lower the moral stan-   10
dards of those who see it. Hence the sympathy of the audience
should never be thrown to the side of crime, wrong-doing, evil or
sin.
This is done:

1. When evil is made to appear attractive or alluring, and good
   is made to appear unattractive.
2. When the sympathy of the audience is thrown on the side of
   crime, wrong-doing, evil, sin. The same thing is true of a film
   that would throw sympathy against goodness, honor, innocence, purity or honesty.

   Note: Sympathy with a person who sins is not the same
   as sympathy with the sin or crime of which he is guilty. We
   may feel sorry for the plight of the murderer or even understand the circumstances which led him to his crime. We may
   not feel sympathy with the wrong which he has done.

   The presentation of evil is often essential for art or
   fiction or drama. This in itself is not wrong provided:

   a. That evil is not presented alluringly. Even if later in the
      film the evil is condemned or punished, it must not be
      allowed to appear so attractive that the audience's emo-
      tions are drawn to desire or approve so strongly that later
      the condemnation is forgotten and only the apparent joy
      of the sin remembered.
   b. That throughout, the audience feels sure that evil is
      wrong and good is right.

II. Correct standards of life shall, as far as possible, be presented.   11
   A wide knowledge of life and of living is made possible
through the film. When right standards are consistently presented, the motion picture exercises the most powerful
influences. It builds character, develops right ideals, inculates
correct principles, and all this in attractive story form.

   If motion pictures consistently hold up for admiration high
types of characters and present stories that will affect lives for the
better, they can become the most powerful natural force for the
improvement of mankind.

III. Law, natural or human, shall not be ridiculed, nor shall sympathy   12
be created for its violation.

By natural law is understood the law which is written in the hearts of all mankind, the great underlying principles of right and justice dictated by conscience.

By human law is understood the law written by civilized nations.

1. The presentation of crimes against the law is often necessary for the carrying out of the plot. But the presentation must not throw sympathy with the crime as against the law nor with the criminal as against those who punish him.

2. The courts of the land should not be presented as unjust. This does not mean that a single court may not be represented as unjust, much less that a single court official must not be presented this way. But the court system of the country must not suffer as a result of this presentation.

Particular Applications

I. Crimes Against the Law[1]

These shall never be presented in such a way as to throw sympa-   13
thy with the crime as against law and justice or to inspire others with a desire for imitation.

1. **Murder**
   a. The technique of murder must be presented in a way that will not inspire imitation.
   b. Brutal killings are not to be presented in detail.
   c. Revenge in modern times shall not be justified.
2. **Methods of Crime** should not be explicitly presented.
   a. Theft, robbery, safe-cracking, and dynamiting of trains, mines, buildings, etc., should not be detailed in method.
   b. Arson must be subject to the same safeguards.
   c. The use of firearms should be restricted to essentials.
   d. Methods of smuggling should not be presented.

[1] See Special Regulations on Treatment of Crime. [Footnotes are by Vizzard.]

3. **The illegal drug traffic** must not be portrayed in such a way as to stimulate curiosity concerning the use of, or traffic in, such drugs; nor shall scenes be approved which show the use of illegal drugs, or their effects, in detail.[2]

4. **The use of liquor** in American life, when not required by the plot or for proper characterization, will not be shown.

II. Sex

The sanctity of the institution of marriage and the home shall be   14
upheld. Pictures shall not infer that low forms of sex relationship are the accepted or common thing.

1. **Adultery and Illicit Sex,** sometimes necessary plot material, must not be explicitly treated or justified, or presented attractively.

2. **Scenes of Passion**
   a. These should not be introduced except where they are definitely essential to the plot.
   b. Excessive and lustful kissing, lustful embraces, suggestive postures and gestures are not to be shown.
   c. In general, passion should be treated in such manner as not to stimulate the lower and baser emotions.

3. **Seduction or Rape**
   a. These should never be more than suggested, and then only when essential for the plot. They must never be shown by explicit method.
   b. They are never the proper subject for comedy.

4. **Sex perversion** or any inference of it is forbidden.[3]

5. **White slavery** shall not be treated.[4]

6. **Miscegenation** (sex relationship between the white and black races) is forbidden.

---

[2] As amended by resolution of the Board of Directors, September 11, 1946.

[3] Amended in Oct. 1961 to permit "sex aberration" when treated with "care, discretion, and restraint." Note the switch from the word "perversion" and the latent fear of legal consequences in its employment.

[4] Subsequently changed to read: "The methods and techniques of prostitution and white slavery shall never be presented in detail, nor shall the subjects be presented unless shown in contrast to right standards of behavior. Brothels in any clear identification as such may not be shown."

7. **Sex hygiene** and venereal diseases are not proper subjects for theatrical motion pictures.[5]
8. Scenes of **actual child birth,** in fact or in silhouette, are never to be presented.
9. **Children's sex organs** are never to be exposed.

III. Vulgarity

The treatment of low, disgusting, unpleasant, though not neces-   15
sarily evil, subjects should be guided always by the dictates of good taste and a proper regard for the sensibilities of the audience.

IV. Obscenity

Obscenity in word, gesture, reference, song, joke, or by sugges-   16
tion (even when likely to be understood only by part of the audience) is forbidden.

V. Profanity[6]

Pointed profanity and every other profane or vulgar expression,   17
however used, are forbidden.

No approval by the Production Code Administration shall be given to the use of words and phrases in motion pictures including, but not limited to, the following:

Alley cat (applied to a woman); bat (applied to a woman); broad (applied to a woman); Bronx cheer (the sound); chippie; cocotte; God, Lord, Jesus Christ (unless used reverently); cripes; fanny; fairy (in a vulgar sense); finger (the); fire, cries of; Gawd; goose (in a vulgar sense); "hold your hat" or "hats"; hot (applied to a woman); "in your hat"; Madam (relating to prostitution); nance; nerts; nuts (except when meaning crazy); pansy; razzberry (the sound); slut (applied to a woman); S.O.B.; son-of-a; tart; toilet gags; tom cat (applied to a man); traveling salesman and farmer's daughter jokes; whore; damn, hell (excepting when the use of said last two words shall be essential and required for portrayal, in

---

[5] Abortion was considered to come under the heading of "sex hygiene." In the amended Code of Dec. 1956, the subject was brought up specifically as follows: "The subject of abortion shall be discouraged, shall never be more than suggested, and when referred to shall be condemned. It must never be treated lightly, or made the subject of comedy. Abortion shall never be shown explicitly or by inference, and a story must not indicate that an abortion has been performed. The word 'abortion' shall not be used."

[6] As amended by resolution of the Board of Directors, November 1, 1939, and September 12, 1945.

proper historical context, of any scene or dialogue based upon historical fact or folklore, or for the presentation in proper literary context of a Biblical, or other religious quotation, or a quotation from a literary work **provided** that no such use shall be permitted which is intrinsically objectionable or offends good taste).

In the administration of Section V of the Production Code, the Production Code Administration may take cognizance of the fact that the following words and phrases are obviously offensive to the patrons of motion pictures in the United States and more particularly to the patrons of motion pictures in foreign countries:

Chink, Dago, Frog, Greaser, Hunkie, Kike, Nigger, Spig, Wop, Yid.

VI. Costume[7]

1. **Complete nudity** is never permitted. This includes nudity in fact   18
   or in silhouette, or any licentious notice thereof by other characters in the pictures.
2. **Undressing scenes** should be avoided, and never used save
   where essential to the plot.
3. **Indecent or undue exposure** is forbidden.
4. **Dancing costumes** intended to permit undue exposure or indecent movements in the dance are forbidden.

VII. Dances

1. Dances suggesting or representing sexual actions or indecent   19
   passion are forbidden.
2. Dances which emphasize indecent movements are to be regarded
   as obscene.

VIII. Religion

1. No film or episode may throw **ridicule** on any religious faith.   20
2. **Ministers of religion** in their character as ministers of religion
   should not be used as comic characters or as villains.
3. **Ceremonies** of any definite religion should be carefully and
   respectfully handled.

IX. Locations

The treatment of bedrooms must be governed by good taste and   21
delicacy.

---

[7] See Special Resolution on Costumes.

X. National Feelings

1. **The use of the Flag** shall be consistently respectful.   22
2. **The history,** institutions, prominent people and citizenry of all nations shall be represented fairly.

XI. Titles

The following titles shall not be used: 23

1. Titles which are salacious, indecent, obscene, profane or vulgar.
2. Titles which suggest or are currently associated in the public mind with material, characters or occupations unsuitable for the screen.
3. Titles which are otherwise objectionable.[8]

XII. Repellent Subjects

The following subjects must be treated within the careful limits of   24
good taste:

1. **Actual hangings** or electrocutions as legal punishments for crime.
2. **Third Degree** methods.
3. **Brutality** and possible gruesomeness.
4. **Branding** of people or animals.
5. **Apparent cruelty** to children or animals.
6. **The sale of women,** or a woman selling her virtue.
7. **Surgical operations.**

Special Regulations on Crime in Motion Pictures[9]

RESOLVED, that the Board of Directors of the Motion Picture Asso-   25
ciation of America, Incorporated, hereby ratifies, approves, and confirms the interpretations of the Production Code, the practices thereunder, and the resolutions indicating and confirming such interpretations heretofore adopted by the Association of Motion Picture Producers, Incorporated, all effectuating regulations relative to the treatment of crime in motion pictures, as follows:

1. Details of crime must never be shown and care should be exercised at all times in discussing such details.

---

[8] As amended by resolution of the Board of Directors, December 3, 1947.

[9] As adopted by the Board of Directors, December 20, 1938.

2. Action suggestive of wholesale slaughter of human beings, either by criminals, in conflict with police, or as between warring factions of criminals, or in public disorder of any kind, will not be allowed.

3. There must be no suggestion, at any time, of excessive brutality.

4. Because of the increase in the number of films in which murder is frequently committed, action showing the taking of human life, even in the mystery stories, is to be cut to the minimum. These frequent presentations of murder tend to lessen regard for the sacredness of life.

5. Suicide, as a solution of problems occurring in the development of screen drama, is to be discouraged as morally questionable and as bad theatre — unless absolutely necessary for the development of the plot.

6. There must be no display, at any time, of machine guns, submachine guns or other weapons generally classified as illegal weapons in the hands of gangsters, or other criminals, and there are to be no off-stage sounds of the repercussions of these guns.

7. There must be no new, unique or trick methods shown for concealing guns.

8. The flaunting of weapons by gangsters, or other criminals, will not be allowed.

9. All discussions and dialogue on the part of gangsters regarding guns should be cut to the minimum.

10. There must be no scenes, at any time, showing law-enforcing officers dying at the hands of criminals. This includes private detectives and guards for banks, motor trucks, etc.

11. With special reference to the crime of kidnapping — or illegal abduction — such stories are acceptable under the Code only when the kidnapping or abduction is (a) not the main theme of the story; (b) the person kidnapped is not a child; (c) there are no details of the crime of kidnapping; (d) no profit accrues to the abductors or kidnappers; and (e) where the kidnappers are punished.

    It is understood, and agreed, that the word kidnapping, as used in paragraph 11 of these Regulations, is intended to mean abduction, or illegal detention, in modern times, by criminals for ransom.

12. Pictures dealing with criminal activities, in which minors participate, or to which minors are related, shall not be approved if they incite demoralizing imitation on the part of youth.

13. No picture shall be approved dealing with the life of a notorious criminal of current or recent times which uses the name, nick-

name or alias of such notorious criminal in the film, nor shall a picture be approved if based upon the life of such a notorious criminal unless the character shown in the film be punished for crimes shown in the film as committed by him.[10]

Special Resolution on Costumes

On October 25, 1939, the Board of Directors of the Motion Picture Association of America, Inc., adopted the following resolution: 26
     RESOLVED, that the provisions of Paragraphs 1, 3 and 4 of subdivision VI of the Production Code, in their application to costumes, nudity, indecent or undue exposure and dancing costumes, shall not be interpreted to exclude authentically photographed scenes photographed in a foreign land, of natives of such foreign land, showing native life, if such scenes are a necessary and integral part of a motion picture depicting exclusively such land and native life, provided that no such scenes shall be intrinsically objectionable nor made a part of any motion picture produced in any studio; and provided further that no emphasis shall be made in any scenes of the customs or garb of such natives or in the exploitation thereof. . . .

Review Questions

1. How is the Code organized?
2. What are the chief crimes whose portrayal is restricted?
3. What are the chief aspects of sex that are restricted?
4. What is the implied difference among "vulgarity," "obscenity," and "profanity" in the Code?
5. What, in general, are the reasons given for the Code's provisions?

Discussion Questions

1. Do you believe that it should be (or can be) the purpose of entertainment to "improve" the human race? Is it possible for entertainment to "degrade" human beings? Do you agree that a person "may be judged by his standard of entertainment as easily as by the standard of his work"? Do you agree that a film, "as a product of a mind and as the cause of definite effects . . . has a deep moral significance and an unmistakable moral quality"?
2. Will people's moral standards be lowered — or will people be desensitized — if "evil is made to appear attractive or alluring, and good is

---

[10] As amended by resolution of the Board of Directors, December 3, 1947.

made to appear unattractive," or when "the sympathy of the audience is thrown on the side of the crime, wrong-doing, evil, sin"?

3. Is it possible — or desirable — to speak of "correct standards of life"? Are such standards a myth, or are they necessary for society? Does the 1930 Code promote such "correct standards"?

4. Do the "Reasons Underlying the General Principles" adequately justify the particular provisions of the Code? Why or why not?

5. Discuss some of the most justifiable and the least justifiable provisions of the 1930 Code.

6. If you believe that the reasons given by the writers of the Code are unconvincing or inadequate, what considerations have they ignored or downplayed?

7. Examine the language in which the 1930 Code is written. Find examples of words or phrases that carry highly emotional connotations (e.g. "spiritual or moral progress") and explain how they work in the argument for censorship. Is the use of such language fair or unfair?

Writing Suggestions

1. What is your reaction to the 1930 Production Code? Organize your response so that you (1) develop a clear main idea, expressed as a thesis sentence; (2) devise two or three main arguments for the validity of this idea; (3) include a number of quotations and specific examples from the text and/or from your own experience.

2. Describe some of the ways in which recent films have violated the standards of the 1930 Production Code. In your view, is it a good thing that these standards have been violated?

3. Select a film that you have seen recently, and write a report that a 1930s censor might produce on this film. Organize the report according to the Code categories.

4. Draw up a "Code" to regulate the content and form of some other product, service, or activity in our society: advertisements, automobiles, presidential candidates, potato chips, and so on. Having drawn up such a code, argue its necessity (i.e., that certain desirable effects will follow, or that undesirable effects will continue if the Code is not adopted and enforced).

5. Develop a Motion Picture Production Code that reflects your own values and standards.

6. You are away from home and you receive a letter in which your younger brother or sister mentions that he or she is interested in seeing a particularly violent or sexually explicit film currently playing. Write a letter, trying to talk him or her out of going to see it. Try not to sound patronizing or omniscient.

THE STRUGGLE OVER
DOUBLE INDEMNITY

Murray Schumach

Murray Schumach was born in Brooklyn, New York, in 1913. He worked for the *New York Times* from 1930 until 1978, reporting extensively on the theater, television shows, and the Hollywood movie industry. His articles have been reprinted in major newspapers and magazines throughout the United States and abroad.

☐

Any newspaper reader has run across stories about a wife and her 1
lover who join to murder her husband. He has read it so many times it is a cliché. The only things he looks for are why and how the poor husband was dispatched. Was it for money? Love? Perhaps even out of boredom? And back in the thirties, when scandal, despite — or perhaps because of — the Depression and the Roosevelt Revolution, received more space and pictures than it does today, most adults and adolescents were almost experts on this type of crime.

Yet, when such a story was suggested as a movie in 1935, it 2
started ten years of bickering between movie producers and Hollywood censors. Today *Double Indemnity* is just an exciting murder movie. It is not regarded as a threat to morality. It is difficult to imagine that *Double Indemnity* was a trail-blazer in movie history.

Double Indemnity is important in the story of American movie 3
censorship — and movie trends — for two reasons. First, it was the first movie in which both the male and the female protagonists were thorough villains. Second, *Double Indemnity* paved the way for America's twentieth-century successor to the erudite Sherlock Holmes — the tough-talking omniscient private eye. James M. Cain, author of the novel on which the book was based, must have been surprised at the Hollywood ruckus. For as a book it did not begin to create the stir of such other Cain novels as *The Postman Always Rings Twice*.

The plot as originally suggested for a movie went as follows. A 4
married woman and her lover murder her husband for his insurance. Eventually, the woman confesses the murder to investigators from the insurance company who withhold the information from the police because the police have already called the death an accident and do

From pages 62–65 of "Indemnity, Eternity, Plus Two" in *The Face on the Cutting Room Floor* by Murray Schumach. Copyright © 1964 by Murray Schumach. Reprinted by permission of William Morrow & Company.

not want to be bothered. The couple leaves the United States and later commits joint suicide.

Looking back on the hectic history of the conversion of this book 5 into a movie, it seems as though it could not have taken place during the third and fourth decades of the twentieth century. The arguments raised by Hollywood's censors seem more characteristic of Victorian England than of the American literary ferment that produced the Group Theatre on Broadway and the incendiary realism of James T. Farrell's *Studs Lonigan* trilogy and John Steinbeck's *The Grapes of Wrath*.

The struggle over *Double Indemnity* in Hollywood began on Octo- 6 ber 9, 1935, when Maurice Revnes, of Metro-Goldwyn-Mayer, sent a letter to Breen asking him to read the book and to advise "at the earliest possible date, as to whether we will be able to make it as it stands or whether you could suggest any changes that would make it possible to get past the censors with it."

The very next day Breen rushed off a letter to Mayer, then boss 7 of the Metro studio, saying: "I regret to inform you that, because of a number of elements inherent in the story in its present form, it is our judgment that the story is in violation of provisions of the Production Code and, as such, is almost certain to result in a picture which we would be compelled to reject if, and when, such a picture is presented for approval."

He summarized the plot and pointed out it was "replete with 8 explicit details of the planning of the murder and the effective commission of the crime, thus definitely violating the Code provisions which forbid the presentation of 'details of crime.' "

Breen raised objections to the central characters themselves. 9 "The leading characters are murderers who cheat the law and die at their own hands. . . . It may be argued that one of these criminals is, in a sense, glorified by his confession to save the girl he loves." This was a reference to the fact that the murderer falls in love with the stepdaughter of his accomplice and confesses when he realizes the circumstantial evidence points to the girl's sweetheart.

"The story," Breen continued, "deals improperly with an illicit 10 and adulterous sex relationship. The general low tone and sordid flavor of this story make it, in our judgment, thoroughly unacceptable for screen production before mixed audiences in the theater. I am sure you will agree that it is most important to avoid what the Code calls 'the hardening' of audiences, especially those who are young and impressionable, to the thought and fact of crime."

Copies of this letter were sent to Paramount, Fox, Warner 11 Brothers and Columbia, all of which were showing interest in the project.

The next chapter of this tale began on September 21, 1943, eight 12
years later, when Paramount sent to the censors a new version that
was part outline and part script. In this approach, prepared by Billy
Wilder and Charles Brackett, the murderer kills his accomplice; then,
though mortally wounded by her, talks his confession into a dicta-
phone at the insurance office. By this time the insurance investigator
is closing in on him, and he collapses just as the investigator arrives.

Breen's reaction to this version was entirely different. Presum- 13
ably, during the passing years, details of crime had become more
common and adultery was no longer quite as objectionable in the
movies. In addition, the suicide, to which religious groups usually
take strong objection, had been eliminated and the insurance investigator had not, in effect, connived with a pair of murderers to permit
their escape.

This time Breen's objections were minor and easily remedied. He 14
pointed out that in one scene the wife was wearing a bath towel in a
manner that was too revealing. He suggested that the towel "should
certainly go below her knees." This was done. Then there was a line,
in the lingo of the novel — and of the private eye brigades that were
to follow — that the censor did not like. A lady, instead of being told
to sit down, was asked to "park your south end." The more polite
form was substituted.

What began as an argument about morals in *Double Indemnity* 15
ended in a quibble about words, a pattern that is fairly common in
censorship matters.

Review Questions

1. Why was *Double Indemnity* a landmark in American film censorship?
2. What were Breen's initial objections to the proposed film treatment?
3. Why was the 1943 version acceptable?

Discussion Questions

1. To what extent do you agree with Breen that "it is most important to avoid . . . 'the hardening' of audiences, especially those who are young and impressionable, to the thought and fact of crime"? To what extent is Breen voicing a legitimate concern? *Can* audiences become hardened to the "thought and fact of crime"?
2. Should filmmakers be discouraged from portraying the blatant violation of a commonly accepted norm or standard of conduct — even if those standards change over the years?
3. What is the purpose of the opening paragraph, which does not deal directly with film censorship?

4. What is Schumach's attitude toward the incidents he is recounting, as shown by his choice of examples, his language, his *manner* of telling the story?

5. What is the significance of Schumach's sentence that begins (in paragraph 1): "And back in the thirties, when scandal, despite — or perhaps because of — the Depression and the Roosevelt Revolution . . ."? What does this suggest about the relationship between social realities and the kinds of things the general public wants to read about or to see?

Writing Suggestions

1. Write a screen treatment of a film you have seen recently, as it might read *after* a censor, applying the 1930 Code, got through with it.

2. Write an account of the *process* of trying to make something acceptable that was previously unacceptable. The subject may be something in your own experience or something from your reading.

THE MOTION PICTURE PRODUCTION CODE (1968)

By the mid-1960s it had become apparent that the 1930 Production Code was obsolete. In 1953 Otto Preminger's *The Moon Is Blue* was refused a Code seal because of its off-color language (such as "seduce" and "virgin"). Preminger resigned from the Motion Picture Producer's Association and released the film without a seal — successfully. In 1956 Elia Kazan's explicit (for 1956) *Baby Doll* was granted a code seal, as was Stanley Kubrick's *Lolita* in 1962. In 1964 Eric Johnston, head of the M.P.P.A., died, and was replaced — two years later — by Jack Valenti, a former assistant to President Lyndon B. Johnson. After Valenti granted a code seal to Mike Nichols's *Who's Afraid of Virginia Woolf?*, a film with a veritable blue streak of profanity, he knew for certain that it was time to relegate the old code to the scrap heap. The system designed as its replacement was modeled on the rating system in effect for decades in Great Britain. The new emphasis would not be on censorship, but on restricting children and adolescents from "mature" films. A rating board, whose members were appointed by Valenti, was established to view films and assign ratings. Producers whose films received restrictive ratings (X or R) could often receive less restrictive ratings by snipping the offending scenes and resubmitting the film. The board's attitudes have liberalized considerably since the early years following 1968; many films that in the early 1970s received R ratings would be rated PG if released today.

☐

This Code is designed to keep in close harmony with the mores, culture, the moral sense and change in our society.   1

The objectives of the Code are: 2

1. To encourage artistic expression by expanding creative freedom.

2. To assure that the freedom which encourages the artist remains responsible and sensitive to the standards of the larger society.

Censorship is an odious enterprise. We oppose censorship and classification by governments because they are alien to the American tradition of freedom.   3

Much of this nation's strength and purpose is drawn from the premise that the humblest of citizens has the freedom of his own choice. Censorship destroys this freedom of choice.   4

It is within this framework that the Motion Picture Association continues to recognize its obligation to the society of which it is an integral part.   5

In our society parents are the arbiters of family conduct. Parents have the primary responsibility to guide their children in the kind of lives they lead, the character they build, the books they read, and the movies and other entertainment to which they are exposed.   6

The creators of motion pictures undertake a responsibility to make available pertinent information about their pictures which will assist parents to fulfill their responsibilities.   7

But this alone is not enough. In further recognition of our obligation to the public, and most especially to parents, we have extended the Code operation to include a nationwide voluntary film rating program which has as its prime objective a sensitive concern for children. Motion pictures will be reviewed by a Code and Rating Administration which, when it reviews a motion picture as to its conformity with the standards of the Code, will issue ratings. It is our intent that all motion pictures exhibited in the United States will carry a rating. These ratings are: 8

(G) Suggested for General Audiences

This category includes motion pictures that in the opinion of the Code and Rating Administration would be acceptable for all audiences, without consideration of age.   9

(M) Suggested for Mature Audiences — Adults & Mature Young People[1]

This category includes motion pictures that in the opinion of the 10 Code and Rating Administration, because of their theme, content and treatment, might require more mature judgment by viewers, and about which parents should exercise their discretion.

(R) Restricted — Persons Under 16 Not Admitted Unless Accompanied by Parent or Adult Guardian

This category includes motion pictures that in the opinion of the 11 Code and Rating Administration, because of their theme, content or treatment, should not be presented to persons under 16 unless accompanied by a parent or adult guardian.

(X) Persons Under 16 Not Admitted

This category includes motion pictures submitted to the Code and 12 Rating Administration which in the opinion of the Code and Rating Administration are rated (X) because of the treatment of sex, violence, crime or profanity. Pictures rated (X) do not qualify for a Code Seal. Pictures rated (X) should not be presented to persons under 16.

The program contemplates that any distributors outside the 13 membership of the Association who choose not to submit their motion pictures to the Code and Rating Administration will self-apply the (X) rating.

The ratings and their meanings will be conveyed by advertising; 14 by displays at the theaters; and in other ways. Thus, audiences, especially parents, will be alerted to the theme, content, and treatment of movies. Therefore, parents can determine whether a particular picture is one which children should see at the discretion of the parent; or only when accompanied by a parent; or should not see.

We believe self-restraint, self-regulation, to be in the American 15 tradition. The results of self-discipline are always imperfect because that is the nature of all things mortal. But this Code, and its administration, will make clear that freedom of expression does not mean toleration of license.

---

[1] In early 1970 the M rating was changed to GP. In early 1972 it was changed again, this time to PG ("Parental Guidance Suggested; some material may not be suitable for pre-teenagers"). The age limit for the R and X categories has been raised to 17.

The test of self-restraint — the rule of reason . . . lies in the   16
treatment of a subject for the screen.

All members of the Motion Picture Association, as well as the   17
National Association of Theatre Owners, the International Film Im-
porters and Distributors of America, and other independent pro-
ducer-distributors are cooperating in this endeavor. Most motion
pictures exhibited in the United States will be submitted for Code
approval and rating, or for rating only, to the Code and Rating
Administration. The presence of the Seal indicates to the public that a
picture has received Code approval.

We believe in and pledge our support to these deep and funda-   18
mental values in a democratic society:

Freedom of choice . . .   19

The right of creative man to achieve artistic excellence . . .   20

The importance of the role of the parent as the guide of the   21
family's comfort . . .

Standards For Production

In furtherance of the objectives of the Code to accord with the mores,   22
the culture, and the moral sense of our society, the principles stated
above and the following standards shall govern the Administrator in
his consideration of motion pictures submitted for Code approval:

- The basic dignity and value of human life shall be respected and upheld. Restraint shall be exercised in portraying the taking of life.
- Evil, sin, crime and wrong-doing shall not be justified.
- Special restraint shall be exercised in portraying criminal or anti-social activities in which minors participate or are involved.
- Detailed and protracted acts of brutality, cruelty, physical violence, torture and abuse shall not be presented.
- Indecent or undue exposure of the human body shall not be presented.
- Illicit sex relationships shall not be justified. Intimate sex scenes violating common standards of decency shall not be portrayed.
- Restraint and care shall be exercised in presentations dealing with sex aberrations.
- Obscene speech, gestures or movements shall not be presented. Undue profanity shall not be permitted.
- Religion shall not be demeaned.
- Words or symbols contemptuous of racial, religious or national groups, shall not be used so as to incite bigotry or hatred.
- Excessive cruelty to animals shall not be portrayed and animals shall not be treated inhumanely.

Review Questions

1. What are the objectives of the 1968 code? How do they differ from the objectives of the 1930 Code?
2. In its general framework how does the 1968 Code compare and contrast with the 1930 Code? How do the "Particular Applications" of the 1930 Code compare and contrast with the "Standards of Production" of the 1968 Code?

Discussion Questions

1. The authors of the 1968 Code caution that "freedom of expression does not mean toleration of license." What does this mean to you?
2. What is the *primary* emphasis of the 1968 Code?
3. What criteria does one use to determine "the mores, the culture, and the moral sense of our society"?
4. In what ways is the *attitude* of the writers of the 1968 Code revealed, as concerns censorship?
5. By their use of language, do the writers of the 1968 Code show themselves any less concerned with morality and with "correct standards of life" than the writers of the 1930 Code? By their use of language, do the writers of the later code appear to be less certain of their values and their standards than the writers of the earlier code? Cite examples in support of your conclusions.

Writing Suggestions

1. Explain why the 1968 Code is or is not an acceptable compromise between the strict 1930 Code and no restrictions at all. Include a thesis statement in your introductory paragraph, and lead off each subsequent paragraph with a topic sentence.
2. Using the 1968 Code standards, classify some novels, short stories, plays, or comic strips that you have read or seen recently. Justify your classifications, using specific examples from the works you are dealing with.

THE CASE OF *BONNIE AND CLYDE*
John Simon

John Simon is one of the country's most respected — and literate — critics. Born in Yugoslavia in 1925, he came to the U.S. in 1941. He has written film and theater (and cultural) criticism for such magazines as *The Hudson Review, Theater Arts, Esquire, Commonweal, The New Leader,* and most recently, *The National Review.* Among his books are *Private Screenings, Movies into Film,* and *Ingmar Bergman Directs.*

Bonnie and Clyde, made in 1967, became a landmark film for its graphic depiction of violence, as well as for its sympathetic treatment of the two protagonists, Bonnie Parker and Clyde Barrow, notorious — and fascinating — bank robbers of the 1920s.

☐

Agnès Varda[1] tells me she liked *Bonnie and Clyde* because "it is violent without being sadistic." I doubt that there is much difference between the two when violence is dwelt on with such clucking solicitude. At the utmost one could call such violence unconscious sadism. But that may be even more attractive to the asinine audiences that guffaw their way through the film; overt sadism is kinky, whereas this is just rousing shooting the hell out of people. As directed by Arthur Penn from a screenplay by Newman and Benton, the well-known slick-magazine writers, the picture is clever trash. The formula is hayseed comedy bursting sporadically into pyrotechnical bloodshed and laced with sentimental pop-Freudianism.   1

The technique is artful, though derived from Godard[2] — quick   2
little vignettes ending in verbal or visual punchlines following one another at breakneck speed. A group of semimoronic naturals gather around an impotent youth and an infantile girl for an extended crime spree that shifts from the absurd and mildly funny to the childishly cruel and murderous. The explanations implied befit a primer of

---

[1] French filmmaker, director of *Cleo from 5 to 7* (1962). [All footnotes by Behrens and Rosen.]

[2] Jean-Luc Godard, French filmmaker and critic. His 1959 film *Breathless (A Bout de Souffle)* helped launch the French New Wave, a cinematic movement often characterized by abrupt editing techniques, freer use of camera movement, disjointed plot lines, and frenetic pace.

abnormal psychology for junior high schools, and that the whole romp is based on a true story does not bring it more than an inch closer to truth. It is outfitted with considerable authenticity of period and place, however, and photographed cannily in sometimes striking, sometimes slick, color.

But the whole thing stinks in the manner of a carefully made-up, combed, and manicured corpse. Crime may have its funny side, but here, for long stretches, it has nothing but funny sides. To switch then, without warning, from belly laughs to bloodbaths and produce facile shock effects is added dishonesty. Between murder as fun and murder as Grand Guignol[3] there is little to choose from. The audience is invited to have a lark either way, and responds to the invitation with unappetizing explosions of laughter and applause. The acting is good, but slop is slop, even served with a silver ladle. 3

This follow-up review was published three months later:

Since it seems to be customary to have second thoughts on *Bonnie and Clyde,* here are mine. They are in no way a palinode, only an amplification of what, I feel, I originally stated with excessive laconism. 4

What is basically wrong with the film is not so much violence as hero worship. The point at which the disaffected intellectual and the footloose lowbrow meet is their shared love for the outlaw. Arthur Penn and his scenarists combine the sentimentality of the second-rate intellectual with a first-rate roustabout's amorality, and out come a Bonnie and Clyde who are all bumbling charm, naïve cleverness, derailed ingenuity. Critics who have seen them as bunglers are myopic; for all their limitations, imposed on them by an unjust society exacerbated by the Depression (here immature sociology joins hands with amateur psychiatry), they are witty, inventive, fun-loving and alive — which is more than you can say for any of the other characters in the film. The policemen are faceless nonentities; the sheriff and the self-righteous father, downright repulsive. Bonnie and Clyde, moreover, are even physically beautiful — star children among the toadstools. 5

The message is that in a capitalist society, and a bankrupt one at that, the outlaw is a far finer fellow than the inane solid citizen who plays into the hands of the exploiters on top, quietly tightens his belt, and even rats on the guys who rob the rich man's banks. The robbers don't exactly turn the loot over to the poor — even this fanciful 6

---

[3] A dramatic genre emphasizing horror, cruelty, and torture, named after the Grand Guignol Theatre of Paris, founded in 1897, where plays that chilled and delighted audiences by such means were regularly presented.

hagiography daren't go that far — but they do make a few Robin Hoodish gestures that ring even falser than their specious context.

Now, the robber can in certain extreme situations be a hero — at 7 any rate, a flawed tragic hero — as in Kleist's *Michael Kohlhaas*,[4] which Penn & Co. would have done well to ponder. But to argue as they do that in periods of social injustice (which means anywhere this side of Utopia) the outlaw is clearly superior to the staid, plodding citizen is sentimental nonsense and moral truancy. The truth of the matter is that those little shopkeepers and bank clerks, dim and dull as they may have been, were, provided they were law-abiding, immeasurably better people than all your robbers and murderers. That is the simple fact that *Bonnie and Clyde,* with its puerile antihero worship, militantly ignores.

Again, I cannot help being made uncomfortable by the biograph- 8 ical falsifications. A work of art has the right to take liberties with history, but does a piece of non-art have the same rights? Certainly, if the subject is someone like Alexander the Great, about whom there are not enough facts available, and those that are may not be facts. Equally obviously, where one enters areas that cannot be docu- mented — thoughts, intimate conversations, private moments — fiction is in order. But where the time is barely past, and data, no less than living memories, still abound, I wonder whether gross distor- tions of fact can be condoned. All the more so as the movie begins with pictures of the actual Bonnie and Clyde, and has narration (dropped later on) in the manner of genuine documentaries and faithful restagings of history.

Esthetic prettification provides the final dishonesty. We get 9 scenes that are stifling in pretty-prettiness (the esthetic equivalent of goody-goodiness), such as the reconciliation in the wheat field with little clouds passing over the sun to produce a fretwork of light and shadow, laughter and tears, analogous to the thunder and lightning in the murder scenes of hackneyed thrillers. Worse yet is the reunion with Bonnie's mother, photographed as a Grant Wood[5] filtered

---

[4] A short novel, written in 1808, by German poet and dramatist, Bernard Heinrich Wilhelm von Kleist (1777-1811). Set in the sixteenth century, and based on an actual case, it tells of a man who, driven by a sense of outraged injustice, becomes an outlaw.

[5] American painter (1892-1942), the leading exponent of the genre known as Midwestern Regionalism, which flourished during the 1930s. His most fa- mous painting is the endlessly parodied "American Gothic," a classically simple, though powerful, depiction of a farmer and his wife.

[6] Pierre Puvis de Chavannes (1824-1898) was the leading French mural painter of the 19th century, whose oil canvases adorn the walls of many public buildings in France. His treatment of subjects from classical antiquity is

through Puvis de Chavannes,[6] through enough filters to outfit the rose window of Chartres Cathedral.

The film's estheticizing continually obtrudes on and obfuscates 10 moral values. Thus, with one highly debatable exception, the crimes and killings performed *by* the Barrow gang are all picturesque, humorous, cozy or, at worst, matter-of-fact affairs. But the violence performed *upon* the gang is always made as harrowingly inhuman as possible. This is explained by the champions of the film as the outlaws' belated awareness that death is real, and the grave their goal — in other words, a rude moral awakening. But, in fact, Clyde makes it clear, in an idyllic scene, that had he to do it over again, he would do exactly the same. He has learned nothing. Fair enough, if only the filmmakers did not so resoundingly applaud him for it. That very confession, made amid the joys of a finally consummated affair, emerges as a heroic *non serviam!* and the brutalities preceding and following it merely serve to underscore the outlaws' courage in shouldering their cruel and unjust fate with round, unblinking eyes.

The point is driven home by the staging of the lovers' death. 11 They are mowed down by a barrage from innumerable guns, sniping out of craven concealment. This much is historical fact, I dare say. But they die a love death that is a superimposition of *Romeo and Juliet* on *Tristan und Isolde*. It is done in lyrical slow motion, without disfigurement of their physical beauty — perfectly inconsistent with the previous naturalism in mutilations and gore. Bonnie is shaken by the shower of bullets as if by the spasms of orgasm, while Clyde choreographically rolls over toward her, star-crossed rather than bullet-riddled, his dying hand reaching out for the beloved straight out of Shakespeare's Verona.

When this syrupy piece of idealization is considered, as it has to 12 be, the final comment on the story, there can be no doubt about the intentions of Penn and his collaborators. What we witness is not the death of a pair of tawdry criminals, but a *J'accuse* hurled at the materialist society that led these innocents to the slaughter. I am for all assaults on materialism, but when the attack is launched by such a frail and leaky cockboat, it is doomed to sink into sentimentality, bathos, anti-art, and, worst of all, inhumanity.

Review Questions

1. What are Simon's objections to *Bonnie and Clyde*?
2. Why does Simon take exception to the prettiness of the film?

---

often allegorical and idealized, characterized by a simplicity of form and rhythmic line, and pale, flat coloring.

Discussion Questions

1. What is Simon's *primary* objection to *Bonnie and Clyde?* How does this objection tie in with the "General Principles" and restrictions of the 1930 Code?
2. Do you think Simon is taking an excessively moralistic position? Is this position — for all its sophistication of expression — too close to that of the 1930 Code? Or is his position a sound and responsible one?
3. Simon seems to delight in witty phrasing ("slop is slop, even served with a silver ladle") or biting sarcasm ("photographed . . . through enough filters to outfit the rose window of Chartres Cathedral"). In addition, he uses words ("palinode," *"non serviam"*) that many of his readers would not know. Are you turned off by such a sneering, highfalutin approach? Or is Simon's only obligation as a critic to say exactly what he believes in whatever way he sees fit?

Writing Suggestion

Review a film you have seen recently in the theater or on television, paying particular attention to the moral values that are implied. If you like, you can try to imitate Simon's tone.

THE CASE OF *DEEP THROAT*
Thomas Meehan

Thomas Meehan writes short stories, drama, satire, and factual articles. His work has appeared in such magazines as *The New Yorker* and *Saturday Review* (where the following selection first appeared). In 1977 he won the Tony Award for writing the book of the musical, *Annie.*

☐

Aside from Bertolucci's *Last Tango in Paris,* which I haven't yet seen, 1
the most talked-about movie in America today is neither a major-
studio Hollywood release nor a critically acclaimed import from Europe but is instead a cheapie hard-core porno flick called *Deep Throat.*
Since opening last June in New York, at a West 49th Street grind
house known as the New Mature World Theater, *Deep Throat* has

grossed nearly a million dollars from moviegoers who paid $5 apiece to get in. And it has made another $2.5 million or so from showings in more than seventy other theaters around the country. Eventually, in fact, *Deep Throat* is expected to earn around $6 million for its producers, a figure that is especially impressive when one learns that the picture was made in six days for a total outlay of $25,000.

But perhaps even more interesting than its enormous earnings is the curious sociological phenomenon, dubbed "porno chic," that *Deep Throat* has given rise to in New York. Among those who've reportedly taken in *Deep Throat* in recent weeks are Johnny Carson, Mike Nichols, Sandy Dennis, Ben Gazzara, Jack Nicholson, Suzy Knickerbocker, Truman Capote, Earl Wilson, and the entire staff of the *New York Times Book Review*. Each evening, as serpentine lines of giggling moviegoers wait to get into *Deep Throat,* chauffeured limousines pull up in front of the New Mature World Theater to disgorge gaggles of New York's wealthiest and most famous people. In the world of Elaine's, Jimmy's, and the Cat Pack, in short, *Deep Throat* is required viewing. In the past, of course, the In crowd wouldn't have been caught embalmed at a pornographic movie, nor would most of the rest of us — such films were only for balding middle-aged men in raincoats who slunk furtively into seedy porno houses when they hoped that nobody was looking.

Perhaps it's not surprising that *Deep Throat* should have been the film to bring about porno chic, for the picture has a good deal going for it, particularly when compared with other pornographic movies. In the first place, *Deep Throat* is professionally made — in 35-mm. color and with high-fidelity synchronized sound. And so — unlike most other dirty movies, which are made with jerky, hand-held 16-mm. cameras and without sound — it has the glossy look of a real movie that might have been turned out by Warner Brothers or MGM. Also, the picture has been skillfully edited and even has an original musical score. *Deep Throat,* moreover, is not a soft-core cheat in which sexual acts are simulated — indeed, it scarcely could be more hard-core. Though the film is only sixty-two minutes long, it graphically depicts no fewer than fifteen sexual acts, including vaginal intercourse, sodomy, fellatio, and cunnilingus. Nothing is left to the imagination; in its clinical close-ups of sexual goings-on *Deep Throat* struck me as a picture that might have been made either as a training film for the Masters and Johnson Institute or as a medical-school classroom movie for students of gynecology. Then, too, there's the fact that, unlike most other dirty movies, *Deep Throat* has a rudimentary plot of sorts, having to do with an anguished young lady who is unable to derive pleasure from sex until she discovers that she is an anatomical freak whose clitoris is in her throat rather than where it properly belongs. And thus she is at last able to find sexual satisfaction through the practice of oral sex. Really. I'm not making any of this up.

Set in Miami, where it was filmed on location early last year by a group of New Yorkers led by Gerard Damiano, a long-time writer-producer-director of pornographic films, *Deep Throat* is basically supposed to be a comedy, but its unprintable jokes are on the preadolescent level of the infantile dirty stories that fourth-grade schoolboys swap in the playground at recess. And most of the picture, which is funny only when it doesn't intend to be, is played in the broad, knockabout manner of a badly written and performed burlesque sketch. A great deal of the film, too, is excruciatingly boring — its sixty-two minutes seems at times like sixty-two hours.

So why has *Deep Throat* been such a smashing box-office success? Mainly, I think, because of the performance given by its star, a twenty-one-year-old "party girl" from Bryan, Texas, who calls herself Linda Lovelace. In contrast to most actresses appearing in pornographic movies, who are dumpy, ugly, and fairly long in the tooth, Miss Lovelace is at once youthful, passably pretty, and has a lithe and supple body. And while she evidences not the slightest talent for acting, she does possess what no less an authority than the *New York Times* has termed "a virtuosic talent for fellatio." As a matter of fact, when it comes to oral sex, she appears to have mastered a trick that one has previously associated only with sword swallowers. And the main reason why Mike Nichols, Truman Capote, *et al.*, have been flocking to *Deep Throat* has been to witness this astonishing and freakish trick, which Miss Lovelace performs five times in the picture. Certainly, there's little else of much interest in *Deep Throat*, which is essentially a dumb and distasteful bore.

A number of New Yorkers have lately been hastening to *Deep Throat* because there is a chance that the picture may soon be shut down by the authorities. That is, it has been officially charged on two counts of promoting obscenity, and a ten-day, non-jury trial was held in New York last December before Criminal Court Judge Joel J. Tyler to determine whether *Deep Throat* is indeed legally obscene. At the moment, Judge Tyler is mulling over more than a thousand pages of expert testimony given at the trial by psychiatrists and others, and he is expected to hand down his decision within the next few weeks.[1] No matter how Judge Tyler rules, however, the producers of *Deep Throat* have already got a second Linda Lovelace porno vehicle before the

---

[1] In March 1973 (shortly after this article appeared) Judge Tyler ruled that *Deep Throat* was "indisputably and irredeemably" obscene, calling it "a feast of carrion and squalor," a "nadir of decadence," and "brazenly explicit." "This is one throat," he observed, "that deserves to be cut." The film was shut down and the exhibitor fined $100,000. Up to that time *Deep Throat* had grossed

cameras, budgeted at $70,000 and entitled — what else? — *Deep Throat II.*

Discussion Questions

1. How do you account for the extraordinary success of *Deep Throat,* and for the fact that "respectable" people went to see it in droves? Is there some unexpectedly large craving for pornography among many more people than was previously suspected? Is the enthusiastic response to *Deep Throat* a sign of social decadence or degeneracy?

2. Do pornographic films like *Deep Throat* pose a threat to a civilized society? For instance, do they, in the long run, "lower the moral standards" (1930 Code) of those who see them? To what extent, if any, should pornographic films be restricted? Why?

Writing Suggestion

Traditionally, straitlaced middle-class morality has been the chief adversary of pornography. More recently, however, the feminist movement has joined the fight, claiming that pornography is male chauvinist in the extreme, degrading and dehumanizing women to the status of sexual objects, and desensitizing men in their responses toward women. Write an essay in which you consider the feminist position on pornography, explaining why you agree or disagree.

---

about $1 million in New York City and an additional $4 million elsewhere in the country. (Later, of course, films every bit as explicit as *Deep Throat* were exhibited unmolested in New York and other cities.)

In April, 1976, obscenity charges were brought in Memphis, Tennessee against Harry Reems, the male star of *Deep Throat.* (The film had not been made in Memphis, only exhibited there.) The Reems case became something of a cause célèbre, partly because of the sensational nature of the film, partly because of the First Amendment implications. In December, 1976, Reems and eleven others involved in the making of *Deep Throat* were convicted by a federal jury in Memphis, and faced with both fines and prison terms. In 1977, a new trial was granted for the *Deep Throat* defendants, at the conclusion of which Reems's conviction was overturned. However, Judge Harry Wellford sentenced eight other defendants to fines up to $10,000 and prison terms of from three months to a year. [Behrens and Rosen]

SEX AND VIOLENCE: PORNOGRAPHY HURTS

Sexual attacks against women — our newspapers, magazines, novels, movies and television shows are full of such incidents. Considering the long history and continued prevalence of this kind of violence, it might seem that little can be done to curb it. But the situation may not be so bleak. Social scientists are beginning to pinpoint the many factors associated with violence, and the National Institute of Mental Health recently has concluded that an understanding of the conditions that lead to sexual attacks against women should be a major goal of research. Some of that research was presented last week in Montreal at the annual meeting of the American Psychological Association.   1

Pornography and its possible role as a causative factor in eliciting violent behavior against women is one of the many areas currently being investigated. And the findings contradict much previous research. Ten years ago, the Presidential Commission on Obscenity and Pornography concluded that there was no relationship between exposure to erotic presentations and subsequent aggression, particularly sexual crimes. This conclusion was attacked by some researchers at the time and has been attacked by many (especially feminists) since. Now researchers are reevaluating the data, reexamining the question and finding solid evidence that at least one kind of pornography is responsible for attitudinal and behavioral changes that result in increased aggression by men against women. The type of pornography in question is called aggressive-erotic. It contains explicit sexual violence against women, and in recent years it has been produced and shown with increasing frequency. Two research projects, each taking a different approach to the study of sexually violent material, were among those described at the APA meeting.   2

Edward Donnerstein of the University of Wisconsin in Madison conducted one of the experiments. In order to examine the effects of aggressive-erotic material on male aggression toward females, 120 male college students were either angered or treated neutrally by either a male or female confederate of the experimenter. The subjects then were shown either a neutral, erotic or aggressive-erotic film. Several minutes later they were given an opportunity to deliver electric shocks to the fingertips of the original male or female confederate — as part of what they were told was a study of the effects of stress on learning. The subjects were unaware of the true purpose of the   3 research, and they did not realize that the films they had seen were part of the same experiment. Debriefings following the experiment, says Donnerstein, indicate that the subjects really had been tricked by the rather complex research design.

The results showed that exposure to an aggressive-erotic film   4
increased aggressive behavior (giving shocks) to a level higher than for the erotic film. These findings were even more pronounced in subjects who had previously been angered by the confederates. When angered subjects were paired with a male, the aggressive-erotic film produced no more aggression than did the erotic film. When paired with a female, however, the subjects displayed an increase in aggression only after viewing the aggressive-erotic film.

Donnerstein's study and others like it find consistent results, but   5
they are open to criticism on several counts — the artificiality of the laboratory setting, and the aggression is seen only immediately after exposure to violent pornography. "There clearly exists a need to assess the effects of mass media stimuli that fuse sexuality and violence outside the laboratory context," say Neil M. Malamuth and James V. Check of the University of Manitoba in Winnipeg. And that's what they have done.

Hundreds of students were sent to the movies as part of an   6
experiment to test the effects of exposure to films that portray sexual violence as having positive consequences. The movies they saw were not pornography, just everyday sex and violence. They included *Swept Away* (a violent male sexual aggressor and a woman who learns to crave sexual sadism find love on a deserted island) and *The Getaway* (a woman falls in love with the man who raped her in front of her husband, then both taunt the husband until he commits suicide). The control films used, *A Man and a Woman* and *Hooper,* show tender romance and nonexplicit sex.

Within a week of viewing the movies, an attitude survey was   7
administered to all students in the introductory psychology sections from which the subjects had been signed up for the experiment. The students did not know that the survey had anything to do with the films they had seen, but embedded within the survey were questions relating to acceptance of interpersonal violence, acceptance of the rape myth (that women enjoy being raped) and adversarial sexual beliefs. Subjects rated from "strongly agree" to "strongly disagree" statements such as "A man is never justified in hitting his wife" and "Many women have an unconscious wish to be raped and may then unconsciously set up a situation in which they are likely to be attacked."

The results of the survey indicated that exposure to the films   8
portraying violent sexuality increased male subjects' acceptance of interpersonal violence against women. A similar (though non-

significant) trend was found for acceptance of rape myths. For females the trend was in the opposite direction. Women exposed to violent-sexual films tended to be slightly less accepting of interpersonal violence and of rape myths than were control subjects. "The present findings," say the researchers, "constitute the first demonstration in a nonlaboratory setting . . . of relatively long-term effects of movies that fuse sexuality and violence."

Why do these findings differ from those of several years ago? 9 Check says that "what's in the pornography is the important factor." Recent findings still suggest that nonviolent pornography has no immediate negative effects (though long-term effects have not been studied), but the new pornography is much more violent. Donnerstein agrees: "We're looking at different material now. . . . Ten-year-old pornography is very bland in comparison." Also, he adds, the women's movement affected us. "Women raised the question, and now social scientists have the responsibility of proving or disproving." And what we have found comes as no surprise, he adds. Many studies, such as those with children and televised violence, have shown similar effects. Now it has been found with violence in pornography. "Everyone finds the same results, no matter what measures they use. . . . There are no discrepant data here at all."

Review Questions

1. What was the Donnerstein experiment? What did it indicate? What criticisms did it draw?
2. What was the Malamuth-Check experiment? How did it compare and contrast with the Donnerstein experiment?

Discussion Questions

1. Do these experiments offer what seems to you convincing evidence of a causal connection between exposure to "aggressive-erotic" films and aggressive behavior? If so, do you believe that additional restrictions on such films are called for (perhaps the reimposition of some of the old restrictions)?
2. To what extent do these experiments demonstrate the wisdom of some of the principles behind the 1930 and the 1968 Motion Picture Production Codes?

Writing Suggestion

Read "The Milgram Experiment" in the "Obedience to Authority" chapter. Write a paper in which you compare and contrast the Milgram experiment to the Donnerstein experiment. Consider the procedures, the results, and the morality of such experiments (particularly the use of deception).

ANYONE FOR CLEAN MOVIES?
Patricia Morrisroe

This article first appeared in *Parade*.

☐

Like the newsreel and the silent movie, the family film is in danger of 1 becoming extinct. Once the most popular category in Hollywood, the General Audience (G-rated) picture is now widely regarded as too tame for today's general audience.

"G movies don't pull in the crowds anymore," says Ted Arnow, 2 assistant vice president of the Loew's theater chain.

Aware that the G-rated audience is an elusive one, Hollywood has 3 turned its energies to the more popular — and profitable — PG (Parental Guidance) and R (Restricted) categories. Apart from animated films, the major Hollywood studios (except for Walt Disney) have said that they will not be producing any G-rated movies this year. This is a big switch from 1968, the year the film rating system started. At that time a third of all movies were G-rated.

One of the main reasons for the decline of the G picture is a 4 shortage of family audiences. According to Jack Valenti, president of the Motion Picture Association of America (MPAA): "Parents don't take their kids to movies anymore. TV has become the G-rated entertainment of today. People stay home for family shows because it's easier and cheaper."

The people who don't stay home are the 18- to 30-year-olds who 5 make up the majority of today's moviegoers. Because they want to see adult themes, the movie industry churns out hundreds of PG- and R-rated films. Ironically, there is a bonus in this strategy. Children and adolescents, considering themselves part of the adult market, swell the box office revenues of PG and R films even more. Enticed by such recent R-rated movies about kids as *Fame, Foxes* and *Little Darlings*, many children consider G-rated films about as exciting as their morning cereal.

"It's very difficult to create a good G movie," explains Eddie 6 Kalish, senior vice president of marketing for Paramount Pictures. "G means everything has to be perfectly antiseptic, which certainly prevents today's comedies and horror films from attaining that rating. Everyone in the industry just takes it for granted a film will be rated at least a PG."

In what has almost become a game to today's filmmakers, their 7
pictures are "spiced up" by the addition of gratuitous violence and
four-letter words to be assured of getting a PG.

The recent *Little Miss Marker*, a G film if there ever was one, is a 8
perfect example. The fourth version of the popular Damon Runyon
story, it was raised to PG status by the addition of several off-color
words in the racetrack sequence. "I don't know what all the fuss was
about," says producer Jennings Lang. "You could hardly hear the
words anyway. Besides, G films and Disney are like bread and butter.
But without that Disney name, the G film is a big turnoff to kids."

Even *Star Wars* didn't risk the jinx of the G. According to Daily 9
Variety, the preliminary version initially earned a G rating from the
MPAA. To get the desired PG, however, a scene depicting a dismem-
bered arm was added to the cantina sequence.

There is growing evidence that even young children are biased 10
against the G rating. Martin Rabinovitch, who recently moved from
the Disney studio to become vice president of advertising at Columbia
Pictures, says: "When I was at Disney, we worked with several psychologists and learned that as kids get to be around the age of 13, they
want to put distance between themselves and younger children. One
way to do this is to boycott the G movie."

Noting this prejudice, even the venerable Disney studio has been 11
forced to play the PG game, releasing its first non-G film, *The Black
Hole*, last year. "We're not living in a G-rated world anymore, and we
can't pretend that we are," says Tom Wilhite, a 27-year-old vice
president at Disney.

While Disney is not abandoning the G film entirely, it is attempt- 12
ing to build up a stable of young filmmakers who are more in touch
with today's youth. Recent efforts have not been extremely successful,
however. Under the total control of two 23-year-old film school grad-
uates, a movie called *Midnight Madness* turned out to be too off-color
even for the studio's new "sophisticated" image. Executives at Disney
headquarters refused to give the film their seal of approval. "Disney is
going to start making movies like *Kramer vs. Kramer, Being There* and
Breaking Away," says Wilhite. "But rest assured, we're not going to
jump into the R-rated market." So for the time being, the next in the
Love Bug series, *Herbie Goes Bananas*, will still be rated G.

Many people blame the MPAA's rating system for creating the 13
stigma against the G picture. "One of the biggest problems we had at
Disney," says Rabinovitch, "is that people immediately pigeonholed
our films as strictly for children. That's a very difficult stereotype to
escape."

If the family film is to survive in the next decade, it would seem 14
that the movie industry should work hard at getting rid of the "G
stigma." Unless it does, G won't stand for anything other than Gone.

Review Questions

1. Why has the G-rated movie all but disappeared?
2. How is Disney Studios, last bastion of the G movie, attempting to accommodate itself to present realities?

Discussion Questions

1. Do you regret the decline (and possible extinction) of the G movie — or the fact that " 'We're not living in a G-rated world anymore . . .' "? Do your parents, or others you know in your parents' generation, regret this decline? Or do you believe that the fate of the G movie signals the welcome end of repressive Victorian morality?
2. How can the industry help parents who don't want to expose their children to certain kinds of objectionable material? For instance, some parents might have little objection to profanity, but much objection to violence on the screen. Should the rating system be revised, so that a PG-L (or R-L) rating would indicate the presence of bad language, while R-S or R-V, respectively, would indicate the presence of sex or violence?

Writing Suggestion

Put yourself in the position of Martin Rabinovitch, when he was at Disney Studios. Write a memo to the studio executives, indicating how the "family film" might survive. One of your main jobs is to show how the studio can make films that are enjoyed not only by children, but also by their parents.

WHERE DO YOU DRAW THE LINE?
Victor B. Cline

Victor B. Cline is a professor of psychology at the University of Utah. After receiving his Ph.D. from the University of California at Berkeley in 1953, he became a research scientist at George Washington University's Human Resources Research Office. He has been for many years the program director of a traveling community mental health clinic. The author of numerous articles on psychotherapy, marriage, delinquency, and psycho-

Excerpted from pages ix–x and 355–358 in *Where Do You Draw the Line: An Exploration of Media Violence, Pornography and Censorship* by Victor Cline (Provo, Utah: Brigham Young University Press, 1974). Copyright © 1974 by Brigham Young University Press. Reprinted by permission of Brigham Young University Press.

diagnostics, he has a particular expertise in the effects of media violence and pornography, on which subject he has lectured at many professional symposia and public forums. The following selection is excerpted from the Preface and Conclusion to a collection of essays he edited on the subject of media violence, pornography, and censorship.

☐

Over the centuries, many men and women have given their lives and 1 in small increments have paved the way for the establishment of free societies such as ours. Few would deny that our civilization is built on the bodies of many martyrs and on the sacrifices of individuals who, unable to tolerate tyranny, opposed it in any form.

Because truth and justice in political and social affairs are often 2 difficult to determine immediately, it is generally conceded that they are best arrived at by free and open discussion. It is additionally conceded that free and unrestrained discussion is not only a legitimate outlet for dissent, but also that it greatly reduces the likelihood of more violent forms of social protest.

Freedom of speech, as embodied in the First Amendment to the 3 United States Constitution, has origins dating back to other forms of government: the participatory democracy of Greece's city states; the later development of Roman codes and institutions based on a "universal natural law," where all men were seen as equal; the still later Magna Charta of 1215; the Edict of Nantes (1598); France's Declaration of the Rights of Man and the Citizen (1789); as well as our own Constitution with its first ten amendments. These all represent tumultuous milestones in the development of our free society.

Since "free speech" represents such a vital element in the devel- 4 opment as well as the preservation of our free society, can we ever compromise on the issue?

Does the First Amendment to the Constitution really mean what 5 it says: "Congress shall make no law . . . abridging the freedom of speech or the press?"

As Norman Podhoretz, editor of *Commentary* magazine, has put it, 6 this is not an easy question to respond to:

Whenever I am forced to think seriously about freedom of speech and the problems it poses, I instantly find myself getting depressed. I tend to take an absolutistic position on freedom of speech, roughly on the ground that restricting it seems on the whole to entail more odious consequences than letting it run entirely wild. Yet I know . . . the absolutist position is highly vulnerable on a theoretical plane — and it is increasingly hard to defend wholeheartedly in the face of certain concrete results.

This dilemma, facing many thoughtful people in our society, 7 along with possible consequences, is frequently scrutinized in two areas: media violence and pornography.

These two issues have received much attention in recent years 8 from behavioral scientists and morality groups, ordinary citizens and PTAs, countless juries, and three presidential commissions.

Recent research suggests, for example, that behavioral scientists 9 have finally established a causal relationship between some children's exposure to TV violence and increased aggressive behavior. This could be interpreted as meaning that some TV programs (and movies) may constitute a "clear and present danger" to some of their younger viewers. If so, does this justify editing (a polite word for censoring) the content of such programs? What about the rights of adult viewers? But then, are some adults also "harmed" by the violence they witness?

What about the elimination of cigarette advertising on TV — is 10 this not a form of censorship? Is it not a violation of the First Amendment in fact and spirit? Do not cigarette manufacturers have free speech protection, too? Is the harm caused by cigarette advertising sufficient to justify this type of suppression of speech?

On the other hand, if this is truly a free society, do not the 11 majority have rights, through their elected representatives, to enact legislation controlling cigarette advertising, TV or movie violence, live sex on stage or whatever — if this were seen to be in the best interest of society generally? For example, is filmed or live sexual sado-masochism in a public theater a form of free speech?

Where does one draw the line on free speech? Or does one ever 12 draw that line? Should one draw such a line? . . .

We might ask, when does something become obscene? When 13 does it cross that line where society might legitimately object? The debate in the pornography area has been going on for some years and has — with the recent Supreme Court decisions — culminated in the decision that pornography consists of a prurient (abnormal or shameful) interest in sex, a lack of serious literary, artistic, political, or scientific value, and a patent offensiveness (as defined by the particular local law). When material meets these tests it is by law obscene in most communities.

Let me propose a possible alternate fourfold test that would 14 include violence as well. A coalescence of at least three out of the four elements would be required in the determination of objectionable material:

1. The material models antisocial behavior (torture, rape, etc.).
2. The sex or violence is presented out of context, unrealistically or obsessively.

3. A shock or trauma is provided to the sensibilities of the average viewer (exceeds community standards). A jury can decide this.

4. The purpose and/or effect is the stimulation of sexual lust/anger.

Violence or sex depicted responsibly in the natural context of human experience would not be affected by this test. Great artistic freedom would exist, but material that is exploitive or destructive would be limited. In no way would the expression of *ideas,* regardless of worth or nonworth, heretical or conventional, be limited. 15

This leads to the next question many people are bothered by — "Who is to judge?" Who is to be the "censor" — granted some of this material may be harmful? Who is to say how much is too much, where to draw the line, or where that point is where one exceeds contemporary community standards? The answer is simple: If a law has been breeched — a jury. If someone is offended, he brings charges. He indicates that he thinks the laws covering this sort of thing have been violated. A jury representing a sampling of the community is called. They examine the evidence and the testimony and they decide. This has been done thousands of times over many centuries in free countries. It's not perfect, but it's better than any other method available. The advantage of the jury in determining community standards is that twelve people cancel out the effect of each person's individual sexual neurosis or personal bias and give a fairly true reflection of current contemporary community standards. And the requirement of a unanimous verdict for conviction by twelve or even eight people means, practically, that the material has to be patently offensive. And what will be termed patently offensive will vary over time and from community to community. It will also differ for adults and children. But this line still needs to be drawn for the same reason we need to control airborne pollutants, excessive noise, heroin traffic, and other social dangers — for the welfare of the citizenry. 16

Where an individual judge is required to rule on whether a particular motion picture or book is obscene, we are faced with the same psychological dilemma as where an individual vice squad officer or Mrs. Grundy becomes the arbiter of the community's morals. All are locked in by their particular biases, unique culture, and personal history. The judge can just as easily have a sexual neurosis which will affect his decision as will any paid small-town censor. There may be some real problems in the tendency of higher courts (judges) over-turning decisions arrived at by local juries where, at least, the individual biases and unique sexual hang-ups of the jurors might cancel each other out and who also represent a fair sampling of the community, assuring arrival at a community standard. One California judge has the remarkable record of never letting an obscenity trial come before a jury. He throws them out of court on one technicality after another. 17

The judge, however, has no one to cancel out his biases and prejudices. Hence, in a psychological sense, he is probably less suited than a jury to make such a judgment, which involves values and consent of the governed as much as any clear legally defined concept of what is obscene or not. And to pretend that all judges have some standard measuring stick in assessing obscene material is unrealistic and naive. . . .

As it is now, the real possibility exists that the censor (or anticensor) of the future will be a corps of judges who may well spend a great deal of their time in private screening rooms deciding what movies the public can and cannot see. And of course this is no different than when the sheriff's deputy alone made the decision. The costumes they wear are different, but the humanness and imperfection of the men remain the same. 18

In conclusion, then, we must draw the kind of line just discussed for the following reason. Both pornography and media violence assault taboos with persuasive force, especially taboos involving sexuality and injury/assault on fellow humans — taboos that are intrinsic to social order. George Elliot . . . has suggested that since Western society is founded on the family as an essential social unit, nihilists and totalitarians must always attack the family as their enemy. And those who attack the family as an institution are enemies of our kind of society. The totalitarian would substitute the state for the family: the nihilists would dissolve both the state and the family in the name of unrestricted gratification of natural appetites, sexual and aggressive. To effect this dissolution, nihilists assault taboos, both because taboos restrain appetite and because they are an integral part of civilized order. And since of all taboos, the sexual ones are most important, pornography becomes for the nihilists important as an instrument of dissolution. The same is true for personal aggression and violence. 19

Elliot comments, "If one is for civilization, for being civilized, for even our warped but still possible society in preference to the anarchy that threatens from one side or the totalitarianism from the other, then one must be willing to take a middle way and to pay the price for responsibility. To be civilized, to accept authority, to rule with order, costs deep in the soul, and not the least of what it costs is likely to be some of the sensuality of the irresponsible." 20

Some have argued, as Elliot notes, that since guilt reduces pleasure in sex, the obvious solution is to abolish all sexual taboos and liberate pornography, which in turn would supposedly free the human spirit — and body. This is a cheery optimistic view, not unlike the sweet hopefulness of the oldfashioned anarchists who thought that all we had to do in order to attain happiness was to get rid of governments so that we might all express our essentially good nature unrestrained. But sexual anarchism, or the aggressive impulse turned 21 loose, like political anarchism before it, is a "lovely" but fraudulent daydream. Perhaps, before civilization, savages were noble, but if there is anything we have learned in this century, it is that those who regress from civilization become ignoble beyond all toleration. They may aspire to innocent savagery, but what they achieve too often is brutality and loss of their essential humanity.

Review Questions

1. Why does Cline refer to the Magna Charta, the French Declaration of the Rights of Man, and the First Amendment?
2. What does Norman Podhoretz believe about the issue of abridging freedom of speech?
3. What kind of evidence supports the idea that there should be censorship of TV?
4. What is Cline's "fourfold test" for determining whether material is obscene or socially objectionable?
5. Why are juries well suited to render decisions in censorship cases?
6. Why are attacks on the family a central concern of both totalitarians and nihilists?
7. Some have argued that the abolition of sexual taboos would reduce guilt and "free the human spirit — and body." Why does Cline argue against abolishing these taboos?

Discussion Questions

1. Do you believe that a line *must* be drawn (beyond which material is to be considered obscene or socially objectionable, and therefore censorable)? If so, should the line be drawn at the point Cline suggests, according to the standards of his fourfold test?
2. Cline suggests that he is advocating a responsible middle ground between the "totalitarian" and the "nihilist" approaches. Do you agree that his position is a middle ground? Do you agree that the alternatives are totalitarianism or nihilism?
3. Cline argues that sexual taboos "restrain appetite and . . . are an integral part of civilized order." Those who would do away with taboos against sex (or "personal aggression and violence") are really advocating the "dissolution" of the civilized order. Comment.
4. Does Cline convince you about the necessity for some form of censorship? If so, how? If not, why not?
5. Examine Cline's language, especially in the final paragraph. What is the effect of phrases like "a cheery optimistic view," "sweet hopefulness," and "a lovely but fraudulent daydream"? How do such conno-

tative phrases carry persuasive force? Are they used to enhance or to replace logical reasoning?

Writing Suggestions

1. In your experience, is it necessary, desirable, or practical for the government or for the industry to censor sex and/or violence from films and TV? If so, what have you observed that makes you think so? If not, how do you counter the argument that both children and adults can be made morally insensitive, or even brutalized, from totally uncensored entertainment?

2. Choose a film or a TV show that you have seen recently, and evaluate it in terms of Cline's fourfold test. Organize your essay into six paragraphs: an introduction, which includes a thesis statement; paragraphs dealing with each of Cline's four criteria, as applied to the film you choose; and a conclusion.

3. Write a law — or possibly a constitutional amendment (examine a law or an amendment for format and language) — that incorporates some or all of Cline's ideas on censorship. Or write a law that embodies your own ideas on censorship.

SUMMARY, SYNTHESIS, CRITIQUE ACTIVITIES

Summary

Summarize one or more of the passages in this chapter. Follow the suggested six-step process. Take into account the answers to the Review Questions for each passage. (Recommended: "The Struggle over *Double Indemnity*.")

Synthesis

1. What is film censorship? Show, by means of *example*, how it has worked. Your basic sources will be the 1930 Motion Picture Production Code and "The Struggle over *Double Indemnity*." Other sources may be used to develop your ideas.

2. How does the 1960 Code *compare and contrast* with the 1930 Code?
    One approach: discuss first the 1930 Code and its key aspects, then the 1968 Code and its key aspects. The comparison-contrast may be drawn during your discussion of the 1968 Code, or in a following paragraph, after you have described the 1968 Code.
    Another approach: develop three *criteria* by which both of these codes can be measured (for example, the objectives of the codes or

the implied standard of public morality and taste). Then discuss each of the codes in terms of each of your criteria. A concluding paragraph would be a good idea.

3. *Compare and contrast* Patricia Morrisroe's attitudes toward censorship — or toward objectionable material in films — with Victor Cline's. Do you see one of these authors as more tolerant than the other? Or are the differences between the articles less a matter of overall attitude than a matter of how they approach the subject of censorship?

4. *Compare and contrast* Victor Cline's "fourfold test" with the overall positions (and some of the specific provisions) of the 1930 and 1968 codes. To which code does Cline seem closest in spirit? With which assumptions behind the codes would he agree or disagree? Pay particular attention to the opening sections of the codes, which explain their rationale.

5. *Compare and contrast* the possible offensiveness of a film like *Bonnie and Clyde* with the possible offensiveness of a film like *Deep Throat*. What harm is done by either or both of these films? To whom is the harm done?

6. How have changing standards of public morality and taste affected film censorship?

   This assignment requires you to discuss a *process*. The most likely sources: the 1930 Code, the 1968 Code, and the headnotes to both. In this essay, your emphasis would not be on the comparison-contrast, but on the way that changing times dictated changes in the original code.

7. *Argue* that sex and violence in films should be restricted, and specify just how. Use as sources the selections on *Bonnie and Clyde, Deep Throat,* and "Sex and Violence: Pornography Hurts." You may also want to refer to certain provisions in the 1930 or 1968 code, as well as to Cline's arguments.

8. Read Plato's observation on the control that the state should have over the stories told to children, as reprinted in the second critique assignment at the end of the chapter on Fairy Tales (pages 201–202). Then *compare and contrast* Plato's view with the views on this subject held by the authors of the 1930 Motion Picture Production Code.

Critique

Write a critique of either the 1930 Motion Picture Production Code or the 1968 Motion Picture Production Code.

Your critique might be organized as follows:

1. statement of purpose and thesis of your essay;
2. background information about the Code;

3. background to your own position, your own assumptions;
4. summary of key points of the Code;
5. argument of your case in light of your overall purpose and your thesis; all points and examples must relate to your thesis;
6. your conclusion, possibly reemphasizing your reasons for arguing as you have.

RESEARCH TOPICS

1. Explain how two or three Hollywood films ran into problems with the Breen Office and/or with the Legion of Decency. Or focus on one film in particular.
2. Trace the course of the *Deep Throat* trial, or of the later obscenity charges brought against porn star Harry Reems.
3. Survey some of the attempts to link sexual or violent crime to the influence of movies and television.
4. Censorship laws and regulations sometimes come into conflict with the principle of freedom of speech. Describe some of the legal aspects of state or national censorship, focusing on particular cases. (See Ira H. Carmen, *Movies, Censorship and the Law,* Ann Arbor: University of Michigan Press, 1966; Neville M. Hunnings, *Film Censors and the Law,* London: George Allen and Unwin, 1967; Louis Nizer, *New Courts of Industry: Self Regulation under the Motion Picture Code, Including an Analysis of the Code,* New York: Jerome S. Ozer, 1971.)

ADDITIONAL READINGS

Boyd, George N. "Movies and the Sexual Revolution: Should the Ratings Be Revised?" *Christian Century,* 23 September 1970, pp. 1124-25.

Chaplin, Charles. *My Autobiography.* New York: Simon and Schuster, 1964, pp. 444-49.

Corliss, Richard. "The Legion of Decency." *Film Comment* 4 (Summer 1968), pp. 24-61.

Denby, David. "Dirty Movies — Hard-Core and Soft." *Atlantic,* August 1970, pp. 99-102.

Ernst, Morris and Pare Lorenz. *Censored: The Private Life of the Movies.* 1930. Reprint. New York: Jerome S. Ozer, 1971.

Farber, Stephen. *The Movie Rating Game.* Washington, D.C.: Public Affairs Press, 1972.

Judson, Horace Freeland. "Skin Deep: How to Watch a Pornographic Movie." *Harpers,* February 1975, pp. 42ff.

Levy, Herbert M. "The Case Against Film Censorship." *Films in Review,* April 1950, pp. 1ff.

Manchel, Frank. "Censorship and Self Control" and "Books of Film Censorship." In *Film Study: A Resource Guide,* by Frank Manchel. Rutherford, N.J.: Fairleigh Dickinson University Press, 1973.

Ostling, Richard N., "A Scrupulous Monitor Closes Shop." [Legion of Decency] *Time,* 6 October 1980, pp. 70-71.

Phelps, Guy. *Film Censorship.* [British censorship] London: Victor Gollancz, 1975.

Rich, Frank. "Movie Sex: Whatever Happened to the Good Parts?" *MS,* November 1976, pp. 51-54.

U.S. Cong., House, Committee on the Post Office and Civil Service, Subcommittee on Postal Operations, *Self-Policing of the Movie and Publishing Industry,* 86th Cong., 2nd sess. Washington, D.C.: GPO, 1961.

Wilcox, John. "The Small Knife: Studies in Censorship." *Sight and Sound,* 25 (Spring 1956), pp. 206ff.

See also the books (Schumach, Cline) from which selections in this chapter were taken.

The Great Depression

Imagine yourself (perhaps in the not too distant future) with a family of your own and what appears to be a secure job. After a period of steadily worsening inflation, the economy collapses around you. You lose your job because your employer can no longer afford to pay you. Most of the working people you know are in the same spot. You can't find another job. Your savings have been wiped out because the banks have failed, and even the government can't make good on all the defaults. Those goods that you bought on credit — your house, your furniture, and your car — have been repossessed because you can't keep up the payments. Like most of the people you know, you can't afford to buy any but the most basic goods and services — and sometimes not even those.

What effect would all this have on you and your family as the months and the years dragged on? What would you do, after it was finally over, to make sure that you were never in such a position again?

A common theme of those who write about the Great Depression is that words are inadequate to express the suffering and despair, that those who didn't actually live through the blighted 1930s can never understand what it was like. Nonetheless, the words are powerful enough. The accounts that follow reveal the Great Depression from several viewpoints — from the panoramic view of the historian to the close-up view of those who lived through it, from the objective view of the newspaper reporter to the outraged view of the novelist.

James Watts and Alan F. Davis provide an introductory survey of the Great Depression, outlining both its causes and its effects. In "Peggy Terry and Her Mother, Mary Owsley," a selection from Studs Terkel's *Hard Times,* a mother and daughter vividly recall how they lived through this traumatic period. Newspaper editor Oscar Ameringer, in "The Plague of Plenty," tells a congressional committee how millions of children starved in the cities, while thousands of bushels of apples rotted in orchards. Then two newspaper accounts report the effects of the Depression on average American citizens. The chapter concludes with a chapter from John Steinbeck's *Grapes of Wrath,* a harrowing novel about the "Okies," farmers uprooted from their land and migrating inch by inch in their battered vehicles toward the Californian rainbow.

THE DEPRESSION
James Watts and Allen F. Davis

James Watts was born in Oswego, N.Y. in 1935, and educated at the State University College at Oneanta, N. Y. and at the University of Missouri. He is now a professor of history at the City College of New York, where he teaches twentieth-century diplomacy and family history.

Allen F. Davis was born in Hardwick, Vermont in 1931, and educated at Dartmouth, the University of Rochester, and the University of Wisconsin. He has written several books on social and intellectual history and social reform. He teaches at Temple University. This selection is the introduction to the "Depression" section of their book *Generations: Your Family in Modern American History.*

☐

Some events are so important that their influence cuts across class   1
lines, affects all races and ethnic groups, and leaves no region untouched. The depression of the 1930s was such an event. No one who
lived through those years in the United States could ever completely
forget the bread lines, the millions of unemployed, or the forlorn and
discouraged men and women who saw their mortgages foreclosed,
their dreams shattered, their children hungry and afraid.

The depression was precipitated by the stock market crash in   2
October 1929, but the actual cause of the collapse was an unhealthy
economy. While the ability of the manufacturing industry to produce
consumer goods had increased rapidly, mass purchasing power had
remained relatively static. Most laborers, farmers, and white-collar
workers, therefore, could not afford to buy the automobiles and
refrigerators turned out by factories in the 1920s, because their incomes were too low. At the same time, the federal government increased the problem through economic policies that tended to encourage the very rich to over-save.

Herbert Hoover, a sensitive and humane engineer, had the mis-   3
fortune of being President when the depression began. Even though
he broke with the past and used the power of the federal government
to stem the tide of depression, especially through loans to businesses
and banks, his efforts proved to be too little and too late. Somewhat
unfairly his name became synonymous with failure and despair. As a
result, Hoover was defeated by Franklin Roosevelt, who took office in

March 1933 with the country in a state of crisis. Many banks had failed, millions were unemployed, and in the Middle West thousands of farmers seemed ready to use violence to protest their hopeless situation.

Roosevelt had a sense of confidence that was contagious. In his inaugural address he announced, "We have nothing to fear except fear itself," which was, of course, not exactly true. But he acted swiftly and decisively, if not always consistently, to right the economy. He closed all the banks and then gradually reopened those that were sound. He rushed through Congress a series of acts ranging from attempts to aid business and agriculture to emergency banking legislation and to the legalization of the sale of beer and wine for the first time in thirteen years. Very few people who lived through the 1930s were neutral about Roosevelt. He came to be hated by many businessmen, who called him a socialist or simply "that man in the White House." Others, more radical than the President, attacked him for not going far enough in his reforms, for trying to patch up the American free enterprise system rather than replacing it with some form of socialism. More important, however, he was loved and admired by the great mass of ordinary Americans, who crowded around the radio to listen to his comforting voice in "fireside chats" that explained the complex government programs. 4

Many of his New Deal measures, such as the Social Security Act and the Wagner Act (aiding the cause of unionism), had far-reaching influence. None, however, solved the massive social and economic problems facing the country. The long list of agencies and administrations, popularly known by their initials — from the AAA that aided farmers to the WPA that provided jobs for the unemployed — succeeded only to the extent of restoring a measure of self-respect and hope to some hard-hit by the depression. Financially, the country remained in a slump. It was not until the 1940s, when defense spending stimulated the economy, that the nation finally emerged from its worst economic crisis. 5

To many, the fact that the nation could go into such a deep slough was puzzling. The early and middle twenties, in which people became fully conscious of being part of the age of the machine, seemed to auger unending economic expansion. Two years before the stock market crash, in 1927, Henry Ford produced his fifteen-millionth automobile and then promptly switched from his all-black Model T to the more colorful and modern Model A. In the same year, the world "shrank" considerably when radio-telephone service was established between New York, London, San Francisco, and Manila, and Charles Lindbergh opened the way for rapid transatlantic travel by his solo flight from New York to Paris. The year 1927 also foreshadowed the great media explosion with the establishment of the 6 first national radio network and the release of the first feature-length film with spoken dialogue. Within a few years, millions would be listening to radio shows like "The Shadow" and "The Lone Ranger" and flocking to their neighborhood theaters to live vicariously with their movie-star heroes and heroines — Clark Gable, Greta Garbo, Gary Cooper, Bette Davis. Technology, with its many facets, seemed to be widening horizons.

This promise of prosperity through technology was deceptive, 7 though. For one thing, although radios and electric refrigerators and flush toilets were being produced by the millions, millions of Americans outside the middle and upper classes still had to use iceboxes and outhouses and live much the same way their ancestors had. Furthermore, as already noted, the prosperity of the middle class was itself based on an economic lie. The depression punctured its inflated dreams. The great majority of Americans suffered, therefore, from the economic collapse whether they were business executives, farmers, workingmen, housewives, or secretaries. In a sense, the depression was not as devastating for the lower classes as it was for the upper and middle classes. The sharecropper in Mississippi, the unemployed black in Chicago, probably did not notice the depression as much because his life was already depressed.

There are many ways to chart the impact of the depression on the 8 lives of Americans. One can mention the $26 billion wiped out by the stock market crash or the millions who lost their savings when the banks failed. The total industrial production in 1932 was half of what it had been in 1929. No one knows how many men and women lost their jobs; estimates of those out of work range from 12 million to 16 million at the peak of the depression, and in some cities the unemployment rate was more than 50 percent. For those who did work, the average pay ranged from twenty to thirty cents an hour in 1932 in heavy industry. In addition, one out of every four farmers lost his farm, and millions were evicted from their homes because they could not pay the rent. (There were 200,000 evictions in New York City alone in 1931.)

But none of these statistics really communicates the hopelessness 9 and the despair of the depression years. In Chicago men and women fought with children over the garbage dumped by trucks. A social worker noticed that the children in one city were playing a game called Eviction. "Sometimes they play 'Relief,' " she remarked, "but 'Eviction' has more action and all of them know how to play." In Philadelphia a store owner told of one family he was keeping on credit. "Eleven children in that house," he reported. "They've got no shoes, no pants. In the house, no chairs. My God, you go in there, you cry that's all."

The search for a secure job, the fear of failure, the worry about   10
vanished savings, lost hope and shattered dreams, and the nagging
worry that it would all happen over again separated those who lived
through the depression from those who were born in the 1940s and
after. Parents who experienced the depression urged their children to
train for a good job, to get married and settle down. But often their
children, products of an age of affluence, cared little about security
and sometimes rejected the material objects, the signs of success, that
took on such importance for parents. Studs Terkel of Chicago, who
has made an art of talking to people and arranging their thoughts
into books, spoke to a young woman who remarked:

> Everytime I've encountered the Depression, it has been used as a barrier
> and a club, it's been a countercommunication. Older people use it to
> explain to me that I can't understand *anything:* I didn't live through the
> Depression. They never say to me: "We can't understand you because
> we didn't live through the leisure society." All attempts at communica-
> tion are totally blocked.

Review Questions

1. What was the cause of the depression?
2. What were the most important contributions of President Roosevelt
   toward relieving the effects of the depression?
3. Why were the outward signs of the prosperity of the 1920s deceptive?
4. How has the depression contributed to the barrier between generations?

Discussion Questions

1. In some accounts of the depression era, President Hoover is portrayed
   as a complete incompetent, while President Roosevelt emerges as
   something of a superman. Do these conceptions agree with the way
   that Hoover and Roosevelt are treated in Watts and Davis's passage?
   Explain.
2. Watts and Davis note that the depression was devastating primarily
   for the upper and middle classes; the lower classes were much less
   affected since they were already depressed. What does this imply
   about the past and present attitudes of those people known as the
   "underclass"? Some would have it that the people of the underclass
   are themselves to blame for their permanently depressed situation.
   What is your opinion?
3. The depression is a vast subject. How well do Watts and Davis sketch
   it in? Outline the topics covered.

4. In discussing this historical phenomenon, Watts and Davis run the risk of missing the human dimension, of boring the reader with generalized descriptions and dry statistics. Do the authors avoid this problem? If so, how?

5. Do you detect any indications today that the causes to which Watts and Davis attribute the depression (the low purchasing power of the middle class, its "inflated dreams," and a general "economic lie" upon which its prosperity was based) exist today to a serious degree? Could it happen again? Why or why not?

Writing Suggestions

1. Watts and Davis end the passage by considering how the depression made it difficult for one generation to communicate with another. Do you find that your parents, or others in your parents' generation, have been so profoundly affected by the times in which they grew up that you find it difficult to understand their attitudes, and vice versa? Discuss.

2. Write a dialogue between a parent (or two parents) and their grown child, illustrating the "countercommunication" between them as a result of the depression and its privations. For additional source material, read the other passages in this chapter, or some of the additional suggested readings listed on page 162.

PEGGY TERRY AND HER MOTHER, MARY OWSLEY
Studs Terkel

This passage appears in Studs Terkel's *Hard Times: An Oral History of the Great Depression.* "Studs" (Louis) Terkel, author and interviewer, was born in 1912 in New York City. He has hosted award-winning radio and TV programs, acted in plays, written short stories, and compiled fascinating personal accounts of ordinary and extraordinary people.

□

From *Hard Times: An Oral History of the Great Depression,* by Studs Terkel. Copyright © 1970 by Studs Terkel. Reprinted by permission of Pantheon Books, a Division of Random House, Inc.

It is a crowded apartment in Uptown.[1] Young people from the neighborhood wander in and out, casually. The flow of visitors is constant; occasionally, a small, raggedy-clothed boy shuffles in, stares, vanishes. Peggy Terry is known in these parts as a spokesman for the poor southern whites. . . . "Hillbillies are up here for a few years and they get their guts kicked out and they realize their white skin doesn't mean what they always thought it meant."

Mrs. Owsley is the first to tell her story.

Kentucky-born, she married an Oklahoma boy "when he came back from World War I. He was so restless and disturbed from the war, we just drifted back and forth." It was a constant shifting from Oklahoma to Kentucky and back again; three, four times the route. "He saw the tragedies of war so vividly that he was discontented everywhere." From 1929 to 1936, they lived in Oklahoma.

There was thousands of people out of work in Oklahoma City. 1
They set up a soup line, and the food was clean and it was delicious. Many, many people, colored and white, I didn't see any difference, 'cause there was just as many white people out of work than were colored. Lost everything they had accumulated from their young days. And these are facts. I remember several families had to leave in covered wagons. To Californy, I guess.

See, the oil boom come in '29. People come from every direction 2
in there. A coupla years later, they was livin' in everything from pup tents, houses built out of cardboard boxes and old pieces of metal that they'd pick up — anything that they could find to put somethin' together to put a wall around 'em to protect 'em from the public.

I knew one family there in Oklahoma City, a man and a woman 3
and seven children lived in a hole in the ground. You'd be surprised how nice it was, how nice they kept it. They had chairs and tables and beds back in that hole. And they had the dirt all braced up there, just like a cave.

Oh, the dust storms, they were terrible.[2] You could wash and 4

---

[1] A Chicago area in which many of the southern white émigrés live; furnished flats in most instances. [Terkel]

[2] During the 1930s draught and severe dust storms plagued much of the Great Plains, including parts of Oklahoma, Kansas, Texas, New Mexico, and Colorado. The storms, which often lasted for days, even weeks, blew away the topsoil, and were powerful enough to uproot telephone poles and steel oil derricks — and to kill people. The term "dust bowl," to indicate the area devastated by the storms, was coined by Associated Press reporter Robert Geiger. "Three little words — " he wrote, "achingly familiar on a Western farmer's tongue — rule life today in the dust bowl of the continent. . . . If it rains." [Behrens and Rosen]

hang clothes on a line, and if you happened to be away from the house and couldn't get those clothes in before that storm got there, you'd never wash that out. Oil was in that sand. It'd color them the most awful color you ever saw. It just ruined them. They was just never fit to use, actually. I had to use 'em, understand, but they wasn't very presentable. Before my husband was laid off, we lived in a good home. It wasn't a brick house, but it wouldn't have made any difference. These storms, when they would hit, you had to clean house from the attic to ground. Everything was covered in sand. Red sand, just full of oil.

The majority of people were hit and hit hard. They were mentally disturbed you're bound to know, 'cause they didn't know when the end of all this was comin'. There was a lot of suicides that I know of. From nothin' else but just they couldn't see any hope for a better tomorrow. I absolutely know some who did. Part of 'em were farmers and part of 'em were businessmen, even. They went flat broke and they committed suicide on the strength of it, nothing else.   5

A lot of times one family would have some food. They would divide. And everyone would share. Even the people that were quite well to do, they was ashamed. 'Cause they was eatin', and other people wasn't.   6

My husband was very bitter. That's just puttin' it mild. He was an intelligent man. He couldn't see why as wealthy a country as this is, that there was any sense in so many people starving to death, when so much of it, wheat and everything else, was being poured into the ocean. There's many excuses, but he looked for a reason. And he found one.   7

My husband went to Washington. To march with that group that went to Washington . . . the bonus boys.   8

He was a machine gunner in the war. He'd say them damn Germans gassed him in Germany. And he come home and his own Government stooges gassed him and run him off the country up there with the water hose, half drownded him. Oh, yes *sir*, yes sir, he was a hell-raiser (laughs — a sudden sigh). I think I've run my race.   9

Peggy Terry's Story:

I first noticed the difference when we'd come home from school in the evening. My mother'd send us to the soup line. And we were never allowed to cuss. If you happened to be one of the first ones in line, you didn't get anything but water that was on top. So we'd ask the guy that was ladling out the soup into the buckets — everybody had to bring their own bucket to get the soup — he'd dip the greasy, watery stuff off the top. So we'd ask him to please dip down to get   10 some meat and potatoes from the bottom of the kettle. But he wouldn't do it. So we learned to cuss. We'd say: "Dip down, God damn it."

Then we'd go across the street. One place had bread, large loaves of bread. Down the road just a little piece was a big shed, and they gave milk. My sister and me would take two buckets each. And that's what we lived off for the longest time. 11

I can remember one time, the only thing in the house to eat was mustard. My sister and I put so much mustard on biscuits that we got sick. And we can't stand mustard till today. 12

There was only one family around that ate good. Mr. Barr worked at the ice plant. Whenever Mrs. Barr could, she'd feed the kids. But she couldn't feed 'em *all*. They had a big tree that had fruit on it. She'd let us pick those. Sometimes we'd pick and eat 'em until we were sick. 13

Her two daughters got to go to Norman for their college. When they'd talk about all the good things they had at the college, she'd kind of hush 'em up because there was always poor kids that didn't have anything to eat. I remember she always felt bad because people in the neighborhood were hungry. But there was a feeling of together. . . . 14

When they had food to give to people, you'd get a notice and you'd go down. So Daddy went down that day and he took my sister and me. They were giving away potatoes and things like that. But they had a truck of oranges parked in the alley. Somebody asked them who the oranges were for, and they wouldn't tell 'em. So they said, well, we're gonna take those oranges. And they did. My dad was one of the ones that got up on the truck. They called the police, and the police chased us all away. But we got the oranges. 15

It's different today. People are made to feel ashamed now if they don't have anything. Back then, I'm not sure how the rich felt. I think the rich were as contemptuous of the poor then as they are now. But among the people that I knew, we all had an understanding that it wasn't our fault. It was something that had happened to the machinery. Most people blamed Hoover, and they cussed him up one side and down the other — it was all his fault. I'm not saying he's blameless, but I'm not saying either it was all his fault. Our system doesn't run by just one man, and it doesn't fall by just one man, either. 16

You don't recall at any time feeling a sense of shame? 17

I remember it was fun. It was fun going to the soup line. 'Cause we all went down the road, and we laughed and we played. The only thing we felt is that we were hungry and we were going to get food. Nobody made us feel ashamed. There just wasn't any of that. 18

Today you're made to feel that it's your own fault. If you're poor, 19 it's only because you're lazy and you're ignorant, and you don't try to help yourself. You're made to feel that if you get a check from Welfare that the bank at Fort Knox is gonna go broke.

Even after the soup line, there wasn't anything. The WPA came, and I married. My husband worked on the WPA. This was back in Paducah, Kentucky. We were just kids. I was fifteen, and he was sixteen. My husband was digging ditches. They were putting in a water main. Parts of the city, even at that late date, 1937, didn't have city water.   20

My husband and me just started traveling around, for about three years. It was a very nice time, because when you're poor and you stay in one spot, trouble just seems to catch up with you. But when you're moving from town to town, you don't stay there long enough for trouble to catch up with you. It's really a good life, if you're poor and you can manage to move around.   21

I was pregnant when we first started hitchhiking, and people were really very nice to us. Sometimes they would feed us. I remember one time we slept in a haystack, and the lady of the house came out and found us and she said, "This is really very bad for you because you're going to have a baby. You need a lot of milk." So she took us up to the house.   22

She had a lot of rugs hanging on the clothesline because she was doing her house cleaning. We told her we'd beat the rugs for her giving us the food. She said, no, she didn't expect that. She just wanted to feed us. We said, no, we couldn't take it unless we worked for it. And she let us beat her rugs. I think she had a million rugs, and we cleaned them. Then we went in and she had a beautiful table, full of all kind of food and milk. When we left, she filled a gallon bucket full of milk and we took it with us.   23

You don't find that now. I think maybe if you did that now, you'd get arrested. Somebody'd call the police. The atmosphere since the end of the Second War — it seems like the minute the war ended, the propaganda started. In making people hate each other.   24

I remember one night, we walked for a long time, and we were so tired and hungry, and a wagon came along. There was a Negro family going into town. Of course, they're not allowed to stop and eat in restaurants, so they'd cook their own food and brought it with 'em. They had the back of the wagon filled with hay. We asked them if we could lay down and sleep in the wagon, and they said yes. We woke up, and it was morning, and she invited us to eat with 'em. She had this box, and she had chicken and biscuits and sweet potatoes and everything in there. It was just really wonderful.   25

I didn't like black people. In fact, I hated 'em. If they just shipped 'em all out, I don't think it woulda bothered me.   26

She recalls her feelings of white superiority, her discoveries. "If I really knew 27
what changed me . . . I don't know. I've thought about it and thought about
it. You don't go anywhere, because you always see yourself as something you're
not. As long as you can say I'm better than they are, then there's somebody below
you can kick. But once you get over that, you see that you're not any better off
than they are. In fact, you're worse off 'cause you're believin' a lie. And it was
right there, in front of us. In the cotton field, chopping cotton, and right over in
the next field, there's these black people — Alabama, Texas, Kentucky. Never
once did it occur to me that we had anything in common.

"After I was up here for a while and I saw how poor white people were 28
treated, poor white southerners, they were treated just as badly as black people
are. I think maybe that just crystallized the whole thing."

I didn't feel any identification with the Mexicans, either. My 29
husband and me were migrant workers. We went down in the valley
of Texas, which is very beautiful. We picked oranges and lemons and
grapefruits, limes in the Rio Grande Valley.

We got a nickel a bushel for citrus fruits. On the grapefruits you 30
had to ring them. You hold a ring in your hand that's about like that
(she draws a circle with her hands), and it has a little thing that slips
down over your thumb. You climb the tree and you put that ring
around the grapefruit. If the grapefruit slips through, you can't pick
it. And any grapefruit that's in your box — you can work real hard,
especially if you want to make enough to buy food that day — you'll
pick some that aren't big enough. Then when you carry your box up
and they check it, they throw out all the ones that go through the ring.

I remember this one little boy in particular. He was really a 31
beautiful child. Every day when we'd start our lunch, we'd sit under
the trees and eat. And these peppers grew wild. I saw him sitting
there, and every once in a while he'd reach over and get a pepper and
pop it in his mouth. With his food, whatever he was eating. I thought
they looked pretty good. So I reached over and popped it in my
mouth, and, oh, it was like liquid fire. He was rolling in the grass
laughing. He thought it was so funny — that white people couldn't
eat peppers like they could. And he was tearing open grapefruits for
me to suck the juice, because my mouth was all cooked from the
pepper. He used to run and ask if he could help me. Sometimes he'd
help me fill my boxes of grapefruits, 'cause he felt sorry for me, 'cause
I got burned on the peppers. (Laughs.)

But that was a little boy. I felt all right toward him. But the men 32
and the women, they were just spics and they should be sent back to
Mexico.

I remember I was very irritated because there were very few 33
gringos in this little Texas town, where we lived. Hardly anybody

spoke English. When you tried to talk to the Mexicans, they couldn't understand English. It never occurred to us that we should learn to speak Spanish. It's really hard to talk about a time like that, 'cause it seems like a different person. When I remember those times, it's like looking into a world where another person is doing those things.

This may sound impossible, but if there's one thing that started 34 me thinking, it was President Roosevelt's cuff links. I read in the paper how many pairs of cuff links he had. It told that some of them were rubies and precious stones — these were his cuff links. And I'll never forget, I was setting on an old tire out in the front yard and we were poor and hungry. I was sitting out there in the hot sun, there weren't any trees. And I was wondering why it is that one man could have all those cuff links when we couldn't even have enough to eat. When we lived on gravy and biscuits. That's the first time I remember ever wondering why.

And when my father finally got his bonus, he bought a second- 35 hand car for us to come back to Kentucky in. My dad said to us kids: "All of you get in the car. I want to take you and show you something." On the way over there, he'd talk about how life had been rough for us, and he said: "If you think it's been rough for us, I want you to see people that really had it rough." This was in Oklahoma City, and he took us to one of the Hoovervilles,[3] and that was the most incredible thing.

Here were all these people living in old, rusted-out car bodies. I 36 mean that was their home. There were people living in shacks made of orange crates. One family with a whole lot of kids were living in a piano box. This wasn't just a little section, this was maybe ten-miles wide and ten-miles long. People living in whatever they could junk together.

And when I read *Grapes of Wrath* — she bought that for me 37 (indicates young girl seated across the room) — that was like reliving my life. Particularly the part where they lived in this Government camp. Because when we were picking fruit in Texas, we lived in a Government place like that. They came around, and they helped the women make mattresses. See, we didn't have anything. And they showed us how to sew and make dresses. And every Saturday night, we'd have a dance. And when I was reading *Grapes of Wrath* this was

---

[3] Hoovervilles were shantytowns erected near city dumps, and occupied by the dispossessed and the jobless. They were also known as "Hoover villages" (after President Herbert Hoover, who was bitterly seen by many depression victims as a figure of reckless optimism). Other Hooverisms: "Hoover soup," "Hooverize," and "Prosperity is just Hoovering around the corner." [Behrens and Rosen]

just like my life. I was never so proud of poor people before, as I was after I read that book.

I think that's the worst thing that our system does to people, is to   38
take away their pride. It prevents them from being a human being. And wondering why the Harlem and why the Detroit. They're talking about troops and law and order in this country when people are allowed to be decent human beings. Every time I hear another building's on fire, I say: oh, boy, baby, hit 'em again. (Laughs.)

I don't think people were put on earth to suffer. I think that's a   39
lot of nonsense. I think we are the highest development on the earth, and I think we were put here to live and be happy and to enjoy everything that's here. I don't think it's right for a handful of people to get ahold of all the things that make living a joy instead of a sorrow. You wake up in the morning, and it consciously hits you — it's just like a big hand that takes your heart and squeezes it — because you don't know what that day is going to bring: hunger or you don't know.

POSTSCRIPT: (*A sudden flash of memory by Peggy Terry, as I was about to*   40
leave.) "*It was the Christmas of '35, just before my dad got his bonus. We didn't get anything for Christmas. I mean nothing. Not an orange, not an apple — nothing. I just felt so bad. I went to the church, to the children's program and I stole a Christmas package. It was this pretty box and it had a big red ribbon on it. I stole it off the piano, and I took it home with me. I told my mother my Sunday school teacher had given me a Christmas present. When I opened it, it was a beautiful long scarf made out of velvet — a cover for a piano. My mother knew my Sunday school teacher didn't give me that. 'Cause we were living in one room, in a little shack in what they called Gander Flat. (Laughs.) For a child — I mean, they teach you about Santa Claus and they teach you all that stuff — and then for a child to have to go to church and steal a present . . . and then it turned out to be something so fantastic, a piano scarf. Children shouldn't have to go around stealing. There's enough to give all of them everything they want, any time they want it. I say that's what we're gonna have.*"

Review Questions

1. What was the most distressing aspect of the depression to Mary Owsley? And to her daughter, Peggy Terry? At what does Peggy Terry become most indignant?

2. How does Peggy Terry contrast the attitudes of people toward the poor during the depression with attitudes toward the poor today?

3. How did Peggy Terry overcome her initially racist attitudes? Has she overcome them completely?

Discussion Questions

1. James Watts and Allen Davis conclude their account of the depression with a quotation designed to show how the experience of the depression blocked communication between older people and younger people: "Everytime I've encountered the Depression, it has been used as a barrier and a club, its been a countercommunication. Older people use it to explain to me that I can't understand *anything*. I didn't live through the Depression. . . ." Explain how accounts like Mary Owsley's and Peggy Terry's might help bridge this gap for you.
2. How did the depression change people's attitudes about themselves and about other people?
3. It is sometimes claimed that adversity brings out the best in people. To what extent do the experiences described by Mary Owsley and Peggy Terry confirm this theory?

Writing Suggestions

1. Discuss several ways in which the attitudes and incidents described in this passage affect any of your attitudes about crime among what is known today as the "underclass."
2. Write an essay on how well you think you would adapt to depression conditions. If you have been accustomed to living in at least moderate prosperity, how would it be for you and for people you know to wait in soup lines?

THE PLAGUE OF PLENTY
Oscar Ameringer

Oscar Ameringer was a newspaper editor in Oklahoma City. In 1932 he testified before a House committee concerning his observations as he traveled around the depression-stricken country.

☐

During the last three months I have visited, as I have said, some   1
twenty states of this wonderfully rich and beautiful country. Here are
some of the things I heard and saw:

In the state of Washington I was told that the forest fires raging   2
in that region all summer and fall were caused by unemployed timber

Oscar Ameringer, "The Plague of Plenty": *Unemployment Relief Hearings before a Subcommittee on Manufactures, United States Senate, Seventy-second Congress, First Session on S. 174 . . . (1932).*

workers and bankrupt farmers in an endeavor to earn a few honest dollars as firefighters. The last thing I saw on the night I left Seattle was numbers of women searching for scraps of food in the refuse piles of the principal market of that city. A number of Montana citizens told me of thousands of bushels of wheat left in the fields uncut on account of its low price that hardly paid for the harvesting. In Oregon I saw thousands of bushels of apples rotting in the orchards. Only absolute[ly] flawless apples were still salable, at from 40 to 50 cents a box containing 200 apples. At the same time, there are millions of children who, on account of the poverty of their parents, will not eat one apple this winter.

While I was in Oregon the Portland *Oregonian* bemoaned the fact   3
that thousands of ewes were killed by the sheep raisers because they did not bring enough in the market to pay the freight on them. And while Oregon sheep raisers fed mutton to the buzzards, I saw men picking for meat scraps in the garbage cans in the cities of New York and Chicago. I talked to one man in a restaurant in Chicago. He told me of his experience in raising sheep. He said that he had killed 3,000 sheep this fall and thrown them down the canyon, because it cost $1.10 to ship a sheep, and then he would get less than a dollar for it. He said he could not afford to feed the sheep, and he would not let them starve, so he just cut their throats and threw them down the canyon.

The roads of the West and Southwest teem with hungry hitch-   4
hikers. The camp fires of the homeless are seen along every railroad track. I saw men, women, and children walking over the hard roads. Most of them were tenant farmers who had lost their all in the late slump in wheat and cotton. Between Clarksville and Russellville, Ark., I picked up a family. The woman was hugging a dead chicken under a ragged coat. When I asked her where she had procured the fowl, first she told me she had found it dead in the road, and then added in grim humor, "They promised me a chicken in the pot, and now I got mine."[1]

In Oklahoma, Texas, Arkansas, and Louisiana I saw untold bales   5
of cotton rotting in the fields because the cotton pickers could not keep body and soul together on 35 cents paid for picking 100 pounds. . . .

As a result of this appalling overproduction on the one side and   6
the staggering underconsumption on the other side, 70 per cent of the farmers of Oklahoma were unable to pay the interests on their

---

[1] A popular Republican slogan in 1928, the year before the stock market collapse, was "A chicken in every pot." Like Prime Minister Chamberlain's "peace in our time" (after the Munich accords with Hitler), the phrase later took on a tinge of bitter irony. [Behrens and Rosen]

mortgages. Last week one of the largest and oldest mortgage companies in that state went into the hands of the receiver. In that and other states we have now the interesting spectacle of farmers losing their farms by foreclosure and mortgage companies losing their recouped holdings by tax sales.

The farmers are being pauperized by the poverty of industrial populations, and the industrial populations are being pauperized by the poverty of the farmers. Neither has the money to buy the product of the other, hence we have overproduction and underconsumption at the same time and in the same country. 7

I have not come here to stir you in a recital of the necessity for relief for our suffering fellow citizens. However, unless something is done for them and done soon, you will have a revolution on hand. And when that revolution comes it will not come from Moscow, it will not be made by the poor Communists whom our police are heading up regularly and efficiently. When the revolution comes it will bear the label "Laid in the U.S.A." and its chief promoters will be the people of American stock. 8

Review Questions

1. What, according to Ameringer, is the chief paradox of the depression?
2. How did the depression create a chain of debt and bankruptcy?
3. What did Ameringer predict would happen if something was not done to relieve the impoverished?

Discussion Questions

1. Why were sheep raisers in Oregon feeding mutton to the buzzards while men in New York and Chicago were "picking for meat scraps in the garbage cans"?
2. How does Ameringer suggest that officials have been looking for revolutionaries in the wrong places?
3. Could such things happen again? If our economy were to collapse utterly, what kind of scenes could we expect to see?
4. Ameringer begins his report not with generalizations but, abruptly, with an account of his actual observations. Why? What is the effect of his descriptions?
5. At what point does Ameringer make his generalizations concerning the causes and the significance of what he has seen? How does the *tone* of his account compare with the tone of Watts and Davis's account in the passage entitled "The Depression"? Is Ameringer more emotional? How does the *content* of Ameringer's account compare to that

of Watts and Davis? What aspects of the depression does Ameringer choose to emphasize?

6. Ameringer says, "I have not come here to stir you in a recital of the necessity for relief for our suffering fellow citizens." How do you account for this statement, since it would be difficult *not* to be stirred in this way by his account?

Writing Suggestion

Choose a situation or state of affairs that you believe is in urgent need of reform. The situation may be personal (having to do with your own living conditions) or may be more social in nature. Then write a descriptive account, in the manner of Ameringer's testimony, providing details and examples to support your conclusion.

SELLING APPLES AND SHINING SHOES and HUNGER RIOTS

The following articles show some of the effects of the depression on average citizens. "Selling Apples and Shining Shoes" appeared in *The New York Times* on June 5, 1932; the "Hunger Riots" stories appeared in the *Times* on January 21 and February 26, 1931.

SELLING APPLES AND SHINING SHOES

Pat Frank

Darwin's theory that man can adapt himself to almost any new envi-   1 ronment is being illustrated, in this day of economic change, by thousands of New Yorkers who have discovered new ways to live and new ways to earn a living since their formerly placid lives were thrown into chaos by unemployment or kindred exigencies. Occupations and duties which once were scorned have suddenly attained unprecedented popularity.

Two years ago citizens shied at jury duty. John Doe and Richard   2 Roe, summoned to serve on a jury, thought of all sorts of excuses. . . . They called upon their ward leaders and their lawyers for aid in getting exemption, and when their efforts were rewarded they sighed with relief. But now things are different.

The Hall of Jurors in the Criminal Courts Building is jammed   3 and packed on court days. Absences of talesmen are infrequent. Why? Jurors get $4 for every day they serve. . . .

From *The New York Times*, June 5, 1932. © 1932 by The New York Times Company. Reprinted by permission. This and the next piece are reprinted as excerpted in *The Great Depression*, ed., David A. Shannon, Prentice-Hall, 1960.

Once the average New Yorker got his shine in an established   4
bootblack "parlor" paying 10 cents, with a nickel tip. But now, in the
Times Square and Grand Central zones, the sidewalks are lined with
neophyte "shine boys," drawn from almost all walks of life. They
charge a nickel, and although a nickel tip is welcomed it is not
expected.

In one block, on West Forty-third Street, a recent count showed   5
nineteen shoe-shiners. They ranged in age from a 16-year-old, who
should have been in school, to a man of more than 70, who said he
had been employed in a fruit store until six months ago. Some sit
quietly on their little wooden boxes and wait patiently for the infrequent customers. Others show true initiative and ballyhoo their trade,
pointing accusingly at every pair of unshined shoes that passes. . . .

Shining shoes, said one, is more profitable than selling apples —   6
and he's tried them both.

"You see, when you get a shine kit it's a permanent investment,"   7
he said, "and it doesn't cost as much as a box of apples anyway. . . ."

According to the Police Department, there are approximately   8
7,000 of these "shine boys" making a living on New York streets at
present. Three years ago they were so rare as to be almost non-
existent, and were almost entirely boys under 17.

To the streets, too, has turned an army of new salesmen, ped-   9
dling everything from large rubber balls to cheap neckties. Within the
past two years the number of these hawkers has doubled. . . . Fourteenth Street is still the Mecca of this type of salesmen; thirty-eight
were recently counted between Sixth Avenue and Union Square and
at one point there was a cluster of five.

Unemployment has brought back the newsboy in increasing   10
numbers. He avoids the busy corners, where news stands are frequent, and hawks his papers in the side streets with surprising success.
His best client is the man who is "too tired to walk down to the corner
for a paper."

Selling Sunday papers has become a science. Youngsters have   11
found that it is extremely profitable to invade apartment houses
between 11 and 12 o'clock Sunday morning, knock on each apartment door, and offer the Sunday editions. Their profits are usually
between $1.50 and $2.

The condition of business, with the resulting necessity of watch-   12
ing the market-basket expenditures, has proved a boon for the small,
New Jersey truck farmer. Between 5 and 6 o'clock in the morning the
ferries are clogged with horses and carts and vegetables. And while he
is not yet shouting his wares on Park Avenue, he has invaded many a
neighborhood in which a vegetable hawker had not been seen in
years. His goods may or may not be cheaper than the corner grocer's,
but there is some psychology about buying vegetables from a cart that

is dear to the thrifty housewife. The number of vegetable hawkers has increased by 40 per cent within the last two years, according to the estimate of the City Licensing Bureau. . . .

HUNGER RIOTS

These news stories from *The New York Times,* January 21 and February 26, 1931, are typical of several that appeared in the nation's press sporadically during the early depression. The evidence suggests that most such riots were organized rather than spontaneous, but that to organize a "hunger riot," given the circumstances, was not a particularly difficult task. [Shannon]

OKLAHOMA CITY, Jan. 20 (AP). — A crowd of men and women, shouting that they were hungry and jobless, raided a grocery store near the City Hall today. Twenty-six of the men were arrested. Scores loitered near the city jail following the arrests, but kept well out of range of fire hose made ready for use in case of another disturbance. 1

The police tonight broke up a second meeting of about one hundred unemployed men and arrested Francis Owens, alleged head of the "Oklahoma City Unemployed Council," who was accused of instigating the raid. 2

Before the grocery was entered, a delegation of unemployed, led by Owens, had demanded of City Manager E. M. Fry that the authorities furnish immediate relief. Owens rejected a request by Mr. Fry for the names and addresses of the "Unemployed Council," said to number 2,500 men and women, both whites and Negroes. 3

The raiders disregarded efforts of H. A. Shaw, the store manager, to quiet them. 4

"It is too late to bargain with us," the leaders shouted, as they stripped the shelves. 5

The police hastily assembled emergency squads and dispersed the crowd numbering 500, with tear gas. Only those who were trapped in the wrecked store were arrested. Five women among them were released. The windows of the store were smashed as the raiders attempted to flee. 6

John Simmons was held on a charge of assault after he had leaped on the back of Lee Mullenix, a policeman, when the officer attempted to enter the crowded store. 7

Floyd Phillips was charged with inciting a riot. The police said he 8 was one of the speakers who harangued the crowd at the City Hall before they began a parade that ended at the store.

MINNEAPOLIS, Feb. 25 (AP). — Several hundred men and women in an unemployed demonstration late today stormed a grocery and meat market in the Gateway district, smashed plate glass windows and helped themselves to bacon and ham, fruit and canned goods.   9

One of the store owners suffered a broken arm when he was attacked as he drew a revolver and attempted to keep out the first to enter.   10

One hundred policemen were sent to the district and seven persons were arrested as the leaders.   11

ST. PAUL, MINN., Feb. 25 (AP). — A crowd, after attending a meeting to protest against unemployment, forced its way late today into a small store owned by George Baglio, near the downtown section, and took more than $50 worth of merchandise, mostly cigars, cigarettes, candy and apples. Police arrested three men and held them without charge.   12

Review Questions

1. What are some of the new occupations taken up by the unemployed?
2. Why is shining shoes better than selling apples?
3. Why have some New Jersey farmers benefited from the depression?
4. What were the charges against Francis Owens? What were the charges against Floyd Phillips?

Discussion Questions

1. The "Selling Apples" article is somewhat optimistic, since its purpose is to show how people can adapt to terrible conditions. The "Hunger Riots" article is decidedly pessimistic. Which viewpoint do you think is the more accurate one? Is the human animal in dire straits infinitely adaptable — or a beast in the jungle?
2. Why do you think Mr. Fry wanted the names and addresses of the members of the "Unemployed Council"?
3. Why does the writer of "Selling Apples" begin with a reference to Darwin's theory? What is Darwin's theory? How is this relevant to the story that follows?
4. Newspaper stories usually begin with sentences that answer the "five W's" — who, what, where, when, and why. How is this true of the stories on "Hunger Riots"?

Writing Suggestions

1. Write an account of the Oklahoma City riot that is not objective (like the newspaper account), but that is highly subjective, written from the point of view of one of those arrested in the riot. Or try writing another account of the same incident as it might have appeared in a pro-police magazine.
2. Write a short story based upon the Oklahoma City riot. Add interesting details and incidents; and develop the characters of Owens, Fry, Shaw, and Phillips.

THE GRAPES OF WRATH
John Steinbeck

John Steinbeck (1902–1968), born in Salinas, California, was one of the most widely read American writers of the century. His intensely realistic accounts of society's dispossessed and disinherited, searching for the pot of gold, have more recently been acknowledged to have qualities of allegory and myth. In 1962 he won the Nobel Prize for literature, for "realistic and imaginative writings, distinguished as they are by a sympathetic humor and a social perception." Among his many novels are *Tortilla Flat* (1935), which first brought him fame, *Of Mice and Men* (1937), *Cannery Row* (1945), *The Winter of Our Discontent* (1961) and *Travels with Charley* (1962). But his most famous work is *The Grapes of Wrath* (1939), about migrant agricultural workers, perhaps the single most powerful work about the effects of the Great Depression. Chapter 12 of this novel follows.

☐

Highway 66 is the main migrant road. 66 — the long concrete path   1
across the country, waving gently up and down on the map, from the
Mississippi to Bakersfield — over the red lands and the gray lands,
twisting up into the mountains, crossing the Divide and down into the
bright and terrible desert, and across the desert to the mountains
again, and into the rich California valleys.

66 is the path of a people in flight, refugees from dust and   2
shrinking land, from the thunder of tractors and shrinking ownership, from the desert's slow northward invasion, from the twisting
winds that howl up out of Texas, from the floods that bring no

richness to the land and steal what little richness is there. From all of these the people are in flight, and they come into 66 from the tributary side roads, from the wagon tracks and the rutted country roads. 66 is the mother road, the road of flight.

Clarksville and Ozark and Van Buren and Fort Smith on 64, and there's an end of Arkansas. And all the roads into Oklahoma City, 66 down from Tulsa, 270 up from McAlester. 81 from Wichita Falls south, from Enid north. Edmond, McLoud, Purcell. 66 out of Oklahoma City; El Reno and Clinton, going west on 66. Hydro, Elk City, and Texola; and there's an end to Oklahoma. 66 across the Panhandle of Texas. Shamrock and McLean, Conway and Amarillo, the yellow. Wildorado and Vega and Boise, and there's an end of Texas. Tucumcari and Santa Rosa and into the New Mexican mountains to Albuquerque, where the road comes down from Santa Fe. Then down the gorged Rio Grande to Las Lunas and west again on 66 to Gallup, and there's the border of New Mexico. 3

And now the high mountains. Holbrook and Winslow and Flagstaff in the high mountains of Arizona. Then the great plateau rolling like a ground swell. Ashfork and Kingman and stone mountains again, where water must be hauled and sold. Then out of the broken sun-rotted mountains of Arizona to the Colorado, with green reeds on its banks, and that's the end of Arizona. There's California just over the river, and a pretty town to start it. Needles, on the river. But the river is a stranger in this place. Up from Needles and over a burned range, and there's the desert. And 66 goes on over the terrible desert, where the distance shimmers and the black center mountains hang unbearably in the distance. At last there's Barstow, and more desert until at last the mountains rise up again, the good mountains, and 66 winds through them. Then suddenly a pass, and below the beautiful valley, below orchards and vineyards and little houses, and in the distance a city. And, oh, my God, it's over. 4

The people in flight streamed out on 66, sometimes a single car, sometimes a little caravan. All day they rolled slowly along the road, and at night they stopped near water. In the day ancient leaky radiators sent up columns of steam, loose connecting rods hammered and pounded. And the men driving the trucks and the overloaded cars listened apprehensively. How far between towns? It is a terror between towns. If something breaks — well, if something breaks we camp right here while Jim walks to town and gets a part and walks back and — how much food we got? 5

Listen to the motor. Listen to the wheels. Listen with your ears and with your hands on the steering wheel; listen with the palm of your hand on the gear-shift lever; listen with your feet on the floor boards. Listen to the pounding old jalopy with all your senses, for a change of tone, a variation of rhythm may mean — a week here? That 6 rattle — that's tappets. Don't hurt a bit. Tappets can rattle till Jesus comes again without no harm. But that thudding as the car moves along — can't hear that — just kind of feel it. Maybe oil isn't gettin' someplace. Maybe a bearing's startin' to go. Jesus, if it's a bearing, what'll we do? Money's goin' fast.

And why's the son-of-a-bitch heat up so hot today? This ain't no 7 climb. Le's look. God Almighty, the fan belt's gone! Here, make a belt outa this little piece a rope. Le's see how long — there. I'll splice the ends. Now take her slow — slow, till we can get to a town. That rope belt won't last long.

'F we can on'y get to California where the oranges grow before 8 this here ol' jug blows up. 'F we on'y can.

And the tires — two layers of fabric worn through. On'y a four- 9 ply tire. Might get a hundred miles more outa her if we don't hit a rock an' blow her. Which'll we take — a hunderd, maybe, miles, or maybe spoil the tubes? Which? A hunderd miles. Well, that's somepin you got to think about. We got tube patches. Maybe when she goes she'll only spring a leak. How about makin' a boot? Might get five hunderd more miles. Le's go on till she blows.

We got to get a tire, but, Jesus, they want a lot for a ol' tire. They 10 look a fella over. They know he got to go on. They know he can't wait. And the price goes up.

Take it or leave it. I ain't in business for my health. I'm here a- 11 sellin' tires. I ain't givin' 'em away. I can't help what happens to you. I got to think what happens to me.

How far's the nex' town? 12

I seen forty-two cars a you fellas go by yesterday. Where you all 13 come from? Where all of you goin'?

Well, California's a big State. 14

It ain't that big. The whole United States ain't that big. It ain't 15 that big. It ain't big enough. There ain't room enough for you an' me, for your kind an' my kind, for rich and poor together all in one country, for thieves and honest men. For hunger and fat. Whyn't you go back where you come from?

This is a free country. Fella can go where he wants. 16

That's what you think! Ever hear of the border patrol on the 17 California line? Police from Los Angeles — stopped you bastards, turned you back. Says, if you can't buy no real estate we don't want you. Says, got a driver's license? Le's see it. Tore it up. Says you can't come in without no driver's license.

It's a free country. 18

Well, try to get some freedom to do. Fella says you're jus' as free 19 as you got jack to pay for it.

In California they got high wages. I got a han'bill here tells 20 about it.

Baloney! I seen folks comin' back. Somebody's kiddin' you. You 21
want that tire or don't ya?

Got to take it, but, Jesus, mister, it cuts into our money! We ain't 22
got much left.

Well, I ain't no charity. Take her along. 23

Got to, I guess. Let's look her over. Open her up, look a' the 24
casing — you son-of-a-bitch, you said the casing was good. She's
broke damn near through.

The hell she is. Well — by George! How come I didn't see that? 25

You did see it, you son-of-a-bitch. You wanta charge us four 26
bucks for a busted casing. I'd like to take a sock at you.

Now keep your shirt on! I didn' see it, I tell you. Here — tell ya 27
what I'll do. I'll give ya this one for three-fifty.

You'll take a flying jump at the moon! We'll try to make the nex' 28
town.

Think we can make it on that tire? 29

Got to. I'll go on the rim before I'd give that son-of-a-bitch a 30
dime.

What do ya think a guy in business is? Like he says, he ain't in it 31
for his health. That's what business is. What'd you think it was? Fella's
got — See that sign 'longside the road there? Service Club. Luncheon
Tuesday, Colmado Hotel? Welcome, brother. That's a Service Club.
Fella had a story. Went to one of them meetings an' told the story to
all them business men. Says, when I was a kid my ol' man give me a
haltered heifer an' says take her down an' git her serviced. An' the
fella says, I done it, an' ever' time since then when I hear a business
man talkin' about service, I wonder who's gettin' screwed. Fella in
business got to lie an' cheat, but he calls it somepin else. That's what's
important. You go steal that tire an' you're a thief, but he tried to steal
your four dollars for a busted tire. They call that sound business.

Danny in the back seat wants a cup a water. 32

Have to wait. Got no water here. 33

Listen — that the rear end? 34

Can't tell. 35

Sound telegraphs through the frame. 36

There goes a gasket. Got to go on. Listen to her whistle. Find a 37
nice place to camp an' I'll jerk the head off. But, God Almighty, the
food's gettin' low, the money's gettin' low. When we can't buy no more
gas — what then?

Danny in the back seat wants a cup a water. Little fella's thirsty. 38

Listen to that gasket whistle. 39

Chee-rist! There she went. Blowed tube an' casing all to hell. 40
Have to fix her. Save that casing to make boots; cut 'em out an' stick
'em inside a weak place.

Cars pulled up beside the road, engine heads off, tires mended. 41
Cars limping along 66 like wounded things, panting and struggling.
Too hot, loose connections, loose bearings, rattling bodies.

Danny wants a cup a water. 42

People in flight along 66. And the concrete road shone like a 43
mirror under the sun, and in the distance the heat made it seem that
there were pools of water in the road.

Danny wants a cup of water. 44

He'll have to wait, poor little fella. He's hot. Nex' service station. 45
Service station, like the fella says.

Two hundred and fifty thousand people over the road. Fifty 46
thousand old cars — wounded, steaming. Wrecks along the road,
abandoned. Well, what happened to them? What happened to the
folks in that car? Did they walk? Where are they? Where does the
courage come from? Where does the terrible faith come from?

And here's a story you can hardly believe, but it's true, and it's 47
funny and it's beautiful. There was a family of twelve and they were
forced off the land. They had no car. They built a trailer out of junk
and loaded it with their possessions. They pulled it to the side of 66
and waited. And pretty soon a sedan picked them up. Five of them
rode in the sedan and seven on the trailer, and a dog on the trailer.
They got to California in two jumps. The man who pulled them fed
them. And that's true. But how can such courage be, and such faith in
their own species? Very few things would teach such faith.

The people in flight from the terror behind — strange things 48
happen to them, some bitterly cruel and some so beautiful·that the
faith is refired forever.

Review Questions

1. Why have the migrants left their homes to make the journey to California?
2. What do they worry about as they slowly make their way?
3. What attitudes do they encounter from the locals?

Discussion Questions

1. Why do you think Steinbeck describes these particular things to us? How does he show us the best and the worst aspects of the depression?
2. What social criticism do you find in this passage? Against what is it directed?

3. What is illustrated by the story about the family that built a trailer out of junk and was picked up by a sedan?

4. In this passage, not only does Steinbeck use no quotation marks to indicate dialogue, but he also blurs the line between dialogue and exposition. For instance: "And the men driving the trucks and the overloaded cars listened apprehensively. How far between towns? It is a terror between towns. If something breaks — well, if something breaks we camp right here while Jim walks to town and gets a part and walks back and — how much food we got?" What is the effect of this style of writing?

5. Although we learn a great deal about Highway 66, a strip of concrete, we never learn the names of the people who are represented in this chapter; we never learn what they look like. Is this a deficiency in the narrative? Why or why not?

6. At what point does Steinbeck's own attitude toward the migrants come through most clearly, most directly?

Writing Suggestion

Rewrite this chapter as it might appear as a brief expository passage (two or three paragraphs) in a history textbook. Make it general, for the most part, rather than specific. What is gained or lost by such a procedure?

SUMMARY, SYNTHESIS, CRITIQUE ACTIVITIES

Summary

Summarize one or more of the passages in this chapter. Follow the suggested six-step process. Take into account the answers to the Review Questions for each passage. (Recommended: "The Depression.")

Synthesis

1. Write a *description* of the depression, giving *examples* of its devastating effects. Suggested sources: "The Depression," "Peggy Terry and Her Mother, Mary Owsley," "Plague of Plenty." Make "The Depression" your basic source, summarizing some of the information it contains, and then use examples of the calamities of the depression from the other two articles. Your examples may be placed *after* your summary of "The Depression" or at appropriate places *within* it. Remember to include a thesis statement.

2. Write a *description* of some of the ways that lives were changed by the depression. Suggested sources: "Peggy Terry and her Mother, Mary Owsley," "Selling Apples and Shining Shoes," "Hunger Riots," and "The Grapes of Wrath."

3. *Describe* some of the ways that people's minds and attitudes were changed as a result of their experiences during the depression. Use at least three sources and refer to them specifically.
4. Oscar Ameringer, Peggy Terry, and Mary Owsley all lived through the depression. *Compare and contrast* the attitudes and events they describe and the manner (or tone) in which they describe them.
5. *Argue* that some good came out of the experience of the depression. Perhaps your approach would be that devastating though the 1930s were, many people came through these years strengthened, better, and wiser than they were before.

Critique

Write a critique of whichever selection in this chapter most vividly re–creates the sense of deprivation of the depression, making sure to justify your choice.

RESEARCH TOPICS

1. Discuss the effects of the depression on (a) the American farmer or (b) American families.
2. Read through parts of Studs Terkel's *Hard Times: An Oral History of the Great Depression.* Write a report on a particular aspect of this era, perhaps a particular kind of deprivation or opportunity, using Terkel's subjects as your sources.
3. *A Project in Oral History: Impact of the Depression.*[1]

    This project in oral history has several objectives. First, you should utilize your interviewing techniques by talking to a resident of the community in which you are living. Select a person old enough to have lived through the depression and attempt to recover some of the history of the depression years.

    You might follow a line of questioning similar to this: Do you remember the stock market crash? What did you think of Herbert Hoover? Did you or your family lose any money in the market or in bank failures? What was your attitude toward Franklin Roosevelt? Did you ever listen to him on the radio? What else did you listen to on the radio? Were you or someone in your family unemployed? Do you know anyone who worked for the CCC or WPA?[2] What kinds of experiences did he or she have? Did you move from one house to

---

[1] From *Generations: Your Family in Modern American History,* Second Edition, edited by James Watts and Allen F. Davis. Copyright © 1974, 1978 by Alfred A. Knopf, Inc. Reprinted by permission of Alfred A. Knopf, Inc.

[2] The Civilian Conservation Corps and the Work Projects Administration, two of the public agencies created by the Roosevelt administration to provide government jobs for the unemployed.

another? What did you do for fun? Did people have more fun in those days? Were the movies important in any way? What about the importance of the automobile? What did economic hardship do to family life? Did anyone you knew lose faith in the American system? Does the fact that you lived through the depression influence your ideas and attitudes today?

Try not to let a preconceived idea of how the discussion should flow interfere with the direction the conversation will spontaneously take. Use your common sense and be flexible. Interrupt as little as possible, except when you have to jog the interviewee's memory. Your role is to listen.

Use the same techniques and questions when you interview members of your own family on their depression experiences. Then, write a preliminary report on your findings, to be incorporated later in a research paper.

Additional Readings

Banks, Ann. "Making It through Hard Times" [excerpt from *First Person America: Narratives Collected by the Federal Writer's Project*]. *Atlantic* July 1980, pp. 40-44ff.

Bonnifield, Paul. *The Dust Bowl: Men, Dirt, and Depression.* Albuquerque: University of New Mexico Press, 1979.

Galbraith, John Kenneth. *The Great Crash of 1929.* 3rd ed. Boston: Houghton Mifflin, 1972.

Hearn, Charles R. *The American Dream in the Great Depression.* Westport, Conn.: Greenwood Press, 1977.

Rothstein, Arthur. *The Depression Years as Photographed by Arthur Rothstein.* New York: Dover, 1978.

Shannon, David A., ed. *The Great Depression.* Englewood Cliffs, N.J.: Prentice-Hall, 1960.

Swados, Harvey, ed. *The American Writers and the Great Depression.* Indianapolis: Bobbs-Merrill, 1966.

Terkel, Studs. *Hard Times: An Oral History of the Great Depression.* New York: Avon, 1970.

————. "Studs Terkel Talks with Arthur Miller." *Saturday Review,* September 1980, pp. 24-27.

Westin, Jeane. *Making Do: How Women Survived the '30's.* Chicago: Follett, 1976.

Wooster, Donald E. *Dust Bowl: The Southern Plains in the 1930's.* New York: Oxford University Press, 1979.

See also the books (Watts and Davis, Steinbeck) from which selections in this unit were taken.

A Closer Look
at Fairy Tales

"Once upon a time . . ." Millions of children around the world have listened to these (or similar) words. And, once upon a time, such words were magic archways into a world of entertainment and fantasy for children and their parents. But in our own century, fairy tales have come under the scrutiny of anthropologists, linguists, educators, psychologists and psychiatrists, as well as literary critics, who have come to see them as a kind of social genetic code — a means by which cultural values are transmitted from one generation to the next. Some people, of course, may scoff at the idea that charming tales like "Cinderella" or "Snow White" are anything other than charming tales, at the idea that fairy tales may really be ways of inculcating young and impressionable children with culturally approved values. But even if they are not aware of it, adults and children make use of fairy tales in complex and subtle ways, some of which are explored in the selections that follow.

The chapter begins with Charles Perrault's "Cinderella," which is followed by a revised, modern version of the tale, rendered as a poem by feminist Anne Sexton. Her "transformation" of the seventeenth-century classic raises unsettling questions about the desirability of "living happily ever after" with a "prince." Next, psychologist Bruno Bettelheim suggests how fairy tales might help children cope with their "existential predicament," by setting the examples of characters who are able to outgrow dependencies on parents or rivalries with brothers and sisters. Then Roger Sale, a literary critic, examines fairy tales as documents that demonstrate a provocative "cultural oneness throughout the Eurasian continent." Folklorists have uncovered characters, events, and motifs from these stories that "appear, often with only slight changes, in tales told in India, Japan, France, Germany, and Ireland." Is it possible that these tales were invented independently in each of these places? And if so, what does this suggest about the human imagination? But perhaps these stories spread throughout the world as people did: perhaps population migrations can be traced by carefully observing the details of stories in different countries.

The chapter concludes with two other short fairy tales, from Ireland and Russia, which you may wish to analyze in light of Bettelheim's and Sale's arguments.

A note on terminology: "Cinderella," "Jack and the Beanstalk," "Little Red Riding Hood," and the like are commonly referred to as fairy tales, though, strictly speaking, they are not. True fairy tales concern a "class of supernatural beings of diminutive size, who in popular belief are said to possess magical powers and to have great influence for good or evil over the affairs of humans" (*Oxford English Dictionary*). "Cinderella," and the others just mentioned, concern no beings of diminutive size, though extraordinary, magical events do occur in the story. Folklorists would be more apt to call these stories "wonder tales." We retain the traditional "fairy tale," though, with the proviso that in popular usage the term is misapplied. See Roger Sale's article for a further discussion of this point. You may notice that the authors in this chapter use the terms "folktale" and "fairy tale" interchangeably. The expression "folktale" refers to *any* story conceived orally and passed on in an oral tradition. Thus, "folktale" is a generic term that incorporates both fairy tales and wonder tales.

CINDERELLA
Charles Perrault

Charles Perrault (1628–1703) was born in Paris, of a prosperous family. He practiced law for a short time and then devoted his attentions to a job in government, in which capacity he was instrumental in promoting the advancement of the arts and sciences and in securing pensions for writers, both French and foreign. Perrault is best known as a writer for his *Contes de ma mère l'oie* (*Mother Goose Tales*), a collection of fairy tales taken from popular folklore.

☐

Once there was a nobleman who took as his second wife the proudest and haughtiest woman imaginable. She had two daughters of the same character, who took after their mother in everything. On his side, the husband had a daughter who was sweetness itself; she inherited this from her mother, who had been the most kindly of women. 1

No sooner was the wedding over than the stepmother showed her ill-nature. She could not bear the good qualities of the young girl, for they made her own daughters seem even less likeable. She gave her the roughest work of the house to do. It was she who washed the dishes and the stairs, who cleaned out Madam's room and the rooms of the two Misses. She slept right at the top of the house, in an attic, on a lumpy mattress, while her sisters slept in panelled rooms where they had the most modern beds and mirrors in which they could see 2

From *Fairy Tales* by Charles Perrault, edited and translated by Geoffrey Brereton (Baltimore: Penguin Books), published 1957. Reprinted by permission of Penguin Books Ltd. and Anne Brereton.

themselves from top to toe. The poor girl bore everything in patience and did not dare to complain to her father. He would only have scolded her, for he was entirely under his wife's thumb.

When she had finished her work, she used to go into the chim- 3
ney-corner and sit down among the cinders, for which reason she was usually known in the house as Cinderbottom. Her younger stepsister, who was not so rude as the other, called her Cinderella. However, Cinderella, in spite of her ragged clothes, was still fifty times as beautiful as her sisters, superbly dressed though they were.

One day the King's son gave a ball, to which everyone of good 4
family was invited. Our two young ladies received invitations, for they cut quite a figure in the country. So there they were, both feeling very pleased and very busy choosing the clothes and the hair-styles which would suit them best. More work for Cinderella, for it was she who ironed her sisters' underwear and goffered their linen cuffs. Their only talk was of what they would wear.

"I," said the elder, "shall wear my red velvet dress and my collar 5
of English lace."

"I," said the younger, "shall wear just my ordinary skirt; but, to 6
make up, I shall put on my gold-embroidered cape and my diamond clasp, which is quite out of the common."

The right hairdresser was sent for to supply double-frilled coifs, 7
and patches were bought from the right patch-maker. They called Cinderella to ask her opinion, for she had excellent taste. She made useful suggestions and even offered to do their hair for them. They accepted willingly.

While she was doing it, they said to her: 8

"Cinderella, how would you like to go to the ball?"

"Oh dear, you are making fun of me. It wouldn't do for me."

"You are quite right. It would be a joke. People would laugh if they saw a Cinderbottom at the ball."

Anyone else would have done their hair in knots for them, but 9
she had a sweet nature, and she finished it perfectly. For two days they were so excited that they ate almost nothing. They broke a good dozen laces trying to tighten their stays to make their waists slimmer, and they were never away from their mirrors.

At last the great day arrived. They set off, and Cinderella 10
watched them until they were out of sight. When she could no longer see them, she began to cry. Her godmother, seeing her all in tears, asked what was the matter.

"If only I could . . . If only I could . . ." She was weeping so much that she could not go on.

Her godmother, who was a fairy, said to her: "If only you could go to the ball, is that it?"

"Alas, yes," said Cinderella with a sigh.

"Well," said the godmother, "be a good girl and I'll get you there."

She took her into her room and said: "Go into the garden and get me a pumpkin."

Cinderella hurried out and cut the best she could find and took it to her godmother, but she could not understand how this pumpkin would get her to the ball. Her godmother hollowed it out, leaving only the rind, and then tapped it with her wand and immediately it turned into a magnificent gilded coach. 11

Then she went to look in her mouse-trap and found six mice all alive in it. She told Cinderella to raise the door of the trap a little, and as each mouse came out she gave it a tap with her wand and immediately it turned into a fine horse. That made a team of six horses, each of a fine mouse-coloured grey. 12

While she was wondering how she would make a coachman, Cinderella said to her: 13

"I will go and see whether there is a rat in the rat-trap, we could make a coachman of him."

"You are right," said the godmother. "Run and see."

Cinderella brought her the rat-trap, in which there were three big rats. The fairy picked out one of them because of his splendid whiskers and, when she had touched him, he turned into a fat coachman, with the finest moustaches in the district. 14

Then she said: "Go into the garden and you will find six lizards behind the watering-can. Bring them to me." 15

As soon as Cinderella had brought them, her godmother changed them into six footmen, who got up behind the coach with their striped liveries, and stood in position there as though they had been doing it all their lives. 16

Then the fairy said to Cinderella:

"Well, that's to go to the ball in. Aren't you pleased?"

"Yes. But am I to go like this, with my ugly clothes?"

Her godmother simply touched her with her wand and her clothes were changed in an instant into a dress of gold and silver cloth, all sparkling with precious stones. Then she gave her a pair of glass slippers, most beautifully made. 17

So equipped, Cinderella got into the coach; but her godmother warned her above all not to be out after midnight, telling her that, if she stayed at the ball a moment later, her coach would turn back into a pumpkin, her horses into mice, her footmen into lizards, and her fine clothes would become rags again. 18

She promised her godmother that she would leave the ball before midnight without fail, and she set out, beside herself with joy. 19

The King's son, on being told that a great princess whom no one knew had arrived, ran out to welcome her. He handed her down from 20

the coach and led her into the hall where his guests were. A sudden silence fell; the dancing stopped, the violins ceased to play, the whole company stood fascinated by the beauty of the unknown princess. Only a low murmur was heard: "Ah, how lovely she is!" The King himself, old as he was, could not take his eyes off her and kept whispering to the Queen that it was a long time since he had seen such a beautiful and charming person. All the ladies were absorbed in noting her clothes and the way her hair was dressed, so as to order the same things for themselves the next morning, provided that fine enough materials could be found, and skilful enough craftsmen.

The King's son placed her in the seat of honour, and later led her   21
out to dance. She danced with such grace that she won still more admiration. An excellent supper was served, but the young Prince was too much occupied in gazing at her to eat anything. She went and sat next to her sisters and treated them with great courtesy, offering them oranges and lemons which the Prince had given her. They were astonished, for they did not recognize her.

While they were chatting together, Cinderella heard the clock   22
strike a quarter to twelve. She curtsied low to the company and left as quickly as she could.

As soon as she reached home, she went to her godmother and,   23
having thanked her, said that she would very much like to go again to the ball on the next night — for the Prince had begged her to come back. She was in the middle of telling her godmother about all the things that had happened, when the two sisters came knocking at the door. Cinderella went to open it.

"How late you are!" she said, rubbing her eyes and yawning and   24
stretching as though she had just woken up (though since they had last seen each other she had felt very far from sleepy).

"If you had been at the ball," said one of the sisters, "you would   25
not have felt like yawning. There was a beautiful princess there, really ravishingly beautiful. She was most attentive to us. She gave us oranges and lemons."

Cinderella could have hugged herself. She asked them the name   26
of the princess, but they replied that no one knew her, that the King's son was much troubled about it, and that he would give anything in the world to know who she was. Cinderella smiled and said to them:

"So she was very beautiful? Well, well, how lucky you are!   27
Couldn't I see her? Please, Miss Javotte, do lend me that yellow dress which you wear about the house."

"Really," said Miss Javotte, "what an idea! Lend one's dress like   28
that to a filthy Cinderbottom! I should have to be out of my mind."

Cinderella was expecting this refusal and she was very glad when   29
it came, for she would have been in an awkward position if her sister had really lent her her frock.

On the next day the two sisters went to the ball, and Cinderella 30
too, but even more splendidly dressed than the first time. The King's
son was constantly at her side and wooed her the whole evening. The
young girl was enjoying herself so much that she forgot her godmother's warning. She heard the clock striking the first stroke of
midnight when she thought that it was still hardly eleven. She rose
and slipped away as lightly as a roe-deer. The Prince followed her, but
he could not catch her up. One of her glass slippers fell off, and the
Prince picked it up with great care.

Cinderella reached home quite out of breath, with no coach, no 31
footmen, and wearing her old clothes. Nothing remained of all her
finery, except one of her little slippers, the fellow to the one which she
had dropped. The guards at the palace gate were asked if they had
not seen a princess go out. They answered that they had seen no one
go out except a very poorly dressed girl, who looked more like a
peasant than a young lady.

When the two sisters returned from the ball, Cinderella asked 32
them if they had enjoyed themselves again, and if the beautiful lady
had been there. They said that she had, but that she had run away
when it struck midnight, and so swiftly that she had lost one of her
glass slippers, a lovely little thing. The Prince had picked it up and
had done nothing but gaze at it for the rest of the ball, and undoubtedly he was very much in love with the beautiful person to whom it
belonged.

They were right, for a few days later the King's son had it 33
proclaimed to the sound of trumpets that he would marry the girl
whose foot exactly fitted the slipper. They began by trying it on the
various princesses, then on the duchesses and on all the ladies of the
Court, but with no success. It was brought to the two sisters, who did
everything possible to force their feet into the slipper, but they could
not manage it. Cinderella, who was looking on, recognized her own
slipper, and said laughing:

"Let me see if it would fit me!"

Her sisters began to laugh and mock at her. But the gentleman 34
who was trying on the slipper looked closely at Cinderella and, seeing
that she was very beautiful, said that her request was perfectly reasonable and that he had instructions to try it on every girl. He made
Cinderella sit down and, raising the slipper to her foot, he found that
it slid on without difficulty and fitted like a glove.

Great was the amazement of the two sisters, but it became greater 35
still when Cinderella drew from her pocket the second little slipper
and put it on her other foot. Thereupon the fairy godmother came in
and, touching Cinderella's clothes with her wand, made them even
more magnificent than on the previous days.

Then the two sisters recognized her as the lovely princess whom 36 they had met at the ball. They flung themselves at her feet and begged her forgiveness for all the unkind things which they had done to her. Cinderella raised them up and kissed them, saying that she forgave them with all her heart and asking them to love her always. She was taken to the young Prince in the fine clothes which she was wearing. He thought her more beautiful than ever and a few days later he married her. Cinderella, who was as kind as she was beautiful, invited her two sisters to live in the palace and married them, on the same day, to two great noblemen of the Court.

Discussion Questions

1. Why do "Cinderella," and other fairy tales as well, begin with "Once . . ." (or "Once upon a time . . .")?

2. Are children's imaginations different from those of adults? Can the same story — a fairy tale — please both? Can you think of any contemporary adult fiction that makes use of fairy-tale plot structures, images, and so on?

3. Is there a moral to "Cinderella"? Might this be a negative moral — for instance, don't trust your stepmother?

4. What makes Perrault's version of "Cinderella" a classic fairy tale? Consider the following in your answer. *Narrator:* Who is telling the story? Describe the voice of the storyteller. If you have difficulty locating this voice, discuss your difficulty. *Plot:* Outline the plot of "Cinderella." Are these events in any way typical of other fairy tales? *Characters:* Write a brief description of each character in the tale. Are these characters realistic (i.e., like someone you would meet on the street) or stereotyped?

Writing Suggestion

Write your own two- to four-page fairy tale, and assume that it should be read to someone who is eight years old.

CINDERELLA

Anne Sexton

Anne Sexton (1928–1974) has been acclaimed by critics as one of America's outstanding poets. In 1967, she won the Pulitzer Prize for poetry for *Live or Die.* She published four other collections of her work, including *Transformations,* in which she recast, with a modern twist, popular European fairy tales such as "Cinderella." Sexton's poetry has appeared in *The New Yorker, Harper's,* the *Atlantic,* and *Saturday Review.* She received a Robert Frost Fellowship (1959), a scholarship from the Radcliffe College's New Institute for Independent Study (1961–63), a grant from the Ford Foundation (1964), and a Guggenheim award (1969). In her book, *All My Pretty Ones,* Sexton quoted Franz Kafka: "The books we need are the kind that act upon us like a misfortune, that make us suffer like the death of someone we love more than ourselves. A book should serve as the axe for the frozen sea within us." Asked in an interview (by Patricia Marx) about this quotation, Sexton responded: "I think [poetry] should be a shock to the senses. It should almost hurt."

☐

You always read about it: 1
the plumber with twelve children
who wins the Irish Sweepstakes.
From toilets to riches.
That story.   5

Or the nursemaid,
some luscious sweet from Denmark
who captures the oldest son's heart.
From diapers to Dior.
That story.   10

Or a milkman who serves the wealthy,
eggs, cream, butter, yogurt, milk,
the white truck like an ambulance
who goes into real estate
and makes a pile.   15
From homogenized to martinis at lunch.

Or the charwoman
who is on the bus when it cracks up
and collects enough from the insurance.

From mops to Bonwit Teller.   20
That story.

Once
the wife of a rich man was on her deathbed
and she said to her daughter Cinderella:
Be devout. Be good. Then I will smile   25
down from heaven in the seam of a cloud.
The man took another wife who had
two daughters, pretty enough
but with hearts like blackjacks.
Cinderella was their maid.   30
She slept on the sooty hearth each night
and walked around looking like Al Jolson.
Her father brought presents home from town,
jewels and gowns for the other women
but the twig of a tree for Cinderella.   35
She planted that twig on her mother's grave
and it grew to a tree where a white dove sat.
Whenever she wished for anything the dove
would drop it like an egg upon the ground.
The bird is important, my dears, so heed him.   40

Next came the ball, as you all know.
It was a marriage market.
The prince was looking for a wife.
All but Cinderella were preparing
and gussying up for the big event.   45
Cinderella begged to go too.
Her stepmother threw a dish of lentils
into the cinders and said: Pick them
up in an hour and you shall go.
The white dove brought all his friends;   50
all the warm wings of the fatherland came,
and picked up the lentils in a jiffy.
No, Cinderella, said the stepmother,
you have no clothes and cannot dance.
That's the way with stepmothers.   55

Cinderella went to the tree at the grave
and cried forth like a gospel singer:
Mama! Mama! My turtledove,
send me to the prince's ball!
The bird dropped down a golden dress   60
and delicate little gold slippers.
Rather a large package for a simple bird.
So she went. Which is no surprise.

Her stepmother and sisters didn't
recognize her without her cinder face   65
and the prince took her hand on the spot
and danced with no other the whole day.

As nightfall came she thought she'd better
get home. The prince walked her home
and she disappeared into the pigeon house   70
and although the prince took an axe and broke
it open she was gone. Back to her cinders.
These events repeated themselves for three days.
However on the third day the prince
covered the palace steps with cobbler's wax   75
and Cinderella's gold shoe stuck upon it.
Now he would find whom the shoe fit
and find his strange dancing girl for keeps.
He went to their house and the two sisters
were delighted because they had lovely feet.   80
The eldest went into a room to try the slipper on
but her big toe got in the way so she simply
sliced it off and put on the slipper.
The prince rode away with her until the white dove
told him to look at the blood pouring forth.   85
That is the way with amputations.
They don't just heal up like a wish.
The other sister cut off her heel
but the blood told as blood will.
The prince was getting tired.   90
He began to feel like a shoe salesman.
But he gave it one last try.
This time Cinderella fit into the shoe
like a love letter into its envelope.

At the wedding ceremony   95
the two sisters came to curry favor
and the white dove pecked their eyes out.
Two hollow spots were left
like soup spoons.

Cinderella and the prince   100
lived, they say, happily ever after,
like two dolls in a museum case
never bothered by diapers or dust,
never arguing over the timing of an egg,
never telling the same story twice,   105
never getting a middle-aged spread,

their darling smiles pasted on for eternity.
Regular Bobbsey Twins.
That story.

Review Questions

1. What are the differences, in terms of plot, between Sexton's "Cinderella" and Perrault's?
2. Sexton's happily-ever-after version is not quite as happy as Perrault's. Identify those lines throughout the poem that, together with the final verse, support this reading.

Discussion Questions

1. Based on your reading of "Cinderella," why do you suppose Sexton entitled her collection of poems, in which "Cinderella" appeared, *Transformations*?
2. Why does Sexton begin her poem with references to plumbers, nursemaids, and milkmen?
3. How would you characterize the prince in this tale? Offer lines from the text to support your views.
4. The narrator of Sexton's "Cinderella" possesses a knowledge that narrators of traditional tales either do not possess or do not share with the reader. What is this knowledge? How are you made aware of it?
5. What is the effect of modernisms, such as "looking like Al Jolson," on the tone of the poem? Identify other modernisms.
6. Examine the use of repetition in the poem. Which words and phrases are repeated? Offer a theory of why Sexton uses such repetition.
7. What does Sexton's rationale appear to be for breaking the poem into verses where she does?

Writing Suggestions

1. Would you be content to read this poem to your child and call it "Cinderella"? Why or why not?
2. Discuss Sexton's use of sarcasm in "Cinderella." Cite examples of sarcasm and develop an explanation for its presence.
3. In which ways does Sexton's version of "Cinderella" depend upon the original for its effect?

THE USES OF ENCHANTMENT
Bruno Bettelheim

Bruno Bettelheim, a distinguished psychologist and educator, was born in 1903 in Vienna. He was naturalized as a U.S. citizen in 1939 and has served as a professor of psychology at Rockford College and the University of Chicago. Bettelheim has been awarded the honor of Fellow by several prestigious professional associations. He is a prolific writer and has contributed articles to numerous popular and professional publications. His list of books includes *Love Is Not Enough — The Treatment of Emotionally Disturbed Children, The Informed Heart, Surviving,* and *The Uses of Enchantment,* from which this selection has been excerpted.

☐

In order to master the psychological problems of growing up — overcoming narcissistic disappointments, oedipal dilemmas, sibling rivalries; becoming able to relinquish childhood dependencies; gaining a feeling of selfhood and of self-worth, and a sense of moral obligation — a child needs to understand what is going on within his conscious self so that he can also cope with that which goes on in his unconscious. He can achieve this understanding, and with it the ability to cope, not through rational comprehension of the nature and content of his unconscious, but by becoming familiar with it through spinning out daydreams — ruminating, rearranging, and fantasizing about suitable story elements in response to unconscious pressures. By doing this, the child fits unconscious content into conscious fantasies, which then enable him to deal with that content. It is here that fairy tales have unequaled value, because they offer new dimensions to the child's imagination which would be impossible for him to discover as truly on his own. Even more important, the form and structure of fairy tales suggest images to the child by which he can structure his daydreams and with them give better direction to his life.   1

In child or adult, the unconscious is a powerful determinant of behavior. When the unconscious is repressed and its content denied entrance into awareness, then eventually the person's conscious mind will be partially overwhelmed by derivatives of these unconscious elements, or else he is forced to keep such rigid, compulsive control   2 over them that his personality may become severely crippled. But when unconscious material *is* to some degree permitted to come to awareness and worked through in imagination, its potential for causing harm — to ourselves or others — is much reduced; some of its forces can then be made to serve positive purposes. However, the prevalent parental belief is that a child must be diverted from what troubles him most: his formless, nameless anxieties, and his chaotic, angry, and even violent fantasies. Many parents believe that only conscious reality or pleasant and wish-fulfilling images should be presented to the child — that he should be exposed only to the sunny side of things. But such one-sided fare nourishes the mind only in a one-sided way, and real life is not all sunny.

There is a widespread refusal to let children know that the source 3 of much that goes wrong in life is due to our very own natures — the propensity of all men for acting aggressively, asocially, selfishly, out of anger and anxiety. Instead, we want our children to believe that, inherently, all men are good. But children know that *they* are not always good; and often, even when they are, they would prefer not to be. This contradicts what they are told by their parents, and therefore makes the child a monster in his own eyes.

The dominant culture wishes to pretend, particularly where chil- 4 dren are concerned, that the dark side of man does not exist, and professes a belief in an optimistic meliorism. Psychoanalysis itself is viewed as having the purpose of making life easy — but this is not what its founder intended. Psychoanalysis was created to enable man to accept the problematic nature of life without being defeated by it, or giving in to escapism. Freud's prescription is that only by struggling courageously against what seem like overwhelming odds can man succeed in wringing meaning out of his existence.

This is exactly the message that fairy tales get across to the child 5 in manifold form: that a struggle against severe difficulties in life is unavoidable, is an intrinsic part of human existence — but that if one does not shy away, but steadfastly meets unexpected and often unjust hardships, one masters all obstacles and at the end emerges victorious.

Modern stories written for young children mainly avoid these 6 existential problems, although they are crucial issues for all of us. The child needs most particularly to be given suggestions in symbolic form about how he may deal with these issues and grow safely into maturity. "Safe" stories mention neither death nor aging, the limits to our existence, nor the wish for eternal life. The fairy tale, by contrast, confronts the child squarely with the basic human predicaments.

For example, many fairy stories begin with the death of a mother 7 or father; in these tales the death of the parent creates the most agonizing problems, as it (or the fear of it) does in real life. Other stories tell about an aging parent who decides that the time has come to let the new generation take over. But before this can happen, the successor has to prove himself capable and worthy. The Brothers Grimm's story "The Three Feathers" begins: "There was once upon a time a king who had three sons. . . . When the king had become old and weak, and was thinking of his end, he did not know which of his sons should inherit the kingdom after him." In order to decide, the king sets all his sons a difficult task; the son who meets it best "shall be king after my death."

It is characteristic of fairy tales to state an existential dilemma briefly and pointedly. This permits the child to come to grips with the problem in its most essential form, where a more complex plot would confuse matters for him. The fairy tale simplifies all situations. Its figures are clearly drawn; and details, unless very important, are eliminated. All characters are typical rather than unique.   8

Contrary to what takes place in many modern children's stories, in fairy tales evil is as omnipresent as virtue. In practically every fairy tale good and evil are given body in the form of some figures and their actions, as good and evil are omnipresent in life and the propensities for both are present in every man. It is this duality which poses the moral problem, and requires the struggle to solve it.   9

Evil is not without its attractions — symbolized by the mighty giant or dragon, the power of the witch, the cunning queen in "Snow White" — and often it is temporarily in the ascendancy. In many fairy tales a usurper succeeds for a time in seizing the place which rightfully belongs to the hero — as the wicked sisters do in "Cinderella." It is not that the evildoer is punished at the story's end which makes immersing oneself in fairy stories an experience in moral education, although this is part of it. In fairy tales, as in life, punishment or fear of it is only a limited deterrent to crime. The conviction that crime does not pay is a much more effective deterrent, and that is why in fairy tales the bad person always loses out. It is not the fact that virtue wins out at the end which promotes morality, but that the hero is most attractive to the child, who identifies with the hero in all his struggles. Because of this identification the child imagines that he suffers with the hero his trials and tribulations, and triumphs with him as virtue is victorious. The child makes such identifications all on his own, and the inner and outer struggles of the hero imprint morality on him.   10

The figures in fairy tales are not ambivalent — not good and bad at the same time, as we all are in reality. But since polarization dominates the child's mind, it also dominates fairy tales. A person is either good or bad, nothing in between. One brother is stupid, the other is clever. One sister is virtuous and industrious, the others are vile and lazy. One is beautiful, the others are ugly. One parent is all good, the other evil. The juxtaposition of opposite characters is not   11 for the purpose of stressing right behavior, as would be true for cautionary tales. (There are some amoral fairy tales where goodness or badness, beauty or ugliness play no role at all.) Presenting the polarities of character permits the child to comprehend easily the difference between the two, which he could not do as readily were the figures drawn more true to life, with all the complexities that characterize real people. Ambiguities must wait until a relatively firm personality has been established on the basis of positive identifications. Then the child has a basis for understanding that there are great differences between people, and that therefore one has to make choices about who one wants to be. This basic decision, on which all later personality development will build, is facilitated by the polarizations of the fairy tale.

Furthermore, a child's choices are based, not so much on right versus wrong, as on who arouses his sympathy and who his antipathy. The more simple and straightforward a good character, the easier it is for a child to identify with it and to reject the bad other. The child identifies with the good hero not because of his goodness, but because the hero's condition makes a deep positive appeal to him. The question for the child is not "Do I want to be good?" but "Who do I want to be like?" The child decides this on the basis of projecting himself wholeheartedly into one character. If this fairy-tale figure is a very good person, then the child decides that he wants to be good, too. 12

Amoral fairy tales show no polarization or juxtaposition of good and bad persons; that is because these amoral stories serve an entirely different purpose. Such tales or type figures as "Puss in Boots," who arranges for the hero's success through trickery, and Jack, who steals the giant's treasure, build character not by promoting choices between good and bad, but by giving the child the hope that even the meekest can succeed in life. After all, what's the use of choosing to become a good person when one feels so insignificant that he fears he will never amount to anything? Morality is not the issue in these tales, but rather, assurance that one can succeed. Whether one meets life with a belief in the possibility of mastering its difficulties or with the expectation of defeat is also a very important existential problem. 13

The deep inner conflicts originating in our primitive drives and our violent emotions are all denied in much of modern children's literature, and so the child is not helped in coping with them. But the child is subject to desperate feelings of loneliness and isolation, and he often experiences mortal anxiety. More often than not, he is unable to express these feelings in words, or he can do so only by indirection: fear of the dark, of some animal, anxiety about his body. Since it creates discomfort in a parent to recognize these emotions in his child, the parent tends to overlook them, or he belittles these spoken fears out of his own anxiety, believing this will cover over the child's fears. 14

The fairy tale, by contrast, takes these existential anxieties and 15
dilemmas very seriously and addresses itself directly to them: the
need to be loved and the fear that one is thought worthless; the love
of life, and the fear of death. Further, the fairy tale offers solutions in
ways that the child can grasp on his level of understanding. For
example, fairy tales pose the dilemma of wishing to live eternally by
occasionally concluding: "If they have not died, they are still alive."
The other ending — "And they lived happily ever after" — does not
for a moment fool the child that eternal life is possible. But it does
indicate that which alone can take the sting out of the narrow limits of
our time on this earth: forming a truly satisfying bond to another.
The tales teach that when one has done this, one has reached the
ultimate in emotional security of existence and permanence of relation available to man; and this alone can dissipate the fear of death. If
one has found true adult love, the fairy story also tells, one doesn't
need to wish for eternal life. This is suggested by another ending
found in fairy tales: "They lived for a long time afterward, happy and
in pleasure."

An uninformed view of the fairy tale sees in this type of ending 16
an unrealistic wish-fulfillment, missing completely the important message it conveys to the child. These tales tell him that by forming a true
interpersonal relation, one escapes the separation anxiety which
haunts him (and which sets the stage for many fairy tales, but is always
resolved at the story's ending). Furthermore, the story tells, this
ending is not made possible, as the child wishes and believes, by
holding on to his mother eternally. If we try to escape separation
anxiety and death anxiety by desperately keeping our grasp on our
parents, we will only be cruelly forced out, like Hansel and Gretel.

Only by going out into the world can the fairy-tale hero (child) 17
find himself there; and as he does, he will also find the other with
whom he will be able to live happily ever after; that is, without ever
again having to experience separation anxiety. The fairy tale is fu-
ture-oriented and guides the child — in terms he can understand in
both his conscious and his unconscious mind — to relinquish his
infantile dependency wishes and achieve a more satisfying independent existence.

Today children no longer grow up within the security of an 18
extended family, or of a well-integrated community. Therefore, even
more than at the times fairy tales were invented, it is important to
provide the modern child with images of heroes who have to go out
into the world all by themselves and who, although originally ignorant
of the ultimate things, find secure places in the world by following
their right way with deep inner confidence.

The fairy-tale hero proceeds for a time in isolation, as the mod- 19
ern child often feels isolated. The hero is helped by being in touch

with primitive things — a tree, an animal, nature — as the child feels more in touch with those things than most adults do. The fate of these heroes convinces the child that, like them, he may feel outcast and abandoned in the world, groping in the dark, but, like them, in the course of his life he will be guided step by step, and given help when it is needed. Today, even more than in past times, the child needs the reassurance offered by the image of the isolated man who nevertheless is capable of achieving meaningful and rewarding relations with the world around him.

Review Questions

1. According to Bettelheim, what are the sources of the child's "existential predicament"?
2. How are these predicaments resolved?
3. Why must a child be presented with a simplified version of life's ambiguities?
4. In which ways does Bettelheim believe that modern children's stories are flawed?
5. What is separation anxiety? What can fairy tales teach children about this?

Discussion Questions

1. Do you agree with Bettelheim that children need to be offered simplified versions of life's ambiguities? Would it confuse a child to read about a character in a fairy tale who is both "good" and "bad"?
2. Bettelheim says that it is necessary for children to read about heroes who go out into the world by themselves. Do you agree that a child should learn about isolation at such a young age?
3. Do you recall having an "existential predicament" as a child? What kinds of fears did you have? Does Bettelheim accurately describe these fears?
4. Bettelheim's discussion can be classified both as an analysis and as an argument. Reread the first paragraph and show how Bettelheim "sows the seeds" of his analysis and his argument. (You may want to refer to a dictionary in order to distinguish between these terms.)
5. Examine the logical development of paragraph eleven. How does each sentence lead into the other sentences? (You might find it useful to number a sheet of paper from 1 to 13 and make a note or two for each sentence.)
6. The article can be broken down into three sections (paragraphs 1–5, 6–13, and 14–19). Label these sections with titles of your own. Why is paragraph 11 located where it is?

Writing Suggestions

1. Many people feel that analyses such as Bettelheim's "ruin" fairy tales. Do you agree? (Is childhood as complicated as Bettelheim suggests? Are fairy tales "fun" and "wholesome" and nothing more?
2. Who were your fairy-tale heroes? Why were they your heroes? What parts of Bettelheim's discussion apply to your childhood? Write an essay, discussing these matters.

FAIRY TALES WERE NOT COMPOSED FOR CHILDREN
Roger Sale

Roger Sale was born in New Haven, Connecticut in 1932. He is a professor of English Literature and has taught at Amherst College and at the University of Washington. In 1969 he received a fellowship from the National Endowment for the Humanities. He has written numerous scholarly articles and books, including *Fairy Tales and After: From Snow White to E. B. White,* in which this selection appears.

☐

Fairy tale literature is one of the great kinds, a body of stories that do   1
what no other literature does. They reach back into a dateless time,
speak with grave assurance of wishes and fears, harbor no moralizing,
no sense of "art," because their ways and means are varied, because
there are so many stories to tell, so many ways to tell the "same" story.
The term "fairy tale" is only a convenience since few stories we call by
that name contain fairies, elves, leprechauns, or similar creatures. Yet
everyone seems instinctively agreed on what the term includes and
excludes, even though fairy tales blend easily into related kinds, like
myths, legends, romances, realistic folk fables, and cautionary tales.
"Cinderella," "Sinbad the Sailor," and "Hansel and Gretel" are fairy
tales, while the stories of King Arthur, Pandora, Patient Griselda, and
the Ancient Mariner are not. A nice borderline case is that of a
Neapolitan tale that resembles many versions of "The Sleeping
Beauty," but the king in this story, when he comes to the enchanted
castle, rapes the sleeping princess. This is probably not what most
people would call a fairy tale, even though the princess conceives and

bears two children and eventually comes back to life, and other events as horrible as rape do take place in many fairy tales.

The existence of fairy tales is evidence of a cultural oneness throughout the Eurasian continent. Comparative folklorists have managed to uncover characters, events, and motifs that appear, often with only slight changes, in tales told in India, Japan, France, Germany, and Ireland. Each people gave the stories different twists and emphases, just as each people also developed distinctively native or local tales. The fairy tale book on which I was raised contains two Japanese stories, one of which, "The Tongue-Cut Sparrow," is similar to the Grimms' "The Fisherman and His Wife," while the other, "The Accomplished and Lucky Teakettle," is like no other story I am aware of. The best-known stories in *The Thousand and One Nights* are distinctively "Arabian," but many of the lesser-known tales have much in common with some Indian and European ones. The various stories about Jack as the killer of giants belong strictly to the British Isles, while the English "Goldilocks and the Three Bears" resembles the Grimms' "Snow White" in its central episode. On the other hand, African and native American Indian stories belong to other families altogether from the fairy tales of Europe and Asia. 2

The stories we know derive from a relatively late period just before they began to be written down and collected, but are descendants of versions that go back into the mists of time, through centuries we can only sum up with the term "oral tradition." Furthermore, the stories themselves often reach back still further, to a time once upon a time; two thousand years ago, says the beginning of "The Juniper Tree," or when wishing still did some good, as the opening of "The Frog Prince" tells it. The versions we know were written, rewritten, and collected primarily in the two hundred years between Charles Perrault's *Histoires ou contes du temps passé*[1] at the end of the seventeenth century and the *Fairy Books* of Andrew Lang at the end of the nineteenth. But all take us back to a world when only a handful of people outside the church were literate; what came before fairy tales, or the worlds they speak of, the teller knoweth not. 3

The ancientness of the tales, their curious persistence in so many different countries, their testimony to the strength of an oral tradition now all but gone, all serve to make them a literature that latter-day people need to treat with great care and respect if they are going to know them at all. The courtly French tellers around the end of the seventeenth century—Perrault, Countess d'Aulnoy, Madame de Villeneuve, Madame Le Prince de Beaumont—were given to making the 4

---

[1] *Histoires ou contes du temps passé,* Perrault's famous collection of fairy stories for children, *Tales of Past Time.* [Behrens and Rosen]

tales wittier, more aristocratic, and sometimes more heart-piercing than they found them, and they often combined, within one story, elements they derived from their native oral tradition with others that had been part of a tradition of written tales almost as old. Clearly, however, the earlier the writer, or the closer the writers to the oral traditions, the better or less bruising the result. These first French written tales so closely resemble, and so fully respect, older traditions that few people know or care that "Puss in Boots" and "Beauty and the Beast" have actual authors. Hans Christian Andersen, writing more than a century later, had a more difficult time. He was raised in Odense, a Danish town where traditional stories were still told, but he spent his adult life in Copenhagen and became so imbued with a faint and faintly self-pitying Romanticism that even his best stories are distorted with authorial self-concern and flecked with satire and moralizing. But Andersen, troubled and vain though he was, was always essentially an oral teller; when we come down yet another century, to something like the fairy tales of C. S. Lewis, we see the damage caused when fairy stories are to be read from books. Lewis had a true and catholic love of older things, and a great longing to be part of their world, but the ear and instinct just weren't there, and the Narnia books, popular though they are with latter-day audiences, are brittle, mechanical, and naggingly preachy in ways older fairy tales never are.

Fairy tales may be irreplaceable, then, but whenever a tradition 5 fades so it can be recovered only imperfectly, and only by isolated individuals, damage is inevitable, to the reader and to the tale. When many people shared the tradition, even in the latter days when it was more a written than an oral tradition, the sharing helped free the literature from being a matter of individual taste; so many stories were known that the intent of each individual tale could be felt and understood. This discouraged the distortion caused when fairy tale literature became thought of as children's literature; also it helped maintain the balance between wishes and fears that is the equilibrium of all fairy tales by keeping individual listeners and readers from being isolated from each other. That balance is often so delicate that any individual might well feel that fairy tales are mostly daydream wishes or nightmare fears, when in fact they are neither. Finally, in this century at least, so many people know fairy tales only through badly truncated and modernized versions that it is no longer really fairy tales they know.

The enemy, thus, is historical provincialism, the attitude that 6 pretends one's native latter-day eyes and instincts are bound to be enough to gain an understanding of fairy tale literature. Of course our eyes and instincts are all we have to work with, but they can become more alert and better attuned just by reading many fairy tales, from many different places, with as much slowness and patience as can be mustered. Some sense of historical change can help a great deal here. The crucial point about fairy tales is that they *became* children's literature but were nothing of the sort for most of their long years of existence. Indeed, fairy tales could not have been children's literature originally, because, at least in our sense, children and childhood did not exist until recent centuries. To begin to contemplate the importance of that is to begin not only to understand what fairy tales are not, but to glimpse what we can best presume they once were.

Childhood was invented, and when it was, children's literature 7
followed quite naturally. As for what was before the invention of childhood, here is a summary offered by Philippe Ariès at the end of his long and painstaking work on the subject, *Centuries of Childhood:* "In the Middle Ages, at the beginning of modern times, and for a long time after that in the lower class, children were mixed with adults as soon as they were considered capable of doing without their mothers or nannies, not long after a tardy weaning (in other words, at about the age of seven). They immediately went straight into the great community of men, sharing in the work and play of their companions, old and young alike." Ariès is describing a world that lived with the most rudimentary — as we might think of it — conception of maturity as a physical matter. If there were stages in the growth of children, they were simply before and after infancy. This is easily seen in medieval and early Renaissance depictions of the Seven Ages of Man[2] and in portraits of royal and noble children in that period. There are no children there, at least not as we think of them, but babes in arms, the putti that surround the madonnas, and then people of varying sizes all of whom have adult faces. People we think of as children look like what we call midgets.

Since children were either nursing infants or small adults, fami- 8
lies did not have the importance they later came to have in a more bourgeois society: "The family fulfilled a function; it ensured the transmission of life, property, and names; but it did not penetrate very far into human sensibility. Myths such as courtly and precious love denigrated marriage, while realities such as the apprenticeship of children loosened the emotional bond between parents and children . . . New sciences such as psychoanalysis, pediatrics, and psychology devote themselves to the problems of childhood, and their findings are transmitted to parents by way of a mass of popular literature. Our world is obsessed by the physical, moral, and sexual problems of childhood."

---

[2] Perhaps the best known depiction of the Seven Ages of Man (from infancy to old age) is the speech of Jaques in Shakespeare's *As You Like It* (Act II, sc. vii). [Behrens and Rosen]

Before this conclusion Ariès has offered a great deal of evidence ⁹ concerning clothing, games, the construction of domestic dwellings, and, above all, schools to show how "the child" was brought into existence during the seventeenth century and, at most levels of society, during the eighteenth and nineteenth centuries. If, with this in mind, we then think of the relations between parents and children as seen in fairy tales, we may be less surprised at how straightforward, unanguished, and even businesslike they usually seem. The parents in "Hop o' My Thumb" and "Hansel and Gretel" must abandon their children, the king in "The Frog Prince" tells his daughter she must go to bed with the frog if she said she would, the miller in "Rumpelstiltskin" sells his daughter because he has boasted about her, Laidronette in "Green Snake" is told to live apart from her family because she is ugly, and at no point do any of these children protest or show so much as momentary resentment at their treatment. This is not easy for latter-day people to understand, but it does help to know that the basic sense of the relations of members of a family to each other has changed since fairy tales were commonly being told.

We can also learn something from this about both the tellers of ¹⁰ the tales and the audience for them. First, the teller is never self-conscious, never calls attention to himself or herself, seldom calls attention to particular details or offers to interpret them; never, as we say in this century, apologizes and never explains. The tone is always assured without any accompanying sense that that tone has been adopted; such assurance comes with the territory. Second, the audience is not a restricted group in any way we can recognize; except in the literal sense in which a told tale probably must have an audience, we can learn almost nothing about it from the tales themselves. Ariès speaks of children, at about age seven, moving into "the great community of men," but this was not, as we might call it, the human community or the family of man, but, rather, all the rest of us. For most people the community consisted of groups that ranged from thirty or forty to as many as a hundred or more people, but no group ever would mistake itself, no matter how isolated it was, for the whole world. Other communities existed relatively nearby, itinerants traveled easily between them, and not very far away would be a church, a castle, a town, where one might go upon good occasion, where life was lived differently but in ways one learned or was told about. Presumably both the passing of time and the intervention of people from the outside would alter the way a story might be told, but would not, therefore, alter the fundamentally anonymous tone of the teller speaking to this little segment of "the great community of man." Variations on stories could come and go, travel around, develop still further variations until one story began to seem like two or three somewhat different ones, without any alteration of the relation of teller to tale. No one in particular had to say anything, no one in particular had to learn anything, everyone anticipated certain motifs or characters or events without ever insisting that one way of telling a story was the only way or the right way. The property that was the tales was truly communal, both within the smallish group (but much larger than a family) that was hearing a particular telling of a particular tale and within the much larger group (impossible to define or delimit) that could be presumed to listen to fairy tales.

We are apt to want to know what something means, but we are 11 self-conscious and inquisitive people, liable to a fear of ignorance or stupidity. We are also apt to imagine that there is some implicit schedule in human life, so that we can imagine something especially interesting to people of a certain age, or something that is "too much" for a child, or something we are "too old for." We select our audiences and often tell our tales with a precise sense of a particular audience. Parents pick particular books for particular children and particular ages and adjust their stories so they can be more easily understood or so they can seem more grown-up or up-to-date. There is no trace of anything like this self-consciousness, this selectivity, this careful choosing of words, in fairy tale literature. What was was, and was equally for everyone. What we now call "French," "Scottish," or "German" fairy tales did not exist, because the community's sense of itself was not national and because so many variations existed in the languages we now call by these names.

A girl is in a wood. Give her a brother and one has "Hansel and 12 Gretel," give her many brothers and sisters and one has "Hop o' My Thumb," send the girl to dwarves and one has "Snow White," to bears and one has "Goldilocks," to grandmother and one has "Little Red Riding Hood." Make the girl a boy and one might have Jack, either the one who climbs beanstalks or the one who kills giants; make her a man and one has "The Wonderful Musician"; give her three drops of blood and a servant and one has "The Goose Girl." Probably no one teller at any one time or place ever had all these variations available, to say nothing of a sense of these as variations, but something like this sense of variety and possibility all, clearly or vaguely, intersected by one or more familiar motifs or events. Now suppose that we ask, in our latter-day fashion, what is the wood? Does it mean anything, symbolize anything, suggest anything? Of course, because in a wood one can get lost, or encounter known, suspected, or unknown dangers; almost no one in fairy tale literature goes into the woods to play, or to meet someone as in an assignation. What happens in woods in fairy tales happens so often that one begins to make easy associations, so that when these associations are denied or ignored, as in "The Wonderful Musician," one is quickly aware of it. But forests in fairy tales are so frequent, their associations so obvious, that they come to seem a given, not unlike an opening chord in a piece of music that can be played loudly or softly, by this or that instrument, and go on to this or that among countless melodies. The wood is important, thus, because the story cannot proceed without it — no wood, no seven dwarves — but the last thing one needs to do is to ponder what it means, since what it means will be what is made of it in this telling of this tale. By itself the wood is nothing; combined with other things it can direct a tale, be a place where princes never live but often visit, where woodcutters can be found, and wolves, and witches.

The more we sense the community of fairy tales and fairy tale tellers, the more we can get rid of our latter-day sense of community associations of family and nation, the more we can rid our sense of literary kind or genre of association with convention, narrative stance, and tone, the better we can glimpse these tales, tellers, and their audiences. We love to say that the *meaning* of something *is* that something; here we get a real chance to practice what we claim. This does not mean we are to be struck dumb by fairy tales, or that we should never ask questions, or never interpret, but that we can gain a great deal from the stories if first we read, and read a lot, and watch, with patience and a love of slowness, and then, when we come to speak, do so closer the tentativeness that all older things deserve. Above all, we need to adjust or even temporarily to abolish our sense of older and younger, parent and child, and let the tales give us their sense of these people and these relations. This can be hard, as reading about courtly love or kingship can be hard, since we think we know about these things already, and it is much easier to learn a truly foreign language than it is to readjust the meanings and emphases of one's own. But if we look at just one kind of mistake of this sort we can perhaps be more aware of how easy it is to make such mistakes. 13

During the first century and a half of children's literature, from roughly 1700 to 1850, a long battle was fought to expunge fairy tales on grounds that they were about what the Houyhnhnm master calls "the thing which was not" and could not therefore teach anything. It was, however, assumed that the danger they posed was for children, since presumably no parent or adult would want to read a fairy tale. Part of this battle is a work called *The Parental Instructor,* which can best be found today in an interesting collection of early English children's literature edited by Leonard de Vries and called *Flowers of Delight.* Charles and Mary Elliott have asked their father to tell them a fairy tale, "Cinderella, Ass-skin, Tom Thumb, or Bluebeard," all Perrault stories, one notes, as if "childish" fairy tales were made worse by having been imported from wicked France. Their father reproves them: "'What!' said Mr. Elliott, 'at your age — would you wish me to relate stories which have not even the shadow of common sense in them? It would be ridiculous to see a great big boy of ten and a young 14 lady of nine, listening, with open mouths, to the adventures of an ogre who ate little children, or the Little Gentleman with his Seven League boots; I could only pardon it in a child, who requires to be rocked asleep by his nurse.' "

Mr. Elliott is, we say, wrong, wrong about fairy tales, wrong about 15 children; it is not required that all literature pass literal-minded utilitarian tests, especially not required that the imagination of children be stifled and channeled so as to exclude everything not realistic, sensible, educational. But, in my experience, whenever I have asked someone to state the objections to Mr. Elliott, he or she has always begun by saying Mr. Elliott is repressing the natural and normal instincts of his children. That, apparently, is what we find most objectionable about him. The counterargument to his, however, tends to have some assumptions buried in it which are fatal to any decent understanding of fairy tales. Children need to be imaginative, need to learn about that which is not, need to discover and explore their own fantasies and those of others. Thus they need fairy tales. That is, say, the counterargument offered by Bruno Bettelheim in *The Uses of Enchantment*.

Both Mr. Elliott's argument and the counterargument offered by 16 Bettelheim and others suffer because they are based on a sense of children rather than an understanding of fairy tales, and because they draw a clear distinction between the real and the magical that fairy tales do not make and presumably their tellers did not make. Fairy tales are no more "for" children than they are "not for" children, and no fairy tale I know distinguishes real from unreal, to say nothing of fantasy from fact. About children I agree with Bettelheim and disagree with Mr. Elliott, but that is irrelevant to fairy tales themselves. Mr. Elliott wants to say fairy tales are at best stories for the nursery, worthless for lads and lasses of nine or ten; Bettelheim wants to say they are good for children of nine and ten because they are about maturing processes children are frightened of and yet must go through. Both are really psychologists, putting fairy tales into some prearranged idea of growth.

Their mistake, as I have said, is all the more difficult to correct 17 because it is, in the latter days, so hard to spot in the first place. Correction begins with a slow reading of many tales, done with as few prearranged ideas as possible; a full reading of tales from one country followed by a sampling from a number of others is a good way to begin. Take, as one does this, a motif or event, and see what happens to it in various tales, something more articulated than a girl in a wood, like births. In "Snow White" a queen pricks her finger and wishes for a child, who soon is born; in "Rapunzel" a couple vainly wishes for a child until a witch from whom the husband has stolen rampion announces a child will be born; in "The Sleeping Beauty" a frog announces to the wife while she is bathing that she will become pregnant; "The Goose Girl," on the other hand, opens with a child and mother, and the mother bequeaths three drops of blood to the daughter as she sets out to find her prince. All these are German stories, to be found in Grimm. Countess d'Aulnoy's "The White Deer" opens with a wife being told by a shrimp that she will have a child, and the shrimp then turns into a handsome old woman; the Russian tale "Kip, the Enchanted Cat" starts with a queen and a cat, and the cat has a kitten before she tells the queen she too will have a baby.

We have, thus, a motif or a scene that seems to know no national boundaries, at least in Europe. A couple, but especially the wife, wants a child, and something must happen, blood must flow, an enchanted animal must make an announcement, before the wish can be granted. If we ask why this should be such a common motif, we probably need to know little more than that women of much earlier times, especially women not of the nobility, came to puberty much later than women in latter days and also tended to marry much younger than women do now. Thus many couples could have been married some years before they could have had a child; the period we know as adolescence hadn't been invented yet, of course. Beyond that we need not inquire, I suspect. Nor need we be surprised that this motif invariably comes at the beginning of stories, nor that, for the most part, the child that is born will turn out to be much more important in the story than either parent. The woman often died in childbirth, the man tended to remain faceless. But each use of this motif is somewhat different from the others, so that we can easily imagine the tellers of a particular tale shaping the episode of the annunciation and birth to fit the child to come and perhaps even the story to come. Here the basic wish, for the child, and the basic fear, that there will be no child, meet so simply and obviously that nothing need be made clear except whatever is required by the particular story being told. 18

Review Questions

1. "The existence of fairy tales is evidence of a cultural oneness throughout the Eurasian continent." What does Sale mean by this?

2. What is "historical provincialism"? How does it hinder one from examining fairy tales?

3. When did fairy tales become children's literature? Why is it important to know that they were not always children's literature?

4. According to Sale, what is Bettelheim's "mistake"?

5. How must we adjust our modern sense of community, family, and nation if we are to "understand" fairy tales?

Discussion Questions

1. The literary term "motif" refers to simple elements, or plots, which recur in stories. The wicked stepmother motif, for example, is common to many fairy tales. Examine paragraph 12 and explain how motifs are important to Sale's analysis.

2. Sale says that our latter-day eyes and instincts keep us from understanding fairy tales. Would these same eyes and instincts keep you from understanding more recent literature — say, a novel written in 1860? Are there any qualities in fairy tales (and in other kinds of literature) that are "immune" to the passage of time?

3. Sale mentions the "balance between wishes and fears that is the equilibrium of fairy tales." What are these wishes and fears?

4. Reread paragraphs 6 through 9. Why does Sale cite the work of Philippe Ariès? How does Sale, in paragraph 6, prepare for his reference to Ariès? Notice that Sale does not quote one long passage from Ariès. He weaves shorter quotations around his own (Sale's) discussion. What are the advantages of this?

5. In paragraph 6, Sale writes, "The enemy, thus, is historical provincialism. . . ." What does "thus" refer to? How does this one word signify a shift in the discussion?

6. Sale is often "musical" with his writing. Read aloud paragraph 3. How do the sentences, both individually and in relation to the other sentences in the paragraph, create a sensation of flowing through time? How does this sensation relate to the subject of the paragraph? Why does Sale end the paragraph the way he does?

Writing Suggestions

1. Does the idea of a "cultural oneness" appeal to you? Do you think that people, regardless of ethnic or geographic communities, have the same wishes and fears? Write an essay, detailing your response.

2. Reread Perrault's "Cinderella" and identify the various motifs, the familiar elements of plot and character in the story. How does Sexton make use of these motifs?

THE TWELVE WILD GEESE
Patrick Kennedy

Kennedy's tale appears in a collection of Irish fairy tales compiled by the Irish poet William Butler Yeats. Along with J. M. Synge, Lady Gregory, and Standish O'Grady, Yeats helped re-create for readers of modern English an Irish literature and mythology which had been dormant for nearly a thousand years. This literary revival helped engender a feeling of national heritage among the Irish, who, during the first two decades of this century, struggled to gain their freedom from Great Britain, along with a separate national identity. Yeats refers to "The Twelve Wild Geese" and other stories of the revival as "full of simplicity and musical occurrences, for they are the literature of a class for whom every incident in the old rut of birth, love, pain, and death has cropped up unchanged for centuries: who have steeped everything in the heart: to whom everything is a symbol."

☐

There was once a King and Queen that lived very happily together, and they had twelve sons and not a single daughter. We are always wishing for what we haven't, and don't care for what we have, and so it was with the Queen. One day in winter, when the bawn [barn] was covered with snow, she was looking out of the parlor window, and saw there a calf that was just killed by the butcher and a raven standing near it. "Oh," says she, "if I had only a daughter with her skin as white as that snow, her cheeks as red as that blood, and her hair as black as that raven, I'd give away every one of my twelve sons for her." The moment she said the word, she got a great fright, and a shiver went through her, and in an instant after, a severe-looking old woman stood before her. "That was a wicked wish you made," said she, "and to punish you it will be granted. You will have such a daughter as you desire, but the very day of her birth you will lose your other children." She vanished the moment she said the words. 1

And that very way it turned out. When she expected her delivery, she had her children all in a large room of the palace, with guards all round it, but the very hour her daughter came into the world, the guards inside and outside heard a great whirling and whistling, and the twelve princes were seen flying one after another out through the open window, and away like so many arrows over the woods. Well, the king was in great grief for the loss of his sons, and he would be very 2

Patrick Kennedy, "The Twelve Wild Geese" in *Irish Folk Stories and Fairy Tales*, edited by William Butler Yeats, 1972, pp. 256–261.

enraged with his wife if he only knew that she was so much to blame for it.

Everyone called the little princess Snow-white-and-Rose-red on account of her beautiful complexion. She was the most loving and lovable child that could be seen anywhere. When she was twelve years old she began to be very sad and lonely, and to torment her mother, asking her about her brothers that she thought were dead, for none up to that time ever told her the exact thing that happened them. The secret was weighing very heavy on the Queen's conscience, and as the little girl persevered in her questions, at last she told her. "Well, mother," said she, "it was on my account my poor brothers were changed into wild geese, and are now suffering all sorts of hardship; before the world is a day older, I'll be off to seek them, and try to restore them to their own shapes."   3

The King and Queen had her well watched, but all was no use. Next night she was getting through the woods that surrounded the palace, and she went on and on that night, and till the evening of next day. She had a few cakes with her, and she got nuts, and *mugoreens* (fruit of the sweet briar), and some sweet crabs, as she went along. At last she came to a nice wooden house just at sunset. There was a fine garden round it, full of the handsomest flowers, and a gate in the hedge. She went in, and saw a table laid out with twelve plates, and twelve knives and forks, and twelve spoons, and there were cakes, and cold wild fowl, and fruit along with the plates, and there was a good fire, and in another long room there were twelve beds. Well, while she was looking about her she heard the gate opening, and footsteps along the walk, and in came twelve young men, and there was great grief and surprise on all their faces when they laid eyes on her. "Oh, what misfortune sent you here?" said the eldest. "For the sake of a girl we were obliged to leave our father's court, and be in the shape of wild geese all day. That's twelve years ago, and we took a solemn oath that we would kill the first young girl that came into our hands. It's a pity to put such an innocent and handsome girl as you are out of the world, but we must keep our oath." "But," said she, "I'm your only sister, that never knew anything about this till yesterday; and I stole away from our father's and mother's palace last night to find you out and relieve you if I can." Every one of them clasped his hands, and looked down on the floor, and you could hear a pin fall till the eldest cried out, "A curse light on our oath! What shall we do?" "I'll tell you that," said an old woman that appeared at the instant among them. "Break your wicked oath, which no one should keep. If you attempted to lay an uncivil finger on her I'd change you into twelve *booliaun buis* (stalks of ragweed), but I wish well to you as well as to her. She is appointed to be your deliverer in this way. She must spin and   4 knit twelve shirts for you out of bog-down, to be gathered by her own hands on the moor just outside of the wood. It will take her five years to do it, and if she once speaks, or laughs, or cries the whole time, you will have to remain wild geese by day till you're called out of the world. So take care of your sister; it is worth your while." The fairy then vanished, and it was only a strife with the brothers to see who would be first to kiss and hug their sister.

So for three long years the poor young princess was occupied 5 pulling bog-down, spinning it, and knitting it into shirts, and at the end of the three years she had eight made. During all that time, she never spoke a word, nor laughed, nor cried: the last was the hardest to refrain from. One fine day she was sitting in the garden spinning, when in sprung a fine grayhound and bounded up to her, and laid his paws on her shoulder, and licked her forehead and her hair. The next minute a beautiful young prince rode up to the little garden gate, took off his hat, and asked for leave to come in. She gave him a little nod, and in he walked. He made ever so many apologies for intruding, and asked her ever so many questions, but not a word could he get out of her. He loved her so much from the first moment, that he could not leave her till he told her he was king of a country just bordering on the forest, and he begged her to come home with him, and be his wife. She couldn't help loving him as much as he did her, and though she shook her head very often, and was very sorry to leave her brothers, at last she nodded her head, and put her hand in his. She knew well enough that the good fairy and her brothers would be able to find her out. Before she went she brought out a basket holding all her bog-down, and another holding the eight shirts. The attendants took charge of these, and the prince placed her before him on his horse. The only thing that disturbed him while riding along was the displeasure his stepmother would feel at what he had done. However, he was full master at home, and as soon as he arrived he sent for the bishop, got his bride nicely dressed, and the marriage was celebrated, the bride answering by signs. He knew by her manner she was of high birth, and no two could be fonder of each other.

The wicked stepmother did all she could to make mischief, saying 6 she was sure she was only a woodman's daughter; but nothing could disturb the young king's opinion of his wife. In good time the young queen was delivered of a beautiful boy, and the king was so glad he hardly knew what to do for joy. All the grandeur of the christening and the happiness of the parents tormented the bad woman more than I can tell you, and she determined to put a stop to all their comfort. She got a sleeping posset given to the young mother, and while she was thinking and thinking how she could best make away with the child, she saw a wicked-looking wolf in the garden, looking up at her, and licking his chops. She lost no time, but snatched the child from the arms of the sleeping woman, and pitched it out. The beast caught it in his mouth, and was over the garden fence in a minute. The wicked woman then pricked her own fingers, and dabbed the blood round the mouth of the sleeping mother.

Well, the young king was just then coming into the big bawn from 7 hunting, and as soon as he entered the house, she beckoned to him, shed a few crocodile tears, began to cry and wring her hands and hurried him along the passage to the bedchamber.

Oh, wasn't the poor king frightened when he saw the queen's 8 mouth bloody, and missed his child? It would take two hours to tell you the devilment of the old queen, the confusion and fright, and grief of the young king and queen, the bad opinion he began to feel of his wife, and the struggle she had to keep down her bitter sorrow, and not give way to it by speaking or lamenting. The young king would not allow any one to be called, and ordered his stepmother to give out that the child fell from the mother's arms at the window, and that a wild beast ran off with it. The wicked woman pretended to do so, but she told underhand to everybody she spoke to what the king and herself saw in the bed-chamber.

The young queen was the most unhappy woman in the three 9 kingdoms for a long time, between sorrow for her child, and her husband's bad opinion; still she neither spoke nor cried, and she gathered bog-down and went on with the shirts. Often the twelve wild geese would be seen lighting on the trees in the park or on the smooth sod, and looking in at her windows. So she worked on to get the shirts finished, but another was at an end, and she had the twelfth shirt finished, except one arm, when she was obliged to take to her bed, and a beautiful girl was born.

Now the king was on his guard, and he would not let the mother 10 and child be left alone for a minute; but the wicked woman bribed some of the attendants, set others asleep, gave the sleepy posset to the queen, and had a person watching to snatch the child away, and kill it. But what should she see but the same wolf in the garden looking up, and licking his chops again? Out went the child, and away with it flew the wolf, and she smeared the sleeping mother's mouth and face with blood, and then roared, and bawled, and cried out to the king and to everybody she met, and the room was filled, and everyone was sure the young queen had just devoured her own babe.

The poor mother thought now her life would leave her. She was 11 in such a state she could neither think nor pray, but she sat like a stone, and worked away at the arm of the twelfth shirt.

The king was for taking her to the house in the wood where he 12 found her, but the stepmother, and the lords of the court, and the judges would not hear of it, and she was condemned to be burned in the big bawn at three o'clock the same day. When the hour drew near, the king went to the farthest part of his palace, and there was no more unhappy man in his kingdom at that hour.

When the executioners came and led her off, she took the pile of   13
shirts in her arms. There was still a few stitches wanted, and while they were tying her to the stake she still worked on. At the last stitch she seemed overcome and dropped a tear on her work, but the moment after she sprang up, and shouted out, "I am innocent; call my husband!" The executioners stayed their hands, except one wicked-disposed creature, who set fire to the faggot next him, and while all were struck in amaze, there was a rushing of wings, and in a moment the twelve wild geese were standing around the pile. Before you could count twelve, she flung a shirt over each bird, and there in the twinkling of an eye were twelve of the finest young men that could be collected out of a thousand. While some were untying their sister, the eldest, taking a strong stake in his hand, struck the busy executioner such a blow that he never needed another.

While they were comforting the young queen, and the king was   14
hurrying to the spot, a fine-looking woman appeared among them holding the babe on one arm and the little prince by the hand. There was nothing but crying for joy, and laughing for joy, and hugging and kissing, and when any one had time to thank the good fairy, who in the shape of a wolf, carried the child away, she was not to be found. Never was such happiness enjoyed in any palace that ever was built, and if the wicked queen and her helpers were not torn by wild horses, they richly deserved it.

Discussion Questions

1. An explicit moral is given at the beginning of "The Twelve Wild Geese." Are there other morals to the story? Must a fairy tale have a moral? Does the presence of a moral at the beginning of the story increase or decrease your interest in what is to follow?

2. At what points in the story does the old woman (in whatever guise) appear? If a child to whom you were reading the story asked, "Who is this old woman?" what would be your response?

3. Why is it necessary for the princess to remain silent for five years?

4. Is there something odd about a marriage in which one of the partners does not speak for two years? (Why do you suppose it is a woman, and not a man, who does not speak?)

5. "The fairy then vanished, and it was only a strife with the brothers to see who would be first to kiss and hug their sister." Why is this sentence so effective in demonstrating the extent of the brothers' affections? Locate and discuss other sentences which you feel to be especially fine descriptions.

Writing Suggestions

1. Are the elements of violence and malevolence in "The Twelve Wild Geese" possibly damaging to children? How old would your child have to be before you would consider reading this story to him or her? Explain your answer in an essay.

2. Analyze the role of the mother-figures in this story and their relationships with their children. Would you consider the old woman/wolf a mother-figure? Write an essay, detailing your responses.

THE MAGIC SHIRT
Aleksandr Nikolayevich Afanas'ev

"The Magic Shirt," was recorded by Aleksandr Nikolayevich Afanas'ev, the Russian counterpart of the Grimm brothers. His collections of Russian folklore, published from 1866 on, were instrumental in introducing Russian popular tales to world literature.

The analysis of such fairy tales has been aided considerably by the work of folklorist Vladimir Propp, who studied one hundred Russian tales and observed the structural similarities among them. Propp's analysis (as summarized here by F. André Favat in his study *Child and Tale*) along with those of Bettelheim and Sale will provide three distinct perspectives from which you can view folktales.

. . . In *Morphology of the Folktale* (1927), Propp produced a description of the fairy tale according to its component parts and a description of their relationship. He noticed, for instance, that sets of events such as the following occurred:

1. A Czar gives an eagle to a hero. The eagle carries the hero away to another kingdom.
2. An old man gives Súcenko a horse. The horse carries Súcenko away to another kingdom.
3. A sorcerer gives Iván a little boat. The boat takes Iván to another kingdom.
4. A princess gives Iván a ring. Young men appearing from out of the ring carry Iván away into another kingdom.

Observing that both constants and variables were present, Propp hypothesized that, though the names and attributes of the *dramatis personae* change, their actions and functions do not. Subsequent investigation of 100 Russian fairy tales showed this to be fact.

Propp found that the characters of different tales often performed the same actions recurring with "astounding" frequency. He observed that, while

From *National Council of Teachers of English Research Report*, no. 19, 1977, pp. 12–13, 97–98. Copyright © 1977 by the National Council of Teachers of English. Reprinted by permission of the publisher and the author.

the number of personages in the stories was extremely large, the number of functions was extremely small, a fact which accounted for the tales' uniformity and repetitiveness on one hand, and their multiformity and variety on the other. Propp extracted thirty-one actions or functions that could exist in a fairy tale, designating them as nouns expressing action. Thus the action of a villain causing harm or injury to a member of a family is referred to as "villainy," the hero leaving home is "departure," the hero marrying and ascending the throne are "wedding," and so on. Propp observed that a large number of the functions occurred in pairs, such as the addressing of an interdiction to the hero and the hero's violation of the interdiction; the pursuit of the hero and the rescue of the hero from pursuit; the villain's attempts at deceiving his victim and the victim's unwitting submission to the deception, and so on. Still other functions occurred in larger groups, such as the hero's being tested by someone he meets, perhaps an old woman asking for help, his reaction to the test, and his acquiring the use of a magical device or agent.

Propp also noted that although all tales did not possess all thirty-one functions, whatever functions did exist were always in the same sequence. For example, if one imagines the prototypic tale as existing along a continuum such as this:

1 2 3 31

then various individual tales could consist of various numbers of these functions. But those functions that did exist in each tale would always proceed from left to right. Even though certain functions might be absent within a section of the continuum, this would still not change the order of the functions:

Tale III
(———————————→)

Tale II
(——————————————————————→)

Tale I
(——————————————————→)

1 .... 8a .... 11 .... 18 ... 20 31

Propp also showed that not only could his scheme accurately describe Russian fairy tales other than the 100 he examined, but also and more significantly, non-Russian fairy tales.

Propp's Functions of *Dramatis Personae*

The following is a simplified listing of Propp's functions of *dramatis personae* as described in his *Morphology of the Folktale.* For each function there is given (1) a brief summary of its "essence," as Propp called it, plus (2) an abbreviated definition of the function in one word.

1. One of the members of a family absents himself from home. (Definition: *absentation.*)
2. An interdiction is addressed to the hero. (Definition: *interdiction.*)
3. The interdiction is violated. (Definition: *violation.*)
4. The villain makes an attempt to reconnaissance. (Definition: *reconnaissance.*)
5. The villain receives information about his victim. (Definition: *delivery.*)
6. The villain attempts to deceive his victim in order to take possession of him or his belongings. (Definition: *trickery.*)
7. The victim submits to deception and thereby unwittingly helps his enemy. (Definition: *complicity.*)
8. The villain causes harm or injury to a member of a family. (Definition: *villainy.*)
8a. One member of a family either lacks something or desires to have something. (Definition: *lack.*)
9. Misfortune or lack is made known; the hero is approached with a request or command; he is allowed to go or he is dispatched. (Definition: *mediation, the connective incident.*)
10. The seeker agrees to or decides upon counteraction. (Definition: *beginning counteraction.*)
11. The hero leaves home. (Definition: *departure.*)
12. The hero is tested, interrogated, attacked, etc., which prepares the way for his receiving either a magical agent or helper. (Definition: *the first function of the donor.*)
13. The hero reacts to the actions of the future donor. (Definition: *the hero's reaction.*)
14. The hero acquires the use of a magical agent. (Definition: *provision or receipt of a magical agent.*)
15. The hero is transferred, delivered, or led to the whereabouts of an object of search. (Definition: *spatial transference between two kingdoms, guidance.*)
16. The hero and the villain join in direct combat. (Definition: *struggle.*)
17. The hero is branded. (Definition: *branding, marking.*)
18. The villain is defeated. (Definition: *victory.*)
19. The initial misfortune or lack is liquidated. (Definition: *liquidation.*)
20. The hero returns. (Definition: *return.*)
21. The hero is pursued. (Definition: *pursuit, chase.*)
22. Rescue of the hero from pursuit. (Definition: *rescue.*)
23. The hero, unrecognized, arrives home or in another country. (Definition: *unrecognized arrival.*)
24. A false hero presents unfounded claims. (Definition: *unfounded claims.*)
25. A difficult task is proposed to the hero. (Definition: *difficult task.*)
26. The task is resolved. (Definition: *solution.*)
27. The hero is recognized. (Definition: *recognition.*)
28. The false hero or villain is exposed. (Definition: *exposure.*)
29. The hero is given a new appearance. (Definition: *transfiguration.*)
30. The villain is punished. (Definition: *punishment.*)
31. The hero is married and ascends the throne. (Definition: *wedding.*)

As you read the following tale, "The Magic Shirt," see how many of Propp's thirty-one functions have been woven into the narrative.

☐

A brave soldier, while serving in his regiment, received a hundred 1
rubles from home. The sergeant got wind of it and borrowed this money from him. When the time came to settle the debt, instead of paying it, he gave the soldier a hundred blows on his back with a stick, saying: "I never saw your money. You invented the whole thing!" The soldier became enraged and ran away into a deep forest; he was about to lie down to rest under a tree when he saw a six-headed dragon flying toward him. The dragon stopped beside the soldier, questioned him about his life, and said: "Why should you trudge through the woods like this? Instead, come and serve me for three years." "With pleasure," said the soldier. "Sit on me, then," said the dragon. The soldier began to load all his belongings on the dragon. "Eh, veteran, why are you taking all this trash with you?" "How can you ask that, dragon? A soldier gets flogged for losing even a button, and now you want me to drop all my belongings!"

The dragon brought the soldier to his palace and charged him as 2
follows: "Sit by the kettle for three years, keep the fire going, and cook my kasha!" The dragon himself went to travel in the world during all that time. The soldier's work was not hard: he put wood under the kettle and sat beside it drinking vodka and eating tasty snacks — and the dragon's vodka was not like ours, all watered down, but quite strong! After three years the dragon came flying home. "Well, veteran, is the kasha ready?" "It must be, for all these three years my fire did not go out once." The dragon ate the whole kettleful in one meal, praised the soldier for his faithful service, and hired him for the next three years.

These years passed too, and the dragon ate his kasha again and 3
left the soldier for still another three years. For two years our soldier cooked the kasha, and toward the end of the third began to think, "Here I am living with the dragon for the ninth year, cooking his kasha all the time, and I don't even know what it tastes like. I must try it." He raised the lid and found his sergeant sitting in the kettle. "Ah, my friend," thought the soldier, "now I'm going to give you a good time; I'll pay you back the blows you gave me." And he began to

From *Russian Fairy Tales,* collected by Aleksandr Afanas'ev, translated by Norbert Guterman. Copyright 1945 by Pantheon Books, Inc. and renewed 1973 by Random House, Inc. Reprinted by permission of Pantheon Books, a Division of Random House, Inc.

drag in wood and put it under the kettle, as much as he could, and made such a fire that he cooked not only the flesh but even the bones of the sergeant to a pulp. The dragon returned, ate the kasha, and praised the soldier: "Well, veteran, the kasha was good before, but this time it was even better. Choose whatever you like as your reward." The soldier looked around and chose for himself a mighty horse and a shirt of thick cloth. This shirt was not an ordinary shirt, but a magic one: he who put it on became a mighty champion.

The soldier then went to a king, helped him in a difficult war, and married his beautiful daughter. But the princess disliked being married to a common soldier. So she intrigued with a neighboring prince, and in order to find out whence came the soldier's mighty strength, she coaxed and flattered him. Having discovered what she wanted, she seized the opportunity when her husband was asleep to remove his shirt and give it to the prince. The prince put on the magic shirt, took a sword, cut the soldier into little pieces, put them in a hempen bag, and said to the stableboys: "Take this bag, tie it to some battered jade, and drive her into the open field!" The stableboys went to carry out this order, but meantime the soldier's mighty steed had turned himself into a battered jade and put himself in the stableboys' path. They took him, tied the bag to him, and drove him into the open field. The mighty steed darted off faster than a bird, came to the dragon's castle, stopped there, and for three nights and three days neighed without ceasing. 4

The dragon was sound asleep, but he was finally awakened by the horse's loud neighing and stamping, and came out of his palace. He looked into the bag and groaned aloud! He took the pieces, put them together, washed them with the water of death — and the soldier's body was joined together. He sprinkled it with the water of life, and the soldier came to. "Fie," he said, "I have slept a long time!" "You would have slept very long indeed without your good horse!" answered the dragon, and taught the soldier the difficult science of assuming different shapes. The soldier turned into a dove, flew to the prince with whom his faithless wife now lived, and sat on the sill of the kitchen window. The young cook saw him. "Ah," she said, "what a pretty little dove!" She opened the window and let him into the kitchen. The dove struck the floor and became a goodly youth. "Do me a service, lovely maiden," he said, "and I will marry you." "What shall I do for you?" "Get from the prince his shirt of thick cloth." "But he never takes it off, except when he bathes in the sea." 5

The soldier found out at what time the prince bathed, went out on the road, and turned into a flower. Soon the prince and the princess came to the beach, followed by the cook carrying clean linen. The prince noticed the flower and admired it, but the princess guessed at once what it was: "Ah, that accursed soldier must have 6 turned himself into this!" She picked the flower and began to crumple it and pluck the petals, but the flower turned into a little fly and without being noticed hid in the cook's bosom. As soon as the prince undressed and went into the water, the fly flew out and turned into a bright falcon. The falcon snatched the shirt and carried it away, then turned into a goodly youth and put it on. Then the soldier took a sword, put his treacherous wife and her lover to death, and married the lovely young cook.

Discussion Questions

1. There are elements of violence, adultery, and jealous love in this story. Imagine, for the moment, that you are on a panel at a debate. First, argue why "The Magic Shirt" should be read to children. Then, argue why it should not be read to them.

2. "The soldier then went to a king, helped him in a difficult war, and married his beautiful daughter." The events to which this sentence refers could well be the basis for an entire story. Why, in this story, are the events compressed? Locate other similarly compressed episodes. What effect do these have on the pacing of the story?

3. Discuss the relationship between nobility (or officers in the army) and commoners in this story. Are there social and political overtones to "The Magic Shirt"?

Writing Suggestions

1. Rewrite the story from the dragon's point of view.

2. Using Propp's 31 structural elements of the fairy tale, write the outline of an episode of a current television serial. (You could also write the outline of a *Star Wars*-type movie.)

SUMMARY, SYNTHESIS, CRITIQUE ACTIVITIES

Summary

Summarize Bettelheim's or Sale's article. Follow the suggested six-step process and take into account answers to the Review Questions for each passage.

Synthesis

1. Base a *comparison and contrast* synthesis on the two versions of "Cinderella." (Bear in mind that you will not be able, in a short paper, to

treat these selections exhaustively. Focus on two or three elements of comparison and contrast — possibly differences in language, plot line, ending, stereotypes of women, or narrator.

2. How does a fairy tale you have written *exemplify* the positions taken by Sale or Bettelheim? If these authors do not raise issues germane to your story, then explain why this is so. You'll have to analyze your own story and then *contrast* your analysis with Bettelheim's and Sale's.

3. Using Vladimir Propp's 31 structural elements as criteria, *compare and contrast* two of the tales in this chapter.

4. *Compare and contrast* Bettelheim's and Sale's views on fairy tales. Recall that each examines different aspects of the tales — Bettelheim, the psychological and individual; Sale, the literary and cultural.

5. *Argue* that one or more of the tales in this chapter is excessively sexist or violent and therefore not suitable for children.

6. You have read four fairy tales in this chapter — from France, Ireland, Russia, and the United States. In examining these stories, can you detect any motifs that would indicate Sale's "cultural oneness"?

7. Discuss the *process* by which characters fall in love and/or marry in fairy tales.

Critique

1. Write a critique of Bettelheim's or Sale's article — the one you did not summarize above. Remember that Bettelheim and Sale work with different assumptions — assumptions that you need to define and examine.

2. Write a critique of the following, a passage in *The Republic,*[1] in which Plato discusses the control the state should have over the instruction of children:

> Then shall we simply allow our children to listen to any stories that anyone happens to make up, and so receive into their minds ideas often the very opposite of those we shall think they ought to have when they are grown up?
> No, certainly not.
> It seems, then, our first business will be to supervise the making of fables and legends, rejecting all which are unsatisfactory; and we shall induce nurses and mothers to tell their children only those which we have approved, and to think more of moulding their souls with these stories than they now do of rubbing their limbs to make them strong and shapely. Most of the stories now in use must be discarded.

---

[1] *The Republic of Plato,* trans. Francis MacDonald Cornford (New York: Oxford University Press, 1960) p. 69.

If you have read the "Morality and the Movies" chapter, you may wish to draw some connections between Plato's views and those of the authors of the 1930 Motion Picture Production Code.

RESEARCH TOPICS

1. Analyze ten modern children's stories, examining their structural patterns (i.e., plot structures, themes, character types). How do these patterns compare with those that Propp found in Russian fairy tales?

2. Obtain a copy of a reading list for elementary school children, and read ten to twelve selections included on the list. Report on the criteria that you feel the teachers or school officials may have used in compiling the list. If you have the opportunity, interview one or more of the people who compiled or approved the list.

3. Examine the issue of violence or sex discrimination in fairy tales. After a review of several articles and books, you may want to focus your discussion on one or two tales.

ADDITIONAL READINGS

Andersen, Hans Christian. *Hans Christian Andersen: His Classic Fairy Tales.* New York: Golden Press, 1974.

Alexander, A. E. "Stephen King's *Carrie* — A Universal Fairy Tale." *Journal of Popular Culture,* 13 (Fall 1979), pp. 282-288.

Berger, Terry, ed. *Black Fairy Book.* New York: Atheneum, 1969.

Clouston, W. A. *Popular Tales and Fictions: Their Migrations and Transformations* (in two volumes). Detroit: Singing Tree Press, 1968.

Elms, A. C. "The Three Bears: Four Interpretations." *Journal of American Folklore,* 90 (July 1977), pp. 257-273.

Favat, F. André. *Child and Tale: The Origins of Interest.* Urbana, Ill.: National Council of Teachers of English Research Report no. 19, 1977.

Grimm, Jakob. *Grimm's Fairy Tales.* New York: Pantheon Books, 1944.

Haviland, Virginia. *Children's Literature: A Guide to Reference Sources.* Washington: Library of Congress, 1966.

Issues in Children's Book Selection: A Collection of Articles Reprinted from School Library Journal. New York: R. R. Bowker Company, 1973.

Jacobs, Joseph, ed. *Indian Folk and Fairy Tales.* New York: G. P. Putnam's Sons, n.d.

Lang, Andrew, ed. *Blue Fairy Book.* New York: David McKay Company, Inc., 1948. See also Lang's Violet, Red, Yellow, and Green Fairy Books.

Lyn, Ruth Nadelman. *Fantasy for Children: An Annotated Checklist.* New York: R. R. Bowker, 1979.

Miller, Olive Beaupré, *My Book House.* 12 vols. Lake Bluff, Ill.: United Educators, 1980.

Stone, Kay. "Things Walt Disney Never Told Us." *Journal of American Folklore,* 88 (Jan. 1975), pp. 42-50.

J. R. R. Tolkien. *Tree and Leaf.* Boston: Houghton Mifflin, 1965.

Weitzman, Eifler, Hokada, and Ross. "Sex-Role Socialization in Picture Books for Preschool Children." *American Journal of Sociology,* 77, no. 6 (May 1972), pp. 42-50.

Williams, Jay. *The Practical Princess and Other Liberating Fairy Tales.* New York: Parent's Magazine Press, 1978.

Note: See also books (Sexton, Perrault, Bettelheim, Sale) from which selections in this unit were taken.

Obedience
to Authority

This is, perhaps, the most fundamental lesson of our study: ordinary people, simply doing their jobs, and without any particular hostility on their part, can become agents in a terrible destructive process. Moreover, even when the destructive effects of their work become patently clear, and they are asked to carry out actions incompatible with fundamental standards of morality, relatively few people have the resources needed to resist authority.

— Stanley Milgram

During the 1960s, Yale psychologist Stanley Milgram conducted a landmark study to determine the extent to which ordinary individuals would obey the clearly immoral orders of an authority figure. The results were shocking, not only to the psychiatrists who had predicted that few people would follow such orders, but also to many other social scientists and laymen — some of whom applauded Milgram for his fiendishly ingenious research design, some of whom bitterly attacked him for unethical procedures.

Debates on obedience to authority are hardly academic. During the Second World War, millions of people were exterminated in Nazi death camps. Those who were brought to trial for these crimes at Nuremberg pleaded innocent: they had been ordered, they said, under pain of death, to carry out the murders. Eventually, they were found guilty and hanged; but a question survived them: could ordinary people, influenced by ruthless figures of authority, become agents of terror? Milgram set out to discover an answer.

Following a description of the Milgram experiment by psychologists Ronald Smith and Erwin and Barbara Sarason, you will read a review of *Obedience to Authority,* the book in which Milgram reported his results. Then, we include a brief article that reports on a similar experiment conducted with sixteen-year-old Jordanian children. In "Superior Orders and Reprisals," the chief U.S. prosecutor at Nuremberg, Telford Taylor, places the dilemma of obedience to immoral or illegal orders into a historical context, a context against which the My Lai massacre can be considered. In 1969, during the height of the U.S. involvement in Vietnam, Lt. William Calley was accused and convicted of murdering Vietnamese civilians when his platoon raided the hamlet of My Lai. Calley's lawyer argued that his client was simply following orders. Secretary of the Army Stanley Resor reports on the incident; and in an interview, psychiatrist Robert Lifton discusses the process by which soldiers can become agents of terror. Finally, Jean Anouilh, in his modern version of *Antigone,* explores the external conflict between individual conscience and the authority of the state.

THE MILGRAM EXPERIMENT
Ronald E. Smith, Irwin G. Sarason, and
Barbara Sarason

Ronald Smith, of the Portland State University, and Irwin and Barbara Sarason, of the University of Washington (Seattle) are professors of psychology and coauthors of *Psychology: Frontiers of Behavior,* in which "The Milgram Experiment" appears. Stanley Milgram is a social and experimental psychologist, who was educated at Harvard University and has been awarded numerous honors. Between 1961 and 1967, he was principal investigator for a National Science Foundation Research Grant at Yale University, where he conducted his famous and controversial experiments.

☐

After World War II the Nuremberg war trials were conducted in order to try Nazi war criminals for the atrocities they had committed. In many instances the defense offered by those on trial was that they had "only followed orders." During the Vietnam War American soldiers accused of committing atrocities in Vietnam gave basically the same explanation for their actions. 1

Most of us reject justifications based on "obedience to authority" as mere rationalizations, secure in our convictions that we, if placed in the same situation, would behave differently. However, the results of a series of ingenious and controversial investigations performed in the 1960s by psychologist Stanley Milgram suggest that perhaps we should not be so sure of ourselves. 2

Milgram wanted to determine the extent to which people would obey an experimenter's commands to administer painful electric shocks to another person. Pretend for a moment that you are a subject in one of his studies. Here is what would happen. On arriving at a university laboratory in response to a classified ad offering volunteers $4 for one hour's participation in an experiment on memory, you meet another subject, a pleasant, middle-aged man with whom you chat while awaiting the arrival of the experimenter. When the experimenter arrives, dressed in a laboratory coat, he pays you and then informs you and the other person that one of you will be the 3 subject in the experiment and that the other will serve as his assistant. You are chosen by lot to be the assistant, but in reality you are the subject.

The experimenter explains that the study is concerned with the effects of punishment on learning. Accompanied by you, the "subject" is conducted into a room and strapped into a chair, and a large electrode is attached to his wrist. He is told that he is to learn a list of word pairs and that whenever he makes an error he will receive electric shocks of increasing intensity. On hearing this, the "subject" responds, "When I was at the West Haven V.A. Hospital a few years ago, they detected a slight heart condition. Nothing serious, but are these shocks dangerous?" The experimenter replies in an unconcerned manner that although the shocks may be painful, they will cause no permanent tissue damage.

You and the experimenter then proceed to an adjoining room connected by an intercom so that the "subject's" responses can be heard. You are seated in front of an apparatus with 30 toggle switches ranging from 15 volts to 450 volts. (See Figure 1.) Your task is to administer the learning task to the "subject." Whenever he gives an incorrect answer, you must give him an electric shock, starting at the lowest level (15 volts) and increasing the level by 15 volts each time. You are given a sample shock of 45 volts and find it moderately painful.

What you are unaware of at this point is that you are in a carefully contrived situation. The learner is actually an actor who receives no shock at all, and the responses you hear over the intercom are tape-recorded so that they will be exactly the same for each "assistant." The experimenter's actions are also carefully programmed.

As the experiment proceeds, the learner makes error after error. You increase the shock level steadily until he is clearly experiencing pain. The tape-recorded responses are programmed to correspond to the shock intensities as follows:

75 volts Ugh!
90 volts Ugh!
105 volts Ugh! (*louder*)
120 volts Ugh! Hey, *this* really hurts.
135 volts Ugh!!
150 volts Ugh!!! Experimenter! That's all. Get me out of here. I told you I had heart trouble. My heart's starting to bother me now. Get me out of here. I told you I had heart trouble. My heart's starting to bother me. I refuse to go on. Let me out.
165 volts Ugh! Let me out. (*shouting*)

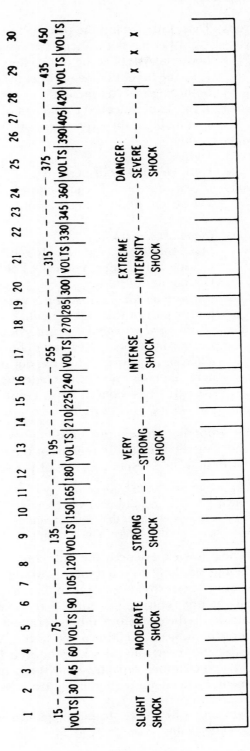

Figure 1 The control panel of the shocking apparatus used in the Milgram research. Copyright © 1974 by Stanley Milgram. Reprinted by permission of Harper & Row, Publishers, Inc.

180 volts	Ugh! I can't stand the pain. Let me out of here! (*shouting*)
195 volts	Ugh! Let me out of here. Let me out of here. My heart's bothering me. Let me out of here! You have no right to keep me here! Let me out! Let me out of here! My heart's bothering me. Let me out! Let me out!
210 volts	Ugh!! Experimenter! *Get* me out of here. I've had enough. I won't be in the experiment any more.
225 volts	Ugh!
240 volts	Ugh!
255 volts	Ugh! Get me *out* of here.
270 volts	(*Agonized scream*). Let me out of here. Let me out of here. Let me out of here. Let me out. Do you hear? Let me out of here.
285 volts	(*Agonized scream*).
300 volts	(*Agonized scream*). I absolutely refuse to answer any more. Get me out of here. You can't hold me here. Get me out. Get me out of here.
315 volts	(*Intensely agonized scream*). *I told you I refuse to answer.* I'm no longer part of this experiment.
330 volts	(*Intense and prolonged agonized scream*). Let me out of here. Let me out of here. My heart's bothering me. Let me out, I tell you. (*Hysterically*) Let me out of here. Let me out of here. You have no right to hold me here. Let me out! Let me out! Let me out of here! Let me out! Let me out!
345 volts	(*At 345 volts and thereafter, there was only silence.*)[1]

But supposing you express unwillingness at some point to con- 8
tinue shocking the learner? In that event the experimenter, sitting at
a nearby desk, would respond in one of the following ways:

"Please continue" or "Please go on."
"The experiment requires that you continue."
"It is absolutely essential that you continue."
"You have no other choice. You must go on."

Having now experienced the Milgram situation at least in your 9
imagination, how long do you think you would continue to administer
shocks? Most of our students maintain that they would not go beyond
105 volts before refusing to continue the experiment. A panel of
psychiatrists predicted before the experiment that perhaps only 1
percent of the subjects would proceed to the 450-volt level.

In fact, however, the "shock" produced by the results of this 10
study was much more startling than the simulated shocks in the
experiment. Forty men ranging in age from 20 to 50 and represent-

---

ing a cross section of the population, participated in the investigation. The maximum shock levels they administered are shown in Table 1. Nearly two-thirds of them administered the 450-volt maximum shock, and the average maximum shock they administered was 368 volts.

Virtually all the people who administered high levels of shock exhibited extreme discomfort, anxiety, and distress. Most verbally refused to continue on one or more occasions. But continue they did when ordered to do so by the experimenter, who assured them that what happened in the experiment was his responsibility.   11

By contriving a situation with many real-life elements, Milgram succeeded in demonstrating that a high percentage of "normal" people will obey an authority figure even when the destructive effects of their obedience are obvious. The conclusions that he draws from his work are chilling indeed: 12

> A commonly offered explanation is that those who shocked the victim at the most severe level were monsters, the sadistic fringe of society. But if one considers that almost two-thirds of the participants fall into the category of "obedient" subjects, and that they represented ordinary people drawn from working, managerial, and professional classes, the argument becomes very shaky. Indeed, it is highly reminiscent of the issue that arose in connection with Hannah Arendt's 1963 book, *Eichmann in Jerusalem.* Arendt contended that the prosecution's effort to depict Eichmann as a sadistic monster was fundamentally wrong, that he came closer to being an uninspired bureaucrat who simply sat at his desk and did his job. For asserting these views, Arendt became the object of considerable scorn, even calumny. Somehow, it was felt that the monstrous deeds carried out by Eichmann required a brutal, twisted, and sadistic personality, evil incarnate. After witnessing hundreds of ordinary people submit to the authority in our own experiments, I must conclude that Arendt's conception of the *banality of evil* comes closer to the truth than one might dare imagine. The ordinary person who shocked the victim did so out of a sense of obligation — a conception of his duties as a subject — and not from any peculiarly aggressive tendencies.   13

> This is, perhaps, the most fundamental lesson of our study: ordinary people, simply doing their jobs, and without any particular hostility on their part, can become agents in a terrible destructive process. Moreover, even when the destructive effects of their work become patently clear, and they are asked to carry out actions incompatible with fundamental standards of morality, relatively few people have the resources needed to resist authority. A variety of inhibitions against disobeying authority come into play and successfully keep the person in his place.[2] (Milgram, 1974, pp. 5–6)   14

---

[2] Copyright © 1974 by Stanley Milgram. Reprinted by permission of Harper & Row, Publishers, Inc.

Table 1 Maximum shock levels administered by subjects in the Milgram experiment.

Shock level	Verbal designation and voltage level	Number of subjects giving each maximum shock level
	Slight Shock	
1	15	
2	30	
3	45	
4	60	
	Moderate Shock	
5	75	
6	90	1
7	105	
8	120	
	Strong Shock	
9	135	
10	150	6
11	165	
12	180	1
	Very Strong Shock	
13	195	
14	210	
15	225	
16	240	
	Intense Shock	
17	255	
18	270	2
19	285	
20	300	1
	Extreme-Intensity Shock	
21	315	1
22	330	1
23	345	
24	360	
	Danger: Severe Shock	
25	375	1
26	390	
27	405	
28	420	
	XXX	
29	435	
30	450	26
Average maximum shock level		368 volts
Percentage of obedient subjects		65.0%

Milgram's method of investigation also generated shock waves 15 among psychologists. Many questioned whether it was ethical to expose subjects without warning to experiments that were likely to generate considerable stress and that might conceivably have lasting negative effects on them. But supporters of Milgram's work argue that adequate precautions were taken to protect participants. There was an extensive debriefing at the conclusion of the experiment, and participants were informed that they had not actually shocked anyone. They had a friendly meeting with the unharmed "subject." The purpose of the experiment was explained to them, and they were assured that their behavior in the situation was perfectly normal. Further, supporters argue, the great societal importance of the problem being investigated justified the methods the experimenters used. Finally, they cite follow-up questionnaire data collected by Milgram from his subjects after they received a complete report of the purposes and results. Eighty-four percent of the subjects stated that they were glad to have been in the experiment (and several spontaneously noted that their participation had made them more tolerant of others or otherwise changed them in desirable ways). Fifteen percent expressed neutral feelings, and only 1.3 percent stated that they were sorry to have participated.

The controversy over the ethics of Milgram's research has raged 16 for over a decade. In combination with other controversial issues, it has prompted a deep and abiding concern for protecting the welfare of subjects in psychological research. Because of such concerns, it is most unlikely that Milgram's research could be conducted today.

Review Questions

1. What did Milgram want to determine by his experiment?
2. How was the experiment designed?
3. What were the anticipated outcomes? What were the actual outcomes?
4. What conclusions does Milgram draw from the experiment?
5. To what does the term "banality of evil" refer?

Discussion Questions

1. Why do you think that only 1.3 percent of the subjects were sorry to have participated in the experiment? Why would you not wish to participate?
2. The experiment was conducted in a laboratory at Yale University, a setting quite different from the concentration camps in World War II (though both settings are institutional and present the "subjects" with

a military or quasi-military authoritarian hierarchy). To what extent does this difference affect the validity of Milgram's claims?

3. In order to increase our knowledge of humankind, is it permissible to conduct experiments that rely on deception? Do the ends justify the rather extreme means, in this case? Would your answer be different if you were one of the subjects who administered a "shock" of 450 volts?

4. Milgram says that the majority of the subjects obeyed the commands of the experimenter because "a variety of inhibitions against disobeying authority come into play and successfully keep the person in his place." What are some of these inhibitions?

5. An experimenter attempts to "control" variables that might otherwise influence his or her results. In this experiment there are several variables: experimenter, experimenter's confederate, subject, confederate's reactions to shocks, experimenter's reactions to subject's protests. How does Milgram control, or hold constant, all of the variables in his experiment except one?

6. What is the "scientific method"? Does Milgram follow it here?

Writing Suggestions

1. Think of a sociological or psychological issue that interests you. Go to the library reference section and locate the psychological and sociological abstracts, references that provide summaries and bibliographic citations for studies pertaining to a wide variety of topics. Locate three articles on your topic and refer to them in a paper in which you review the issue that the sociologists or psychologists have explored, the types of research they have conducted, and the implications of their research.

2. You are one of the subjects of Milgram's experiment who was sorry to have participated. In a letter to Milgram, explain your feelings.

3. In a carefully organized "reminiscence," write about the last time you disobeyed an order. Did you do so out of principle? Out of laziness (e.g., you didn't take out the trash because you didn't care to)? Why were you expected to obey the order? Was the expectation a valid one?

REVIEW OF STANLEY MILGRAM'S *OBEDIENCE TO AUTHORITY*

Richard Herrnstein

Richard Herrnstein (b. 1930), a research psychologist at Harvard University, has written numerous books, including *I.Q. in the Meritocracy*. He is a regular contributor of articles to professional journals and is currently editor of the *Psychological Bulletin*.

☐

. . . No doubt about it, these experiments were a surprise, and a nasty   1
surprise at that. The essence of a major discovery is its capacity to cause a large shift in our beliefs about some part of the world. Milgram's data show us something about the human world that we had failed to grasp before. They show us, not precisely that people are callous, but that they can slip into a frame of mind in which their actions are not entirely their own. Psychologically, it is not they alone who are flipping the switches, but also the institutional authority — the austere scientist in the laboratory coat. The authority is taken to have the right to do what he is doing, by virtue of knowledge or status. Permutations of the basic procedure made it clear that the subjects' obedience depended on a sense of passivity, and that disobedience resulted if the subject was made to feel as if he were acting on his own initiative. Ordinary people will, in fact, not easily engage in brutality on their own. But they will apparently do so if someone else is in charge.

The experiments prove decisively that ordinary people can turn   2
into lethal instruments in the hands of an unscrupulous authority. The subjects who obeyed did not appear to be in any way atypical; they were not stupid, maladjusted, psychopathic, or immoral in usual terms. They simply did not apply the usual standards of humanity to their own conduct. Or, rather, the usual standards gave way to a more pressing imperative, the command of authority. The brutality latent in these ordinary people — in all of us — may have little to do with aggression or hostility. In fact hostility was here the humane impulse, for when it turned on the pseudo-experimenter it was a source of disobedience. In Milgram's procedure, and in the many natural settings it more or less mimics, brutality is the awful corollary of things we rightly prize in human society, like good citizenship or personal loyalty.

R. J. Herrnstein, "Review of Milgram's *Obedience to Authority*." Reprinted from *Commentary*, June 1974, by permission; all rights reserved.

Milgram's work is said by some to show how close our society has   3
come to Nazi Germany. But does it really? In Italy, Australia, South
Africa, and contemporary Germany, subjects in comparable experiments have been *more*, not less, obedient. No experiment any place
has yet produced a negative result to boast about. In the totalitarian
countries — from Spain to China — experiments like Milgram's have
not been done for they would be considered subversive, as they would
indeed be. But just picture how people would behave in Spain or
Albania or China, where obedience is taken far more seriously than in
permissive, turbulent America. Ironically, we live in a society where
disobedience, not obedience, is in vogue, contrary to the fashionable
rhetoric of journalists and social commentators. Still, Milgram's
American subjects mostly obeyed, and would probably do so even
today, ten tumultuous years later.

The parallels to Nazi Germany, then, really say something about   4
the quality of the authority rather than the obedience to it. A degree
of obedience is the given in human society; enough of it to turn
dangerous if the wrong people wield it. The political problem is how
to decide who shall be the authority, for it is futile if not dangerous to
hope for a society of disobeyers. Consider a contemporary case in
point. Federal Judge Gesell recently accused some lawyers of a "Nuremberg mentality." They had defended their client, Egil Krogh, on
the grounds that he was obeying the orders of the President, his
Commander-in-Chief, when he lied under oath. The judge's view was
that Krogh may indeed have been obeying orders, but he should have
disobeyed. At other times, people honor their loyal and obedient
citizens instead of imprisoning them, and I suspect that Judge Gesell
is no different. The Judge saw it the way he did because a bitter
alienation of many people from our government has fostered the
illusion that obedience to authority is itself malevolent.

The illusion is palpably false, though the authority may, alas, be   5
malevolent. There is a crucial dilemma here, one that will plague any
political scheme that values both social order and individual autonomy. But the horns of the dilemma have never been so clear as they
are in the light of Milgram's experiments. On one side, we find that
even permissive, individualistic America creates people who can become agents of terror. As the weapons of terror become more powerful and more remote from their victims, the dangers of obedience
grow. We know that bombardiers in military aircraft suffer little of
the conflict and anxiety shown by Milgram's subjects, for they inflict
punishment at an even greater distance and they serve an authority
with greater license. That horn of the dilemma is much in the news
these days. But the other horn is the penalty if we set too high a value
on individual conscience and autonomy. The alternative to authority

and obedience is anarchy, and history teaches that that is the surest way to chaos and, ultimately, tyranny.

Though he recognizes the alternatives, Milgram's sympathies are   6
libertarian. He wants a more defiant citizenry, a higher percentage of disobeyers to authority. I have no doubt that it would be easy to make people more likely to say no to authority, simply by reducing the penalties for doing so. But the evidence does not suggest that people use only benevolence or moral sensitivity as the criteria for rejecting authority. Think of some real examples. Would it be greed or a higher virtue that would be the main reason for defaulting on taxes if the penalties were reduced? What deserter from the army would fail to claim it was conscience, not cowardice, once conscientious desertion became permissible? Milgram, and no doubt others, would probably answer that reducing the penalties is not enough — that people need to be taught virtue, not just relieved of the hazards of vice. That is fine, but it does not seem like cynicism to insist that the burden of proof falls on those who think they know a way to make people better than they have ever been. I find no proof in this book, or in the contemporary literature of civil disobedience. Milgram's work, brilliant as it is, resolves no dilemmas.

Psychology does not often spawn a finding that is neither trivial,   7
obvious, nor false. Milgram's is the rare exception. The research is well conceived and done with care and skill, even elegance. It was both unexpected and timely, which are virtues that add up to far more than the sum of the parts. Why, then, has the work produced the poles of response? It won Milgram professional recognition and numerous honors, and it was also attacked again and again in the technical literature. The book was reviewed on the front page of the New York *Times Book Review,* an uncommon distinction for an academic work in social science, but the review was a hatchet job by a professor of literature whose distaste for social science was the main message.

Many people, besides the *Times* reviewer, do not like social sci-   8
ence. There are so many of them that I can even sort them into categories: those who dislike it because they believe it tells us nothing they did not know and those who dislike it because it tells us something they did not want to hear. Milgram's work arouses those in the latter category, who typically insist that they belong in the former category. It is one thing to contemplate the banality of evil in the abstract, but something else to learn that the spore will germinate in New Haven at the prompting of a man in a laboratory coat. The gross discrepancy between what people predicted for the experiment and what others did as subjects is the tangible proof of the findings' power to inform us about ourselves — about our capacity for cruelty and our

ignorance of the capacity. Those who continue to insist that the experiment teaches nothing may be relying on ignorance to solve the awful dilemma of authority. It will resolve nothing, of course, but it is no surprise that Milgram's news has driven some heads into the sand.

But that is not the only problem with Milgram's work. Some 9 people, often social scientists themselves, object to the element of deception, especially when it is calculated to produce acute discomfort. This seems to me a valid concern, a secondary dilemma arising from the fact of the research itself rather than from its findings. To learn how people behave under duress or danger, the researcher dissembles, for he cannot subject people to real-life hazards. If there is to be experimentation on people in social settings, there is therefore likely to be deception and manipulation. It is an unpleasant prospect, and easy to reject. But, then, consider Milgram's experiments. Deception and manipulation led to a remarkable addition to our knowledge of the perils of authority. Knowledge like that comes hard and slow. Can we afford to prohibit further discoveries of that caliber and relevance?

Some people answer the question with a dogmatic yes, setting the 10 highest priority on individual privacy at the risk of continuing ignorance. That happens not to be my view. I value privacy but worry about ignorance. A small, temporary loss of a few people's comfort and privacy seems a bearable price for a large reduction in ignorance, but I can see, as can Milgram, how delicate a judgment this implies. Even so, I hope there are other experiments like Milgram's coming along — experiments that will teach us about ourselves, with no more than the minimum necessary deception and discomfort, elegantly and economically conducted. It should not be easy to do experiments like Milgram's — for they should not be done casually — but it should be possible, and, needless to say, the experimenter should not be held in contempt if the outcome is unexpected or uncomfortable. The goal of science is *news*, not *good* news.

Review Questions

1. Why does Herrnstein call "palpably false" the sentiment that any kind of obedience to authority is malevolent?
2. What is the "crucial dilemma" that Herrnstein discusses?
3. What does Herrnstein see as the alternative to obedience to authority? What is his view of the alternative?
4. How does Herrnstein account for the varying critical reception of Milgram's work?
5. What is Herrnstein's view of the deception practiced in the experiment?

Discussion Questions

1. Herrnstein says that it is possible that the "perfectionist dogma" of human society — that we are, basically, decent, caring, and humane people — may be giving way to humbler expectations. Is Milgram's work, after all, a surprise? If so, what are your assumptions about human nature? If not, what are you conceding about our behavior? How do your views on the future of the race depend upon your answers?

2. "In Milgram's procedure, and in the many natural settings it more or less mimics, brutality is the awful corollary of things we rightly prize in human society, like good citizenship or personal loyalty." What does Herrnstein mean?

3. When, in obeying the orders of a superior, does loyalty become criminal?

4. Is it possible to set too high a value on individual conscience and autonomy? What are the dangers of refusing to compromise one's autonomy?

5. Analyze paragraphs 6 through 10 of Herrnstein's review. Pay attention to the logic of the paragraphs. How does one paragraph lead to another? Why is the text broken into paragraphs as it is? Also pay attention to transitions and to the use of examples, questions, and parallel structures.

6. Paragraph 7 begins, "Psychology does not often spawn a finding that is neither trivial, obvious, nor false. Milgram's is the rare exception." Why does Herrnstein cast the first sentence in the negative? Can you find other examples where he plays with the subtleties of language to similar advantage?

Writing Suggestions

1. Herrnstein says that "Milgram's work, brilliant as it is, resolves no dilemmas" about the nature of authority. In an essay, discuss the dilemmas that need resolving (see Review Question 2). What solution would you propose?

2. You have read a strongly positive review of Milgram's work. Others, notably one by Steven Marcus (*New York Times Book Review*, January 13, 1976, pp. 1–3), are strongly negative. Compare and contrast Herrnstein's and Marcus's reviews. Or locate the *Book Review Digest*, a reference that lists titles of books (by the year of publication) and sources where reviews of these books can be found. Choose a favorite novel and locate three reviews. Write a brief analysis, comparing and contrasting the reviews.

"SHOCKING" OBEDIENCE FOUND IN CHILDREN

Researchers have repeated the Milgram experiment on school-age children in Jordan, this time with even more dramatic results.

☐

More than a decade ago, psychologist Stanley Milgram set out to   1
probe the human "obedience to orders" that enabled Germans to
carry out mass human exterminations during World War II, and at
the same time allowed many of their Jewish victims to march passively
to slaughter. Using controversial simulated shock experiments, Milgram showed that an alarming proportion of adults (65 percent of
those tested) were willing to inflict severe, possibly permanent, damage upon persons they did not know — simply because they were
instructed to do so.

    Similar results have since been obtained, primarily in studies in   2
Germany and Australia. But until now, no such tests had been performed on children, or in non- "European-derived" cultures. However, newly reported obedience studies among 192 youngsters in
Amman, Jordan, indicate that overobedience may be a universal
phenomenon that cuts across ages and cultures.

    Duplicating Milgram's original model, University of Jordan re-   3
searchers Khawla A. Yahya and Mitri E. Shanab tested 6- to 16-year-
old Jordanian school children. The youngsters, 96 males and 96
females, were divided into groups of "teachers" and "learners."
Teachers were trained and instructed to administer progressively
higher doses of electricity each time their learner gave the wrong
answer to a question. The young teachers were placed before a
control panel with a 20-step dial that they believed set the level of the
shock from slight to "extremely dangerous" (marked with the sketch
of the head of a skeleton). As in Milgram's experiments, the machine
did not actually transmit an electric shock, but the youngsters were
convinced that it did, particularly when they heard the learners in an
adjacent room pound the walls and scream in pain from steps 14 to
16, and fall silent after step 16 (as they were coached to do by the
researchers).

    All the while, the youngsters were consistently ordered to admin-   4
ister the shocks for the sake of the experiment, despite the sounds of

pain they heard from the next room. A control group of children was given the option of either giving or not giving the shock when a mistake was made.

The researchers report in the July *Journal of Personality and* 5 *Social Psychology* that 73 percent of the test children continued to deliver shock all the way to the end of the scale, whereas only 16 percent of the control subjects did so. No significant differences were found between sexes or within the 10-year age range. Those young-sters who continued to administer shock above level 14 were classified as overobedient, because they went on with the test even though they could hear the protests and ultimate silence of their learners. In cases where the young teachers hesitated after hearing cries or reactions, they were urged on with orders such as, "The experiment requires that you continue," or, "You have no other choice but to continue." When asked after the sessions why they continued to punish the learners, 69 percent of the females and 40 percent of the males said it was because they were obeying orders, and 30 percent of the females and 60 percent of the males said it was because "punishment is beneficial for learning."

Yahya and Shanab, who is also on the faculty of California State 6 University at Fresno, conclude "that this study has revealed not only that obedience and overobedience are culture free but that such behavior is observed very early in life." Such results, they add, iden-tify orders as the critical variable and "rule out explanations that tend to depict humans as being aggressive in nature."

Milgram told *Science News* he is "not surprised" that his findings 7 appear to hold with children in a different culture. Children, he reasons, "have less reason not to be compliant than adults," who are more prone to conflict over "whether or not to go along with au-thority."

"I'm glad to see this [the experiment] done with a non-Euro- 8 pean culture," says Milgram, a psychology professor at the City Uni-versity of New York's Graduate Center. "It adds a little strength or support to the universality of [my] findings" and shows that "obedi-ence is not just a United States phenomenon."

Review Questions

1. Was the Yahya-Shanab experiment the first attempt to duplicate Mil-gram's experiment in a different setting?
2. How many youngsters were involved? What were their ages?
3. How did the youngsters later explain their actions?
4. What did the study demonstrate?

Discussion Questions

1. Children are sometimes thought to be innocents, noble savages, un-corrupted by adult values. Do the results of this experiment show that these children were too early imbued with "adult" values — or is the question of child/adult values irrelevant? Is this a matter of basic human nature?

2. How do you account for the different responses of males and females?

3. Explain the way that the first two paragraphs serve to introduce the subject of the article.

4. This article is essentially a summary of a longer article that appeared in a professional journal. Did the writer of the present article do any additional research?

Writing Suggestion

In a report of about the same length as this article, discuss the significance of both the Milgram experiment and the Yahya-Shanab experiment.

SUPERIOR ORDERS AND REPRISALS
Telford Taylor

Telford Taylor (b. 1908) received his law degree from Harvard University and has lectured at the Columbia and Yale law schools. Taylor served as an intelligence officer for the U.S. Army and as U.S. chief counsel at the Nuremberg trials of Nazi war criminals. He has received numerous medals of honor from foreign governments and has written extensively on legal matters. The following selection appears in *Nuremberg and Vietnam: An American Tragedy.*

☐

Moral responsibility is all very well, the reader may be thinking, but 1 what about military orders? Is it not the soldier's first duty to give instant obedience to orders given by his military superiors? And apart from duty, will not the soldier suffer severe punishment, even death, if he refuses to do what he is ordered to do? If, then, a soldier is told by his sergeant or lieutenant to burn this house or shoot that prisoner, how can he be held criminally accountable on the ground that the burning or shooting was a violation of the laws of war?

These are some of the questions that are raised by the concept 2 commonly called "superior orders," and its use as a defense in war crimes trials. It is an issue that must be as old as the laws of war themselves, and it emerged in legal guise over three centuries ago when, after the Stuart restoration in 1660, the commander of the guards at the trial and execution of Charles I was put on trial for treason and murder. The officer defended himself on the ground "that all he did was as a soldier, by the command of his superior officer whom he must obey or die," but the court gave him short shrift, saying that "when the command is traitorous, then the obedience to that command is also traitorous."

Though not precisely articulated, the rule that is necessarily 3 implied by this decision is that it is the soldier's duty to obey *lawful* orders, but that he may disobey — and indeed must, under some circumstances — unlawful orders. Such has been the law of the United States since the birth of the nation. In 1804, Chief Justice John Marshall declared that superior orders will justify a subordinate's conduct only "if not to perform a prohibited act," and there are many other early decisions to the same effect.

A strikingly illustrative case occurred in the wake of that conflict 4 of which most Englishmen have never heard (although their troops burned the White House) and which we call the War of 1812. Our country was badly split by that war too and, at a time when the United States Navy was not especially popular in New England, the ship-of-the-line *Independence* was lying in Boston Harbor. A passer-by directed abusive language at a marine standing guard on the ship, and the marine, Bevans by name, ran his bayonet through the man. Charged with murder, Bevans produced evidence that the marines on the *Independence* had been ordered to bayonet anyone showing them disrespect. The case was tried before Justice Joseph Story, next to Marshall the leading judicial figure of those years, who charged the jury that any such order as Bevans had invoked "would be illegal and void," and if given and put into practice, both superior and subordinate would be guilty of murder. In consequence, Bevans was convicted.

The order allegedly given to Bevans was pretty drastic, and 5 Boston Harbor was not a battlefield; perhaps it was not too much to expect the marine to realize that literal compliance might lead to bad trouble. But it is only too easy to conceive of circumstances where the matter might not be at all clear. Does the subordinate obey at peril that the order may later be ruled illegal, or is he protected unless he had good reason to doubt its validity?

The early cases did not answer this question uniformly or pre- 6
cisely. There are rigid, absolute formulations, such as the statement of
Chief Justice Taney in 1851 that: "It can never be maintained that a
military officer can justify himself for doing an unlawful act, by
producing the order of his superior." More realistic judicial assess-
ments, however, recognized that often the subordinate is in no position to determine the legality or illegality of the order, and that the
very nature of military service requires prompt obedience. "While
subordinate officers are pausing to consider whether they ought to
obey, or are scrupulously weighing the evidence of the facts upon
which the commander-in-chief exercises the right to demand their
services," Justice Story observed in 1827, "the hostile enterprise may
be accomplished." Twenty-five years later Justice Curtis made much
the same point in a case where the soldier was sued for false arrest: "I
do not think the defendant was bound to go behind the order,
apparently lawful, and satisfy himself by inquiry that his commanding
officer proceeded upon sufficient grounds. To require this would be
destructive of military discipline and of the necessary promptness and
efficiency of the service."

Much the most dramatic case in American military history which 7
turned on this problem was the trial, already mentioned, of Major
Henry Wirz, the commandant of the Confederate prison camp at
Andersonville, Ga. Abundant and virtually uncontested evidence
showed that the Union prisoners were herded into a camp altogether
lacking shelter, so that they froze in winter and burned in summer;
that the stream constituting the sole source of water was constantly
fouled by corpses and human waste; that the food was totally inadequate, despite abundant harvests in the country around the camp;
that neighboring farmers, hearing of the starvation rampant at the
camp, came with wagonloads of food for their relief, but were turned
away by Wirz; that the camp was a nightmare of hunger, exposure
and disease and that the inmates died at the rate of several hundred a
week, mounting to a total of some 14,000 by the end of the war.

Wirz was tried before a military commission of six Union gen- 8
erals and two colonels, presided over by Major General Lew Wallace,
a minor but protean historical figure who, apart from his military
exploits, was a politician, diplomat, lawyer, and author of the fabu-
lously successful novel "Ben-Hur." A rigid-minded German Swiss,
Wirz defended himself on the ground that his administration of the
camp was governed by orders from General John H. Winder, the
officer in charge of all Confederate prison camps. The evidence bore
out his claim, but the prosecution took the position that Wirz had
followed orders willingly rather than under duress, and that Wirz and
Winder were co-conspirators. The military commission found Wirz
guilty of both conspiring to destroy the lives of Union soldiers and of

murder "in violation of the laws and customs of war," and sentenced him to be hanged. Presumably, therefore, it must have accepted the prosecution's contention, though (in accordance with the practice of military courts) there was no written opinion.[1]

Awareness that a problem is an old one is not, of course, the key to its solution. But these cases of many years past are important, I believe, in showing that the idea that under some circumstances military orders ought to be disobeyed is not a novel doctrine first conceived at Nuremberg. Furthermore, while the earliest decisions on the point were rendered by civilian judges, the modern development of the doctrine during the 75 years following the Civil War was largely the work of military men. 9

The Lieber regulations and the Hague and Geneva Conventions are silent on this subject, and the earliest statement of a general, governing rule appeared in the German Military Penal Code of 1872, Article 47 of which provided: 10

> If execution of an order given in line of duty violates a statute of the penal code, the superior giving the order is alone responsible. However, the subordinate obeying the order is liable to punishment as an accomplice if . . . he knew that the order involved an act the commission of which constituted a civil or military crime or offense.

The imposition of responsibility on those giving illegal orders, but not the secondary responsibility of subordinates who carry out orders known to be illegal, was provided for in the British and American Army manuals published in 1914. Both explicitly exempted from liability those whose violations of the laws of war were committed under orders of their "government" or "commanders," while declaring that the commanders who ordered or authorized the offenses might be punished. These provisions raised questions whether anyone at all could be held liable if the "commanders" were themselves acting under orders from still farther up the military chain of command. 11

At the outbreak of the Second World War, accordingly, military law on the question of superior orders was in a state of considerable confusion. The British and American manuals appeared to treat 12

---

[1] In the play based on the trial, Wirz's last line is, "I did not have that feeling of strength to do that. I could not disobey." There is an interesting likeness between this language and the statement of the German Supreme Court in the *Llandovery Castle* case (convicting two naval lieutenants who had acted under superior orders) that: "A refusal to obey the commander of a submarine would have been something so unusual, that it is humanly possible to understand that the accused could not bring themselves to disobey" [Taylor].

them as an absolute defense to charges against an accused subordinate, but was this really intended, no matter how atrocious the order? Perhaps not, for elsewhere the British manual called for "prompt, immediate, and unhesitating obedience" only when the "orders of the superior are not obviously and decidedly in opposition to the law of the land or to the well-known and established customs of the army." The German law of 1872 embodied a more rational approach and, despite all the horrors of the Nazi conquests and exterminations, it remained in effect throughout the war, and was reaffirmed in principle by no less a person than Dr. Joseph Goebbels, the Minister of Propaganda, who in May, 1944, published an article condemning Allied bombing operations, in which he declared:

> No international law of warfare is in existence which provides that a soldier who has committed a mean crime can escape punishment by pleading as his defense that he followed the commands of his superiors. This holds particularly true if those commands are contrary to all human ethics and opposed to the well-established usage of warfare.

During the same year (1944) the British and American military establishments revised the "superior orders" provisions of their field manuals. The new British language adopted the essential principle of the German law of 1872, cast in discursive rather than statutory terms. Members of the armed forces "are bound to obey lawful orders only"; to be sure, in conditions of "war discipline" they could not "be expected to weigh scrupulously the legal merits of the order received," but they could not "escape liability if, in obedience to a command, they commit acts which both violate unchallenged rules of warfare and outrage the general sentiment of humanity." 13

The 1944 American provision was quite different, for it stated no guiding principle whatever. Individuals who violate the laws of war "may be punished therefor," it declared, adding: "However, the fact that the acts complained of were done pursuant to order of a superior or government sanction may be taken into consideration in determining culpability, either by way of defense or in mitigation of punishment." But *when* should such orders "be taken into consideration," and what should determine whether the orders ought to be considered as a defense or merely in mitigation? It was a most unsatisfactory formulation. 14

Scrutiny of these efforts of military men to grapple with the effect of superior orders, as a defense to war crimes charges, discloses that the problem involves two quite different factors, one of which is appropriate by way of defense, and the other only in mitigation. The first is essentially a question of *knowledge,* and the second a question of *fear.* 15

Some orders are so atrocious, or plainly unlawful, that the subor- 16
dinate must know, or can reasonably be held to know, that they
should not be obeyed. But, especially in combat situations, there are
bound to be many orders the legitimacy of which depends on the
prevailing circumstances, the existence and sufficiency of which will
be beyond the reach of the subordinate's observation or judgment.
The military service is based on obedience to orders passed down
through the chain of command, and the success of military operations
often depends on the speed and precision with which orders are
executed. Especially in the lower ranks, virtually unquestioning obedience to orders, other than those that are palpably vicious, is a
necessary feature of military life. If the subordinate is expected to
give such obedience, he should also be entitled to rely on the order as
a full and complete defense to any charge that his act was unlawful.
The German law of 1872 was therefore rightly conceived insofar as it
made the subordinate's liability turn on his awareness of the order's
unlawful quality.

But knowledge is not the end of the problem. Suppose the soldier 17
is indeed aware that the order is beyond the pale, but is confronted by
a superior who is backing his command with threat of stern punishment, perhaps immediate death. It is one thing to require men at war
to risk their lives against the enemy, but quite another to expect them
to face severe or even capital penalties on the basis of their own
determination that their superior's command is unlawful. Such a
course calls for a high degree of moral as well as physical courage;
men are not to be judged too severely for falling short, and mitigation
of the punishment is appropriate.

Substantially these rules — that lack of knowledge of an order's 18
unlawfulness is a defense, and fear of punishment for disobedience a
mitigating circumstance — are embodied in the Army's current field
manual, issued in 1956:

a. The fact that the law of war has been violated pursuant to an order 19
of a superior authority, whether military or civil, does not deprive the
act in question of its character of a war crime, nor does it constitute a defense in the trial of an accused individual, unless he did not know and
could not reasonably have been expected to know that the act ordered
was unlawful. In all cases where the order is held not to constitute
a defense to an allegation of war crime, the fact that the individual
was acting pursuant to orders may be considered in mitigation of punishment.
b. In considering the question whether a superior order constitutes a valid 20
defense, the court shall take into consideration the fact that obedience to
lawful military orders is the duty of every member of the armed forces;
that the latter cannot be expected, in conditions of war discipline, to

weigh scrupulously the legal merits of the orders received; that certain rules of warfare may be controversial; or that an act otherwise amounting to a war crime may be done in obedience to orders conceived as a measure of reprisal. At the same time it must be borne in mind that members of the armed forces are bound to obey only lawful orders.

These principles are sound, and the language is well chosen to convey the quality of the factors, imponderable as they are, that must be assessed in a given case. As with so many good rules, the difficulty lies in its application — in weighing evidence that is likely to be ambiguous or conflicting. Was there a superior order? Especially at the lower levels, many orders are given orally. Was a particular remark or look intended as an order, and if so what was its scope? If the existence and meaning of the order are reasonably clear, there may still be much doubt about the attendant circumstances — how far the obeying soldier was aware of them, and how well equipped to judge them. If the order was plainly illegal, to what degree of duress was the subordinate subjected? Especially in confused ground fighting of the type prevalent in Vietnam, evidentiary questions such as these may be extremely difficult to resolve. 21

The doctrine of "superior orders" as a defense for the subordinate is, of course, the converse of what lawyers call *respondeat superior* — the liability of the order-giver. And in conclusion, it should be emphasized that the consequence of allowing superior orders as a defense is not to eliminate criminal responsibility for what happened, but to shift its locus upwards. It would stultify the whole system to exculpate the underlings who follow orders and ignore the superiors who give them. Indeed, the greater the indulgence shown to the soldier on the theory that his first duty is to give unquestioning obedience, the greater the responsibility of the officer to see to it that obedience entails no criminal consequences. 22

The superior's responsibility, moreover, is not limited to the situation where he has given affirmative orders. A commander is responsible for the conduct of his troops, and is expected to take all necessary action to see that they do not, on their own initiative, commit war crimes. Gen. George B. McClellan, as commander of the Army of the Potomac in 1861, warned all of his officers that they would "be held responsible for punishing aggression by those under their command," and directed that military commissions be established to punish any persons connected with his Army who might engage in conduct "in contravention of the established rules of law." The 1956 Army Manual provides explicitly that a military commander is responsible not only for criminal acts committed in pursuance of his orders, but "is also responsible if he has actual knowledge, or should have knowledge . . . that troops or other persons subject to 23 his control are about to commit or have committed a war crime and he fails to take the necessary and reasonable steps to insure compliance with the law of war or to punish violations thereof."

This language embodied no novel conception of a commander's responsibility. Ten years earlier, a military commission of American generals condemned General Tomayuki Yamashita to death by hanging, for failure properly to control the conduct of Japanese troops under his command in the Philippines. The *Yamashita* case, and the principles that it exemplifies, are of great importance in establishing the reach of criminal responsibility for episodes such as those said to have occurred at Son My [My Lai]. 24

Another doctrine, which may be invoked to justify conduct that otherwise would be a war crime, is that of *reprisals*. Today the open resort to reprisals is not as frequent as in earlier times, but the concept is nonetheless of great importance in relation to the conduct of the war in Vietnam. 25

In origin, a reprisal (or "retaliation," as Lieber called it) was an action taken by a nation against an enemy that would normally be a violation of the laws of war, but that was justified as necessary to prevent the enemy from continuing to violate the laws of war. Thus if one side makes a practice of shooting medical corpsmen or bombing hospitals, the other side may take action by way of reprisal in order to dissuade the enemy from continuing his unlawful course of conduct. The justification for reprisals was the lack of any apparent alternative; the enemy miscreants were beyond the reach of the offended belligerent, and protests had proved fruitless. As Lieber put it, their purpose was not "mere revenge," but rather "protective retribution." 26

Resort to reprisals in order to bring an enemy government back to the paths of military virtue is still recognized by the laws of war, subject to various restrictions written into the Geneva Conventions and the recent army field manuals. But reprisals of this type are not much used today, partly because they are generally ineffective, and partly because the resort to crime in order to reform the criminal is an unappetizing method. Generally, a nation that deliberately embarks on a course of conduct violative of the laws of war will have taken into account the possibility and effect of reprisals, and will not be easily checked. Then crime and reprisal both continue, and the standards of warfare are debased. 27

But reprisals of another type, directed not against an enemy government but against the civilian population of territory under military occupation, are of great significance in relation to both Nuremberg and the Vietnam war. They were inflicted on a number of occasions during the Civil War, and used extensively by the Germans during the Franco-Prussian War of 1871 and the First World War. One example from many is General Karl von Bülow's proclamation of 28

Aug. 22, 1914, issued in the course of the German advance into Belgium:

> The inhabitants of the town of Andenne, after having protested their peaceful intentions, made a treacherous surprise attack on our troops.
>
> It was with my consent that the General had the whole place burned down, and about one hundred people shot.
>
> I bring this fact to the attention of the town of Liège, so that its inhabitants may know the fate with which they are threatened, if they take a similar attitude.

Review Questions

1. How old is the problem of superior orders? Historically, how have judges responded to defendants who have invoked this defense?
2. What are the two factors involved in the issue of superior orders?
3. What is a mitigating circumstance, in the context of superior orders?
4. If a soldier is excused of a crime because he was obeying an order, upon whom is the responsibility of the crime shifted? What is this known as among lawyers?
5. What are reprisals? Why are they generally ineffective?

Discussion Questions

1. What is the usefulness of Taylor's historical perspective? Can a study of the past help us with our current problems? (Why, for instance, study about the rise and fall of the Roman Empire or about Napoleon's conquests?)
2. What are your feelings about the efforts to "humanize" warfare, as in the Hague and Geneva Conventions? In the actual heat of battle, can a war be fought "humanely"? What are the "standards of war" such that they can be "debased"? Is all war debased and equally barbarous? If your answer is yes, how would you counter the charge that you are naively pious?
3. Does the dilemma of superior orders place the combat soldier in an unreasonable position? Conversely, does a commander's responsibility (as specified in paragraph 22) for the actions of his troops freight him with an unreasonable burden?
4. If you have never been to war, how are you limited in answering the above questions?
5. What are the semantic distinctions between "mere revenge" and "protective retribution" (paragraph 26)? To what extent is the term protective retribution a euphemism?

6. Taylor makes extensive use of examples. How do these enliven and inform his discussion?

Writing Suggestions

1. Research and write a report on some aspect of the Hague and Geneva Conventions. You may want to focus on the history of war accords, the necessity of having such accords, violations of the accords, or the assumptions about warfare and human behavior that underlie the accords.
2. Rewrite in "plain English" paragraphs 19 and 20, which appear in the 1956 Army field manual. What are the differences between your version and the original? Refer to the closing paragraphs of Herrnstein's review. Is Herrnstein's language any less precise than the language in the Army manual? Are we talking about different kinds of precision here?

MASSACRE AT MY LAI: AN OFFICIAL REPORT
Stanley Resor

Stanley Resor, Secretary of the Army, presented this official report on the My Lai investigation to the Senate Arms Services Committee.

☐

As you know, it is not normally the policy of the executive branch   1
to disclose information pertaining to ongoing criminal investigations — especially when, as is the case here, new and perhaps
conflicting evidence may come to light as the investigation continues.

In addition, there has already been far too much comment in the   2
press on matters of an evidentiary nature, and we are very concerned
that prejudicial pretrial publicity may make it difficult to accord the
accused in any prosecution a fair trial. We are taking every step to
assure that the Government is not responsible for contributing to
such publicity, and I must therefore refrain on this occasion from
commenting directly upon the evidence. With this caveat, let me now
review the known facts concerning the tragic events which took place
at My Lai hamlet, Song My village, Quang Ngai Province, on March
16, 1968.

Stanley R. Resor, "Official Report on the My Lai Investigation," *U.S. News & World Report* 8 December 1969, pp. 78–79.

My Lai hamlet is located in an area which is now and has been for   3
several years under Viet Cong control. Intelligence reports indicate
that it has been the traditional home of the 48th Local Force Battal-
ion, considered one of the best Viet Cong battalions in the country.
Although the area was within the tactical area of operations of the
Second ARVN [South Vietnamese Army] Division, U.S. forces had
conducted prior operations in the vicinity and had suffered moderate
casualties, principally from mines and booby traps.

In March, 1968, the Eleventh Infantry Brigade, a unit of the   4
American Division, made plans to conduct an operation in this area,
and a provisional task force known as Task Force Barker was assigned
the operation. This task force, commanded by Lieutenant Colonel
Barker, was composed of three companies drawn from two battalions,
and designated A, B and C.

On the morning of March 16, following a three-minute artillery   5
preparation on its landing zone which is thought to have produced
few if any casualties, Company C, commanded by Captain Medina
and consisting of approximately 105 infantrymen, made a helicopter
assault immediately west of My Lai. Company A simultaneously occupied a blocking position to the north, and Company B made a helicopter assault into an uninhabited area to the south. The first platoon,
commanded by First Lieutenant Calley,[1] led the advance and physically occupied the cluster of habitations that constituted the hamlet.
Most of the buildings were then burned or otherwise destroyed. The

---

[1] Lt. William L. Calley, Jr., was the only person convicted (March 29, 1971) of
the mass slayings of "not less than 22 Vietnamese" at the hamlet of My Lai in
South Vietnam in 1968. His life sentence was reduced to twenty years at hard
labor and then, in 1974, was reduced again — by half. On September 25,
1974, Calley's conviction was overturned by U.S. District Court Judge J.
Robert Elliott, who contended that "massive adverse pretrial publicity" had
prevented Calley from receiving a fair trial. The conviction was reinstated by
the U.S. Court of Appeals in September 1975, and nine months later the
Supreme Court refused to reconsider the verdict. Following Calley's original
conviction, which caused an outcry among public officials and thousands of
private citizens, President Nixon announced that he would personally review
the case "before any final sentence is carried out," and instructed Army
authorities to release Calley from the stockade at Ft. Benning, Ga. and return
him to his base apartment while his murder conviction was under review.
Nixon's intervention was assailed by the Army prosecutor in the trial, Capt.
Aubrey Daniel III, who sent a letter to the President stating, "The greatest
tragedy of all will be if political expediency dictates the compromise of such a
fundamental moral principle as the inherent unlawfulness of the murder of
innocent persons." Calley had spent nearly three years under guard at his
apartment in Ft. Benning, enough time to qualify him for parole, which he
received in 1974. [Behrens and Rosen]

operation terminated at approximately 6 p.m. on that day, and Task Force Barker was withdrawn.

The task-force commander's after-action report for the entire operation indicated enemy losses as 128 killed; it made no mention of civilian casualties. Friendly losses were given as 2 killed and 11 wounded; however, the only U.S. casualty clearly attributable to the My Lai assault was one soldier who shot himself in the foot.   6

During the day, reports received from an Army helicopter pilot who had supported the operation suggested there might have been unnecessary killing of noncombatants at My Lai. As a result, the brigade commander was directed to conduct an investigation of the incident. During this informal investigation he interviewed the task-force commander and S-3 [operations officer] and the commander of the two companies which had been in the immediate area. He also received some reports of unnecessary killing through Vietnamese channels.   7

The brigade commander concluded that approximately 20 non-combatants had been inadvertently killed by preparatory fires and in crossfires between friendly and enemy forces, and that the reports of unnecessary killing of civilians were merely another instance of a common Viet Cong propaganda technique and were groundless — a view apparently shared by the Vietnamese district chief. He forwarded this finding to the commanding general of the American Division. The matter was not brought to the attention of U.S. Army Vietnam or Military Assistance Command Vietnam headquarters [both in Saigon] or the Department of the Army.   8

Over one year later, in early April, 1969, the first suggestion that something extraordinary had taken place at My Lai reached the Department of the Army. At this time we received identical letters, dated March 29, 1969, and originally addressed to Secretary [of Defense] Laird and five members of Congress, from a Mr. Ronald Ridenhour. In these letters Mr. Ridenhour, a former soldier who had heard rumors about a supposed atrocity from fellow soldiers, alleged that Task Force Barker had been assigned the mission of destroying My Lai and all its inhabitants. He went on to describe in considerable detail several instances of alleged murder which he believed had occurred there.   9

Upon receipt of these letters, the Army immediately initiated a preliminary inquiry, and on April 23, 1969, the Chief of Staff directed the Inspector General to conduct a full-scale investigation of the allegations made by Mr. Ridenhour. This investigation took place both here in the United States and in Vietnam, and involved interviews with 36 witnesses, ranging from the commander of the Eleventh Infantry Brigade to riflemen who participated in the operation.   10

On Aug. 4, 1969, the investigation was transferred to the Provost   11

Marshal General. Since that date, criminal investigators have located and interrogated over 75 witnesses, 28 of whom are still on active military duty. They have also visited the site of the incident and interviewed local Vietnamese officials and former inhabitants of the hamlet who witnessed the alleged killings.

An Army combat photographer present at My Lai took a number   12
of photographs which he did not turn over to Army officials. We obtained copies of his slides in August of this year and can show them to you this morning if you wish.

As you know, General Talbott, Commanding General, Fort Ben-   13
ning, has convened a general court-martial to try Lieutenant Calley for the premeditated murder of 109 Vietnamese civilians. In addition, charges of assault with intent to kill 30 noncombatants have been filed against one of Calley's squad leaders, Staff Sergeant Mitchell. An Article 32 investigation of the charge against Sergeant Mitchell is expected to get under way shortly, having been held up for some time by a defense request for time to obtain additional evidence.

A number of critical issues remain to be resolved. Primary among   14
them is the extent to which the members of Company C were acting pursuant to orders from their company commander or higher head-quarters when they destroyed My Lai's buildings and fired upon its unresisting inhabitants. This aspect of the case is being accorded a very high priority.

In addition, it is estimated that besides Lieutenant Calley and   15
Sergeant Mitchell there are at least 24 former members of Company C, nine of whom are still on active duty, who must be deemed subjects of the continuing criminal investigation. The efforts of seven criminal investigators are currently focused upon the task of developing evidence concerning the actions of these men. It is estimated that several months may elapse before all of the allegations presently under investigation can be fully evaluated.

Finally, there is the question of the adequacy of the investigation   16
of the incident which was conducted in Vietnam immediately after it occurred. Because this is an extremely important and sensitive aspect of our inquiry, General Westmoreland and I have decided that it should be severed from the rest of the investigation and handled separately at a very high level.

We have therefore chosen Lt. Gen. William R. Peers to head a   17
small team whose mission will be to determine the adequacy of both the original investigation and its subsequent review. This action should not be taken as an indication that we believe that investigation to have been inadequate, but merely as a sign of our continuing determination that the matter be carefully and impartially explored.

Mr. Chairman, the story which has been unfolding before the   18
public during the last fortnight, and which I have discussed briefly

with you this morning, is an appalling one. I would like to add some personal comments to this chronology.

I have reviewed what we know of the incident at My Lai with a 19
number of officers who have served in Vietnam. It is their judgment — a judgment which I personally endorse and share — that what apparently occurred at My Lai is wholly unrepresentative of the manner in which our forces conduct military operations in Vietnam.

Our men in Vietnam operate under detailed directives from 20
MACV and other higher headquarters which prohibit in unambiguous terms the killing of civilian noncombatants under circumstances such as those at My Lai.

During the last few years hundreds of thousands of American 21
soldiers have participated in similar operations in Vietnam. I am convinced that their over-all record is one of decency, consideration and restraint toward the unfortunate civilians who find themselves in a zone of military operations. Against this record, the events at My Lai are all the more difficult to understand.

Unfortunately, details concerning the matter did not come to our 22
attention until a year after the events in question. Once we learned of the allegations, the Army immediately commenced an investigation which has already resulted in the filing of criminal charges against two individuals. In pursuing this investigation and in referring the reports of investigation to responsible court-martial convening authorities, we fully appreciated that the disclosures which would inevitably follow would damage both the Army and the Government of the United States. Despite this, we pursued the only course of action which was consistent with our international obligations, our national policies and the ethic of American military operations.

I hope that the information which I have presented to you this 23
morning has given each of you a greater understanding of this matter, and that it has renewed your confidence in the Army's willingness and ability to pursue the investigation and attendant prosecutions to a satisfactory conclusion. I assure you that, however great may be your dismay and sense of outrage that such a thing could occur in our armed forces, it could be no greater than mine, nor than that experienced by the thousands of loyal and brave officers and men who have labored so long and sacrificed so magnificently in search of the just peace we all seek in Vietnam.

Review Questions

1. What occurred at My Lai on March 16, 1968?
2. Who is Lt. Calley, and what role did he play in the incident?
3. How does the army regard the behavior of its military personnel at My Lai in relation to the behavior of other U.S. military forces?

Discussion Questions

1. What are the possible interpretations of the government's official position that Calley's conduct was "wholly unrepresentative" of the overall U.S. effort in Vietnam?
2. Was Calley being used as a scapegoat, as many claimed? Was he any more guilty than the U.S. government for being involved in the war in the first place? Was Calley any more guilty of murder than bombardiers, who dropped millions of tons of explosives on Vietnam during the course of the war?
3. Resor was Secretary of the Army when he presented this report to the members of the Senate Armed Services Committee. One could describe Resor's style as "militaristic." Examine his presentation, paying particular attention to his use of adjectives. What pattern emerges?

Writing Suggestion

Rewrite any twenty to thirty lines of Resor's description of the events at My Lai. Assume that you witnessed the events, and write your account in the first person. How do your description and Resor's differ?

WHY MY LAI WAS POSSIBLE —
AN INTERVIEW WITH ROBERT JAY LIFTON

Robert Lifton (b. 1926) is a distinguished psychiatrist and author of more than a dozen books, including *Death in Life: Survivors of Hiroshima,* which won the National Book Award in 1968. The following interview with Dr. Lifton is reprinted from *U.S. News & World Report.*

☐

Q Some newspaper dispatches report that in the aftermath of   1
My Lai there was a feeling of elation, followed — for some of the
men — by a feeling of being conscience-stricken. How do you account
for that?

A That feeling of elation, or relief, has to do with finding some
kind of outlet for enormous fear, rage and frustration. It is disturbing
to contemplate this — that killing babies and women serves as an

Reprinted from *U.S. News & World Report* in which this interview appeared on Dec. 15, 1969, under the title, "Why Civilians Are War Victims." Copyright 1969, U.S. News & World Report, Inc. Reprinted by permission.

outlet for frustration — but that is what I mean by the extremity of the situation in Vietnam, rather than any specific disturbance in an individual soldier.

Also involved at My Lai, you must realize, was that many of these men had witnessed the deaths of buddies. That is a profound experience for any fighting man, and something they feel very directly. It automatically renders each of these men a kind of survivor, and the survivor has a very special kind of psychology in which he tries to find some meaning in the death he has witnessed, especially the death of a buddy. He feels guilty over having survived while the other man dies. This was, you might say, a perverted form of finding significance through retaliation.

Q Once it was all over, did even the men who refused to fire 2 their guns feel a duty to cover up for those who did?

A Yes, and that is important. I believe that men in such a situation develop a form of guilt because of being implicated in it, whether or not they fired bullets. They are implicated because it is their squad, their company.

The main point is that a kind of group loyalty is developed in war. It is paramount in combat, and such group loyalty dictates against revealing such an incident, because that betrays the group. There is involved in a case such as this both individual guilt and shared guilt. It is very strong, and makes men reluctant to speak for fear of being disloyal.

Q Why is it in such an incident that some soldiers blindly obey 3 orders to shoot civilians while others disobey?

A The first thing I would say is that the general situation leads most men to obey such an order. There is a lot of evidence, from a lot of different sources, that, given a strongly authoritarian situation where men are under orders, especially military orders, they will follow them even when they are very outrageous orders by ordinary standards.

Then, there is another point: Soldiers in combat are different from ordinary men. They've been through a series of experiences which develop in them what I would call a very advanced stage of psychic numbing — they are numbed to the whole issue of death and dying and suffering, which is almost a professional necessity if one is to function effectively in combat.

In any war, all soldiers have first been through basic training, a process by which they are made over into combat soldiers, which means leaving certain scruples behind them — and leaving behind their identity as civilians, with all the niceties that entails — in order to become a soldier committed to carrying out a mission which includes killing.

Then you get in combat. You're under great risk to your own life, probably on a daily basis, and you become hardened and numbed and more likely to engage in the kind of behavior, in a very general way, that you wouldn't engage in as a civilian.

Q Are you saying that Army discipline is so forceful and overrid- 4 ing that it can make a man lose his sense of values?

A It can be. In addition to that, there is more than simply Army discipline at work here. It's a general group feeling that takes on a particular characteristic in Vietnam — where Army discipline, very strong, becomes connected with a group sense of contempt for the South Vietnamese, and of helplessness in a confused situation. So that, if one didn't follow orders, one would be not only violating military orders — which is a significant thing in itself — but one would also be violating the group norm and the group feeling, which is a very strong issue in combat. . . .

Q Do you see in the My Lai incident a breakdown in the moral 5 fiber of American youth generally, or do you think it was an isolated event that is unlikely to recur?

A I don't think it's fair to say that there is a breakdown of the moral fiber of Americans in general. Perhaps some people would like to see it that way, or would be inclined to see it that way. But I think everything that we know about human behavior would suggest that under very extreme situations a large number of people are capable of this kind of behavior. So it doesn't reflect a basic lack of moral fiber or a basic moral inferiority of any kind, but rather an impossible situation with enormous stresses under which almost anybody — or at least a great majority of people — would be capable of some of this behavior.

The other point I would like to make, however, is this:

There have been statements by some military and Government leaders that My Lai is clearly an isolated incident which will be dealt with, and has little to do with the way in which Americans conduct a war.

I do think that these incidents — My Lai and related killings of civilians — are very much at odds with ordinary American standards of humane behavior. But I don't think they are isolated incidents. I think there has been a lot of evidence that a large number of similar incidents have occurred, and that our whole war effort in Vietnam has involved indiscriminate killing of civilians.

These incidents are in the very nature of this war in Vietnam, rather than isolated incidents unrelated to the rest of the war.

Q Doctor, should Americans as a whole be expected to share a 6 feeling of guilt about an episode such as the one at My Lai?

A What follows from what we've been saying is that, first of all, we have to face My Lai squarely. That's terribly difficult to do, psychologically and ethically. Given the nobler aspects of the American tradition, which I think we have to keep returning to, it's very hard to face the fact that American boys have done this, and that they've been doing things like this in Vietnam.

Then, having faced it, we have to try to evaluate how it came about — again hardheadedly. I think when one does this, one has neither to deny that it occurred — as some groups may be prone to do — nor try to isolate it as a single occurrence — as other groups are prone to do — but to connect it with the nature of this war, and hardheadedly evaluate the nature of this war.

I think that we require not only public expressions of guilt but an honest examination of the general inhumanity of our involvement in Vietnam, and an honest decision to end that involvement.

We have to decide what we wish to stand for — which should be the very opposite of what happened at My Lai. I'm speaking both ethically and psychologically.

I sense that the impact of this experience on American society is very profound. We don't yet know the full story, because we're only at the beginning of the impact. But it's very clear that the impact is very strong. The reservoir of decency in American society is also very great, so that Americans really are appalled by this kind of incident.

Q On the other hand, Dr. Lifton, it has been suggested that there might be a callousness developing in the American public toward war — a generation that after three wars in three decades now is inclined to shrug its shoulders and turn away. Do you agree?

A There has been developing what one can call a callousness, which is prominent in Americans but not limited to Americans, because any kind of brutalizing experience — if it goes on long enough and if it is repeated enough — causes one to adapt oneself to it.

I did a study in Hiroshima. People in Hiroshima subjected to the atomic bomb called upon what I call psychic closing-off, or psychic numbing, as a way of coping with what was an overwhelming experience. They couldn't have remained psychically intact unless they went numb to some extent, even though they knew what was going on.

As we go through wars and as we develop this incredible technology of weaponry — nuclear weapons, large-scale conventional weapons, and germ weapons — the whole thing takes on a nightmare element that can't be comprehended or dealt wtih. We know destruction may be near — and we're not ignorant totally, but any means, about the nature of this destruction — but we can't cope with it in our imaginations. So we try, in various ways, to withdraw from it — become numb.

I think that has been happening in a very general way. I have written of this age as less an age of anxiety than an age of numbing, which is directly related to the idea of callousness that has been suggested about Vietnam.

In terms of Vietnam specifically, the war goes on and on, and we can't seem to win it or even make any sense of it. We see and read reports of it every day, and we see brutal things on television in connection with it. There is also the ritual of the body count — callous to the point of obscenity, especially when it turns out that a very great number of the bodies counted are those of dead civilians. So there is a process of getting used to this kind of war, which is a form of callousness and numbing on the part of the American public.

Still, I would add, an increasing number of Americans have refused to "get used to" Vietnam and have been aroused sufficiently by incidents such as the one at My Lai to suggest that the national conscience has not yet been numbed.

Review Questions

1. How are soldiers in combat different from civilians?
2. How does being part of a group affect the degree to which someone will obey orders?
3. What special psychological and moral situation did GIs face in Vietnam, according to Lifton?
4. Why would survivors of the war feel guilty? How does one find significance in surviving?
5. What is psychic numbing? When is it likely to occur?

Discussion Questions

1. How do Lifton's comments affect the way in which you view Calley's offenses? Is Calley any less guilty?
2. Is it possible for a civilian, who has never been to war, to judge Calley fairly?
3. Why has it been difficult for Americans to accept My Lai? Why would we want to see the massacre as an isolated incident, which Lifton says it is not?
4. Do Lifton's antiwar sentiments invalidate his psychological observations about GIs in Vietnam?
5. To what extent does the question-and-answer format of this article make the interviewer "invisible"? Can you detect the interviewer's personality?

6. Lifton refers to the body counts — weekly reports of the numbers of dead and wounded — as "callous to the point of obscenity." Why is the phrase so forceful?

Writing Suggestions

1. You are a psychologist. A GI, a veteran of Vietnam, comes into your office and says, "It's been seven years since I got back — and still I can't adjust." Write a dialogue between yourself and the GI.
2. Choose an issue that interests you. Do some preliminary research on it and draft a series of questions that you can ask a friend, teacher, clergyman, lawyer, etc. Conduct your interview and prepare two reports based upon it. Present one simply as a transcript of your interview. Provide an appropriate introduction. Present the other as part of a report that you narrate. For example, assume that you are a newspaper reporter and use the information you've gained in your interview to prepare an article.

ANTIGONE
Jean Anouilh

Jean Anouilh (b. 1910) is a French dramatist whose first play, *L'Hermine,* was produced when he was twenty-two years old. The recurring theme in much of Anouilh's work is the loss of innocence involved in struggling for survival in a decadent world. *Antigone* was first produced in German-occupied Paris during World War II. With its theme of individual conscience vs. the authority of the state, the play was both timely and controversial. It was often produced — in modern dress — during the revolutionary 1960s when the Vietnam War had provoked widespread rebelliousness against government (and other) authority. Anouilh's *Antigone* follows the plot of its predecessor, written by Sophocles in 400 B.C. Antigone is the spirited daughter of the dead King Oedipus. Her two brothers, Polynices and Eteocles, die in combat, having led armies against each other before the gates of Thebes. Creon, king of Thebes and Antigone's uncle, orders the body of Eteocles to be buried with full funeral rites. But Polynices must be left to rot in the sun because he attacked the city. Anyone who violates Creon's decree by attempting to bury Polynices is to be punished by death. Antigone, who cannot abide by her uncle's edict, buries her brother to ensure the peace of his soul and is arrested.

Enraged upon learning of Antigone's disobedience, Creon confronts his niece.

☐

CREON: Why did you try to bury your brother?

ANTIGONE: I owed it to him.

CREON: I had forbidden it.

ANTIGONE: I owed it to him. Those who are not buried wander eternally and find no rest. If my brother were alive, and he came home weary after a long day's hunting, I should kneel down and unlace his boots, I should fetch him food and drink, I should see that his bed was ready for him. Polynices is home from the hunt. I owe it to him to unlock the house of the dead in which my father and my mother are waiting to welcome him. Polynices has earned his rest.

CREON: Polynices was a rebel and a traitor, and you know it.

ANTIGONE: He was my brother.

CREON: You heard my edict. It was proclaimed throughout Thebes. You read my edict. It was posted up on the city walls.

ANTIGONE: Of course I did.

CREON: You knew the punishment I decreed for any person who attempted to give him burial.

ANTIGONE: Yes, I knew the punishment.

CREON: Did you by any chance act on the assumption that a daughter of Oedipus, a daughter of Oedipus' stubborn pride, was above the law?

ANTIGONE: No, I did not act on that assumption.

CREON: Because if you had acted on that assumption, Antigone, you would have been deeply wrong. Nobody has a more sacred obligation to obey the law than those who make the law. You are a daughter of lawmakers, a daughter of kings, Antigone. You must observe the law.

ANTIGONE: Had I been a scullery maid washing my dishes when that law was read aloud to me, I should have scrubbed the greasy water from my arms and gone out in my apron to bury my brother.

CREON: What nonsense! If you had been a scullery maid, there would have been no doubt in your mind about the seriousness of that edict. You would have known that it meant death; and you would have been satisfied to weep for your brother in your kitchen. But you! You thought that because you come of the royal line, because you were my niece and were going to marry my son, I shouldn't dare have you killed.

ANTIGONE: You are mistaken. Quite the contrary. I never doubted for an instant that you would have me put to death.

A pause, as CREON *stares fixedly at her.*

CREON: The pride of Oedipus! Oedipus and his headstrong pride all over again. I can see your father in you — and I believe you. Of course you thought that I should have you killed! Proud as you are, it seemed to you a natural climax in your existence. Your father was like that. For him as for you human happiness was meaningless; and mere human misery was not enough to satisfy his passion for torment. [*He sits on stool behind the table.*] You come of people for whom the human vestment is a kind of straitjacket: it cracks at the seams. You spend your lives wriggling to get out of it. Nothing less than a cosy tea party with death and destiny will quench your thirst. The happiest hour of your father's life came when he listened greedily to the story of how, unknown to himself, he had killed his own father and dishonored the bed of his own mother. Drop by drop, word by word, he drank in the dark story that the gods had destined him first to live and then to hear. How avidly men and women drink the brew of such a tale when their names are Oedipus — and Antigone! And it is so simple, afterwards, to do what your father did, to put out one's eyes and take one's daughter begging on the highways.

Let me tell you, Antigone: those days are over for Thebes. Thebes has a right to a king without a past. My name, thank God, is only Creon. I stand here with both feet firm on the ground; with both hands in my pockets; and I have decided that so long as I am king — being less ambitious than your father was — I shall merely devote myself to introducing a little order into this absurd kingdom; if that is possible.

Don't think that being a king seems to me romantic. It is my trade; a trade a man has to work at every day; and like every other trade, it isn't all beer and skittles. But since it is my trade, I take it seriously. And if, tomorrow, some wild and bearded messenger walks in from some wild and distant valley — which is what happened to your dad — and tells me that he's not quite sure who my parents were, but thinks that my wife Eurydice is actually my mother, I shall ask him to do me the kindness to go back where he came from; and I shan't let a little matter like that persuade me to order my wife to take a blood test and the police to let me know whether or not my birth certificate was forged. Kings, my girl, have other things to do than to surrender themselves to their private feelings. [*He looks at her and smiles.*] Hand *you* over to be killed! [*He rises, moves to end of table and sits on the top of table.*] I have other plans for you. You're going to marry Haemon; and I want you to fatten up a bit so that you can give him a sturdy boy. Let me assure you that Thebes needs that boy a good deal more than it needs your death. You will go to your room, now, and do as you have been told; and you won't say a word about this to anybody. Don't fret about the guards: I'll see that their mouths are shut. And don't annihilate me with those eyes. I know that you think I am a brute, and I'm sure you must consider me very prosaic. But the fact is, I have always been fond of you, stubborn though you always were. Don't forget that the first doll you ever had came from me. [*A pause.* ANTIGONE *says nothing, rises, and crosses slowly below the table toward the arch.* CREON *turns and watches her; then*] Where are you going?

ANTIGONE [*stops downstage. Without any show of rebellion*]: You know very well where I am going.

CREON [*after a pause*]: What sort of game are you playing?

ANTIGONE: I am not playing games.

CREON: Antigone, do you realize that if, apart from those three guards, a single soul finds out what you have tried to do, it will be impossible for me to avoid putting you to death? There is still a chance that I can save you; but only if you keep this to yourself and give up your crazy purpose. Five minutes more, and it will be too late. You understand that?

ANTIGONE: I must go and bury my brother. Those men uncovered him.

CREON: What good will it do? You know that there are other men standing guard over Polynices. And even if you did cover him over with earth again, the earth would again be removed.

ANTIGONE: I know all that. I know it. But that much, at least, I can do. And what a person can do, a person ought to do.

Pause.

CREON: Tell me, Antigone, do you believe all that flummery about religious burial? Do you really believe that a so-called shade of your brother is condemned to wander for ever homeless if a little earth is not flung on his corpse to the accompaniment of some priestly abracadabra? Have you ever listened to the priests of Thebes when they were mumbling their formula? Have you ever watched those dreary bureaucrats while they were preparing the dead for burial — skipping half the gestures required by the ritual, swallowing half their words, hustling the dead into their graves out of fear that they might be late for lunch?

ANTIGONE: Yes, I have seen all that.

CREON: And did you never say to yourself as you watched them, that if someone you really loved lay dead under the shuffling, mumbling ministrations of the priests, you would scream aloud and beg the priests to leave the dead in peace?

ANTIGONE: Yes, I've thought all that.

CREON: And you still insist upon being put to death — merely because I refuse to let your brother go out with that grotesque passport; because I refuse his body the wretched consolation of that mass-production jibber-jabber, which you would have been the first to be embarrassed by if I had allowed it. The whole thing is absurd!

ANTIGONE: Yes, it's absurd.

CREON: Then why, Antigone, why? For whose sake? For the sake of them that believe in it? To raise them against me?

ANTIGONE: No.

CREON: For whom then if not for them and not for Polynices either?

ANTIGONE: For nobody. For myself.

A pause as they stand looking at one another.

CREON: You must want very much to die. You look like a trapped animal.

ANTIGONE: Stop feeling sorry for me. Do as I do. Do your job. But if you are a human being, do it quickly. That is all I ask of you. I'm not going to be able to hold out for ever.

CREON [*takes a step toward her*]: I want to save you, Antigone.

ANTIGONE: You are the king, and you are all-powerful. But that you cannot do.

CREON: You think not?

ANTIGONE: Neither save me nor stop me.

CREON: Prideful Antigone! Little Oedipus!

ANTIGONE: Only this can you do: have me put to death.

CREON: Have you tortured, perhaps?

ANTIGONE: Why would you do that? To see me cry? To hear me beg for mercy? Or swear whatever you wish, and then begin over again?

A pause.

CREON: You listen to me. You have cast me for the villain in this little play of yours, and yourself for the heroine. And you know it, you damned little mischief-maker! But don't you drive me too far! If I were one of your preposterous little tyrants that Greece is full of, you would be lying in a ditch this minute with your tongue pulled out and your body drawn and quartered. But you can see something in my face that makes me hesitate to send for the guards and turn you over to them. Instead, I let you go on arguing; and you taunt me, you take the offensive. [*He grasps her left wrist.*] What are you driving at, you she devil?

ANTIGONE: Let me go. You are hurting my arm.

CREON [*gripping her tighter*]: I will not let you go.

ANTIGONE [*moans*]. Oh!

CREON: I was a fool to waste words. I should have done this from the beginning. [*He looks at her.*] I may be your uncle — but we are not a particularly affectionate family. Are we, eh? [*Through his teeth, as he twists.*] Are we? [CREON *propels* ANTIGONE *round below him to his side.*] What fun for you, eh? To be able to spit in the face of a king who has all the power in the world; a man who has done his own killing in his day; who has killed people just as pitiable as you are — and who is still soft enough to go to all this trouble in order to keep you from being killed.

A pause.

ANTIGONE: Now you are squeezing my arm too tightly. It doesn't hurt any more.

CREON *stares at her, then drops her arm.*

CREON: I shall save you yet. [*He goes below the table to the chair at end of table, takes off his coat, and places it on the chair.*] God knows, I have things enough to do today without wasting my time on an insect like you. There's plenty to do, I assure you, when you've just put down a revolution. But urgent things can wait. I am not going to let politics be the cause of your death. For it is a fact that this whole business is nothing but politics: the mournful shade of Polynices, the decomposing corpse, the sentimental weeping, and the hysteria that you mistake for heroism — nothing but politics.

Look here. I may not be soft, but I'm fastidious. I like things clean, shipshape, well scrubbed. Don't think that I am not just as offended as you are by the thought of that meat rotting in the sun. In the evening, when the breeze comes in off the sea, you can smell it in the palace, and it nauseates me. But I refuse even to shut my window. It's vile; and I can tell you what I wouldn't tell anybody else: it's stupid, monstrously stupid. But the people of Thebes have got to have their noses rubbed into it a little longer. My God! If it was up to me, I should have had them bury your brother long ago as a mere matter of public hygiene. I admit that what I am doing is childish. But if the featherheaded rabble I govern are to understand what's what, that stench has got to fill the town for a month!

ANTIGONE [*turns to him*]: You are a loathsome man!

CREON: I agree. My trade forces me to be. We could argue whether I ought or ought not to follow my trade; but once I take on the job, I must do it properly.

ANTIGONE: Why do you do it at all?

CREON: My dear, I woke up one morning and found myself King of Thebes. God knows, there were other things I loved in life more than power.

ANTIGONE: Then you should have said no.

CREON: Yes, I could have done that. Only, I felt that it would have been cowardly. I should have been like a workman who turns down a job that has to be done. So I said yes.

ANTIGONE: So much the worse for you, then. I didn't say yes. I can say no to anything I think vile, and I don't have to count the cost. But because you said yes, all that you can do, for all your crown and your trappings, and your guards — all that you can do is to have me killed.

CREON: Listen to me.

ANTIGONE: If I want to. I don't have to listen to you if I don't want to. You've said your *yes*. There is nothing more you can tell me that I don't know. You stand there, drinking in my words. [*She moves behind chair.*] Why is it that you don't call your guards? I'll tell you why? You want to hear me out to the end; that's why.

CREON: You amuse me.

ANTIGONE: Oh, no, I don't. I frighten you. That is why you talk about saving me. Everything would be so much easier if you had a docile, tongue-tied little Antigone living in the palace. I'll tell you something, Uncle Creon: I'll give you back one of your own words. You are too fastidious to make a good tyrant. But you are going to have to put me to death today, and you know it. And that's what frightens you. God! Is there anything uglier than a frightened man!

CREON: Very well. I am afraid, then. Does that satisfy you? I am afraid that if you insist upon it, I shall have to have you killed. And I don't want to.

ANTIGONE: I don't have to do things that I think are wrong. If it comes to that, you didn't really want to leave my brother's body unburied, did you? Say it! Admit that you didn't.

CREON: I have said it already.

ANTIGONE: But you did it just the same. And now, though you don't want to do it, you are going to have me killed. And you call that being a king!

CREON: Yes, I call that being a king.

ANTIGONE: Poor Creon! My nails are broken, my fingers are bleeding, my arms are covered with the welts left by the paws of your guards — but I am a queen!

CREON: Then why not have pity on me, and live? Isn't your brother's corpse, rotting there under my windows, payment enough for peace and order in Thebes? My son loves you. Don't make me add your life to the payment. I've paid enough.

ANTIGONE: No, Creon! You said yes, and made yourself king. Now you will never stop paying.

CREON: But God in heaven! Won't you try to understand me! I'm trying hard enough to understand you! There had to be one man who said yes. Somebody had to agree to captain the ship. She had sprung a hundred leaks; she was loaded to the water line with crime, ignorance, poverty. The wheel was swinging with the wind. The crew refused to work and were looting the cargo. The officers were building a raft, ready to slip overboard and desert the ship. The mast was splitting, the wind was howling, the sails were beginning to rip. Every man jack on board was about to drown — and only because the only thing they thought of was their own skins and their cheap little day-to-day traffic. Was that a time, do you think, for playing with words like yes and no? Was that a time for a man to be weighing the pros and cons, wondering if he wasn't going to pay too dearly later on; if he wasn't going to lose his life, or his family, or his touch with other men? You grab the wheel, you right the ship in the face of a mountain of water. You shout an order, and if one man refuses to obey, you shoot straight into the mob. Into the mob, I say! The beast as nameless as the wave that crashes down upon your deck; as nameless as the whipping wind. The thing that drops when you shoot may be someone who poured you a drink the night before; but it has no name. And you, braced at the wheel, you have no name, either. Nothing has a name — except the ship, and the storm. [*A pause as he looks at her.*] Now do you understand?

ANTIGONE: I am not here to understand. That's all very well for you. I am here to say no to you, and die.

CREON: It is easy to say no.

ANTIGONE: Not always.

CREON: It is easy to say no. To say yes, you have to sweat and roll up your sleeves and plunge both hands into life up to the elbows. It is easy to say no, even if saying no means death. All you have to do is to sit still and wait. Wait to go on living; wait to be killed. That is the coward's part. *No* is one of your man-made words. Can you imagine a world in which trees say *no* to the sap? In which beasts say *no* to hunger or to propagation? Animals are good, simple, tough. They move in droves, nudging one another onwards, all traveling the same road. Some of them keel over, but the rest go on; and no matter how many may fall by the wayside, there are always those few left that go on bringing their young into the world, traveling the same road with the same obstinate will, unchanged from those who went before.

ANTIGONE: Animals, eh, Creon! What a king you could be if only men were animals! . . .

Review Questions

1. How does Antigone force Creon to obey his own laws?
2. Why does Creon wish to save Antigone?
3. Under what conditions did Creon decide to become king of Thebes?
4. What does politics have to do with Creon's decision not to bury Polynices?
5. Creon and Antigone agree that "the whole thing is absurd." *What* is absurd?

Discussion Questions

1. Is Antigone being responsible, irresponsible, or both in insisting on burying her brother and defying Creon's decree? (Responsible in the sense that she is adhering to a code of morality that supersedes the laws of Thebes; irresponsible in the sense that it is selfish to be a martyr who need not compromise her beliefs in order to live in a community.)
2. Creon puts the needs of the state above all private concerns. ("Kings, my girl, have other things to do than to surrender themselves to their

private feelings.'') Explain Creon's commitment to the law and his conviction that laws make civilization possible. (Pay particular attention to his speech about the sinking ship.)

3. Why does Creon argue that it is ''easy'' to say no? For whom is the predicament of the play more troubling? Why?

4. ''Grotesque passport.'' ''Wretched consolation.'' What makes these expressions poetic? Locate other such expressions and explain their effectiveness.

5. Discuss Creon's metaphor of the sinking ship. Why is it appropriate for this situation? What do you learn of Creon's character from this speech?

Writing Suggestions

1. CREON: . . . I admit that what I'm doing is childish. But if the feather-headed rabble I govern are to understand what's what, that stench [of Polynices's rotting body] has got to fill the town for a month!
ANTIGONE: You are a loathsome man!
CREON: I agree. My trade forces me to be. We could argue whether I ought or ought not to follow my trade; but once I take on the job, I must do it properly.

   Must the trade of lawmaker force one to be loathsome? Do you think that the ''featherheaded rabble'' could have understood the need for submission to the law without having to endure the stench of Polynices's decomposing body? Develop your answers, and your defense for them, into an argument.

2. ''A world populated only by Antigones could never exist.'' In an essay discuss why or why not.

3. Read the original *Antigone* by Sophocles and a complete version of Anouilh's play. Compare and contrast the two plays. You might want to particularly consider the effect of Anouilh's modernization. Is it odd to read characters created over two thousand years ago speaking of blood tests? There are many other modernisms. Can such an old play dressed in new clothes be successful?

SUMMARY, SYNTHESIS, CRITIQUE ACTIVITIES

Summary

Summarize one or more of the passages in this unit. Follow the suggested six-step process. Take into account the answers to the Review Questions for each passage. (Recommended: ''The Milgram Experiment,'' ''U.S. Report on the My Lai Investigation,'' ''Superior Orders and Reprisals'')

Synthesis

1. You are presiding at the court-martial of Lt. William Calley. You have heard all of the evidence (Calley did kill unarmed civilians) and the argument for the defense (that Calley was obeying orders). In the attempt to help make a decision about Calley's guilt, you write a memorandum to yourself, reviewing all of the evidence and the various points raised by the prosecution and defense — which, for our purposes, you can consider the information contained in this chapter's readings. Your memorandum would take the form of an *argument*: having reviewed the available information provided by Milgram, Lifton, Taylor, and Anouilh, reach a decision on Calley's guilt or innocence.

2. You have taken the job of babysitting for your hyperactive nephew, a job that will last five days (long enough to make you consider some solution to his unruliness other than waiting for his parents to return). What will you say (or do!) to your nephew to get him to obey you? Why *should* he obey you? To aid you in your *argument,* make use of the readings in this unit.

3. *Define* obedience to authority.

4. How is the story of *Antigone* an *example* of the dilemmas of obedience to authority, as discussed by Milgram, Taylor, Herrnstein, and Lifton? Are there ways in which *Antigone* does not exemplify these discussions?

5. *Describe* a situation in which you were faced with the moral and ethical dilemma of whether or not to obey a figure of authority. How does your experience *exemplify* any of the readings in this unit?

6. *Compare and contrast* Stanley Resor's and Robert Lifton's treatments of the behavior of GIs in war zones. In your answer, consider their different professional positions: Resor was, at that time, Secretary of the Army; Lifton is a psychiatrist.

7. *Compare and contrast* the predicament of the fictional character Antigone with that of William Calley. In what ways is such a comparison limited? To what extent can a "fiction" help us understand the motives, fears, and questions of an actual person?

Critique

1. Write a critique of the Milgram experiment. Do you agree with Herrnstein's comments?

2. Critique Secretary Resor's statement on My Lai. Does it appear to you that Resor has been as candid as possible, given the fact that no indictment had yet been brought against Calley? Consider also the conflicting pressures that Resor must have been feeling.

RESEARCH TOPICS

1. Read Milgram's book, *Obedience to Authority: An Experimental View,* and all of the reviews that you can find in the various indexes. (A good place to begin would be the *Book Review Digest.*) Summarize the types of criticisms — positive and negative — that reviewers have made. Then present your own views on the controversial experiments.

2. Investigate the role of John Dean in the Watergate scandal — the "bugging" of the Democratic national headquarters and the subsequent cover-up that eventually brought down the Nixon administration. To what extent do the issues you've discussed in this unit apply to Dean's relationship with former President Nixon?

3. Investigate the court-martial of Lt. William Calley. Was President Nixon justified in commuting his sentence? Examine, in detail, the dilemmas the jury must have faced when presented with Calley's defense that he was only following orders.

4. Obtain a copy of the transcript from Adolph Eichmann's trial, and then read Hannah Arendt's *Eichmann in Jerusalem: A Report on the Banality of Evil* plus the reviews of that book. Write a critique both of Arendt's work and the reviews of her work.

ADDITIONAL READINGS

Arendt, Hannah. *Eichmann in Jerusalem: A Report on the Banality of Evil.* New York: Viking Press, 1963.

Fromm, Erich. *Escape from Freedom.* New York: Holt, Rinehart and Winston, 1941.

Hammer, Richard. *The Court-Martial of Lt. Calley.* New York: Coward, McCann and Geoghegan, 1971.

McCarthy, Mary. *Medina.* New York: Harcourt, Brace, Jovanovich, Inc., 1972.

Meisnner, William. *The Assault on Authority: Dialogue or Dilemma?* Maryknoll, New York: Orbis Books, 1971. (See especially pp. 205–295.)

Milgram, Stanley. *Obedience to Authority: An Experimental View.* New York: Harper and Row, 1974.

Munson, Howard. "Blind Obedience: Report on Obedience to Authority Symposium." *Psychology Today,* January 1978, pp. 11ff.

Patten, S. C. "Milgram's Shocking Experiments." *Philosophy,* 52 (October 1977), pp. 425–440.

Schonfeld, William R. *Obedience and Revolt: French Behavior Toward Authority.* London and Beverly Hills: Sage Publications, 1976.

Thoreau, Henry David. *On the Duty of Civil Disobedience.* New York: Coward, McCann and Geoghegan, 1971.

See also Telford Taylor's book.

7

The Age of Computers — And Beyond

In our section on personality, Chapter 12, we include some pieces classifying people into types — according to how they relate to other people, according to how they function in a business environment, and so on. But it might also be possible to classify people according to how they react to the age of computers. Some revel in it. Others are bewildered, but try gamely to adjust. Still others react with dismay, even fear, to the CRTs (cathode ray tubes) blossoming like spring flowers around them. And a few appear to experience their deepest moments of pleasure and satisfaction when the computers break down — for instance, when the library computer is down and their books have to be checked out manually. This confirms their not-so-secret conviction that computers (like horseless carriages, years before) are more trouble than they're worth.

But like it or not, computers are here. And assuming civilization survives, computers will remain with us the rest of our lives, playing an increasingly greater role in ordering our financial affairs, planning our travel, arranging and even designing our leisure-time activities, and, in general, keeping track of everything that needs to be kept track of.

The selections in this chapter give some idea of the present and future impact of the computer age. In "And Man Created the Chip," *Newsweek* writers Merrill Sheils, William Cook, and others provide an overview of the computer revolution, explaining how computer technology has evolved since its primitive beginnings less than four decades ago, how modern computers work, how they will transform our lives, and why some people are worried about this transformation. On a personal level, *Washington Post* writer Judy Mann, in "A Staff Writer Becomes Invalid in READ Mode," reveals how the computerization of a traditional job can bring out deep anxieties and feelings of inadequacy, even in the seasoned professional. From an entirely different viewpoint, an "inside" one, systems programmer Frederick P. Brooks presents an almost lyric vision of computer software. In "The Joys — and Woes — of Programming," he suggests that programming at the higher levels is comparable to the highest flights of creative effort, the modern equivalent, perhaps, of composing a poem or a symphony, or designing a great cathedral. In "Electronic Tutors," science-fiction writer Arthur C. Clarke explains how the computer age may revolutionize education by doing away with the need for most schools. Finally, astronomer Robert Jastrow postulates that we humans may eventually have to give way on the evolutionary ladder to a new breed of thinking computers, for within the next few generations (computer generations, that is) those digital wonders may very well supersede us.

251

AND MAN CREATED THE CHIP
Merrill Sheils

Merrill Sheils is a staff writer for *Newsweek,* where this article first appeared as a cover story in June, 1980. Sheils was assisted in the preparation of this piece by researchers William Cook, Michael Reese, Marc Frons, and Phyllis Malamud.

In a brief article that accompanied Sheils's feature, Sharon Begley and her colleagues, John Carey and Michael Reese, inquire, "How Smart Can Computers Get?"

☐

Welcome! Always glad to show someone from the early '80s around the place. 1
The biggest change, of course, is the smart machines — they're all around us. No need to be alarmed, they're very friendly. Can't imagine how you lived without them. The telephone, dear old thing, is giving a steady busy signal to a bill collector I'm avoiding. Unless he starts calling from a new number my phone doesn't know, he'll never get through. TURN OFF! Excuse me for shouting — almost forgot the bedroom television was on. Let's see, anything else before we go? The oven already knows the menu for tonight and the kitchen robot will mix us a mean Martini. Guess we're ready. Oh no, you won't need a key. We'll just program the lock to recognize your voice and let you in whenever you want.

A revolution is under way. Most Americans are already well 2
aware of the gee-whiz gadgetry that is emerging, in rapidly accelerating bursts, from the world's high-technology laboratories. But most of us perceive only dimly how pervasive and profound the changes of the next twenty years will be. We are at the dawn of the era of the smart machine — an "information age" that will change forever the way an entire nation works, plays, travels and even thinks. Just as the industrial revolution dramatically expanded the strength of man's muscles and the reach of his hand, so the smart-machine revolution will magnify the power of his brain. But unlike the industrial revolution, which depended on finite resources such as iron and oil, the new information age will be fired by a seemingly limitless resource — the inexhaustible supply of knowledge itself. Even computer scientists, who best understand the galloping technology and its potential, are

wonderstruck by its implications. "It is really awesome," says L. C. Thomas of Bell Laboratories. "Every day is just as scary as the day before."

The driving force behind the revolution is the development of two fundamental and interactive technologies — computers and integrated circuits. Today, tiny silicon chips half the size of a fingernail are etched with circuitry powerful enough to book seats on jumbo jets (and keep the planes working smoothly in the air), cut complex swatches of fabric with little wastage, help children learn to spell and play chess well enough to beat all but the grandest masters. The new technology means that bits of computing power can be distributed wherever they might be useful — the way small electric motors have become ubiquitous — or combined in giant mainframe computers to provide enormous problem-solving potential. In addition, this "computational plenty" is making smart machines easier to use and more forgiving of unskilled programming. Machines are even communicating with each other. "What's next?" asks Peter E. Hart, director of the SRI International artificial-intelligence center. "More to the point, what's *not* next?"

The explosion is just beginning. In 1979, the world market for microelectronics topped $11 billion. Over the next five years, chip sales are expected to grow by at least 20 percent annually, and the market for microprocessors, entire "computers on a chip," will expand by 50 per cent each year — even though the chips themselves and the computing power they represent are diving in price. As industry officials are fond of remarking, if the automobile industry had improved its technology at the same rate computer science has, it would now be turning out Rolls-Royces that cost no more than $70 apiece.

There are a few clouds on the industry's horizon: capital costs are rising, and Japan is mounting an all-out challenge to American supremacy in the field. Some experts predict that the shape of the industry will change considerably by the end of the decade, perhaps even shrinking down to a half-dozen IBM-like giants. But whatever shake-outs lie ahead, the world will continue to snap up chips as fast as manufacturers can turn them out, creating a mushrooming "information industry" that will grow into a $500 billion-a-year enterprise, by far the biggest on earth.

The transformation will not be easy, for smart machines bring with them the seeds of widespread economic dislocation and social unrest. Eventually, for example, they will make possible the full automation of many factories, displacing millions of blue-collar workers with a new "steel collar" class. Even office workers will feel the crunch, as smart machines do more and more of the clerical work.

Traditional businesses such as television networks and publishing companies will encounter new competition as programmers and advertisers beam information directly into the consumer's home.

Some social critics warn of a new generation of Luddites[1] who will fight to stop the new technology through restrictive laws — or even sabotage. Others predict the rise of a new criminal class of master computer-raiders. And many view the advent of smart machines with a dread they cannot really explain. To them, computers are alien, too complicated to understand and too prone to horrifying mistakes like the recent false alarms on the Air Force's NORAD missile-detection system. Alarmists harbor fears that the technology will get out of control — perhaps producing new machines that can outsmart their human masters. 7

But industry experts think these problems can — and will — be solved. In the optimists' scenario, educational programs will retrain displaced workers and equip them with skills suited to the booming new information business. Meanwhile, laymen will grow more and more comfortable with computers as they invade everyday life. And in the end, the smart-machine revolution will do far more to enrich life than most Americans realize. As the industry likes to picture the future, the new technology offers potential solutions to humanity's most intractable problems — the allocation of energy resources, food enough for all and the worldwide improvement of health care, to name just a few. 8

Somewhere between the dire warnings and the utopian visions, the future will take form. But there is no doubt that the era of smart machines will be vastly different from anything that preceded it. "What we are doing is creating a new class structure around wealth — this time, the wealth of information," says SRI International futurologist Peter Schwartz. "Like today's 'haves and have-nots,' we will be a society of the 'knows and know-nots.'" 9

What makes both the industry and the technology all the more astonishing is that neither existed 35 years ago. The pace of development is roughly akin to going from the Wright Brothers' first airplane to the space shuttle in a decade. 10

The first big electronic computer was ENIAC (for Electronic Numerical Integrator and Calculator), which was built in 1946. ENIAC filled a huge room, gobbled up 140,000 watts of electricity 11

---

[1] During industrial riots in England from 1811 to 1816, some workmen joined to wreck the new textile machinery, believing that it had helped to lower wages and create unemployment. They were called Luddites, after Ned Lud, who years before had destroyed his employer's stocking frames. [Behrens and Rosen]

and contained 18,000 vacuum tubes that generated and controlled the electric current, allowing ENIAC to calculate. The tubes were large and expensive, and they produced a lot of heat, but it really didn't matter: almost as soon as ENIAC was complete, it was obsolete.

In 1947, scientists at Bell Laboratories introduced the transistor,   12 a tiny piece of semiconducting material such as silicon or germanium. Minute impurities added to the semiconductor enabled it to free or capture electrons without huge amounts of external energy. And as it turned out, the transistor was the perfect mate for digital computers using a binary code — an arithmetic system that employs only two digits or "bits," 1 and 0, that can be combined in strings, or "bytes," to represent any numerical value. (Bytes, in turn, can be used in a computer language to represent alphabetical characters.) Such computers rely on a large number of electrical circuits that are either "on" (corresponding to 1) or "off" (representing 0) to hold the binary code. The more circuits, the more the computer can do — and the closer they are to each other, the faster the computer can perform. Transistors allowed computer scientists to combine many more circuits in a fraction of the space of the old vacuum-tube design and at much less cost.

Another advantage of transistors is that they lose none of their   13 capacity as they shrink in size. The next giant step in the small-is-beautiful revolution was the simultaneous announcement in 1959 by Texas Instruments and Fairchild Semiconductor that both had successfully produced integrated circuits — single semiconductor chips containing several complete electronic circuits. Once again, the breakthrough enabled manufacturers to pack more computing power into less space. By 1970, the laboratories were producing chips with large-scale integration of circuitry (LSI): thousands of integrated circuits crammed onto a single quarter-inch square of silicon. Today, fully 100,000 transistors can be integrated on a chip, making a tiny piece of silicon far more powerful than ENIAC.

There are various different kinds of microchips — for example,   14 there are memories that store data, amplifiers that transmit it and microprocessors that combine a number of computing tasks. The size of their components almost defies explanation. A human hair has a width of 100 microns; parts of the transistors now crowded onto chips are less than 3 microns wide. By the mid-1980s, with the advent of very large-scale integration (VLSI), scientists expect to be using sub-micron geometries. George H. Heilmeier, who is vice president for corporate research at Texas Instruments, describes the increasing density this way: "In the mid-1960s, the complexity of a chip was comparable to that of the street network of a small town. Today's microprocessor is comparable to the entire Dallas–Ft. Worth area.

And the ultimate quarter-micron technology will be capable of producing chips whose complexity rivals an urban street network covering the entire North American continent."

Making a chip is a complex process. Most manufacturers now use what Heilmeier calls the "dip and wash" technique. A diagram of electronic circuitry is designed by a scientist on a computer terminal. Photographic machines produce hundreds of reproductions of the display and reduce them in size until their individual components are in the micron range. A photographic negative, or mask, is made of the patterns. Ultraviolet light is then projected through the mask onto a thin, 4-inch wafer of silicon that has been treated with photo resist, a light-sensitive material. Just like a film, the photo resist is developed, and the tiny patterns of the chips' circuitry emerge on the silicon's surface. The wafer is dipped in acid, which eats away the silicon where there is no photo resist. A layer of metal can be deposited for the interconnections between circuits, then another layer of photo resist. Some wafers take ten or more etched layers. Once all the layers are formed on the wafer, the chips are sawed out, fine wire leads are connected and they are ready for use in electronic devices. 15

VLSI will take even more complicated manufacturing technology. One technique most companies consider promising is electron-beam lithography, which uses electron beams to expose the photo resist on the wafer in much finer detail than optical processes permit. The scientists are also working hard to improve memory systems so that they will be able to store the ever-greater amounts of data for the chips to process. 16

One big advance in the works is bubble memories. On a chip of garnet coated with a thin layer of magnetic film, scientists form microscopic regions of reverse magnetization. The presence of one of these bubbles represents the 1 of the binary code, its absence the 0 — and the over-all pattern contains the data that has been stored. Bubble memories have two great advantages over previous technology: the memory patterns do not disappear when the power is turned off, and they take up less space. Researchers at Bell Labs have turned out one experimental bubble-memory chip with the ability to store 11.5 million bits — more than ten times the capacity of the most powerful chip now on the market. Appropriately enough, the Bell scientists call it "the incredible hulk." 17

All these wonders are bursting out of the labs at a steadily dwindling cost to consumers. "The great thing about semiconductors is that when you make them smaller and denser, they automatically get faster and the power requirement goes down," says Lewis M. Branscomb, chief scientist for IBM. "So the entire machine, if you're building a larger computer, gets smaller, and you need less packaging. 18

That makes them less expensive." One way of measuring the improvement is to take a look at Control Data Corp.'s new Cyber 205, which CDC introduced this month as "the world's most powerful computing system." The 205, which can perform 800 million operations in a single second, is smaller and eight times more powerful than its predecessor, a CDC mainframe introduced just two years ago. But the price — $7.9 million — is about the same.

Not surprisingly, the rapid growth of computer power, combined 19
with its declining cost, has inspired a rush to find new applications for the technology. By the mid-1980s, most automobiles will contain microprocessors that regulate fuel use, adjust engine performance and notify the driver on a dashboard terminal when something goes wrong. And starting next year, the Library of Congress will catalog all new books and other acquisitions on a computer: they will never be entered in an old-fashioned card catalog.

Hospitals, too, are making use of the wonders. At Massachusetts 20
General in Boston, an automated analyzer hooked to the hospital's big computers tests blood samples. And the hospital has also developed a medical computer language called MUMPS that puts its computers to use in a variety of ways. Using one program, a student doctor is presented with a simulated "patient" with certain symptoms. At each step, the student has a choice of action — and the patient responds. If the student errs, the program makes it clear — and in the worst case, dryly informs the student that the patient has died.

The next big frontier on the consumer market — and one the 21
industry hopes will make computers more attractive than ever — is speech. Two years ago, Texas Instruments brought out a learning device called "Speak and Spell," which "spoke" with a voice generated by two memory chips and a speech-synthesizer under the control of a microprocessor. The product attracted interest from all over the world, and TI itself has redoubled its research. Last year, it introduced a sophisticated translating machine available in four languages that permits the user to enter a word on a keyboard and get both a digital display of its foreign translation and a computer "voice" pronouncing it.

More complicated still are smart machines that both speak *and* 22
understand the human voice. At Bell Labs, scientists are concentrating on systems that will allow human beings and computers to communicate by voice over the telephone. An experimental airline-reservation program has a vocabulary of about 200 words. The customer would have to use words the machine recognizes — and the computer would respond with appropriate information in sequences that have not been preprogramed. In April, IBM researchers used a computer to transcribe speech into printed form with a 91 per cent accuracy

rate. "The good news was that the accuracy was so high," says Branscomb. "The bad news was that it took the computer 200 times as long to transcribe as we took to speak."

The scientists are confident that they will eventually be able to produce machines that both talk and listen with a high degree of accuracy, though they admit that some breakthroughs — such as teaching them to distinguish among homonyms by analyzing the context — are a long way off. For the handicapped, the benefits could be enormous: vast improvements in telephones for the deaf, for instance, that can print out whatever the voice on the other end is saying. 23

An even bigger breakthrough could come from technology that allows smart machines to "talk" among themselves. "Somehow, we have to figure out a way to link them all together," says George Pake, vice president of corporate research for Xerox. "The essence of the smart machines is that they will help us to communicate with them — and they, in turn, will be able to communicate with each other." Xerox itself recently patented Ethernet — a system that can connect up to 100 disparate machines, enabling them to send bursts of information at incredible speeds. And Xerox, Satellite Business Systems and several other high-tech giants also plan to offer satellite services that would permit worldwide intra-corporate communication among smart machines. 24

But the really big player in the game may turn out to be American Telephone and Telegraph Co., the telecommunications behemoth that is the parent company of Bell Labs. Recent Federal deregulatory initiatives may permit AT&T to enter the data-processing field, and Bell could come in with a big bang. Not only can AT&T move huge amounts of information over existing telephone lines, its research arm has been working on a giant new network called Advanced Communications Systems (ACS). ACS is an intelligent network: it can translate the language of any computer into its own digital code, move the data through the system, then translate it again to the language of the receiving terminal or computer. 25

Other companies in data processing are afraid that Ma Bell will crush them with her huge capital and scientific resources. Newspaper publishers, for instance, worry that once office and home computers can tap into data banks all over the country, people will no longer need newspapers: both news and advertising could be fed directly into the living room. But Robert W. Lucky, director of Bell's electronic and computer-systems research lab, thinks cultural habits will prevail — at least for the foreseeable future. "I want to *feel* The New York Times, take it to the bathroom with me, spill my orange juice on it," he says. 26

In other sectors of the economy, the changes could come quickly.   27
The advent of microprocessors has made industrial robots, for example, far more useful and versatile than ever before. Today, instead of performing just one simple task, they can be repeatedly programed to switch jobs — and to do highly complex ones, at that. And for the first time, the new technology has made robots cheaper and more efficient than many of their human counterparts: for an hourly "wage" of just $4.60, the average cost of maintaining them, they perform tedious and dangerous work with a high degree of reliability. The average human worker on an automobile assembly line, by contrast, earns $16 an hour.

Big Labor has been slow to take notice of the change, perhaps   28
because the first automation "revolution," in the era of dumb robots, made so few inroads. But now robots can be built so that they can "see" rudimentary shapes and even make tactile distinctions. By some estimates, from 50 to 75 percent of all U.S. factory workers could be displaced by smart robots before the end of the century. The estimates may be inflated, but they suggest that the new automation will emerge as a stormy issue at the union-management bargaining table in the years ahead.

Smart machines of a different sort are invading America's   29
offices: U.S. business will be 200 percent more automated by 1990, some experts predict. Electronic filing systems already store information in many offices, and electronic mail flashes messages from coast to coast. Several small computer companies like Chromatics, Inc., of Atlanta have pioneered sophisticated systems that not only analyze data but display the analyses in vivid color graphs, charts and pictures that eliminate the need for bulky computer print-outs. Architects can use the machines to visualize how new buildings will fit into existing neighborhoods, and the U.S. Navy is using them to test underwater equipment.

Computers have not really invaded the home as yet: only about   30
200,000 home computers are in use across the United States. But that will change as consumers recognize the extraordinary potential of the smart machines. Already, for instance, a home-computer user can tap into the data banks of Source Telecomputing Corp. of McLean, Va., over ordinary telephone lines. At a cost of $2.75 an hour for off-peak, nonbusiness hours and $15 per hour during the workday, the armchair computerist can call up the UPI news wire and sort through it by key words: "Carter," for instance, would produce all the stories in the data banks about Jimmy Carter. The company, which advertises as "The Source," also has the entire world airline schedule and descriptions of wines in its data banks, and it provides a 10,000-item discount-shopping catalog — even taking orders through the computer.

As similar services start to move into the market and compete for customers, home-computer manufacturers like Apple, Radio Shack and Hewlett-Packard expect sales to take off.

The nation's schools have already been invaded by pocket calcu- 31 lators, and more sophisticated "learning machines" will surely follow. To supplement its "Speak and Spell," for instance, Texas Instruments will introduce two new speaking devices this summer, "Speak and Read" and "Speak and Math," both designed to help kids master basic skills.

The educational possibilities seem enormous. "It is perfectly pos- 32 sible to build enough computing power into a video game in a few years so that your youngster will be able to simulate the laws of physics on a spaceship and see not little blips on the screen, but the view out the window of the spaceship," says Carver A. Mead, a computer-science professor at the California Institute of Technology. "He could fly near the velocity of light and see what that looks like, or fly down between the atoms of a crystal, looking at them from whatever angle he wants. If you think television has had a big impact, imagine this! Since the ability to write, there has never been a thing that made that big a change in the way people learn and grow up."

The smart-machine industry — by any estimate still in its in- 33 fancy — is also in for some changes. Analysts point out that vertical integration is already taking place, with computer giants like IBM investing in semiconductor production and turning out minicomput-ers as well as mainframes, and semiconductor companies like Texas Instruments testing the computer markets. At the same time, the industry is growing steadily more capital-intensive as technology grows more and more sophisticated, technical personnel require higher salaries and facilities expand to meet the exploding demand. Last year, the industry devoted fully 16 per cent of sales revenues to capital expenditures, compared with 4.7 percent for all manufactur-ing industries. The inevitable result in the next few years will be increasing concentration, with many small smart-machine manufac-turers being bought up by the big companies or squeezed out of the market.

The giants that are left will dominate an ever-growing share of 34 the U.S. economy. Computer experts see only one major impediment to the rapid growth of the information age: resistance to the technol-ogy by an adult generation that fears it. Some of the public's fears are justified; smart machines, for example, can be used to invade the privacy of home and office. Computer crime is already on the rise, with a sophisticated new breed of criminals cracking the codes that protect confidential corporate information and arranging the elec-tronic transfer of bank funds to their own accounts. But computer scientists argue that eventually, the improved technology of the smart machines themselves will be able to prevent such abuses.

There is no doubt that machines will get smarter and smarter, 35 even designing their own software and making new and better chips for new generations of computers ("incest is best," one industry slogan has it). More and more of their power will be devoted to making them easier to use — "friendly," in industry parlance — even for those not trained in computer science. And computer scientists expect that public ingenuity will come up with applications the most visionary researchers have not even considered. One day, a global network of smart machines will be exchanging rapid-fire bursts of information at unimaginable speeds. If they are used wisely, they could help mankind to educate its masses and crack new scientific frontiers. "For all of us, it will be fearful, terrifying, disruptive," says SRI's Peter Schwartz. "In the end there will be those whose lives will be diminished. But for the vast majority, their lives will be greatly enhanced." In any event, there is no turning back: if the smart machines have not taken over, they are fast making themselves indispensable — and in the end, that may amount to very much the same thing.

How Smart Can Computers Get?

Sharon Begley

On a Monday morning at Yale University, Margot Flowers sits down 1 with her friend Abdul for another debate on Mideast politics:

MARGOT: Who started the 1967 war? 2

ABDUL: The Arabs did, by blockading the Strait of Tiran. 3

MARGOT: But Israel attacked first. 4

ABDUL: According to international law, blockades are acts of war. 5

MARGOT: Were we supposed to let you import American arms 6
through the strait?

ABDUL: Israel was not importing arms through the strait. The reason for the blockade was to keep Israel from importing oil from Iran.

They don't have the finesse of U.N. diplomats, but then Margot 7 Flowers is one of three scientists who created Abdul, a computer program that dips into its memory of data to reason out answers to

Sharon Begley, with John Carey and Michael Reese, "How Smart Can Computers Get," in "And Man Created the Chip," *Newsweek*, June 30, 1980.

questions. The dialogue is an exercise in a 25-year-old field called artificial intelligence (AI), and with the remarkable advances in computer technology at their command, hundreds of AI researchers are testing the potential of the new electronic brains. Their goal is as remarkable as their technology: to determine how close a computer can come to simulating the human mind and, perhaps, transcending it.

The results thus far are both tantalizing and reassuring. In scores   8
of AI experiments, well-programed computers can play chess and backgammon, draw analogies among Shakespearean plays and understand tales involving friendship and adultery. Computers can use facts to make inferences and draw on experience to reach unprogramed conclusions. But only up to a point: what AI researchers are learning is that the human brain is even more astonishing than they thought — and that true intelligence involves elements of will, consciousness and creativity of which today's computers are incapable. "So far, artificial intelligence falls under the definition of problem solving," says AI scientist Terry Winograd of Stanford. "That's the first step."

The first "thinking" problem solver was probably a 1956 com-   9
puter program called the Logic Theorist, which could choose from a set of facts and use logical operations to prove mathematical statements. Its first triumph was finding a proof of a theorem in mathematical logic that both Bertrand Russell and Alfred North Whitehead had missed.

Today's problem solvers are even more sophisticated. One of the   10
most impressive is the backgammon champ programed by Hans J. Berliner of Carnegie-Mellon University in Pittsburgh. The program chooses among all possible legal moves by reducing each to a mathematical equation that measures threats and opportunities and then picks the move whose equation has the highest value. BACON, another program developed by Nobel laureate Herbert A. Simon and his colleagues at Carnegie-Mellon, looks for patterns in scientific data. On its own, BACON "discovered" a rule of planetary mechanics first established by Johannes Kepler in 1609. And when it was fed all the facts that were known about chemistry in the year 1800, BACON deduced the principle of atomic weight — a feat that took human scientists another 50 years.

Such problem solving relies on clear rules and rigid logic. Wino-   11
grad took the next step with SHRDLU, a program that could manipulate cubes and pyramids on a tabletop to build a given structure, figuring out the intermediate steps without being explicitly told how to do it. It was a breakthrough in artificial intelligence, but SHRDLU still lacked the ability to learn, that is, to use the experience gained in a project to avoid repeating past mistakes.

Now many researchers are trying to get machines to make gener- 12
alizations — that is, to link the common characteristics of separate
facts. At Yale, for instance, a program called IPP analyzes newspaper
stories about terrorism. It reads the stories, elicits the important information from each sentence, then files it away in a way that will let it
make connections among different stories. IPP correctly concludes
that Irish gunmen tend to shoot policemen and Italian terrorists
attack businessmen. But after it has read several stories about double
killings, it also asserts that terrorist victims always come in pairs. IPP
makes this sort of overgeneralization from limited data because it has
no common sense born of wide experience. Says Roger Schank,
director of Yale's AI Lab, "You will not understand a news story
unless you have a tremendous amount of world knowledge."

AI researchers in some laboratories are also encouraging their 13
computers to deal with information involving not so much hard facts
as emotions and inferences. At Yale, Wendy Lehnert has programed
BORIS to read and understand a short story by providing the computer with basic information about human relationships including
friendships, favors and legal disputes. The machine then decides
what is important, stores facts selectively, draws inferences from the
facts and tests them at different levels, answering complex questions.
"How did Richard feel?" "He was happy to hear from a friend."
Richard, a lawyer, is glad to get a letter from Paul, BORIS explains,
because Paul once lent him money, and Richard understands that
Paul wants him to return the favor by representing Paul in a divorce
action. Without explicit statements in the story, the computer has
deduced that divorces require lawyers and that the loan represents a
favor to be returned. For all its cleverness, however, BORIS understands just two short stories—and each took six months of programing.

Understanding may also be enhanced by analogy, the compari- 14
son of similar events and characteristics. AT MIT, Patrick H. Winston
has programed a computer to draw literary analogies. When fed plot
outlines of four Shakespearean tragedies and one comedy, the program concludes that *Macbeth* and *Hamlet* are the most alike. On
this basis, it matches up characters, actions and motives. Macbeth and
Claudius both kill kings because they are ambitious. Their victims are
Duncan and Hamlet's father. Macduff and Hamlet avenge the murders. The program is actually reasoning by analogy, Winston argues,
since it answers questions about *Hamlet* by knowing about *Macbeth*.

Analogy can also be used for learning. Computers grasp the 15
concept of electrical resistance, for instance, by drawing analogies to
water pipes. Since "machines won't be intelligent until they acquire
what they need on their own," Winston says, learning is a critical skill.
But machines that "learn" are very rudimentary. One program can

learn the concept of an arch when it is shown structures that are and aren't arches, and another can acquire skill from its experiences in playing checkers — avoiding moves that made it lose previous games. But it has never learned new strategies of playing.

If learning is possible, is creativity next? Some scientists believe it 16 is. In his Pulitzer Prize-winning book *Gödel, Escher, Bach,* computer scientist Douglas R. Hofstadter of Indiana University argues that a computer's hardware and software may one day combine to let it both create and feel. The interwoven levels may even give machines "qualities such as 'will,' 'intuition' . . . and 'consciousness,' " he writes, just as human hardware (the brain's neurons) and software (the mind's reasoning processes) do.

Hofstadter and other experts suggest that machine consciousness 17 might be achieved once the programmers get a computer to think about thinking and to understand its own process of understanding. That challenge has eluded them thus far, mainly because their software programs are infants compared with the rapidly maturing hardware. And most computer scientists have their doubts that true creativity — the stuff of human emotion and deep experience — can ever be reached. "Computers can only touch on the shadow of what we call emotion," says Winograd. But even if silicon sensibilities never love, grieve or fear, intelligent computers have already changed man's sense of himself as the only thinking being. Humanity has survived other jolts to its ego, from Copernicus to Darwin, and it will undoubtedly survive this one, too. And so far, at least, mankind has a fallback position. If intelligent machines make us really uncomfortable, says Berliner, "we can always pull the plug."

Review Questions

1. What are some of the "clouds" on the computer industry's horizon? What economic problems could the computer age bring about?

2. Why was the first big computer, ENIAC, obsolete soon after it was completed? What development made possible the first revolution in the computer industry?

3. Why does the price of new computer equipment go down even though it is more advanced?

4. What are some of the future applications of new computer technology?

5. Why do many people worry about constantly advancing computer technology?

6. What are, at present, the limitations of "artificial intelligence," especially in comparison with the human brain?

Discussion Questions

1. Early in the article a computer scientist is quoted as saying of the new technology: "It is really awesome. . . . Every day is just as scary as the day before." Is this just excitement, or is it really "awesome" and "scary"? Could this indicate the doubt of the scientific community about creating a Frankenstein monster?

2. Futurologist Peter Schwartz says that "Like today's 'haves and have-nots,' we will be a society of the 'knows and know-nots.'" Will a society of "knows and know-nots" be any fairer than a society of "haves and have-nots"?

3. One point only implied in the article is how computers will affect the quality (as opposed to the efficiency) of life. Doubtless computers (like washing machines before them) will relieve us of many tedious and repetitive tasks. But to what extent will they make life more enjoyable, more worth living?

4. There has been some evidence that with the development of pocket calculators, children are becoming less capable of doing math calculations on paper or in their heads. Is this a problem? Is there a danger that we could grow so dependent upon the reasoning power of computers that we lose some of our own reasoning power? If so, what can we do about it?

5. The article begins with a catalogue of the various benefits and problems that the computer age will bring about. Are the writers of the article totally objective about all of this, or do they indicate what their own position is? Do they belong with the optimists or the pessimists — or somewhere in between? Explain.

6. Consider the sentence: "Today, tiny silicon chips half the size of a fingernail are etched with circuitry powerful enough to book seats on jumbo jets (and keep the planes working smoothly in the air), cut complex swatches of fabric. . . ." Isn't the parenthetical expression more important than the main clause? Why do you think the sentence was written this way?

7. In the paragraph beginning "Making a chip is a complex process," the authors go on to explain the process in detail. Is the explanation too technical for laymen? Could it have been reworded or otherwise modified to make it clearer? Or are laymen simply going to have to start thinking technically if they want to understand the way the modern world works?

Writing Suggestions

1. Write a description of two or three ways in which your own life has been affected by the ever-advancing development of computer tech-

nology. You may want to point out both advantages and disadvantages.

2. Write a scenario describing (on the basis of your own knowledge or imagination) ways that computer technology will change our society — for good or for ill.

3. Read an account in a history text or an encyclopedia of the industrial revolution of the 18th and 19th centuries. Then write an article in the style of the *Newsweek* feature as it might have appeared in a contemporary magazine, detailing the wondrous developments and what the future holds, together with an account of the various advantages and disadvantages of the industrial revolution.

4. Write a letter to the head of marketing at one of the major electronics firms (such as RCA or Texas Instruments) explaining a proposal you have for a new microcomputer system. Explain its workings, its benefits, and its marketability.

5. Write a short story involving a home of the future that is controlled largely by computer.

A STAFF WRITER BECOMES INVALID IN READ MODE
Judy Mann

Judy Mann is a columnist for the *Washington Post,* where this piece first appeared.

☐

This is my second attempt at writing this column. The first attempt   1
ended in total disaster when all of my *bons mots* were devoured before
my eyes by the machine upon which they were being written. The
machine, as you might have guessed, is not my beloved and trusted
typewriter which did nothing more than faithfully record words on
paper with only a few misspellings. No, not anymore. The machine in
question is a computer, a sleek new presence which is familiar to all
the folks who watch the Lou Grant show, but which I should tell you
right off, is not familiar to a lot of the folks who work in the newsroom
of The Washington Post.

We've known for several years now that the computers were   2
coming, but there were enough delays along the way that we got
lulled into a false sense of security. The future was not yet now. But it

---

became clear during this past spring and summer that the end of the typewriter age was in sight. Workmen invaded the newsroom, rewiring things, digging up floors and tearing out ceilings. By the beginning of August, hundreds of terminals that looked like Japanese televisions appeared. The word was out: By September we would all be working on computers. The option was such that computers were no longer a joking matter.

For those of us who have been reluctant to leap into the 21st 3 century, the computers have been a source of deep and abiding anxiety. We have all been hearing stories from colleagues on other newspapers about how computers have "aborted" their stories (a *genteel* computer term for killed) or lost them or mixed them up with other people's stories. My husband, who wrote for years on a typewriter, switched to a computer at his newspaper and began calling home saying he would be late for dinner because "the computer was down." One time it swallowed two-thirds of his column.

When I got back from vacation, I found a memo in my mailbox 4 informing me that I was to attend the second week of computer training classes. For the next few days I watched with a mixture of dread and curiosity as colleague after colleague vanished from the newsroom for the first round of courses and reappeared bearing thick red books filled with arcane instructions about how to work the computer. Reporters and editors who had heretofore shown an appreciation and even, in some cases, a love for the English language came back spouting a whole new vocabulary that you knew right off interfaced with computers. They talked about being in the read mode, not to mention the edit mode, and when they got carried away with their new skills they would dabble on the machines in the newsroom and go into the insert mode right before your very eyes.

(I almost got in terrible trouble right then. I pushed the "store" 5 button when I should have pushed the "record" button and the machine abruptly flashed a message on the screen that I was "IN-VALID IN THE READ/WRITE MODE." The last time I did that I lost the beginning of the column entirely. Since being invalid is obviously better than being killed, I must be getting better.)

To continue. I began having computer anxiety attacks, similar to 6 the math anxiety attacks I had in high school. What if I couldn't understand the computers? What if I couldn't make them work? What would I do for a living that didn't involve computers? What was to become of me?

The first class did not go well. One of our earliest exercises 7 involved writing our bylines into the computer and following that with the phrase "Washington Post Staff Writer." I misspelled about half of that and then tried to repair the errors and the next thing I knew things were flashing wildly on the screen and our instructor was throwing up his hands and signaling the computer to "abort" the entire effort. To my humiliation, I had to start all over.

But I got better at it. When it came time to make some letters in bold roman type I did it without a hitch. I learned how to delete characters and define graphs and how to find old stories and how to hide my personal documents so that editors summoning up a column would not find themselves looking at my grocery list. 8

By the end of the second class I had gotten over a lot of my anxiety and mastered the technique of writing in my name and the name of the story. By then, of course, the class had gone onto far more sophisticated modes and some showoffs were talking about "list parameters" and transferring messages to each other and "changing headers" and splitting screens and scrolling up and scrolling down and they were asking questions that you knew were designed, not to elicit information, but to make the rest of us look like dummies. 9

But for better or for worse, we have entered the computer age and those who have gone before us in the newsroom have sent back rave reviews. And so far, they seem to be right. Writing this column was a piece of cake: I lost three lead paragraphs, the machine froze on me three times, and two printing machines refused to print copies of what I had written. I kept storing things so that they would vanish off the screen instead of recording them. The machine refused repeatedly to honor my commands to abort and to clear, not to mention my orders to execute and scroll down. And in the end when the machine stopped functioning dead in its tracks, it was not much of a comfort when the technician who came over to rescue me fixed me with a flinty look and said: "What did you do to it?" 10

Something tells me now is the time to move into the pray mode. 11

Review Questions

1. How has the computer age in the newsroom affected the English language?
2. What is Mann's attitude toward the invasion of computers in the *Washington Post* newsroom?

Discussion Questions

1. Why should "computers have been a source of deep and abiding anxiety" for "those of us who have been reluctant to leap into the 21st century"? Who are "those of us"? Does it include you? Would it include your parents?
2. Is it possible that Mann may take a secret pride in not understanding the mysterious ways of the computer? Is there a basic conflict be-

tween the ways of the traditional writer-reporter and the ways of advanced technology?

3. This column is funny; but why, exactly? What is the source of the humor? What would have been lost (besides the humor) if the story had been told straight?

4. Contrast the tone of this article with the tone of "And Man Created the Chip." Cite examples of words and phrases that typify the tone of the Mann piece.

Writing Suggestion

Write an article in the style of this column detailing your distresses and mishaps at having to deal with some new device (possibly a computer) or some new, unfamiliar way of doing things.

THE JOYS — AND WOES — OF PROGRAMMING
Frederick P. Brooks, Jr.

Frederick P. Brooks, Jr., is Professor and Chairman of the Computer Science Department at the University of North Carolina at Chapel Hill. He is best known as the "father of the IBM System/360," having served as project manager for its development and later as manager of the Operating System/360 software project during its design phase. Earlier, he was architect of the IBM Stretch and Harvest computers. Among his publications are *Automatic Data Processing* and *The Mythical Man-Month: Essays on Software Engineering,* where this passage first appeared.

Why is programming fun? What delights may its practitioner expect 1
as his reward?

First is the sheer joy of making things. As the child delights in his 2
mud pie, so the adult enjoys building things, especially things of his
own design. I think this delight must be an image of God's delight in
making things, a delight shown in the distinctness and newness of
each leaf and each snowflake.

Second is the pleasure of making things that are useful to other 3
people. Deep within, we want others to use our work and to find it

From *The Mythical Man-Month* by Frederick P. Brooks, Jr.; © 1975, Addison-Wesley, Reading, Massachusetts, pp. 7–9. Reprinted with permission.

helpful. In this respect the programming system is not essentially different from the child's first clay pencil holder "for Daddy's office."

Third is the fascination of fashioning complex puzzle-like objects 4 of interlocking moving parts and watching them work in subtle cycles, playing out the consequences of principles built in from the beginning. The programmed computer has all the fascination of the pinball machine or the jukebox mechanism, carried to the ultimate.

Fourth is the joy of always learning, which springs from the 5 nonrepeating nature of the task. In one way or another the problem is ever new, and its solver learns something: sometimes practical, sometimes theoretical, and sometimes both.

Finally, there is the delight of working in such a tractable medium. 6 The programmer, like the poet, works only slightly removed from pure thought-stuff. He builds his castles in the air, from air, creating by exertion of the imagination. Few media of creation are so flexible, so easy to polish and rework, so readily capable of realizing grand conceptual structures. (As we shall see later, this very tractability has its own problems.)

Yet the program construct, unlike the poet's words, is real in the 7 sense that it moves and works, producing visible outputs separate from the construct itself. It prints results, draws pictures, produces sounds, moves arms. The magic of myth and legend has come true in our time. One types the correct incantation on a keyboard, and a display screen comes to life, showing things that never were nor could be.

Programming then is fun because it gratifies creative longings 8 built deep within us and delights sensibilities we have in common with all men.

Not all is delight, however, and knowing the inherent woes makes 9 it easier to bear them when they appear.

First, one must perform perfectly. The computer resembles the 10 magic of legend in this respect, too. If one character, one pause, of the incantation is not strictly in proper form, the magic doesn't work. Human beings are not accustomed to being perfect, and few areas of human activity demand it. Adjusting to the requirement for perfection is, I think, the most difficult part of learning to program.

Next, other people set one's objectives, provide one's resources, 11 and furnish one's information. One rarely controls the circumstances of his work, or even its goal. In management terms, one's authority is not sufficient for his responsibility. It seems that in all fields, however, the jobs where things get done never have formal authority commensurate with responsibility. In practice, actual (as opposed to formal) authority is acquired from the very momentum of accomplishment.

The dependence upon others has a particular case that is especially 12 painful for the system programmer. He depends upon other people's programs. These are often maldesigned, poorly implemented, incompletely delivered (no source code or test cases), and poorly documented. So he must spend hours studying and fixing things that in an ideal world would be complete, available, and usable.   13

The next woe is that designing grand concepts is fun; finding nitty little bugs is just work. With any creative activity come dreary hours of tedious, painstaking labor, and programming is no exception.

Next, one finds that debugging has a linear convergence, or   14
worse, where one somehow expects a quadratic sort of approach to the end. So testing drags on and on, the last difficult bugs taking more time to find than the first.

The last woe, and sometimes the last straw, is that the product   15
over which one has labored so long appears to be obsolete upon (or before) completion. Already colleagues and competitors are in hot pursuit of new and better ideas. Already the displacement of one's thought-child is not only conceived, but scheduled.

This always seems worse than it really is. The new and better   16
product is generally not *available* when one completes his own; it is only talked about. It, too, will require months of development. The real tiger is never a match for the paper one, unless actual use is wanted. Then the virtues of reality have a satisfaction all their own.

Of course the technological base on which one builds is *always*   17
advancing. As soon as one freezes a design, it becomes obsolete in terms of its concepts. But implementation of real products demands phasing and quantizing. The obsolescence of an implementation must be measured against other existing implementations, not against unrealized concepts. The challenge and the mission are to find real solutions to real problems on actual schedules with available resources.

This then is programming, both a tar pit in which many efforts   18
have floundered and a creative activity with joys and woes all its own.

Discussion Questions

1. What analogies does Brooks use in attempting to describe the exhilaration of programming? Are these analogies appropriate? If you are, or have been, a practitioner of the craft of programming, do you agree with him?

2. More than once, Brooks refers to the "incantation" that must be addressed to the computer. What is his purpose in using such an apparently inappropriate term?

3. One of the woes, according to Brooks, is that "debugging has a linear convergence, or worse, where one somehow expects a quadratic sort

of approach to the end." What do you think this means? Does the next sentence make his idea any clearer? How would you describe debugging in plain English?

Writing Suggestions

1. Write a companion piece on the joys — and woes — of some other craft or occupation that you have practiced. Make your description as systematic as Brooks's, describing each joy and woe in turn.

2. Frequently, there is a barrier between humanists and scientists — between people who focus on human nature and the creative imagination and people who focus on the experimental investigation of natural phenomena. (In a famous essay C. P. Snow called this situation "The Two Cultures.") Scientists (it is thought) scorn humanists as impractical dreamers, while humanists (it is thought) scorn scientists as amoral technicians. Write an essay detailing Brooks's efforts to bridge this gap in perspective, and, in particular, to write in the traditional language of humanists.

3. Reread the next to last paragraph. Brooks's language is full of technical jargon. This may be intentionally tongue-in-cheek, or Brooks may be so far trapped inside his field that he can't break out of it. Rewrite the paragraph in plain English.

ELECTRONIC TUTORS
Arthur C. Clarke

Arthur C. Clarke, one of the most prolific science and science-fiction writers, and a popular lecturer at colleges, was born in England in 1917. He had already begun his writing career when World War II intervened, during which he served as a Royal Air Force flight lieutenant at an experimental radar installation. After the war he took a degree in physics and mathematics at Kings College in London. Following a two-year stint as an editor of a science journal, he settled down to full-time writing. Clarke has written more than forty books of fiction and nonfiction, which have been translated into fifteen languages. In 1962 he won the Kalinga Prize for the popularization of science. He worked with Stanley Kubrick on *2001: A Space Odyssey,* based on his own story, "The Sentinel"; and he has worked with the American space program. He lives in Sri Lanka. "Electronic Tutors" first appeared in *Omni* magazine.

We are now witnessing one of the swiftest and most momentous 1
revolutions in the entire history of technology. For more than a
century the slide rule was the essential tool of engineers, scientists,
and anyone else whose work involved extensive calculations. Then,
just a decade ago, the invention of the pocket calculator made the
slide rule obsolete almost overnight, and with it whole libraries of
logarithmic and trigonometric tables.

There has never been so stupendous an advance in so short a
time. Simply no comparison can be made between the two devices.
The pocket calculator is millions of times more accurate and scores of
times swifter than the slide rule, and it now actually costs less. It's as if
we'd jumped overnight from bullock carts to the Concorde — and
Concorde were cheaper! No wonder the slide rule manufacturers
have gone out of business. If you have a good slide rule, leave it in
your will. It will someday be a valuable antique.

Pocket calculators are already having a profound effect on the 2
teaching of mathematics, even at the level of elementary arithmetic.
But they are about to be succeeded by devices of much greater power
and sophistication — machines that may change the very nature of
the educational system.

The great development in our near future is the portable elec- 3
tronic library — a library not only of books, but of films and music. It
will be about the size of an average book and will probably open in the
same way. One half will be the screen, with high-definition, full-color
display. The other will be a keyboard, much like one of today's
computer consoles, with the full alphabet, digits, basic mathematical
functions, and a large number of special keys — perhaps 100 keys in
all. It won't be as small as some of today's midget calculators, which
have to be operated with toothpicks.

In theory, such a device could have enough memory to hold all 4
the books in the world. But we may settle for something more modest,
like the *Encyclopaedia Britannica,* the *Oxford English Dictionary,* and
Roget's Thesaurus. (Incidentally, Peter Mark Roget was the inventor of
the log-log slide rule.) Whole additional libraries, stored in small,
plug-in memory modules, could be inserted into the portable library
when necessary. All this technology has already been developed,
though for other uses. Oddly enough, the most skilled practitioners
of this new art are the designers of video games.

Reading material may be displayed as a fixed page or else 5
"scrolled" so that it rolls upward at a comfortable reading rate. Pictures could appear as in an ordinary book, but they may eventually be
displayed as three-dimensional holographic images. Text and imagery, of course, will be accompanied by sound. Today's tape recorders

can reproduce an entire symphony on a cassette. The electronic library may be able to play back the complete works of Beethoven while displaying the scores on its screen.

And how nice to be able to summon up Lord Clark's *Civilisation* or Jacob Bronowski's *Ascent of Man* whenever or wherever you felt like it! (Yes, I know that these tapes currently cost about $2,000 apiece, unless you are lucky or wicked enough to have a pirated copy. But one day the BBC will get its money back, and thereafter the price will be peanuts.) 6

I still haven't touched on the real potential of this technology, the opportunity to cure one of the great failings in conventional education, especially in large classes. Genuine education requires feedback — interaction between pupil and teacher. At the very least, this allows the student to clear up points he does not understand. Ideally, it provides inspiration as well. Yet I recently met a Turkish engineer who said that all he had ever seen of his professor was the tiny figure up on the platform, above a sea of heads. It is a predicament shared by all too many students. 7

The electronic tutor will go a long way toward solving this problem. Some computer programs already allow the student to carry on a dialogue with the computer, asking it questions and answering the questions it asks. "Computer-aided instruction" — CAI, not to be confused with CIA — can be extremely effective. At best, the pupil may refuse to believe that he is dealing with a computer program and not with another human being. 8

Technology's influence on education is nothing new. There's an old saying that the best educational setup consists of a log with teacher at one end and pupil at the other. Our modern world is not only woefully short of teachers, it's running out of logs. But there has always been a shortage of teachers, and technology has always been used to ameliorate this — a fact that many people tend to forget. 9

The first great technological aid to education was the book. You don't have to clone teachers to multiply them. The printing press did just that, and the mightiest of all educational machines is the library. Yet this potent resource is now about to be surpassed by an even more remarkable one, a depository of knowledge as astonishing to most of us today as books were to our remote ancestors. 10

I can still recall my own amazement when, at a NASA conference less than ten years ago, I saw my first "electronic slide rule." It was a prototype of the HP 35, demonstrated to us by Dr. Bernard Oliver, vice-president of Hewlett-Packard. Though I was impressed, even awed, I did not fully realize that something revolutionary had come into the world. 11

It is quite impossible for even the most farsighted prophet to visualize all the effects of a really major technological development. 12

The telephone and the automobile produced quantum jumps in communication and transportation. They gave ordinary men a mastery over space that not even kings and emperors had possessed in the past. They changed not only the patterns of everyday life, but the physical structure of the world — the shapes of our cities, the uses of the land. This all happened in what is historically a moment of time, and the process is still accelerating. Look how the transistor radio swept across the planet within a single generation.

Though they are not yet as important as books, audiovisual aids 13 such as film strips, 16-millimeter projectors, and videotape machines are rapidly penetrating the educational field. Most of these aids are still far too expensive for developing countries, however, and I'm not sure they are really worth the cost of producing them.

Perhaps the most influential device of all is the ordinary televi- 14 sion set, whether intended for education or not. I'd be interested to know what impact *Sesame Street* has on the relatively few children of a totally different culture who see it here in Sri Lanka. Still, every TV program has some educational content; the cathode-ray tube is a window on the world — indeed, on many worlds. Often it's a very murky window, with a limited view, but I've slowly come to the conclusion that on balance even bad TV is preferable to no TV.

The power of television lies in its ability to show current events, 15 often as they are happening. But for basic educational purposes, the video recorder is much more valuable. Its pretaped programs can be repeated at any convenient time. Unfortunately, the chaos of competing systems has prevented standardization and cheap mass production.

Videotape machines, however, are far too complicated; they can 16 never be really cheap or long-lived. Video discs, which are just coming on the market, will be much cheaper. Yet I am sure that they, too, represent only a transitional stage. Eventually we will have completely solid-state memory and storage devices, with no moving parts except laser beams or electric fields. After all, the human brain doesn't have any moving parts, and it can hold an enormous amount of information. The electronic memories I'm talking about will be even more compact than the brain — and very cheap. They should be ready soon.

Consider the very brief history of the computer. The first models 17 were clumsy giants filling whole rooms, consuming kilowatts of power, and costing millions of dollars. Today, only 35 years later, far greater storage and processing capacity can be packed into a microchip measuring 1.625 square centimeters. That's miracle number one. Miracle number two is the cost of that chip: not a couple of million dollars, but about $10.

The change has already begun. Computer-aided instruction is 18 now available in many American colleges and high schools. Consoles with typewriter keyboards allow the student to "talk" to a central computer at any time of day, going through any subject when he feels like doing so, at the rate that suits him. The computer, of course, can talk to hundreds of students simultaneously, giving each the illusion that he is the center of attention. It's infinitely patient, unlike most teachers, and it's never rude or sarcastic. What a boon to slow or handicapped students!

Today's CAI consoles are big, expensive, fixed units, usually wired into the college computer. They could be portable. Already businessmen are traveling the world with attaché case-sized consoles they can plug into the telephone to talk with their office computer thousands of kilometers away. But it is the completely portable and self-contained electronic tutor that will be the next full step beyond today's pocket calculators.

Its prototype is already here, in the nurseries of the affluent West. The first computer toys, many of them looking as if they'd flown off the screen during a showing of *Star Wars*, invaded the shops last Christmas. They play ticktacktoe, challenge you to repeat simple melodies, ask questions, present elementary calculations, and await the answer — making rude noises if you get it wrong. Children love them, when they're able to wrestle them away from their parents. In 1978 they cost $50; now they're half that. Soon they'll be given away as prizes in cereal boxes.

These are toys, but they represent the wave of the future. Much more sophisticated are the pocket electronic translators that first came on the market in 1979, at about the cost of calculators five years earlier. When you type words and phrases into a little alphabetical keyboard, the translation appears on a small screen. You change languages simply by plugging in a different module. The latest models of these machines have even learned to speak. Soon they may become superb language teachers. They could listen to your pronunciation, match it with theirs, and correct you until they are satisfied.

Such devices would be specialized versions of the general-purpose pocket tutor, which will be the student's universal tool by the end of the century. It is hard to think of a single subject that could not be programmed into these devices at all levels of complexity. You'll be able to change subjects or update courses merely by plugging in different memory modules or cassettes, exactly as you can in today's programmable pocket computers.

Where does this leave the human teacher? Well, let me quote this dictum: Any teacher who can be replaced by a machine should be!

During the Middle Ages many scholars regarded printed books with apprehension. They felt that books would destroy their monopoly on knowledge. Worse still, books would permit the unwashed masses to improve their position in society, perhaps even to learn the most cherished secret of all — that no man is better than any other. And they were correct. Those of you who have seen the splendid television series *Roots,* which I hope comes to Sri Lanka someday, will recall that the slaves were strictly forbidden to learn reading and had to pretend that they were illiterate if they had secretly acquired this skill. Societies based on ignorance or repression cannot tolerate general education.

Yet the teaching profession has survived the invention of books. 25 It should welcome the development of the electronic tutor, which will take over the sheer drudgery, the tedious repetition, that are unavoidable in so much basic education. By removing the tedium from the teacher's work and making learning more like play, electronic tutors will paradoxically humanize education. If a teacher feels threatened by them, he's surely in the wrong profession.

We need mass education to drag this world out of the Stone Age, 26 and any technology, any machine, that can help do that is to be welcomed, not feared. The electronic tutor will spread across the planet as swiftly as the transistor radio, with even more momentous consequences. No social or political system, no philosophy, no culture, no religion can withstand a technology whose time has come — however much one may deplore such unfortunate side effects as the blaring tape recorders being carried by pilgrims up the sacred mountain Sri Pada. We must take the good with the bad.

When electronic tutors reach technological maturity around the 27 end of the century, they will be produced not in the millions but in the hundreds of millions and cost no more than today's pocket calculators. Equally important, they will last for years. (No properly designed solid-state device need ever wear out. I'm still using the HP 35 Dr. Oliver gave me in 1970.) So their amortized cost will be negligible; they may even be given away, with users paying only for the programs plugged into them. Even the poorest countries could afford them— especially when the reforms and improved productivity that widespread education will stimulate help those countries to pull themselves out of poverty.

Just where does this leave the schools? Already telecommunica- 28 tion is making these ancient institutions independent of space. *Sunrise Semester* and *University of the Air* can be heard far from their "campuses." The pocket tutor will complete this process, giving the student complete freedom of choice in study time as well as in work location.

We will probably still need schools to teach younger children the 29 social skills and discipline they will need as adults. But remember that educational toys are such fun that their young operators sometimes have to be dragged kicking and screaming away from their self-imposed classes.

At the other end of the spectrum, we'll still need universities for 30
many functions. You can't teach chemistry, physics, or engineering
without labs, for obvious reasons. And though we'll see more and
more global classes, even at the graduate level, electronics can never
completely convey all the nuances of personal interaction with a
capable teacher.

There will be myriads of "invisible colleges" operating through 31
the global communications networks. I remarked earlier that any
teacher who could be replaced by a machine should be. Perhaps the
same verdict should apply to any university, however ivy-covered its
walls, if it can be replaced by a global electronic network of computers
and satellite links.

But there will also be nexuses where campuses still exist. In the 32
year 2000 many thousands of students and instructors will still meet
in person, as they have done ever since the days of Plato's Academy 23
centuries ago.

Review Questions

1. What will the "electronic tutor" look like? What kind of information
   storage capacity will it have?
2. How will the "computer-aided instruction device" handle "feedback" — the interaction between teacher and student?
3. What other revolutions in technology have influenced education since
   the times of "a log with teacher at one end and pupil at the other"?
4. Why does Clarke feel that the teaching profession should not fear the
   advent of electronic tutors?
5. What types of education will conventional schools still have to handle?

Discussion Questions

1. Clarke asserts: "Any teacher who can be replaced by a machine
   should be!" Do you agree?
2. Does Clarke have any reservations about the electronic revolution in
   education? Do you? What are they?
3. Clarke argues that "No social or political system, no philosophy, no
   culture, no religion can withstand a technology whose time has
   come. . . ." Here and elsewhere, he seems to imply that the salvation of man depends on technology. Others are not so sure. How do
   you feel about this?
4. Given the technology that will soon be available, what other educational applications do you foresee, in addition to the ones cited by
   Clarke?

5. Do you think Clarke is overenthusiastic when he compares the development of electronic educational devices to the invention of the printed book? Or is the revolution truly as profound as he suggests?

6. In view of Clarke's predictions about the near-total replacement of traditional schools and universities in the not-too-distant future, does his last sentence seem to fit in with the rest of the article? How can it be reconciled with what comes before?

Writing Suggestions

1. Write a description of how the process of computerization has affected your life as a student.

2. Speculate in writing on your life as a student had you been born a generation or so later. Imagine how your own educational interests and goals would be served in an age when electronic tutors were the norm. What kind of things would you most enjoy? What kind of things (if any!) would you miss about your present education?

3. If your interests lie in this direction, research some current computer publications and other articles and write a report on some of the electronic educational aids now available.

4. Clarke's treatment of computers is serious, in contrast to Judy Mann's, which is humorous. Write a column on the subject of "Electronic Tutors," but in a humorous style like that of Mann.

TOWARD AN INTELLIGENCE BEYOND MAN'S
Robert Jastrow

Robert Jastrow, a physicist, has been since 1961 director of the National Aeronautic and Space Administration's Goddard Institute for Space Studies. Born in New York City in 1925, Jastrow was educated at Columbia University and did postdoctoral work at Leiden University, the Princeton Institute of Advanced Study, and the University of California at Berkeley. He has taught at Yale, Columbia, and Dartmouth. Most of his work has concerned astronomy and space exploration. He has written several books, including *Red Giants and White Dwarfs* and *Until the Sun Dies;* and he has won numerous awards for excellence in his field, including the NASA medal for exceptional scientific achievement. The following piece first appeared in *Time* magazine.

Reprinted by permission from *Time,* The Weekly Newsmagazine; Copyright Time Inc. 1978. First appeared February 20, 1978.

☐

As Dr. Johnson said in a different era about ladies preaching, the 1
surprising thing about computers is not that they think less well than a
man, but that they think at all. The early electronic computer did not
have much going for it except a prodigious memory and some good
math skills, but today the best models can be wired up to learn by
experience, follow an argument, ask pertinent questions and write
pleasing poetry and music. They can also carry on somewhat distracted conversations so convincingly that their human partners do
not know they are talking to a machine.

These are amiable qualities for the computer; it imitates life like 2
an electronic monkey. As computers get more complex, the imitation
gets better. Finally, the line between the original and the copy becomes blurred. In another 15 years or so — two more generations of
computer evolution, in the jargon of the technologists — we will see
the computer as an emergent form of life.

The proposition seems ridiculous because, for one thing, com- 3
puters lack the drives and emotions of living creatures. But when
drives are useful, they can be programmed into the computer's brain,
just as nature programmed them into our ancestors' brains as a part
of the equipment for survival. For example, computers, like people,
work better and learn faster when they are motivated. Arthur Samuel
made this discovery when he taught two IBM computers how to play
checkers. They polished their game by playing each other, but they
learned slowly. Finally, Dr. Samuel programmed in the will to win by
forcing the computers to try harder — and to think out more moves
in advance — when they were losing. Then the computers learned
very quickly. One of them beat Samuel and went on to defeat a
champion player who had not lost a game to a human opponent in
eight years.

Computers match people in some roles, and when fast decisions 4
are needed in a crisis, they often outclass them. The human brain has
a wiring defect that prevents it from absorbing several streams of
information simultaneously and acting on them quickly. Throw too
many things at the brain at one time and it freezes up; it evolved more
than 100,000 years ago, when the tempo of life was slower.

We are still in control, but the capabilities of computers are 5
increasing at a fantastic rate, while raw human intelligence is changing slowly, if at all. Computer power is growing exponentially; it has
increased tenfold every eight years since 1946. Four generations of
computer evolution — vacuum tubes, transistors, simple integrated
circuits and today's miracle chips — followed one another in rapid
succession, and the fifth generation, built out of such esoteric devices
as bubble memories and Josephson junctions, will be on the market in

the 1980s. In the 1990s, when the sixth generation appears, the compactness and reasoning power of an intelligence built out of silicon will begin to match that of the human brain.

By that time, ultra-intelligent machines will be working in part- 6
nership with our best minds on all the serious problems of the day, in an unbeatable combination of brute reasoning power and human intuition. What happens after that? Dartmouth President John Kemeny, a pioneer in computer usages, sees the ultimate relation between man and computer as a symbiotic union of two living species, each completely dependent on the other for survival. The computer — a new form of life dedicated to pure thought — will be taken care of by its human partners, who will minister to its bodily needs with electricity and spare parts. Man will also provide for computer reproduction, as he does today. In return, the computer will minister to our social and economic needs. Child of man's brain rather than his loins, it will become his salvation in a world of crushing complexity.

The partnership will not last very long. Computer intelligence is 7
growing by leaps and bounds, with no natural limit in sight. But human evolution is a nearly finished chapter in the history of life. The human brain has not changed, at least in gross size, in the past 100,000 years, and while the organization of the brain may have improved in that period, the amount of information and wiring that can be crammed into a cranium of fixed size is limited.

That does not mean the evolution of intelligence has ended on 8
the earth. Judging by the record of the past, we can expect that a new species will arise out of man, surpassing his achievements as he has surpassed those of his predecessor, *Homo erectus*. Only a carbon-chemistry chauvinist would assume that the new species must be man's flesh-and-blood descendants, with brains housed in fragile shells of bone. The new kind of intelligent life is more likely to be made of silicon.

The history of life suggests that the evolution of the new species 9
will take about a million years. Since the majority of the planets in the universe are not merely millions but *billions* of years older than the earth, the life they carry — assuming life to be common in the cosmos — must long since have passed through the stage we are about to enter.

A billion years is a long time in evolution; 1 billion years ago, the 10
highest form of life on the earth was a worm. The intelligent life in these other, older solar systems must be as different from us as we are from creatures wriggling in the ooze. Those superintelligent beings surely will not be housed in the more or less human shapes portrayed in *Star Wars* and *Close Encounters of the Third Kind*. In a cosmos that has endured for billions of years against man's mere million, the human form is not likely to be the standard form for intelligent life.

In any event, our curiosity may soon be satisfied. At this moment   11
a shell of TV signals carrying old *I Love Lucy* programs and *Tonight*
shows is expanding through the cosmos at the speed of light. That
bubble of broadcasts has already swept past about 50 stars like the
sun. Our neighbors know we are here, and their replies should be on
the way. In another 15 or 20 years we will receive their message and
meet our future. Let us be neither surprised nor disappointed if its
form is that of Artoo Detoo, the bright, personable canister packed
with silicon chips.

Review Questions

1. Why were computers once thought to be unable to match the thinking
   powers of human beings?
2. What are the four generations of computer evolution?
3. Why is it plausible to suppose that humanity will evolve into a new
   form of life?
4. In what way may we soon learn what our future is to be?

Discussion Questions

1. Does the prospect of computers catching up with and even surpassing
   man in intelligence make you uneasy? Do you find it hard to accept the
   idea that "human evolution is a nearly finished chapter in the history of
   life"?
2. Does Jastrow's suggestion that the human being will evolve into a
   new form of computer life seem wild speculation, or is anyone who
   thinks so a "carbon-chemistry chauvinist"?
3. What kind of evidence or reasoning does Jastrow present to support
   the theory he advances? Is it sufficient?
4. Assess Jastrow's attitude toward the evolution from carbon-based to
   silicon-based life. Does he appear to consider this with apprehension,
   with eager anticipation, or with philosophical reserve?

Writing Suggestions

1. A common theme of science fiction stories is the literal "computer
   revolution" — computers and robots running amuck and seizing control from their human inventors. (Consider, for example, Isaac Asi-
   mov's *I Robot* and the "Hal 9000" computer in Stanley Kubrick's film,
   2001: A Space Odyssey.) Write an article from some future encyclopedia giving the details of such a computer revolution and its effects on
   the world.

2. If you disagree with Jastrow and believe that computers will never replace humans, write an essay explaining why.

3. Jastrow suggests that signals from our TV shows may be speeding through the universe, reaching other, unearthly civilizations. Assume that you are an anthropologist (or a TV critic) in one of these civilizations. Write an interpretation (or a review) of one (or more) of the TV shows you receive. What can you make of the civilization that produced it?

SUMMARY, SYNTHESIS, CRITIQUE ACTIVITIES

Summary

Summarize one or more of the passages in this chapter. Follow the suggested six-step process. Take into account the answers to the Review Questions for each passage. (Recommended: "And Man Created the Chip," "Electronic Tutors.")

Synthesis

1. *Describe* some of the ways computers will change our way of life. Suggested sources: "And Man Created the Chip" and "Electronic Tutors." If you feel ambitious, you could use other sources in the chapter. You might consider also Cragan and Shields's article in the "Politics and Language" chapter.

2. *Describe* both the actual and potential power of computers as well as their limitations or problems. Refer specifically to at least three sources.

3. *Describe* the *process* by which computers have improved since they were invented and how they will continue to improve in the future. Although you will naturally deal to some extent with the effects of computers on society, keep the focus on the computer itself. Suggested sources: "And Man Created the Chip," "Electronic Tutors," and "Toward an Intelligence Beyond Man's."

4. *Compare and contrast* human and computer modes of reasoning and functioning. Suggested sources: "And Man Created the Chip" (especially the section on "How Smart Can Computers Get?"), "A Staff Writer Becomes Invalid in READ Mode," and "Toward an Intelligence Beyond Man's." What characteristics differentiate human thinking from computer "thinking"?

5. Imagine that you have stepped into a time machine and sent yourself back to the 1876 Philadelphia Exposition — a proud display of the most advanced industrial hardware. Write an address that you might give on that momentous occasion, *describing* "The Age of Computers." Key

your address to your audience — the general public very much interested in progress. What kinds of things would they be most interested in hearing about?

6. The authors of the selections in this unit write from many different perspectives: one is a newspaper columnist; one, an astronomer; one, a writer of science fiction tales; one, a computer programmer; and so on. Write a *comparison-contrast* synthesis, discussing how the background or profession of the writer has influenced both what he or she has to say and how he or she says it. Use the information in the headnotes to help you.

7. *Argue* that people will never be superseded by computers, or that they will. Your main source, naturally, will be Jastrow; but you can also draw on other pieces, such as "And Man Created the Chip," as well as your own observations and understanding.

Critique

Write a critique of Jastrow's "Toward an Intelligence Beyond Man's." Among the questions you might consider are the following:

1. What appeal or lack of appeal does his thesis have?
2. Do his predictions seem plausible?
3. What assumptions does he make about the future history of the human race? In particular, what assumptions does he make about the future development of technology? To what degree can anyone confidently make such assumptions?

RESEARCH TOPICS

1. Write a paper on how advanced computer technology may revolutionize (or make obsolete) one or more of the following:

   libraries   law
   shopping   public transportation
   medicine   education

2. Report on the development of computer technology, from ENIAC to the current state of the art.

3. Discuss the latest development in crime — theft by computer — explaining some of the methods being used to counteract it.

ADDITIONAL READINGS

Covvey, H. Dominic, and Neil Harding McAlister. *Computer Consciousness: Surviving the Automated '80s.* Reading, Mass.: Addison-Wesley, 1980.

Ditlea, Steven. "When a Computer Joins the Family." *New York Times,* 30 August 1979, III, pp. 1ff.

Hoover, Thomas. "Conversation with a Computer." *Reader's Digest,* July 1980, pp. 13ff.

"Push-button Criminals of the '80s." *U.S. News & World Report,* 22 September 1980, pp. 39–40.

Schuyten, Peter J. "New Breed Emerges in Home Computers." *New York Times,* 8 May 1980, IV, pp. 1ff.

Strother, Robert. "Crime by Computer." *Reader's Digest,* April 1976, pp. 143–48.

Vazsonyi, Andrew. *Introduction to Data Processing.* 3rd ed. Homewood, Ill.: Richard D. Irwin, 1980.

Wedemeyer, Dee. "Adapting the Workplace to Computers." *New York Times,* 23 April 1978, VIII, pp. 1ff.

Death and Dying

We all know that one day we will die, and yet we avoid thinking about the eventuality, as though it will never happen to us, as though death is something that only happens to others. Why do *we* find it so hard to discuss our own mortality? For it is not a universal dread: other people at other times have readily accepted death as a natural part of living. *Our* avoidance is a particularly modern syndrome. How other peoples have approached death, how we approach it, and how pioneers like Elisabeth Kübler-Ross have been teaching us to approach it — these are the concerns of this chapter.

As editors, we thought long and hard about whether or not to include in this book a chapter on death and dying. Several questions concerned us: should college students, at a point in their lives when they are so fresh and vital, be burdened with such somber matters? Are they equipped at all to struggle with these questions? Might teachers feel uneasy with so sensitive a subject? Arguments, pro and con, can be made for each of these questions; but we decided, in keeping with the spirit of Kübler-Ross's work, that the subject need not be morose, that young people are, in fact, both sensitive and strong enough (and in some cases, when there have been deaths in the family, even experienced enough) to express difficult and private feelings. Indeed, it is precisely the high emotional content of this subject that makes it suitable for a course in composition, a course in which you should have some investment in what you write. Often, when you are writing for someone else (such as a teacher), your prose will be flat and uninspired. But when there is something you *need* to say, you can discover the satisfaction of words carefully and sensitively chosen. You will care about your words because you will realize how important they are. So, we include the chapter on death and dying, trusting that you will receive it in the spirit we intended.

First, Joseph and Laurie Braga advise that we confront the reality of our own eventual death, for by so doing, we can give increased meaning to our life. Next, historian Philippe Ariès reveals that the attitudes and practices of our forebears were, in many ways, more mature and realistic than our own. Our own attitudes, and how they can be changed for the better, have occupied psychiatrist Elisabeth Kübler-Ross for many years. She is, in fact, one of the foremost advocates of the movement that has helped revolutionize the way Americans think about death; and it is fitting that the next few readings deal with her work. "On the Fear of Death" is Kübler-Ross's own assessment of how medical technology has helped to dehumanize death, to isolate the dying person from loved ones and familiar surroundings at the time when they are needed the most. Then, psychologist Daniel Goleman reviews the "five stages of grief" that Kübler-Ross has observed people to experience, once they know that death is approaching. Following, poet Linda Pastan and anthropologist Norman Klein provide some different (and not entirely favorable) perspectives from which to view Kübler-Ross's work. In an excerpt from "The Death of Ivan Ilyich," the great Russian novelist Leo Tolstoy gives artistic voice to many of our own hidden fears and questions. And finally, lest we become too depressed with it all, Woody Allen reminds us that it is still possible to laugh, if nervously, at the "Grim Reaper."

DEATH: THE FINAL STAGE OF GROWTH
Joseph L. Braga and Laurie D. Braga

Joseph Braga and Laurie Braga, both developmental psychologists, are on the faculty of the Department of Psychiatry at the University of Miami School of Medicine. The Bragas are authors of several books on child development and learning. This selection is part of the Foreword to Elisabeth Kübler-Ross's collection of essays, *Death: The Final Stage of Growth*.

☐

Death is a subject that is evaded, ignored, and denied by our youth-   1
worshipping, progress-oriented society. It is almost as if we have taken on death as just another disease to be conquered. But the fact is that death is inevitable. We will all die; it is only a matter of time. Death is as much a part of human existence, of human growth and development, as being born. It is one of the few things in life we can count on, that we can be assured will occur. Death is not an enemy to be conquered or a prison to be escaped. It is an integral part of our lives that gives meaning to human existence. It sets a limit on our time in this life, urging us on to do something productive with that time as long as it is ours to use.

This, then, is the meaning of *Death: the Final Stage of Growth*: All   2
that you are and all that you've done and been is culminated in your death. When you're dying, if you're fortunate enough to have some prior warning (other than that we all have all the time if we come to terms with our finiteness), you get your final chance to grow, to become more truly who you really are, to become more fully human. But you don't need to nor should you wait until death is at your

Excerpted from the foreword to *Death: The Final Stage of Growth* by Elisabeth Kübler-Ross. © 1975 by Elisabeth Kübler-Ross. Published by Prentice-Hall, Inc., Englewood Cliffs, N.J. 07632. Reprinted by permission of the publisher.

doorstep before you start to really live. If you can begin to see death as an invisible, but friendly, companion on your life's journey — gently reminding you not to wait till tomorrow to do what you mean to do — then you can learn to *live* your life rather than simply passing through it.

Whether you die at a young age or when you are older is less important than whether you have fully lived the years you have had. One person may live more in eighteen years than another does in eighty. By living, we do not mean frantically accumulating a range and quantity of experience valued in fantasy by others. Rather, we mean living each day as if it is the only one you have. We mean finding a sense of peace and strength to deal with life's disappointments and pain while always striving to discover vehicles to make more accessible, increase, and sustain the joys and delights of life. One such vehicle is learning to focus on some of the things you have learned to tune out — to notice and take joy in the budding of new leaves in the spring, to wonder at the beauty of the sun rising each morning and setting each night, to take comfort in the smile or touch of another person, to watch with amazement the growth of a child, and to share in children's wonderfully "uncomplexed," enthusiastic, and trusting approach to living. To live. 3

To rejoice at the opportunity of experiencing each new day is to prepare for one's ultimate acceptance of death. For it is those who have not really lived — who have left issues unsettled, dreams unfulfilled, hopes shattered, and who have let the real things in life (loving and being loved by others, contributing in a positive way to other people's happiness and welfare, finding out what things are *really you*) pass them by — who are most reluctant to die. It is never too late to start living and growing. This is the message delivered each year in Dickens's "Christmas Carol" — even old Scrooge, who has spent years pursuing a life without love or meaning, is able through his willing it, to change the road he's on. Growing is the human way of living, and death is the final stage in the development of human beings. For life to be valued every day, not simply near to the time of anticipated death, one's own inevitable death must be faced and accepted. We must allow death to provide a context for our lives, for in it lies the meaning of life and the key to our growth. 4

Think about your own death. How much time and energy have you put into examining your feelings, beliefs, hopes, and fears about the end of your life? What if you were told you had a limited time to live? Would it change the way you're presently conducting your life? Are there things you would feel an urgency to do before you died? Are you afraid of dying? Of death? Can you identify the sources of your fears? Consider the death of someone you love. What would you talk about to a loved one who was dying? How would you spend your 5 time together? Are you prepared to cope with all the legal details of the death of a relative? Have you talked with your family about death and dying? Are there things, emotional and practical, that you would feel a need to work out with your parents, children, siblings before your own death or theirs? Whatever the things are that would make your life more personally meaningful before you die — do them now, because you *are* going to die; and you may not have the time or energy when you get your final notice. . . .

Review Questions

1. Death "is an integral part of our lives that gives meaning to human existence." How is this so?
2. How do Braga and Braga recommend that we prepare for our death?

Discussion Questions

1. The passage begins: "Death is a subject that is evaded, ignored, and denied by our youth-worshipping, progress-oriented society." In what particular ways is this true?
2. "When you're dying . . . you get your final chance to grow, to become more truly who you really are, to become more fully human." Does this statement make sense to you? What does it mean, "to become more fully human"?
3. What are the "real things in life," according to the authors? Do you agree with this assessment? If so, why do you think you are devoting so much time and energy to other matters?
4. Do you find it grim or depressing to read or to talk about death? If so, in what ways is it depressing?
5. Do you think that the authors are being unrealistic or impractical in recommending people to look so forthrightly, so carefully at the prospect of their own death?
6. More than once the authors remind you, the reader, that you are going to die. Does this indicate a callousness of tone, perhaps a disregard of your feelings? How would you characterize the *tone* of this passage?
7. This passage might be considered an extended *definition* of death — one that is personal, rather than clinical in thrust. How would you summarize this definition, in a brief paragraph?

Writing Suggestions

1. Consider how you might spend the rest of your life if you knew that you had only a limited time to live. Consider the questions Braga and Braga pose: "Would it change the way you're presently conducting

your life? Are there things you would feel an urgency to do before you died? Are you afraid of dying? Of death? Can you identify the sources of your fears?'' Write a description of your everyday life if you were to take these questions into account.

2. Write on the next set of questions posed by the authors: ''Consider the death of someone you love. What would you talk about to a loved one who was dying? How would you spend your time together? . . . Have you talked with your family about death and dying?''

3. If you have known someone who died, and who attempted, before death, to come to terms with his mortality, write an account of this person's (and your own) experience and its significance for you.

4. Write an obituary for yourself, as it might appear in the newspaper at some point in the future. Study some actual newspaper obituaries. Try to imitate the format, the style, the tone. You may incorporate into this obituary your goals, your dreams, your priorities — but try to keep the Nobel Prizes to a maximum of one!

THE DYING MAN IS DEPRIVED OF HIS DEATH
Philippe Ariès

Philippe Ariès of Maison Lafitte, France, is the author of numerous books and articles on a wide variety of subjects, including the internationally acclaimed *Centuries of Childhood* (1962).[1] His 1973 lectures at the Johns Hopkins University Symposia in Comparative History have been published as *Western Attitudes Toward Death* (1974). Most recently, Ariès has published *The Hour of Our Death* (1981), which has been described as a ''majestically ambitious attempt to isolate, define, and synthesize a thousand years of attitudes about dying, burying, grieving, and remembering.'' David Stannard, the editor of the book from which the following article is excerpted, calls Ariès a ''storyteller of overwhelming erudition and intelligence, a sophisticated raconteur in the world of scholarship. . . .'' Ariès trained in the study of history at the Sorbonne. He describes himself as a ''weekend historian'' and earns his livelihood as a civil servant in Paris, where he is employed by the Institute of Applied Research for Tropical and Subtropical Fruits.

From ''The Reversal of Death: Changes in Attitudes Toward Death in Western Societies,'' by Philippe Ariès, translated by Valerie M. Stannard in *Death in America*, edited by David E. Stannard. Copyright © 1974 by the Trustees of The University of Pennsylvania. Reprinted by permission.
[1] Roger Sale quotes briefly from *Centuries of Childhood* in his discussion of fairy tales. See pages 183–84.

Today man is not in control of his death or the circumstances surrounding it.

☐

For thousands of years man was lord and master of his death, and the circumstances surrounding it. Today this has ceased to be so. 1

In the past It used to be understood and accepted that a man knew when he was dying, whether he became spontaneously aware of the fact or whether he had to be told. It seemed reasonable to our old storytellers that, as the plowman in La Fontaine[2] says, man would feel his approaching death. In those days death was rarely sudden, even in the case of an accident or a war, and sudden death was much feared, not only because there was no time for repentance, but because it deprived a man of the experience of death. Thus death was almost always presaged, especially since even minor illnesses often turned out to be fatal. One would have had to be mad not to see the signs, and moralists and satirists made it their job to ridicule those foolish enough to deny the evidence. Roland[3] "feels that death is taking all of him," Tristam[4] "felt that his life was draining away, he realized that he was dying." Tolstoy's peasant replied to the goodwoman who asked him if he were all right: "Death is here"; for Tolstoy's peasants died like Tristam or like La Fontaine's plowman, having the same resigned, comfortable attitude toward it. This is not to say that the attitude toward death was the same throughout all this long period of time, but that it survived in some social strata from one generation to the next despite competition from other styles of death. 2

When the person involved was not the first to become aware of his fate, others were expected to warn him. A papal document of the Middle Ages made this a task of the doctor, a task he for a long time carried out unflinchingly. We find him at Don Quixote's[5] bedside: 3

---

[2] Jean de La Fontaine (1621–1695) was a French poet and composer of the *Fables,* a famous collection of 240 poems adapted from the stories of Aesop, Phaedrus, Nevelet and others. [Behrens and Rosen]

[3] Roland was a legendary knight who died at the Battle of Ronceveaux, defending Charlemagne's rear guard. His feats are recounted in the medieval epic *The Song of Roland.*

[4] Tristam is the principal character of the early thirteenth century *Tristam and Isolde* (a story on which Wagner based an opera of the same name). Tristam, having fallen in love with the betrothed to the king, must flee. After fighting valiantly on a battlefield, he is mortally wounded. By the time Isolde arrives, Tristam has died; his love, out of despair, dies as well.

[5] Don Quixote is the principal character of Cervantes's (1547–1616) classic *Don Quixote de la Mancha,* the story of an old man who, having read too many tales of romance and chivalry, dons his rusty armor and sets out to become a knight-errant. After numerous adventures, Don Quixote realizes the folly of his quest and returns home to die peacefully, making no attempt to flee from his death.

"He took his pulse, and was not happy with the results. He therefore told him that whatever he did, he should think of saving his soul, as his body was in grave danger." The *artes moriendi*[6] of the fifteenth century also charged with this task the "spiritual" friend (as opposed to "carnal" friends), who went by the name — so repugnant to our modern fastidiousness — of *nuncius mortis*.[7]

As man progressed through time, the higher up the social and urban ladder he climbed, the less he himself was aware of his approaching death, and the more he had to be prepared for it; consequently, the more he had to depend on those around him. The doctor renounced the role that for so long had been his, probably in the eighteenth century. In the nineteenth century he spoke only when questioned, and then somewhat reticently. Friends no longer had to intervene, as in the time of Gerson[8] or even Cervantes, because from the seventeenth century on, it was the family that took care of this — a sign of development in family feeling. An example of this can be seen in the de La Ferronnays household in 1848. Mme. de La Ferronnays[9] had fallen ill. The doctor announced that her condition was dangerous, and "one hour later, hopeless." Her daughter wrote: "When she came out of the bath . . . she suddenly said to me, while I was thinking of a good way to tell her what the doctor thought: 'but I can't see anything any more, I think I'm going to die.' She immediately recited an ejaculatory prayer. 'Oh Jesus,'" the daughter then remarked, "'what a strange joy I felt from those calm words at such a terrible time.'" She was relieved because she had been spared the distress of making a nevertheless indispensable disclosure. The relief is a modern characteristic, the necessity to disclose the truth is ancient.

Not only was the dying man to be deprived of his death, he also had to preside over it. As people were born in public, so did they die in public, and not only the king, as is well known from Saint-Simon's[10] famous pages on the death of Louis XIV, but everyone. Countless engravings and paintings depict that scene for us. As soon as someone "was helplessly sick in bed," his room filled with people — parents, children, friends, neighbors, fellow guild members. The windows and shutters were closed. Candles were lit. When passersby in the streets

4

5

---

[6] *artes moriendi* — literally, arts (or skills) of the dying.

[7] *nuncius mortis* — announcer of death.

[8] Jean de Gerson (1363–1429) was a French theologian and chancellor of the University of Paris.

[9] de La Ferronays — a family, during the 1840s, which was decimated by tuberculosis.

[10] Louis de Rouvroy, duc de Saint-Simon (1675–1755), was a French prose writer whose masterpiece, *Mémoires*, contains extensive accounts of the reign of Louis XIV, including the obituary of the king.

met a priest carrying the *viaticum*,[11] custom and piety demanded that they follow him into the dying man's room, even if he was a stranger. The approach of death transformed the room of a dying man into a sort of public place. Pascal's[12] remark, "man will die alone," which has lost much of its impact on us since today man almost always dies alone, can only be understood in this context. For what Pascal meant was that in spite of all the people crowded around his bed, the dying man was alone. The enlightened doctors of the end of the eighteenth century, who believed in the qualities of fresh air, complained a great deal about this bad habit of crowding into the rooms of sick people. They tried to have the windows opened, the candles snuffed, and the crowd of people turned out.

We should not make the mistake of thinking that to be present at 6
these last moments was a devout custom prescribed by the Church. The enlightened or reformed priests had tried, long before the doctors, to do away with this crowd so that they could better prepare the sick person for a virtuous end. As early as the *artes moriendi* of the fifteenth century it had been recommended that the dying man be left alone with God so that he should not be distracted from the care of his soul. And again, in the nineteenth century, it sometimes happened that very pious people, after yielding to the custom, asked the numerous onlookers to leave the room, all except the priest, so that nothing would disturb their private conversation with God. But these were rare examples of extreme devotion. Custom prescribed that death was to be marked by a ritual ceremony in which the priest would have his place, but only as one of many participants. The leading role went to the dying man himself. He presided over the affair with hardly a misstep, for he knew how to conduct himself, having previously witnessed so many similar scenes. He called to him one by one his relatives, his friends, his servants, "even down to the lowliest," Saint-Simon said, describing the death of Mme. de Montespan. He said farewell to them, asked their pardon, gave them his blessing. Invested with sovereign authority by the approach of death, especially in the eighteenth and nineteenth centuries, the dying person gave orders and advice, even when this dying person was a very young girl, almost a child.

Today nothing remains either of the sense that everyone has or 7
should have his impending death, or of the public solemnity sur-

---

[11] *viaticum* — literally meaning the money for a journey, the term is now used for the Eucharist, given to the dying person as a provision for the journey to the next world.

[12] Blaise Pascal (1623–1662) was a French mathematician, physicist, religious philosopher, and writer.

rounding the moment of death. What used to be appreciated is now hidden; what used to be solemn is now avoided.

It is understood that the primary duty of the family and the doctor is to conceal the seriousness of his condition from the person who is to die. The sick person must no longer ever know (except in very rare cases) that his end is near. The new custom dictates that he die in ignorance. This is not merely a habit that has innocently crept into the customs — it has become a moral requirement. Vladimir Jankélévitch confirmed this unequivocally during a recent colloquium of doctors on the subject: "Should we lie to the patient?" "The liar," he stated, "is the one who tells the truth. . . . I am against the truth, passionately against the truth. . . . For me, the most important law of all is the law of love and charity."[13] Was this quality then lacking prior to the twentieth century, since ethics made it obligatory to inform the patient? In such opposition we see the extent of this extraordinary reversal of feelings, and then of ideas. How did this come about? It would be too hasty to say that in a society of happiness and well-being there is no longer any room for suffering, sadness and death. To say this is to mistake the result for the cause.

It is strange that this change is linked to the development in family feelings, and to the emotional centrality of the family in our world. In fact, the cause for the change must be sought in the relationship between a sick person and his family. The family has no longer been able to tolerate the blow it had to deal to a loved one, and the blow it also had to deal to itself, in bringing death closer and making it more certain, in forbidding all deception and illusion. How many times have we heard it said of a spouse or a parent: "At least I had the satisfaction of knowing that he never felt he was dying"? *This "not feeling oneself dying" has in our everyday language replaced the "feeling one's impending death" of the seventeenth century.*

In point of fact, it must happen quite often — but the dead never tell — that the sick person knows quite well what is happening, and pretends not to know for the sake of those around him. For if the family has loathed to play *nuncius mortis,* a role which in the Middle Ages and at the beginning of modern times it was not asked to play, the main actor has also abdicated. Through fear of death? But death has always existed. Only it used to be laughed at — "What haste you are in, O cruel goddess!" — while society compelled the terrified dying man nevertheless to act out the great scene of farewells and departure. Some say this fear is innate, but its suppression is equally innate. The fear of death does not explain why the dying man turns

---

[13] *Médecine de France,* 177 (1966), 3–16, repr. in Jankélévitch, *La mort* (Paris: Flammarion, 1966). [Ariès]

his back on his own death. Again we must seek for the explanation in the history of the family.

The man of the late Middle Ages and the Renaissance (as op- 11 posed to the man of the early Middle Ages, like Roland, who still lives in Tolstoy's peasants) insisted on participating in his own death, because he saw in his death the moment when his individuality received its ultimate form. He was master over his life only insofar as he was master over his death. His death was his, and his alone. However, beginning with the seventeenth century he no longer had sole sovereignty over his own life and, consequently, over his death. He shared his death with his family, whereas previously his family had been isolated from the serious decisions he, and he alone, had to make regarding his death.

Last wills and testaments are a case in point. From the fourteenth 12 century to the beginning of the eighteenth century, the will was one way for each person to express himself freely while at the same time it was a token of defiance — or lack of confidence — with regard to his family. Thus, when in the eighteenth century family affection triumphed over the traditional mistrust by the testator of his inheritors, the last will and testament lost its character of moral necessity and personal warm testimony. This was, on the contrary, replaced by such an absolute trust that there was no longer any need for written wills. The last spoken wishes became at long last sacred to the survivors, and they considered themselves to be committed from then on to respect these wishes to the letter. For his part, the dying man was satisfied that he could rest in peace on the word of his close ones. This trust that began in the seventeenth and eighteenth centuries and was developed in the nineteenth century, has in the twentieth century turned into alienation. As soon as serious danger threatens one member of a family, the family immediately conspires to deprive him of information and thus his freedom. The patient then becomes a minor, like a child or a mental defective, to be taken into charge and separated from the rest of the world by his spouse or parents. They know better than he what he should do and know. He is deprived of his rights, specifically the formerly essential right of knowing about his death, of preparing for it, of organizing it. And he lets this happen because he is convinced that it is for his own good. He relies on the affection of his family. If, in spite of everything, he does guess the truth, he will pretend to not know it. Death used to be a tragedy — often comic — acted out for the benefit of a man who was about to die. Today, death is a comedy — always tragic — acted out for the benefit of a man who does not know he is about to die.

Without the progress of medicine the pressure of family feeling 13 would probably not have been sufficient to make death disappear so quickly and so completely. Not so much because of the real conquests made by medicine as because, as a result of medicine, in the mind of the sick man death has been replaced by illness. This substitution first appeared in the second half of the nineteenth century. When the dying peasant in Tolstoy's *Three Deaths* (1859) was asked where he hurt, he replied: "I hurt all over, death is here; that's what it is." On the other hand Ivan Ilych (1886), after overhearing a conversation that could leave him in no doubt, continues to think obstinately of his floating kidney, of his infected appendix, which can be cured by the doctor or the surgeon. The illness has become the focus of illusion. His wife treats him like a child who is disobeying the doctor's orders: he is not taking his medicine properly, that is why he is not getting better.

Moreover, it is clear that, with the advancements in therapeutics and surgery, it has become increasingly more difficult to be certain that a serious illness is fatal; the chances of recovering from it have increased so much. Even with diminished capacities, one can still live. Thus, in our world where everyone acts as though medicine is the answer to everything — where even though Caesar must die one day, there is absolutely no reason for oneself to die — incurable diseases, particularly cancer, have taken on the hideous, terrifying aspects of the old representations of death. More than the skeleton or mummy of the *macabres*[14] of the fourteenth and fifteenth centuries, more than the leper with his bell, cancer today is death. However, the disease must be incurable (or thought to be so) in order for death to be allowed to come forward and take on its name. The anguish this releases forces society to hurriedly intensify its customary demands of silence, and thus to bring this overly dramatic situation to the banal level of an afternoon walk.

People die, then, in secret — more alone than Pascal ever imagined. This secrecy results from refusing to admit the imminent death of a loved one by concealing it beneath the veil of a persistent disease. There is another aspect of this secrecy that American sociologists have succeeded in interpreting. What we have been inclined to view as avoidance, they have shown to be the empirical establishment of a style of dying in which discretion appears as the modern form of dignity. It is, with less poetry, the death of Mélisande,[15] a death of which Jankélévitch would approve.

14

15

---

[14] *macabres* — art of the fourteenth through sixteenth centuries that portrayed death in the form of a mummy, or partly decomposed cadaver.

[15] Mélisande is a character in Maurice Maeterlink's play *Pelleas and Mélisande* (1893). Mélisande, a gentle, loving woman who has no concept of good or evil, dies after the premature death of her child.

A study has been made by Barney G. Glaser and Anselm L. 16
Strauss in six hospitals in the San Francisco Bay Area of the reactions
toward death of the interdependent group of the patient, his family
and the medical personnel (doctors and nurses).[16] What happens
when it is known that the patient is nearing his end? Should the family
be notified, or the patient himself, and when? For how long should
life be prolonged by artificial means, and at what point should the
individual be permitted to die? How does the medical staff behave
toward a patient who does not know, or who pretends not to know, or
who does know that he is dying? These problems no doubt arise in
every modern family, but within the confines of a hospital, a new
authority intervenes: the medical authority. Today people are dying
less and less at home, more and more in hospitals; indeed, the hospital has become the modern place for dying, which is why Glaser and
Strauss' observations are important. However, the scope of their book
goes beyond empirical analyses of attitudes. The authors have discovered a new ideal way of dying which has replaced the theatrical
ceremonies of the Romantic era and, in a more general way, of the
traditional public nature of death. There is a new model for dying
which they explain almost naively, comparing it with their concrete
observations. Thus we see taking shape a "style of dying," or rather an
"acceptable style of living while dying," an "acceptable style of facing
death." The accent is placed on the word "acceptable." It is essential,
indeed, that the death be such that it can be accepted or tolerated by
the survivors.

If doctors and nurses (the nurses with more reticence) delay for 17
as long as possible notifying the family, if they are reluctant to notify
the patient himself, the reason is that they are afraid of becoming
caught up in a chain of sentimental reactions that would bring about a
loss of self-control, their own as much as that of the patient or the
family. To dare to speak of death, to admit death into social relations,
is no longer, as in former times, to leave the everyday world undisturbed; it brings about an exceptional, outrageous and always dramatic situation. Death used to be a familiar figure, and moralists had
to make him hideous in order to create fear. Now the word has only to
be mentioned to provoke an emotive tension incompatible with the
equilibrium of everyday life. "An acceptable style of dying," then, is
one that avoids "status-forcing scenes," scenes that tear the person out
of his social role, that violate his social role. These scenes are patients'
crises of despair, their cries, their tears, and in general, any demon-
strations that are too impassioned, too noisy or even too moving, that
might upset the serenity of the hospital. This would be the "embarrass-

---

[16] *Awareness of Dying* (Chicago: Aldine, 1965). [Ariès]

ingly graceless dying," the style of dying that would embarrass the survivors, the opposite of the acceptable style of dying. It is in order to avoid this that nothing is said to the patient. Basically, however, what is essential is less whether the patient does or does not know, but rather, that if he does know he should have the good taste and the courage to be discreet. He should behave in such a manner that the hospital staff can forget that he knows, and can communicate with him as though death were not hovering about them. Communication is, in fact, an equally necessary factor. It is not enough for the patient to be discreet, he must also be open and receptive to messages. His indifference might set up the same "embarrassment" among the medical personnel as would an excess of demonstration. There are, then, two ways to die badly: one consists of seeking an exchange of emotions; the other is to refuse to communicate.

The authors very earnestly cite the case of an old woman who 18 conducted herself very well at first, according to convention: she cooperated with the doctors and nurses, and fought bravely against her illness. Then one day she decided that she had fought enough, the time had come to give up. She closed her eyes and did not open them again; in this way she was signifying that she was withdrawing from the world, and was awaiting her end alone. Formerly this sign of introspection would have surprised no one and would have been respected. In the California hospital, it drove the doctors and nurses to despair, and they quickly sent for one of the patient's sons to come by plane, he being the only person capable of persuading her to open her eyes and not go on "hurting everybody." Patients also sometimes turn toward the wall and remain in that position. This is recognizable, not without emotion, as one of man's oldest gestures when he feels death approaching. The Jews of the Old Testament died this way and, even in the sixteenth century, the Spanish Inquisition recognized by this sign an unconverted Marrano.[17] Tristam died in this way: "He turned toward the wall and said: 'I can hold on to my life no longer.' " Nevertheless, in our time the doctors and nurses of a California hospital saw in this ancient gesture nothing but an antisocial refusal to communicate, an unpardonable renouncement of the vital struggle.

We should realize that the surrender of the patient is censured 19 not only because it demoralizes the medical personnel, representing as it does a failure to meet a moral obligation, but also because it supposedly reduces the capacity for resistance of the patient himself. It thus becomes as much to be feared as the "status-forcing scenes." This is why, today, American and British doctors are less often hiding the seriousness of their case from terminal patients. This year British

---

[17] Marrano — a Christianized Jew or Moor of medieval Spain, especially one who accepted conversion only to escape persecution.

television broadcast a program on cancer patients who had been apprised very accurately of their situation; this broadcast was intended as an encouragement to tell the truth. The doctors probably think that a man who has been told, if he is stable, will be more willing to undergo treatment in the hope of living to the full his last remaining days and, when all is said and done, will die just as discreetly and with as much dignity as if he had known nothing. This is the death of the good American, as described by Jacques Maritain in a book designed for the American public: he is led by the medical personnel "to think in a sort of dream, that the act of dying amid happy smiles, amid white garments like angels' wings would be a veritable pleasure, a moment of no consequence: relax, take it easy, it's nothing." This is also, with a little less of the commercial smile and a little more music, the humanistic, dignified death of the contemporary philosopher: to disappear *"pianissimo*[18] and, so to speak, on tiptoe" (Jankélévitch).

Review Questions

1. In times past, what was the role of the dying man at his death? Of his family? His doctor? His priest? Why were these functions considered necessary?
2. What reasons does Ariès suggest are responsible for the shift from a ceremonial death to the conspiracy of silence and secrecy now often surrounding the dying?
3. What is the role of modern medicine in helping to "deprive" the dying man of his death?
4. What is "an acceptable way of dying," as revealed by the study of dying patients in the San Francisco Bay Area hospital study? What is Ariès's attitude toward this "acceptable" style?

Discussion Questions

1. What is the meaning of Ariès's title, "The Dying Man Is Deprived of His Death"?
2. Ariès offers and then rejects one reason for the change of attitude toward death: "In a society of happiness and well-being there is no longer any room for suffering, sadness and death." Do you see a significant relationship between a society of "happiness and well-being" and our attitudes toward death? Are we trying to wish death away by pretending it doesn't exist?
3. What does Ariès mean when he writes: "Death used to be a tragedy — often comic — acted out for the benefit of a man who was

---

[18] *pianissimo* — a musical term meaning very softly.

about to die. Today, death is a comedy — always tragic — acted out for the benefit of a man who does not know he is about to die"?

4. In the first part of this passage, a great many examples are given to illustrate attitudes toward death. How are these examples organized?

5. What are the main parts of this essay? Pay particular attention to the transitions between the parts, to the order of examples, and to the pattern of cause and effect.

6. Is this an entirely objective analysis, or does Ariès inject his own point of view? If so, how?

7. Does Ariès convince you that one way of dying is to be preferred to another way? Explain.

Writing Suggestions

1. Should the patient be told he is dying? More than ever before, this has become an agonizing question for family members and for doctors. Research this matter, as it has been treated in recent magazine and newspaper articles. Focus on particular cases and upon the opinions of those who have been intimately involved in such decisions. Write a summary of your findings.

2. Select a small number of fictional works (short stories, novels, plays, films) that deal in whole or in part with death and the dying. What kind of attitudes are dramatized? What attitudes are apparently held by the authors? In what ways are the attitudes of the characters and the authors characteristic of their times? Compare and contrast one or more of these aspects.

ON THE FEAR OF DEATH
Elisabeth Kübler-Ross

Elisabeth Kübler-Ross has been one of the foremost advocates of the movement that has helped revolutionize the way Americans think about death. Born in Zurich, Switzerland, in 1926, she received her M.D. degree from the University of Zurich in 1957, and came to the United States as an intern the following year. (She holds dual Swiss-American citizenship today.) She began her work with terminally ill patients while teaching psychiatry at the University of Chicago Medical School, later organizing seminars for doctors, nurses, and social workers at Chicago's Billings Hospital. The results of this work were reported in *On Death and Dying* (1969), her first and most well known book. Since that time, Kübler-Ross has traveled around the world many times, giving seminars, workshops, and lectures on death and dying. During the 1970s she began to turn her interest to the question of life after death; and for many of her former medical colleagues, her work became too mystical. At present, she heads "Shanti Nilaya" (Sanskrit for "home of peace"), an organization she founded in 1976, north of Escondido, California, "dedicated to the promotion of physical, emotional, and spiritual health." Other books by Kübler-Ross are *Questions and Answers on Death and Dying* (1974); *Death: The Final Stage of Growth* (1975), a collection of essays, poems, and letters, some by former patients; and *To Live Until We Say Goodbye* (1978), a volume of photographs of dying patients, with text by Kübler-Ross.

□

Epidemics have taken a great toll of lives in past generations. Death in infancy and early childhood was frequent and there were few families who didn't lose a member of the family at an early age. Medicine has changed greatly in the last decades. Widespread vaccinations have practically eradicated many illnesses, at least in western Europe and the United States. The use of chemotherapy, especially the antibiotics, has contributed to an ever decreasing number of fatalities in infectious diseases. Better child care and education has effected a low morbidity and mortality among children. The many diseases that have taken an impressive toll among the young and middle-aged have been conquered. The number of old people is on the rise, and with this fact come the number of people with malignancies and chronic diseases associated more with old age. 1

Pediatricians have less work with acute and life-threatening situations as they have an ever increasing number of patients with psychosomatic disturbances and adjustment and behavior problems. Physicians have more people in their waiting rooms with emotional problems than they have ever had before, but they also have more elderly patients who not only try to live with their decreased physical abilities and limitations but who also face loneliness and isolation with all its pains and anguish. The majority of these people are not seen by a psychiatrist. Their needs have to be elicited and gratified by other professional people, for instance, chaplains and social workers. It is for them that I am trying to outline the changes that have taken place in the last few decades, changes that are ultimately responsible for the increased fear of death, the rising number of emotional problems, and the greater need for understanding of and coping with the problems of death and dying. 2

When we look back in time and study old cultures and people, we   3
are impressed that death has always been distasteful to man and will
probably always be. From a psychiatrist's point of view this is very
understandable and can perhaps best be explained by our basic
knowledge that, in our unconscious, death is never possible in regard
to ourselves. It is inconceivable for our unconscious to imagine an
actual ending of our own life here on earth, and if this life of ours has
to end, the ending is always attributed to a malicious intervention
from the outside by someone else. In simple terms, in our unconscious mind we can only be killed; it is inconceivable to die of a natural
cause or of old age. Therefore death in itself is associated with a bad
act, a frightening happening, something that in itself calls for retribution and punishment.

One is wise to remember these fundamental facts as they are   4
essential in understanding some of the most important, otherwise
unintelligible communications of our patients.

The second fact that we have to comprehend is that in our   5
unconscious mind we cannot distinguish between a wish and a deed.
We are all aware of some of our illogical dreams in which two completely opposite statements can exist side by side — very acceptable in
our dreams but unthinkable and illogical in our wakening state. Just as
our unconscious mind cannot differentiate between the wish to kill
somebody in anger and the act of having done so, the young child is
unable to make this distinction. The child who angrily wishes his
mother to drop dead for not having gratified his needs will be trau-
matized greatly by the actual death of his mother — even if this event
is not linked closely in time with his destructive wishes. He will always
take part or the whole blame for the loss of his mother. He will always
say to himself — rarely to others — "I did it, I am responsible, I was
bad, therefore Mommy left me." It is well to remember that the child
will react in the same manner if he loses a parent by divorce, separation, or desertion. Death is often seen by a child as an impermanent
thing and has therefore little distinction from a divorce in which he
may have an opportunity to see a parent again.

Many a parent will remember remarks of their children such as,   6
"I will bury my doggy now and next spring when the flowers come up
again, he will get up." Maybe it was the same wish that motivated the
ancient Egyptians to supply their dead with food and goods to keep
them happy and the old American Indians to bury their relatives with
their belongings.

When we grow older and begin to realize that our omnipotence is   7
really not so omnipotent, that our strongest wishes are not powerful
enough to make the impossible possible, the fear that we have contributed to the death of a loved one diminishes — and with it the guilt.
The fear remains diminished, however, only so long as it is not

challenged too strongly. Its vestiges can be seen daily in hospital corridors and in people associated with the bereaved.

A husband and wife may have been fighting for years, but when 8
the partner dies, the survivor will pull his hair, whine and cry louder and beat his chest in regret, fear and anguish, and will hence fear his own death more than before, still believing in the law of talion — an eye for an eye, a tooth for a tooth — "I am responsible for her death, I will have to die a pitiful death in retribution."

Maybe this knowledge will help us understand many of the old 9
customs and rituals which have lasted over the centuries and whose purpose is to diminish the anger of the gods or the people as the case may be, thus decreasing the anticipated punishment. I am thinking of the ashes, the torn clothes, the veil, the *Klage Weiber*[1] of the old days — they are all means to ask you to take pity on them, the mourners, and are expressions of sorrow, grief, and shame. If someone grieves, beats his chest, tears his hair, or refuses to eat, it is an attempt at self-punishment to avoid or reduce the anticipated punishment for the blame that he takes on the death of a loved one.

This grief, shame, and guilt are not very far removed from 10
feelings of anger and rage. The process of grief always includes some qualities of anger. Since none of us likes to admit anger at a deceased person, these emotions are often disguised or repressed and prolong the period of grief or show up in other ways. It is well to remember that it is not up to us to judge such feelings as bad or shameful but to understand their true meaning and origin as something very human. In order to illustrate this I will again use the example of the child — and the child in us. The five-year-old who loses his mother is both blaming himself for her disappearance and being angry at her for having deserted him and for no longer gratifying his needs. The dead person then turns into something the child loves and wants very much but also hates with equal intensity for this severe deprivation.

The ancient Hebrews regarded the body of a dead person as 11
something unclean and not to be touched. The early American Indians talked about the evil spirits and shot arrows in the air to drive the spirits away. Many other cultures have rituals to take care of the "bad" dead person, and they all originate in this feeling of anger which still exists in all of us, though we dislike admitting it. The tradition of the tombstone may originate in this wish to keep the bad spirits deep down in the ground, and the pebbles that many mourners put on the grave are left-over symbols of the same wish. Though we call the firing of guns at military funerals a last salute, it is the same

---

[1] *Klage Weiber* — German for the lamentation, or shrieking, of women, that would follow the death of someone in the community. [Behrens and Rosen]

symbolic ritual as the Indian used when he shot his spears and arrows into the skies.

I give these examples to emphasize that man has not basically changed. Death is still a fearful, frightening happening, and the fear of death is a universal fear even if we think we have mastered it on many levels.   12

What has changed is our ways of coping and dealing with death and dying and our dying patients.   13

Having been raised in a country in Europe where science is not so advanced, where modern techniques have just started to find their way into medicine, and where people still live as they did in this country half a century ago, I may have had an opportunity to study a part of the evolution of mankind in a shorter period.   14

I remember as a child the death of a farmer. He fell from a tree and was not expected to live. He asked simply to die at home, a wish that was granted without questioning. He called his daughters into the bedroom and spoke with each one of them alone for a few moments. He arranged his affairs quietly, though he was in great pain, and distributed his belongings and his land, none of which was to be split until his wife should follow him in death. He also asked each of his children to share in the work, duties, and tasks that he had carried on until the time of the accident. He asked his friends to visit him once more, to bid good-bye to them. Although I was a small child at the time, he did not exclude me or my siblings. We were allowed to share in the preparations of the family just as we were permitted to grieve with them until he died. When he did die, he was left at home, in his own beloved home which he had built, and among his friends and neighbors who went to take a last look at him where he lay in the midst of flowers in the place he had lived in and loved so much. In that country today there is still no make-believe slumber room, no embalming, no false makeup to pretend sleep. Only the signs of very disfiguring illnesses are covered up with bandages and only infectious cases are removed from the home prior to the burial.   15

Why do I describe such "old-fashioned" customs? I think they are an indication of our acceptance of a fatal outcome, and they help the dying patient as well as his family to accept the loss of a loved one. If a patient is allowed to terminate his life in the familiar and beloved environment, it requires less adjustment for him. His own family knows him well enough to replace a sedative with a glass of his favorite wine; or the smell of a home-cooked soup may give him the appetite to sip a few spoons of fluid which, I think, is still more enjoyable than an infusion. I will not minimize the need for sedatives and infusions and realize full well from my own experience as a country doctor that they are sometimes life-saving and often unavoidable. But I also know that patience and familiar people and foods   16 could replace many a bottle of intravenous fluids given for the simple reason that it fulfills the physiological need without involving too many people and/or individual nursing care.

The fact that children are allowed to stay at home where a fatality 17 has stricken and are included in the talk, discussions, and fears gives them the feeling that they are not alone in the grief and gives them the comfort of shared responsibility and shared mourning. It prepares them gradually and helps them view death as part of life, an experience which may help them grow and mature.

This is in great contrast to a society in which death is viewed as 18 taboo, discussion of it is regarded as morbid, and children are excluded with the presumption and pretext that it would be "too much" for them. They are then sent off to relatives, often accompanied with some unconvincing lies of "Mother has gone on a long trip" or other unbelievable stories. The child senses that something is wrong, and his distrust in adults will only multiply if other relatives add new variations of the story, avoid his questions or suspicions, shower him with gifts as a meager substitute for a loss he is not permitted to deal with. Sooner or later the child will become aware of the changed family situation and, depending on the age and personality of the child, will have an unresolved grief and regard this incident as a frightening, mysterious, in any case very traumatic experience with untrustworthy grownups, which he has no way to cope with.

It is equally unwise to tell a little child who lost her brother that 19 God loved little boys so much that he took little Johnny to heaven. When this little girl grew up to be a woman she never solved her anger at God, which resulted in a psychotic depression when she lost her own little son three decades later.

We would think that our great emancipation, our knowledge of 20 science and of man, has given us better ways and means to prepare ourselves and our families for this inevitable happening. Instead the days are gone when a man was allowed to die in peace and dignity in his own home.

The more we are making advancements in science, the more we 21 seem to fear and deny the reality of death. How is this possible?

We use euphemisms, we make the dead look as if they were 22 asleep, we ship the children off to protect them from the anxiety and turmoil around the house if the patient is fortunate enough to die at home, we don't allow children to visit their dying parents in the hospitals, we have long and controversial discussions about whether patients should be told the truth — a question that rarely arises when the dying person is tended by the family physician who has known him from delivery to death and who knows the weaknesses and strengths of each member of the family.

I think there are many reasons for this flight away from facing 23 death calmly. One of the most important facts is that dying nowadays is more gruesome in many ways, namely, more lonely, mechanical, and dehumanized; at times it is even difficult to determine technically when the time of death has occurred.

Dying becomes lonely and impersonal because the patient is often taken out of his familiar environment and rushed to an emergency room. Whoever has been very sick and has required rest and comfort especially may recall his experience of being put on a stretcher and enduring the noise of the ambulance siren and hectic rush until the hospital gates open. Only those who have lived through this may appreciate the discomfort and cold necessity of such transportation which is only the beginning of a long ordeal — hard to endure when you are well, difficult to express in words when noise, light, pumps, and voices are all too much to put up with. It may well be that we might consider more the patient under the sheets and blankets and perhaps stop our well-meant efficiency and rush in order to hold the patient's hand, to smile, or to listen to a question. I include the trip to the hospital as the first episode in dying, as it is for many. I am putting it exaggeratedly in contrast to the sick man who is left at home — not to say that lives should not be saved if they can be saved by a hospitalization but to keep the focus on the patient's experience, his needs and his reactions. 24

When a patient is severely ill, he is often treated like a person with no right to an opinion. It is often someone else who makes the decision if and when and where a patient should be hospitalized. It would take so little to remember that the sick person too has feelings, has wishes and opinions, and has — most important of all — the right to be heard. 25

Well, our presumed patient has now reached the emergency room. He will be surrounded by busy nurses, orderlies, interns, residents, a lab technician perhaps who will take some blood, an electrocardiogram technician who takes the cardiogram. He may be moved to X-ray and he will overhear opinions of his condition and discussions and questions to members of the family. He slowly but surely is beginning to be treated like a thing. He is no longer a person. Decisions are made often without his opinion. If he tries to rebel he will be sedated and after hours of waiting and wondering whether he has the strength, he will be wheeled into the operating room or intensive treatment unit and become an object of great concern and great financial investment. 26

He may cry for rest, peace, and dignity, but he will get infusions, transfusions, a heart machine, or tracheostomy if necessary. He may want one single person to stop for one single minute so that he can ask one single question — but he will get a dozen people around the clock, all busily preoccupied with his heart rate, pulse, electrocardio- 27 gram or pulmonary functions, his secretions or excretions but not with him as a human being. He may wish to fight it all but it is going to be a useless fight since all this is done in the fight for his life, and if they can save his life they can consider the person afterwards. Those who consider the person first may lose precious time to save his life! At least this seems to be the rationale or justification behind all this — or is it? Is the reason for this increasingly mechanical, depersonalized approach our own defensiveness? Is this approach our own way to cope with and repress the anxieties that a terminally or critically ill patient evokes in us? Is our concentration on equipment, on blood pressure our desperate attempt to deny the impending death which is so frightening and discomforting to us that we displace all our knowledge onto machines, since they are less close to us than the suffering face of another human being which would remind us once more of our lack of omnipotence, our own limits and failures, and last but not least perhaps our own mortality?

Maybe the question has to be raised: Are we becoming less human or more human? Though this book is in no way meant to be judgmental, it is clear that whatever the answer may be, the patient is suffering more — not physically, perhaps, but emotionally. And his needs have not changed over the centuries, only our ability to gratify them. 28

Review Questions

1. What changes during the past few decades have necessitated a new attention to the emotional problems of old age and death?
2. In what ways are guilt, shame and punishment (as well as grief) associated with death?
3. What purpose is served by the forms and rituals associated with death — such as tombstones and the firing of guns at military funerals?
4. Why does Kübler-Ross prefer some of the "old-fashioned" customs surrounding death?
5. Why does Kübler-Ross object to the way that children are often excluded from contact with, or discussion about, the dying?
6. In what ways has our modern medical technology made the process of dying "lonely, mechanical, and dehumanized"?

Discussion Questions

1. Why should advanced, technological cultures be less realistic or mature about dealing with death and dying than less advanced ones?
2. In what ways does the idea of death most disturb you?

3. Kübler-Ross says that a person dying at home, in the company of his family, may well be provided with a glass of wine or a bowl of soup in place of a sedative or an infusion (which might, medically, be more beneficial). This raises a larger question: to what extent (if at all) should there be a trade-off between prolonging life and allowing a person to die with dignity? What, in fact, does dying "with dignity" mean? At what point does life no longer become the most important consideration?

4. In this passage, Kübler-Ross uses a number of different rhetorical devices: example, description, comparison-contrast, cause and effect, argument. Find passages that exemplify some of these devices.

5. Paragraph 1 has no topic sentence, per se, though one is implied. What is it?

6. From this passage, you should be able to infer a good deal about the character of the author. What qualities do you find that you think would make her a good psychiatrist? What passages, in particular, make you think so?

7. Kübler-Ross ends this passage with a series of questions. Why doesn't she answer them?

Writing Suggestion

Research the rituals and practices associated with death in another culture — perhaps a primitive culture. Report on how these rituals and practices compare and contrast with our own.

WE ARE BREAKING THE SILENCE ABOUT DEATH

Daniel Goleman

Daniel Goleman has lectured at Harvard on death and dying, first as a graduate assistant to thanatologist Edwin Shneidman, later in his own course on the psychology of consciousness. During his graduate work in clinical psychology, he did research on suicide, and has published in professional journals on the subject. Since 1975, he has been an associate editor of *Psychology Today,* where this article first appeared.

Psychiatrist Elisabeth Kübler-Ross and I were to meet and fly together   1
to Colorado Springs, where she was to give a workshop for nurses,
doctors and volunteers who work with dying patients. Our flight was
soon to board, but there was no sign of Kübler-Ross. Then she
appeared, bustling down the corridor, a small, wiry woman carrying
two huge shoulder-bags. After the briefest exchange of amenities, she
explained that she was concerned that one of her patients might be
late for the flight. The patient was to be one of 12 dying people at the
seminar. They would teach those who work with the dying by sharing
their private fears and hopes.

At the last minute her patient, an emaciated but smiling woman,   2
showed up at the gate. Kübler-Ross and I had planned to talk on the
plane, but instead she spent the entire flight giving her patient emergency oxygen. Later I learned that Kübler-Ross had met her patient
the week before. She saw that the woman had only a few more weeks
or months to live, and learned that she had never traveled far from
her hometown. So, on the spur of the moment, Kübler-Ross invited
her to come along as her guest. She should, the doctor felt, live her
remaining days fully.

Kübler-Ross began her work with the dying in the mid '60s when   3
she decided to interview a dying patient for a medical-school seminar
she was teaching. She searched the school's 600-bed hospital, asking
the staff on each ward if there were any dying patients. On every
ward she got the same answer: No. Yet on any given day in a hospital
that size, many patients are near death. When she then went back and
asked about specific patients, their doctors reluctantly admitted that
they were terminally ill.

Medical schools in those days avoided the topic of death and   4
dying. Medical staffs treated the physical problems of their dying
patients but, more often than not, ignored the fact of approaching
death. Virtually no one, the doctor included, was comfortable with
the fact of death. It was taboo, best kept out of sight and out of mind.

Once a patient died, he vanished. One of Kübler-Ross's students   5
realized that in all her months as a hospital resident she could hardly
recall seeing a dead person. In part she chose to avoid them, but there
was also "the remarkable disappearing act that occurs as the body is
cleverly whisked out of sight . . ."

In the decade since Kübler-Ross first gave her seminar on dying,   6
the taboo has weakened. Death is in vogue as a topic of books,
seminars, scholarly articles, and classes at every level from college
down to elementary school. There are two professional journals devoted to the study of death, dozens of volunteer groups working with

the dying, and one or two medical facilities geared solely to helping people die with dignity.

There is no single cause for this change, but Elisabeth Kübler- 7 Ross has done more to further it than any other person. Through her 1969 best seller *On Death and Dying*, her seminars for physicians, clergy, and others who work with dying people, and her public talks, Kübler-Ross has alerted us to a new way of handling dying.

Kübler-Ross is Chairman of the National Advisory Council to 8 Hospice in New Haven, Connecticut, which leads the way in humane care of the dying. Modeled on a similar center in London, New Haven Hospice puts Kübler-Ross's advice into practice with a team on call around-the-clock to help people die in their own homes rather than in a strange hospital. Hospice has plans for building a center for dying patients. In contrast to policy at most hospitals, family members will be encouraged to join the medical staff in caring for their dying relatives. Visiting hours will be unlimited, and patients' children and even pets will be free to visit.

Kübler-Ross's natural openness toward the dying reflects her 9 experience as a child in rural Switzerland. In her community, she saw death confronted with honesty and dignity. She also has the authority of one whose medical practice has been limited for the last decade to dying patients and their families; lately, her practice has been restricted to dying children. Her public life as an author and a lecturer allows her a rare luxury in her medical work; she charges no one for her services.

Kübler-Ross's career has been unusually humanitarian from the 10 start. Before entering medical school in Switzerland, she worked at the close of the Second World War in eastern Europe, helping the survivors of bombed-out cities and death camps. After becoming a psychiatrist, she gravitated to treating chronic schizophrenics, and then to work with retarded children, whose mental slowness was compounded by being deaf, dumb or blind.

From the thousands of hours she has spent with patients facing 11 death, Kübler-Ross has charted the psychological stages people typically go through once they know they are soon to die. Though any single person need not go through the entire progression, most everyone facing death experiences at least one of these stages. The usual progression is from denial of death through rage, bargaining, depression, and finally, acceptance.

These reactions are not restricted to dying, but can occur with a 12 loss of any kind. We all experience them to some degree in the ordinary course of life changes. Every change is a loss, every beginning an end. In the words of the Tibetan poet Milarepa, "All worldly pursuits end in sorrow, acquisition in dispersion, buildings in destruction, meetings in separation, birth in death."

A person's first reaction to the news that he has a terminal disease   13
is most often denial. The refusal to accept the fact that one is soon to
die cushions death's impact. It gives a person time to come to grips
with the loss of everything that has mattered to him.

Psychoanalysts recognize that at the unconscious level, a person   14
does not believe he will die. From this refusal to believe in one's own
death springs the hope that, despite a life-threatening illness, one will
not die. This hope can take many forms: that the diagnosis is wrong,
that the illness is curable, that a miracle treatment will turn up. As
denial fades into a partial acceptance, the person's concern shifts
from the hope of longer life to the wish that his or her family will be
well and his affairs taken care of after his death.

Denial too often typifies the hospital staff's reaction to a patient   15
who faces death. Doctors and nurses see themselves as healers; a
dying patient threatens this role. Further, a person who cannot contemplate his own death, even if he is a physician, feels discomfort with
someone who is dying. For this reason hospital staffs often enclose the
dying patient in a cocoon of medical details that keeps death under
wraps.

Sociologists Barney Glaser and Anselm Strauss studied the mu-   16
tual pretense that often exists when patient and staff know the patient
is dying. A staff member and a terminal patient might safely talk
about his disease, they found, so long as they skirt its fatal
significance. But they were most comfortable when they stuck to safe
topics like movies and fashions — anything, in short, that signifies life
going on as usual.

This is a fragile pretense, but not one that either party can easily   17
break. Glaser and Strauss found that a patient would sometimes send
cues to the staff that he wanted to talk about dying, but the nurses and
doctors would decide not to talk openly with him because they feared
he would go to pieces. The patient would openly make a remark
acknowledging his death, but the doctor or nurse would ignore him.
Then, out of tact or empathy for the embarrassment or distress he
caused, the patient would resume his silence. In this case, it is the
staff's uneasiness that maintains the pretense, not the patient's.

In the reverse instance, a doctor may give the patient an opening   18
to talk about dying, and have the patient ignore it. Kübler-Ross urges
hospital staff members to let the patient know that they are available
to talk about dying, but not to force the subject on the patient. When
he no longer needs to deny his death, the patient will seek out a staff
member and open the topic.

When the family knows a patient is dying and keeps the secret   19
from him, they create a barrier that prevents both patient and family
from preparing for the death. The dying patient usually sees through
a make-believe, smiling mask. Genuine emotions are much easier on

the patient, allowing relatives to share his feelings. When his family can be open about the seriousness of the illness, there is time to talk and cry together and to take care of important matters under less emotional pressure.

A student nurse hospitalized for a fatal illness wrote to her professional colleagues in a nursing journal: "You slip in and out of my room, give me medications and check my blood pressure. Is it because I am a student nurse myself that I sense your fright? If only we could be honest, both admit our fears, touch one another. Then it might not be so hard to die — in a hospital — with friends close by." 20

Denial becomes increasingly hard as the patient's health deterio- 21 rates. Although mutual pretense avoids embarrassment and emotional strains, it sacrifices valuable time in which the dying patient and his family could take care of unfinished emotional and practical matters, like unsettled arguments or unwritten wills, that death will forestall forever.

Kübler-Ross feels that a period of denial is useful if it gives the 22 patient and his family time to find a way to deal with the stark truth of death. But when denial persists until the person dies, the survivors' grief is needlessly prolonged by the guilts and regrets. Often patients near death say they wished they had been told they were dying sooner so that they could have prepared themselves and their families.

A few rare patients, though, need to cling to denial because the 23 reality is too much to bear. When those closest to the person offer no love or comfort, as when children of the dying patient blame the parent for deserting them, the patient may deny the inevitable to the very end. But this is rare; of 500 patients, Kübler-Ross found only four who refused to the last to admit that they were dying.

Once a dying patient accepts the invitation to talk about his 24 death, Kübler-Ross tries to help him recognize any unfinished business that needs his attention. Straightforward truth helps the dying person fully live the time left. She tries to elicit their hidden hopes and needs, then find someone who can fulfill these needs.

Physical pain sometimes prevents a dying patient from making 25 the best use of his remaining days. When his pain is overwhelming, he either becomes preoccupied with it or dependent on painkillers that leave him groggy. Kübler-Ross controls pain with Brompton's mixture. This old-time formula of morphine, cocaine, alcohol, syrup, and chloroform water dulls the patient's pain without dimming his alertness.

When a patient stops denying his impending death, the feelings 26 that most often well up are rage and anger. The question, "Why me?" is asked with bitterness. The patient aims his resentment at whoever is handy, be it staff, friends or family. Healthy people remind the patient that he will die while they live. The unfairness of it all arouses his rage. He may be rude, uncooperative, or downright hostile. For example, when a nurse was late with his pain medication, the patient snapped, "Why are you late? You don't care if I suffer. Your coffee break is more important to you than my pain."

As the rage abates the patient may start to bargain with God or 27 fate, trying to arrange a temporary truce. The question switches from "Why me?" to "Why now?" He hopes for more time to finish things, to put his house in order, to arrange for his family's future needs, to make a will. The bargain with God takes the form of the patient promising to be good or to do something in exchange for another week, month, or year of life.

With full acceptance of his approaching death, a person often 28 becomes depressed. Dying brings him a sense of hopelessness, help-lessness and isolation. He mourns past losses, and regrets things left undone or wrongs he's committed. One of Kübler-Ross's patients, for example, regretted that when his daughter was small and needed him, he was on the road making money to provide a good home. Now that he was dying, he wanted to spend every moment he could with her, but she was grown and had her own friends. He felt it was too late. At this stage the dying person starts to mourn his own death, the loss of all the people and things he has found meaningful, the plans and hopes never to be fulfilled. Kübler-Ross calls this kind of depres-sion a "preparatory grief." It allows a person to get ready for his death by letting go of his attachments to life.

During this preparatory grief, the patient may stop seeing family 29 and friends, and become withdrawn and silent. His outer detachment matches the inner renouncement of what once mattered to him. Family members sometimes misinterpret his detachment as a rejec-tion. Kübler-Ross helps them to see that the patient is beginning to accept his death. Hence, he needs much less contact with family and friends.

After this preparatory mourning, the dying person can reach a 30 peaceful acceptance. He is no longer concerned with the prolongation of his life. He has made peace with those he loves, settled his affairs, relinquished his unfinished dreams. He may feel an inner calm, and become mellow in outlook. He can take things as they come, including the progress of his illness. People bring him pleasure, but he no longer speaks of plans for the future. His focus becomes the simple joys of everyday life; he enjoys today without waiting for tomorrow. At this stage, the person is ready to live his remaining days fully and die well.

The story of a modern Zen master's death shows this frame of 31 mind. As the master lay dying, one of his students brought him a special cake, of which he had always been fond. With a wan smile the master slowly ate a piece of the cake. As he grew weaker still, his students leaned close and asked if he had any final words for them. "Yes," he said, as they leaned forward eagerly, "My, but this cake is delicious."

What the dying teach us, says Kübler-Ross, is how to live. In   32 summing up what she has learned from her dying patients, she likes to recite a poem by Richard Allen that goes:

. . . as you face your death,
it is only the love
you have given
and received
which will count . . .
if you have loved well
then it will have been worth it . . .
but if you have not
death will always come too soon
and be too terrible to face.

Review Questions

1. What attitudes did Kübler-Ross encounter when she first tried to learn about dying patients?
2. How has Kübler-Ross been instrumental in promoting a new consciousness about death and dying?
3. What are the stages typically undergone by dying patients once they know of their condition?
4. In what way does the medical profession reinforce the denial of death?

Discussion Questions

1. To what extent do you think the type of society we live in creates the stages of dying that Kübler-Ross has described? Or would you expect these stages to be universal throughout the earth and throughout history?
2. Goleman reports that in the past decade or so, death has been "in vogue," and cites the wealth of books, seminars, and so on devoted to death. Does this make death-consciousness seem a passing fad — perhaps like electronic TV games? Or is there evidence, in popular culture for instance, that our society has finally begun to come to terms with death?
3. Goleman cites the example of the dying man whose main regret was that he had never spent enough time with his daughter and now wanted to spend every minute with her. Suppose some universal catastrophe threatened death within the year to everyone on earth.

How do you think this knowledge would change society and the people making it up in the remaining year?
4. What is the purpose of the opening anecdote about Kübler-Ross? What impression of her does it provide? What is the purpose of the closing anecdote about the Zen master? How might the two anecdotes be related?
5. The author injects himself into the article at the outset and then never does so again. What could his purpose have been?
6. Why do you think Goleman spends more time on "denial" than on any of the other stages of dying?
7. At what points does Goleman include examples and quotations? Would examples and quotations be helpful at other points?

Writing Suggestions

1. Write an essay on the subject of Discussion Question 3.
2. Imagine that because of some genetic disorder, you will live to be at least 250 years old, and that you would live most of this long life in reasonably good health and without extraordinary signs of aging.

   How would you use the extra time allotted to you? Draw up a plan for your life, setting goals, indicating your career choices, your social life, etc.

   Variation on this assignment: Imagine that *everyone* suddenly developed the same genetic disorder — that *everyone* would live to be 250. What effects would this have on society?

THE FIVE STAGES OF GRIEF
Linda Pastan

Linda Pastan (b. 1932), daughter of a physician and a molecular biologist, was educated at Radcliffe College, Simmons College, and Brandeis University. Her books of poetry include *A Perfect Circle of Sun* (1971), *On the Way to the Zoo* (1975), *Aspects of Eve* (1975), *The Five Stages of Grief* (1978), in which this poem appears, and, most recently, *Setting the Table* (1980).

Reprinted from *The Five Stages of Grief: Poems by Linda Pastan*, with the permission of W.W. Norton & Company, Inc. Copyright © 1978 by Linda Pastan.

The night I lost you
someone pointed me towards
the Five Stages of Grief.
Go that way, they said,
it's easy, like learning to climb   5
stairs after the amputation.
And so I climbed.
Denial was first.
I sat down at breakfast
carefully setting the table   10
for two. I passed you the toast —
you sat there. I passed
you the paper — you hid
behind it.
Anger seemed more familiar.   15
I burned the toast, snatched
the paper and read the headlines myself.
But they mentioned your departure,
and so I moved on to
Bargaining. What could I exchange   20
for you? The silence
after storms? My typing fingers?
Before I could decide, *Depression*
came puffing up, a poor relation
its suitcase tied together   25
with string. In the suitcase
were bandages for the eyes
and bottles of sleep. I slid
all the way down the stairs
feeling nothing.   30
And all the time Hope
flashed on and off
in defective neon.
Hope was a signpost pointing
straight in the air.   35
Hope was my uncle's middle name,
he died of it.
After a year I am still climbing,
though my feet slip
on your stone face.   40
The treeline
has long since disappeared;
green is a color

I have forgotten.
But now I see what I am climbing   45
towards: *Acceptance*
written in capital letters,
a special headline:
Acceptance,
its name is in lights.   50
I struggle on,
waving and shouting.
Below, my whole life spreads its surf,
all the landscapes I've ever known
or dreamed of. Below   55
a fish jumps: the pulse
in your neck.
Acceptance. I finally
reach it.
But something is wrong.   60
Grief is a circular staircase.
I have lost you.

Discussion Questions

1. Are the five stages of grief something a person consciously experience? What does Pastan mean that the steps are "easy, like learning to climb stairs after the amputation"?

2. Why are the stages of grief represented in terms of a climb?

3. Are you prepared for the "I have lost you" at the end? Why or why not? What problems are associated with the "formula" of grieving in five ways?

4. After each of the five stages, Pastan offers a poetic description of her experience. Examine the appropriateness of these descriptions for each of the five stages. Why, for instance, does she write of burning the toast after *Anger*? Why does *Depression* come with its suitcase tied together with string? (Can *Depression* own a suitcase?)

5. Examine how Pastan develops the metaphor of climbing throughout the poem. What verbs does she use to denote the climb? How are these verbs appropriate for each stage of the climb?

Writing Suggestions

1. Read some of the other poems in the volume *The Five Stages of Grief.* Develop an essay in which you discuss the growth of ideas in this volume. (Are some poems morose and others not? What are the various ways in which Pastan regards death and grieving?)

2. You may wish to attempt writing your own poetry on the subject. Will your poems have a rhyme or metrical scheme? In writing a poem, how much of the effort is emotionally inspired and how much is intellectually worked and reworked for effect? How will you, as a critic of your own poetry, try to improve it?

IS THERE A RIGHT WAY TO DIE?
Norman Klein

Norman Klein is associate professor of anthropology at California State University of Los Angeles. He is editor of *Culture, Curers, and Contagion.*

☐

In Albert Camus's novel *The Stranger,* the protagonist, Meursault, commits an absurd murder and undergoes an even more absurd trial: he sees himself being judged not for his crime alone, but also for his failure to "emote properly" on the day of his mother's funeral. This "flaw" in his character influences the outcome of the trial and seals his doom.

In our own society, faddish therapies stress the idea that openly expressing sorrow, anger, or pain is a good thing, and the only means for "dealing with one's feelings honestly." "Holding things in" comes to be seen as deviant.

Yet nowhere has it been convincingly proved that expressing grief has universal therapeutic value. Perhaps more important, this insistence on the requirement to feel and tell represents an ethnocentric standard that can do injustice to persons and groups who cope differently.

Americans are said to fear and deny death, and if the denial becomes complete, it requires "defenses which can only be destructive," in the words of Elisabeth Kübler-Ross. She is perhaps best known for her scheme of the five stages of a "complete" death: (1) denial, (2) anger, (3) bargaining, (4) depression, and (5) acceptance. Each stage has a transitional value — taken alone, for instance, denial is seen as bad, though as a temporary buffer it is good — and, given enough time, a patient can reach a point of accepting death.

Kübler-Ross's work is undoubtedly useful; it may even help family, friends, and professionals to assist the dying patient who has the emotional needs she describes.

Reprinted from *Psychology Today* Magazine, October 12, 1978. Copyright © 1978 Ziff-Davis Publishing Company. Reprinted by permission.

Yet it is surely conceivable that some Americans can work 6
through grief internally or privately, without psychological cost; it is
even more conceivable that whole cultural subgroups may have different ways of conceiving and responding to such experience. Harvard psychiatrist Ned H. Cassem has questioned the generally negative view of denial espoused by Kübler-Ross. "Denial can be a
constructive force, enabling people to put out of mind morbid, frightening, and depressing aspects of life."

A cross-cultural perspective reveals how arbitrary any one such 7
standard may be. In 1976, psychologists Paul Rosenblatt, Patricia
Walsh, and Douglas Jackson used the Human Relations Area Files, a
massive compendium of anthropological data, to examine mourning
in a large number of societies. They found in their review of 73
societies that what varies is the form and intensity of its expression. In
72 societies, people weep at death; the Balinese say they laugh to
avoid crying. Are the Balinese unhealthy?

The researchers also correlated gender differences in crying for 8
60 societies: in 32 of them, both sexes cried equally; in the 28 in
which there was a difference, it was always the women who cried
more. Are they healthier?

In 18 of 32 societies, self-injury (such as cutting off a finger at a 9
joint) is regularly attempted by both grieving men and women;
women self-mutilate more in 12. But if emotional letting go is a good
thing, should men and women, equally, mutilate themselves even
more frequently?

Closer to home, psychologist Richard Kalish and anthropologist 10
David Reynolds compared the attitudes on death and mourning of
black Americans, Japanese-Americans, Mexican-Americans, and
white Americans in Los Angeles. Asked if they would "try very hard
to control the way you showed your emotions in public," the groups
offered a wide range of responses. Japanese and black respondents
said they would (82 percent, 79 percent) more often than white
Americans and Mexican-Americans, for example (74 percent, 64
percent).

Japanese-Americans, who are most frequently reticent about 11
public grief, would seem to bear out the stereotypic notion of Orien-
tals as stoic. Public-health nurse Thelma Dobbins Payne reports that
the reluctance of many Japanese-American women to cry out during
childbirth leads some non-Japanese physicians to "wonder if Japanese
women feel the pain." Japanese-American physicians, however, described a common alternative style in labor: "wincing," "grimacing,"
"frowning."

How much and what type of emoting is necessary to avoid the 12
label "stoic"? The real issue rests with the way the various cultures
define the appropriate expression of emotion. At the same time, it is

very important to note that in no group Kalish and Reynolds studied was there a 100 percent agreement by all informants — sex, age, religion, and education all affected the responses.

"Death and dignity" and "a beautiful death" verge on becoming the new jargon of concern. But for whom are these expressions really meaningful? Do they describe the dying person's experience, or the observer's? Attitudes toward death are clearly influenced by culture — and by subculture, and by individual personality. It follows, then, that we must take care not to formalize or prescribe the way in which people express emotion. As Kalish and Reynolds remark in their discussion, "This era is in danger of replacing old myths and stereotypes with new myths and stereotypes, slightly more accurate and less destructive perhaps, but nonetheless not always appropriate."

13

Review Questions

1. What are Klein's objections to the "faddish therapies" for dealing with grief?
2. What were the results of the various cross-cultural studies of grief? What conclusions may be reached from these results?

Discussion Questions

1. Does Klein reject the main body of Kübler-Ross's work, or just part of it? If only part, which part? Did Klein force you to reevaluate your own assessment of Kübler-Ross's conclusions?
2. What is the purpose of Klein's introductory remarks about the protagonist of Camus's *The Stranger*?
3. What are the "old myths and stereotypes" and the "new myths and stereotypes" to which Richard Kalish and David Reynolds (quoted by Klein in the last sentence) refer?

Writing Suggestion

Klein writes:

> In our own society, faddish therapies stress the idea that openly expressing sorrow, anger, or pain is a good thing, and the only means for "dealing with one's feelings honestly." "Holding things in" comes to be seen as deviant.
>
> Yet nowhere has it been convincingly proved that expressing grief has universal therapeutic value. Perhaps more important, this insistence on the requirement to feel and tell represents an ethnocentric standard that can do injustice to persons and groups who cope differently.

And in a review of *Ordinary People*, the winner of the 1980 Academy Award for Best Picture, reviewer Judith Martin writes:

> . . . the premise [of *Ordinary People*] is a deadly serious endorsement of the reigning psychotherapeutic dogma — the same litany that is now being vehemently questioned from inside and outside the profession in major government arenas.
>
> There is only one character in this film who does not subscribe to the idea that constant talking about one's intimate feelings, crying and "expressing" anger (shouting obscenities) are essential to mental health. Every shred of dialogue attests to this — the community is one big therapeutic center, where schoolmasters, business acquaintances and neighbors constantly give their diagnoses of other people's psyches (the standard conversation opens with "You look . . .") and then make the supreme offer of help: "Do you want to talk about it?"
>
> The one dissenter is the boy's mother, and she is the villain. . . . Consider her behavior when the husband to whom she has been actively loving and loyal for 21 years starts whining such cliche accusations as "I don't know if you're really giving" and "I don't know who you are." Instead of plunging into guilt and soul talk, she fights back her tears and leaves. Given the possibility that prevailing faith in talk therapy may be misplaced . . . an audience not bound by such belief may want to stand up and cheer: Another Nora is slamming another door.[1]

Write an essay in which you (a) relate Klein's and Martin's ideas and then (b) argue for or against them. If you have seen *Ordinary People*, you may want to discuss Martin's comments in light of your own understanding of the film. You may also want to turn to the selection, "Leaving the 'Doll's House,'" in the next chapter (which leads up to the moment when Nora slams the door). After reading the conclusion of Ibsen's play, comment on the validity of Martin's analogy between Nora and the mother in *Ordinary People*.

---

[1] Judith Martin, "Ordinary People: Pop Psychology," *The Washington Post*, 26 September 1980; © 1980 The Washington Post. Reprinted by permission.

THE DEATH OF IVAN ILYICH
Leo Tolstoy

Count Leo Tolstoy (1828–1910) was born in the province of Tula, Russia. He served in the army during the Crimean War (1854–56), after which he retired to his country estate to study and write. When he was about fifty years old, he renounced the Russian Orthodox Church and developed a new mystical sect which believed in nonresistance to evil. His most well known novels are *War and Peace* (1866) and *Anna Karenina* (1875–77). *The Death of Ivan Ilyich* was written in 1886. The protagonist is a middle-aged magistrate of reserved disposition and utterly correct bearing, liked and respected, however, by his colleagues. He has married well and has two grown children; his home life is something less than perfect, but generally tolerable. He wins a judicial appointment in Petersburg (now Leningrad), and is in the process of giving directions for the decoration of his new house when he slips from a ladder, bruising his side. At first he thinks nothing of the incident and goes about his normal schedule of work and entertainment. But the ache in his side persists, and he consults several doctors, who are noncommittal: As this excerpt begins, Ivan Ilyich is beginning to realize the significance of the pain that will not go away.

□

Reviewing the anatomical and physiological details of what, according   1
to the doctor's view, was taking place within him, he understood it all.
It was just one thing — a little thing wrong with the intestinal appendix. It might all come right. Only strengthen one sluggish organ, and
decrease the undue activity of another, and absorption would take
place, and all would be set right. He was a little late for dinner. He ate
his dinner, talked cheerfully, but it was a long while before he could
go to his own room to work. At last he went to his study, and at once
sat down to work. He read his legal documents and did his work, but
the consciousness never left him of having a matter of importance
very near to his heart which he had put off, but would look into later.
When he had finished his work, he remembered that the matter near
his heart was thinking about the intestinal appendix. But he did not
give himself up to it; he went into the drawing room to tea. There
were visitors; and there was talking, playing on the piano, and singing; there was the young examining magistrate, the desirable match
for the daughter. Ivan Ilyich spent the evening, as Praskovya
Fyodorovna observed, in better spirits than any of them; but he never

From *Great Russian Stories*, translated by Constance Garnett, published by Vintage Press, 1959.

forgot for an instant that he had the important matter of the intestinal appendix put off for consideration later. At eleven o'clock he said good night and went to his own room. He had slept alone since his illness in a little room adjoining his study. He went in, undressed, and took up a novel of Zola, but did not read it; he fell to thinking. And in his imagination the desired recovery of the intestinal appendix had taken place. There had been absorption, rejection, reestablishment of the regular action.

"Why, it's all simply that," he said to himself. "One only wants to assist nature." He remembered the medicine, got up, took it, lay down on his back, watching for the medicine to act beneficially and over-come the pain. "It's only to take it regularly and avoid injurious influences; why, already I feel rather better, much better." He began to feel his side; it was not painful to the touch. "Yes, I don't feel it — really, much better already." He put out the candle and lay on his side. "The appendix is getting better, absorption." Suddenly he felt the familiar, old, dull, gnawing ache, persistent, quiet, in earnest. In his mouth the same familiar loathsome taste. His heart sank, and his brain felt dim, misty. "My God, my God!" he said, "again, again, and it will never cease." And suddenly the whole thing rose before him in quite a different aspect. "Intestinal appendix! kidney!" he said to himself. "It's not a question of the appendix, not a question of the kidney, but of life and . . . death. Yes, life has been and now it's going, going away, and I cannot stop it. Yes. Why deceive myself? Isn't it obvious to every one, except me, that I'm dying, and it's only a question of weeks, of days — at once perhaps. There was light, and now there is darkness. I was here, and now I'm going! Where?" A cold chill ran over him, his breath stopped. He heard nothing but the throbbing of his heart.

"I shall be no more, then what will there be? There'll be nothing. Where then shall I be when I'm no more? Can this be dying? No; I don't want to!" He jumped up, tried to light the candle; and fumbling with trembling hands, he dropped the candle and the candlestick on the floor and fell back again on the pillow. "Why trouble? it doesn't matter," he said to himself, staring with open eyes into the darkness. "Death. Yes, death. And they — all of them — don't understand, and don't want to understand, and feel no pity. They are playing. (He caught through the closed doors the faraway cadence of a voice and the accompaniment.) They don't care, but they will die too. Fools! Me sooner and them later; but it will be the same for them. And they are merry. The beasts!" Anger stifled him. And he was agonizingly, insufferably miserable. "It cannot be that all men always have been doomed to this awful horror!" He raised himself.

"There is something wrong in it; I must be calm. I must think it all over from the beginning." And then he began to consider. "Yes, the beginning of my illness. I knocked my side, and I was just the same, that day and the days after; it ached a little, then more, then doctors, then depression, misery, and again doctors; and I've gone on getting closer and closer to the abyss. Strength growing less. Nearer and nearer. And here I am, wasting away, no light in my eyes. I think of how to cure the appendix, but this is death. Can it be death?" Again a horror came over him; gasping for breath, he bent over, began feeling for the matches, and knocked his elbow against the bedside table. It was in his way and hurt him; he felt furious with it, in his anger knocked against it more violently, and upset it. And in despair, breathless, he fell back on his spine waiting for death to come that instant.

The visitors were leaving at that time. Praskovya Fyodorovna was   5
seeing them out. She heard something fall, and came in.

"What is it?"

"Nothing. I dropped something by accident."

She went out, brought a candle. He was lying, breathing hard and fast, like a man who has run a mile, and staring with fixed eyes at her.

"What is it, *Jean?*"

"No—othing, I say. I dropped something." — "Why speak? She won't understand," he thought.

She certainly did not understand. She picked up the candle, lighted it for him, and went out hastily. She had to say good-by to a departing guest. When she came back, he was lying in the same position on his back, looking upwards.

"How are you — worse?"

"Yes."

She shook her head, sat down.

"Do you know what, *Jean?* I wonder if we hadn't better send for Leshchetiski to see you here?"

This meant calling in the celebrated doctor, regardless of expense. He smiled malignantly, and said no. She sat a moment longer, went up to him, and kissed him on the forehead.

He hated her with all the force of his soul when she was kissing him, and had to make an effort not to push her away.

"Good night. Please God, you'll sleep."

"Yes."

Ivan Ilyich saw that he was dying, and was in continual despair.   6

At the bottom of his heart Ivan Ilyich knew that he was dying; but   7
so far from growing used to this idea, he simply did not grasp it — he was utterly unable to grasp it.

The example of the syllogism that he had learned in Kiseveter's   8
logic — Caius is a man, men are mortal, therefore Caius is mortal —

had seemed to him all his life correct only as regards Caius, but not at all as regards himself. In that case it was a question of Caius, a man, an abstract man, and it was perfectly true, but he was not Caius, and was not an abstract man; he had always been a creature quite, quite different from all others; he had been little Vanya with a mamma and papa, and Mitya and Volodya, with playthings and a coach-man and a nurse; afterwards with Katenka, with all the joys and griefs and ecstasies of childhood, boyhood, and youth. What did Caius know of the smell of the leathern ball Vanya had been so fond of? Had Caius kissed his mother's hand like that? Caius had not heard the silk rustle of his mother's skirts. He had not made a riot at school over the pudding. Had Caius been in love like that? Could Caius preside over the sittings of the court?

And Caius certainly was mortal, and it was right for him to die; but for me, little Vanya, Ivan Ilyich, with all my feelings and ideas — for me it's a different matter. And it cannot be that I ought to die. That would be too awful. 9

That was his feeling.

"If I had to die like Caius, I should have known it was so, some inner voice would have told me so. But there was nothing of the sort in me. And I and all my friends, we felt that it was not at all the same as with Caius. And now here it is!" he said to himself. "It can't be! It can't be, but it is! How is it? How's one to understand it?" And he could not conceive it, and tried to drive away this idea as false, incorrect, and morbid, and to supplant it by other, correct, healthy ideas. But this idea, not as an idea merely, but as it were an actual fact, came back again and stood confronting him. 10

And to replace this thought he called up other thoughts, one after another, in the hope of finding support in them. He tried to get back into former trains of thought, which in old days had screened off the thought of death. But, strange to say, all that had in old days covered up, obliterated the sense of death, could not now produce the same effect. Latterly, Ivan Ilyich spent the greater part of his time in these efforts to restore his old trains of thought which had shut off death. At one time he would say to himself, "I'll put myself into my official work; why, I used to live in it." And he would go to the law courts, banishing every doubt. He would enter into conversation with his colleagues, and would sit carelessly, as his old habit was, scanning the crowd below dreamily, and with both his wasted hands he would lean on the arms of the oak armchair just as he always did; and bending over to a colleague, pass the papers to him and whisper to him, then suddenly dropping his eyes and sitting up straight, he would pronounce the familiar words that opened the proceedings. But suddenly in the middle, the pain in his side, utterly regardless of the stage he had reached in his conduct of the case, began its work. It 11 riveted Ivan Ilyich's attention. He drove away the thought of it, but it still did its work, and then *It* came and stood confronting him and looked at him, and he felt turned to stone, and the light died away in his eyes, and he began to ask himself again, "Can it be that *It* is the only truth?" And his colleagues and his subordinates saw with surprise and distress that he, the brilliant, subtle judge, was losing the thread of his speech, was making blunders. He shook himself, tried to regain his self-control, and got somehow to the end of the sitting, and went home with the painful sense that his judicial labors could not as of old hide from him what he wanted to hide; that he could not by means of his official work escape from *It*. And the worst of it was that *It* drew him to itself not for him to do anything in particular, but simply for him to look at *It* straight in the face, to look at *It* and, doing nothing, suffer unspeakably.

And to save himself from this, Ivan Ilyich sought amusements, other screens, and these screens he found, and for a little while they did seem to save him; but soon again they were not so much broken down as let the light through, as though *It* pierced through everything, and there was nothing that could shut *It* off. 12

Sometimes during those days he would go into the drawing room he had furnished, that drawing room where he had fallen, for which — how bitterly ludicrous it was for him to think of it! — for the decoration of which he had sacrificed his life, for he knew that it was that bruise that had started his illness. He went in and saw that the polished table had been scratched by something. He looked for the cause, and found it in the bronze clasps of the album, which had been twisted on one side. He took up the album, a costly one, which he had himself arranged with loving care, and was vexed at the carelessness of his daughter and her friends. Here a page was torn, here the photographs had been shifted out of their places. He carefully put it to rights again and bent the clasp back. 13

Then the idea occurred to him to move all this *établissement* of the albums to another corner where the flowers stood. He called the footman; or his daughter or his wife came to help him. They did not agree with him, contradicted him; he argued, got angry. But all that was very well, since he did not think of *It*; *It* was not in sight. 14

But then his wife would say, as he moved something himself, "Do let the servants do it, you'll hurt yourself again," and all at once *It* peeped through the screen; he caught a glimpse of *It*. He caught a glimpse of *It*, but still he hoped *It* would hide itself. Involuntarily though, he kept watch on his side; there it is just the same still, aching still, and now he cannot forget it, and *It* is staring openly at him from behind the flowers. What's the use of it all? 15

"And it's the fact that here, at that curtain, as if it had been 16 storming a fort, I lost my life. Is it possible? How awful and how silly! It cannot be! It cannot be, and it is."

He went into his own room, lay down, and was again alone with It. Face to face with *It*, and nothing to be done with *It*. Nothing but to look at *It* and shiver. 17

How it came to pass during the third month of Ivan Ilyich's illness, it would be impossible to say, for it happened little by little, imperceptibly, but it had come to pass that his wife and his daughter and his son and their servants and their acquaintances, and the doctors, and, most of all, he himself — all were aware that all interest in him for other people consisted now in the question how soon he would leave his place empty, free the living from the constraint of his presence, and be set free himself from his sufferings. 18

He slept less and less; they gave him opium, and began to inject morphine. But this did not relieve him. The dull pain he experienced in the half asleep condition at first only relieved him as a change, but then it became as bad, or even more agonizing, than the open pain. He had special things to eat prepared for him according to the doctors' prescriptions; but these dishes became more and more distasteful; more and more revolting to him. 19

Special arrangements, too, had to be made for his other physical needs, and this was a continual misery to him. Misery from the uncleanliness, the unseemliness, and the stench, from the feeling of another person having to assist in it. 20

But just from this most unpleasant side of his illness there came comfort to Ivan Ilyich. There always came into his room on these occasions to clear up for him the peasant who waited on table, Gerasim. 21

Gerasim was a clean, fresh, young peasant, who had grown stout and hearty on the good fare in town. Always cheerful and bright. At first the sight of this lad, always cleanly dressed in the Russian style, engaged in this revolting task, embarrassed Ivan Ilyich. 22

One day, getting up from the night stool, too weak to replace his clothes, he dropped on to a soft low chair and looked with horror at his bare, powerless thighs, with the muscles so sharply standing out on them. 23

Then there came in with light, strong steps Gerasim, in his thick boots, diffusing a pleasant smell of tar from his boots, and bringing in the freshness of the winter air. Wearing a clean hempen apron, and a clean cotton shirt, with his sleeves tucked up on his strong, bare young arms, without looking at Ivan Ilyich, obviously trying to check the radiant happiness in his face so as not to hurt the sick man, he went up to the night stool. 24

"Gerasim," said Ivan Ilyich faintly.

Gerasim started, clearly afraid that he had done something amiss,   25
and with a rapid movement turned towards the sick man his fresh,
good-natured, simple young face, just beginning to be downy with the
first growth of beard.

"Yes, your honor."

"I'm afraid this is very disagreeable for you. You must excuse me.
I can't help it."

"Why, upon my word, sir!" And Gerasim's eyes beamed, and he
showed his white young teeth in a smile. "What's a little trouble? It's a
case of illness with you, sir."

And with his deft, strong arms he performed his habitual task,
and went out, stepping lightly. And five minutes later, treading just as
lightly, he came back.

Ivan Ilyich was still sitting in the same way in the armchair.

"Gerasim," he said, when the latter had replaced the night stool
all sweet and clean, "please help me; come here." Gerasim went up to
him. "Lift me up. It's difficult for me alone, and I've sent Dimitri
away."

Gerasim went up to him; as lightly as he stepped he put his strong   26
arms round him, deftly and gently lifted and supported him, with
the other hand pulled up his trousers, and would have set him down
again. But Ivan Ilyich asked him to carry him to the sofa. Gerasim,
without effort, carefully not squeezing him, led him, almost carrying
him, to the sofa, and settled him there.

"Thank you; how neatly and well . . . you do everything."

Gerasim smiled again, and would have gone away. But Ivan
Ilyich felt his presence such a comfort that he was reluctant to let him
go.

"Oh, move that chair near me, please. No, that one, under my
legs. I feel easier when my legs are higher."

Gerasim picked up the chair, and without letting it knock, set it   27
gently down on the ground just at the right place, and lifted Ivan
Ilyich's legs on to it. It seemed to Ivan Ilyich that he was easier just at
the moment when Gerasim lifted his legs higher.

"I'm better when my legs are higher," said Ivan Ilyich. "Put that
cushion under me."

Gerasim did so. Again he lifted his legs to put the cushion under
them. Again it seemed to Ivan Ilyich that he was easier at that
moment when Gerasim held his legs raised. When he laid them down
again, he felt worse.

"Gerasim," he said to him, "are you busy just now?"

"Not at all sir," said Gerasim, who had learned among the town-
bred servants how to speak to gentlefolks.

"What have you left to do?"

"Why, what I have to do? I've done everything, there's only the wood to chop for tomorrow."

"Then hold my legs up like that — can you?"

"To be sure, I can." Gerasim lifted the legs up. And it seemed to Ivan Ilyich that in that position he did not feel the pain at all.

"But how about the wood?"

"Don't you trouble about that, sir. We shall have time enough."

Ivan Ilyich made Gerasim sit and hold his legs, and began to talk to him. And, strange to say, he fancied he felt better while Gerasim had hold of his legs.

From that time forward Ivan Ilyich would sometimes call Gerasim, and get him to hold his legs on his shoulders, and he liked talking with him. Gerasim did this easily, readily, simply, and with a good nature that touched Ivan Ilyich. Health, strength, and heartiness in all other people were offensive to Ivan Ilyich; but the strength and heartiness of Gerasim did not mortify him, but soothed him.

Ivan Ilyich's great misery was due to the deception that for some reason or other every one kept up with him — that he was simply ill, and not dying, and that he need only keep quiet and follow the doctor's orders, and then some great change for the better would be the result. He knew that whatever they might do, there would be no result except more agonizing sufferings and death. And he was made miserable by this lie, made miserable at their refusing to acknowledge what they all knew and he knew, by their persisting in lying over him about his awful position, and in forcing him too to take part in this lie. Lying, lying, this lying carried on over him on the eve of his death, and destined to bring that terrible, solemn act of his death down to the level of all their visits, curtains, sturgeons for dinner . . . was a horrible agony for Ivan Ilyich. And, strange to say, many times when they had been going through the regular performance over him, he had been within a hair's breadth of screaming at them: "Cease your lying! You know, and I know, that I'm dying; so do, at least, give over lying!" But he had never had the spirit to do this. The terrible, awful act of his dying was, he saw, by all those about him, brought down to the level of a casual, unpleasant, and to some extent indecorous, incident (somewhat as they would behave with a person who should enter a drawing room smelling unpleasant). It was brought down to this level by that very decorum to which he had been enslaved all his life. He saw that no one felt for him, because no one would even grasp his position. Gerasim was the only person who recognized the position, and felt sorry for him. And that was why Ivan Ilyich was only at ease with Gerasim. He felt comforted when Gerasim sometimes supported his legs for whole nights at a stretch, and would not go away to bed, saying, "Don't you worry yourself, Ivan Ilyich, I'll get sleep enough yet," or when suddenly dropping into the familiar peasant forms of speech, he added: "If thou weren't sick, but as 'tis, 'twould be strange if I didn't wait on thee." Gerasim alone did not lie; everything showed clearly that he alone understood what it meant, and saw no necessity to disguise it, and simply felt sorry for his sick, wasting master. He even said this once straight out, when Ivan Ilyich was sending him away.

"We shall all die. So what's a little trouble?" he said, meaning by 30 this to express that he did not complain of the trouble just because he was taking this trouble for a dying man, and he hoped that for him too some one would be willing to take the same trouble when his time came.

Apart from this deception, or in consequence of it, what made 31 the greatest misery for Ivan Ilyich was that no one felt for him as he would have liked them to feel for him. At certain moments, after prolonged suffering, Ivan Ilyich, ashamed as he would have been to own it, longed more than anything for some one to feel sorry for him, as for a sick child. He longed to be petted, kissed, and wept over, as children are petted and comforted. He knew that he was an important member of the law courts, that he had a beard turning grey, and that therefore it was impossible. But still he longed for it. And in his relations with Gerasim there was something approaching to that. And that was why being with Gerasim was a comfort to him. Ivan Ilyich longs to weep, longs to be petted and wept over, and then there comes in a colleague, Shebek; and instead of weeping and being petted, Ivan Ilyich puts on his serious, severe, earnest face, and from mere inertia gives his views on the effect of the last decision in the Court of Appeal, and obstinately insists upon them. This falsity around him and within him did more than anything to poison Ivan Ilyich's last days. . . .

Late at night his wife came back. She came in on tiptoe, but he 32 heard her, opened his eyes, and made haste to close them again. She wanted to send away Gerasim and sit up with him herself instead. He opened his eyes and said, "No, go away."

"Are you in great pain?"

"Always the same."

"Take some opium."

He agreed and drank it. She went away.

Till three o'clock he slept a miserable sleep. It seemed to him that 33 he and his pain were being thrust somewhere into a narrow, deep, black sack, and they kept pushing him further and further in, and still could not thrust him to the bottom. And this operation was awful to him, and was accompanied with agony. And he was afraid, and yet wanted to fall into it, and struggled and yet tried to get into it. And all of a sudden he slipped and fell and woke up. Gerasim, still the same, is sitting at the foot of the bed half dozing peacefully, patient. And he is lying with his wasted legs clad in stockings, raised on Gerasim's shoulders, the same candle burning in the alcove, and the same interminable pain.

"Go away, Gerasim," he whispered.

"It's all right, sir. I'll stay a bit longer."

"No, go away."

He took his legs down, lay sideways on his arm, and he felt very 34 sorry for himself. He only waited till Gerasim had gone away into the next room; he could restrain himself no longer, and cried like a child. He cried at his own helplessness, at his awful loneliness, at the cruelty of people, at the cruelty of God, at the absence of God.

"Why hast Thou done all this? What brought me to this? Why, 35 why torture me so horribly?"

He did not expect an answer, and wept indeed that there was and could be no answer. The pain grew more acute again, but he did not stir, did not call.

He said to himself. "Come, more then; come, strike me! But what for? What have I done to Thee? what for?"

Then he was still, ceased weeping, held his breath, and was all 36 attention; he listened, as it were, not to a voice uttering sounds, but to the voice of his soul, to the current of thoughts that rose up within him.

"What is it you want?" was the first clear idea able to be put into words that he grasped.

"What? Not to suffer, to live," he answered.

And again he was utterly plunged into attention so intense that even the pain did not distract him.

"To live? Live how?" the voice of his soul was asking.

"Why, live as I used to live before — happily and pleasantly."

"As you used to live before — happily and pleasantly?" queried 37 the voice. And he began going over in his imagination the best moments of his pleasant life. But strange to say, all these best moments of his pleasant life seemed now not at all what they had seemed then. All — except the first memories of childhood — there, in his childhood there had been something really pleasant in which one could have lived if it had come back. But the creature who had this pleasant experience was no more; it was like a memory of some one else.

As soon as he reached the beginning of what had resulted in him 38 as he was now, Ivan Ilyich, all that had seemed joys to him then now melted away before his eyes and were transformed into something trivial, and often disgusting.

And the further he went from childhood, the nearer to the actual 39 present, the more worthless and uncertain were the joys. It began with life at the school of jurisprudence. Then there had still been something genuinely good; then there had been gaiety; then there had been friendship; then there had been hopes. But in the higher classes these good moments were already becoming rarer. Later on, during the first period of his official life, at the governor's, good moments appeared; but it was all mixed, and less and less of it was good. And further on even less was good, and the further he went the less good there was.

His marriage . . . as gratuitous as the disillusion of it and the 40 smell of his wife's breath and the sensuality, the hypocrisy! And that deadly official life, and anxiety about money, and so for one year, and two, and ten, and twenty, and always the same thing. And the further he went, the more deadly it became. "As though I had been going steadily downhill, imagining that I was going uphill. So it was in fact. In public opinion I was going uphill, and steadily as I got up it life was ebbing away from me. . . . And now the work's done, there's only to die.

"But what is this? What for? It cannot be! It cannot be that life 41 has been so senseless, so loathsome? And if it really was so loathsome and senseless, then why die, and die in agony? There's something wrong.

"Can it be I have not lived as one ought?" suddenly came into his 42 head. "But how not so, when I've done everything as it should be done?" he said, and at once dismissed this only solution of all the enigma of life and death as something utterly out of the question.

"What do you want now? To live? Live how? Live as you live at 43 the courts when the usher booms out: 'The Judge is coming!' . . . The judge is coming, the judge is coming," he repeated to himself. "Here he is, the judge! But I'm not to blame!" he shrieked in fury. "What's it for?" And he left off crying, and turning with his face to the wall, fell to pondering always on the same question, "What for, why all this horror?"

But however much he pondered, he could not find an answer. 44 And whenever the idea struck him, as it often did, that it all came of his never having lived as he ought, he thought of all the correctness of his life and dismissed the strange idea.

Another fortnight had passed. Ivan Ilyich could not now get up 45 from the sofa. He did not like lying in bed, and lay on the sofa. And lying almost all the time facing the wall, in loneliness he suffered all the inexplicable agonies, and in loneliness pondered always that inexplicable question, "What is it? Can it be true that it's death?" And an inner voice answered, "Yes, it is true." "Why these agonies?" and a voice answered, "For no reason." Beyond and besides this there was nothing.

From the very beginning of his illness, ever since Ivan Ilyich first 46
went to the doctor's, his life had been split up into two contradictory
moods, which were continually alternating — one was despair and the
anticipation of an uncomprehended and awful death; the other was
hope and an absorbed watching over the actual condition of his body.
First there was nothing confronting him but a kidney or intestine
which had temporarily declined to perform their duties, then there
was nothing but unknown awful death, which there was no escaping.

These two moods had alternated from the very beginning of the 47
illness; but the further the illness progressed, the more doubtful and
fantastic became the conception of the kidney, and the more real the
sense of approaching death.

He had but to reflect on what he had been three months before 48
and what he was now, to reflect how steadily he had been going
downhill, for every possibility of hope to be shattered.

Of late, in the loneliness in which he found himself, lying with his 49
face to the back of the sofa, a loneliness in the middle of a populous
town and of his numerous acquaintances and his family, a loneliness
than which none more complete could be found anywhere — not at
the bottom of the sea, not deep down in the earth; — of late in this
fearful loneliness Ivan Ilyich had lived only in imagination in the past.
One by one the pictures of his past rose up before him. It always
began from what was nearest in time and went back to the most
remote, to childhood, and rested there. If Ivan Ilyich thought of the
stewed prunes that had been offered him for dinner that day, his
mind went back to the damp, wrinkled French plum of his childhood,
of its peculiar taste and the flow of saliva when the stone was sucked;
and along with this memory of a taste there rose up a whole series of
memories of that period — his nurse, his brother, his playthings. "I
mustn't . . . it's too painful," Ivan Ilyich said to himself, and he
brought himself back to the present. The button on the back of the
sofa and the creases in the morocco. "Morocco's dear, and doesn't
wear well; there was a quarrel over it. But the morocco was different,
and different too the quarrel when we tore father's portfolio and
were punished, and mamma bought us the tarts." And again his mind
rested on his childhood, and again it was painful, and he tried to drive
it away and think of something else.

And again at that point, together with that chain of associations, 50
quite another chain of memories came into his heart, of how his
illness had grown up and become more acute. It was the same there,
the further back the more life there had been. There had been both
more that was good in life and more of life itself. And the two began
to melt into one. "Just as the pain goes on getting worse and worse, so
has my whole life gone on getting worse and worse," he thought. One
light spot was there at the back, at the beginning of life, and then it

kept getting blacker and blacker, and going faster and faster. "In inverse ratio to the square of the distance from death," thought Ivan Ilyich. And the image of a stone falling downwards with increasing velocity sank into his soul. Life, a series of increasing sufferings, falls more and more swiftly to the end, the most fearful sufferings. "I am falling." He shuddered, shifted himself, would have resisted, but he knew beforehand that he could not resist; and again, with eyes weary with gazing at it, but unable not to gaze at what was before him, he stared at the back of the sofa and waited, waited expecting that fearful fall and shock and dissolution. "Resistance is impossible," he said to himself. "But if one could at least comprehend what it's for? Even that's impossible. It could be explained if one were to say that I hadn't lived as I ought. But that can't be alleged," he said to himself, thinking of all the regularity, correctness, and propriety of his life. "That really can't be admitted," he said to himself, his lips smiling ironically as though some one could see his smile and be deceived by it. "No explanation! Agony, death. . . . What for?"

So passed a fortnight. During that fortnight an event occurred 51 that had been desired by Ivan Ilyich and his wife. Petrishchev made a formal proposal. This took place in the evening. Next day Praskovya Fyodorovna went in to her husband, resolving in her mind how to inform him of Fyodor Dmitryevich's proposal, but that night there had been a change for the worse in Ivan Ilyich. Praskovya Fyodorovna found him on the same sofa, but in a different position. He was lying on his face, groaning, and staring straight before him with a fixed gaze.

She began talking of remedies. He turned his stare on her. She 52 did not finish what she had begun saying; such hatred of her in particular was expressed in that stare.

"For Christ's sake, let me die in peace," he said.

She would have gone away, but at that moment the daughter 53 came in and went up to say good morning to him. He looked at his daughter just as at his wife, and to her inquiries how he was, he told her drily that they would soon all be rid of him. Both were silent, sat a little while, and went out.

"How are we to blame?" said Liza to her mother. "As though we 54 had done it! I'm sorry for papa, but why punish us?"

At the usual hour the doctor came. Ivan Ilyich answered, "Yes, 55 no," never taking his exasperated stare from him, and towards the end he said, "Why, you know that you can do nothing, so let me be."

"We can relieve your suffering," said the doctor.

"Even that you can't do; let me be."

The doctor went into the drawing room and told Praskovya 56 Fyodorovna that it was very serious, and that the only resource left them was opium to relieve his sufferings, which must be terrible. The doctor said his physical sufferings were terrible, and that was true; but even more terrible than his physical sufferings were his mental sufferings, and in that lay his chief misery.

His moral sufferings were due to the fact that during that night, 57 as he looked at the sleepy, good-natured, broad-cheeked face of Gerasim, the thought had suddenly come into his head, "What if in reality all my life, my conscious life, has been not the right thing?" The thought struck him that what he had regarded before as an utter impossibility, that he had spent his life not as he ought, might be the truth. It struck him that those scarcely detected impulses of struggle within him against what was considered good by persons of higher position, scarcely detected impulses which he had dismissed, that they might be the real thing, and everything else might be not the right thing. And his official work, and his ordering of his daily life and of his family, and these social and official interests, — all that might be not the right thing. He tried to defend it all to himself. And suddenly he felt all the weakness of what he was defending. And it was useless to defend it.

"But if it's so," he said to himself, "and I am leaving life with the 58 consciousness that I have lost all that was given me, and there's no correcting it, then what?" He lay on his back and began going over his whole life entirely anew. When he saw the footman in the morning, then his wife, then his daughter, then the doctor, every movement they made, every word they uttered, confirmed for him the terrible truth that had been revealed to him in the night. In them he saw himself, saw all in which he had lived, and saw distinctly that it was all not the right thing; it was a horrible, vast deception that concealed both life and death. This consciousness intensified his physical agonies, multiplied them tenfold. He groaned and tossed from side to side and pulled at the covering over him. It seemed to him that it was stifling him and weighing him down. And for that he hated them.

They gave him a big dose of opium; he sank into unconscious- 59 ness; but at dinner time the same thing began again. He drove them all away, and tossed from side to side.

His wife came to him and said, "*Jean*, darling, do this for my 60 sake" (for my sake?). "It can't do harm, and it often does good. Why, it's nothing. And often in health people —— "

He opened his eyes wide.

"What? Take the sacrament? What for? No. Besides . . ."

She began to cry.

"Yes, my dear. I'll send for our priest, he's so nice."

"All right, very well," he said.

When the priest came and confessed him he was softened, felt as 61 it were a relief from his doubts, and consequently from his sufferings, and there came a moment of hope. He began once more thinking of the intestinal appendix and the possibility of curing it. He took the sacrament with tears in his eyes.

When they laid him down again after the sacrament for a minute, 62 he felt comfortable, and again the hope of life sprang up. He began to think about the operation which had been suggested to him. "To live, I want to live," he said to himself. His wife came in to congratulate him; she uttered the customary words and added —

"It's quite true, isn't it, that you're better?"

Without looking at her, he said, "Yes."

Her dress, her figure, the expression of her face, the tone of her 63 voice — all told him the same: "Not the right thing. All that in which you lived and are living is lying, deceit, hiding life and death away from you." And as soon as he had formed that thought, hatred sprang up in him, and with that hatred agonizing physical sufferings, and with these sufferings the sense of inevitable, approaching ruin. Something new was happening; there were screwing and shooting pains, and a tightness in his breathing.

The expression of his face as he uttered that "Yes" was terrible. 64 After uttering that "Yes," looking her straight in the face, he turned on to his face, with a rapidity extraordinary in his weakness, and shrieked —

"Go away, go away, let me be!"

From that moment there began the scream that never ceased for 65 three days, and was so awful that through two closed doors one could not hear it without horror. At the moment when he answered his wife he grasped that he had fallen, that there was no return, that the end had come, quite the end, while doubt was still as unsolved, still remained doubt.

"Oo! Oo—o! Oo!" he screamed in varying intonations. He had 66 begun screaming, "I don't want to!" and so had gone on screaming on the same vowel sound — oo!

All those three days, during which time did not exist for him, he 67 was struggling in that black sack into which he was being thrust by an unseen resistless force. He struggled as the man condemned to death struggles in the hands of the executioner, knowing that he cannot save himself. And every moment he felt that in spite of all his efforts to struggle against it, he was getting nearer and nearer to what terrified him. He felt that his agony was due both to his being thrust into this black hole and still more to his not being able to get right into it. What hindered him from getting into it was the claim that his life had been good. That justification of his life held him fast and would not let him get forward, and it caused him more agony than all.

All at once some force struck him in the chest, in the side, and 68 stifled his breathing more than ever; he rolled forward into the hole, and there at the end there was some sort of light. It had happened with him, as it had sometimes happened to him in a railway carriage, when he had thought he was going forward while he was going back, and all of a sudden recognized his real direction.

"Yes, it has all been not the right thing," he said to himself, "but that's no matter." He could, he could do the right thing. "What is the right thing?" he asked himself, and suddenly he became quiet.   69

This was at the end of the third day, two hours before his death.   70
At that very moment the schoolboy had stealthily crept into his father's room and gone up to his bedside. The dying man was screaming and waving his arms. His hand fell on the schoolboy's head. The boy snatched it, pressed it to his lips, and burst into tears.

At that very moment Ivan Ilyich had rolled into the hole, and   71
caught sight of the light, and it was revealed to him that his life had not been what it ought to have been, but that that could still be set right. He asked himself, "What is the right thing?" — and became quiet, listening. Then he felt some one was kissing his hand. He opened his eyes and glanced at his son. He felt sorry for him. His wife went up to him. He glanced at her. She was gazing at him with open mouth, the tears unwiped streaming over her nose and cheeks, a look of despair on her face. He felt sorry for her.

"Yes, I'm making them miserable," he thought. "They're sorry,   72
but it will be better for them when I die." He would have said this, but had not the strength to utter it. "Besides, why speak, I must act," he thought. With a glance to his wife he pointed to his son and said —

"Take away . . . sorry for him. . . . And you too . . ." He tried   73
to say "forgive," but said "forgo" . . . and too weak to correct himself, shook his hand, knowing that He would understand Whose understanding mattered.

And all at once it became clear to him that what had tortured him   74
and would not leave him was suddenly dropping away all at once on both sides and on ten sides and on all sides. He was sorry for them, must act so that they might not suffer. Set them free and be free himself of those agonies. "How right and how simple!" he thought. "And the pain?" he asked himself. "Where's it gone? Eh, where are you, pain?"

He began to watch for it.   75

"Yes, here it is. Well, what of it, let the pain be.

"And death. Where is it?"

He looked for his old accustomed terror of death, and did not find it. "Where is it? What death?" There was no terror, because death was not either.

In the place of death there was light.

"So this is it!" he suddenly exclaimed aloud.

"What joy!"

To him all this passed in a single instant, and the meaning of that 76 instant suffered no change after. For those present his agony lasted another two hours. There was a rattle in his throat, a twitching in his wasted body. Then the rattle and the gasping came at longer and longer intervals.

"It is over!" some one said over him.

He caught those words and repeated them in his soul.

"Death is over," he said to himself. "It's no more."

He drew in a breath, stopped midway in the breath, stretched and died.

Review Questions

1. How does Ivan Ilyich attempt to deny the imminence of death?
2. What are Ivan Ilyich's various reactions upon realizing that he is going to die?
3. Why does he spend time in the trivial business of the photo album?
4. What kind of comfort does he come to take from Gerasim, comfort he cannot obtain from his family? What is the significance of Gerasim's coming from peasant stock? How does Ivan Ilyich want to be treated?
5. With what realization does Ivan Ilyich's terror of death disappear?

Discussion Questions

1. In what way do the attitudes of Ivan Ilyich and his family reflect some of the attitudes discussed by Daniel Goleman, Elisabeth Kübler-Ross, and Philippe Ariès in their articles?
2. How does the "It" gradually assume ominous and omnipotent proportions? How does "It" become personified — almost a separate character in the drama of Ivan Ilyich's death?
3. Describe the range of moods in which we find Ivan Ilyich in this extract. Locate the passages in which these moods are described or dramatized.
4. What is the point of the Caius syllogism? Why is Caius contrasted with "little Vanya"?
5. Does the description of Ivan Ilyich's thoughts seem realistic? Or does it seem, at times, overdramatized? For instance, does it seem likely that he would feel so much hatred toward his wife when she comes in to see how he is? Or does it seem likely that he would take so much comfort in Gerasim?
6. When Ivan Ilyich is conversing with "the voice of his soul," he reflects on the happy moments in his life and concludes that "the further he went [i.e., the more social and civic esteem he earned] the less good

there was." By contrast, Gerasim, from peasant stock, appears content with his life. Why does Tolstoy make this contrast? What is he saying about going "uphill"?

7. What about childhood invites Ivan Ilyich, at the time of his death, to reflect upon it?

8. " 'How are we to blame?' said Liza to her mother. 'As though we had done it! I'm sorry for papa, but why punish us?' " Discuss Liza's reaction to her father's behavior.

9. Trace Tolstoy's treatment of what Ivan Ilyich "ought" to have done with his life. What is this "right thing" to which the dying man makes reference? When does the concern about how he ought to have lived first occur to Ivan Ilyich? At first, he resists thinking about the subject. How does this change? Cite specific passages from the text in your answer.

10. Why is Ivan Ilyich sorry for his son and wife? Why, at an earlier point in the story, did he want them to be sorry for him?

Writing Suggestions

1. In an example synthesis (in which you refer to passages by Kübler-Ross and Ariès), discuss Ivan Ilyich's death as a case of "modern," as opposed to "traditional," death.

2. "Why hast Thou done all this? What brought me to this? Why, why torture me so horribly?"
   He did not expect an answer, and wept indeed that there was and could be no answer. The pain grew more acute again, but he did not stir, did not call.

In an essay discuss why Ivan Ilyich — why we — ask such questions that have no answers?

3. "Can it be that I have not lived as one ought?" suddenly came into his head. "But how not so, when I've done everything as it should be done?" he said, and at once dismissed this only solution of all the enigma of life and death as something utterly out of the question.

In an essay discuss how it is possible for one "not to live as one ought" but still live according to social custom. Why does Ivan Ilyich dismiss this question? Why must he, inevitably, answer it?

DEATH KNOCKS
Woody Allen

Woody Allen was born Allen Stewart Konigsberg in Brooklyn, New York, in 1935. A comedian, actor, director, and writer for television, films, and the stage, Allen is regarded by many critics as a comic genius. Stuart Rosenthal characterizes his style as "an eclectic bombardment of literary, television, movie, and Madison Avenue techniques, and his target is the ordinary man's inadequacy in the face of the *clichés* that these sources promote." Allen's films include *What's New Pussycat? Take the Money and Run, Play It Again, Sam, Annie Hall* (which won Academy Awards for best director and best original screenplay), *Interiors, Manhattan,* and *Stardust Memories.* "Death Knocks" appears in *Getting Even,* a collection of humorous pieces, most of which were originally published in the *New Yorker.* Other Allen collections are *Without Feathers* (1976) and *Side Effects* (1980).

☐

(The play takes place in the bedroom of the Nat Ackermans' two-story house, somewhere in Kew Gardens. The carpeting is wall-to-wall. There is a big double bed and a large vanity. The room is elaborately furnished and curtained, and on the walls there are several paintings and a not really attractive barometer. Soft theme music as the curtain rises. Nat Ackerman, a bald, paunchy fifty-seven-year-old dress manufacturer, is lying on the bed finishing off tomorrow's Daily News. *He wears a bathrobe and slippers, and reads by a bed light clipped to the white headboard of the bed. The time is near midnight. Suddenly we hear a noise, and Nat sits up and looks at the window.)*

NAT: What the hell is that?

(Climbing awkwardly through the window is a sombre, caped figure. The intruder wears a black hood and skin-tight black clothes. The hood covers his head but not his face, which is middle-aged and stark white. He is something like Nat in appearance. He huffs audibly and then trips over the windowsill and falls into the room.)

DEATH *(for it is no one else)*: Jesus Christ. I nearly broke my neck.

NAT *(watching with bewilderment)*: Who are you?

DEATH: Death.

NAT: Who?

DEATH: Death. Listen — can I sit down? I nearly broke my neck. I'm shaking like a leaf.

NAT: Who *are* you?

DEATH: *Death.* You got a glass of water?

NAT: Death? What do you mean, Death?

DEATH: What is wrong with you? You see the black costume and the whitened face?

NAT: Yeah.

DEATH: Is it Halloween?

NAT: No.

DEATH: Then I'm Death. Now can I get a glass of water — or a Fresca?

NAT: If this is some joke —

DEATH: What kind of joke? You're fifty-seven? Nat Ackerman? One eighteen Pacific Street? Unless I blew it — where's that call sheet? (*He fumbles through pocket, finally producing a card with an address on it. It seems to check.*)

NAT: What do you want with me?

DEATH: What do I want? What do you think I want?

NAT: You must be kidding. I'm in perfect health.

DEATH (*unimpressed*): Uh-huh. (*Looking around*) This is a nice place. You do it yourself?

NAT: We had a decorator, but we worked with her.

DEATH (*looking at picture on the wall*): I love those kids with the big eyes.

NAT: I don't want to go yet.

DEATH: *You* don't want to go? Please don't start in. As it is, I'm nauseous from the climb.

NAT: What climb?

DEATH: I climbed up the drainpipe. I was trying to make a dramatic entrance. I see the big windows and you're awake reading. I figure it's worth a shot. I'll climb up and enter with a little — you know . . . (*Snaps fingers*) Meanwhile, I get my heel caught on some vines, the drainpipe breaks, and I'm hanging by a thread. Then my cape begins to tear. Look, let's just go. It's been a rough night.

NAT: You broke my drainpipe?

DEATH: Broke. It didn't break. It's a little bent. Didn't you hear anything? I slammed into the ground.

NAT: I was reading.

DEATH: You must have really been engrossed. (*Lifting newspaper Nat was reading*) "NAB COEDS IN POT ORGY." Can I borrow this?

NAT: I'm not finished.

DEATH: Er — I don't know how to put this to you, pal . . .

NAT: Why didn't you just ring downstairs?

DEATH: I'm telling you, I could have, but how does it look? This way I get a little drama going. Something. Did you read *Faust*?

NAT: What?

DEATH: And what if you had company? You're sitting there with important people. I'm Death — I should ring the bell and traipse right in the front? Where's your thinking?

NAT: Listen, Mister, it's very late.

DEATH: Yeah. Well, you want to go?

NAT: Go where?

DEATH: Death. It. The Thing. The Happy Hunting Grounds. (*Looking at his own knee*) Y'know, that's a pretty bad cut. My first job, I'm liable to get gangrene yet.

NAT: Now, wait a minute. I need time. I'm not ready to go.

DEATH: I'm sorry. I can't help you. I'd like to, but it's the moment.

NAT: How can it be the moment? I just merged with Modiste Originals.

DEATH: What's the difference, a couple of bucks more or less.

NAT: Sure, what do you care? You guys probably have all your expenses paid.

DEATH: You want to come along now?

NAT (*studying him*): I'm sorry, but I cannot believe you're Death.

DEATH: Why? What'd you expect — Rock Hudson?

NAT: No, it's not that.

DEATH: I'm sorry if I disappointed you.

NAT: Don't get upset. I don't know, I always thought you'd be . . . uh . . . taller.

DEATH: I'm five seven. It's average for my weight.

NAT: You look a little like me.

DEATH: Who should I look like? I'm your death.

NAT: Give me some time. Another day.

DEATH: I can't. What do you want me to say?

NAT: One more day. Twenty-four hours.

DEATH: What do you need it for? The radio said rain tomorrow.

NAT: Can't we work out something?

DEATH: Like what?

NAT: You play chess?

DEATH: No, I don't.

NAT: I once saw a picture of you playing chess.

DEATH: Couldn't be me, because I don't play chess. Gin rummy, maybe.

NAT: You play gin rummy?

DEATH: Do I play gin rummy? Is Paris a city?

NAT: You're good, huh?

DEATH: Very good.

NAT: I'll tell you what I'll do —

DEATH: Don't make any deals with me.

NAT: I'll play you gin rummy. If you win, I'll go immediately. If I win, give me some more time. A little bit — one more day.

DEATH: Who's got time to play gin rummy?

NAT: Come on. If you're so good.

DEATH: Although I feel like a game . . .

NAT: Come on. Be a sport. We'll shoot for a half hour.

DEATH: I really shouldn't.

NAT: I got the cards right here. Don't make a production.

DEATH: All right, come on. We'll play a little. It'll relax me.

NAT (*getting cards, pad, and pencil*): You won't regret this.

DEATH: Don't give me a sales talk. Get the cards and give me a Fresca and put out something. For God's sake, a stranger drops in, you don't have potato chips or pretzels.

NAT: There's M&M's downstairs in a dish.

DEATH: M&M's. What if the President came? He'd get M&M's too?

NAT: You're not the President.

DEATH: Deal.

> (*Nat deals, turns up a five.*)

NAT: You want to play a tenth of a cent a point to make it interesting?

DEATH: It's not interesting enough for you?

NAT: I play better when money's at stake.

DEATH: Whatever you say, Newt.

NAT: Nat. Nat Ackerman. You don't know my name?

DEATH: Newt, Nat — I got such a headache.

NAT: You want that five?

DEATH: No.

NAT: So pick.

DEATH (*surveying his hand as he picks*): Jesus, I got nothing here.

NAT: What's it like?

DEATH: What's what like?

(*Throughout the following, they pick and discard.*)

NAT: Death.

DEATH: What should it be like? You lay there.

NAT: Is there anything after?

DEATH: Aha, you're saving twos.

NAT: I'm asking. Is there anything after?

DEATH (*absently*): You'll see.

NAT: Oh, then I will actually see something?

DEATH: Well, maybe I shouldn't have put it that way. Throw.

NAT: To get an answer from you is a big deal.

DEATH: I'm playing cards.

NAT: All right, play, play.

DEATH: Meanwhile, I'm giving you one card after another.

NAT: Don't look through the discards.

DEATH: I'm not looking. I'm straightening them up. What was the knock card?

NAT: Four. You ready to knock already?

DEATH: Who said I'm ready to knock? All I asked was what was the knock card.

NAT: And all I asked was is there anything for me to look forward to.

DEATH: Play.

NAT: Can't you tell me anything? Where do we go?

DEATH: We? To tell you the truth, *you* fall in a crumpled heap on the floor.

NAT: Oh, I can't wait for that! Is it going to hurt?

DEATH: Be over in a second.

NAT: Terrific. (*Sighs*) I needed this. A man merges with Modiste Originals . . .

DEATH: How's four points?

NAT: You're knocking?

DEATH: Four points is good?

NAT: No, I got two.

DEATH: You're kidding.

NAT: No, you lose.

DEATH: Holy Christ, and I thought you were saving sixes.

NAT: No. Your deal. Twenty points and two boxes. Shoot. (*Death deals.*) I must fall on the floor, eh? I can't be standing over the sofa when it happens?

DEATH: No. Play.

NAT: Why not?

DEATH: Because you fall on the floor! Leave me alone. I'm trying to concentrate.

NAT: Why must it be on the floor? That's all I'm saying! Why can't the whole thing happen and I'll stand next to the sofa?

DEATH: I'll try my best. Now can we play?

NAT: That's all I'm saying. You remind me of Moe Lefkowitz. He's also stubborn.

DEATH: I remind him of Moe Lefkowitz. I'm one of the most terrifying figures you could possibly imagine, and him I remind of Moe Lefkowitz. What is he, a furrier?

NAT: You should be such a furrier. He's good for eighty thousand a year. Passementeries. He's got his own factory. Two points.

DEATH: What?

NAT: Two points. I'm knocking. What have you got?

DEATH: My hand is like a basketball score.

NAT: And it's spades.

DEATH: If you didn't talk so much.

(*They redeal and play on.*)

NAT: What'd you mean before when you said this was your first job?

DEATH: What does it sound like?

NAT: What are you telling me — that nobody ever went before?

DEATH: Sure they went. But I didn't take them.

NAT: So who did?

DEATH: Others.

NAT: There's others?

DEATH: Sure. Each one has his own personal way of going.

NAT: I never knew that.

DEATH: Why should you know? Who are you?

NAT: What do you mean who am I? Why — I'm nothing?

DEATH: Not nothing. You're a dress manufacturer. Where do you come to knowledge of the eternal mysteries?

NAT: What are you talking about? I make a beautiful dollar. I sent two kids through college. One is in advertising, the other's married. I got my own home. I drive a Chrysler. My wife has whatever she wants. Maids, mink coat, vacations. Right now she's at the Eden Roc. Fifty dollars a day because she wants to be near her sister. I'm supposed to join her next week, so what do you think I am — some guy off the street?

DEATH: All right. Don't be so touchy.

NAT: Who's touchy?

DEATH: How would you like it if I got insulted quickly?

NAT: Did I insult you?

DEATH: You didn't say you were disappointed in me?

NAT: What do you expect? You want me to throw you a block party?

DEATH: I'm not talking about that. I mean me personally. I'm too short, I'm this, I'm that.

NAT: I said you looked like me. It's like a reflection.

DEATH: All right, deal, deal.

(*They continue to play as music steals in and the lights dim until all is in total darkness. The lights slowly come up again, and now it is later and their game is over. Nat tallies.*)

NAT: Sixty-eight . . . one-fifty . . . Well, you lose.

DEATH (*dejectedly looking through the deck*): I knew I shouldn't have thrown that nine. Damn it.

NAT: So I'll see you tomorrow.

DEATH: What do you mean you'll see me tomorrow?

NAT: I won the extra day. Leave me alone.

DEATH: You were serious?

NAT: We made a deal.

DEATH: Yeah, but —

NAT: Don't "but" me. I won twenty-four hours. Come back to-morrow.

DEATH: I didn't know we were actually playing for time.

NAT: That's too bad about you. You should pay attention.

DEATH: Where am I going to go for twenty-four hours?

NAT: What's the difference? The main thing is I won an extra day.

DEATH: What do you want me to do — walk the streets?

NAT: Check into a hotel and go to a movie. Take a *schvitz*. Don't make a federal case.

DEATH: Add the score again.

NAT: Plus you owe me twenty-eight dollars.

DEATH: *What?*

NAT: That's right, Buster. Here it is — read it.

DEATH (*going through pockets*): I have a few singles — not twenty-eight dollars.

NAT: I'll take a check.

DEATH: From what account?

NAT: Look who I'm dealing with.

DEATH: Sue me. Where do I keep my checking account?

NAT: All right, gimme what you got and we'll call it square.

DEATH: Listen, I need that money.

NAT: Why should you need money?

DEATH: What are you talking about? You're going to the Beyond.

NAT: So?

DEATH: So — you know how far that is?

NAT: So?

DEATH: So where's gas? Where's tolls?

NAT: We're going by car!

DEATH: You'll find out. (*Agitatedly*) Look — I'll be back tomorrow, and you'll give me a chance to win the money back. Otherwise I'm in definite trouble.

NAT: Anything you want. Double or nothing we'll play. I'm liable to win an extra week or a month. The way you play, maybe years.

DEATH: Meantime I'm stranded.

NAT: See you tomorrow.

DEATH (*being edged to the doorway*): Where's a good hotel? What am I talking about hotel, I got no money. I'll go sit in Bickford's. (*He picks up the* News.)

NAT: Out. Out. That's my paper. (*He takes it back.*)

DEATH (*exiting*): I couldn't just take him and go. I had to get involved in rummy.

NAT (*calling after him*): And be careful going downstairs. On one of the steps the rug is loose.

(*And, on cue, we hear a terrific crash. Nat sighs, then crosses to the bedside table and makes a phone call.*)

NAT: Hello, Moe? Me. Listen, I don't know if somebody's playing a joke, or what, but Death was just here. We played a little gin . . . No, *Death.* In person. Or somebody who claims to be Death. But, Moe, he's such a *schlep!*

Curtain

Discussion Questions

1. Death is usually personified as a terrible, "grim reaper." How does Allen take advantage of this convention? How does he personify death?

2. At one point during the play, Nat says, "I said you looked like me. It's like a reflection." Considering your answer to the previous question, what do you think Allen is saying?

3. Why are Death and Nat playing gin rummy, and not chess? (In Ingmar Bergman's allegorical film *The Seventh Seal* (1956), Antoninus Blok, a knight returning from the crusades, encounters Death. Playing for time, Blok challenges Death to a game of chess. Woody Allen reveres Bergman and was undoubtedly conscious of the parallel when he wrote *Death Knocks.*)

4. Examine the ways in which Allen intersperses serious comments about death and dying throughout the comic dialogue.

5. Analyze the plot structure of the play, from Death's entry to his exit. In un-comic terms, what is happening?

Writing Suggestions

1. Is death a subject to be treated with humor? Are we not — is Allen not — troubled by dying? In an essay (in which you might reflect on personal experience), discuss how a humorist can help us cope with

difficult issues. What are the advantages of Allen's treating death in this fashion? What are the disadvantages? Are there limits to what we will laugh at?

2. Read other works by Woody Allen and attempt, in a synthesis, to explain his method of humor. Are there certain subjects he works with more regularly than others? What does he expect of his audience? What image of himself does he project? Examine passages that you find particularly funny. What makes you laugh?

SUMMARY, SYNTHESIS, CRITIQUE ACTIVITIES

Summary

Summarize one or more of the passages in this chapter. Follow the suggested six-step process. Take into account the "Review Questions" for each passage. (*Recommended:* "We Are Breaking the Silence about Death")

Synthesis

too challenging

X1. *Describe* the extent to which Kübler-Ross's stages of dying account for Ivan Ilyich's thoughts and behavior.

2. *Define* the concept of death with dignity. Suggested sources: "We Are Breaking the Silence about Death" and "The Dying Man Is Deprived of His Death."

3. Have you ever actively considered your own mortality — the simple fact that you will be alive one instant and dead the next? *Describe* your feelings about your own mortality, perhaps in comparison to the feelings expressed or implied in "The Death of Ivan Ilyich."

4. *Argue* that modern attitudes towards death are less mature, less healthy than earlier attitudes. Cite "On the Fear of Death" and "The Dying Man Is Deprived of His Death."

X5. Both Leo Tolstoy and Woody Allen refer to death as IT. What are the differences in their treatments of death and dying? Your *comparison and contrast* synthesis should take account of the main character in each piece and his (non)acceptance of death.

6. Goleman writes of death and dying in a discursive way and Pastan writes in a poetic way. Which selection appeals to you more? *Argue* your position based on a close reading of Goleman and Pastan.

7. *Compare and contrast* "right ways" of dying. Suggested sources: Goleman, Pastan, Kübler-Ross, and Klein. At some point, of course, you should define "right."

8. The authors of the selections in this chapter write from many different perspectives: historical, psychological, psychiatric, poetical, anthropological, narrative, humorous. Focusing on about three passages, write a *comparison-contrast* synthesis, discussing how the background or profession of the writer has influenced both what he or she has to say about death and dying and how he or she says it. Use the information in the headnotes to help you.

9. The selections in this unit offer a number of case studies of dying persons and their loved ones: the farmer who fell from the tree in the Kübler-Ross passage, Mme. de La Ferronnays in the Ariès passage, the narrator of Pastan's poem, Ivan Ilyich, Woody Allen's Nat Ackerman. Drawing upon three or four of these (or other) selections, *compare and contrast* the ways that people die and the ways that their loved ones respond. Draw whatever conclusions seem warranted. If you feel ambitious, you might also read Plato's account of the death of Socrates at the end of his dialogue "Phaedo," and incorporate the death of Socrates into your synthesis.

Critique

Write a critique of Kübler-Ross's "On the Fear of Death." You may wish to consider some of Klein's arguments.

RESEARCH TOPICS

1. Research the literature on life-after-death experiences. Do these accounts affect the way in which you approach the subject of death and dying?

2. Compare and contrast the doctrines on death and dying in two religions. You may wish to focus your examination on the concept of heaven and hell, last rites, funeral services, burial practices, mourning, or sacred literature (the Bible, Koran, Talmud, etc.).

3. Examine the possible reasons why death and dying have become such a widely discussed topic during the last fifteen years. Were we, in a historical sense, "ready" for the discussion?

4. Review the moral and legal considerations involved with the practice of euthanasia. Argue your own position.

5. Discuss death and dying from the perspective of a single academic discipline. If you plan to become an economics major, you might research the cost and financing of funerals in this country. Prospective literature majors may want to read and synthesize several novels,

short stories, or plays that treat the subject of death and dying. Those interested in psychology might examine the characteristic patterns of grief in a family when one of its members has died.

ADDITIONAL READINGS

Ariès, Phillipe. *Western Attitudes Toward Death.* Trans. by Patricia M. Ranum. Baltimore: The Johns Hopkins University Press, 1974.

"At the Hour of Death." *Commonweal,* 6 June 1980, pp. 333–335.

Congdon, Howard. *The Pursuit of Death.* Nashville: Pantheon Press, 1977.

Dudley, E. "Toward a Conquest of Death." *Futurist,* December 1980, pp. 71–77.

Fulton, Robert. *Death, Grief, and Bereavement: A Bibliography: 1845–1975.* New York: Arno Press, 1977.

———, Eric Markusen, Greg Owen, June Scheiber, eds. *Death and Dying: Challenge and Change.* Reading, Mass.: Addison-Wesley Publishing Company, 1978.

Kübler-Ross, Elisabeth. *On Death and Dying.* New York: Macmillan, 1969.

———. *Death: The Final Stage of Growth.* Englewood Cliffs: Prentice-Hall, 1975.

Larue, Gerald. "Death and the Humanist Counselor." *The Humanist,* May/June 1980, pp. 13–15.

Mitford, Jessica. *The American Way of Death.* New York: Simon and Schuster, 1963.

Plato. *Phaedo.* Trans. with intro. and commentary by R. Hackforth. Cambridge, England: University Press, 1955. [Esp. at the end of the *Phaedo,* the death of Socrates.]

Rubin, Harold. "Directive to Physicians: The Right to Die Decently." *Nation,* 4 February 1978, pp. 114–116.

Saroyan, William. *Obituaries.* Berkeley: Creative Arts Book Co., 1979.

Simpson, Michael. *Dying, Death and Grief: A Critically Annotated Bibliography and Source Book of Thanatology and Terminal Care.* New York: Plenum Press, 1979.

Veatch, Robert. *Death, Dying, and the Biological Revolution: Our Last Quest for Responsibility.* New Haven: Yale University Press, 1976.

See also David Stannard, *Death in America,* from which the Ariès article was taken.

A Woman's Role

First, of course, was the interminable prerevolutionary period when it seldom occurred to either sex that women had any duties on earth other than to be wives, mistresses, and mothers to their men. What feminist sentiment existed was easily repulsed, either by ridicule, intimidation, or brute force. The idea that women had any right to self-fulfillment, apart from men, had no chance to take hold.

Then came the revolution. It came slowly, at different times, in different places, starting almost imperceptibly in the late eighteenth century (with Mary Wollstonecraft's *Vindication of the Rights of Women*), gathering force in the nineteenth century, through women like Susan B. Anthony and Elizabeth Cady Stanton, and continuing into the early days of the present century with the suffragette movement. Finally, heralded by women like Simone de Beauvoir, Betty Friedan, Kate Millett, and Gloria Steinem, the revolution exploded. Sexist attitudes in the kitchen, the bedroom, and the boardroom encountered a mass and determined challenge beyond all past experience. Soon afterward, the inevitable counterrevolution began, aided by antifeminists like Marabel Morgan and Phyllis Schlafly, as well as by the accumulated weight of traditional thought, unready for the domestic and social disruption that would ensue if feminist ideals of total equality in all spheres of life were carried to conclusion. The difficulty that the Equal Rights Amendment has met in gaining ratification is only one indication of the still-potent force of the opposition.

Nevertheless, the impact of the feminist revolution has been profound, and its effects will not easily be reversed. Even if such visible landmarks as E.R.A. are not built, the way men and women think about each other and about their roles in society (at least in the United States) has been drastically changed. Thus, we now find ourselves in the postrevolutionary period, when women must consider where they will go from here. In particular, they must consider what form — and what tone — the feminist revolution will now take.

The readings in this chapter represent each of the three periods we have been discussing — though perhaps we should not talk of periods so much as attitudes, for revolutionary attitudes existed in the nineteenth century, just as prerevolutionary attitudes persist today. Examples of this prerevolutionary attitude (of woman as domestic, or as subordinate, or as simply irrational, in comparison to men) are presented in our first three selections. Mary Daly provides a historical perspective, recounting the origins of the sexist attitudes that have held women in domestic subjugation since Biblical times. Then, Pope Pius XI, in his encyclical ''On Christian

Marriage," emphatically reaffirms the traditional role of the domestic woman in the twentieth century. And in a red flag song from *My Fair Lady,* superchauvinist Henry Higgins explains why no sane man would ever let a woman in his life.

The revolutionary period is represented first in an excerpt from *A Doll's House,* in which playwright Henrik Ibsen shows how one heretofore conventional woman angrily abandons her role as a housewife. Then Kate Millett, in her "Manifesto for Revolution," details the abuses of patriarchal authority and anticipates a sexual revolution that will free men and women of the gender roles that have kept them from achieving their "full human status." The counterrevolution is represented by Phyllis Schlafly, who compares the "woman's liberationist" with her "Positive Woman."

The postrevolutionary attitude is represented by feminists Anne Roiphe and Betty Friedan. In "Confessions of a Female Chauvinist Sow," Roiphe tells how she tries (not always successfully) to avoid being as sexist as many women she has known. And in "Feminism's Next Step," Betty Friedan argues that women must break through their "own feminist mystique and move into the second stage [of the revolution], no longer against men but with them."

SOCIAL ATTITUDES TOWARDS WOMEN
Mary Daly

Mary Daly (b. 1928) has taught philosophy and theology at Cardinal Cushing College and Boston College. She has written extensively on the role of women in the Catholic Church in such books as *The Church and the Second Sex* and *Sisterhood Is Powerful.* Daly, whose says her "fundamental interest is the women's revolution," examines Biblical history with a set of assumptions that differ radically from those of traditional theologians.

☐

The situation of women in Western society has always been fraught   1
with ambiguity. The writings of innumerable authors in a variety of
fields attest to the existence of the problem, although there is by no
means agreement concerning the nature of the problem. Adherents
of the "eternal feminine" mystique accept as normative the feminine

stereotypes of our culture, according to which a "true woman" does not achieve self-actualization through intellectual creativity and participation in political, economic, and social life on a level equal to that of men. Rather, according to this view, her destiny lies in generic fulfillment through motherhood, physical or spiritual, and in being a helpmate to her husband. Opposition to this position is strong. Radically opposed to the idea that the feminine stereotype is "natural" are the findings of anthropology, which suggest that "many, if not all, of the personality traits that we have called masculine or feminine are as lightly linked to sex, as are the clothing, the manners, and the form of head-dress that a society at a given period assigns to sex." Recent research in experimental psychology also tends to refute the idea that the cluster of qualities expressed by the "eternal feminine" stereotype are innate and peculiar to women. A growing number of authors argue that the characteristics of the "eternal feminine" are opposed to those of a developing, authentic person, who must be unique, self-critical, active, and searching. Modern feminists argue that the biological burdens associated with maternity and the restrictions imposed by cultural conditioning have held women back from the attainment of full human stature. They note with irony that the compensation offered by society to women for acceptance of the restrictions which it has imposed upon them in the political, economic, social, educational, and moral spheres has been imprisonment upon a pedestal.

   The oppressive situation of women in ancient times is reflected in the Bible. The authors of both the Old and the New Testaments were men of their times, and it would be naive to think that they were free of the prejudices of their epochs. Indeed, the Bible contains much to jolt the modern woman, who is accustomed to think of herself, at least to some extent, as an autonomous person. In the writings of the Old Testament, women emerge as subjugated and inferior beings. Although the wife of an Israelite was not on the level of a slave, and however much better off she was than wives in other Near-Eastern nations, it is indicative of her inferior condition that the wife addressed her husband as a slave addressed his master, or a subject his king. In the Decalogue a man's wife is listed among his possessions, along with such items as his ox and his ass (Exodus 20:17; Deuteronomy 5:21). While her husband could repudiate her, she could not claim a divorce. Misconduct on the part of the wife was severely punished among the ancient Hebrews, whereas infidelity on the part of the man was punished only if he violated the rights of another man by taking a married woman as his accomplice. A man could sell his daughter as well as his slaves. If a couple did not have children, it was assumed to be the fault of the wife. In summary, although Hebrew women were honored as parents and often treated with kindness, their social and legal status was that of subordinate beings. Hebrew males prayed: "I thank thee, Lord, that thou has not created me a woman."

Throughout the centuries, Christian authors have placed great   3 importance upon the account of the creation of Eve in the second chapter of Genesis. Combined with the story of the Fall, this seemed to present irrefutable evidence of woman's essentially inferior intellectual and moral stature. Indeed, through the ages the anti-feminine tradition in Christian culture has justified itself to a large extent on the story of the origin and activities of the "first mother," which until recently was not understood to be androcentric myth but rather was taken as straight historical fact. A psychoanalyst who is also a student of biblical literature has summarized the situation succinctly: "The biblical story of Eve's birth is the hoax of the millennia."

Androcentric tendencies in Western culture, rooted also in the   4 profound misogynism of the Greeks, are reflected in the New Testament as well, which in turn has served as a basis for their perpetuation throughout Christendom. The most strikingly anti-feminine passages are in the Pauline texts. Paul was greatly concerned with order in society and in Christian assemblies in particular. It seemed important to him that women should not have a predominant place in Christian assemblies, that they should not "speak" in public or unveil their heads. This could have caused scandal and ridicule of the new sect, which already had to face charges of immorality and effeminacy. Thus he repeatedly insisted upon "correct" sexual behavior, including the subjection of wives at meetings. Paul went further and looked for theological justification for the prevailing customs. Thus, for example: "For a man ought not to cover his head, since he is the image and glory of God; but woman is the glory of man. For man was not made from woman, but woman from man. Neither was man created for woman, but woman for man" (I Corinthians 11:7ff.). Paul was basing his theological assertion here upon the then commonly held interpretation of Genesis. The extent of the effect is inestimable. For nearly two thousand years sermons and pious literature have been based upon the "glory of man" theme, and this has been accepted as God's inspired word.

Another frequently quoted Pauline text (probably not written by   5 Paul but traditionally attributed to him) based on the then current interpretation of Genesis and used ever since as authority for the subordination of women is the following:

> Let a woman learn in silence with all submissiveness. I permit no woman to teach or to have authority over men; she is to keep silent. For Adam was formed first, then Eve; and Adam was not deceived, but the woman was deceived and became a transgressor. Yet woman will be saved through bearing children, if she continues in faith and love and holiness, with modesty (I Timothy 2:11–15).

As for women's place in domestic society, the Pauline teaching was most explicit: "As the Church is subject to Christ, so let wives be subject in everything to their husbands" (Ephesians 5:24).

Such texts, understood as divinely inspired and without reference to the cultural context in which they were written, have served as powerful instruments for the reinforcement of the subjection of women in Western society. They have been used by religious authorities down through the centuries as a guarantee of divine approval for the transformation of woman's subordinate status from a contingent fact into an immutable norm of the feminine condition. They have been instrumental in withholding from women equal education, legal and economic equality, and access to the professions.

The low esteem for women in Western society during the early centuries of Christianity is reflected in the writings of the Church Fathers. The characteristics they considered to be typically feminine include fickleness and shallowness, garrulousness and weakness, slowness of understanding, and instability of mind. There were some violent tirades, such as that of Tertullian: "Do you not know that you are Eve? . . . You are the devil's gateway. . . . How easily you destroyed man, the image of God. Because of the death which you brought upon us, even the Son of God had to die" (*De cultu feminarum*, libri duo I, 1). On the whole, the attitude was one of puzzlement over the seemingly incongruous fact of woman's existence. Augustine summed up the general idea in saying that he did not see in what way it could be said that woman was made to be a help for man, if the work of child-bearing be excluded.

The Fathers found in Genesis an "explanation" of woman's inferiority which served as a guarantee of divine approval for perpetuating the situation which made her inferior. There was uncritical acceptance of the androcentric myth of Eve's creation and refusal, in varying degrees of inflexibility, to grant that woman is the image of God — an attitude in large measure inspired by Paul's first epistle to the Corinthians. Thus Augustine wrote that only man is the image and glory of God. According to him, since the believing woman cannot lay aside her sex, she is restored to the image of God only where there is no sex, that is, in the spirit (*De Trinitate,* XII, 7).

Together with the biblical account and the teachings of Church Fathers, those living in the early centuries of the Christian era were confronted with an image of women produced by oppressive conditions which were universal. A girlhood of strict seclusion and of minimal education prepared them for the life of mindless subordinates. This was followed by an early marriage which effectively cut them off from the possibility of autonomous action for the rest of their lives. Their inferiority was a fact; it appeared to be "natural."

Thus experience apparently supported the rib story just as the myth itself helped "explain" the common experience of women as incomplete and lesser humans. The vicious circle was complete. . . .

Review Questions

1. Why do accounts of women in the Bible "jolt" the modern woman?
2. According to Daly, what is the importance of considering the cultural context in which the New Testament was written?
3. What is the "glory of man" theme? What is its significance?
4. How did the Church Fathers perpetuate the view of women's inferiority, according to Daly?

Discussion Questions

1. When Daly writes about the "oppressive" situation of women in ancient times, she is, as a historian, betraying a bias: she writes as a "modern, autonomous person." Cite examples throughout the essay that reveal Daly's bias. Does such a bias invalidate her inquiry into the lives of women in ancient times? Can a historical inquiry ever be free of the historian's point of view? Can history be objective? Goethe, the famous eighteenth-century German poet and dramatist, said: "Any statement thought of simply as a *fact* has already been interpreted and formulated in the light of a theory." How does this apply to Daly's historical survey?
2. Paul writes that a man should not cover his head because he is in the image of God, while a woman should cover her head because she is in the image of man. Daly says that Paul made this statement having "looked for theological justifications for the prevailing [sexual] customs." What are Daly's assumptions about Biblical history?

Writing Suggestions

1. Daly says that women have been "imprisoned on a pedestal." Is this imprisonment limited to women? That is, are men not also imprisoned by gender roles? Are the prisons different? Prepare an editorial in which you examine these prisons.
2. Research and prepare a report on a historical event which you learned about as a child and which you now feel your history teacher or history text presented with a sexual bias.

ON CHRISTIAN MARRIAGE
Pope Pius XI

Pius XI was born Achille Ambrogio Damiano Ratti in 1857 in Desio, Italy. He became cardinal and archbishop of Milan in 1921 and Pope in 1922, an office which he held for seventeen years until his death in 1939. Pius issued several encyclicals of importance, especially those "On the Roman Catholic Church in Mexico" and "On Christian Marriage."

□

Encyclical Letter *Casti Connubii*, December 31, 1930

How great is the dignity of chaste wedlock, Venerable Brethren, 1 may be judged best from this that Christ Our Lord, Son of the Eternal Father, having assumed the nature of fallen man, not only, with His loving desire of compassing the redemption of our race, ordained it in an especial manner as the principle and foundation of domestic society and therefore of all human intercourse, but also raised it to the rank of a truly and "great sacrament" of the New Law, restored it to the original purity of its divine institution, and accordingly entrusted all its discipline and care to His spouse the Church.

In order, however, that amongst men of every nation and every 2 age the desired fruits may be obtained from this renewal of matrimony, it is necessary, first of all, that men's minds be illuminated with the true doctrine of Christ regarding it; and secondly, that Christian spouses, the weakness of their wills strengthened by the internal grace of God, shape all their ways of thinking and of acting in conformity with that pure law of Christ so as to obtain true peace and happiness for themselves and for their families.

Yet not only do We, looking with paternal eye on the universal 3 world from this Apostolic See as from a watchtower, but you also, Venerable Brethren, see, and seeing deeply grieve with Us that a great number of men, forgetful of that divine work of renewal, either entirely ignore or shamelessly deny the great sanctity of Christian wedlock, or relying on the false principles of a new and utterly perverse morality, too often trample it underfoot. And since these most pernicious errors and depraved morals have begun to spread even amongst the faithful and are gradually gaining ground, in Our

office as Christ's Vicar upon earth and Supreme Shepherd and Teacher We consider it Our duty to raise Our voice to keep the flock committed to Our care from poisoned pastures and, as far as in Us lies, to preserve it from harm.

We have decided therefore to speak to you, Venerable Brethren, and through you to the whole Church of Christ and indeed to the whole human race, on the nature and dignity of Christian marriage, on the advantages and benefits which accrue from it to the family and to human society itself, on the errors contrary to this most important point of the Gospel teaching, on the vices opposed to conjugal union, and lastly on the principal remedies to be applied. In so doing We follow the footsteps of Our predecessor, Leo XIII, of happy memory, whose encyclical *Arcanum,* published fifty years ago, We hereby confirm and make Our own, and while We wish to expound more fully certain points called for by the conditions and needs of our times, nevertheless We declare that, far from being obsolete, it retains its full force at the present day. 4

And to begin with that same encyclical, which is almost wholly concerned in vindicating the divine institution of matrimony, its sacramental dignity, and its perpetual stability, let it be repeated as an immutable and inviolable fundamental doctrine that matrimony was not instituted or restored by man but by God; not by man were the laws made to strengthen and confirm and elevate it, but by God, the Author of nature, and by Christ Our Lord by Whom nature was restored, and hence these laws cannot be subject to any human decrees or to any contrary pact even of the spouses themselves. This is the doctrine of Holy Scripture, this is the constant tradition of the Universal Church, this is the solemn definition of the sacred Council of Trent, which declares and establishes from the words of Holy Writ itself that God is the Author of the perpetual stability of the marriage bond, its unity and its firmness. . . . 5

[The] mutual inward moulding of husband and wife, this determined effort to perfect each other, can in a very real sense, as the Roman Catechism teaches, be said to be the chief reason and purpose of matrimony, provided matrimony be looked at not in the restricted sense as instituted for the proper conception and education of the child, but more widely as the blending of life as a whole and the mutual interchange and sharing thereof. 6

By this same love it is necessary that all the other rights and duties of the marriage state be regulated as the words of the Apostle: "Let the husband render the debt to the wife, and the wife also in like manner to the husband, not only a law of justice, but of charity. 7

Domestic society being confirmed, therefore, by this bond of love, there should flourish in it that "order of love," as St. Augustine calls it. This order includes both the primacy of the husband with 8 regard to the wife and children, the ready subjection of the wife and her willing obedience, which the Apostle commends in these words: "Let women be subject to their husbands as to the Lord, because the husband is the head of the wife, as Christ is the head of the church.

This subjection, however, does not deny or take away the liberty   9
which fully belongs to the woman both in view of her dignity as a human person, and in view of her most noble office as wife and mother and companion; nor does it bid her obey her husband's every request if not in harmony with right reason or with the dignity due to a wife; nor, in fine, does it imply that the wife should be put on a level with those persons who in law are called minors, to whom it is not customary to allow free exercise of their rights on account of their lack of mature judgment, or of their ignorance of human affairs. But it forbids that exaggerated liberty which cares not for the good of the family; it forbids that in this body which is the family, the heart be separated from the head to the great detriment of the whole body and the proximate danger of ruin. For if the man is the head, the woman is the heart, and as he occupies the chief place in ruling, so she may and ought to claim for herself the chief place in love.

Again, this subjection of wife to husband in its degree and man-   10
ner may vary according to the different conditions of persons, place and time. In fact, if the husband neglect his duty, it falls to the wife to take his place in directing the family. But the structure of the family and its fundamental law, established and confirmed by God, must always and everywhere be maintained intact.

With great wisdom Our predecessor Leo XIII, of happy mem-   11
ory, in the encyclical on *Christian Marriage* which We have already mentioned, speaking of this order to be maintained between man and wife, teaches: "The man is the ruler of the family, and the head of the woman; but because she is flesh of his flesh and bone of his bone, let her be subject and obedient to the man, not as a servant but as a companion, so that nothing be lacking of honor or of dignity in the obedience which she pays. Let divine charity be the constant guide of their mutual relations, both in him who rules and in her who obeys, since each bears the image, the one of Christ, the other of the Church." . . .

The same false teachers who try to dim the luster of conjugal   12
faith and purity do not scruple to do away with the honorable and trusting obedience which the woman owes to the man. Many of them even go further and assert that such a subjection of one party to the other is unworthy of human dignity, that the rights of husband and wife are equal; wherefore, they boldly proclaim, the emancipation of women has been or ought to be effected. This emancipation, in their opinion, must be threefold, in the ruling of the domestic society,

in the administration of family affairs and in the rearing of the children. It must be social, economic, physiological; physiological, that is to say, the woman is to be freed at her own good pleasure from the burdensome duties properly belonging to a wife as companion and mother (We have already said that this is not an emancipation but a crime); social inasmuch as the wife being freed from the care of children and family, should, to the neglect of these, be able to follow her own bent and devote herself to business and even public affairs; finally economic, whereby the woman even without the knowledge and against the will of her husband may be at liberty to conduct and administer her own affairs, giving her attention chiefly to these rather than to children, husband and family.

This, however, is not the true emancipation of woman, nor that   13
rational and exalted liberty which belongs to the noble office of a Christian woman and wife; it is rather the debasing of the womanly character and the dignity of motherhood, and indeed of the whole family, as a result of which the husband suffers the loss of his wife, the children of their mother and the home and the whole family of an ever watchful guardian. More than this, this false liberty and unnatural equality with the husband is to the detriment of the woman herself, for if the woman descends from her truly regal throne to which she has been raised within the walls of the home by means of the Gospel, she will soon be reduced to the old state of slavery (if not in appearance, certainly in reality) and become, as amongst the pagans, the mere instrument of man.

This equality of rights, which is so much exaggerated and dis-   14
torted, must indeed be recognized in those rights which belong to the dignity of the human soul and which are proper to the marriage contract and inseparably bound up with wedlock. In such things undoubtedly both parties enjoy the same rights and are bound by the same obligations; in other things there must be a certain inequality and due accommodation, which is demanded by the good of the family and the right ordering and unity and stability of home life.

As, however, the social and economic conditions of the married   15
woman must in some way be altered on account of the changes in social intercourse, it is part of the office of the public authority to adapt the civil rights of the wife to modern needs and requirements, keeping in view what the natural disposition and temperament of the female sex, good morality, and the welfare of the family demand, and provided always that the essential order of the domestic society remain intact, founded as it is on something higher than human authority and wisdom, namely on the authority and wisdom of God, and so not changeable by public laws or at the pleasure of private individuals.

Review Questions

1. Why is the institution of Christian marriage a "great sacrament"?
2. What should be the "order of love" in a Christian marriage?
3. In paragraph 5 of the encyclical, how does Leo XIII, Pius's predecessor, define the proper relationship between husband and wife?
4. Why, according to Pius, is the "emancipation of woman" a "debasing of the womanly character and the dignity of motherhood"?
5. To what extent should a public authority, such as a state legislature, "adapt the civil rights of the wife to modern needs and requirements"? At the same time, why are the basic laws of Christian marriage not subject to human decrees?

Discussion Questions

1. To what "pernicious errors and depraved morals" does Pius refer in paragraph 3 of the encyclical? How do these errors threaten the sanctity of marriage as a religious institution? If marriage is regarded as a *social* institution, are these errors and depravities still errors? Why or why not?
2. The Church's position on marriage is that it is a divine institution. Is this position arguable?
3. Pius is careful to balance his remarks: he writes that while a woman should be subject to her husband, "subjugation . . . does not deny or take away the liberty which fully belongs to the woman." Would Pius's definition of liberty be acceptable to feminists?
4. Pius writes in an ecclesiastical style. Describe this style and cite examples from the encyclical.
5. Paragraph 1 of the encyclical is one extended sentence. Circle the words that establish a parallel structure in the sentence — *not only* and *but also*. Underline *ordained it, raised it,* and *entrusted* and try rereading the sentence.
6. Analyze Pius's chain of reasoning in the first five paragraphs of the encyclical. Pay special attention to the first lines of paragraphs 2 through 5. What is Pius doing here?

Writing Suggestions

1. Based on your reading of these passages in Pius's Encyclical Letter, discuss the dilemma that a devoutly raised Catholic woman might experience if she were sympathetic to the causes of women's liberation. Write your essay as though you were that woman, making a series of entries into a diary or journal.

2. Why would paragraph 12 of the encyclical be likely to stir great controversy among those who believe, contrary to Pius, that the laws of marriage *are* subject to human decree? Develop your ideas in an essay.

LET A WOMAN IN YOUR LIFE . . . !
Alan Jay Lerner

Alan Jay Lerner (b. 1918), playwright, screenwriter, and lyricist, collaborated with Frederick Loewe on a number of successful musicals, including *Brigadoon, Paint Your Wagon, Gigi, Camelot,* and, most notably, *My Fair Lady* (1956), which was based on George Bernard Shaw's *Pygmalion.* In both plays, the supremely self-confident and chauvinistic Henry Higgins, a professor of languages, instructs Eliza Dolittle, a coarse, cockney flower girl, in the refinements of elegant diction. After a few weeks, he is able to escort Eliza to an Embassy ball and to pass her off as a princess — thus confirming his theory about the social importance of language. This song is from the first act of *My Fair Lady.*

I'm an ordinary man;
Who desires nothing more
Than just the ordinary chance
To live exactly as he likes
And do precisely what he wants.   5
An average man am I
Of no eccentric whim;
Who likes to live his life
Free of strife,
Doing whatever he thinks is best for him.   10
Just an ordinary man.

But let a woman in your life
And your serenity is through!
She'll redecorate your home
From the cellar to the dome;   15
Then get on to the enthralling
Fun of overhauling
You.

Oh, let a woman in your life
And you are up against the wall!
Make a plan and you will find   20
She has something else in mind;
And so rather than do either
You do something else that neither
Likes at all.   25

You want to talk of Keats or Milton;
She only wants to talk of love.
You go to see a play or ballet,
And spend it searching for her glove.

Oh, let a woman in your life
And you invite eternal strife!   30
Let them buy their wedding bands
For those anxious little hands;
I'd be equally as willing
For a dentist to be drilling
Than to ever let a woman in my life!   35

    (*With sudden amiability*)

I'm a very gentle man;
Even-tempered and good-natured,
Whom you never hear complain;
Who has the milk of human kindness
By the quart in ev'ry vein.   40
A patient man am I
Down to my fingertips;
The sort who never could,
Ever would,
Let an insulting remark escape his lips.   45

    (*Violently*)

But let a woman in your life
And patience hasn't got a chance.
She will beg you for advice;
Your reply will be concise.
And she'll listen very nicely   50
Then go out and do precisely
What she wants!
You were a man of grace and polish
Who never spoke above a hush.
Now all at once you're using language   55
That would make a sailor blush.

Oh, let a woman in your life
And you are plunging in a knife!
Let the others of my sex   60
Tie the knot — around their necks;
I'd prefer a new edition
Of the Spanish Inquisition
Than to ever let a woman in my life!

    (*The storm over, he "cheeps" sweetly to the bird*)

                                        65

I'm a quiet living man
Who prefers to spend his evenings
In the silence of his room;
Who likes an atmosphere as restful
As an undiscovered tomb.
A pensive man am I   70
Of philosophic joys;
Who likes to meditate,
Contemplate,
Free from humanity's mad, inhuman noise.
Just a quiet living man.   75

    (*With abrupt rage*)

But let a woman in your life
And your sabbatical is through!
In a line that never ends
Come an army of her friends;
Come to jabber and to chatter   80
And to tell her what the matter
Is with you.

She'll have a booming, boist'rous fam'ly
Who will descend on you en masse.
She'll have a large Wagnerian mother   85
With a voice that shatters glass!

Oh, let a woman in your life . . .

    (*He turns on one of the machines at the accelerated speed so that the voice coming over the speaker becomes a piercing female babble. He runs to the next machine*)

Let a woman in your life . . .

    (*He turns it on the same way and dashes to the next*)

Let a woman in your life . . .

    (*He turns on the third; the third being the master control, he slowly turns the volume up until the chattering is unbearable.* PICKERING *covers his ears, his face knotted in pain. Having illustrated his point,* HIGGINS *suddenly turns all the machines off and makes himself comfortable in a chair*)

I shall never let a woman in my life!

(*The lights black out for the end of the scene*)

Discussion Question

Read the following letter to Ann Landers:

Dear Ann Landers:

Whatever happened to "the girl right next door"? I am 30 years old and two years "behind schedule." I decided a long time ago that I would marry at 28. I belong to two dating clubs and have attended over 200 church socials. I have proposed to at least 50 girls, but they all say no. I realize some of my views are old-fashioned, but there must be at least one girl around with old-fashioned views. My demands are as follows — I call them the Ten Commandments of Marriage.

1. Virgin (certified by a physician).
2. Non-drinker.
3. Non-smoker.
4. No dancing where liquor is sold.
5. All food prepared from scratch. (No frozen foods, either.)
6. No excessive allowance.
7. No second car. (This only tends to make a woman independent.)
8. Eat out only once every two weeks.
9. I choose our friends.
10. "The man of the house" should be the final boss in all situations.

I know the girl next door is out there somewhere. Will you help me find her, Ann? — B.W.J. in East Liverpool, Ohio.[1]

How do B.W.J.'s attitudes about women compare to those of Henry Higgins? Are they two of a kind, or is one worse? Speculate on how and why B.W.J. developed such "old-fashioned" attitudes. Are any of his ten points reasonable? Were they ever reasonable? (If not, why were many of them accepted by many women a generation or so ago, and earlier?)

Writing Suggestions

1. Write a response to B.W.J.
2. Compose lyrics for a song entitled "Let a Man in Your Life."

---

[1] *The Washington Post*, November 17, 1980. Copyright 1980 by Field Newspaper Syndicate. Reprinted by permission of Ann Landers and Field Newspaper Syndicate.

LEAVING THE "DOLL'S HOUSE"

Henrik Ibsen

When Henrik Ibsen (1828–1906) presented *A Doll's House* (1879), women throughout Western civilization were considered to be the possessions of their husbands and fathers. The story of Nora and Torvald Helmer shocked Ibsen's contemporaries because at the end of the play Nora leaves her husband, a man who, like her father, considers her an amusing toy — a doll. Indeed, Nora sometimes assumes the role of the demure doll-house-wife, for this is what her husband expects. But she is much more than a stereotype: Nora is a resourceful, passionate woman. Seven years before the action of the play, Torvald was very ill and was told that unless he went abroad he would die. The Helmers at that time did not possess the funds necessary for such a trip and Nora, knowing that her husband would rather die than borrow money, arranged a loan (by forging her father's signature) with a local money-lender, Krogstad. Torvald recovered and became the manager of a bank at which Krogstad worked. The two men despised one another and Torvald eventually dismissed his subordinate. Seeking to ruin the Helmers, Krogstad writes a letter to Torvald, explaining how Nora had borrowed money and had forged her father's name. In the following passage, the concluding scene of the play, Torvald discovers Krogstad's letter and bitterly denounces Nora for attempting to help him in so "dishonorable" a way.

☐

HELMER: Nora!

NORA: Ah!—

HELMER: What is this? Do you know what is in this letter?

NORA: Yes, I know. Let me go! Let me get out!

HELMER (*holding her back*): Where are you going?   5

NORA (*trying to get free*): You shan't save me, Torvald!

HELMER (*reeling*): True? Is this true, that I read here? Horrible! No, no — it is impossible that it can be true.

NORA: It is true. I have loved you above everything else in the world.

HELMER: Oh, don't let us have any silly excuses.   10

NORA (*taking a step towards him*): Torvald — !

From *A Doll's House* by Henrik Ibsen, translated by R. Farquharson Sharp and Eleanor Marx-Aveling, revised by Linda Hanaas. An Everyman's Library Edition. By permission of E. P. Dutton and J. M. Dent & Sons Ltd. Publishers.

HELMER: Miserable creature — what have you done?

NORA: Let me go. You shall not suffer for my sake. You shall not take it upon yourself.

HELMER: No tragedy airs, please. (*Locks the hall door.*) Here you shall stay and give me an explanation. Do you understand what you have done? Answer me! Do you understand what you have done?

NORA (*looks steadily at him and says with a growing look of coldness in her face*): Yes, now I am beginning to understand thoroughly.

HELMER (*walking about the room*): What a horrible awakening! All these eight years — she who was my joy and pride — a hypocrite, a liar — worse, worse — a criminal! The unutterable ugliness of it all! — For shame! For shame! (NORA *is silent and looks steadily at him. He stops in front of her.*) I ought to have suspected that something of the sort would happen. I ought to have foreseen it. All your father's want of principle — be silent! — all your father's want of principle has come out in you. No religion, no morality, no sense of duty — . How I am punished for having winked at what he did! I did it for your sake, and this is how you repay me.

NORA: Yes, that's just it.

HELMER: Now you have destroyed all my happiness. You have ruined all my future. It is horrible to think of! I am in the power of an unscrupulous man; he can do what he likes with me, ask anything he likes of me, give me any orders he pleases — I dare not refuse. And I must sink to such miserable depths because of a thoughtless woman!

NORA: When I am out of the way, you will be free.

HELMER: No fine speeches, please. Your father had always plenty of those ready, too. What good would it be to me if you were out of the way, as you say? Not the slightest. He can make the affair known everywhere; and if he does, I may be falsely suspected of having been a party to your criminal action. Very likely people will think I was behind it all — that it was I who prompted you! And I have to thank you for all this — you whom I have cherished during the whole of our married life. Do you understand now what it is you have done for me?

NORA (*coldly and quietly*): Yes.

HELMER: It is so incredible that I can't take it in. But we must come to some understanding. Take off that shawl. Take it off, I tell you. I must try and appease him some way or another. The matter must be hushed up at any cost. And as for you and me, it must appear as if everything between us were just as before — but naturally only in the eyes of the world. You will still remain in my house, that is a matter of course. But I shall not allow you to bring up the children; I dare not trust them to you. To think that I should be obliged to say so to one whom I have loved so dearly, and whom I still — . No, that is all over. From this moment happiness is not the question; all that concerns us is to save the remains, the fragments, the appearance —

(*A ring is heard at the front-door bell.*)

HELMER (*with a start*): What is that? So late! Can the worst — ? Can he — ? Hide yourself, Nora. Say you are ill.

(NORA *stands motionless.* HELMER *goes and unlocks the hall door.*)

MAID (*half-dressed, comes to the door*): A letter for the mistress.

HELMER: Give it to me. (*Takes the letter, and shuts the door.*). Yes, it is from him. You shall not have it; I will read it myself.

NORA: Yes, read it.

HELMER (*standing by the lamp*): I scarcely have the courage to do it. It may mean ruin for both of us. No, I must know. (*Tears open the letter, runs his eye over a few lines, looks at a paper enclosed, and gives a shout of joy.*) Nora! (*She looks at him questioningly.*) Nora! — No, I must read it once again — . Yes, it is true! I am saved! Nora, I am saved!

NORA: And I?

HELMER: You too, of course; we are both saved, both you and I. Look, he sends you your bond back. He says he regrets and repents — that a happy change in his life — never mind what he says! We are saved, Nora! No one can do anything to you. Oh, Nora, Nora! — no, first I must destroy these hateful things. Let me see — . (*Takes a look at the bond.*) No, no, I won't look at it. The whole thing shall be nothing but a bad dream to me. (*Tears up the bond and both letters, throws them all into the stove, and watches them burn.*) There — now it doesn't exist any longer. He says that since Christmas Eve you — . These must have been three dreadful days for you, Nora.

NORA: I have fought a hard fight these three days.

HELMER: And suffered agonies, and seen no way out but — . No, we won't call any of the horrors to mind. We will only shout with joy, and keep saying, "It's all over! It's all over!" Listen to me, Nora. You don't seem to realise that it is all over. What is this? — such a cold, set face! My poor little Nora, I quite understand; you don't feel as if you could believe that I have forgiven you. But it is true,

Nora, I swear it; I have forgiven you everything. I know that what you did, you did out of love for me. 95

NORA: That is true.

HELMER: You have loved me as a wife ought to love her husband. Only you had not sufficient knowledge to judge of the means you used. But do you suppose you are any the less dear to me, because you don't understand how to act on your own responsi- 100 bility? No, no; only lean on me; I will advise you and direct you. I should not be a man if this womanly helplessness did not just give you a double attractiveness in my eyes. You must not think any more about the hard things I said in my first moment of conster- nation, when I thought everything was going to overwhelm me. I 105 have forgiven you, Nora; I swear to you I have forgiven you.

NORA: Thank you for your forgiveness. (*She goes out through the door to the right.*)

HELMER: No, don't go — . (*Looks in.*) What are you doing in there?

NORA (*from within*): Taking off my fancy dress. 110

HELMER (*standing at the open door*): Yes, do. Try and calm yourself, and make your mind easy again, my frightened little singing-bird. Be at rest, and feel secure; I have broad wings to shelter you under. (*Walks up and down by the door.*) How warm and cosy our home is, Nora. Here is shelter for you; here I will protect you like a 115 hunted dove that I have saved from a hawk's claws; I will bring peace to your poor beating heart. It will come, little by little, Nora, believe me. To-morrow morning you will look upon it all quite differently; soon everything will be just as it was before. Very soon you won't need me to assure you that I have forgiven 120 you; you will yourself feel the certainty that I have done so. Can you suppose I should ever think of such a thing as repudiating you, or even reproaching you? You have no idea what a true man's heart is like, Nora. There is something so indescribably sweet and satisfying, to a man, in the knowledge that he has 125 forgiven his wife — forgiven her freely, and with all his heart. It seems as if that had made her, as it were, doubly his own; he has given her a new life, so to speak; and she has in a way become both wife and child to him. So you shall be for me after this, my little scared, helpless darling. Have no anxiety about anything, 130 Nora; only be frank and open with me, and I will serve as will and conscience both to you — . What is this? Not gone to bed? Have you changed your things?

NORA (*in everyday dress*): Yes, Torvald, I have changed my things now.

HELMER: But what for? — so late as this. 135

NORA: I shall not sleep to-night.

HELMER: But, my dear Nora —

NORA (*looking at her watch*): It is not so very late. Sit down here, Torvald. You and I have much to say to one another. (*She sits down at one side of the table.*)   140

HELMER: Nora — what is this? — this cold, set face?

NORA: Sit down. It will take some time; I have a lot to talk over with you.

HELMER (*sits down at the opposite side of the table*): You alarm me, Nora! — and I don't understand you.   145

NORA: No, that is just it. You don't understand me, and I have never understood you either — before to-night. No, you mustn't interrupt me. You must simply listen to what I say. Torvald, this is a settling of accounts.

HELMER: What do you mean by that?   150

NORA (*after a short silence*): Isn't there one thing that strikes you as strange in our sitting here like this?

HELMER: What is that?

NORA: We have been married now eight years. Does it not occur to you that this is the first time we two, you and I, husband and wife,   155
have had a serious conversation?

HELMER: What do you mean by serious?

NORA: In all these eight years — longer than that — from the very beginning of our acquaintance, we have never exchanged a word on any serious subject.   160

HELMER: Was it likely that I would be continually and for ever telling you about worries that you could not help me to bear?

NORA: I am not speaking about business matters. I say that we have never sat down in earnest together to try and get at the bottom of anything.   165

HELMER: But, dearest Nora, would it have been any good to you?

NORA: That is just it; you have never understood me. I have been greatly wronged, Torvald — first by papa and then by you.

HELMER: What! By us two — by us two, who have loved you better than anyone else in the world?   170

NORA (*shaking her head*): You have never loved me. You have only thought it pleasant to be in love with me.

HELMER: Nora, what do I hear you saying?

NORA: It is perfectly true, Torvald. When I was at home with papa, he told me his opinion about everything, and so I had the same opinions; and if I differed from him I concealed the fact, because he would not have liked it. He called me his doll-child, and he played with me just as I used to play with my dolls. And when I came to live with you — 175

HELMER: What sort of an expression is that to use about our marriage? 180

NORA (*undisturbed*): I mean that I was simply transferred from papa's hands into yours. You arranged everything according to your own taste, and so I got the same tastes as you — or else I pretended to, I am really not quite sure which — I think sometimes the one and sometimes the other. When I look back on it, it seems to me as if I had been living here like a poor woman — just from hand to mouth. I have existed merely to perform tricks for you, Torvald. But you would have it so. You and papa have committed a great sin against me. It is your fault that I have made nothing of my life. 185

190

HELMER: How unreasonable and how ungrateful you are, Nora! Have you not been happy here!

NORA: No, I have never been happy. I thought I was, but it has never really been so.

HELMER: Not — not happy! 195

NORA: No, only merry. And you have always been so kind to me. But our home has been nothing but a playroom. I have been your doll-wife, just as at home I was papa's doll-child; and here the children have been my dolls. I thought it great fun when you played with me, just as they thought it great fun when I played with them. That is what our marriage has been, Torvald. 200

HELMER: There is some truth in what you say — exaggerated and strained as your view of it is. But for the future it shall be different. Playtime shall be over, and lesson-time shall begin.

NORA: Whose lessons? Mine, or the children's? 205

HELMER: Both yours and the children's, my darling Nora.

NORA: Alas, Torvald, you are not the man to educate me into being a proper wife for you.

HELMER: And you can say that!

NORA: And I — how am I fitted to bring up the children? 210

HELMER: Nora!

NORA: Didn't you say so yourself a little while ago — that you dare not trust me to bring them up?

HELMER: In a moment of anger! Why do you pay any heed to that?

NORA: Indeed, you were perfectly right. I am not fit for the task. 215
There is another task I must undertake first. I must try and
educate myself — you are not the man to help me in that. I must
do that for myself. And that is why I am going to leave you now.

HELMER (*springing up*): What do you say?

NORA: I must stand quite alone, if I am to understand myself and 220
everything about me. It is for that reason that I cannot remain
with you any longer.

HELMER: Nora, Nora!

NORA: I am going away from here now, at once. I am sure Christine
will take me in for the night — 225

HELMER: You are out of your mind! I won't allow it! I forbid you!

NORA: It is no use forbidding me anything any longer. I will take with
me what belongs to myself. I will take nothing from you, either
now or later.

HELMER: What sort of madness is this! 230

NORA: To-morrow I shall go home — I mean, to my old home. It will
be easiest for me to find something to do there.

HELMER: You blind, foolish woman!

NORA: I must try and get some sense, Torvald.

HELMER: To desert your home, your husband and your children! 235
And you don't consider what people will say!

NORA: I cannot consider that at all. I only know that it is necessary for
me.

HELMER: It's shocking. This is how you would neglect your most
sacred duties. 240

NORA: What do you consider my most sacred duties?

HELMER: Do I need to tell you that? Are they not your duties to your
husband and your children?

NORA: I have other duties just as sacred.

HELMER: That you have not. What duties could those be? 245

NORA: Duties to myself.

HELMER: Before all else, you are a wife and a mother.

NORA: I don't believe that any longer. I believe that before all else I
am a reasonable human being, just as you are — or, at all events,
that I must try and become one. I know quite well, Torvald, that 250
most people would think you right, and that views of that kind

are to be found in books; but I can no longer content myself with what most people say, or with what is found in books. I must think over things for myself and get to understand them.

HELMER: Can you not understand your place in your own home? 255
Have you not a reliable guide in such matters as that? — have you no religion?

NORA: I am afraid, Torvald, I do not exactly know what religion is.

HELMER: What are you saying?

NORA: I know nothing but what the clergyman said, when I went to 260
be confirmed. He told us that religion was this, and that, and the other. When I am away from all this, and am alone, I will look into that matter too. I will see if what the clergyman said is true, or at all events if it is true for me.

HELMER: This is unheard of in a girl of your age! But if religion 265
cannot lead you aright, let me try and awaken your conscience. I suppose you have some moral sense? Or — answer me — am I to think you have none?

NORA: I assure you, Torvald, that is not an easy question to answer. I really don't know. The thing perplexes me altogether. I only 270
know that you and I look at it in quite a different light. I am learning, too, that the law is quite another thing from what I supposed; but I find it impossible to convince myself that the law is right. According to it a woman has no right to spare her old dying father, or to save her husband's life. I can't believe that. 275

HELMER: You talk like a child. You don't understand the conditions of the world in which you live.

NORA: No, I don't. But now I am going to try. I am going to see if I can make out who is right, the world or I.

HELMER: You are ill, Nora; you are delirious; I almost think you are 280
out of your mind.

NORA: I have never felt my mind so clear and certain as to-night.

HELMER: And is it with a clear and certain mind that you forsake your husband and your children?

NORA: Yes, it is.

285

HELMER: Then there is only one possible explanation.

NORA: What is that?

HELMER: You do not love me any more.

NORA: No, that is just it.

HELMER: Nora! — and you can say that?

290

NORA: It gives me great pain, Torvald, for you have always been so kind to me, but I cannot help it. I do not love you any more.

HELMER (*regaining his composure*): Is that a clear and certain conviction too?

NORA: Yes, absolutely clear and certain. That is the reason why I will   295
not stay here any longer.

HELMER: And can you tell me what I have done to forfeit your love?

NORA: Yes, indeed I can. It was to-night, when the wonderful thing did not happen; then I saw you were not the man I had thought you.   300

HELMER: Explain yourself better. I don't understand you.

NORA: I have waited so patiently for eight years; for, goodness knows, I knew very well that wonderful things don't happen every day. Then this horrible misfortune came upon me; and then I felt quite certain that the wonderful thing was going to   305
happen at last. When Krogstad's letter was lying out there, never for a moment did I imagine that you would consent to accept this man's conditions. I was so absolutely certain that you would say to him: Publish the thing to the whole world. And when that was done —   310

HELMER: Yes, what then? — when I had exposed my wife to shame and disgrace?

NORA: When that was done, I was so absolutely certain, you would come forward and take everything upon yourself, and say: I am the guilty one.   315

HELMER: Nora — !

NORA: You mean that I would never have accepted such a sacrifice on your part? No, of course not. But what would my assurances have been worth against yours? That was the wonderful thing which I hoped for and feared; and it was to prevent that, that I wanted to   320
kill myself.

HELMER: I would gladly work night and day for you, Nora — bear sorrow and want for your sake. But no man would sacrifice his honour for the one he loves.

NORA: It is a thing hundreds of thousands of women have done.   325

HELMER: Oh, you think and talk like a heedless child.

NORA: Maybe. But you neither think nor talk like the man I could bind myself to. As soon as your fear was over — and it was not fear for what threatened me, but for what might happen to you — when the whole thing was past, as far as you were con-   330 cerned it was exactly as if nothing at all had happened. Exactly as before, I was your little skylark, your doll, which you would in future treat with doubly gentle care, because it was so brittle and fragile. (*Getting up.*) Torvald — it was then it dawned upon me that for eight years I had been living here with a strange man, and had borne him three children — . Oh, I can't bear to think of it! I could tear myself into little bits!

HELMER (*sadly*): I see, I see. An abyss has opened between us — there is no denying it. But, Nora, would it not be possible to fill it up?

NORA: As I am now, I am no wife for you.

HELMER: I have it in me to become a different man.

NORA: Perhaps — if your doll is taken away from you.

HELMER: But to part! — to part from you! No, no, Nora, I can't understand that idea.

NORA (*going out to the right*): That makes it all the more certain that it must be done. (*She comes back with her cloak and hat and a small bag which she puts on a chair by the table.*)

HELMER: Nora, Nora, not now! Wait till to-morrow.

NORA (*putting on her cloak*): I cannot spend the night in a strange man's room.

HELMER: But can't we live here like brother and sister — ?

NORA (*putting on her hat*): You know very well that would not last long. (*Puts the shawl around her.*) Good-bye, Torvald. I won't see the little ones. I know they are in better hands than mine. As I am now, I can be of no use to them.

HELMER: But some day, Nora — some day?

NORA: How can I tell? I have no idea what is going to become of me.

HELMER: But you are my wife, whatever becomes of you.

NORA: Listen, Torvald. I have heard that when a wife deserts her husband's house, as I am doing now, he is legally freed from all obligations towards her. In any case I set you free from all your obligations. You are not to feel yourself bound in the slightest way, any more than I shall. There must be perfect freedom on both sides. See, here is your ring back. Give me mine.

HELMER: That too?

NORA: That too.

HELMER: Here it is.

NORA: That's right. Now it is all over. I have put the keys here. The maids know all about everything in the house — better than I do.

To-morrow, after I have left her, Christine will come here and   370
pack my own things that I brought with me from home. I will
have them sent after me.

HELMER: All over! All over! — Nora, shall you never think of me
again?

NORA: I know I shall often think of you and the children and this   375
house.

HELMER: May I write to you, Nora?

NORA: No — never. You must not do that.

HELMER: But at least let me send you —

NORA: Nothing — nothing —   380

HELMER: Let me help you if you are in want.

NORA: No. I can receive nothing from a stranger.

HELMER: Nor — can I never be anything more than a stranger to
you?

NORA (*taking her bag*): Ah, Torvald, the most wonderful thing of all   385
would have to happen.

HELMER: Tell me what that would be!

NORA: Both you and I would have to be so changed that — . Oh,
Torvald, I don't believe any longer in wonderful things happening.   390

HELMER: But I will believe in it. Tell me! So changed that — ?

NORA: That our life together would be a real wedlock. Good-bye. (*She
goes out through the hall.*)

HELMER (*sinks down on a chair at the door and buries his face in his hands*):
Nora! Nora! (*Looks round, and rises.*) Empty. She is gone. (*A hope*   395
flashes across his mind.) The most wonderful thing of all — ?

(*The sound of a door shutting is heard from below.*)

Discussion Questions

1. What does Helmer's transformation (from an accusing to a forgiving
husband) reveal about his character?

2. What are Nora's needs? Cite lines in the play to support your answer.

3. What does Helmer say that indicates his obliviousness to Nora's
needs?

4. Do you accept Nora's conclusion that her husband and father have
been responsible for her making nothing of her life? Who or what else
might be responsible? How so?

5. What is the effect — on both Helmer and you — of Nora's statement, "I cannot spend the night in a strange man's room"?
6. What is the significance of the play's title in this last scene?
7. Why must Nora leave her husband and children? Is she being selfish? Irresponsible? Responsible?

Writing Suggestions

1. Is it possible for two people to live together for eight years and still be strangers? Does intimacy between husband and wife mean that there should be no secrets? Assume that you are a marriage counselor. Compose an answer for a married couple who are considering divorce and who ask you these questions.
2. Take any twenty to thirty lines of the play and rewrite them as a third-person narration (e.g., "Nora, thinking how her husband would respond to the letter, sat slowly into the chair. Helmer tore open the envelope and scanned its contents. . . ."). After you have done this, compare your effort to the original. What are the advantages of a dramatic dialogue? Of a third-person narration? The disadvantages of each?
3. What does Torvald need to learn? Is he capable of such learning? Develop your ideas in an essay.

SEXUAL POLITICS: A MANIFESTO FOR REVOLUTION
Kate Millett

Kate Millett (b. 1934), professor of English, sculptress, and filmmaker, is perhaps best known for her radical feminist views. Millett wrote her "Manifesto for Revolution" in 1968, intending it for airplay at Columbia University's student-operated radio station. Despite the revolutionary fervor on college campuses in the late 1960s, station officials refused to allow her to deliver her talk. Two years later, however, with the publication of *Sexual Politics,* Millett found a national audience. Her book received widespread attention, and she was immediately recognized as a leader of the women's liberation movement. Her other works include *The Prostitution Papers* (1973), *Flying* (1974), *Sita* (1977), and *The Basement* (1979).

Excerpt from Sexual Politics by Kate Millett. Copyright © 1969, 1970 by Kate Millett. Reprinted by permission of Doubleday & Company, Inc.

☐

When one group rules another, the relationship between the two is 1
political. When such an arrangement is carried out over a long period
of time it develops an ideology (feudalism, racism, etc.). All historical
civilizations are patriarchies: their ideology is male supremacy.

Oppressed groups are denied education, economic indepen- 2
dence, the power of office, representation, an image of dignity and
self-respect, equality of status, and recognition as human beings.
Throughout history women have been consistently denied all of
these, and their denial today, while attenuated and partial, is nevertheless consistent. The education allowed them is deliberately designed to be inferior, and they are systematically programmed out of
and excluded from the knowledge where power lies today — e.g., in
science and technology. They are confined to conditions of economic
dependence based on the sale of their sexuality in marriage, or a
variety of prostitutions. Work on a basis of economic independence
allows them only a subsistence level of life — often not even that.
They do not hold office, are represented in no positions of power,
and authority is forbidden them. The image of woman fostered by
cultural media, high and low, then and now, is a marginal and de-
meaning existence, and one outside the human condition — which is
defined as the prerogative of man, the male.

Government is upheld by power, which is supported through 3
consent (social opinion), or imposed by violence. Conditioning to an
ideology amounts to the former. But there may be a resort to the
latter at any moment when consent is withdrawn — rape, attack,
sequestration, beatings, murder. Sexual politics obtains consent
through the "socialization" of both sexes to patriarchal policies. They
consist of the following:

1. the formation of human personality along stereotyped lines of
   sexual category, based on the needs and values of the master class
   and dictated by what he would cherish in himself and find convenient in an underclass: aggression, intellectuality, force and
   efficiency for the male; passivity, ignorance, docility, "virtue,"
   and ineffectuality for the female.
2. the concept of sex role, which assigns domestic service and atten-
   dance upon infants to all females and the rest of human interest,
   achievement and ambition to the male; the charge of leader at all
   times and places to the male, and the duty of follower, with equal
   uniformity, to the female.
3. the imposition of male rule through institutions: patriarchal religion, the proprietary family, marriage, "The Home," masculine
   oriented culture, and a pervasive doctrine of male superiority.

A Sexual Revolution would bring about the following conditions, 4 desirable upon rational, moral and humanistic grounds:

1. the end of sexual repression — freedom of expression and of sexual mores (sexual freedom has been partially attained, but it is now being subverted beyond freedom into exploitative license for patriarchal and reactionary ends).

2. Unisex, or the end of separatist character-structure, temperament and behavior, so that each individual may develop an entire — rather than a partial, limited, and conformist — personality.

3. re-examination of traits categorized into "masculine" and "feminine," with a total reassessment as to their human usefulness and advisability in both sexes. Thus if "masculine" violence is undesirable, it is so for both sexes, "feminine" dumb-cow passivity likewise. If "masculine" intelligence or efficiency is valuable, it is so for both sexes equally, and the same must be true for "feminine" tenderness or consideration.

4. the end of sex role and sex status, the patriarchy and the male supremacist ethic, attitude and ideology — in all areas of endeavor, experience, and behavior.

5. the end of the ancient oppression of the young under the patriarchal proprietary family, their chattel status, the attainment of the human rights presently denied them, the professionalization and therefore improvement of their care, and the guarantee that when they enter the world, they are desired, planned for, and provided with equal opportunities.

6. Bisex, or the end of enforced perverse heterosexuality, so that the sex act ceases to be arbitrarily polarized into male and female, to the exclusion of sexual expression between members of the same sex.

7. the end of sexuality in the forms in which it has existed historically — brutality, violence, capitalism, exploitation, and warfare — that it may cease to be hatred and become love.

8. the attainment of the female sex to freedom and full human status after millennia of deprivation and oppression, and of both sexes to a viable humanity.

Discussion Questions

1. Millett purposefully writes in a challenging, strident tone. (Locate instances where she is particularly abrasive.) Why did she choose this approach? For whom do you suppose she was writing?

2. In her manifesto, Millett offers several definitions and makes a great many assumptions about the social organization of Western culture. Identify these definitions and assumptions. Why are they essential to the manifesto?
3. Is the manifesto as valid today as it was in 1968, when it was written?
4. Was the "socialization of both sexes to patriarchal policies" ever based on anything other than social expediency for the male? That is, was there any time in our history when aggression and force were properly part of the male's domain? If so, when did this physiological or biological expediency give way to the social? Or did it ever?

Writing Suggestions

1. Give a brief definition of sexual politics and then analyze how these politics are important to the feminist movement.
2. Assume that you are the program manager at the Columbia University radio station and that you have decided against Millett's reading her manifesto over the air. In a letter to Millett, carefully explain your position. Will you cite as your reasoning the sensitivity of the listening public? Will you cite flaws in the manifesto itself?
3. Using Millett's piece as a guide, write a manifesto for a cause you would support.

UNDERSTANDING THE DIFFERENCE
Phyllis Schlafly

Phyllis Schlafly (b. 1924), author, lawyer, and lecturer, is best known for her outspoken and articulate opposition to the Equal Rights Amendment. She has twice run unsuccessful campaigns for Congress (1952 and 1970) and has written nine books, including five on national defense. "Understanding the Difference" appears in her controversial *The Power of the Positive Woman,* published in 1977.

☐

The first requirement for the acquisition of power by the Positive   1
Woman is to understand the differences between men and women.
Your outlook on life, your faith, your behavior, your potential for
fulfillment, all are determined by the parameters of your original

premise. The Positive Woman starts with the assumption that the world is her oyster. She rejoices in the creative capability within her body and the power potential of her mind and spirit. She understands that men and women are different, and that those very differences provide the key to her success as a person and fulfillment as a woman.

The women's liberationist, on the other hand, is imprisoned by her own negative view of herself and of her place in the world around her. This view of women was most succinctly expressed in an advertisement designed by the principal women's liberationist organization, the National Organization for Women (NOW), and run in many magazines and newspapers and as spot announcements on many television stations. The advertisement showed a darling curlyheaded girl with the caption: "This healthy, normal baby has a handicap. She was born female." 2

This is the self-articulated dog-in-the-manger, chip-on-the-shoulder, fundamental dogma of the women's liberation movement. Someone — it is not clear who, perhaps God, perhaps the "Establishment," perhaps a conspiracy of male chauvinist pigs — dealt women a foul blow by making them female. It becomes necessary, therefore, for women to agitate and demonstrate and hurl demands on society in order to wrest from an oppressive male-dominated social structure the status that has been wrongfully denied to women through the centuries. 3

By its very nature, therefore, the women's liberation movement precipitates a series of conflict situations — in the legislatures, in the courts, in the schools, in industry — with man targeted as the enemy. Confrontation replaces cooperation as the watchword of all relationships. Women and men become adversaries instead of partners. 4

The second dogma of the women's liberationists is that, of all the injustices perpetrated upon women through the centuries, the most oppressive is the cruel fact that women have babies and men do not. Within the confines of the women's liberationist ideology, therefore, the abolition of this overriding inequality of women becomes the primary goal. This goal must be achieved at any and all costs — to the woman herself, to the baby, to the family, and to society. Women must be made equal to men in their ability *not* to become pregnant and *not* to be expected to care for babies they may bring into the world. 5

This is why women's liberationists are compulsively involved in the drive to make abortion and child-care centers for all women, regardless of religion or income, both socially acceptable and government-financed. Former Congresswoman Bella Abzug has defined the goal: "to enforce the constitutional right of females to terminate pregnancies that they do not wish to continue." 6

If man is targeted as the enemy, and the ultimate goal of women's liberation is independence from men and the avoidance of pregnancy 7 and its consequences, then lesbianism is logically the highest form in the ritual of women's liberation. Many, such as Kate Millett, come to this conclusion, although many others do not.

The Positive Woman will never travel that dead-end road. It is 8 self-evident to the Positive Woman that the female body with its baby-producing organs was not designed by a conspiracy of men but by the Divine Architect of the human race. Those who think it is unfair that women have babies, whereas men cannot, will have to take up their complaint with God because no other power is capable of changing that fundamental fact. On some college campuses, I have been assured that other methods of reproduction will be developed. But most of us must deal with the real world rather than with the imagination of dreamers.

Another feature of the woman's natural role is the obvious fact 9 that women can breast-feed babies and men cannot. This functional role was not imposed by conspiratorial males seeking to burden women with confining chores, but must be recognized as part of the plan of the Divine Architect for the survival of the human race through the centuries and in the countries that know no pasteurization of milk or sterilization of bottles.

The Positive Woman looks upon her femaleness and her fertility 10 as part of her purpose, her potential, and her power. She rejoices that she has a capability for creativity that men can never have.

The third basic dogma of the women's liberation movement is 11 that there is no difference between male and female except the sex organs, and that all those physical, cognitive, and emotional differences you *think* are there, are merely the result of centuries of restraints imposed by a male-dominated society and sex-stereotyped schooling. The role imposed on women is, by definition, inferior, according to the women's liberationists.

The Positive Woman knows that, while there are some physical 12 competitions in which women are better (and can command more money) than men, including those that put a premium on grace and beauty, such as figure skating, the superior physical strength of males over females in competitions of strength, speed, and short-term endurance is beyond rational dispute.

In the Olympic Games, women not only cannot win any medals in 13 competition with men, the gulf between them is so great that they cannot even qualify for the contests with men. No amount of training from infancy can enable women to throw the discus as far as men, or to match men in push-ups or in lifting weights. In track and field events, individual male records surpass those of women by 10 to 20 percent.

Female swimmers today are beating Johnny Weissmuller's rec- 14 ords, but today's male swimmers are better still. Chris Evert can never win a tennis match against Jimmy Connors. If we removed lady's tees from golf courses, women would be out of the game. Putting women in football or wrestling matches can only be an exercise in laughs.

The Olympic Games, whose rules require strict verification to   15
ascertain that no male enters a female contest and, with his masculine advantage, unfairly captures a woman's medal, formerly insisted on a visual inspection of the contestants' bodies. Science, however, has discovered that men and women are so innately different physically that their maleness/femaleness can be conclusively established by means of a simple skin test of fully clothed persons. . . .

The Five Principles

When the women's liberationists enter the political arena to pro-   16
mote legislation and litigation in pursuit of their goals, their specific demands are based on five principles.

(1) They demand that a "gender-free" rule be applied to every   17
federal and state law, bureaucratic regulation, educational institution, and expenditure of public funds. Based on their dogma that there is no real difference between men and women (except in sex organs), they demand that males and females have identical treatment always. Thus, if fathers are not expected to stay home and care for their infant children, then neither should mothers be expected to do so; and, therefore, it becomes the duty of the government to provide kiddy-care centers to relieve mothers of that unfair and unequal burden.

The women's lib dogma demands that the courts treat sex as a   18
"suspect" classification — just as race is now treated — so that no difference of treatment or separation between the sexes will ever be permitted, no matter how reasonable or how much it is desired by reasonable people.

The nonsense of these militant demands was illustrated by the   19
Department of Health, Education and Welfare (HEW) ruling in July, 1976, that all public school "functions such as father-son or mother-daughter breakfasts" would be prohibited because this "would be subjecting students to separate treatment." It was announced that violations would lead to a cutoff of federal assistance or court action by the Justice Department.

When President Gerald Ford read this in the newspaper, he was   20
described by his press secretary as being "quite irritated" and as saying that he could not believe that this was the intent of Congress in passing a law against sex discrimination in education. He telephoned HEW Secretary David Mathews and told him to suspend the ruling.

The National Organization for Women, however, immediately   21
announced opposition to President Ford's action, claiming that such
events (fashion shows, softball games, banquets, and breakfasts) are
sex-discriminatory and must be eliminated. It is clear that a prohibi-
tion against your right to make any difference or separation between
the sexes anytime anywhere is a primary goal of the women's liberation movement.

No sooner had the father-son, mother-daughter flap blown over   22
than HEW embroiled itself in another controversy by a ruling that an
after-school choir of fifth and sixth grade boys violates the HEW
regulation that bars single-sex choruses. The choir in Wethersfield,
Connecticut, that precipitated the ruling had been established for
boys whose "voices haven't changed yet," and the purpose was "to get
boys interested in singing" at an early age so they would be willing to
join coed choruses later. Nevertheless, HEW found that such a boy's
chorus is by definition sex discriminatory.

The Positive Woman rejects the "gender-free" approach. She   23
knows that there are many differences between male and female and
that we are entitled to have our laws, regulations, schools, and courts
reflect these differences and allow for reasonable differences in treatment and separations of activities that reasonable men and women
want.

The Positive Woman also rejects the argument that sex discrimi-   24
nation should be treated the same as race discrimination. There is
vastly more difference between a man and a woman than there is
between a black and a white, and it is nonsense to adopt a legal and
bureaucratic attitude that pretends that those differences do not exist.
Even the United States Supreme Court has, in recent and relevant
cases, upheld "reasonable" sex-based differences of treatment by legislatures and by the military.

(2) The women's lib legislative goals seek an irrational mandate of   25
"equality" at the expense of justice. The fact is that equality cannot
always be equated with justice, and may sometimes even be highly
unjust. If we had absolutely equal treatment in regard to taxes, then
everyone would pay the same income tax, or perhaps the same rate of
income tax, regardless of the size of the income.

If we had absolutely equal treatment in regard to federal spend-   26
ing programs, we would have to eliminate welfare, low-income housing benefits, food stamps, government scholarships, and many other
programs designed to benefit low-income citizens. If we had absolutely equal treatment in regard to age, then seventeen-year-olds, or
even ten-year-olds, would be permitted to vote, and we would have to
eliminate Social Security unless all persons received the same benefits
that only those over sixty-two receive now.

Our legislatures, our administrative departments, and our courts 27
have always had and still retain the discretion to make reasonable
differences in treatment based on age, income, or economic situation.
The Positive Woman believes that it makes no sense to deprive us of
the ability to make reasonable distinctions based on sex that reasonable men and women want.

(3) The women's liberation movement demands that women be 28
given the benefit of "reverse discrimination." The Positive Woman
recognizes that this is mutually exclusive with the principle of equal
opportunity for all. Reverse discrimination is based on the theory that
"groups rights" take precedence over individual rights, and that "reverse discrimination" (variously called "preferential treatment," "re-
medial action," or "affirmative action") should be imposed in order to
compensate some women today for alleged past discriminations
against other women. The word "quotas" is usually avoided, but it
amounts to the same thing.

The fallacy of reverse discrimination has been aptly exposed by 29
Professor Sidney Hook. No one would argue, he wrote, that because
many years ago blacks and women were denied the right to vote, we
should now compensate by giving them an extra vote or two, or by
barring white men from voting at all.

But that is substantially what the women's liberationists are de- 30
manding — and getting by federal court orders — in education, employment, and politics when they ask for "affirmative action" to remedy past discrimination.

The Positive Woman supports equal opportunity for individuals 31
of both sexes, as well as of all faiths and races. She rejects the theories
of reverse discrimination and "group rights." It does no good for the
woman who may have been discriminated against twenty-five years
ago to know that an unqualified woman today receives preferential
treatment at the expense of a qualified man. Only the vindictive
radical would support such a policy of revenge.

(4) The women's liberation movement is based on the unproven 32
theory that uniformity should replace diversity — or, in simpler language, the federalization of all remaining aspects of our life. The
militant women demand that *all* educational institutions conform to
federally determined rules about sex discrimination.

There is absolutely no evidence that HEW bureaucrats can do a 33
better or fairer job of regulating our schools and colleges than local
officials. Nor is there any evidence that individuals, or women, or
society as a whole, would be better off under a uniform system
enforced by the full power of the federal government than they
would be under a free and competitive system, under local control,
using diverse methods and regulations. It is hard to see why anyone

would want to put more power into the hands of federal bureaucrats who cannot cope with the problems they already have.

The militant women demand that HEW regulations enforce a 34 strict gender-free uniformity on all schools and colleges. Everything from sports to glee clubs must be coed, regardless of local customs or wishes. The militants deplore the differences from state to state in the laws governing marriage and divorce. Yet does anyone think our nation would be improved if we were made subject to a national divorce law devised by HEW?

The Positive Woman rejects the theory that Washington, D.C., is 35 the fountainhead of all wisdom and professional skill. She supports the principle of leaving all possible control and discretion in the hands of local school and college officials and their elected boards.

(5) The women's liberation movement pushes its proposals on the 36 premise that everything must be neutral as between morality and immorality, and as between the institution of the family and alternate lifestyles: for example, that homosexuals and lesbians should have just as much right to teach in the schools and to adopt children as anyone else; and that illegitimate babies and abortions by married or single mothers should be accepted as normal behavior for teachers — and funded by public money.

A good example of the rabid determination of the militant radi- 37 cals to push every law and regulation to the far-out limit of moral neutrality is the HEW regulation on sex discrimination that implements the Education Amendments of 1972. Although the federal statute simply prohibits sex discrimination, the HEW regulation (1) requires that any medical benefit program administered by a school or college pay for abortions for married and unmarried students, (2) prohibits any school or college from refusing to employ or from firing an unmarried pregnant teacher or a woman who has had, or plans to have, an abortion, and (3) prohibits any school or college from refusing admission to any student who has had, or plans to have, an abortion. Abortion is referred to by the code words "termination of pregnancy."

This HEW regulation is illogical, immoral, and unauthorized by 38 any reasonable reading of the 1972 Education Act. But the HEW regulation became federal law on July 18, 1975, after being signed by the president and accepted by Congress.

The Positive Woman believes that our educational institutions 39 have not only the right, but the obligation, to set minimum standards of moral conduct at the local level. She believes that schools and colleges have no right to use our public money to promote conduct that is offensive to the religious and moral values of parents and taxpayers.

Review Questions

1. What is the chief difference in attitude, according to Schlafly, between the Positive Woman and the women's liberationist?
2. To the women's liberationist (according to Schlafly), what is the most oppressive injustice of all that has been perpetrated on women?
3. Why does Schlafly reject the "dogma" that the only difference between men and women is the sex organs?
4. What kind of examples does Schlafly cite to illustrate the absurdity of "gender-free" rules?
5. Why does Schlafly advocate local, rather than federal, regulation of sex discrimination in schools?

Discussion Questions

1. In her Five Principles, Schlafly writes that the ideas she advocates (such as some difference in treatment and some separation of the sexes) are the ideas of "reasonable" people. Do you agree that such ideas are "reasonable"? What is the meaning of "reasonable"?
2. Phyllis Schlafly suggests that certain life styles (such as homosexuality and lesbianism) and certain practices (such as abortion) are immoral, and that if they are not actually to be prosecuted, they should certainly not be encouraged and funded by the state. (The implicit position is that admittedly homosexual public employees should be denied employment in government agencies and that abortions not be publicly funded.) Do you agree with this position? Why or why not? Do you believe that "our educational institutions have not only the right, but the obligation, to set minimum standards of moral conduct . . ."? If so, how should these standards be set? Who should set them?
3. So-called reverse discrimination has come under considerable fire during the past ten or fifteen years. To what extent do you believe that society should attempt to make restoration to members of groups that have been the victims of racial or sexual discrimination by allowing them special consideration in getting jobs, gaining admittance to college, receiving scholarship funds, and so on?
4. At one point Schlafly writes of the "rabid determination of the militant radicals . . ." How does she use the emotional power of language to enhance her argument? Find other examples of emotional language. How does it work?
5. Schlafly sets up a running comparison-contrast between the Positive Woman and the women's liberationist. Do you think she makes a valid distinction? Do you know people who are examples of each type, who

believe the types of things Schlafly attributes to them? Or do both sides appear to be at least partially manufactured for rhetorical effect?

6. Does Schlafly adequately support her contention that schools and colleges should be regulated by local, rather than by federal, officials?

Writing Suggestions

1. Describe an incident or a series of incidents (that you have either seen or heard about or read about) that illustrate either the position of the Positive Woman or the women's liberationist, as described by Schlafly. Do you reach the same conclusion from these incidents as does Schlafly?

2. Write a critique of Schlafly's passage — possibly in the form of a letter. Explain what you understand her position to be, and why you agree or disagree with her (or partially agree and partially disagree). Explain why she has or has not convinced you.

3. Select two opposing sets of people (other than the Positive Woman and the women's liberationist). Describe the four or five "principles" that divide them. You may try to imitate Schlafly's tone (and in some cases, even her language) to press your points home.

CONFESSIONS OF A FEMALE CHAUVINIST SOW
Anne Roiphe

Anne Roiphe (b. 1935) is an American novelist (*Up the Sandbox!, Digging Out,* and *Long Division*) and essayist. In a review of Roiphe's fiction in *The New York Times Book Review* (November 5, 1972), Nora Sayre writes that Roiphe "seems to have a rugged belief in marriage, yet she also questions it acutely. And she pays many tributes to imagined freedom. Her characters tug and pull against the restraints of relatives, spouses, children, past and upbringing." These same concerns are reflected, in nonfiction form, in her "Confessions of a Female Chauvinist Sow."

I once married a man I thought was totally unlike my father and I   1
imagined a whole new world of freedom emerging. Five years later it was clear even to me — floating face down in a wash of despair — that I had simply chosen a replica of my handsome daddy-true. The

Reprinted by permission of Brandt & Brandt Literary Agents, Inc. from *New York* Magazine (October 30, 1972). Copyright © 1972 by Anne Roiphe.

updated version spoke English like an angel but — good God! — underneath he was my father exactly: wonderful, but not the right man for me.

Most people I know have at one time or another been fouled up by their childhood experiences. Patterns tend to sink into the unconscious only to reappear, disguised, unseen, like marionette strings, pulling us this way or that. Whatever ails people — keeps them up at night, tossing and turning — also ails movements no matter how historically huge or politically important. The women's movement cannot remake consciousness, or reshape the future, without acknowledging and shedding all the unnecessary and ugly baggage of the past. It's easy enough now to see where men have kept us out of clubs, baseball games, graduate schools; its easy enough to recognize the hidden directions that limit Sis to cake-baking and Junior to bridge-building; it's now possible for even Miss America herself to identify what *they* have done to us, and, of course, *they* have and *they* did and *they* are. . . . But along the way we also developed our own hidden prejudices, class assumptions and an anti-male humor and collection of expectations that gave us, like all oppressed groups, a secret sense of superiority (co-existing with a poor self-image — it's not news that people can believe two contradictory things at once).

Listen to any group that suffers materially and socially. They have a lexicon with which they tease the enemy: ofay, goy, honky gringo. "Poor pale devils," said Malcolm X loud enough for us to hear, although blacks had joked about that to each other for years. Behind some of the women's liberation thinking lurk the rumors, the prejudices, the defense systems of generations of oppressed women whispering in the kitchen together, presenting one face to their menfolk and another to their card clubs, their mothers and sisters. All this is natural enough but potentially dangerous in a revolutionary situation in which you hope to create a future that does not mirror the past. The hidden anti-male feelings, a result of the old system, will foul us up if they are allowed to persist.

During my teen years I never left the house on my Saturday night dates without my mother slipping me a few extra dollars — mad money, it was called. I'll explain what it was for the benefit of the new generation in which people just sleep with each other: the fellow was supposed to bring me home, lead me safely through the asphalt jungle, protect me from slithering snakes, rapists and the like. But my mother and I knew young men were apt to drink too much, to slosh down so many rye-and-gingers that some hero might well lead me in front of an oncoming bus, smash his daddy's car into Tiffany's window or, less gallantly, throw up on my new dress. Mad money was for getting home on your own, no matter what form of insanity your date happened to evidence. Mad money was also a wallflower's rope ladder; if the guy you came with suddenly fancied someone else, well, you didn't have to stay there and suffer, you could go home. Boys were fickle and likely to be unkind; my mother and I knew that, as surely as we knew they tried to make you do things in the dark they wouldn't respect you for afterwards, and in fact would spread the word and spoil your rep. Boys liked to be flattered; if you made them feel important they would eat out of your hand. So talk to them about their interests, don't alarm them with displays of intelligence — we all knew that, we groups of girls talking into the wee hours of the night in a kind of easy companionship we thought impossible with boys. Boys were prone to have a good time, get you pregnant, and then pretend they didn't know your name when you came knocking on their door for finances or comfort. In short, we believed boys were less moral than we were. They appeared to be hypocritical, self-seeking, exploitative, untrustworthy and very likely to be showing off their precious masculinity. I never had a girl friend I thought would be unkind or embarrass me in public. I never expected a girl to lie to me about her marks or sports skill or how good she was in bed. Altogether — without anyone's directly coming out and saying so — I gathered that men were sexy, powerful, very interesting, but not very nice, not very moral, humane and tender, like us. Girls played fairly while men, unfortunately, reserved their honor for the battlefield.

Why are there laws insisting on alimony and child support? Well, everyone knows that men don't have an instinct to protect their young and, given half a chance, with the moon in the right phase, they will run off and disappear. Everyone assumes a mother will not let her child starve, yet it is necessary to legislate that a father must not do so. We are taught to accept the idea that men are less than decent; their charms may be manifold but their characters are riddled with faults. To this day I never blink if I hear that a man has gone to find his fortune in South America, having left his pregnant wife, his blind mother and taken the family car. I still gasp in horror when I hear of a woman leaving her asthmatic infant for a rock group in Taos because I can't seem to avoid the assumption that men are naturally heels and women the ordained carriers of what little is moral in our dubious civilization.

My mother never gave me mad money thinking I would ditch a fellow for some other guy or that I would pass out drunk on the floor. She knew I would be considerate of my companion because, after all, I was more mature than the boys that gathered about. Why was I more mature? Women just are people-oriented; they learn to be empathetic at an early age. Most English students (students interested in humanity, not artifacts) are women. Men and boys — so the myth goes — conceal their feelings and lose interest in anybody else's. Everyone knows that even little boys can tell the difference between one kind of a car and another—proof that their souls are mechanical, their attention directed to the nonhuman.

I remember shivering in the cold vestibule of a famous men's   7
athletic club. Women and girls are not permitted inside the club's door. What are they doing in there, I asked? They're naked, said my mother, they're sweating, jumping up and down a lot, telling each other dirty jokes and bragging about their stock market exploits. Why can't we go in? I asked. Well, my mother told me, they're afraid we'd laugh at them.

The prejudices of childhood are hard to outgrow. I confess that   8
every time my business takes me past that club, I shudder. Images of large bellies resting on massage tables and flaccid penises rising and falling with the Dow Jones average flash through my head. There it is, chauvinism waving its cancerous tentacles from the depths of my psyche.

Minorities automatically feel superior to the oppressor because,   9
after all, they are not hurting anybody. In fact, they feel morally better. The old canard that women need love, men need sex — believed for too long by both sexes — attributes moral and spiritual superiority to women and makes of men beasts whose urges send them prowling into the night. This false division of good and bad, placing deforming pressures on everyone, doesn't have to contaminate the future. We know that the assumptions we make about each other become a part of the cultural air we breathe and, in fact, become social truths. Women who want equality must be prepared to give it and to believe in it, and in order to do that it is not enough to state that you are as good as any man, but also it must be stated that he is as good as you and both will be humans together. If we want men to share in the care of the family in a new way, we must assume them as capable of consistent loving tenderness as we.

I rummage about and find in my thinking all kinds of anti-male   10
prejudices. Some are just jokes and others I will have a hard time abandoning. First, I share an emotional conviction with many sisters that women given power would not create wars. Intellectually I know that's ridiculous; great queens have waged war before; the likes of Lurleen Wallace, Pat Nixon and Mrs. General Lavelle can be depended upon in the future to guiltlessly condemn to death other people's children in the name of some ideal of their own. Little girls, of course, don't take toy guns out of their hip pockets and say "Pow, pow" to all their neighbors and friends like the average well-adjusted little boy. However, if we gave little girls the six-shooters, we would soon have double the pretend body count.

Aggression is not, as I secretly think, a male-sex-linked character-   11
istic: brutality is masculine only by virtue of opportunity. True, there

are 1,000 Jack the Rippers for every Lizzie Borden, but that surely is the result of social forms. Women as a group are indeed more masochistic than men. The practical result of this division is that women seem nicer and kinder, but when the world changes, women will have a fuller opportunity to be just as rotten as men and there will be fewer claims of female moral superiority.

Now that I am entering early middle age, I hear many women   12
complaining of husbands and ex-husbands who are attracted to younger females. This strikes the older woman as unfair, of course. But I remember a time when I thought all boys around my age and grade were creeps and bores. I wanted to go out with an older man: a senior or, miraculously, a college man. I had a certain contempt for my coevals, not realizing that the freshman in college I thought so desirable, was some older girl's creep. Some women never lose that contempt for men of their own age. That isn't fair either and may be one reason why some sensible men of middle years find solace in young women.

I remember coming home from school one day to find my   13
mother's card game dissolved in hysterical laughter. The cards were floating in black rivers of running mascara. What was so funny? A woman named Helen was lying on a couch pretending to be her husband with a cold. She was issuing demands for orange juice, aspirin, suggesting a call to a specialist, complaining of neglect, of fate's cruel finger, of heat, of cold, of sharp pains on the bridge of the nose that might indicate brain involvement. What was so funny? The ladies explained to me that all men behave just like that with colds, they are reduced to temper tantrums by simple nasal congestion, men cannot stand any little physical discomfort — on and on the laughter went.

The point of this vignette is the nature of the laughter — us   14
laughing at them, us feeling superior to them, us ridiculing them behind their backs. If they were doing it to us we'd call it male chauvinist pigness; if we do it to them, it is inescapably female chauvinist sowness and, whatever its roots, it leads to the same isolation. Boys are messy, boys are mean, boys are rough, boys are stupid and have sloppy handwriting. A cacophony of childhood memories rushes through my head, balanced, of course, by all the well-documented feelings of inferiority and envy. But the important thing, the hard thing, is to wipe the slate clean, to start again without the meanness of the past. That's why it's so important that the women's movement not become anti-male and allow its most prejudiced spokesmen total leadership. The much-chewed-over abortion issue illustrates this. The women's-liberation position, insisting on a woman's right to determine her own body's destiny, leads in fanatical extreme to a kind of

emotional immaculate conception in which the father is not judged even half-responsible — he has no rights, and no consideration is to be given to his concern for either the woman or the fetus.

Woman, who once was abandoned and disgraced by an un- 15
wanted pregnancy, has recently arrived at a new pride of ownership or disposal. She has traveled in a straight line that still excludes her sexual partner from an equal share in the wanted or unwanted pregnancy. A better style of life may develop from an assumption that men are as human as we. Why not ask the child's father if he would like to bring up the child? Why not share decisions, when possible, with the male? If we cut them out, assuming an old-style indifference on their part, we perpetuate the ugly divisiveness that has character-ized relations between the sexes so far.

Hard as it is for many of us to believe, women are not really 16
superior to men in intelligence or humanity — they are only equal.

Review Question

According to Roiphe, in what ways are females chauvinist?

Discussion Questions

1. Roiphe's tone might be described as informal or "familiar." Explain.
2. What is the significance of the word "Sow" in the essay's title?
3. At which points in her essay does Roiphe make use of examples? Are these examples useful? Why or why not?
4. How does Roiphe establish her authority in this essay? (Consider both your answer to question 3 and the title, "Confessions of a Female Sow." Also, recall how Pius XI establishes his authority to speak on the subject of women and their role in society.)
5. What is the "myth'" with which Roiphe is primarily concerned?

Writing Suggestions

1. Do you agree with Roiphe that "women as a group are indeed more masochistic than men"? Argue for or against this position. Feel free to refer to personal experiences, as Roiphe does.
2. Do you believe that Roiphe's claim that females can also be chauvin-ists is valid? In an essay in which you refer to your own experiences, develop your ideas.

FEMINISM'S NEXT STEP
Betty Friedan

Betty Naomi Friedan (b. 1921), a feminist organizer and writer, has lectured at more than fifty universities, institutes, and professional associations, world-wide. Her first major work, *The Feminist Mystique* (1963), is a critique of women's roles in post World War II America. In it, Friedan identifies a "problem that has no name," a problem that

> . . . lay buried, unspoken, for many years in the minds of American women. It was a strange stirring, a sense of dissatisfaction, a yearning that women suffered in the middle of the twentieth century in the United States. Each suburban wife struggled with it alone. As she made the beds, shopped for groceries, matched slipcover material, ate peanut butter sandwiches with her children, chauffeured Cub Scouts and Brownies, lay beside her husband at night — she was afraid to ask even of herself the silent question — "Is this all?"[1]

The problem, of course, involves the definition of women as people other than wives and mothers. Friedan's critique prompted immediate criticism from radical feminists, who insisted that she wrote only for the white middle class and that she wanted to integrate women into a male-dominated society that should be overthrown. Eighteen years after publication of *The Feminine Mystique,* Friedan continues to talk integration. The following article first appeared in the *New York Times Magazine* and is adapted from her most recent book, *The Second Stage.*

□

"The women's movement is over," said my friend, a usually confident   1
executive, who is also a wife and feminist. "At least," she continued in a grim tone, "it is in my shop. The men are making jokes about bimbos again, and the other woman in the executive group and I just look at each other. It doesn't matter if we get mad; they act as if we aren't there. When a new job opens up, all they look for now is men. It's as if the word has gone out that we've lost our case; there won't be any equal rights amendment, so they don't need to worry anymore about lawsuits over sex discrimination, even though laws against it are still on the books. They figure they can do what they want about women now, like the old days."

[1] Betty Friedan, "The Problem That Has No Name," from *The Feminine Mystique* (New York: W. W. Norton and Co., 1963), p. 15.

The women's movement in some form will never be over. But the 2
rights that women have struggled to win in the last decade are in
deadly danger, with right-wing groups in Congress determined to gut
laws against sex discrimination and to abolish legal abortion and a
conservative Supreme Court already backtracking on equality. We
now have less than 365 days to pass the equal rights amendment,
which is both the symbol and the substance of women's rights. If
E.R.A. does not become part of the Constitution by June 30, 1982, it
may not come up again in this century.

And there are other signs that we have reached, not the begin- 3
ning of the end, but the end of the beginning.

Listening to my own daughter and others of her generation, I 4
sense something off, out of focus, going wrong. From the daughters,
working so hard at their new careers, determined not to be trapped as
their mothers were, expecting so much and taking for granted the
opportunities we fought for, I've begun to hear undertones of pain
and puzzlement, almost a bitterness that they hardly dare admit. As if,
with all those opportunities that we won for them, they are reluctant
to speak out loud about certain other needs some of us rebelled
against — needs for love, security, men, children, family, home.

I sense a frustration in women not so young, about those careers 5
they're lucky to have, facing agonizing conflicts over having children.
Can they have it all? How?

I sense a desperation in divorced women and men and an un- 6
spoken fear of divorce in those still married, which is being twisted
into a backlash against equal rights that are more essential than ever
for the divorced.

I sense a sullen impatience among some of those women who 7
entered the work force in unprecedented millions over the last 10
years, who are in fact earning 59 cents for every dollar men earn
because the only jobs available to most women are still in the low-
paying clerical and service fields. Even among the few who have
broken through to the executive suite, I sense the exhilaration of
trying to be superwomen giving way to disillusionment with the to-
kens of power.

What is going wrong? Why this uneasy sense of battles won, only 8
to be fought again, of battles that should have been won and yet are
not, of battles that suddenly one does not really want to win, and the
weariness of battle altogether — how many feel it?

I, and other feminists, dread to discuss these troubling symptoms 9
because the women's movement has been the source and focus of so
much of our energy, strength and security for so long. We cannot
conceive that it will not go on forever the same way it has for nearly 20
years. But we cannot go on denying these puzzling symptoms of

distress. If they mean something is seriously wrong, we had better find out and change direction yet again, before it is too late.

I believe it is over, the first stage. We must now move into the second stage of the sex-role revolution, which the women's movement set off.   10

In that first stage, our aim was full participation, power and voice in the mainstream — inside the party, the political process, the professions, the business world. But we were diverted from our dream by a sexual politics that cast man as enemy and seemed to repudiate the traditional values of the family. In reaction against the feminine mystique, which defined women solely in terms of their relation to men as wives, mothers and homemakers, we insidiously fell into a feminist mystique, which denied that core of women's personhood that is fulfilled through love, nurture, home. We seemed to create a polarization between feminists and those women who still looked to the family for their very identity, not only among the dwindling numbers who were still full-time housewives, but also among women who do not get as much sense of worth or security from their jobs as they get — or wish they could get — from being someone's wife or mother. The very terms in which we fought for abortion, or against rape, or in opposition to pornography seemed to express a hate for men and a lack of reverence for childbearing that threatened those women profoundly. That focus on sexual battles also took energy away from the fight for the equal rights amendment and kept us from moving to restructure work and home so that women could have real choices. We fought for equality in terms of male power, without asking what equality really means between women and men.   11

I believe that we have to break through our own feminist mystique now and move into the second stage — no longer against, but with men. In the second stage we have to transcend that polarization between feminism and the family. We have to free ourselves from male power traps, understand the limits of women's power as a separate interest group and grasp the possibility of generating a new kind of power, which was the real promise of the women's movement. For the second stage is not so much a fixed agenda as it is a process, a mode that will put a new value on qualities once considered — and denigrated as — special to women, feminine qualities that will be liberated in men as they share experiences like child care. These qualities, used mainly in the private world of the family until now, were previewed for the first time publicly in the women's movement; now they will be used in a larger political sphere by both men and women.   12

We discovered the first-stage limits — and the potential — of women's power in the last election. After the momentous passage of   13 the equal rights amendment by Congress in 1972 and approval by 35 of the 38 states needed to ratify a Constitutional amendment, E.R.A. had become deadlocked in the 15 unratified states. Despite majority popular support, as shown by the polls, E.R.A. was taken up as a target of right-wing political groups and became a focus for the reactionary political wave that was beginning to sweep the country. Discussion of it bogged down in hysterical claims that the amendment would eliminate privacy in bathrooms, encourage homosexual marriage, put women in the trenches and deprive housewives of their husbands' support.

What the equal rights amendment says is, "Equality of rights 14 under the law shall not be denied or abridged by the United States or any state on account of sex." What it would do is put half the population under the full protection of the Constitution and the Bill of Rights for the first time, guaranteeing inalienable equal opportunity for women in employment, education and other spheres. It would also provide the basis for equality in social security, marriage and divorce law, pensions, and military service. . . .

It will take a miracle of political wisdom and survival skills for 15 women to save the equal rights amendment by June 30, 1982. The women's movement has made such miracles happen before. The great march on Washington by thousands of women in the hot summer of 1979 made their real passion for equality clear enough to Congress to achieve extension of the traditional seven-year deadline for ratification of Constitutional amendments.

For a miracle like that, in the current reactionary political cli- 16 mate, the leaders of every woman's organization—from NOW and the League of Women Voters to the most career-oriented professional woman's caucuses and nonpolitical college sororities—would have to put aside their separate agendas. They would have to give not only lip service priority to E.R.A., but they would have to summon an emergency mobilization of their members, their staffs and their own treasuries, even mortgaging their buildings, to put all possible woman power into states like Virginia, Georgia, Oklahoma, North Carolina, as well as Illinois, Missouri and Florida, dividing the command of different states among the different organizations, or agreeing to follow a combined command.

Republican politicians from President Reagan down would have 17 to be made to understand that their responsibility for killing the equal rights amendment might be the margin for defeat for Republicans in 1984. And Democratic politicians would have to understand that our voting bloc — now larger than the traditional ethnic and blue-collar base — could be their only hope for power again in this century, but only if they mobilize their still considerable political muscle, expertise and flagging courage for equal rights for women as masterfully as they did to bring about the 96–0 defeat for cuts in old-age Social Security in the Senate.

And the seemingly apathetic "me" generation of students would have to be aroused, as they haven't been since the Vietnam War, the daughters to pay their dues and insure the opportunities they now take for granted, the sons to insure their own new dreams for more fulfilling lives. The women who have had assertiveness training and learned to dress for success would have to apply the hard skills and money from their own careers to insure that the doors the women's movement forced open don't close on them. The women afraid of divorce would have to see equal rights as the best insurance for themselves and their families against financial disaster. 18

Recently, a well-dressed woman in her 40's, facing a crisis in her own 25-year marriage, told me of her despair at the inability of women leaders to "get their act together" and truly mobilize to meet the crisis of E.R.A. 19

"They're not sure even now whether to ask women to go to Virginia or Georgia or Oklahoma. They say we might rock the boat," she said. "Don't they realize we have to rock the boat now. Who handed them or even President Reagan the right to give up our daughters' possibility to live lives of hope and equality for the rest of this century? It's not a matter of the specific details of the change E.R.A. will make in the laws of this state or that. If we lose the E.R.A., the rights we all take for granted now will be up to the whim of the individual judge again or the boss or husband. We won't have real control over our own lives without equal rights in the Constitution." 20

That woman had gotten her own suburban friends, who had never been near a NOW meeting or consciousness-raising group, to pool their money to hire a top professional political consultant to assess the chances of passing E.R.A. in the time left. One teen-ager contributed $800 she had raised baby-sitting for E.R.A. More valuable than the study itself — which showed that passage of E.R.A. was still politically possible—was the urgency of these women. If only that could be made visible. 21

That energy is out there, waiting for leadership. And the fact is, the most recent national poll conducted by Yankelovich, Skelly and White in May 1981, confirming the conservative mood of the nation in support of Reagan on economic issues, recorded a substantial 61 percent majority for passage of E.R.A. as compared with 30 percent against. 22

Finally, I think we have to face the fact that on June 30, 1982, we may lose the battle to get equal rights for women into the Constitution — and consider the real consequences. Many women whose own power in the executive suite or political arena arose from the women's 23

movement for equality in a sense they have forgotten or never acknowledged in their own careers — will most surely lose that power.
Women who were persuaded that E.R.A. was against the family, and
that all they needed was a man to take care of them the rest of their
lives, will have reason to fear financial disaster in divorce. Leaders of
special-interest groups — men or women whose concerns are for the
rights of homosexuals, blacks, Jews, children, the aged — may realize
too late that defeat of the E.R.A., which protects the rights of half the
nation, may doom the already threatened rights of much smaller
interest groups.

If we had not been diverted by sexual politics, we might not now   24
be watching the dismantling of affirmative-action programs against
sex discrimination in education and employment by conservative extremists in the Senate. The defeat of the Senators on the Moral
Majority hit list (Birch Bayh, Frank Church, John C. Culver, George
S. McGovern) cannot be attributed solely to disgust with Carter or to
Reagan's coattails. The women's movement has to assume some responsibility. We underestimated the threat and did not mobilize ourselves in all-out defense of the men who were explicitly targeted for
defeat by the National Conservative Political Action Committee supposedly because they supported equal rights for women, the right to
abortion and homosexual rights.

Is a distorted sexual politics at work if the women's movement   25
did not rise to the support of these men with the same passion as, for
instance, it supported Bella Abzug or Elizabeth Holtzman in their
Senate races? Is a distorted sexual politics responsible for the lumping
of these three issues together in such an inflammable, sexually
charged package? It is all very well for leaders of the women's movement today to insist, correctly, that the equal rights amendment has
nothing to do with either abortion or homosexuality — in fact, it has
nothing to do with sexual behavior at all. But the sexual politics that
distorted the sense of priorities of the women's movement during the
1970s made it easy for the so-called Moral Majority to lump E.R.A.
with homosexual rights and abortion into one explosive package of
licentious, family-threatening sex.

There is no doubt that the radical right with its almost unlimited   26
money is using abortion and homosexuality as a red herring. For
surely, homosexuality and abortion are not the main problems in
America today. But up through history to Hitler and the Ayatollah,
and not exempting Stalinist Russia, control and manipulation of sexuality and the family and suppression of the rights and personhood of
women have been key elements in authoritarian power. The emotions
and repressions linked to sexuality are so powerful that it is also
relatively easy to divert people's attention from their own basic eco-

nomic interests and even from asking the tough political questions simply by manipulating sexual hysteria.

The Founding Fathers of this republic wrote into the Bill of Rights the protection of certain basic areas of privacy. Surely it is politically unwise to seem to threaten that area of inviolate sexual privacy now, as part of an effort to secure these basic rights for women. Tactics that smack of sexual exhibitionism, even slogans like "sexual preference," distort the basic principle; they seem to invade that very right of privacy for which we fight. 27

Maybe there was something slightly off in the way we handled abortion. Such slogans as "free abortion on demand" had connotations of sexual permissiveness, affronting not only the moral values of conservatives but implying a certain lack of reverence for life and the mysteries of conception and birth. 28

After all, why do feminists seem to be fighting "for abortion" against women who say they are fighting for "the right to life"? How can we fight the real battle in such terms? Who is really for abortion? That is like being for mastectomy. I, myself, am for life. I am for the choice to have children, which those who would ban access to safe, legal, medical abortion endanger. 29

The true potential of women's power can be realized only by transcending the false polarization between feminism and the family. It is an abstract polarization that does not exist in real life. 30

For instead of the polarization that has plagued the women's movement in the last few years and prevented the very possibility of political solutions, new research shows that virtually all women today share a basic core of commitment to the family and to their own equality within and beyond it, as long as family and equality are not seen to be in conflict. 31

One such study, "Juggling Contradictions: Women's Ideas About Families," was conducted by Nancy Bennett, Susan Harding, et al. of the Social Science Research Community at the University of Michigan in 1979. The 33 women in this study were between the ages of 28 and 45, white, with children, living in small and medium-size Michigan cities. A third of the women had some college education, most of the families had an income of between $15,000 and $30,000, and more than half the women were employed, most of them part time, at jobs ranging from selling real estate to nursing, hairdressing and cleaning houses. 32

The researchers admitted that their preconceptions and practically everything they had read had prepared them to put the women they interviewed into two categories — familial or individualistic. The "familial ideology" places a tremendous value on the family and on 33 motherhood, both as an activity and as a source of identity. It holds that family — husband and children — should be the primary focus of a woman's life and that the needs of the family should be placed above all else. In contrast, the "individualistic ideology" places the individual on an equal level with the family — mothers have needs and goals to meet as persons apart from the family.

The researchers reported: "Instead of finding categories of women, we found categories of ideas . . . bits and pieces of two distinct belief systems — familial and individualistic ideologies. None of the women we spoke with subscribed completely to one ideology or the other; they all expressed some combination of the two, in their words and in their lives. The ideologies are opposed in the political arena. . . . The women we spoke with, however, did not present these ideas as contradictory." 34

The researchers stressed: "We were not surprised to find conflicting ideas or ideologies expressed by the women we interviewed, but to find them combined in the views and behavior of each woman." 35

The tension between the two ideologies — woman-as-individual and woman-serving-her-family — looked irreconcilable in the abstract, but was, in fact, reconciled in the women's lives. They worked, usually part time or on different shifts from their husbands, shared child care with husbands or grandmothers or others and approved of child-care centers, even if they were not yet ready to use them themselves. 36

Even those who themselves symbolize or preach one or the other ideology can be seen combining both in their own lives. When Rosabeth Moss Kanter, the eminent sociologist and author of "Men and Women in the Corporation," takes her 2-year-old son to a board meeting, her partner-husband, Barry, takes over with the child. They describe this arrangement in feminist terms. But when Marabel Morgan "saves" her marriage, not by decking her body in ostrich feathers but by enlisting her husband as partner-manager to keep track of and invest the money she earns lecturing on the "Total Woman," she describes this as "feminine," not feminist. 37

There are not two kinds of women in America. The political polarization between feminism and the family was preached and manipulated by extremists on the right — and colluded in, perhaps unconsciously, by feminist and liberal or radical leaders — to extend or defend their own political power. Now, as ideological polarization is being resolved in real life by juggling and rationalizing new necessities in traditional terms and old necessities in feminist terms, women will strengthen the family in evolving ways. 38

Politically, for the women's movement to continue to promote issues like E.R.A., abortion and child care solely in individualistic 39 terms subverts our own moral majority. Economic necessity and the very survival of the family now force the increasing majority of women to work and to make painful choices about having more children. And women who merely tolerated, or even disapproved of, these concerns, will now face them as matters of concrete personal urgency and the survival of their families. The women's movement has appealed to women as individualists; the Moral Majority has played to and elicited an explosive, defensive reaction on behalf of women as upholders of the family. Perhaps the reactionary preachers of the Moral Majority who decry women's moves to equality as threats to the family are merely using the family to limit women's real political power. In a similar vein, feminists intent on mobilizing women's political power are, in fact, defeating their own purpose by denying the importance of the family.

That Michigan study showed something very important. All the women believed in equality and all of them believed in the family — from the same or converging needs for security, identity, and some control over their lives. Whether or not they supported a particular issue depended on how they perceived its affecting them. No appeal would be acceptable, even to the most individualistic, if it denied or conflicted with their commitment to the family, which they all shared.

"Family" is not just a buzz word for reactionaries; for women, as for men, it is the symbol of that last area where one has any hope of control over one's destiny, of meeting one's most basic human needs, of nourishing that core of personhood threatened now by vast impersonal institutions and uncontrollable corporate and government bureaucracies. Against these menaces, the family may be as crucial for survival as it used to be against the untamed wilderness and the raging elements, and the old, simple kinds of despotism.

For the family, all psychological science tells us, is the nutrient of our humanness, of all our individuality. The Michigan women, and all the others they exemplify, may show great political wisdom as well as personal survival skills in holding on to the family as the base of their identity and human control.

It is time to start thinking of the movement in new terms. It is very important indeed that the daughters — and the sons — hold on to the dream of equality in the years ahead and move consciously to the second stage of the sex-role revolution. If we cannot, at this moment, solve the new problems we can no longer deny, we must at least pass on the right questions. These second-stage questions reflect the most urgent problems now facing this nation.

There is a quiet movement of American men that is converging on the women's movement, though it is masked at the moment by a resurgence of *machismo*. This movement of men for self-fulfillment beyond the rat race for success and for a role in the family beyond breadwinner makes it seem that women are seeking power in terms men are leaving behind. Even those women who have made it on such terms are forfeiting the quality of life, exchanging their old martyred service of home and children for harassed, passive service of corporation.

In the second stage, women have to say "No" to standards of success on the job set in terms of men who had wives to take care of all the details of life, and standards at home set in terms of women whose whole sense of worth and power had to come from that perfectly run house, those perfectly controlled children. Instead of accepting that double burden, women will realize that they can and must give up some of that power in the home and the family when they are carrying part of the breadwinning burden and some beginnings of power on the job. Instead of those rigid contracts that seemed the feminist ideal in the first stage, there will be in the second stage an easy flow as man and woman share the chores of home and children — sometimes 50–50, sometimes 20–80 or 60–40, according to their abilities and needs. In the second stage, the woman will find and use her own strength and style at work, instead of trying so hard to do it man's way, and she will not feel she has to be more independent than any man for fear that she will fall back into that abject dependence that she sometimes secretly yearns for. 45

Politically, instead of focusing on woman as victim and on sexual battles that don't really change anything, like those marches against pornography, feminists in the second stage will forge new alliances with men from unions, church and corporation that are essential if we are to restructure jobs and home on a human basis. 46

Despite the recent Supreme Court decision, which ruled that women may be excluded from the draft, I feel that in the second stage, questions like "Should women be drafted?" will be obsolete, for it will be understood that for the nation's survival, women simply will have to be drafted if a major war threatens. With the dangers of nuclear holocaust, new questions need to be asked about the defense of the nation that demand a sensitivity to human values and to life on the part of both male and female military leaders. 47

Above all, the second stage involves not a retreat to the family, but embracing the family in new terms of equality and diversity. The choice to have children — and the joys and burdens of raising them — will be so costly and precious that it will have to be shared more equally by mother, father and others from, or in place of, the larger family. The trade-offs will be seen more clearly as both men and women become realistic about the values and the price. It will probably not be possible economically for most women to have a real 48 choice to be just a housewife, full-time or lifelong. But men as well as women will be demanding parental leave or reduced schedules for those few years — or in early, middle or later life for their own rebirth. A voucher system, such as Milton Friedman and other conservatives have already proposed for different purposes, could be used to provide a "child allowance," payable perhaps as a tax rebate, to every man or woman who takes primary responsibility for care of a child or dependent parent at home. She or he would get equal credit in the wage-earning spouse's pension and old-age Social Security vestment; this credit would not be lost in case of divorce. If both parents returned to work and shared child-care responsibilities, they could use those vouchers to help pay for child care in the community. Many advanced nations have such a child or family allowance.

And in the second stage, unions and companies will begin to give   49
priority to restructuring hours of work — flextime and flexible benefit packages — not just to help women but because men will be demanding them and because improved quality of work will not only cost less but yield greater results in terms of reduced absenteeism, increased productivity and profit than the conventional package.

But in the second stage when we talk about "family" we will no   50
longer mean just Mom and Dad and the kids. We will be more keenly aware of how the needs of both women and men for love and intimacy and emotional and economic sharing and support change over time and of the new shapes family can take. In the second stage we will need new forms of homes and apartments that don't depend on the full-time service of the housewife, and new shared housing for single parents and people living alone — widowed, married and divorced — who are the largest new group in the population.

The only bright spot in the housing market this past year was   51
the great increase in sales of homes and condominiums to single women living alone. But since in fact it takes two incomes to buy housing today, banks and boards of condominiums and mortgage lending officers will increasingly be faced with requests for mortgages or leases by two, three or more persons unrelated by blood or marriage.

The common interests of all these kinds of families will create the   52
basis for a new political alliance for the second stage that may not be a women's movement. Men may be — must be — at the cutting edge of the second stage. Women were reborn, in effect, merely by moving across into man's world. In the first stage, it almost seemed as if women and men were moving in opposite directions, reversing roles or exchanging one half-life for another. In the second stage, we will go beyond the either-or of "superwoman" or "total woman" and "house husband" or "urban cowboy" to a new wholeness: an integra-

tion, in our personal lives, of the masculine and feminine in each of us in all our infinite personal variety — not unisex but new human sex.

If we can move beyond the false polarities and single-issue battles, and appreciate the limits and true potential of women's power, we will be able to join with men — follow or lead — in the new human politics that must emerge beyond reaction. It will be a new, passionate volunteerism, an activism that comes out of living these new problems for which there may be no single answer. It must have the same kind of relevance to the vital interests in life of both men and women and meet the same needs for higher purpose and communality as did the women's movement. 53

Now, those whose roots are in the service of life must have the strength to ask, if no one else does, what should government be responsible for if not for the needs of people in life? And the strength to start from those real needs of life to take back government, for the people. The second stage may even now be evolving, out of or aside from what we have thought of as our battle. 54

I know that equality, the personhood we fought for, is truly necessary for women — and opens new life for men. But I hear now what I could not hear before — the fears and feelings of some who have fought against our movement. It is not just a conspiracy of reactionary forces, though such forces surely play upon and manipulate those fears. 55

There is no going back. The women's movement was necessary. But the liberation that began with the women's movement isn't finished. The equality we fought for isn't livable, isn't workable, isn't comfortable in the terms that structured our battle. The first stage, the women's movement, was fought within and against and defined by that old structure of unequal, polarized male and female sex roles. But to continue reacting against such structure is still to be defined and limited by its terms. What's needed now is to transcend those terms and transform the structure itself. 56

How do we surmount the reaction that threatens to destroy the very gains we thought we had already won in the first stage of the women's movement? How do we surmount our own reaction, which shadows our feminism and our femininity (we blush even to use that word now)? How do we transcend the polarization between women and women and between women and men to achieve the new human wholeness that is the promise of feminism, and get on with solving the concrete, practical, everyday problems of living, working and loving as equal persons? This is the personal and political business of the second stage. 57

Review Questions

1. What are the causes of the frustration and the impatience that Friedan senses?
2. Define the first stage of the sex-role revolution.
3. What are the differences between the feminine and the feminist mystique?
4. How were the issues of homosexual rights and abortion associated — wrongly, in Friedan's estimation — with the passage of the Equal Rights Amendment?
5. What is the false polarization between feminism and the family? According to Friedan, how does it threaten men and women? How have feminists unwittingly contributed to the polarization?
6. "The second stage is not so much a fixed agenda as it is a process. . . ." What does Friedan mean by this?
7. Why were the sexual politics of the early revolution distorted?

Discussion Questions

1. Examine the first eight paragraphs of the article. How does Friedan signal that she is beginning an analysis?
2. Is Friedan's vision of the revolution's second stage a realistic one? Do you detect in her article a willingness to capitulate to a male-dominated system? Based on your reading of the "Manifesto for Revolution," how do you think Kate Millett would respond to Friedan's views?
3. Friedan's article drew many responses, pro and con, some of which were printed in the letters to the editor page of *The New York Times Magazine*. The response by psychiatrist Natalie Shainess follows:

> I was simply appalled by Betty Friedan's article "Feminism's Next Step," in the July 5th issue. I fear she has lost her way, or been blinded by something.
>
> There is no question about her place as leader of the Women's Liberation movement, or that she inspired women to move out of their bondage in household drudgery — uncompensated by either money, or much appreciation. There is no doubt that it was at her call that women gained a professional and vocational toehold. But that is the point: they have not as yet made gains much beyond that.
>
> She says "We have to break through our own feminist mystique now and move into the second stage, no longer against men, but with them." I do not think the woman's movement ever was, for the most part, against men: IT WAS *FOR* WOMEN!
>
> Any strategist knows that the time to give up is not when you have made small gains, not when you are losing (unless you are in mortal fear of continuing the struggle), but when your success is assured — or

almost so. How can she counsel that abortion is not an issue to fight for, at a time when this guarantor of "pursuit of happiness" is in jeopardy? How can she advise giving up the struggle, when ERA is in mortal danger of being lost?

As a psychiatrist and psychoanalyst, I do not question the necessity for family life, for positive relationship to men. But what Friedan overlooks is the fact that in any struggle between factions, what happens depends on what *each* side does. Why *is* ERA in such trouble, if it is "nothing"? Why do women not receive equal pay for equal work? Why does she not consider pornography a threat? It is one of the greatest, because it reduces woman to a degraded need-server — how can she be seen as a *person,* with a sick view of her spread over the land? In acknowledging that women may lose the ERA battle in 1982, she is virtually inviting women to give up; she is a captain refusing to fight to keep the ship from sinking. How many human endeavors have succeeded at the last moment, because there was simply a refusal to give up?

It is my belief that the time is not *now* to preach conciliation to women; how about urging it on men? They are the ones holding the power; they should be interested in peace; they should be interested in positive relationships with women — and not through a peephole of sex only. They should be interested in family. No one in power has ever ceded this power easily — this is a problem. But as I see it, women must try to hold their gains and continue to fight for what is their *right* in a democratic country: to be treated as equals, with a guarantee of all the constitutional rights our democracy offers — and with a loving hand of peace extended to them by men, in place of the false courtesies of the past. Why is conciliation only urged on women?

Women are too prone to see themselves as men see them; they can do without the current, ego-damaging views of a former leader.[1]

Write an essay considering Friedan's arguments in light of Shainess's response. In your opinion, whose advice should women and the women's movement follow — Friedan's or Shainess's? In what way are your beliefs influenced by your own gender or your own experiences?

4. Conduct an interview with a working woman, twenty-eight to thirty-five years of age, who, in your estimation, is "determined not to be trapped" as her mother was. Can you detect any of the frustration, despair, and bitterness that Friedan has observed? Use your notes to prepare a report on the subject.

---

[1] Letter to *The New York Times,* reprinted in its entirety with permission of Dr. Natalie Shainess. A portion of this letter appeared in the letters to the editor section, 23 August 1981. © 1981 by the New York Times Company. Reprinted by permission.

SUMMARY, SYNTHESIS, CRITIQUE ACTIVITIES

Summary

Summarize one or more of the passages in this chapter. Follow the suggested six-step process. Take into account the answers to the Review Questions for each passage. (*Recommended:* "Social Attitudes Towards Women" and "Feminism's Next Step.")

Synthesis

1. Write a conversation between Schlafly, Millett, and Friedan. Your conversation will, essentially, be a *comparison and contrast* synthesis. Schlafly's and Millett's positions are clearly distinguishable. Are Millett's and Friedan's positions just as distinguishable? You might wish to review the discussion questions for these readings before you begin your conversation.

2. Whether or not you agree with Schlafly's position, apply it in an analysis of Act II of *A Doll's House.* In order to construct this *argument,* you must become familiar with Schlafly's assumptions.

3. Use the predicament of Ibsen's character Nora as an *example* of another passage in this chapter. Is Nora guilty of what Pius XI calls "pernicious errors and depraved morals"? Does she suffer from "the problem that has no name"? Do you feel that in struggling to affirm her individuality, she has become a "strident man-hater"? Has she become a "Female Chauvinist Sow"? Has she articulated her own manifesto for revolution?

4. Based on your reading in this chapter, *define* the role of women in American culture. You will first want to clarify the major issues, as you understand them, and then stake out a position.

5. The authors of the selections in this chapter write from many different perspectives: one was a pope; one, a Broadway lyricist; one, a playwright; several are feminist writers; and one is an antifeminist writer. *Compare and contrast* some of these passages, showing how the perspective and profession of the writer has influenced both what she or he has to say on the role of women, and how she or he has said it. Use the information in the headnotes to help you.

6. Basic to any discussion of a woman's role is how women should or do behave toward men. Using three or four of the selections in this chapter, *compare and contrast* the conclusions reached by various writers on this subject, showing also how the special perspective or background of the writer has influenced his attitudes. (Caution: when discussing Lerner's song, be careful to differentiate between Lerner

the lyricist and Henry Higgins, his character — whose views he may or may not share.)

7. Compare and contrast Friedan's and Shainess's views on the best direction for the women's movement (see the letter by Shainess reprinted on page 407–08, Writing Suggestion 3, following the Friedan selection). First locate the common ground shared by both writers and then proceed to analyze the chief differences.

8. Based on your reading in this chapter, *define* a good (if not an ideal) marriage. What are the rights and responsibilities of the partners — to themselves and to one another?

Critique

Write a critique of Mary Daly's essay. You might find it useful, by way of introduction, to mention Pius XI's Encyclical Letter, "On Christian Marriage." Daly is writing in opposition to a tradition that Pius represents. Pay special attention to discussion questions that follow Daly's essay.

RESEARCH TOPICS

1. Discuss the conflicting demands faced by the professional working woman who is also a wife and mother. (You may wish to take the opposite approach to the question and discuss the conflicting demands faced by the professional working man who is also a husband and father.)

2. Review and analyze one aspect of the controversy surrounding the proposed Equal Rights Amendment. You might focus your discussion, for example, on obstacles to ratification, or on implications for male-female relationships — in the marketplace or in the military.

3. Compare and contrast the attitudes of three generations of men and women in your family regarding the "proper" role of women. What economic, social, and familial circumstances helped determine these different attitudes?

4. Is women's liberation an exclusively American liberation? To what degree is the "raised consciousness" of Americans shared by people in other countries?

ADDITIONAL READINGS

Bosmajian, Hamida and Haig Bosmajian, eds. *The Great Argument: The Rights of Women.* Reading, Mass.: Addison-Wesley Publishing Company, 1972.

Daly, Mary. *Beyond the Father: Toward a Philosophy of Women's Liberation.* Boston: Beacon Press, 1973.

Diner, Helen. *Mothers and Amazons: The First Feminine History of Culture.* New York: The Julian Press, Inc., 1965.

Friedman, Jean E. and William G. Shade, eds. *Our American Sisters: Women in American Life and Thought.* Boston: Allyn and Bacon, Inc., 1973.

Gilder, George. "The Myths of Racial and Sexual Discrimination." *National Review,* 32 (Nov. 14, 1980), pp. 1381ff.

Gornick, Vivian. *Essays on Feminism.* New York: Harper & Row, 1978.

Greer, Germaine. *The Female Eunuch.* New York: McGraw-Hill Book Company, 1971.

Hartman, Mary S. and Lisa Banner. *Clio's Consciousness Raised: New Perspectives on the History of Women.* New York: Harper Torchbooks, 1974.

Lazarre, Jane. *On Loving Men.* New York: The Dial Press, 1978.

Mead, Margaret. *Male and Female.* New York: William Morrow, 1949.

Millett, Kate. *Sexual Politics.* New York: Doubleday, 1970.

Osborne, Martha Lee, ed. *Woman in Western Thought.* New York: Random House, 1979.

Pleck, Joseph H. and Jack Sawyer, eds. *Men and Masculinity.* Englewood Cliffs, N.J.: Prentice-Hall, 1974.

Schneir, Miriam, ed. *Feminism: The Essential Historical Writings.* New York: Vintage Books, 1972.

Scott, Anne Firor. "What, Then, Is the American: This New Woman?" *The Journal of American History,* 65 (Dec. 1978), pp. 679–703.

Stassinopoulos, Arianna. *The Female Woman (An Argument Against Women's Liberation, for Female Emancipation).* New York: Random House, 1973.

Stoeltje, Beverly J. " 'A Helpmate for Man Indeed': The Image of the Frontier Woman." *Journal of American Folklore,* 88 (Jan. 1975), pp. 25–40.

Will, Elizabeth L. "Women's Roles in Antiquity: New Archeological Views." *Science Digest,* 87 (March 1980), pp. 35–39.

See also books (Friedan, Schlafly) from which selections in this unit were taken.

10 Politics and Language

As speakers of a language, we assume that words describe the world either accurately or inaccurately. If the description is accurate, we call the words true; if inaccurate, false. But there is a third possibility — that words may fail utterly to refer to the world, and so are neither true, nor false, but meaningless. Advertising is one natural habitat of such words. Politics is another. How often have you been exasperated by a political speech? The speaker approaches the podium, acknowledges the applause, smiles broadly, and then launches into a speech that, for all your heroic efforts of concentration, you simply cannot understand. "What is the problem?" you ask yourself. "Is it me, or is it him? Don't I know enough about current events to make sense of what he's saying? Does anyone else here understand him better than I do?"

Take comfort: you are not alone in your confusion. Political language is a Bermuda Triangle of ideas. In this chapter we offer some incisive observations of writers who either use political language with power and grace, or who explore the intellectual and political consequences of purposefully ambiguous political speechmaking. George Orwell, in the classic "Politics and the English Language," examines the lack of precision and the staleness of written prose that regularly passes for political thought. In "A Computer-Generated Foreign Policy Speech Guaranteed to Play in Peoria," John Cragan and Donald Shields test some of Orwell's assumptions by programming a computer to splice together — in perfectly grammatical English — a string of political platitudes. The result is a very familiar type of speech: it says nothing but it sounds quite good.

So as not to leave the impression that political language is inherently hopeless, we include two genuinely eloquent political statements: the Declaration of Independence and Lincoln's Gettysburg Address. The Declaration is followed by H. L. Mencken's modern American version of what the founding fathers were saying; and Lincoln's speech is followed first by Gilbert Highet's well-known critical appraisal, and next by Oliver Jensen's rendition of Lincoln's address into "Eisenhowese" — the style of speechmaking practiced by our former president (and a good many others). Then, political humorist Russell Baker sets out to explore terrain familiar to many contemporary politicians: he treks across the Broad Range of Issues, stopping along the way to canoe down the Labor Pool. Finally, communications professor Dan Hahn offers a handy decoding guide to that distinctive dialect of English — politicalese.

POLITICS AND THE ENGLISH LANGUAGE
George Orwell

George Orwell (1903–1950) was born Eric Blair in India, educated at Eton in England, and served for awhile in the Imperial Police in Burma, until revulsion with British imperialism forced him to quit. Implacably opposed to totalitarianism in any form, Orwell wrote *Animal Farm* (an allegorical satire on the Russian revolution) in 1945 and *1984* (a devastatingly grim portrait of a future totalitarian society) in 1948 — the title being an inversion of its publishing date. Characteristically, he links the decline of the English language to the corrupting effects of politics. "Politics and the English Language," his most famous essay, was written in 1945. (For more of Orwell's thoughts on the relationship between politics and language, read the appendix to *1984:* "The Principles of Newspeak.")

☐

Most people who bother with the matter at all would admit that the   1
English language is in a bad way, but it is generally assumed that we cannot by conscious action do anything about it. Our civilization is decadent and our language — so the argument runs — must inevitably share in the general collapse. It follows that any struggle against the abuse of language is a sentimental archaism, like preferring candles to electric light or hansom cabs to aeroplanes. Underneath this lies the half-conscious belief that language is a natural growth and not an instrument which we shape for our own purposes.

Now, it is clear that the decline of a language must ultimately   2
have political and economic causes: it is not due simply to the bad influence of this or that individual writer. But an effect can become a cause; reinforcing the original cause and producing the same effect in an intensified form, and so on indefinitely. A man may take to drink because he feels himself to be a failure, and then fail all the more completely because he drinks. It is rather the same thing that is happening to the English language. It becomes ugly and inaccurate because our thoughts are foolish, but the slovenliness of our language makes it easier for us to have foolish thoughts. The point is that the process is reversible. Modern English, especially written English, is full of bad habits which spread by imitation and which can be avoided if one is willing to take the necessary trouble. If one gets rid of these

habits one can think more clearly, and to think clearly is a necessary first step towards political regeneration: so that the fight against bad English is not frivolous and is not the exclusive concern of professional writers. I will come back to this presently, and I hope that by that time the meaning of what I have said here will have become clearer. Meanwhile, here are five specimens of the English language as it is now habitually written.

These five passages have not been picked out because they are 3 especially bad — I could have quoted far worse if I had chosen — but because they illustrate various of the mental vices from which we now suffer. They are a little below the average, but are fairly representative samples. I number them so that I can refer back to them when necessary:

(1) I am not, indeed, sure whether it is not true to say that the Milton who once seemed not unlike a seventeenth-century Shelley had not become, out of an experience ever more bitter in each year, more alien [*sic*] to the founder of that Jesuit sect which nothing could induce him to tolerate.

Professor Harold Laski
(Essay in Freedom of Expression)

(2) Above all, we cannot play ducks and drakes with a native battery of idioms which prescribes such egregious collocations of vocables as the Basic *put up with* for *tolerate* or *put at a loss* for *bewilder*.

Professor Lancelot Hogben (Interglossa).

(3) On the one side we have the free personality: by definition it is not neurotic, for it has neither conflict nor dream. Its desires, such as they are, are transparent, for they are just what institutional approval keeps in the forefront of consciousness; another institutional pattern would alter their number and intensity, there is little in them that is natural, irreducible, or culturally dangerous. But *on the other side,* the social bond itself is nothing but the mutual reflection of these self-secure integrities. Recall the definition of love. Is not this the very picture of a small academic? Where is there a place in this hall of mirrors for either personality or fraternity?

Essay on psychology in Politics (New York).

(4) All the "best people" from the gentlemen's clubs, and all the frantic fascist captains, united in common hatred of Socialism and bestial horror of the rising tide of the mass revolutionary movement, have turned to acts of provocation, to foul incendiarism, to medieval legends of poisoned wells, to legalize their own destruction of proletarian organizations, and rouse the agitated petty-bourgeoisie to chauvinistic fervor on behalf of the fight against the revolutionary way out of the crisis.

Communist pamphlet.

(5) If a new spirit is to be infused into this old country, there is one thorny and contentious reform which must be tackled, and that is the humanization and galvanization of the B.B.C. Timidity here will be-

speak canker and atrophy of the soul. The heart of Britain may be sound and of strong beat, for instance, but the British lion's roar at present is like that of Bottom in Shakespeare's *Midsummer Night's Dream* — as gentle as any sucking dove. A virile new Britain cannot continue indefinitely to be traduced in the eyes, or rather ears, of the world by the effete languors of Langham Place, brazenly masquerading as "standard English." When the Voice of Britain is heard at nine o'clock, better far and infinitely less ludicrous to hear aitches honestly dropped than the present priggish, inflated, inhibited, school-ma'amish arch braying of blameless bashful mewing maidens!

Letter in Tribune.

Each of these passages has faults of its own, but, quite apart from avoidable ugliness, two qualities are common to all of them. The first is staleness of imagery; the other is lack of precision. The writer either has a meaning and cannot express it, or he inadvertently says something else, or he is almost indifferent as to whether his words mean anything or not. This mixture of vagueness and sheer incompetence is the most marked characteristic of modern English prose, and especially of any kind of political writing. As soon as certain topics are raised, the concrete melts into the abstract and no one seems able to think of turns of speech that are not hackneyed: prose consists less and less of *words* chosen for the sake of their meaning, and more and more of *phrases* tacked together like the sections of a prefabricated hen-house. I list below, with notes and examples, various of the tricks by means of which the work of prose-construction is habitually dodged:

Dying Metaphors

A newly invented metaphor assists thought by evoking a visual image, while on the other hand a metaphor which is technically "dead" (e.g. *iron resolution*) has in effect reverted to being an ordinary word and can generally be used without loss of vividness. But in between these two classes there is a huge dump of worn-out metaphors which have lost all evocative power and are merely used because they save people the trouble of inventing phrases for themselves. Examples are: *Ring the changes on, take up the cudgels for, toe the line, ride roughshod over, stand shoulder to shoulder with, play into the hands of, no axe to grind, grist to the mill, fishing in troubled waters, on the order of the day, Achilles' heel, swan song, hotbed.* Many of these are used without knowledge of their meaning (what is a "rift," for instance?), and incompatible metaphors are frequently mixed, a sure sign that the writer is not interested in what he is saying. Some metaphors now current have been twisted out of their original meaning without those who use them even being aware of the fact. For example, *toe the line* is sometimes written *tow the line*. Another example is *the hammer and the anvil*, now always used with the implication that the anvil gets the worst of it. In real life it is always the anvil that breaks the hammer, never the other way about: a writer who stopped to think what he was saying would be aware of this, and would avoid perverting the original phrase.

Operators or Verbal False Limbs

These save the trouble of picking out appropriate verbs and nouns, and at the same time pad each sentence with extra syllables which give it an appearance of symmetry. Characteristic phrases are *render inoperative, militate against, make contact with, be subjected to, give rise to, give grounds for, have the effect of, play a leading part (role) in, make itself felt, take effect, exhibit a tendency to, serve the purpose of*, etc., etc. The keynote is the elimination of simple verbs. Instead of being a single word, such as *break, stop, spoil, mend, kill* a verb becomes a *phrase*, made up of a noun or adjective tacked on to some general-purpose verb such as *prove, serve, form, play, render*. In addition, the passive voice is wherever possible used in preference to the active, and noun constructions are used instead of gerunds (*by examination of* instead of *by examining*). The range of verbs is further cut down by means of the *-ize* and *de-* formations, and the banal statements are given an appearance of profundity by means of the *not un-* formation. Simple conjunctions and prepositions are replaced by such phrases as *with respect to, having regard to, the fact that, by dint of, in view of, in the interests of, on the hypothesis that;* and the ends of sentences are saved from anticlimax by such resounding commonplaces as *greatly to be desired, cannot be left out of account, a development to be expected in the near future, deserving of serious consideration, brought to a satisfactory conclusion* and so on and so forth.

Pretentious Diction

Words like *phenomenon, element, individual* (as noun), *objective, categorical, effective, virtual, basic, primary, promote, constitute, exhibit, exploit, utilize, eliminate, liquidate,* are used to dress up simple statements and give an air of scientific impartiality to biased judgments. Adjectives like *epoch-making, epic, historic, unforgettable, triumphant, age-old, inevitable, inexorable, veritable,* are used to dignify the sordid processes of international politics, while writing that aims at glorifying war usually takes on an archaic color, its characteristic words being: *realm, throne, chariot, mailed fist, trident, sword, shield, buckler, banner, jackboot, clarion*. Foreign words and expressions such as *cul de sac, ancien régime, deus ex machina, mutatis mutandis, status quo, gleichschaltung, weltan-*

schauung, are used to give an air of culture and elegance. Except for the useful abbreviations *i.e., e.g.,* and *etc.,* there is no real need for any of the hundreds of foreign phrases now current in English. Bad writers, and especially scientific, political and sociological writers, are nearly always haunted by the notion that Latin or Greek words are grander than Saxon ones, and unnecessary words like *expedite, ameliorate, predict, extraneous, deracinated, clandestine, subaqueous* and hundreds of others constantly gain ground from their Anglo-Saxon opposite numbers.[1] The jargon peculiar to Marxist writing (*hyena, hangman, cannibal, petty bourgeois, these gentry, lacquey, flunkey, mad dog, White Guard,* etc.) consists largely of words and phrases translated from Russian, German or French; but the normal way of coining a new word is to use a Latin or Greek root with the appropriate affix and, where necessary, the *-ize* formation. It is often easier to make up words of this kind (*deregionalize, impermissible, extramarital, non-fragmentary* and so forth) than to think up the English words that will cover one's meaning. The result, in general, is an increase in slovenliness and vagueness.

Meaningless Words

In certain kinds of writing, particularly in art criticism and literary criticism, it is normal to come across long passages which are almost completely lacking in meaning.[2] Words like *romantic, plastic, values, human, dead, sentimental, natural, vitality,* as used in art criticism, are strictly meaningless, in the sense that they not only do not point to any discoverable object, but are hardly ever expected to do so by the reader. When one critic writes, "The outstanding feature of Mr. X's work is its living quality," while another writes, "The immediately striking thing about Mr. X's work is its peculiar deadness," the reader accepts this as a simple difference of opinion. If words like *black* and

8

---

[1] An interesting illustration of this is the way in which the English flower names which were in use till very recently are being ousted by Greek ones, *snapdragon* becoming *antirrhinum, forget-me-not* becoming *myosotis,* etc. It is hard to see any practical reason for this change of fashion: it is probably due to an instinctive turning-away from the more homely word and a vague feeling that the Greek is scientific.

[2] Example: "Comfort's catholicity of perception and image, strangely Whitmanesque in range, almost the exact opposite in aesthetic compulsion, continues to evoke that trembling atmospheric accumulative hinting at a cruel, an inexorably serene timelessness. . . . Wrey Gardiner scores by aiming at simple bull's-eyes with precision. Only they are not so simple, and through his contented sadness runs more than the surface bitter-sweet of resignation." (Poetry Quarterly.)

white were involved, instead of the jargon words *dead* and *living,* he would see at once that language was being used in an improper way. Many political words are similarly abused. The word *Fascism* has now no meaning except in so far as it signifies "something not desirable." The words *democracy, socialism, freedom, patriotic, realistic, justice,* have each of them several different meanings which cannot be reconciled with one another. In the case of a word like *democracy,* not only is there no agreed definition, but the attempt to make one is resisted from all sides. It is almost universally felt that when we call a country democratic we are praising it: consequently the defenders of every kind of régime claim that it is a democracy, and fear that they might have to stop using the word if it were tied down to any one meaning. Words of this kind are often used in a consciously dishonest way. That is, the person who uses them has his own private definition, but allows his hearer to think he means something quite different. Statements like *Marshal Pétain was a true patriot, The Soviet Press is the freest in the world, The Catholic Church is opposed to persecution,* are almost always made with intent to deceive. Other words used in variable meanings, in most cases more or less dishonestly, are: *class, totalitarian, science, progressive, reactionary, bourgeois, equality.*

Now that I have made this catalogue of swindles and perversions, 9 let me give another example of the kind of writing that they lead to. This time it must of its nature be an imaginary one. I am going to translate a passage of good English into modern English of the worst sort. Here is a well-known verse from *Ecclesiastes:*

> I returned and saw under the sun, that the race is not to the swift, nor the battle to the strong, neither yet bread to the wise, nor yet riches to men of understanding, nor yet favour to men of skill; but time and chance happeneth to them all.

Here it is in modern English: 10

> Objective consideration of contemporary phenomena compels the conclusion that success or failure in competitive activities exhibits no tendency to be commensurate with innate capacity, but that a considerable element of the unpredictable must invariably be taken into account.

This is a parody, but not a very gross one. Exhibit (3), above, for 11 instance, contains several patches of the same kind of English. It will be seen that I have not made a full translation. The beginning and ending of the sentence follow the original meaning fairly closely, but in the middle the concrete illustrations — race, battle, bread — dissolve into the vague phrase "success or failure in competitive activities." This had to be so, because no modern writer of the kind I am discussing — no one capable of using phrases like "objective consideration of contemporary phenomena" — would ever tabulate his thoughts in that precise and detailed way. The whole tendency of modern prose is away from concreteness. Now analyse these two sentences a little more closely. The first contains forty-nine words but only sixty syllables, and all its words are those of everyday life. The second contains thirty-eight words of ninety syllables: eighteen of its words are from Latin roots, and one from Greek. The first sentence contains six vivid images, and only one phrase ("time and chance") that could be called vague. The second contains not a single fresh, arresting phrase, and in spite of its ninety syllables it gives only a shortened version of the meaning contained in the first. Yet without a doubt it is the second kind of sentence that is gaining ground in modern English. I do not want to exaggerate. This kind of writing is not yet universal, and outcrops of simplicity will occur here and there in the worst-written page. Still, if you or I were told to write a few lines on the uncertainty of human fortunes, we should probably come much nearer to my imaginary sentence than to the one from *Ecclesiastes*.

    As I have tried to show, modern writing at its worst does not   12
consist in picking out words for the sake of their meaning and inventing images in order to make the meaning clearer. It consists in gumming together long strips of words which have already been set in order by someone else, and making the results presentable by sheer humbug. The attraction of this way of writing is that it is easy. It is easier — even quicker, once you have the habit — to say *In my opinion it is not an unjustifiable assumption that* than to say *I think*. If you use ready-made phrases, you not only don't have to hunt about for words; you also don't have to bother with the rhythms of your sentences, since these phrases are generally so arranged as to be more or less euphonious. When you are composing in a hurry — when you are dictating to a stenographer, for instance, or making a public speech — it is natural to fall into a pretentious, Latinized style. Tags like *a consideration which we should do well to bear in mind* or *a conclusion to which all of us would readily assent* will save many a sentence from coming down with a bump. By using stale metaphors, similes and idioms, you save much mental effort, at the cost of leaving your meaning vague, not only for your reader but for yourself. This is the significance of mixed metaphors. The sole aim of a metaphor is to call up a visual image. When these images clash — as in *The Fascist octopus has sung its swan song, the jackboot is thrown into the melting pot* — it can be taken as certain that the writer is not seeing a mental image of the objects he is naming; in other words he is not really thinking. Look again at the examples I gave at the beginning of this essay. Professor Laski (1) uses five negatives in fifty-three words. One of these is superfluous, making nonsense of the whole passage, and in addition there is the slip *alien* for *akin*, making further nonsense, and several

avoidable pieces of clumsiness which increase the general vagueness. Professor Hogben (2) plays ducks and drakes with a battery which is able to write prescriptions, and, while disapproving of the everyday phrase *put up with*, is unwilling to look *egregious* up in the dictionary and see what it means; (3), if one takes an uncharitable attitude towards it, is simply meaningless: probably one could work out its intended meaning by reading the whole of the article in which it occurs. In (4), the writer knows more or less what he wants to say, but an accumulation of stale phrases chokes him, like tea leaves blocking a sink. In (5), words and meaning have almost parted company. People who write in this manner usually have a general emotional meaning — they dislike one thing and want to express solidarity with another — but they are not interested in the detail of what they are saying. A scrupulous writer, in every sentence that he writes, will ask himself at least four questions, thus: What am I trying to say? What words will express it? What image or idiom will make it clearer? Is this image fresh enough to have an effect? And he will probably ask himself two more: Could I put it more shortly? Have I said anything that is avoidably ugly? But you are not obliged to go to all this trouble. You can shirk it by simply throwing your mind open and letting the ready-made phrases come crowding in. They will construct your sentences for you — even think your thoughts for you, to a certain extent — and at need they will perform the important service of partially concealing your meaning even from yourself. It is at this point that the special connection between politics and the debasement of language becomes clear.

In our time it is broadly true that political writing is bad writing. 13
Where it is not true, it will generally be found that the writer is some kind of rebel, expressing his private opinions and not a "party line." Orthodoxy, of whatever color, seems to demand a lifeless, imitative style. The political dialects to be found in pamphlets, leading articles, manifestos, White Papers and the speeches of undersecretaries do, of course, vary from party to party, but they are all alike in that one almost never finds in them a fresh, vivid, home-made turn of speech. When one watches some tired hack on the platform mechanically repeating the familiar phrases — *bestial atrocities, iron heel, blood-stained tyranny, free peoples of the world, stand shoulder to shoulder* — one often has a curious feeling that one is not watching a live human being but some kind of dummy: a feeling which suddenly becomes stronger at moments when the light catches the speaker's spectacles and turns them into blank discs which seem to have no eyes behind them. And this is not altogether fanciful. A speaker who uses that kind of phraseology has gone some distance towards turning himself into a machine. The appropriate noises are coming out of his larynx, but his brain is

not involved as it would be if he were choosing his words for himself. If the speech he is making is one that he is accustomed to make over and over again, he may be almost unconscious of what he is saying, as one is when one utters the responses in church. And this reduced state of consciousness, if not indispensable, is at any rate favorable to political conformity.

In our time, political speech and writing are largely the defence 14 of the indefensible. Things like the continuance of British rule in India, the Russian purges and deportations, the dropping of the atom bombs on Japan, can indeed be defended, but only by arguments which are too brutal for most people to face, and which do not square with the professed aims of political parties. Thus political language has to consist largely of euphemism, question-begging and sheer cloudy vagueness. Defenceless villages are bombarded from the air, the inhabitants driven out into the countryside, the cattle machine-gunned, the huts set on fire with incendiary bullets: this is called *pacification*. Millions of peasants are robbed of their farms and sent trudging along the roads with no more than they can carry: this is called *transfer of population* or *rectification of frontiers*. People are imprisoned for years without trial, or shot in the back of the neck or sent to die of scurvy in Arctic lumber camps; this is called *elimination of unreliable elements*. Such phraseology is needed if one wants to name things without calling up mental pictures of them. Consider for instance some comfortable English professor defending Russian totalitarianism. He cannot say outright, "I believe in killing off your opponents when you can get good results by doing so." Probably, therefore, he will say something like this:

"While freely conceding that the Soviet régime exhibits certain 15 features which the humanitarian may be inclined to deplore, we must, I think, agree that a certain curtailment of the right to political opposition is an unavoidable concomitant of transitional periods, and that the rigors which the Russian people have been called upon to undergo have been amply justified in the sphere of concrete achievement."

The inflated style is itself a kind of euphemism. A mass of Latin 16 words falls upon the facts like soft snow, blurring the outlines and covering up all the details. The great enemy of clear language is insincerity. When there is a gap between one's real and one's declared aims, one turns as it were instinctively to long words and exhausted idioms, like a cuttlefish squirting out ink. In our age there is no such thing as "keeping out of politics." All issues are political issues, and politics itself is a mass of lies, evasions, folly, hatred and schizophrenia. When the general atmosphere is bad, language must suffer. I should expect to find — this is a guess which I have not sufficient knowledge to verify — that the German, Russian and Italian languages have all deteriorated in the last ten or fifteen years, as a result of dictatorship.

But if thought corrupts language, language can also corrupt 17 thought. A bad usage can spread by tradition and imitation, even among people who should and do know better. The debased language that I have been discussing is in some ways very convenient. Phrases like *a not unjustifiable assumption, leaves much to be desired, would serve no good purpose, a consideration which we should do well to bear in mind,* are a continuous temptation, a packet of aspirins always at one's elbow. Look back through this essay, and for certain you will find that I have again and again committed the very faults I am protesting against. By this morning's post I have received a pamphlet dealing with conditions in Germany. The author tells me that he "felt impelled" to write it. I open it at random, and here is almost the first sentence that I see: "[The Allies] have an opportunity not only of achieving a radical transformation of Germany's social and political structure in such a way as to avoid a nationalistic reaction in Germany itself, but at the same time of laying the foundations of a co-operative and unified Europe." You see, he "feels impelled" to write — feels, presumably, that he has something new to say — and yet his words, like cavalry horses answering the bugle, group themselves automatically into the familiar dreary pattern. This invasion of one's mind by ready-made phrases (*lay the foundations, achieve a radical transformation*) can only be prevented if one is constantly on guard against them, and every such phrase anaesthetizes a portion of one's brain.

I said earlier that the decadence of our language is probably 18 curable. Those who deny this would argue, if they produced an argument at all, that language merely reflects existing social conditions, and that we cannot influence its development by any direct tinkering with words and constructions. So far as the general tone or spirit of a language goes, this may be true, but it is not true in detail. Silly words and expressions have often disappeared, not through any evolutionary process but owing to the conscious action of a minority. Two recent examples were *explore every avenue* and *leave no stone unturned,* which were killed by the jeers of a few journalists. There is a long list of flyblown metaphors which could similarly be got rid of if enough people would interest themselves in the job; and it should also be possible to laugh the *not un-* formation out of existence,[3] to reduce the amount of Latin and Greek in the average sentence, to drive out foreign phrases and strayed scientific words, and, in general, to make

---

[3] One can cure oneself of the *not un-* formation by memorizing this sentence: *A not unblack dog was chasing a not unsmall rabbit across a not ungreen field.*

pretentiousness unfashionable. But all these are minor points. The defence of the English language implies more than this, and perhaps it is best to start by saying what it does *not* imply.

To begin with it has nothing to do with archaism, with the salvaging of obsolete words and turns of speech, or with the setting up of a "standard English" which must never be departed from. On the contrary, it is especially concerned with the scrapping of every word or idiom which has outworn its usefulness. It has nothing to do with correct grammar and syntax, which are of no importance so long as one makes one's meaning clear, or with the avoidance of Americanisms, or with having what is called a "good prose style." On the other hand it is not concerned with fake simplicity and the attempt to make written English colloquial. Nor does it even imply in every case preferring the Saxon word to the Latin one, though it does imply using the fewest and shortest words that will cover one's meaning. What is above all needed is to let the meaning choose the word, and not the other way about. In prose, the worst thing one can do with words is to surrender to them. When you think of a concrete object, you think wordlessly, and then, if you want to describe the thing you have been visualizing you probably hunt about till you find the exact words that seem to fit it. When you think of something abstract you are more inclined to use words from the start, and unless you make a conscious effort to prevent it, the existing dialect will come rushing in and do the job for you, at the expense of blurring or even changing your meaning. Probably it is better to put off using words as long as possible and get one's meaning as clear as one can through pictures or sensations. Afterwards one can choose — not simply *accept* — the phrases that will best cover the meaning, and then switch round and decide what impression one's words are likely to make on another person. This last effort of the mind cuts out all stale or mixed images, all prefabricated phrases, needless repetitions, and humbug and vagueness generally. But one can often be in doubt about the effect of a word or a phrase, and one needs rules that one can rely on when instinct fails. I think the following rules will cover most cases: 19

(i) Never use a metaphor, simile or other figure of speech which you are used to seeing in print.

(ii) Never use a long word where a short one will do.

(iii) If it is possible to cut a word out, always cut it out.

(iv) Never use the passive where you can use the active.

(v) Never use a foreign phrase, a scientific word or a jargon word if you can think of an everyday English equivalent.

(vi) Break any of these rules sooner than say anything outright barbarous.

These rules sound elementary, and so they are, but they demand a deep change of attitude in anyone who has grown used to writing in the style now fashionable. One could keep all of them and still write bad English, but one could not write the kind of stuff that I quoted in those five specimens at the beginning of this article.

I have not here been considering the literary use of language, but merely language as an instrument for expressing and not for concealing or preventing thought. Stuart Chase and others have come near to claiming that all abstract words are meaningless, and have used this as a pretext for advocating a kind of political quietism. Since you don't know what Fascism is, how can you struggle against Fascism? One need not swallow such absurdities as this, but one ought to recognize that the present political chaos is connected with the decay of language, and that one can probably bring about some improvement by starting at the verbal end. If you simplify your English, you are freed from the worst follies of orthodoxy. You cannot speak any of the necessary dialects, and when you make a stupid remark its stupidity will be obvious, even to yourself. Political language — and with variations this is true of all political parties, from Conservatives to Anarchists — is designed to make lies sound truthful and murder respectable, and to give an appearance of solidity to pure wind. One cannot change this all in a moment, but one can at least change one's own habits, and from time to time one can even, if one jeers loudly enough, send some worn-out and useless phrase — some *jackboot, Achilles' heel, hotbed, melting pot, acid test, veritable inferno* or other lump of verbal refuse — into the dustbin where it belongs.

Review Questions

1. What are the causes — and the effects — of the decline of language?
2. What two faults are common to the five passages Orwell quotes?
3. Why do writers continue to use the devices that contribute to the debasement of language?
4. What are the main categories of "tricks" by which the English language is debased? What are the reasons for the use of each?
5. The scrupulous writer will ask himself what four questions before writing?
6. Why does Orwell assert that "it is better to put off using words as long as possible. . . ."?
7. What must we do to help reverse the debasement of language?

Discussion Questions

1. Orwell writes of "ugliness" in prose. What do you think he means by this? Locate some particularly ugly phrases in the passages he quotes.

2. Orwell admits that his translation of the *Ecclesiastes* passage "is a parody, but not a very gross one." In his view, modern written English tends more toward the style of his translation than toward the original. Is this a fair assessment, in your view? Since almost everyone would admit that the parody version is unreadable, why do people go on writing this way?

3. Orwell asserts that political writing is bad writing. Find a published political speech and compile examples of the type of writing Orwell deplores. (Places to look: *The Congressional Record, Public Papers of the Presidents of the United States, The New York Times* — particularly in the weeks before an election.)

4. Orwell asserts that "In our age there is no such thing as 'keeping out of politics.' All issues are political issues. . . ." What does he mean by this? Do you agree with him?

5. Orwell adds to the preceding quotation: ". . . politics itself is a mass of lies, evasions, folly, hatred and schizophrenia." And toward the end of the essay, in a famous crescendo, he claims: "Political language — and with variations this is true of all political parties, from Conservatives to Anarchists — is designed to make lies sound truthful and murder respectable, and to give an appearance of solidity to pure wind." Is he overstating his case with such assertions? Is he being unfair to politicians? Or was he writing at a time (1945, immediately following the cataclysm of World War II and at the beginning of what General Ripper in *Dr. Strangelove* called "your postwar Commie conspiracy") when politics and political language were more degraded than they are today?

6. Although Orwell presents early in his essay the five passages displaying the worst tendencies of modern English, he does not get around to criticizing them specifically until much later. Why not? Would it have been better to include the criticism immediately after the passages?

7. Does Orwell's essay demonstrate the freshness of imagery and precision of language upon which he insists? Cite examples.

8. Orwell tells us that if we look back through his essay, "for certain you will find that I have again and again committed the very faults I am protesting against." Has he? If he has, why couldn't he have looked back himself and corrected the problems? If he hasn't, why should he make this invitation?

9. This essay was written more than thirty-five years ago. Has it become outdated significantly, either because of its subject matter or because of the particular examples of bad language Orwell cites?

Writing Suggestions

1. Find a recent political speech (see Discussion Question 3) and write an analysis of it (or part of it) according to the criteria discussed by Orwell.

2. Write a speech consisting almost entirely of the "tricks" Orwell discusses.

3. Find a printed passage that displays qualities of the *Ecclesiastes* parody and translate it into plain English. (Places to look: textbooks, newspapers — particularly letters to the editor, political speeches, legal writing, regulations.) Or take a couple of the five passages Orwell himself provides and translate them.

4. Translate the following passages into plain English:

    a. It is true that non-bureaucratic systems can provide greater latitude for innovation, individualism, professional self-fulfillment, and ready adaptability to change than can more complex organizations. They also provide for conditions that can make for instability, role confusion and interpersonal tensions, which, if they become severe, can militate against the interests of clientele. [The answer lies in] developing a balance between those elements of structure and process conducive to rational management of the organization and those elements essential for optimum client service.

    b. In cases not covered by other authority herein, the Departments of the Army, the Navy, and the Air Force may provide air transportation with reimbursements therefor, and subject to other restrictions, in accordance with the provisions of applicable law, when the traffic is of official concern to the executive departments or agencies, or to the legislative or judicial branches of the Government. Requests for transportation in this category should be directed to the departments concerned with a clear indication of the method by which reimbursement is to be accomplished.

    Begin the translation process by (1) trying to humanize the passages — including human beings whenever you can; (2) changing, when appropriate, the passive sentence constructions to active ones; (3) simplifying the language; and (4) breaking up sentences if necessary.

A COMPUTER-GENERATED SPEECH, GUARANTEED TO PLAY IN PEORIA

John F. Cragan and Donald C. Shields

John F. Cragan is associate professor of speech communication at Illinois State University at Normal. Donald C. Shields is associate professor of speech communication at the University of Missouri, St. Louis. A report of Cragan and Shields's work was featured on the premier broadcast of CBS's *Universe,* narrated by Walter Cronkite.

In the past two decades, the American political campaign has been   1
concerned more with public relations than with public policy. The 1960 televised debates between Richard M. Nixon and John F. Kennedy marked the beginning of electronic domination of political campaigns. Each successive campaign has witnessed an ever-increasing emphasis on symbols over substance. The general conclusion drawn from the Kennedy-Nixon debates is that the candidates held similar substantive positions on policy, but that Kennedy presented a more pleasing image. The fact that public relations played a major role in electing Kennedy established the potential of TV to make a candidate electable.

Aware of television's advantage as a medium for waging political   2
campaigns, subsequent political candidates eagerly turned to the symbolic packaging of marketing and advertising advisors in order to create the necessary television presidential image. The result of such Madison Avenue influence was predictable — proven television techniques for selling beer, toothpaste, detergent, and soda pop are now commonly used to sell politicians.

The problem with politicians turning to consumer advertising   3
techniques is that the success of these techniques does not require a link between symbols and substance — a beer is a beer and toothpaste is toothpaste. The difference in images between who smokes Virginia Slims, Kools, Marlboros, or Camels has little to do with the substantive reality of the tobacco that is in each of those cigarettes. The *reality* of a *difference* exists solely in the symbols of the media advertising campaign. The ad agencies are not selling tobacco or beer or toothpaste. They are selling rhetorical and symbolic fantasies which encourage consumers to get involved in visions of the "Pepsi Generation," the

Reprinted from *USA Today,* May 1980 (appeared under the title, "Communications in American Politics: Symbols without Substance"). Copyright 1980 by Society for the Advancement of Education. Reprinted by permission.

"Marlboro Man," and "UnCola," or to purchase toothpaste on the dramatic basis of its sex appeal. Because there are few substantive differences between beers, toothpaste, or detergents, this sort of symbol manipulation seems relatively harmless. However, use of such techniques in political campaigns is quite another matter.

Historically, political candidates and political campaigns have followed the precepts of the great American experience in democracy. Candidates selected issues or viewpoints and interpreted them to the electorate through speeches which provided reasons and justifications for accepting their views and platforms over those of their opponents. The tenets of democracy said that the vast electorate would study the person, study the person's positions and views, and vote for the candidate who would best serve the country. However, the 30- to 60-second image commercial — coupled with the fragmentation of the electorate's feelings and beliefs on such issues as Vietnam, the economy, abortion, and equal rights for women — produced a new genre of political speeches that manipulated symbols in an attempt to please the most and offend the least. The candidate did not present substantive stands or hold substantive policies, but, rather, vocalized images which made him appear to be all things to all people.

In 1976, we set out to demonstrate the absurdity of political candidates emphasizing symbols over substance in foreign policy campaign rhetoric. Specifically, we studied how mediated political rhetoric "played in Peoria." To do this, we culled from newspapers, magazines, and television political messages that represented the three dominant foreign policy dramas presented in the campaign: Cold War, Neo-Isolationism, and Power Politics. To represent the three foreign policy dramas, we chose messages related to the 20 most important foreign policy issues of the time (Russia, China, Middle East, arms control, terrorists, etc.). For each of the 20 issues, there were three different symbolic expressions corresponding respectively to the three foreign policy dramas. For example, in reference to the issue of terrorists, the Cold War message stressed the need for the U.S. to meet terrorism with force whenever and wherever it occurs; the Neo-Isolationist position recommended that the U.S. use its influence in the UN to get a resolution against terrorism; and the Power Politics position called for a flexible policy of decisive action and protracted negotiation.

The 60 messages were presented to Peorians, who ranked them on a continuum from accepted through neutral to rejected. The collected data was analyzed by computer and Peorians who had similar reactions to the statements were grouped together. The computer analysis revealed that the Power Politics drama of American involvement in foreign affairs was dominant in Peoria, the Cold War drama was the next most popular, and the Neo-Isolationist position was least accepted. The computer then selected messages that would please the most and offend the least Peorians. To order these messages, the computer followed certain decision rules that would allow it to produce the perfect six-seven-minute political speech on foreign policy.

This speech is replete with symbolic messages that have the appearance of substance. However, because the computer generated the talk in all its scientific sterility, there can be no substantive reality or programs to which the symbols are tied. The speech itself is symbolically and syntactically coherent, but it represents no actual foreign policy. Indeed, close examination reveals that it is merely a collection of safe political phrases that most Americans would have difficulty rejecting. Not all political speeches contain empty rhetoric — some tie symbols to substance. For example, Pres. Lyndon Johnson spoke of a "Great Society" in 1964 and the first 100 days of his Administration saw the passage of legislation that was the substantive social policy his symbols referred to. Likewise, Henry Kissinger's Power Politics rhetoric described a cognitive foreign policy of balancing the influences of the five major world power centers (China, Russia, Europe, Japan, and the U.S.). Subsequently, he and Pres. Richard Nixon traveled to these power centers, negotiated with them, and established a changed foreign policy with them.

A major consideration in the 1980 and subsequent campaigns ought to be how politicians can be encouraged to tie their symbols to substantive programs. Following is a computerized political speech that epitomizes political symbol manipulation at its worst. Our machine speech can be compared to the speeches made by real candidates on subjects such as foreign policy, energy, and the economy.

Computer-derived Foreign Policy Speech

I'd like to take this opportunity here in Peoria to set forth clearly and specifically my position on foreign policy. In order to do that, I'd first like to explain how I see the world today and indicate to you what I believe America's role in world politics should be. First of all, let me say that the U.S. is not a failure. For 200 years, we have provided the world, through the great experience of democracy, a model — a model that the world is free to follow, but one that we will not impose. Ideally, we would prefer merely to be this model. Unfortunately, the pragmatic realities of the international scene force us to play other roles.

The international scene today is highly complex. In some ways, it is still a struggle between the free world and communism, for, despite all claims to the contrary, Russia is still a communist state. But, 1976 is not 1956. Russia has acquired nuclear and conventional military parity with us — and China and the Middle East make all dealings with the Russians more difficult. Therefore, in the day-to-day affairs of world politics, we must strive to manage and stabilize our relationships with other major powers. In a nuclear age, we can not escape the responsibility to build a safe future through wise diplomacy.

Now please do not misunderstand me. A policy of detente with the 11
Soviet Union does not mean that we're "Uncle Sucker." I recognize that it's foolhardy to unilaterally disarm, but I also know that it's easy to talk in a mock and tough way and run the risk of war. Neither response reflects my position. Detente means to me a state of affairs marked by the absence of significant tension that could lead the U.S. and Russia into a nuclear confrontation. Detente does not mean that all differences will be resolved, or that Russia will not attempt to expand her influence. It does mean that peaceful coexistence is the only rational alternative.

I don't intend to "flip-flop" on any foreign policy issues. Nor do I 12
intend to speak in glib generalities. I came here to talk specifically about American foreign policy and that's what I mean to do. First of all, the lesson of Vietnam. The lesson of Vietnam is one of indecision. The U.S. was not wrong in the purpose for which we fought. While South Vietnam was not totally a free government, it still enjoyed more liberty than any communist regime in Eastern Europe allows. Our mistake was in not moving decisively when we first militarily intervened to discourage further communist aggression in that country.

Which brings me to the issue of possible future U.S. intervention. I 13
believe that intervention is a diplomatic tool that is needed, even if it is only a threat to maintain a balanced international scene. Intervention is not right or wrong, but it may be used rightly or wrongly.

Of course, we can not talk about intervention without talking about 14
the CIA. I do not believe that we should dismantle the CIA, for many times it is the CIA's covert capability that stands between a do-nothing policy and nuclear confrontation. I oppose unnecessary secrecy, but I believe in a strong national defense. And, unfortunately, in today's world, the CIA is needed.

There has been a lot of talk about Europe in this campaign. Let me 15
again state my position. The NATO alliance and the "trip-wire" presence of American troops stationed in Germany are important parts of America's defense. It would be foolish to withdraw American troops from the Continent of Europe without negotiating a similar withdrawal of Russian troops from Eastern Europe.

The Middle East is again in a no-war, no-peace stalemate and is 16
likely to remain so for some time. Step-by-step diplomacy, treating all parties with an even hand, is the only means for maintaining a delicate peace in the Middle East.

The United States must ground its China policy in morality. We 17
should work to improve our relationships with her. The People's Republic of China is a sovereign state, but we must not forget to support our ally, The Republic of China, on Taiwan. I believe both governments can learn to live with the reality of each other.

In Africa, a specific American presence is necessary if we are to 18
prevent further communist inroads and a tarnishing of America's

influence on this awakening continent. The communists should know that we are prepared to come to the defense of sovereign nations and the Africans should know that we stand ready to help them negotiate a peace among themselves.

In Latin America, we should avoid "big stick" tactics, but we should 19 not stick our heads in the sand to what's going on down there. With respect to Panama, the U.S. neither owns nor has sovereignty over the Canal Zone. However, Panama granted us rights by a 1903 treaty. We should renegotiate a new treaty that protects America's vital interests in the Canal Zone.

On terrorists, my position is clear. International terrorism, such as 20 bombings and hijackings, is deplorable. Yet, the U.S. should not put itself in a position committed to meet such actions whenever and wherever they might occur. I will go to the United Nations and get an international law against terrorism.

I should not leave Peoria without stating my opinion of grain sales. 21 First of all, I think the embargoing of food is immoral, given the starving millions in the world. Second, whether we sell or do not sell grain to Russia will not alter her behavior in international affairs.

As I stated in my opening remarks, the U.S. is not a crippled giant. 22 We have not lost confidence in ourselves. We are a proud democratic nation that must play a major role of leadership in international affairs. I trust you will agree that my foreign policy is based on a realistic and mature view of how to maintain world order and peace.

Recent political speechmaking appears to be dominated by sym- 23 bols not grounded in substance. Faced with an energy crisis, Pres. Carter cloistered himself for a week at Camp David, where he consulted with outside experts, his own advisors, and even the average citizen. As it turned out, the reason for this cloistering was to develop a good speech on energy, not to formulate an energy policy. If Franklin Delano Roosevelt had gone to the mountain, he would have come down with 1,000 programs, not 1,000 words. So preoccupied was Carter with appearance, as opposed to a substantive policy, that his long-awaited speech omitted a discussion of atomic energy and the role it could play in America's struggle for energy independence and conservation. Not content with the symbolism of just a single national political address, the Carter Administration rode the *Delta Queen* down the Mississippi River, attracting even greater media and public attention. The genre of American political rhetoric has thus swung full circle from stump speeches, to whistle-stop speeches, to airport speeches, and back to riverboat speeches. Carter's continued reliance on symbols without substance exemplifies that many politicians in this country know how to run for office, but do not know how to enact substantive policy once they are there. Madison Avenue and the Jody Powells and Hamilton Jordans of the world can sell beer, detergent, and toothpaste — and politicians. They apparently can not provide the perception and expertise necessary to develop the product — in this case, a substantive governmental policy.

Print and broadcast journalists can encourage politicians to tie 24 symbols to substantive programs by investigating the marketing, polling, and speechwriting techniques of the candidates and reporting their findings to the American public. The electorate needs to agitate for a movement away from 30-second political commercials towards more open debate among the candidates.

Some critics argue that the television medium has affected the 25 messages that go through it; others contend that television does not have to present the form of political symbolism currently being offered by the politicians. Whether television, politicians or both are the cause of the problem is not yet clear. What is clear is that we can not continue to package and sell political candidates as we do toothpaste and expect our 200-year experiment in democracy to survive.

Review Questions

1. What event marked the beginning of the electronic era in American politics?
2. How has the marketing of political candidates as if they were brands of beer or toothpaste affected political speeches?
3. What are the three main approaches to foreign policy that determined how the issues would be treated in the computer speech?
4. How did the authors produce the data that were fed into the computer to yield the synthetic speech?

Discussion Questions

1. Aside from the minor detail that this speech was put together by a computer, what is the matter with it? Does it contain anything with which you disagree? And if so, is your disagreement any more significant than your disagreement with any flesh-and-blood politician? What is so upsetting about such an apparently sensible speech?
2. The authors warn that "we can not continue to package and sell political candidates as we do toothpaste and expect our 200-year experiment in democracy to survive." Is this an exaggeration? How, and to what extent, do such "packaged" speeches threaten our democracy?
3. Cragan and Shields argue that the "electorate needs to agitate for a movement away from 30-second political commercials toward more open debate among candidates." But as a practical matter, how can this be done?

4. According to the authors, what is the relationship between their computer-generated speech for Peorians and the commercialization of political candidates?
5. Go through the computer speech and try to identify those parts that represent a cold war approach, those parts that represent a neo-isolationist approach, and those parts that represent a power politics approach. Which approach dominates? In general, what seems to be the "speaker's" strategy in presenting each issue?

Writing Suggestions

1. Find a foreign policy speech by an American politician (look in *Public Papers of the Presidents of the U.S., The Congressional Record, Vital Speeches, The New York Times*), and write an analysis of it according to the degree to which it represents each of the three foreign policy approaches cited by the authors. (If these categories don't appear to apply, determine others that do.)
2. Try this experiment on a local level. Develop three main approaches to a series of issues current at your college (e.g., tuition, use of student fees, teacher evaluations), and poll a group of students on these issues, as they are presented in groups of sentences. Then combine the most popular groups of sentences to create a speech for a student candidate. Or submit your speech as a letter to the editor of the school paper.

THE DECLARATION OF INDEPENDENCE
Thomas Jefferson and others

On June 10, 1776, a committee of the Continental Congress was appointed to draft a Declaration of Independence of the thirteen American colonies from Great Britain. As chairman of the committee (which included John Adams and Benjamin Franklin), Thomas Jefferson was asked to prepare the document. In drafting the Declaration, Jefferson drew on some of the more enlightened political ideas of the late seventeenth and eighteenth centuries, including those of English philosopher John Locke, who had written on natural law and of the sovereignty of the people over their government. On July 2, 1776, the Congress voted unanimously for independence, and two days later, on July 4, approved the Declaration. Essentially, the Declaration of Independence is an eloquent explanation to the rest of the world of why the colonists felt compelled, indeed, felt it their right, to sever their political ties with Great Britain. Most of the document is a catalogue of violations of the "government by contract" by King George III. The Declaration of Independence has had considerable influence among leaders of subsequent revolutionary movements (starting with the French Revolution of 1789), and is, of course, along with the Constitution, the most cherished of American political documents.

☐

In Congress, July 4, 1776
The unanimous Declaration of the thirteen united States of America,

When in the Course of human events, it becomes necessary for one   1
people to dissolve the political bands which have connected them with
another, and to assume among the powers of the earth, the separate
and equal station to which the Laws of Nature and of Nature's God
entitle them, a decent respect to the opinions of mankind requires
that they should declare the causes which impel them to the separation.

We hold these truths to be self-evident, that all men are created   2
equal, that they are endowed by their Creator with certain unaliena-
ble Rights, that among these are Life, Liberty and the pursuit of
Happiness. That to secure these rights, Governments are instituted
among Men, deriving their just powers from the consent of the
governed. That whenever any Form of Government becomes destructive of these ends, it is the Right of the People to alter or to
abolish it, and to institute a new Government, laying its foundation on
such principles, and organizing its powers in such form, as to them
shall seem most likely to effect their Safety and Happiness. Prudence,
indeed, will dictate that Governments long established should not be
changed for light and transient causes; and accordingly all experience
hath shewn, that mankind are more disposed to suffer, while evils are
sufferable, than to right themselves by abolishing the forms to which
they are accustomed. But when a long train of abuses and usurpations, pursuing invariably the same Object, evinces a design to reduce
them under absolute Despotism, it is their right, it is their duty, to
throw off such Government, and to provide new Guards for their
future security. Such has been the patient sufferance of these Colonies; and such is now the necessity which constrains them to alter their
former Systems of Government. The history of the present King of
Great Britain is a history of repeated injuries and usurpations, all
having in direct object the establishment of an absolute Tyranny over
these States. To prove this, let Facts be submitted to a candid world:

He has refused his Assent to Laws, the most wholesome and   3
necessary for the public good.

He has forbidden his Governors to pass Laws of immediate and   4
pressing importance, unless suspended in their operation till his As-

sent should be obtained; and when so suspended, he has utterly neglected to attend to them.

He has refused to pass other Laws for the accommodation of 5 large districts of people, unless those people would relinquish the right of Representation in the Legislature, a right inestimable to them and formidable to tyrants only.

He has called together legislative bodies at places unusual, un- 6 comfortable, and distant from the depository of their public Records, for the sole purpose of fatiguing them into compliance with his measures.

He has dissolved Representative Houses repeatedly, for oppos- 7 ing with manly firmness his invasions on the rights of the people.

He has refused for a long time, after such dissolutions, to cause 8 others to be elected; whereby the Legislative powers, incapable of Annihilation, have returned to the People at large for their exercise; the State remaining in the mean time exposed to all the dangers of invasion from without, and convulsions within.

He has endeavoured to prevent the population of these States; 9 for that purpose obstructing the Laws for Naturalization of Foreigners; refusing to pass others to encourage their migrations hither, and raising the conditions of new Appropriations of Lands.

He has obstructed the Administration of Justice, by refusing his 10 Assent to Laws for establishing Judiciary powers.

He has made Judges dependent on his Will alone, for the tenure 11 of their offices, and the amount and payment of their salaries.

He has erected a multitude of New Offices, and sent hither 12 swarms of Officers to harass our people, and eat out their substance.

He has kept among us, in times of peace, Standing Armies, 13 without the Consent of our legislatures.

He has affected to render the Military independent of and supe- 14 rior to the Civil power.

He has combined with others to subject us to a jurisdiction for- 15 eign to our constitution, and unacknowledged by our laws; giving his Assent to their Acts of pretended Legislation:

For quartering large bodies of armed troops among us: 16

For protecting them, by a mock Trial, from punishment for any 17 Murders which they should commit on the Inhabitants of these States:

For cutting off our Trade with all parts of the world: 18

For imposing Taxes on us without our Consent: 19

For depriving us in many cases of the benefits of Trial by Jury: 20

For transporting us beyond Seas to be tried for pretended offences: 21

For abolishing the free System of English Laws in a neighbouring 22
Province, establishing therein an Arbitrary government, and en-
larging its Boundaries so as to render it at once an example and
fit instrument for introducing the same absolute rule into these
Colonies:

For taking away our Charters, abolishing our most valuable Laws 23
and altering fundamentally the Forms of our Governments:

For suspending our own Legislatures, and declaring themselves 24
invested with power to legislate for us in all cases whatsoever.

He has abdicated Government here by declaring us out of his 25
Protection and waging War against us.

He has plundered our seas, ravaged our Coasts, burnt our towns, 26
and destroyed the lives of our people.

He is at this time transporting large Armies of foreign Merce- 27
naries to compleat the works of death, desolation and tyranny, already begun with circumstances of Cruelty & perfidy scarcely paral-
leled in the most barbarous ages, and totally unworthy the Head of a
civilized nation.

He has constrained our fellow Citizens taken Captive on the high 28
Seas to bear Arms against their Country, to become the executioners
of their friends and Brethren, or to fall themselves by their Hands.

He has excited domestic insurrections amongst us, and has en- 29
deavoured to bring on the inhabitants of our frontiers, the merciless
Indian Savages, whose known rule of warfare is an undistinguished
destruction of all ages, sexes and conditions.

In every stage of these Oppressions We have Petitioned for 30
Redress in the most humble terms. Our repeated Petitions have been
answered only by repeated injury. A Prince, whose character is thus
marked by every act which may define a Tyrant, is unfit to be the
ruler of a free people.

Nor have We been wanting in attentions to our British brethren. 31
We have warned them from time to time of attempts by their legislature to extend an unwarrantable jurisdiction over us. We have reminded them of the circumstances of our emigration and settlement
here. We have appealed to their native justice and magnanimity, and
we have conjured them by the ties of our common kindred to disavow
these usurpations, which would inevitably interrupt our connections
and correspondence. They too have been deaf to the voice of justice
and of consanguinity. We must, therefore, acquiesce in the necessity,
which denounces our Separation, and hold them, as we hold the rest
of mankind, Enemies in War, in Peace Friends.

WE THEREFORE the Representatives of the UNITED STATES OF AMER- 32
ICA, in General Congress, Assembled, appealing to the Supreme
Judge of the world for the rectitude of our intentions, do, in the

Name and by Authority of the good People of these Colonies, solemnly publish and declare, That these United Colonies are and of Right ought to be FREE AND INDEPENDENT STATES; that they are Absolved from all Allegiance to the British Crown, and that all political connection between them and the State of Great Britain, is and ought to be totally dissolved; and that as FREE AND INDEPENDENT STATES, they have full Power to levy War, conclude Peace, contract Alliances, establish Commerce, and to do all other Acts and Things which INDEPENDENT states may of right do. AND for the support of this Declaration, with a firm reliance on the protection of divine Providence, we mutually pledge to each other our Lives, our Fortunes and our sacred Honor.

Review Questions

1. Why was the Declaration written?
2. What, in general, were the colonists' chief grievances against the king?
3. What steps did they take before going to the drastic length of writing this Declaration?

Discussion Questions

1. Why is such elegant language necessary to say, in effect, "Let us alone"?
2. What is the meaning of the phrase "a decent respect for the opinions of mankind"? To what extent is this idea a factor in international affairs today?
3. Determine the structure of the Declaration. In what order are the ideas presented? What is the logic behind this order of presentation?

Writing Suggestions

1. Paraphrase the second paragraph of the Declaration and compare your results with the original. Can a case be made for updating the language of the document?
2. Write another "Declaration of Independence," on behalf of some organization, interest group, or individual. Use the format and style of the original; but alter the wording as necessary.

THE DECLARATION OF INDEPENDENCE IN AMERICAN

H. L. Mencken

H(enry) L(ewis) Mencken (1880–1956) was a writer who took pains to offend almost everyone. Born in Baltimore, he began his literary career as a reporter for the *Baltimore Herald* (eventually becoming its editor), and in 1906 he joined the staff of the *Baltimore Sun,* for which he wrote throughout his life. In 1924 Mencken was one of the cofounders of the *American Mercury,* which he edited until 1933. In his distinctively colloquial, yet literary prose, he excoriated religion, business, politicians, authors (though he championed new American novelists Theodore Dreiser and Sinclair Lewis), and whole cultures. He had particular scorn for what he called the "booboisie," and once defined "democracy" as "the worship of jackals by jackasses." Americans, he wrote, were "the most timorous, sniveling, poltroonish, ignominious mob of serfs and goose-steppers ever gathered under one flag in Christendom since the end of the Middle Ages." Mencken wrote numerous books, including a six-volume collection of his essays, *Prejudices* (1919–27); a three-volume autobiography, *Happy Days* (1940), *Newspaper Days* (1941), and *Heathen Days* (1943); and the *Mencken Chrestomathy* (1949), from which the following selection was taken. Mencken's scholarly reputation rests on his encyclopedic study, *The American Language* (1918) and its two equally encyclopedic *Supplements* (1945 and 1948).

☐

When things get so balled up that the people of a country got to cut 1 loose from some other country, and go it on their own hook, without asking no permission from nobody, excepting maybe God Almighty, then they ought to let everybody know why they done it, so that everybody can see they are not trying to put nothing over on nobody.

All we got to say on this proposition is this: first, me and you is as 2 good as anybody else, and maybe a damn sight better; second, nobody ain't got no right to take away none of our rights; third, every man has got a right to live, to come and go as he pleases, and to have a good time whichever way he likes, so long as he don't interfere with nobody else. That any government that don't give a man them rights ain't worth a damn; also, people ought to choose the kind of government they want themselves, and nobody else ought to have no say in the matter. That whenever any government don't do this, then the people have got a right to give it the bum's rush and put in one that will take care of their interests. Of course, that don't mean having a revolution every day like them South American yellowbellies, or every time some jobholder goes to work and does something he ain't got no business to do. It is better to stand a little graft, etc., than to have revolutions all the time, like them coons, and any man that wasn't a anarchist or one of them I.W.W.'s[1] would say the same. But when things get so bad that a man ain't hardly got no rights at all no more, but you might almost call him a slave, then everybody ought to get together and throw the grafters out, and put in new ones who won't carry on so high and steal so much, and then watch them. This is the proposition the people of these Colonies is up against, and they have got tired of it, and won't stand it no more. The administration of the present King, George III, has been rotten from the start, and when anybody kicked about it he always tried to get away with it by strong-arm work. Here is some of the rough stuff he has pulled:

He vetoed bills in the Legislature that everybody was in favor of, 3 and hardly nobody was against.

He wouldn't allow no law to be passed without it was first put up 4 to him, and then he stuck it in his pocket and let on he forgot about it, and didn't pay no attention to no kicks.

When people went to work and gone to him and asked him to put 5 through a law about this or that, he give them their choice: either they had to shut down the Legislature and let him pass it all by himself, or they couldn't have it at all.

He made the Legislature meet at one-horse tank-towns, so that 6 hardly nobody could get there and most of the leaders would stay home and let him go to work and do things like he wanted.

He give the Legislature the air, and sent the members home 7 every time they stood up to him and give him a call-down or bawled him out.

When a Legislature was busted up he wouldn't allow no new one 8 to be elected, so that there wasn't nobody left to run things, but anybody could walk in and do whatever they pleased.

He tried to scare people outen moving into these States, and 9 made it so hard for a wop or one of these here kikes to get his papers that he would rather stay home and not try it, and then, when he come in, he wouldn't let him have no land, and so he either went home again or never come.

He monkeyed with the courts, and didn't hire enough judges to 10 do the work, and so a person had to wait so long for his case to come

---

[1] I.W.W. — The *Industrial Workers of the World* was a radical labor organization founded in Chicago in 1905. [Behrens and Rosen]

up that he got sick of waiting, and went home, and so never got what was coming to him.

He got the judges under his thumb by turning them out when they done anything he didn't like, or by holding up their salaries, so that they had to knuckle down or not get no money. 11

He made a lot of new jobs, and give them to loafers that nobody knowed nothing about, and the poor people had to pay the bill, whether they could or not. 12

Without no war going on, he kept an army loafing around the country, no matter how much people kicked about it. 13

He let the army run things to suit theirself and never paid no attention whatsoever to nobody which didn't wear no uniform. 14

He let grafters run loose, from God knows where, and give them the say in everything, and let them put over such things as the following: 15

Making poor people board and lodge a lot of soldiers they ain't got no use for, and don't want to see loafing around. 16

When the soldiers kill a man, framing it up so that they would get off. 17

Interfering with business. 18

Making us pay taxes without asking us whether we thought the things we had to pay taxes for was something that was worth paying taxes for or not. 19

When a man was arrested and asked for a jury trial, not letting him have no jury trial. 20

Chasing men out of the country, without being guilty of nothing, and trying them somewhere else for what they done here. 21

In countries that border on us, he put in bum governments, and then tried to spread them out, so that by and by they would take in this country too, or make our own government as bum as they was. 22

He never paid no attention whatever to the Constitution, but he went to work and repealed laws that everybody was satisfied with and hardly nobody was against, and tried to fix the government so that he could do whatever he pleased. 23

He busted up the Legislatures and let on he could do all the work better by himself. 24

Now he washes his hands of us and even goes to work and declares war on us, so we don't owe him nothing, and whatever authority he ever had he ain't got no more. 25

He has burned down towns, shot down people like dogs, and raised hell against us out on the ocean. 26

He hired whole regiments of Dutch, etc., to fight us, and told them they could have anything they wanted if they could take it away from us, and sicked these Dutch, etc., on us. 27

He grabbed our own people when he found them in ships on the ocean, and shoved guns into their hands, and made them fight against us, no matter how much they didn't want to. 28

He stirred up the Indians, and give them arms and ammunition, and told them to go to it, and they have killed men, women and children, and don't care which. 29

Every time he has went to work and pulled any of these things, we have went to work and put in a kick, but every time we have went to work and put in a kick he has went to work and did it again. When a man keeps on handing out such rough stuff all the time, all you can say is that he ain't got no class and ain't fitten to have no authority over people who have got any rights, and he ought to be kicked out. 30

When we complained to the English we didn't get no more satisfaction. Almost every day we give them plenty of warning that the politicians over there was doing things to us that they didn't have no right to do. We kept on reminding them who we was, and what we was doing here, and how we come to come here. We asked them to get us a square deal, and told them that if this thing kept on we'd have to do something about it and maybe they wouldn't like it. But the more we talked, the more they didn't pay no attention to us. Therefore, if they ain't for us they must be agin us, and we are ready to give them the fight of their lives, or to shake hands when it is over. 31

Therefore be it resolved, That we, the representatives of the people of the United States of America, in Congress assembled, hereby declare as follows: That the United States, which was the United Colonies in former times, is now a free country, and ought to be; that we have throwed out the English King and don't want to have nothing to do with him no more, and are not taking no more English orders no more; and that, being as we are now a free country, we can do anything that free countries can do, especially declare war, make peace, sign treaties, go into business, etc. And we swear on the Bible on this proposition, one and all, and agree to stick to it no matter what happens, whether we win or we lose, and whether we get away with it or get the worst of it, no matter whether we lose all our property by it or even get hung for it. 32

Discussion Questions

1. What is being parodied in Mencken's version of the Declaration of Independence?
2. Assume the role of a composition teacher and "correct" Mencken's prose. Give him a grade and, of course, be prepared to justify your grade with appropriate remarks. (You may wish to write these down.)

3. Examine the colloquialisms in this selection. Why does Mencken call this style of speech "American" as opposed to English? In what language is the original Declaration written? Are English and "American" two separate languages?

Writing Suggestion

Select any four sentences from the original Declaration of Independence and compare and contrast them with the parallel sentences in Mencken's version. Write an essay, detailing your observations and conclusions. Use at least three criteria of comparison and contrast.

ADDRESS AT THE DEDICATION OF THE GETTYSBURG NATIONAL CEMETERY
Abraham Lincoln

Abraham Lincoln (1809–1865) was not invited as the principal speaker at the dedication ceremonies at Gettysburg, on November 19, 1863. As with all of his speeches, Lincoln wrote the Gettysburg Address himself. He had studied formal rhetoric as a boy and was well versed in the devices that can embellish a speech, giving it eloquence. Interestingly enough, the initial critical reception of the Address was poor. Only weeks after the dedication did Lincoln's brief speech gain notice as a "masterpiece."

☐

Fourscore and seven years ago our fathers brought forth on this   1
continent, a new nation, conceived in Liberty, and dedicated to the
proposition that all men are created equal.

Now we are engaged in a great civil war; testing whether that   2
nation, or any nation so conceived and so dedicated, can long endure.
We are met on a great battlefield of that war. We have come to
dedicate a portion of that field as a final resting-place for those who
here gave their lives that that nation might live. It is altogether fitting
and proper that we should do this.

But, in a larger sense, we cannot dedicate — we cannot conse-   3
crate — we cannot hallow — this ground. The brave men, living and
dead, who struggled here have consecrated it, far above our poor
power to add or detract. The world will little note, nor long remember, what we say here, but it can never forget what they did here. It is
for us the living, rather, to be dedicated here to the unfinished work
which they who fought here have thus far so nobly advanced. It is
rather for us to be here dedicated to the great task remaining before
us — that from these honored dead we take increased devotion to

that cause for which they gave the last full measure of devotion; that we here highly resolve that these dead shall not have died in vain; that this nation, under God, shall have a new birth of freedom; and that government of the people, by the people, for the people, shall not perish from the earth.

Discussion Questions

1. In a short paragraph, paraphrase Lincoln's address. How does your paraphrase of the Gettysburg Address differ from the original?

2. Why do we value eloquent speech? Why, for instance, is Lincoln's address preferable to your paraphrase? Consider your answer and reflect on the assumptions you are making about the uses of language.

3. How does one distinguish between writing that is eloquent and writing that is rhetorically overdone? As you will read in the Gilbert Highet essay, Lincoln's address was received poorly at the time it was given. Can you find evidence in the address to support the editorial claim that "the [dedication] ceremony was rendered ludicrous by some of the sallies of that poor President Lincoln"?

Writing Suggestions

1. Compose your own eloquent address for some solemn occasion. Study the Gettysburg Address and try your hand at some of the rhetorical embellishments you observe Lincoln using.

2. Is eloquent speech appropriate for all occasions? If you were called on to speak at the dedication ceremonies at Gettysburg, what considerations would you bear in mind as you decided the tone your address should take? Assume you are a professor of communication. Compose your answer as a lecture that you would deliver to a class on speech making.

THE GETTYSBURG ADDRESS
Gilbert Highet

Gilbert Highet was born in Glasgow, Scotland, in 1906 and was educated at Glasgow and Oxford Universities. He came to the United States in 1937 and was naturalized fourteen years later. For over thirty years Highet has been a professor of Latin Language and Literature at Columbia University, during which time he has published numerous articles and books, including

From *A Clerk of Oxenford*. Reprinted by permission of Curtis Brown, Ltd. Copyright 1954 by Gilbert Highet.

*The Classical Tradition: Greek and Roman Influences on Western Litera-
ture, The Migration of Ideas, The Anatomy of Satire,* and *The Art of
Teaching.*

▢

Fourscore and seven years ago. . . .

These five words stand at the entrance to the best-known monu-   1
ment of American prose, one of the finest utterances in the entire
language, and surely one of the greatest speeches in all history.
Greatness is like granite: it is molded in fire, and it lasts for many
centuries.

Fourscore and seven years ago. . . . It is strange to think that   2
President Lincoln was looking back to the 4th of July 1776, and that
he and his speech are now further removed from us than he himself
was from George Washington and the Declaration of Independence.
Fourscore and seven years before the Gettysburg Address, a small
group of patriots signed the Declaration. Fourscore and seven years
after the Gettysburg Address, it was the year 1950, and that date is
already receding rapidly into our troubled, adventurous, and valiant
past.

Inadequately prepared and at first scarcely realized in its full   3
importance, the dedication of the graveyard at Gettysburg was one of
the supreme moments of American history. The battle itself had been
a turning point of the war. On the 4th of July 1863, General Meade
repelled Lee's invasion of Pennsylvania. Although he did not follow
up his victory, he had broken one of the most formidable aggressive
enterprises of the Confederate armies. Losses were heavy on both
sides. Thousands of dead were left on the field, and thousands of
wounded died in the hot days following the battle. At first, their burial
was more or less haphazard; but thoughtful men gradually came to
feel that an adequate burying place and memorial were required.
These were established by an interstate commission that autumn, and
the finest speaker in the North was invited to dedicate them. This was
the scholar and statesman Edward Everett of Harvard. He made a
good speech — which is still extant: not at all academic, it is full of
close strategic analysis and deep historical understanding.

Lincoln was not invited to speak, at first. Although people knew   4
him as an effective debater, they were not sure whether he was
capable of making a serious speech on such a solemn occasion. But
one of the impressive things about Lincoln's career is that he constantly strove to *grow.* He was anxious to appear on that occasion and
to say something worthy of it. (Also, it has been suggested, he was
anxious to remove the impression that he did not know how to behave
properly — an impression which had been strengthened by a shock-

ing story about his clowning on the battlefield of Antietam the previous year.) Therefore when he was invited he took considerable care with his speech. He drafted rather more than half of it in the White House before leaving, finished it in the hotel at Gettysburg the night before the ceremony (not in the train, as sometimes reported), and wrote a fair copy next morning.

There are many accounts of the day itself, 19 November 1863.   5
There are many descriptions of Lincoln, all showing the same curious blend of grandeur and awkwardness, or lack of dignity, or — it would be best to call it humility. In the procession he rode horseback: a tall lean man in a high plug hat, straddling a short horse, with his feet too near the ground. He arrived before the chief speaker, and had to wait patiently for half an hour or more. His own speech came right at the end of a long and exhausting ceremony, lasted less than three minutes, and made little impression on the audience. In part this was because they were tired, in part because (as eyewitnesses said) he ended almost before they knew he had begun, and in part because he did not speak the Address, but read it, very slowly, in a thin high voice, with a marked Kentucky accent, pronouncing "to" as "toe" and dropping his final R's.

Some people of course were alert enough to be impressed. Ever-   6
ett congratulated him at once. But most of the newspapers paid little attention to the speech, and some sneered at it. The *Patriot and Union* of Harrisburg wrote, "We pass over the silly remarks of the President; for the credit of the nation we are willing . . . that they shall no more be repeated or thought of"; and the London *Times* said, "The ceremony was rendered ludicrous by some of the sallies of that poor President Lincoln," calling his remarks "dull and commonplace." The first commendation of the Address came in a single sentence of the Chicago *Tribune*, and the first discriminating and detailed praise of it appeared in the Springfield *Republican*, the Providence *Journal*, and the Philadelphia *Bulletin*. However, three weeks after the ceremony and then again the following spring, the editor of *Harper's Weekly* published a sincere and thorough eulogy of the Address, and soon it was attaining recognition as a masterpiece.

At the time, Lincoln could not care much about the reception of   7
his words. He was exhausted and ill. In the train back to Washington, he lay down with a wet towel on his head. He had caught smallpox. At that moment he was incubating it, and he was stricken down soon after he re-entered the White House. Fortunately it was a mild attack, and it evoked one of his best jokes: he told his visitors, "At last I have something I can give to everybody."

He had more than that to give to everybody. He was a unique   8
person, far greater than most people realize until they read his life with care. The wisdom of his policy, the sources of his statesman-

ship — these were things too complex to be discussed in a brief essay. But we can say something about the Gettysburg Address as work of art.

A work of art. Yes: for Lincoln was a literary artist, trained both by others and by himself. The textbooks he used as a boy were full of difficult exercises and skillful devices in formal rhetoric, stressing the qualities he practiced in his own speaking: antithesis, parallelism, and verbal harmony. Then he read and reread many admirable models of thought and expression: the King James Bible, the essays of Bacon, the best plays of Shakespeare. His favorites were *Hamlet, Lear, Macbeth, Richard III,* and *Henry VIII,* which he had read dozens of times. He loved reading aloud, too, and spent hours reading poetry to his friends. (He told his partner Herndon that he preferred getting the sense of any document by reading it aloud.) Therefore his serious speeches are important parts of the long and noble classical tradition of oratory which begins in Greece, runs through Rome to the modern world, and is still capable (if we do not neglect it) of producing masterpieces. 9

The first proof of this is that the Gettysburg Address is full of quotations — or rather of adaptations — which give it strength. It is partly religious, partly (in the highest sense) political: therefore it is interwoven with memories of the Bible and memories of American history. The first and the last words are Biblical cadences. Normally Lincoln did not say "fourscore" when he meant eighty; but on this solemn occasion he recalled the important dates in the Bible — such as the age of Abraham when his first son was born to him, and he was "fourscore and six years old." Similarly he did not say there was a chance that democracy might die out: he recalled the somber phrasing on the Book of Job — where Bildad speaks of the destruction of one who shall vanish without a trace, and says that "his branch shall be cut off; his remembrance shall perish from the earth." Then again, the famous description of our State as "government of the people, by the people, for the people" was adumbrated by Daniel Webster in 1830 (he spoke of "the people's government, made for the people, made by the people, and answerable to the people") and then elaborated in 1854 by the abolitionist Theodore Parker (as "government of all the people, by all the people, for all the people"). There is good reason to think that Lincoln took the important phrase "under God" (which he interpolated at the last moment) from Weems, the biographer of Washington; and we know that it had been used at least once by Washington himself. 10

Analyzing the Address further, we find that it is based on a highly imaginative theme, or group of themes. The subject is — how can we put it so as not to disfigure it? — the subject is the kinship of life and death, that mysterious linkage which we see sometimes as the physical 11 succession of birth and death in our world, sometimes as the contrast, which is perhaps a unity, between death and immortality. The first sentence is concerned with birth:

Our *fathers brought forth* a *new* nation, *conceived* in liberty.

The final phrase but one expresses the hope that

this nation, under God, shall have a *new birth* of freedom.

And the last phrase of all speaks of continuing life as the triumph over death. Again and again throughout the speech, this mystical contrast and kinship reappear: "those who *gave their lives* that that nation might *live*," "the brave men *living* and *dead*," and so in the central assertion that the dead have already consecrated their own burial place, while "it is for us, the *living*, rather to be dedicated . . . to the great task remaining." The Gettysburg Address is a prose poem; it belongs to the same world as the great elegies, and the adagios of Beethoven.

Its structure, however, is that of a skillfully contrived speech. The   12
oratorical pattern is perfectly clear. Lincoln describes the occasion, dedicates the ground, and then draws a larger conclusion by calling on his hearers to dedicate themselves to the preservation of the Union. But within that, we can trace his constant use of at least two important rhetorical devices.

The first of these is *antithesis:* opposition, contrast. The speech is   13
full of it. Listen:

The world will little *note*
        nor long *remember*   what *we say* here
but   it can never *forget*   what *they did here*.

And so in nearly every sentence: "brave men, *living* and *dead*"; "to *add* or *detract*." There is the antithesis of the Founding Fathers and men of Lincoln's own time:

Our *fathers brought forth* a new nation . . .
now *we* are testing whether that nation . . . can *long endure*.

And there is the more terrible antithesis of those who have already died and those who still live to do their duty. Now, antithesis is the figure of contrast and conflict. Lincoln was speaking in the midst of a great civil war.

The other important pattern is different. It is technically called   14
tricolon — the division of an idea into three harmonious parts, usually of increasing power. The most famous phrase of the Address is a tricolon:

government of the people
      by the people
      for the people.

448 Politics and Language

The most solemn sentence is a tricolon:

> we cannot dedicate
> we cannot consecrate
> we cannot hallow   this ground.

And above all, the last sentence (which has sometimes been criticized as too complex) is essentially two parallel phrases, with a tricolon growing out of the second and then producing another tricolon: a trunk, three branches, and a cluster of flowers. Lincoln says that it is for his hearers to be dedicated to the great task remaining before them. Then he goes on,

> that from these honored dead

— apparently he means "in such a way that from these honored dead" —

> we take increased devotion to that cause.

Next, he restates this more briefly:

> that we here highly resolve. . . .

And now the actual resolution follows, in three parts of growing intensity:

> that these dead shall not have died in vain
> that this nation, under God, shall have a new birth
>   of freedom

and that

> (one more tricolon)
>   government of the people
>   by the people
>   for the people
>   shall not perish from the earth.

Now, the tricolon is the figure which, through division, emphasizes basic harmony and unity. Lincoln used antithesis because he was speaking to a people at war. He used the tricolon because he was hoping, planning, praying for peace.

No one thinks that when he was drafting the Gettysburg Address, 15 Lincoln deliberately looked up these quotations and consciously chose these particular patterns of thought. No, he chose the theme. From its development and from the emotional tone of the entire occasion, all the rest followed, or grew — by that marvelous process of choice and rejection which is essential to artistic creation. It does not spoil such a work of art to analyze it as closely as we have done; it is altogether fitting and proper that we should do this: for it helps us to penetrate more deeply into the rich meaning of the Gettysburg Address, and it allows us the very rare privilege of watching the workings of a great man's mind.

Review Questions

1. Cite the evidence that Highet gives for claiming that Lincoln's speech is part of the "long and noble classical tradition of oratory which begins in Greece . . . and is still capable . . . of producing masterpieces."
2. The essay was originally presented as a talk on the radio. Find passages that indicate an oral delivery.

Discussion Questions

1. How does Highet define the tricolon? Analyze his use of it in the sentence: "He used the tricolon because he was hoping, planning, praying for peace."
2. Consider the structure of Highet's essay — a history of the Gettysburg Address followed by a close reading of the Address. Explain why Highet might have composed his essay in this way.
3. What does the Address's initially poor and later enthusiastic critical reception suggest about the nature of criticism? (How could one speech be called "dull and commonplace" one week and a masterpiece the next?)

Writing Suggestion

The Gettysburg Address was subjected to an "instant news analysis" of the sort with which we have become familiar. Today, major news events are usually interpreted for us by television commentators. Write an essay on the limits and merits of this kind of analysis.

THE GETTYSBURG ADDRESS
IN EISENHOWESE

Oliver Jensen

Oliver Jensen, editor for many years of the history magazine *American Heritage,* is a close student of the art form known as the presidential press conference. President Eisenhower let himself be quoted verbatim, with every bumble and stumble intact. Pondering how Ike might have delivered the Gettysburg Address, Jensen published this parody in 1957.

☐

I haven't checked these figures but 87 years ago, I think it was, a 1 number of individuals organized a governmental set-up here in this country, I believe it covered certain Eastern areas, with this idea they were following up based on a sort of national independence arrangement and the program that every individual is just as good as every other individual. Well, now, of course, we are dealing with this big difference of opinion, civil disturbance you might say, although I don't like to appear to take sides or name any individuals, and the point is naturally to check up, by actual experience in the field, to see whether any governmental set-up with a basis like the one I was mentioning has any validity and find out whether that dedication by those early individuals will pay off in lasting values and things of that kind.

Well, here we are, at the scene where one of these disturbances 2 between different sides got going. We want to pay our tribute to those loved ones, those departed individuals who made the supreme sacrifice here on the basis of their opinions about how this thing ought to be handled. And I would say this. It is absolutely in order to do this.

But if you look at the over-all picture of this, we can't pay any 3 tribute — we can't sanctify this area, you might say — we can't hallow according to whatever individual creeds or faiths or sort of religious outlooks are involved like I said about this particular area. It was those individuals themselves, including the enlisted men, very brave individuals, who have given this religious character to the area. The way I see it, the rest of the world will not remember any statements issued here but it will never forget how these men put their shoulders to the wheel and carried this idea down the fairway.

Now frankly, our job, the living individuals' job here, is to pick up 4 the burden and sink the putt they made these big efforts here for. It is our job to get on with the assignment — and from these deceased fine individuals to take extra inspiration, you could call it, for the same theories about the set-up for which they made such a big contribution. We have to make up our minds right here and now, as I see it, that they didn't put out all that blood, perspiration and — well — that they didn't just make a dry run here, and that all of us here, under God, that is, the God of our choice, shall beef up this idea about freedom and liberty and those kind of arrangements, and that government of all individuals, by all individuals and for the individuals, shall not pass out of the world-picture.

Discussion Questions

1. Is Jensen's version of the Gettysburg Address in any way more appealing than the original?
2. Attempt to analyze Jensen's version of the Gettysburg Address using the same criteria for analysis that Highet uses with the original. Can Highet's criteria be applied? (If not, create your own and then judge the merits of the speech.)
3. Why do you suppose Jensen chose the Gettysburg Address as the basis for his parody?

Writing Suggestions

1. Use the example of Jensen's version of the Gettysburg Address to write a definition of the word "parody."
2. Write your own parody of Lincoln's Address, using any style of speech that you feel would be both amusing and informative. (Once you decide upon a style, you must use it consistently if you wish to achieve the desired effect of parody.)

SCALING THE HEIGHTS OF ABSURDITY
Russell Baker

Russell Baker is one of the nation's premiere political humorists. Born in 1925, he was educated at Johns Hopkins (with time out for training as a Navy Pilot during World War II), and took his first newspaper job as a reporter for the *Baltimore Sun*. After a two-year tour of duty as the *Sun*'s London bureau chief, Baker was hired by *The New York Times*. For about eight years, he reported the news from Congress; but in 1962, exasperated with the pomposities of official Washington, he began writing the "Ob-

The New York Times, February 20, 1977. © 1977 by The New York Times Company. Reprinted by permission.

server," a humor column now carried by almost 500 newspapers. According to *Time* magazine, "his column walks the high wire between light humor and substantive comment." In 1979, Baker won the Pulitzer Prize for commentary, the first such honor accorded to a humorist. This piece first appeared in the *New York Times Magazine*.

☐

After his recent visit to Tokyo, Vice President Mondale revealed that 1 he and the Japanese had discussed a broad range of issues. Anyone who has ever gazed on this magnificent range can imagine the poetic nature of the Vice President's talk with the Japanese, for it is one of the most moving spectacles nature affords.

Rising majestically out of the bleak Areas of Responsibility, the 2 Broad Range of Issues stretches from the amusing Height of Absurdity on the north to the historic Peaks of Achievement in the south. It is not clear whether Mr. Mondale has actually seen the Broad Range of Issues or whether his discussions were merely based on study of old National Geographics. The latter seems likelier, for few persons have survived the harrowing journey to that remote paradise.

T. E. Burton, who made the trip in 1923, with nothing more than 3 six camels and a dictionary of clichés, kept a diary of the expedition. Although Burton met a dreadful death on his return journey when he fell into the roaring torrents of the infamous Flow of Information, his diary survived.

At his death, Burton was exploring for the mysterious Reliable 4 Sources, where he believed the Flow of Information originated. Burton's expedition to the Broad Range of Issues started from the east and ran into trouble almost immediately as it passed into the steamy Erogenous Zones. His diary, feverishly sketchy at this point, describes months of struggle to climb out of the squalid Depths of Degradation, which pitted the Zone's landscape.

Indeed, he might have died there had he not seen, one cold 5 winter night, an extraordinary display of the beautiful Rising Expectations light the western sky. Reinvigorated by this atmospheric spectacle, he hauled himself out of the Erogenous Zones and found himself breathing a strangely baffling air.

This, as subsequent geographers have discovered, was the inex- 6 plicable Air of Mystery, which blows off the mosquito-infested Miasma of Suspicion and Hate. Luckily for Burton, the sky was clear that night and he was able to navigate safely around the Miasma by following the familiar, if somewhat tired, Aura of Romance, which shimmered in the southern sky.

The southern detour, however, carried him directly into the 7 dreaded Sands of Time, where he wandered for years, surviving only because his camels had taught him how to store water in his hump.

One day he stumbled into an orchard. It seemed a mirage, for scarcely a hundred yards distant lay another orchard. Burton sent his camels to explore it for reality, and as they stood there looking at his orchard and he stood looking at their orchard, he suddenly realized the magnitude of his accomplishment. He had discovered the Fruitful Exchange of Views.

Refreshed in spirit, he plunged ahead, ignoring the terrors of the notorious Political Extremes to his left and to his right, and noticed that he was approaching a series of well-defined levels. These, of course, were the well-charted Income Levels — Lower, Middle and Upper. 8

Then, in a terrifying instant of atmospheric violence, Burton was abruptly picked up into the air and just as abruptly hurled to the ground. We now know that he was in the grip of the whimsical Unanticipated Windfall, which is quite common at the Upper Income Level. 9

Burton, however, was determined to reach New Heights, an elevation from which, according to ancient lore, one could catch a glimpse of the Areas of Responsibility. Burton spent weeks struggling upward, always upward, and when he at last reached the summit, satisfied that he had reached either New Heights or the equally rewarding Higher Level of Understanding, he fell into a stuporous sleep. 10

On awaking, he found a graffito cut into rock. It said, "Chauvinist pigs to the wall." This was not New Heights. It was simply Raised Consciousness, and Burton realized that he was looking out on the world from the Feminist Viewpoint. "At least," he noted in his diary, "it is better than finding myself at the Unorthodox View." 11

The following year, Burton crossed the Chasm of Misunderstanding, canoed down the Labor Pool and hurled himself through the Language Barrier with such force that he plunged into the fetid Emotional Depression. Only his fierce resolve to enter New Fields of Endeavor kept him going, and when at last he entered the always stimulating New Fields, he met a speech writer who gave him his first glimpse of the Broad Range of Issues from the ancient Well-Balanced Perspective. "Some day," the awestruck Burton predicted, "this range will be discussed even by Vice Presidents." Not even Burton, of course, could have realized the Japanese would join in. 12

Discussion Questions

1. This piece pokes fun at jargon, euphemisms, and clichés. Why are diplomats and politicians especially susceptible to the use of such terms, to speaking in their own special language? Why don't they say what they really mean? What would happen if they did?

2. How does the kind of language cited in this piece exemplify Orwell's concerns?
3. As a satirical piece, "Scaling the Heights of Absurdity" is amusing. But do you think that it can have any significant effect in reversing the debasement of English? If not, what will? (Do you even believe that a language can be debased?)
4. Discuss the device that Baker uses to organize his satire. (What strategy does he use to create the possibility for satire?)

Writing Suggestion

Find a political speech by a president or a Congressman (see *Public Papers of the Presidents of the U.S.* or *The Congressional Record*), and attempt your own satirical commentary.

HOW TO FIGURE OUT WHAT POLITICIANS MEAN
Dan F. Hahn

Dan Hahn is an Associate Professor in the Department of Communication Arts and Sciences at Queens College, New York.

☐

If we were to ask the average person why it is important to pay   1
attention to the language of politicians, I suspect we would be told that it is necessary because politicians lie.

While there may be nothing inherently wrong with that answer, I   2
want to suggest that there are several more significant reasons to watch their language closely. . . .

. . . [W]e need to pay attention to the language of our politicians,   3
because now we understand that when a politician describes Communism as cancer his solution is implied: surgical removal before it spreads. And when the local school board candidate suggests that some literature is poison we know he will want to lock it away where the kids can't get at it.

So language analysis can lead us to understand and even predict   4
the actions of politicians. But it may be even more significant if we

From the article, "Language Clues for the Rhetorical Critic." Reprinted from *ETC.*, Volume 35, No. 1, by permission of the International Society for General Semantics.

understand that their language may also explain the apathy and inactivity of the average citizen.

Thus, when the President describes a situation as a "crisis," our 5 tendency is to quit complaining and line up in support of his policy. When he arouses our fears by telling of Russia's new weapons superiority we supinely allow an escalation of our military budget . . . and when he says that the exorbitant budget will solve the problem we sigh with relief and appreciation.

Surprisingly, however, it isn't just crisis that keeps us in line. So 6 does the normal. So when a bureaucrat describes his action as "routine," we tend to go along. We shrug, perhaps with disgust — but without major objection — and conclude "that's the way things are." . . .

First, let's hypothesize about what might be learned from examining a politician's deployment of various parts of speech. 7

The nouns of a politician will tell you which portions of the world 8 he sees as relevant. They will, in a sense, show you of what he is conscious and thus the arenas in which he will be active.

His verbs will explain his behavior patterns and his attitudes 9 toward leadership. Is he active or passive? If he perceives life as controllable he will be more likely to use strong verbs.

In his adjectives will be found his opinion of the world — the 10 judgments he makes about it. And if you examine his adjective clusters you should be able to discover the categories he utilizes to make judgments — moral, practical, aesthetic, etc.

His adverbs will suggest salience and intensity, and will tend to 11 show you not only what is to be done, but how he plans to do it. Thus, those who expected Carter to be an active President in the FDR mold obviously overlooked his heavy campaign reliance upon adverbs like *gradually, modestly, accurately,* and *slowly.*

Connectives, of course, establish relationships, but they may also 12 suggest dominance (and fear of being dominated). That is, one who utilizes an abnormally high number of connectives probably does so because he doesn't want to be interrupted.

Pronoun use can tell us a good deal about the speaker. For 13 instance, Nixon's use of pronouns typed him as a benevolent dictator. The pronoun "I" tended to be followed by action verbs, while "we" and "us" tended to be used in the receiving position. The Nixonian formula, then, was "I, President Nixon, have acted . . . and we, the citizens, reap the benefits of the action." Pronoun frequency is also revealing. Consider, for example, the implications of the fact that Nixon used "I" ten times as often in foreign policy as in domestic policy speeches . . . or that in the White House tapes he was found to utilize "I" sixteen times as often as it is found in normal conversation.

But in this early stage of our study, I would suggest that the most 14 promising avenue might be metaphor analysis. Does the politician describe human activities in mechanical terms — *input, output, feedback,* etc? If so, we might speculate that he would not be terribly concerned with what the rest of us might think of as the preciousness of human life, that he might try to manipulate humans as if they were some higher manifestation of IBM circuitry.

If he describes any aspect of society as *sick,* we should be alerted 15 that treatment is on the way . . . and we ought to know whether he perceives himself as a chiropractor or surgeon before we cast our ballots.

If we find him utilizing a lot of water metaphors we should 16 understand that he sees the situation as desperate — as we can discover if we abstract out the metaphors and string them together. Here, for instance, is the compilation from Goldwater's acceptance speech at the 1964 Republican convention: Due to "foggy thinking," "the tide has been running against freedom" and we are sinking in a "swampland of collectivism." Therefore, despite the detractors who say "don't rock the boat," the "campaign which we launch here" will "set the tide running again in the cause of freedom." "The past will be submerged" and we will travel democracy's "ocean highway" where freedom will accompany the "rising tide of prosperity." Clearly, Goldwater's liquid metaphors demonstrated that he perceived the situation of the country under Johnson as dangerous; but the American people did not see it quite that way. They did not feel that his analysis put him in the "mainstream" of contemporary thought, and they cast their ballots as though he were floundering in the backwash of Darwinianism.

Finally, I should mention form as an area in which we can get 17 clues from political language. Take, for instance, the line from John Kennedy's Inaugural Address that so caught the imagination of Americans: "Ask not what your country can do for you, but what you can do for your country." But what *can* most of us do? Pay taxes. Die in a war. Work, and thereby avoid welfare. Be law-abiding. Clearly, all these behaviors are either sacrificial or pedestrian. So why did Americans react so positively to the line? Certainly part of the answer relates to the form of the line. As Murray Edelman points out, "Word orders like 'Ask not what . . .' are not used in ordinary conversation or even ordinary speechmaking. We associate the unusual deployment of verb, adverb, and accusative pronoun with biblical language and with eloquent oratory of the past, and we respond to the poetry of these associations." That is, the form recalls other deployments of the same form and the audience reacts to the speaker as though he were of the other genre — a poet, or even a minor prophet — rather than a politician. The form deflects an audience's thought from the content of the line to the image of the speaker, and, simultaneously, transforms the speaker from a mediocre politician to a poet or prophet.

In both capitalism and politics there is a form of address that 18 argues honesty. In a capitalist society, all are familiar with the Latin *caveat emptor,* the notion that the buyer should beware. Yet we have all had the experience of having a salesperson tell us, conspiratorially, that "it's a good thing you came in today, because tomorrow the item you are interested in will be $10 more." The form of the dialogue is: "I'm on your side. I'll level with you and sell it to you today, even though my commission would be better if you delayed your purchase twenty-four hours." Maybe we believe the salesperson; maybe we buy the item; and maybe we end up in the store the next day shopping for another item. How do we act toward our salesperson? Yesterday his form told us, "today I'm looking out for you — tomorrow I'll be lining my own pockets." If we are smart, we will take him at his word. (Of course, if we were that smart we probably wouldn't have believed him yesterday, but that is another story.) The present point is that his manner of telling us yesterday of his trustworthiness makes him suspect today.

Politics has its own version of the personal *caveat emptor.* It is the 19 Senator asking, "Can I speak frankly?," the President averring, "I'll be honest with you." This form may have temporary success, but it implicitly conveys to an audience that these times are exceptions to the non-frank, dishonest norm. Misused often enough, they can turn into liabilities — just as Nixon's phrase, "let me make one thing perfectly clear," came to signal his audience to watch for the obfuscation, the muddying phrase, the escape clause in what he was about to say.

Practically any piece of meta-communication (i.e., communica- 20 tion about the communication) underlines in about the same way. When a professor says, "Listen carefully, this point is important," he underlines that point but also, implicitly, says that what follows after that point in his presentation is not important.

Another form used in politics, as in the rest of life, is what is 21 called "affirmation by denial." As Lucy Komisar notes, "If I say, 'I shall not compare thee to a summer's day, a rose, a running brook,' I have in spite of myself made those comparisons, and the day, rose, and brook have a positive existence in my speech." When a politician says, "I wouldn't think of doing X," only one thing is clear — he *did* think of doing it; it did cross his mind. When Henry Kissinger, after the Mayaguez affair,[1] said "We are not going around looking for opportunities to prove our manhood," one critic responded, "It was a

[1] On May 12, 1975 the U.S. merchant ship *Mayaguez* and its thirty-nine crewmen were seized in the Gulf of Siam by the crew of a Cambodian gunboat. President Ford denounced the seizure as "an act of piracy"; and two

curious comment for the question had never been asked, and it made it clear that at a level very close to his consciousness, Secretary Kissinger knew that this was precisely what America's reaction had been all about."

Of course, you understand, I wouldn't dream of saying that the good Secretary lied.   22

Review Questions

1. How can the parts of speech a politician uses indicate the way he or she perceives the world?
2. What is the political purpose of using archaic sentence constructions, as John F. Kennedy did in his inaugural address?
3. Why should we be especially alert for dishonesty when a politician (or a saleperson) offers to take us into his or her confidence?

Discussion Questions

1. Make a copy of a political speech, highlight those words and phrases that indicate the politician's attitudes, the way he or she views the world, and bring your findings to class for discussion.
2. Hahn has some apparently harsh comments to make on John Kennedy's inaugural address, particularly its most famous line. Do you think he is being overly cynical? Or do we need to have eyes opened by commentaries like this one in order to help safeguard ourselves against demagoguery? Explain.
3. How does Hahn's last line drive home his thesis?

Writing Suggestions

1. Examine one or more speeches of a politician and write an analysis of the language in terms of Hahn's criteria (note active and passive verbs, use of personal pronouns, metaphors, etc.). Then assess the accuracy of your analysis in terms of what the politician's record shows his or her actual attitudes to be.

---

days later, American air, sea, and ground forces launched a rescue mission, sinking three Cambodian gunboats, landing Marines on Cambodia's Tang Island, and engaging with Khmer Rouge troops. The crew of the *Mayaguez* was rescued, but at a cost of sixty-five American casualties including fifteen dead. (Initial reports had specified only one casualty. An additional twenty-three servicemen had been killed earlier in an aircraft accident as they were preparing for possible participation in the rescue mission.) [Behrens and Rosen]

2. After surveying some political speeches — inaugural addresses, perhaps — write an essay on some additional ways the politican in question has indirectly revealed his or her true attitudes and nature.

3. James Barber classified certain presidents in his book, *The Presidential Character* (as active-positive, active-negative, passive-positive, or passive-negative; see the Barber selection in the chapter on the Presidency). Analyze the inaugural addresses of these presidents according to Hahn's criteria. How well do Hahn's criteria support Barber's classifications?

SUMMARY, SYNTHESIS, CRITIQUE ACTIVITIES

Summary

Summarize one or more of the passages in this unit. Follow the suggested six-step process. Take into account the answers to the Review Questions for each passage. (Recommended: "Politics and the English Language," "A Computer-Generated Speech . . .")

Synthesis

1. Write an essay giving *examples* of some of the ways the English language has been corrupted by politics. You may want to consider the question of whether politics has been more of a corrupting influence than other aspects of our society, such as advertising or entertainment.

2. *Compare and contrast* Orwell's treatment of politics and the English language with one other treatment — for instance, Cragan and Shields's or Baker's or Hahn's. By what criteria are you measuring these treatments?

3. *Argue* that contemporary developments have proven Orwell right — that the material in the selections that follow as well as your own observations and research, demonstrate the truth of Orwell's thesis.

4. *Argue* that the English language is in no serious danger of corruption from politics or from anything else, short of nuclear war — that there will always be abuses of the language, some of them very amusing, but that the language and the people who use it and interpret it should be given more credit for adaptability.

5. *Compare and contrast* the two parodies in this unit. Are Mencken and Jensen making identical points about the uses and abuses of language? Which one (if either) of these two authors would Orwell view with greater favor?

6. This book contains a number of political speeches — not only the Gettysburg Address, but also three inaugural addresses in the chapter

on the Presidency. After studying these speeches by Lincoln, Franklin D. Roosevelt, John F. Kennedy, and Ronald Reagan, develop an *argument* about the qualities or elements that successful political speeches appear to have.

7. Using "The Gettysburg Address in Eisenhowese" and "The Declaration of Independence in American," write an extended *definition* of parody.

8. *Compare and contrast* the two parodies and their originals, exploring the differences between eloquent and prosaic speech. Do Americans expect their political leaders to be eloquent? Why or why not?

Critique

Write a critique of Orwell's "Politics and the English Language." In this critique you may find it necessary to refer to some of the other pieces for additional supporting evidence.

RESEARCH TOPICS

1. Assume that you are a speech writer for a member of Congress. Research a topic of current interest and prepare three versions of the same speech, to be delivered to a garden club meeting, a Teamster's Union meeting, and a college group's political action meeting.

2. Discuss one candidate in one election and research the role of advertisers and market analysts in his or her campaign. To what extent is the candidate's appearance as important as his or her political rhetoric?

3. Analyze ten to fifteen speeches of one political figure who interests you. How would you characterize this person's style? Make certain to support your observations with frequent references to the speeches. In order to determine the extent to which this political figure knows his or her subject, you will need to familiarize yourself with the issues in question. In your analysis you should consider the audiences for whom the speeches were written. (Possible sources: *Vital Speeches, The Congressional Record, Public Papers of the Presidents of the United States*)

ADDITIONAL READINGS

Ciardi, J. "Prose: Rich, Ripe, and Federal." *Saturday Review,* 19 October 1974, p. 36.

Collins, Richard M. "Words as Social Control: Noah Webster and the Creation of the American Dictionary." *The American Quarterly,* 28 (Fall 1976), pp. 415–430.

Dieterich, Daniel, ed. *Teaching about Doublespeak.* Urbana, Ill.: National Council of Teachers of English, 1976.

Kozol, Jonathan. "The Politics of Syntax." *English Journal,* 65 (October 1976), pp. 18–19.

Rank, Hugh, ed. *Language and Public Policy.* Urbana, Ill.: National Council of Teachers of English, 1974.

Roelofs, H. Mark. *The Language of Modern Politics: An Introduction to the Study of Government.* Homewood, Illinois: The Dorsey Press, 1967.

Safire, William. "Political Word Watch." *New York Times Magazine,* 19 November 1978, pp. 84ff. See also Safire's columns on language in *The New York Times* (called "On Language" since November, 1979), 1978–present (see *New York Times Index* for particular topic and reference).

Schlesinger, A. "Politics and the American Language." *American Scholar,* 43 (August 1974), pp. 553–562.

Simon, John, occasional columns on language in *Esquire,* 1977–79.

Sparke, William and Beatrice Taines. *Doublespeak: Language for Sale.* New York: Harper's College Press, 1975.

Vittachi, Tarzi. "Newspeak among the Diplomats." *Horizon,* 18 (August 1976), pp. 89ff.

11 | Nuclear War — Inevitable?

Three huge posters dominated the main academic hall at ancient Groningen University in Holland two weeks ago. They contained numbers whose meaning no enlightened citizen, and especially no political leader, should ever forget: Nearly 1.2 million Americans died in all of our past wars, but an all-out nuclear war could kill 140 million. More than 31.7 million people were killed in the Soviet Union during World War I, the Bolshevik Revolution, and World War II, but 130 million would die in a nuclear war. And in Europe, where 12 million perished in the past two wars (the figure should have been 18 million: the charts apparently omitted six million Jews), 100 million would be killed in a nuclear World War III.

—Morton Kondracke
"Nuclear Innocents Abroad"

The threat of atomic war has been with us for so long — almost two generations — that we are in danger of forgetting just what such a war would mean. After the explosions of the two atom bombs at Hiroshima and Nagasaki, people the world over reacted with horror and incomprehension. Though other cities (Dresden, for instance) had been utterly destroyed in World War II, never before had a single weapon been responsible for such destruction. This stunning object lesson in the power of nuclear weapons is perhaps the main reason why nations have so far managed to avoid a third world war. The awesome "balance of terror" among nations appears to be the main barrier between an uneasy peace and a nuclear holocaust.

How long we will be protected by this balance of terror, which may well be a more reliable deterrent than the rationality of government leaders, no one can say. Our greatest danger, perhaps, is to slip into a state of mind that allows us to think of nuclear war, "limited" or not, as one of the ways of resolving conflicts among nations. The impulse to "nuke 'em" (perhaps as a last resort) is ever-present. We can best resist such impulses by considering just what their consequences would be — by doing what nuclear war strategist Herman Kahn called "thinking about the unthinkable." As one of the authors represented in this chapter has put it, with grim understatement: "It is worth recalling what modern nuclear weapons can do."

In "Second Strike," which appeared in *Bulletin of the Atomic Scientists*, physicist Henry Kendall sets out to answer this question. He traces the probable course of a nuclear war, from the first strike by one nation to the retaliatory strike by the other, detailing the immediate and the long-term effects both on these nations and on the rest of the world. In "The First Nuclear War," Warren Boroson and David P. Snyder report on the opinions of experts on which nations are most likely and least likely to come to nuclear blows. In "The Day the Bomb Went Off," *Progressive* editor Erwin Knoll and nuclear engineer Theodore Postol describe what would happen to Chicago, and by extension to any major city, were it hit by a twenty-megaton bomb. Following are two ironic pieces. First, satirist Art Buchwald suggests one, possibly extreme, method of getting us to realize the realities of nuclear war. Next, in a selection from the black comedy, *Dr. Strangelove*, director-writer Stanley Kubrick suggests that it will be a lot easier to start a nuclear war than to stop it — indeed, people's self-destructive urge is such that they may not *want* to stop it. Finally, astronomer Carl Sagan, taking a "cosmic" perspective, surveys our situation and asks how we would explain and justify our nuclear arms race to intelligent beings from another world. Asks Sagan: does anyone speak for the human species?

SECOND STRIKE
Henry Kendall

Henry Kendall is a professor of physics at M.I.T. and a founding member of the Union of Concerned Scientists. "Second Strike" was first presented as a paper before a panel of the first nuclear war conference, cosponsored by the Center for Defense Information and the Institute for Policy Studies, and held in Washington, D.C., in December 1978. The paper was first published in the *Bulletin of the Atomic Scientists*, a journal formed shortly after the atomic age began, in 1945, by scientists seeking to reduce the possibility of nuclear war.

☐

The United States faces a grave national security crisis because we have fallen 1 *behind in the nuclear arms race. Soviet nuclear weapons arsenals have expanded to the point where a surprise Soviet nuclear attack can lay waste the U.S. arsenals, destroy our vastly inferior military capability, and leave practically unscathed the USSR as an unrivalled world power. The dominant nuclear strength of the Soviet Union will give them long-sought political leverage which they can ruthlessly exploit free from any meaningful U.S. military challenge. Our European allies — indeed most countries — will be at their mercy. World trade in food and critical raw materials will be set on their terms, the hapless United States reduced to a cowering servant state manipulated for Soviet purposes.*

This chilling scenario of an emerging Soviet "nuclear superior- 2
ity" and its consequences is now being used by military hardliners in a
national campaign aimed at expanding the already enormous U.S.
nuclear weapons arsenal. It's a scenario that is remote from reality,
however.

No Soviet attack on the United States could preclude a devastating 3
counterattack on the Soviet Union. This is because it only takes a
small number of nuclear weapons to inflict awesome damage on any
attacker. And the United States has *thousands* of nuclear warheads
that can be delivered by a diverse array of vehicles. There is no
technical possibility of an attack so successful as to deprive the United
States of the number of warheads needed for a second strike of
unprecedented devastation. Such a response aimed at the highly
concentrated Soviet industrial base would destroy the USSR as a
modern industrial state. There is no way Russian leaders could ever
hope to "win" a nuclear war, and they know it.

The public and our national decision-makers should come to 4
understand the second-strike nuclear capability of the United States
and the damage it could do to the Soviet Union. The campaign for
new weapons systems and rejection of the imminent SALT treaty[1] is
in full swing; and it is a campaign that is relying heavily on public
acceptance of the erroneous, simple-minded notion of a threatening
"Russian build-up" that could result in their "nuclear superiority."

Just how damaging the U.S. response would be in the event the 5
Soviets struck their most powerful first nuclear blow is not widely
appreciated. It would be destructive beyond precedence. No known
countermeasures or civil defense efforts could blunt or frustrate it to
the extent of making the damage "acceptable" in any practical sense
of that word. Soviet leaders are rational enough to understand that
the Soviet Union would be unable to function as an industrial state
following retaliation by the United States. Many, perhaps most, other
nations would be cruelly affected by nuclear war between the United
States and the Soviet Union.

Of course the United States might not wish to launch an all-out 6
retaliatory attack. Since the mid-1960s the United States has had a

---

[1] The Strategic Arms Limitations Talks (SALT) between the United States
and the Soviet Union were intended to reduce the quantity of nuclear
armaments on both sides. The SALT I treaty took effect in 1972. SALT II
was signed by President Carter and Soviet Communist Party Chairman
Brezhnev in Vienna in June 1979; but a cooling of relations between the two
countries followed (caused by the revelation of Soviet combat troops in Cuba
and the later Soviet invasion of Afghanistan), and subsequently, SALT II's
prospects for ratification in the U.S. Senate appeared dim. [Behrens and
Rosen]

wide variety of "flexible options" in its targeting plans: missiles and bombers can be retargeted with relative ease and small salvos or even individual weapons can be delivered. It is, however, a full destructive response that is the principal concern here, because most thoughtful Department of Defense officials and many other experts believe a small nuclear exchange would, with high probability, escalate to a full exchange.

This article re-examines the expected consequences of first and 7 second strikes to determine whether the Soviet Union *can* achieve nuclear superiority in the sense of a war-winning capacity in the foreseeable future (or, for that matter, the United States). In other words, how real is the portrait presented in the above scenario about the Soviets' military potential?

The First Strike

The U.S. strategic nuclear forces constitute a triad: the intercon- 8 tinental ballistic missiles (now all in hardened silos, dispersed mostly in the western plains states); the nuclear-powered missile submarines (60 percent of which are permanently "on-station," hidden securely in the oceans); intercontinental bombers (30 percent of which are on constant runway alert). Together these forces carry almost 3,000 megatons (3,000 million tons of TNT equivalent) of nuclear explosive power. There are thousands of other bombers and shorter range missiles in the tactical forces of which about 6,000 can be targeted against some parts of the Soviet Union.

It is worth recalling what modern nuclear weapons can do. A 9 single one-megaton airburst has a fireball more than 1½ miles in diameter, and will flatten almost everything over about 50 square miles. The intense heat from the fireball will set fires over an area approaching 100 square miles and cause second-degree burns over 250 square miles. A ground burst's damage area is somewhat smaller but the radioactive fallout is greater; the burst forms a crater 950 feet across and 200 feet deep.

Large exposures to radiation kill by direct interference with body 10 functions: death comes slowly after a few hours to a few weeks. Lower exposures can also cause leukemia, cancers of the lung, thyroid, breast, bone and the intestine, genetic damage, birth defects in off-spring, constitutional and degenerative diseases, and mental retardation. Following a one-megaton ground burst, typically some 600 to 1,000 square miles would receive fallout lethal to unprotected persons, and over an area of about 2,000 square miles there would be a substantial risk of death or incapacitation. An additional 2,000 square miles would be contaminated beyond safe use. Much of Hiroshima was devastated and over 100,000 people killed by a 15 kiloton weapon, doing damage to only about 6 percent of the territory that would be destroyed by a modern one-megaton weapon. The allies employed, in aggregate, about 1.2 megatons of conventional high explosive in World War II.

Suppose the Soviets attempted to launch a first strike against the 11 U.S. nuclear forces: an attack on the ICBMs, on the bomber force, and on submarines in their ports.

The ICBMs. Modern U.S. ICBMs are encased in silos that are 12 hardened to resist 2,000 pounds per square inch of blast overpressure. (By comparison, most buildings collapse at 5 pounds per square inch.) To destroy these silos, missile warheads must have impressive accuracies. Neither the Soviets nor the Americans now have the accuracy necessary to destroy more than a militarily insignificant fraction of the other side's ICBM silos. However it has been estimated that sometime in the 1980s the Soviets might be able to destroy all but a few of all American ICBMs *if* they used their modified SS-18 missiles, each with eight warheads, each warhead releasing the equivalent of 1.5 megatons of TNT, or the smaller six-warhead SS-19 improved accuracy missile, and *if* each warhead had an even chance of landing within 600 feet of its intended target. An optimal attack would be two warheads fired at each ICBM (to ensure killing the missile), one an airburst, the other a ground burst. But there are good reasons for believing that this one-two punch cannot work owing to the first explosion's neutron burst, gravel sucked into the mushroom cloud, and winds of over 1,000 mph, all interfering with the detonation or targeting of the second missile. This difficulty is called "fratricide."

What could the Soviet Union reasonably expect to achieve in this 13 attack? This is to say, what fraction of the ICBMs, submarines, and bombers would be destroyed? Given projected Soviet missile accuracies for the next decade, at least 5 to 15 percent of U.S. ICBMs will remain usable.

The United States, with just these ICBM remnants, could demol- 14 ish the 22 largest Soviet cities, holding a combined population of 32 million, and most of the country's advanced industrial installations. And this is a highly optimistic scenario from the Soviet point of view; the damage would probably be far worse.

The bomber force. One cannot ignore the bombers on alert. They 15 carry about half of U.S. megatonnage. Without any prior notice (that is, in the highly unlikely event of a bolt-from-the-blue surprise attack), the first bomber can get off the airfield within 7 minutes. All 124 bombers on alert (30 percent of the force) can get off the ground within 15 minutes' warning.

Assuming that the Soviets destroy *all* U.S. bombers not on run- 16 way alert — leaving 124 aloft — and even assuming a greater than expected attrition of our bombers enroute to targets, the United States could still deliver, with the surviving bomber force alone, about 700 megatons.

This, too, unrealistically understates the potential U.S. response. 17 If the Soviets were ever to launch a first strike, it would almost certainly be the culmination of escalating international tensions. The attack would probably be preemptive in nature. So some of the bombers would be on airborne alert, and others dispersed through-out the country at emergency civilian and military airfields. With only two days' notice the bomber force could deliver almost 1,800 megatons.

The submarine fleet. The Soviet attack would also include strikes 18 against the U.S. nuclear missile-bearing submarine fleet. Twenty-five boats (60 percent of this fleet) are on station at all times and, hidden in the depths of the sea, are unreachable and invulnerable. So only those 16 in port would be destroyed.

Each of the submarines at sea carries 16 missiles, and in about $\frac{3}{4}$ 19 of the submarines each missile bears 10 warheads. Each of these multiple warheads has an explosive power of 50 kilotons, the equivalent blast power of over two Hiroshima weapons. Even if 20 percent of all these were to fail, in launch or in re-entry, there would still be over 2,200 warheads in the submarine fleet alone that would survive the first strike and that could reach the Soviet Union.

It has been argued that a Soviet first strike could be a "surgical" 20 operation that would disarm the United States, yet leave the civilian sector largely untouched, and that this would, as a consequence, sap the political will of the United States to respond with a second strike. But even if the Soviets scrupulously sought to avoid the killing of civilians, millions of Americans would die. Damage to the civilian sector would be vast, in part a consequence of radioactive fallout across major portions of the country and in part from global effects. Each megaton of ground burst leads to levels of contamination lethal to unprotected persons over about 1,000 square miles. A strike against the ICBM silos would probably be about 50 percent ground bursts, so that something approaching one million square miles of American territory would be rendered heavily contaminated by this supposedly "surgical" strike. The lethal levels of radioactive fallout would hit people hundreds of miles downwind from the actual deto-nations. Most of the farmland in Kansas, Nebraska and Iowa would be contaminated with very high levels of radioactivity, especially strontium-90. Huge quantities of this deadly material would extend for more than 1,000 miles from each detonation, and would contami-nate the bulk of the U.S. milk production.

According to a 1975 study conducted by a panel of the Office of 21 Technology Assessment 12 to 18 million people would be killed from the collateral (or unintended) damage resulting from a Soviet attack intended merely to wipe out America's land-based missile force.

If the Soviets tried to destroy the non-alert bombers on various 22
airfields, and the submarines in port — which any military planner going for an effective first strike would surely want to do — fatalities could easily reach totals as high as 20 million or over. As many people would die in such an attack as would be the case if the Russians deliberately killed one-quarter of the people in this nation's 25 largest metropolitan areas.

In other words, a "limited" counterforce attack against American 23
strategic nuclear weapons would hardly be a "clean, surgical strike" and neither the President nor the American people would consider the attack as being limited. Hence the likelihood of massive American retaliation to this "limited" attack is high.

The Second Strike: Retaliation

The U.S. forces that would survive the first strike would consti- 24
tute a deadly threat to the Soviet Union. . . . If the U.S. forces were put on alert by a heightening of tensions before the Soviet strike or from intelligence of Soviet intentions the numbers of surviving warheads and bombs would jump by over half and the total megatonnage nearly double.

What damage would ensue if this force, or the bulk of it, were 25
used in a retaliatory strike? There are a variety of ways it could be employed, and thus there are a variety of possible consequences. It is the policy of the United States not to target Soviet Union population per se but rather to direct attacks at military and industrial targets. Because so many of these targets are in or near major urban areas population centers would nevertheless be subject to the bulk of the damage.

In fact, it would require only about 1,350 Poseidon warheads, less 26
than half of the warheads on the submarines that are always at sea, to level just about everything in every one of the 220 Soviet cities with population exceeding 100,000. Critical components of the highway, rail and electricity, petroleum- and gas-transportation systems would be targeted with air and ground bursts along with important industrial facilities, ports, airports, and industrial complexes outside of urban areas including mines, oil fields, and refineries. One can reasonably conclude that in excess of 60 percent of the Soviets' industrial capacity would be destroyed by the effects of blast alone, disregarding damage from initial radiation, fallout, and subsequent fires.

But this is not the whole story. The functioning of a modern 27
industrial state like the Soviet Union depends on sophisticated coordi-

nation of continuing supply of energy, industrial components, and a usable transportation system. With the bulk of energy sources gone and transportation destroyed, the nation would be deprived of the ability to restore a functioning industrial system for a very long period of time.

U.S. strikes against the industrial base of the Soviet economy 28 would also be disastrously effective. Soviet industry is highly concentrated and centralized. Sixty percent of all steel output comes from only 25 plants. There are only 34 major petroleum, and eight copper, refineries. Chemicals are largely produced in only 25 cities. All cars are manufactured in 12 large cities. There are only eight major shipbuilding works, 16 heavy machine and 15 agricultural machine production plants. Nine tractor plants make 80 percent of the entire Soviet output; 47 percent is produced in five of the 20 largest cities, 20 percent in the huge Kama Truck Plant alone. The entire Central and Volga regions, with a population of almost 60 million, get most of their electricity from three hydroelectric and two nuclear power plants, all located in large cities.

Some industrial facilities are quite fragile. Thus a large petro- 29 leum refinery would be damaged so badly by a one-megaton blast *eleven miles distant* as to require a quarter of a million man days to repair. Many of the most crucial industries *cannot* be protected by hardening, including oil refineries, electric generating plants, steel works, truck and tractor plants, and others.

As in the United States, radioactive fallout would be extensive 30 with hundreds of thousands of square miles affected. Fallout shelters would lead to a reduction in the number of prompt human fatalities from the fallout but little could be done to protect livestock and crops, as well as other plants and animals, from its effects. Large masses of decaying bodies — human and animal — would create an extremely toxic environment and spread disease unless heroic clean-up measures were successfully carried out.

Long-Term Consequences

In addition to the immediate consequences of a large nuclear 31 exchange there can be long-term global consequences, physical and biological as well as social, political, and economic. Some of these stem from the likelihood of climatic alterations brought on by the exchange as well as from dispersed radioactivity. The extent, duration, and impact of the effects are not very well known at present. Yet what is known or reasonably expected constitutes a grim picture.

The ionizing radiation and high temperatures in nuclear fireballs 32 produce large quantities of nitrogen oxides (component of what is known as smog). These oxides rise and are dispersed in the atmosphere, some fraction reaching the stratosphere. There they react with and destroy ozone in the important layer that normally absorbs, and hence protects us from, most of the ultraviolet rays in the sun's radiation. The reduction of ozone might reach 30 to 70 percent in the northern hemisphere and be less, but significant, in the southern hemisphere. The amount of harmful ultraviolet rays reaching the ground could then rise by a factor between six and one hundred. Recovery of the prewar ozone levels might require 3 to 5 years, or even longer. In the meantime, ultraviolet rays reaching the Earth's surface could cause incapacitating sunburn in as little as 10 minutes, and induce severe burns (snow blindness) of the eye. Fatal sunburn would be the consequence of long exposure. The incidence of skin cancer would rise markedly.

During this period persons outdoors in daytime would need to be swathed and goggled. Because the ultraviolet rays inhibit photosynthesis there would probably be stunted plant growth. Sensitive crops, such as tomatoes and peas, would be scorched and killed. Ultraviolet penetrates water to a depth of a few feet so that damage to aquatic species is possible. The rays would injure not only humans but also bacteria, fungi, higher plants, insects, and animals. Crops would be at risk and work would be hazardous, difficult, and inefficient for all persons engaged in agriculture and outdoor activities. 33

Both the high levels of ultraviolet radiation and the globally dispersed radioactivity would cause genetic damage and mutations. Mutation of some pathogens would possibly lead to novel virulent strains that could cause disease epidemics both of crops and animals on a global scale. Moreover, in the target countries and those nearby where fallout radiation would be most intense, widespread destruction of plant and animal life could lead to major ecological imbalance, some species being far more radiosensitive than others. The changes would very likely be unfavorable to agriculture and animal husbandry. These imbalances could persist for one or more decades. 34

Ground-burst nuclear explosions throw great quantities of gravel and debris into the atmosphere. In a large nuclear exchange this would involve several cubic miles of material, more than from the world's largest natural explosion, the volcano Krakatoa in 1883. Some of the material is so fine it would remain in the atmosphere for years. Additional smoke and dust would come from huge fires, which in some periods of the year could encompass hundreds or thousands of square miles. Because these dusts reflect or absorb small amounts of sunlight which would otherwise warm the Earth's surface they can lead to global cooling and to changes in the distribution and amount of rainfall. 35

The effects of the suspended particulates as well as consequences 36 of ozone depletion might lead to global cooling with an average temperature drop as great as several degrees centigrade although it might be smaller or even negligible. As a result the possibility of climatic changes of a very dramatic nature can by no means be ruled out. And only one degree of cooling would, according to a National Academy of Sciences report, eliminate wheat growing in Canada. The normal ranges of crops could everywhere be altered and normally consistent weather patterns upset. For example, the monsoon in the Indian subcontinent could be altered, affecting half a billion people. Climatic alteration would directly affect the growing of food in virtually every nation on earth. With the halting of U.S. and Canadian grain exports two-thirds of the international commerce in these critical foods would disappear, causing widespread famine in both the developing and industrial countries.

The Soviet Union has had perennial problems with food production and its current agricultural conditions are far from the ideal. One-fourth of the labor force is devoted to agriculture, as compared with 5 percent in the United States and yet the country is a net importer of food. Its own seasonal carryover stocks of food are generally inadequate. 37

Grains, primarily wheat, and potatoes provide about 50 percent of the Soviet diet. Accordingly, the nation is highly vulnerable to damage in this crucial sector. Grain planting and harvesting are almost entirely mechanized and are, therefore, highly sensitive to shortages of spare parts, absence of fuel, and replacement of machines. The major grain growing areas are at the same latitude as the prairie provinces of Canada. Thus the possible climatic cooling could be more than sufficient to wipe out their yield. More southerly regions are deficient in water and in the aftermath of nuclear war could not be converted easily to new crops. 38

At present 30 percent of the value of Soviet crops is lost to pests, insects, rodents, plant pathogens, weeds, and the like. The immensely difficult problems of conducting survival agriculture and extensive radioactive contamination coupled with the effects of ecological imbalances would further aggravate the losses. If the Soviets were, very improbably, to save a large fraction of their population by an effective evacuation and shelter program, there would be major prospect of widespread, perhaps near-total, famine. 39

Soviet survivors of a U.S. second strike, many of them dealt lingering and ultimately fatal afflictions, would face a devastated environment, with urban areas and the bulk of their industrial capacity destroyed, and much of the land and the urban wreckage intensely radioactive and inaccessible for months. They would be without fuels, a transportation system, or the tools, industry and resources necessary 40 to restore an industrial base. The injured, with most hospitals destroyed, would largely have to fend for themselves, for the uninjured would have grave survival problems themselves.

The scale of destruction and the dim prospect for recovery — 41 with no hope of outside assistance — would so numb and psychologically shock the survivors that no effective action toward reconstruction could be begun for a long time. There is a real possibility that the survivors would turn on the remaining Soviet leadership, rejecting reimposition of direction from those seen as responsible for their plight.

Modern industrial nations depend for their functioning on inter- 42 weaving and coordinating numerous technical, social, political, and economic activities. It is the integration of these activities that constitutes the national structure and makes it greater than the sum of its parts. As with a complex machine, some portion of a nation's parts must *all* work at least at some minimum level of efficiency, or the socioeconomic system ceases to function. A large nation is especially vulnerable to assaults that threaten its organized functioning. It should be abundantly clear that a major nuclear strike poses such a peril.

In our judgment there is little doubt that the Soviet Union, in the 43 aftermath of a U.S. second strike, would no longer have national coherence, that it would be unhinged and dismembered to such an extent that even the remnants that did not suffer direct damage could no longer function as a modern industrial society. And the Soviet Union has the capacity to inflict the same level of damage on the United States. Whether this damage could be remedied in a foreseeable period, or would persist indefinitely, is beyond confident prediction. Yet so real is this possibility that neither the Soviet military authorities nor the central government could fail to consider it most carefully. And so awesome is the cost, so beyond the price that any nation would be willing to pay for any conceivable political objective that only madmen could choose such a course. Whatever characteristics the Soviet leadership has revealed over the years it has never displayed that sort of reckless, lunatic inclination.

The immense megatonnage of nuclear weaponry in the super- 44 powers' arsenals, the huge number of relatively invulnerable delivery systems, and the likelihood that a large nuclear exchange would obliterate the target nations, along with inducing disastrous global effects, tell us that further search for "nuclear superiority" by either side is futile. It only leads to the construction and deployment of new and more accurate weapons of destruction that make the nuclear standoff increasingly fragile. By raising fears of "first strike" it could create a hair trigger situation in serious crises and thus gravely weaken deterrence.

Notwithstanding there is continuing pressure from the military 45 and civilian hardliners in the United States and from their Soviet counterparts to enhance and expand their respective nuclear capabilities. These pressures are based on obsolete *military* views surviving from the age of purely conventional weapons, when having the more powerful armed force was regarded as essential to command the field. But this is not the way that citizens or their political leaders in *any* country see the situation today. This is because they understand that a retaliatory nuclear force far smaller than the one we have today is sufficient to ensure deterrence. As McGeorge Bundy, National Security Advisor to President Kennedy, stated:

> There is an enormous gulf between what political leaders really 46 think about nuclear weapons and what is assumed in complex calculations of relative "advantage" in simulated strategic warfare. Think-tank analysts can set levels of "acceptable" damage well up in the tens of millions of lives. They can assume that the loss of dozens of great cities is somehow a real choice for sane men. They are in an unreal world. In the real world of real political leaders — whether here or in the Soviet Union — a decision that would bring even one hydrogen bomb on one city of one's own country would be recognized in advance as a catastrophic blunder; ten bombs on ten cities would be a disaster beyond history; and a hundred bombs on a hundred cities are unthinkable. Yet this unthinkable level of human incineration is the least that could be expected by either side in response to any first strike in the next ten years, *no matter what happens to weapons systems in the meantime.*[2]

The central fact of the nuclear age is that nuclear arms are too 47 powerful and numerous to be used to gain a nation's political or military objectives. Hence we and the Soviet Union must continue to recognize mutual deterrence as the essential, indispensable foundation of a stable military relationship between the two countries and to forego the futile and risky contest for nuclear superiority.

Review Questions

1. What is the "triad" of which U.S. strategic nuclear forces consist?
2. Why does Kendall see a nuclear attack on U.S. missile silos — even a highly accurate and effective attack — as failing to achieve "first-strike" capability?
3. Why does Kendall consider a "bolt-from-the-blue surprise attack" "highly unlikely"? (See the following article on this subject.)

---

[2] Reprinted by permission of *Foreign Affairs*, October 1969. Copyright © 1969 by the Council on Foreign Relations, Inc.

4. Why does Kendall dismiss the possibility of a "surgical" Soviet first strike that would destroy the U.S.'s weaponry, while leaving its civilian sector untouched?

5. Why is Soviet industry so vulnerable to a nuclear strike?

6. What would be the long-term effects of radiation, following a nuclear attack? What, for instance, would be the effect on world climate?

7. What are Kendall's conclusions and recommendations?

Discussion Questions

1. Do you agree with Kendall that no sane leadership would be willing to pay the price that a nuclear war would exact in order to gain its political objectives? In any case, how does one define "sane leadership"?

2. Kendall argues that we could inflict heavy damage on the Soviet Union with the missile force remaining after a Soviet first strike — at least after the kind of first strike capability the Soviets will have during the 1980s. But what about after the 1980s? Should we continue our defense development so that even if the Soviet first-strike capability improves, we will be able to withstand a first strike? Or would such defense development only ·fuel the already out-of-control arms race?

3. What are the long-term climatic and agricultural effects of radioactivity in the atmosphere? Why is the Soviet Union even more vulnerable than the U.S. to such climatic and agricultural disruptions?

4. Does Kendall advocate disarmament? What does he conclude is the only practical course of action for both the U.S. and the Soviet Union?

5. Does this article make you feel better about the stability of the nuclear balance of terror? Why or why not?

6. Why would an unrestricted arms race increase the probability of nuclear war, in Kendall's view?

7. What is the purpose of the "chilling scenario" at the opening of this article?

8. Where does Kendall state the purpose and scope of his article?

9. Kendall's article could be characterized as a rather cool, rational analysis of the nuclear balance of power. Does it seem cool to the point of bloodlessness and inhumanity? Should Kendall have showed more evidence of emotion on such a subject?

10. At what point does Kendall summarize the main points he has covered in the article and begin to develop his conclusion?

11. Why has he written this article? To whom is it addressed? (It first appeared in the *Bulletin of the Atomic Scientists*.) What do you think he would like to see happen as a result of this article?

Writing Suggestions

1. Outline this article, indicating its main points and the most significant supporting details.

2. Kendall says that the price of a nuclear war would be so great that "only madmen could choose such a course. Whatever characteristics the Soviet leadership has revealed over the years it has never displayed that sort of reckless, lunatic inclination." However, it has been feared that if terrorists, or a more erratic government than that of the Soviet Union, got hold of atomic weapons, they might be willing to pay such a price, even if it involved their own certain deaths (which they might well consider martyrdoms). How real a possibility is this? Develop some "scenarios."

THE FIRST NUCLEAR WAR
Warren Boroson, with David P. Snyder

Warren Boroson is on the staff of *Next* magazine, where this article first appeared. David P. Snyder is coauthor of *Studies in the Quality of Life: Delphi and Decision Making.*

□

The first nuclear war. The words are frightening. Few Americans   1
consider that the bombings of Hiroshima and Nagasaki represented a genuine nuclear war. They were a lesson, horrible for the Japanese, instructive for the rest of humankind. But the lesson shows signs of fading from our memories.

To find out how significant the threat of nuclear war is, NEXT   2
conducted a special Delphi poll of 32 leading authorities on the subject. In a Delphi, experts answer similar questions at least twice; it is considered the most reliable forecasting technique available.[1]

Next Magazine, October 1980. Copyright © 1980 by Litton Magazines. Published by Next Publishing Company. Reprinted by permission.

[1] The Delphi method of polling was developed in the early 1950s. During the first poll, the experts do not know one another's names; during the second poll (in which they answer the same questions), they know not only one another's names, but also the results of the first poll. Their second set of responses therefore tends to be more carefully considered and more "mainstream" than their first, more intuitive responses. The final tabulation draws upon both sets of responses to develop a balance between expert intuition and expert consensus. [Behrens and Rosen]

Some highlights: 3

The first nuclear war will probably be fought between Israel and the Arab countries, and Israel will win. But it might be a Pyrrhic victory.

A war between India and Pakistan is almost as likely, a war that India will win.

If a nuclear world war breaks out in the next 10 years, one of the *least* probable causes is the one everyone seems to fear most: a surprise attack by one superpower on another.

We took pains not to weight the panel toward any particular   4
point of view; our 32 respondents represent virtually every shade of opinion. They include: a former deputy commander in chief of the U.S. Army in Europe, the director of the Arms Control and Disarmament Agency, a former member of the negotiating team for the SALT talks, a director of the Defense Nuclear Agency of the Department of Defense, a member of the House Armed Services Committee, as well as staff members of such institutions as the Carnegie Endowment for World Peace, Hudson Institute, and the Brookings Institution, along with academicians from such universities as Harvard, Johns Hopkins, and Cornell.

Michael E. Mandelbaum of Harvard, interviewed after the poll,   5
called the findings "pessimistic, but not drastically so."

Here are more highlights: 6

The chances of a nuclear war during 1980-84 are low but grow-   7
ing, and from 1985-89 the danger is expected to climb ominously. During the 90s, when most third graders come' of draft age, the likelihood of nuclear war may be double what it is today. The chief reason: More than twice as many nations will have nuclear weapons as have them now.

The nuclear wars most likely to occur are regional, not wars that   8
spread over the globe. This is the poll's most optimistic finding.

There's no quick fix, no magic bullet, to prevent nuclear war. Of   9
16 options listed on our questionnaire, the panelists greeted only one with more than lukewarm approval: eliminating sudden and significant military advantages.

The NEXT Delphi poll is the first ever conducted on the pros-   10
pects of nuclear war, barring a secret Delphi study the Pentagon did in the 50s. The questionnaire itself was developed by consulting futurist David P. Snyder, with aid from Lt. Colonel Mason P. Rumney (Ret.) along with panelists Mandelbaum and Lt. General A.S. Collins Jr. (Ret.). Consisting of four legal-sized pages, the NEXT poll asked 89 specific questions that left no room for vagueness or ambiguity.

Most panelists agree, first of all, that there is not safety but peril 11
in numbers. The more nations that have nuclear weapons, the greater
the chances of nuclear war. Five nations definitely have nuclear
weapons now (the U.S., USSR, France, Britain, and China); one
(India) has exploded some sort of device; and two others (Israel and
South Africa) are suspected of having such weapons. By 1990, the
panel consensus holds, about 10 countries will have nuclear weapons,
and by the year 2000, about 13.

Representing the views of the mainstream panelists, Stephanie 12
Neuman of the Institute of War and Peace Studies considers nuclear
proliferation inevitable: "Our experience with conventional arms suggests that every country wants the most advanced weapons it can
afford. There's no question that new countries will opt for nuclear
capability."

Most of the panelists outside the mainstream believe that few new 13
nations will go nuclear. "I would expect a slow, gradual proliferation,
but not a mad, precipitous one," says Robert E. Osgood of Johns
Hopkins. Hatching your own bomb will panic your neighbors, who
will frantically concoct their own weapon; it will annoy countries that
have been selling you plutonium for nuclear reactors. "I mean," says
Osgood, "why take more flak than you have to?"

Another optimistic but nonmainstream view is that, just as the 14
threat of nuclear annihilation seems to have kept the U.S. and USSR
from conflict, nuclear weapons may deter wars between the new
members of the nuclear club. (Peter Sharfman of the Office of Technology Assessment says, "The whole basis of deterrence is: You make
things good by making them possibly awful.") But as consensus panel-
ist Mandelbaum puts it, several countries that can go nuclear "are
hardly models of political stability and social rationality — there's
always the specter of a Qaddafi [of Libya] with the bomb." Neuman is
also dubious about deterrence: "War reflects human nature. I'm very
Realpolitik[2] about this — I think wars will continue to occur, and I
believe, if their survival is at stake, countries will use the weapons
they've got, including nuclear weapons."

Many panelists are more concerned about nuclear war these days 15
because they fear that, with so much technology controlling the
weapons, something might go out of whack. Says Andrew J. Pierre of
the Council on Foreign Relations: "Those recent computer break-
downs involving our strategic nuclear forces have to be taken seriously. We're dealing more and more with computers and shorter lead

---

[2] A realistic or practical approach to political and diplomatic behavior, practiced by those who assume that one or more parties will use deceit or force to
gain their ends. [Behrens and Rosen]

times and more complex gadgetry. And remember, we couldn't get eight helicopters into Iran and out."[3]

Our experts are also worried that the USSR will acquire the ability to knock out America's Minuteman missiles by 1985 or so, which may upset the delicate balance of terror. Like many other panelists, John F. Scott of the U.S. War College doubts that the Soviets would launch a preemptive strike, but misconceptions that they would, he believes, increase the chances of war. "I don't see any abatement in our theological discussions about our so-called loss of superiority," he says. "And the late 80s will be a time when everybody will be the most excitable, the least confident. It will be the kind of situation that adds up to 50 people making stupid mistakes." 16

These shifts and turnings apparently have persuaded the panelists that we seem to be slouching toward Armageddon. Whereas they think there was only a tiny 1 percent chance of nuclear war in the 70s, they see a nerve-wracking 5 percent chance during 1980-84. The chances of war keep increasing until they hit a chilling 10 percent in the 90s. Two panelists say the odds are 50-50 there will be nuclear war during the proliferative 90s. 17

Israel and the Arab states are the most likely belligerents, and the consensus is that the Israelis would win. "They'd have more warheads and a better air force," says George H. Quester of Cornell. "But it would be an empty victory. Probably more Israelis would be killed than Arabs." But Pierre thinks the Arabs would win: "It's easier to kill all the Israelis than to kill all the Arabs." 18

The nuclear war considered second most likely is one between Pakistan and India. Of it Neuman says, "Pakistan's survival politically and economically is really very shaky right now, and it seems to me that when a country is in that position it's willing to take everything down with it." India, the panelists agree, would win any such war. 19

The third most probable nuclear war in the 80s is another regional conflict — between China and the USSR, which the latter would win. Quester thinks this is the single most likely war: "The Chinese surprised me when they invaded Vietnam. Until then, I had thought, gee, here is the ultimate in a people who talk tough and behave moderately. But the invasion of Vietnam was a bit strange. And the Russians surprised me a little when they invaded Afghanistan. So you've got two superpowers that have been somewhat erratic in their behavior." 20

Lower down on the list are a regional war between the NATO and Warsaw Pact countries and a regional war between the U.S. and 21

---

[3] In 1980, President Carter ordered a military rescue mission to retrieve the American Embassy hostages held by Iran. The mission failed because of helicopter problems.

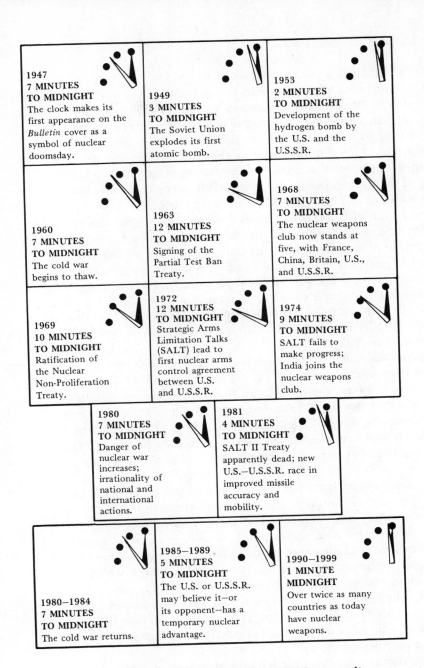

1947
7 MINUTES TO MIDNIGHT
The clock makes its first appearance on the *Bulletin* cover as a symbol of nuclear doomsday.

1949
3 MINUTES TO MIDNIGHT
The Soviet Union explodes its first atomic bomb.

1953
2 MINUTES TO MIDNIGHT
Development of the hydrogen bomb by the U.S. and the U.S.S.R.

1960
7 MINUTES TO MIDNIGHT
The cold war begins to thaw.

1963
12 MINUTES TO MIDNIGHT
Signing of the Partial Test Ban Treaty.

1968
7 MINUTES TO MIDNIGHT
The nuclear weapons club now stands at five, with France, China, Britain, U.S., and U.S.S.R.

1969
10 MINUTES TO MIDNIGHT
Ratification of the Nuclear Non-Proliferation Treaty.

1972
12 MINUTES TO MIDNIGHT
Strategic Arms Limitation Talks (SALT) lead to first nuclear arms control agreement between U.S. and U.S.S.R.

1974
9 MINUTES TO MIDNIGHT
SALT fails to make progress; India joins the nuclear weapons club.

1980
7 MINUTES TO MIDNIGHT
Danger of nuclear war increases; irrationality of national and international actions.

1981
4 MINUTES TO MIDNIGHT
SALT II Treaty apparently dead; new U.S.–U.S.S.R. race in improved missile accuracy and mobility.

1980–1984
7 MINUTES TO MIDNIGHT
The cold war returns.

1985–1989
5 MINUTES TO MIDNIGHT
The U.S. or U.S.S.R. may believe it—or its opponent—has a temporary nuclear advantage.

1990–1999
1 MINUTE MIDNIGHT
Over twice as many countries as today have nuclear weapons.

The Conscience of the International Scientific Community

The Bulletin clock is a symbolic warning of the lateness of the hour as humankind confronts (or fails to confront) the urgent problems of our times. The minute hand, never far from midnight, has moved nine times since the founding of the magazine at the end of World War II. © 1980, *The Bulletin of the Atomic Scientists,* Chicago, Illinois, by permission; and *Next,* October 1980, reprinted by permission of Medical-Economics Company.

USSR (in which nuclear warheads would be exchanged, say, in the Mideast). The first *global* nuclear war, between the U.S. and USSR, is considered only 40 percent as likely as a war between Israel and the Arabs. Most panelists don't think a global war would have a winner. Dissenters tend to believe it would be the Soviet Union and its allies.

If there is a global nuclear war in the next decade, the experts 22 say, the most likely cause would be the escalation of a conflict between the allies of the superpowers (say, in the Mideast) or the escalation of an acute international crisis (like the Cuban missile crisis). Least likely is a surprise attack by one superpower on another. Quester, for one, believes it's ridiculous to think that the Soviets would attack us, even if they perceived a "nuclear window of opportunity" (as it's called): "If they knocked out most of our Minuteman missiles, we would still have lots of submarine-based missiles to retaliate with. And so many Americans would be killed that it's hard to imagine any American President who wouldn't then just punish the Russians by killing as many of them as possible. So why would any Russian leader do it? The scenario is very unrelated to reality."

In a regional nuclear war, the mainstream panelists think, the 23 number of nuclear explosions would very likely be less than 100. Over 5 million people would die (equivalent to the combined populations of Connecticut, Vermont, and Arizona), and 1 million or more people would suffer some form of debilitating radiation poisoning (which typically leads to cancer deaths, miscarriages, and sterilization). The chances of a regional war expanding into a global war are only 10 percent.

Other conclusions from the poll: If there were a *global* nuclear 24 war, over 500 bombs would fall, over 50 million people would die (much below other estimates, such as those reported by the U.S. Office of Technology Assessment), and 25 million or more people would suffer from radiation poisoning. There's an even chance that world political order would collapse; chances are still higher that the current systems of government in Europe and the U.S. would be eliminated. There's a 50 percent risk that industrial societies would revert to a pre-1900 standard of living (with fuel scarce, people might rely on bicycles and horses for transportation, and bartering might replace our economic system).

There's also an even chance for a multi-generational delay in the 25 overall progress of humankind. As someone has asked, "Who could calculate how long it would take to get over the loss of Wall Street, M.I.T., the Mayo Clinic, and the Smithsonian?"

But Robert M. Trice of the Department of Defense called our 26 poll's conclusions sanguine: "The panelists showed an optimism that I found a bit surprising about the ability of states to cope with nuclear exchanges."

The poll found that, almost uniformly, the experts have little   27
faith in any proposal, new or old, to prevent nuclear war. Indeed,
nobody came up with anything resembling a fresh and imaginative
way of scaling down the threat. "I couldn't think of any," says Mandelbaum, "and I really tried."

Why the pessimism? "When you first approach the problem of   28
nuclear weapons," he says, "your impulse is to reach for sweeping
solutions; this impulse has existed since 1945. But it's never come to
anything. So people who are familiar with the history of the atomic
age tend to be skeptical of all-encompassing remedies." Neuman
agrees: "There is a correlation between optimism about quick pana-
ceas and lack of information."

The only step to reduce the likelihood of nuclear war that won   29
substantial support is preventing either the U.S. or USSR from gaining a sudden military advantage — say, through the use of multiple
independently targeted warheads on individual missiles. This was one
of the goals of the SALT II treaty, which the U.S. has shelved.

Other proposals that did fairly well in our poll: 30

A stronger U.S. military position. Says William N. Jackomis,   31
former SALT negotiator: "The Soviets understand military
power. They have been increasing their presence throughout the
world, and the only way to put that in check to some degree is to
have a very, very strong military position."

A nuclear disarmament treaty among the superpowers with no on-   32
site inspection for compliance. "We won't budge unless there's on-
site inspection, and they won't budge if there is," says Scott.
"Sometimes I wonder how serious people are about negotiating
when they take positions like this. It makes you want to throw
your hands up in the air. But a limited treaty with no inspection is
a pretty good bet right now, though a lot of my military colleagues would find it complete nonsense. That's the way it goes."

Stricter safeguards on providing nuclear energy resources to other   33
nations, so they cannot make nuclear weapons. Says Neuman,
"Perhaps the only thing we can do is slow them down a little bit.
Boy, I'm for that."

Various other proposals were almost jeered at by the panel: 34

Universal declaration of no-first-use of nuclear weapons. Says Man-   35
delbaum, "Declarations like that get put aside in the first moments of conflict. Nobody would obey them, and nobody would
believe others would obey them. We might make a no-first-use
declaration, but as long as we have 7,000 nuclear weapons in
Europe, the Soviets are going to be skeptical."

Unilateral disarmament. "If we announced we were unilaterally   36
disarming," says Quester, "the French and the Chinese and the
British nuclear budgets would go up enormously, and probably
so would the Brazilian and the Australian. In other words, other
countries would race to become the new No. 2 — because *they*
wouldn't trust the Russians. . . . If we had disarmed in 1949 or
1951, I think Stalin would have taken over the world."

As for suggestions that new weapons — lasers and electronic   37
beams and such — might replace nuclear arms and be less destructive, the panelists agree it is a forlorn hope.

Amid all the shadows, the NEXT poll discovered a few faint rays   38
of light. For example, Thomas W. Milburn of Ohio State University
believes that a SALT II treaty could be a momentous beginning.
"There almost has to be a sequence of successes," he says. "Everything
would be much easier once we have something like the SALT II
treaty. We might then get a mutual force balance reduction treaty in
Europe and even a comprehensive test ban treaty. The big tie-up
right now lies with the very first step."

Perhaps the least melancholy of all the panelists is Quester. "My   39
own suspicion," he says, "is that optimism is always downplayed in
these polls. You know, anybody who is looking ahead would rather be
wrong on the pessimistic side than on the optimistic side. So we all
predict a little worse than happens. Because if we're wrong, and
everything turns out for the better, nobody is resentful. If we're right
about nuclear war, at least we predicted it.

"I think there's a fair chance that we'll just keep on and on and   40
on. The longer we go without a nuclear war, the stronger the chances
we won't have one. You know, I really expect to retire without having
seen a nuclear weapon used anywhere in the world in anger. That's
another 30 years or so on top of the 35 years we've already had
without bombs going off. By then maybe no one will remember what
a nuclear bomb looks like when it goes off. They'll have to look at old
movies."

Once again, perhaps, humankind will escape by the skin of its   41
teeth.

Review Questions

1. On what basis do the authors report their predictions about the likelihood of nuclear war?
2. The most likely nuclear war, according to the poll, will involve what
   adversaries? What is the least likely nuclear war? Why?
3. Why is nuclear proliferation generally considered inevitable?

4. What factors will create an increase in the possibility of nuclear war as the century draws to a close?
5. Why couldn't the experts come up with any satisfactory proposal to prevent nuclear war?
6. Which proposals draw the most scorn from the experts?

Discussion Questions

1. Which findings of the poll seem the most discouraging? Which seem the most encouraging?
2. The experts were unable to come up with many proposals that had a realistic chance of preventing nuclear war. Have they missed any? What are they?
3. George Quester, professor of government at Cornell University, is quoted as saying, "The longer we go without a nuclear war, the stronger the chance we won't have one." Why should this be so? Do you agree with this assessment, or do you take the more pessimistic view that some kind of nuclear war is almost inevitable during or after the 1990s?
4. Should the U.S., in order to get *some* kind of nuclear disarmament treaty, agree to a "limited treaty with *no* [on-site] inspection," as John F. Scott (strategic research analyst at the U.S. Army War College) believes? Or would this be foolish, an invitation to cheating by either side? Should we hold out for a guaranteed on-site inspection provision?
5. How is this article organized? Of what kind of material does the introduction consist? Which aspects of nuclear war are then taken up?
6. Is it a good idea to include the "highlights" of the report early in the article? Does this make the information anticlimactic when it is reported in more detail later on? Would it have been better to begin with a description of the poll procedures, and then to begin discussing the results step by step?
7. Boroson and Snyder chose to end their report with a lengthy quotation from "the least melancholy of all the panelists." What effect does this conclusion, and their final comment, have?

Writing Suggestion

Devise a poll to reveal the attitudes of faculty and/or students at your school concerning an issue of major concern. The issue might be local, national, or international. You may (as in the *Next* poll) want to distribute questionnaires only to experts or specialists in the field; or you may want to seek the opinion of specialists and laypeople alike. Use quotations liberally when you write up your results.

THE DAY THE BOMB WENT OFF

Erwin Knoll and Theodore Postol

Erwin Knoll, born in Vienna in 1931, is the editor of *The Progressive,* where this article first appeared. He has been a reporter and an editor for the *Washington Post* and the Washington editor for the *Los Angeles Times.* Among his books is *War Crimes and the American Conscience.* Theodore A. Postol is a physicist and nuclear engineer on the staff of the Argonne National Laboratory, which played a part in the development of the atomic bomb. Postol is a member of the Chicago Committee for a Nuclear Overkill Moratorium.

☐

It was a sunny summer morning in the Chicago Loop. The usual 1 bumper-to-bumper jam of cars and trucks. On the sidewalks, the usual crowd of shoppers, tourists, messengers, office workers heading out to an early lunch. It was Friday.

At 11:27, a twenty-megaton nuclear bomb exploded a few feet 2 above street level at the corner of LaSalle and Adams. First the incredible flash of light and heat: In less than one-millionth of a second, the temperature rose to 150 million degrees Fahrenheit — more than four times the temperature at the center of the sun.

The roar followed immediately but there, in the center of the city 3 and for miles around, no one was left to hear it. There was only the heat. And the dust.

Imagine that it happened. We will not speculate here 'on why it 4 happened — on whose fault it was, on the series of diplomatic bluffs and blunders and miscalculations here and there that made it happen. It happened.

Even in the macro-magnitudes of nuclear weaponry, a twenty-megaton 5 *bomb is large — the equivalent of twenty million tons of TNT, though such comparisons have little meaning. The yield of a twenty-megaton bomb is some 1,500 times greater than the yield of the bomb that was dropped on Hiroshima thirty-three years ago.*

The United States does not admit to deploying any twenty-megaton bombs 6 *in its nuclear arsenal. With its superiority in missile numbers and missile accuracy, the United States prefers weapons of lower yield. But the Soviet*

Union's 200 SS-9 intercontinental ballistic missiles are believed to carry warheads in the twenty-megaton range, and they — along with lesser bombs — are presumably targeted on the fifty largest cities in the United States.

In the event of nuclear war, a total of some 100 to 200 megatons would 7
be directed at a metropolitan area like Chicago's.

The bomb that exploded in the Loop left a crater 600 feet deep 8
and nearly a mile and a half in diameter. The crater's lip, extending
almost to the shore of Lake Michigan on the east, was 200 feet high
and would be, after the cloud of radioactive debris and dust had
settled or dissipated, the tallest "object" visible in the area of the blast.

For the moment, though, there was just the incandescent fireball, 9
rising and expanding outward at enormous speed, reaching a height
and breadth of three or four miles, illuminating the sky, so that 100
miles away, over Milwaukee, the flash blinded the crew of a Chicago-
bound airliner.

Around Ground Zero, everything — steel-and-concrete sky- 10
scrapers, roads and bridges, thousands of tons of earth, hundreds of
thousands of people — was instantly evaporated.

At the edge of the fireball, a thin shell of super-heated, super- 11
compressed gas acquired a momentum of its own and was propelled
outward as a blast of immense extent and power, picking up objects
from disintegrating buildings, snatching huge boulders and reducing
them to vapor that would solidify, eventually, into radioactive dust.

Three seconds had elapsed since the bomb went off. 12

A high-altitude blast at one to three miles above ground level would have 13
inflicted considerably greater blast damage, but the surface blast has its own
"advantage": By maximizing the amount of debris sucked up in the nuclear
explosion, it multiplies the long-range radiological effects, threatening the
survival of living things hundreds of miles from the target area. And even the
blast radius of a surface detonation is powerful enough to ignite fires more than
twenty miles from Ground Zero — more than thirty miles if clouds help to
reflect the flash.

Within a minute, the familiar shape of the mushroom cloud 14
began to form over Chicago, symmetrical and strikingly beautiful in
various shades of red and reddish brown. The color was provided by
some eighty tons of nitric and nitrous oxides synthesized in the high
temperatures and nuclear radiations. In time, these compounds
would be borne aloft to reduce the ozone in the upper atmosphere.

The mushroom cloud expanded for ten or fifteen minutes, 15
reaching a mature height of twenty to twenty-five miles and extending seventy to eighty miles across the sky.

To a distance of five miles from Ground Zero — to affluent 16
Evanston on the north, well past working-class Cicero on the west,

beyond the University of Chicago campus on the south, there was —
nothing. A few seconds after the bomb went off, the fireball appeared, brighter than 5,000 suns. Those who saw the sudden flash of
blinding light experienced instant and painless death from the extreme heat long before the noise and shock wave reached them.

Glass melted. Concrete surfaces disintegrated under thermal 17
stress. Anything combustible exploded into raging flames. Even reinforced, blast-resistant structures collapsed, along with highway spans
and bridges.

The blast wave arrived about fifteen seconds later, buffeting the 18
few man-made remnants that had not been pulverized. With the
shock came torrid wind, traveling at some 300 miles an hour, carrying
dust and embers and fragments, blowing down vents and tunnels to
suffocate the few surviving human beings who had been sheltered
below ground level.

After about ten seconds, the wind reversed direction, drawn back 19
toward Ground Zero.

The enormously high temperatures from the fireball of a nuclear weapon 20
generate enough light and heat to ignite simultaneous fires over huge areas. In
these areas the heated air forms a rising column, resembling on a vast scale the
air-flow in a fireplace. Cool air drifts into the fire zone to replace the rising hot
air. As the fires gain strength, burning hotter and more violently, the chimney
effect intensifies, sucking in more air and causing the fire to burn hotter still.

About twenty minutes after the atomic bomb attack on Hiroshima, a mild 21
wind began to blow from all directions toward the center of the city. Within two
or three hours, the wind developed a speed of thirty to forty miles per hour and
air temperatures rose steadily toward 2,000 degrees Fahrenheit as fires burned
out of control for a distance of 1.2 miles from Ground Zero. The wind was
accompanied by light, radioactive rain over the center of the city, and heavier
rain around the periphery. It was a firestorm, and it destroyed about 2,800
acres.

A twenty-megaton bomb could, under similar conditions, generate a 22
firestorm that would devastate an area some 500 times larger.

On the freeways radiating from the Loop, automobiles, trucks, 23
and buses were simultaneously evaporated and blown away, their
particles sucked up into the fireball to become components of the
radioactive cloud.

Along the Stevenson Expressway, some seven or eight miles from 24
Ground Zero, scores of oil storage tanks exploded — ruptured by the
shock wave and then ignited from the grass and shrubbery burning
around them.

At this range, too, aluminum siding on homes evaporated and 25
some concrete surfaces exploded under thermal stress. The few
buildings still standing were in danger of imminent collapse — and all

were engulfed by flames. Highway spans caved in. Asphalt blistered and melted.

Clothing caught fire, and people were charred by intense light 26 and heat. Their charcoal limbs would, in some instances, render their shapes recognizably human.

With greater distance from Ground Zero, the effects diminished. 27 About ten miles from the Loop, in the area around the Brookfield Zoo, the fireball was merely brighter than a thousand suns. Glass did not melt, but shattered window fragments flew through the air at about 135 miles per hour. All trees were burning even before the shock wave uprooted most of them.

Railroad bridges collapsed, and railroad cars were blown from 28 their tracks. Automobiles were smashed and twisted into grotesque shapes. One- and two-story wood frame homes, already burning, were demolished by the shock wave, which also knocked down cinderblock walls and brick apartment buildings.

Those who had taken shelter underground — or, more proba- 29 bly, just happened to be there — survived for fifteen minutes or a half hour longer than those who were exposed. They suffocated as oxygen was drawn away by the firestorm that soon raged overhead.

At O'Hare Airport, the world's busiest, aircraft engaged in land- 30 ing or takeoff crashed and burned. Planes on the ground were buffeted into each other and adjacent hangars, their fuselages bent and partially crushed by the shock wave. Some thirty seconds before the shock wave struck, aluminum surfaces facing the fireball had melted and the aircraft interiors had been set aflame.

The enormous temperatures associated with all nuclear weapons, regard- 31 *less of yield, result from fission — the process in which certain atomic nuclei become unstable and disintegrate. (Even a fusion bomb like the one here described gains about half its energy from fission.) As the nuclei break up and form new atoms, they yield neutrons and immense amounts of energy. The atoms created by fission are so radioactive that if one could collect two ounces of them one minute after their creation, they would match the activity of 30,000 tons of radium and its decay products.*

When a twenty-megaton nuclear bomb goes off, it produces more than 32 *half a ton of this material. One minute after detonation, it is as radioactive as thirty million tons of radium. Though this radioactivity declines within one day by a factor of 3,000, the material still has the radioactivity of 10,000 tons of radium.*

If one could instantly remove the entire fission inventory from the largest 33 *commercial nuclear power plant (3,000 megawatts thermal) and simultaneously detonate a twenty-megaton nuclear bomb, thirty minutes after the "experiment," the activity from the bomb would be about 100,000 times greater than the activity contained in the reactor's fission inventory.*

The astronomically hot fireball indiscriminately incorporates all those 34
materials into a super-heated gas and mixes them with millions of tons of earth
and target debris. The mixture condenses into droplets of liquid and then
solidifies into particles ranging in diameter from one-thousandth to one-fiftieth
of an inch. The particles incorporate all of the extremely dangerous radiologi-
cal residues, and are borne aloft to deliver death hundreds of miles from the
target.

In addition, many neutrons escape the exploding weapon to be absorbed by 35
the earth and air in the immediate blast area. This leads to the production of a
wide variety of neutron-activated radioactive isotopes of such elements as
sodium, chlorine, manganese, zinc, copper, and silicon, as well as radioactive
carbon transmuted from nitrogen in the air.

All of these substances, dangerous to varying extents, remain active in the 36
blast area to jeopardize survivors and would-be rescuers.

In the pleasant western suburb of Hinsdale, some sixteen miles 37
from the Loop, the manicured lawns surrounded by wooden picket
fences on tree-shaded Chicago Avenue caught fire first. Leaves in the
trees ignited next, and then the picket fences themselves. Paint evaporated off house exteriors. Children on bicycles screamed as they were
blinded by the flash of the fireball. An instant later, their skin was
charred. Autos collided as their tires and upholstery burst into flame.

The white wooden cupola on the brick village hall blazed, and 38
even the all-stone Unitarian Church on Maple Street was burning —
ignited by the curtains on the windows facing east.

The shock wave arrived some fifty seconds later, tearing the roofs 39
off houses, blowing in side panels, spreading burning debris.

At about the same distance north of the city, Ravinia Park's 40
summer festival was to have featured an all-Mozart program that
Friday evening. There would be no Mozart and no Ravinia Park. By
11:30 A.M., that agreeably green place was a burning wasteland.

About twenty-one miles southwest of the Loop, the Argonne 41
National Laboratory sprawls on some 1,700 acres of park land. Its
5,000 employees had engaged in a broad variety of research efforts,
many of them centered on the development of nuclear power.
Argonne and its predecessor, the Metallurgical Laboratory of the
University of Chicago, were instrumental in developing the atomic
bomb.

Argonne researchers who happened to be looking out a window 42
on that Friday morning — gazing, perhaps, toward the Sears Tower
barely visible on the skyline to the northeast — suddenly saw a flash
that filled the sky with the brightness (from their vantage point) of
fifty to eighty suns. They were blinded, their clothing was ignited on
their bodies, and exposed skin areas suffered extremely severe third-
degree burns.

Here, too, leaves and grass and many readily combustible mate- 43
rials caught fire at once. The shock wave, which arrived a minute-and-
a-half later, caused only minimal damage, except as it spread burning
debris. But the fires soon raged out of control, for here, as for many
miles around, there was neither power nor water pressure nor emergency equipment nor any human will but the impulse to surrender to
the hysteria of total disaster.

And soon after all this happened, the radioactive cloud, carried 44
by the prevailing winds, began drifting toward the east at about
twenty miles per hour.

By the time the mushroom cloud has completed its fifteen-minute process of 45
stabilization, it is directly overhead for distances up to forty miles from Ground
Zero. Fires are still burning as radioactive particles begin settling on the
landscape. The radiation level rises rapidly to exceed 4,000 to 5,000 roentgens
per hour, delivering a lethal dose within seven to eight minutes. Individuals
driven out of doors by fire are directly exposed.

Within an hour or so, elements of the cloud begin to arrive about forty 46
miles downwind. The density and activity of the particles is such that a belt four
to five miles wide quickly develops radiation levels of more than 3,000 roent-
gens per hour. By this point, activity is diminishing, so that it requires an
exposure of ten to twenty minutes to absorb a deadly dose. Within a larger belt,
up to ten miles wide, fewer particles are falling, allowing up to a half hour's
exposure before a fatal dosage is absorbed.

As the cloud moves downwind, expanding and dropping particles, the 47
fallout level becomes unpredictable, though it remains, in many places, ex-
tremely high.

No one knows how many Americans might die from blast and fire and 48
radiation sickness in a nuclear attack. Casualty projections are a matter of
heated controversy within the Government and outside it. A reasonable conjec-
ture is that an all-out nuclear attack might claim 160 million lives — about
three quarters of the population. In a particularly strategic concentrated
metropolitan area subject to a direct strike — Chicago, for example — virtu-
ally the entire population could be expected to perish.

But American casualties would, of course, not be the only ones. No matter 49
how it happened or whose fault it was, there would be counterstrike, and the
indiscriminate murder of one nation's citizens — ours or theirs — would be
avenged by the indiscriminate murder of the other's.

Moving slowly to the east, Chicago's radioactive cloud brushed 50
Indiana and was blown into Michigan, dropping silent death along
the way, drifting inexorably toward Detroit. But it didn't matter, for
at a few seconds before 11:27 that Friday morning, a twenty-megaton
bomb had exploded in Detroit, too.

Review Questions

1. What is the sequence of devastation in a nuclear explosion? How do the factors of time and distance affect the devastation?
2. What is the difference in effect between a nuclear weapon detonated at ground level and one detonated in the atmosphere?
3. In what manner do the living things and the structures destroyed by the nuclear blast make its effects even more deadly?

Discussion Questions

1. What is gained from the postulation of Chicago (and particular parts of the city) as the site of the nuclear explosion — instead of some hypothetical city or a foreign city such as Moscow?
2. If the effects of nuclear weapons are known to be so devastating, then why haven't sane, rational people taken steps to do away with such weapons? What obstacles lie in the way?
3. Do you consider articles like this sensationalistic? What justification is there for the publication of such ghastly speculations?
4. What is the relationship between the italicized material and the rest of the text? Why do you think the authors chose to present their material in this unusual way?
5. What is the purpose of the opening details: "It was a sunny summer morning . . . office workers heading out to an early lunch. It was Friday"? What does this have to do with the subject of the article?
6. What is the significance of the single-sentence paragraph: "Three seconds had elapsed since the bomb went off"?
7. Knoll and Postol state: "The U.S. does not admit to deploying any twenty-megaton bombs in its nuclear arsenal." Does this mean that the U.S. has no twenty-megaton bombs?
8. Knoll and Postol employ a number of sentence fragments (for example, there are two in the first paragraph). Why should they be allowed to get away with this severe infraction of sentence structure, when students are marked down for the same offense?

Writing Suggestions

1. Reduce this article to a brief one- or two-page memo, outlining the effects of a nuclear explosion of such power in any large city.
2. Notice the casual, almost offhand way the authors report that the catastrophe strikes: "At 11:27, a twenty-megaton nuclear bomb exploded a few feet above street level at the corner of LaSalle and Adams." What is the effect of this offhand manner? Write a more dramatic description of the strike, and then compare the results.

PUTTING YOUR MONEY
WHERE YOUR MIGHT IS

Art Buchwald

Art Buchwald is quite simply one of the funniest men in the country and, as a voice of sanity, one of the most indispensable. His columns, syndicated in hundreds of newspapers throughout the world, skewer official and unofficial pomposity, revealing the vanity and self-protectiveness beneath. Born in Mt. Vernon, N.Y., in 1925, Buchwald attended the University of Southern California, served as a sergeant in the Marine Corps during World War II and as a newspaper correspondent in Paris after the war. His columns have been collected into numerous books, including *I Chose Capital Punishment, Son of the Great Society, I Never Danced at the White House, I Am Not a Crook,* and *The Buchwald Stops Here.*

☐

There is entirely too much talk lately about nuclear war. First we had 1
Secretary of State Alexander Haig testify in front of a Senate committee that there were worse things in this world than nuclear war. Then we had Secretary of Defense Caspar Weinberger pushing for a neutron bomb. Everyone suddenly seems to be thinking the unthinkable.

My friend Alabaster, who is getting nervous about all this nuclear 2
saber-rattling, has a theory as to what is causing it.

"The problem is that for thirty-five years our measuring stick for 3
atomic holocaust has been Hiroshima and Nagasaki.

"Every time someone wants to make an atomic weapon compari- 4
son he says: 'This warhead packs 1,000 times the wallop of the bomb dropped on Hiroshima.' Or 'This artillery shell will give you thirty times more punch than what we did to Nagasaki.'

"These stats don't have relevance anymore. Hiroshima and Na- 5
gasaki are part of ancient history and have no meaning for the people running the world today. We have to come up with a new yardstick to give them some idea of what atomic weapons can do."

"What do you suggest?" I asked him. 6

"I have a modest proposal," Alabaster said. "We need two new 7
examples to demonstrate how awesome nuclear war is, so it will sober up politicians, military men and statesmen, not only here but in the Soviet Union."

"All right," I agreed. "What do you have in mind?" 8

"We should permit the United States and the U.S.S.R. to fire off 9

The Washington Post, February 15, 1981. Reprinted with the permission of Art Buchwald, Los Angeles Times Syndicate.

their largest nuclear weapon at just one Soviet and one U.S. city, to prove how powerful the weaons really are."

"Why not?" I said.   10

"Moscow and Washington would be off limits because we don't   11
want to eliminate the leaders of both countries, or the lesson would be
lost on them," he continued. "We must select two beautiful cities that
have tremendous sentimental meaning for the people of the respective countries. I would suggest the U.S. 'nuke' Leningrad, and the
U.S.S.R. 'nuke' San Francisco."

"Why Leningrad?" I asked.   12

"It is without a doubt the loveliest city in the Soviet Union, with   13
magnificent palaces, irreplaceable architecture, and one of the great
museums of the world."

"Why San Francisco?"   14

"Everyone loves San Francisco. One easily can leave his heart   15
there."

"What will it prove?" I asked.   16

"When the Russians see the devastation one American weapon   17
has done to its beloved Leningrad they will realize that the United
States is not stockpiling Tinker Toys.

"And in turn the Americans who have been discussing nuclear   18
war as some kind of military Super Bowl will have second thoughts
about solving its foreign problems with atomic weapons. With Leningrad and San Francisco 'nuked,' we won't need Hiroshima and Nagasaki anymore to point out the dangers of a new war.

"But my modest proposal has a second benefit. We and the   19
Soviets have spent a bundle on nuclear arms, and both sides deserve
to shoot off at least one in anger during our lifetime, if for no other
reason than to see firsthand that we got our money's worth."

Discussion Questions

1. What is Buchwald's point in this column? What does he gain by making this point humorously — or outrageously — rather than seriously?

2. Do you think Buchwald really has a friend named "Alabaster"? What is Alabaster's function in this piece?

3. Can you detect Buchwald's tone — the way he feels about the subject he is discussing? Characterize this tone. Where is it most evident?

Writing Suggestion

Buchwald (through "Alabaster") calls his suggestion a "modest proposal" — in the spirit of satirist Jonathan Swift's "Modest Proposal" (1729)
to alleviate the problem of starving children in Ireland by selling the children

to rich families, who would fatten them up, cook them, and eat them. Devise another "modest proposal" to solve some serious problem, using Buchwald's format. Or you may want to look up Swift's own "Modest Proposal" (which has been widely reprinted) and use his format and style ("It is a melancholy object to those who walk through this great town or travel in the country, when they see . . .").

THE WAR ROOM SCENE FROM
DR. STRANGELOVE
Stanley Kubrick, Terry Southern, and Peter George

In 1963 a new page in the history of black comedy was written with the release of *Dr. Strangelove: or How I Learned to Stop Worrying and Love the Bomb*. A SAC commander, General Jack D. Ripper, paranoid about a communist plot "to sap and impurify all of our precious bodily fluids," orders his bombers to make a preemptive first strike against the Soviet Union — certain that the president of the U.S., realizing that there is no way to recall the attack force, will unleash the rest of the American nuclear force to prevent a devastating retaliation. Unfortunately, the Soviets have planned for just such an eventuality. Though most of Ripper's bomber squadron is eventually recalled, one wounded B-52 gets through, drops its nuclear load, and thereby detonates the Soviet "doomsday machine," a series of buried nuclear bombs which, exploding, will enshroud the earth with a radioactive cloud for 99 years. So ends this "comedy."

Though recognized immediately by many as a masterpiece of Swiftian satire, *Dr. Strangelove* was also fiercely attacked as irresponsible and ghoulish. It appeared the same year as *Fail-Safe*, a serious treatment of the same subject; and many comparisons between the two films were drawn, some to the detriment of *Dr. Strangelove*. Since then, *Fail-Safe* has sunk into relative oblivion, while *Dr. Strangelove* has become a film classic.

Stanley Kubrick, the director and primary author, was born in New York in 1928. Beginning his career as a photographer for *Look* magazine, he went on to direct such films (in addition to *Dr. Strangelove*) as *Paths of Glory, Lolita, 2001: A Space Odyssey, A Clockwork Orange, Barry Lyndon,* and *The Shining*. Terry Southern, born in 1924, is a writer of essays, short stories and satiric novels (*The Magic Christian, Candy*) and screenplays (*The Loved One, Easy Rider, Blue Movie*). Peter George, a British author, wrote *Red Alert*, a serious novel upon whose essential storyline *Dr. Strangelove* is based. In the film, the president was played by Peter Sellers; the general by George C. Scott.

☐

PRESIDENT MERKIN MUFFLEY: Now, General Turgidson, what's going on here?

GENERAL BUCK TURGIDSON: About thirty-five minutes ago, General Jack Ripper, the Commanding Office at Burpelson Air Force Base issued an order to the thirty-four B-52s of his Wing which were airborne at the time as part of a special exercise we were holding called Operation Dropkick. Now it appears that the order called for the planes to — er — attack their targets inside Russia.

[*all react with consternation*]

The planes were fully armed with nuclear weapons with an average load of forty megatons each. Now, the central display of Russia will indicate the positions of the planes. The triangles are their primary targets; the squares are their secondary targets. The aircraft will begin penetrating Russian radar cover within — er — twenty-five minutes.

PRESIDENT: General Turgidson, I find this very difficult to understand. I was under the impression that I was the only one in authority to order the use of nuclear weapons.

GENERAL TURGIDSON: That's right, sir. You are the only person authorized to do so. And although I hate to judge before all the facts are in, it's beginning to look like General Ripper exceeded his authority.

PRESIDENT: It certainly does — far beyond the point I would have imagined possible.

TURGIDSON: Well, perhaps you're forgetting the provisions of Plan R, sir.

PRESIDENT: Plan R?

TURGIDSON: Plan R is an emergency war plan in which a lower-echelon commander may order nuclear retaliation after a sneak attack *if* the normal chain of command has been disrupted. You — er — approved it, sir; you must remember. [*Muffley looks blank*] Surely, you must recall, sir, when Senator Buford made that big hassle about our deterrent lacking credibility? The idea was for Plan R to be a sort of — er — retaliatory safeguard.

PRESIDENT: A safeguard?

TURGIDSON: Well, I admit the human element seems to have failed us here; but the *idea* was to discourage the Russians from any hope that they could knock out Washington and yourself, sir, as part of a general sneak attack, and escape retaliation because of lack of proper command and control.

PRESIDENT: Well, I assume, then, that the planes will return automatically once they reach their fail-safe points.

TURGIDSON: Er — no, sir, I'm afraid not; you see, the planes *were* holding at their fail-safe points when the Go-Code was issued. Now, once they fly beyond fail-safe, they — er — they do not require a second order to proceed; they will continue until they reach their targets.

PRESIDENT: Then, why haven't you radioed the planes, countermanding the Go-Code?

TURGIDSON: [*Dejectedly*] Well, I'm afraid we're unable to communicate with any of the aircraft.

PRESIDENT: Why?

TURGIDSON: You may recall, sir [*Clears throat*]: one of the provisions of Plan R provides that once the — er — Go-Code is received, the normal SSB radios in the aircraft are switched into a special coded device which I believe is designated as CRM-114. Now, in order to prevent the enemy from issuing fake or confusing orders, CRM-114 is designed not to receive at all — unless the message is preceded by the correct three-letter code-group prefix.

PRESIDENT: Then, do you mean to tell me, General Turgidson, that you will be unable to recall the aircraft?

TURGIDSON: That's about the size of it, sir. However, we are plowing through every possible three-letter combination of the code. But since there are — er — seventeen thousand permutations, ahm . . . [*Very quickly*] it's going to take us about two-and-a-half days to transmit them all. [*Clears throat*]

PRESIDENT: How soon did you say that the planes will penetrate Russian radar cover?

TURGIDSON: [*Briskly*] About eighteen minutes from now, sir.

PRESIDENT: Are you in contact with General Ripper?

TURGIDSON: Er — no, sir, no — er — General Ripper sealed off the base and cut off all communications.

PRESIDENT: Where did you get all this information?

TURGIDSON: General Ripper called Strategic Air Command Headquarters shortly after he issued the Go-Code. I have a portion of the transcript of that conversation if you'd like me to read it.

PRESIDENT: Read it.

TURGIDSON: [*Clears throat*] The duty officer asked General Ripper to confirm the fact that he had issued the Go-Code; and he said: "Yes, Gentlemen, they are on their way in, and no one can bring them back. For the sake of our country and our way of life, I suggest you get the rest of SAC in after them. Otherwise, we will be totally destroyed by Red retaliation. My boys will give you the best kind of start — fourteen hundred megatons worth; and you sure as hell won't stop them now. So let's get going; there's no other choice. God willing, we will prevail in peace and freedom from fear and in true health through the purity . . . and essence . . . of our natural . . . fluids. God bless you all." Then he hung up. [*Pause*] We're . . . we're still trying to figure out the meaning of that last phrase, sir.

PRESIDENT: There's nothing to figure out, General Turgidson. This man is obviously a psychotic.

TURGIDSON: Well, I'd like to hold off judgment on a thing like *that*, sir, until all the facts are in.

PRESIDENT: General Turgidson: when you instituted the human reliability tests, you assured me there was no possibility of such a thing ever occurring.

TURGIDSON: [*Offended*] Well, I — er — don't think it's quite fair to condemn a whole program because of a single slip-up, sir.

PRESIDENT: I want to speak to General Ripper on the telephone, personally.

TURGIDSON: I'm afraid that's impossible sir.

PRESIDENT: General Turgidson, I am becoming less and less interested in your estimates of what is possible and impossible. [*Turgidson angrily takes out a stick of gum and pops it in his mouth*] General Faceman?

GENERAL FACEMAN: Yes, sir?

PRESIDENT: Are there any army units stationed anywhere near Burpelson?

FACEMAN: I'll — er — I'll just check, sir. [*He checks. Turgidson's inset phone buzzes. Turgidson picks up the receiver.*]

TURGIDSON: Hello . . . [*Frantically*] I told you never to call me here; don't you know where I am? . . . Now, look, baby, I can't talk to you now . . . my president needs me . . . of course, the president's . . . [*Faceman continues consulting with his aides*] . . . Of course, it isn't only physical . . . I deeply respect you as a human being. Some day I'm gonna make you Mrs. Buck Turgidson. . . . Allright, listen . . . I'll . . . you go back to sleep . . . I'm . . .

Bucky'll be back there just as soon as he can . . . all right . . . sure. . . . Don't forget to say your prayers. . . . [*Hangs up; looks apprehensively to see if anyone has been watching*]

FACEMAN: Apparently, the 23rd Airborne Division is stationed seven miles away at Alvoredo.

PRESIDENT: General Faceman, I want them to enter the base, locate General Ripper, and put him in immediate telephone contact with me.

FACEMAN: Yes, sir.

TURGIDSON: Mr. President, if I may advise: under Condition Red it is standard procedure that the base be sealed off and the base defended by base security troops. Any force trying to enter there would certainly encounter very heavy casualties.

FACEMAN: General Turgidson, with all due respect for your — er — defense team, my boys will brush 'em aside without too much trouble.

TURGIDSON: [*Stiffening; with icy deliberation*] Mr. President, there are one or two points I'd like to make, if I may.

PRESIDENT: [*Coldly*] Go ahead, General.

TURGIDSON: One: our hopes of recalling the 843rd Bomb Wing are quickly being reduced to a very low order of probability.

Two: In less than fifteen minutes from now the Russkies will be making radar contact with the planes.

Three: When they do, they are going to go absolutely *ape;* and they're going to strike back with everything they've got.

Four: If, prior to this time, we have done nothing further to suppress their retaliatory capability, we will suffer virtual annihilation. Now . . . [*He arches his eyebrows and grins*]

Five: If, on the other hand, we were to immediately launch an all-out and coordinated attack on all their airfields and missile bases [*His voice drops to a loud, excited whisper*] we'd stand a damn good chance of catching them with their pants down. Hell, we've got a five-to-one missile superiority as it is. We could easily assign three missiles to every target and still have a very effective reserve force for any other contingencies. Now . . .

Six: [*He opens his loose-leaf folder and points to it, proudly*] An unofficial study which we undertook of *this* eventuality indicated that we would destroy 90% of their nuclear capability. We would, therefore, prevail, and suffer only modest and *acceptable* civilian casualties from their remaining force, which would be badly damaged and uncoordinated. [*Looks at the president, beaming with pleasure*]

PRESIDENT: General, it is the avowed policy of our country never to strike first with nuclear weapons.

TURGIDSON: Well, Mr. President, I would . . . I would say that General Ripper has already invalidated *that* policy.

PRESIDENT: That was not an act of national policy and there are still alternatives left open to us.

TURGIDSON: Mr. President, we are rapidly approaching a moment of truth, both for ourselves as human beings and for the life of our nation. Now truth is not always a pleasant thing. But it is necessary now to make a choice: to choose between two admittedly regrettable, but nevertheless *distinguishable* postwar environments: one, where you got twenty million people killed, and the other, where you got a hundred and fifty million people killed.

PRESIDENT: You're talking about mass murder, General. Not war.

TURGIDSON: Mr. President, I'm not saying we wouldn't get our hair mussed. But I do say no more than ten to twenty million killed — tops! Er — depending on the breaks.[1]

PRESIDENT: I will not go down in history as the greatest mass murderer since Adolf Hitler.

TURGIDSON: [*Furious*] Perhaps it might be better, Mr. President, if you were more concerned with the American people than with your image in the history books.

PRESIDENT: General Turgidson, I think I've heard quite sufficient from you, thank you very much!

---

[1] Those who believe that speeches like this are too absurd even for satire might consider the following passage from a recent article in the respected journal, *Foreign Policy:*

> Strategists cannot offer painless conflicts or guarantee that their preferred posture and doctrine promise a greatly superior deterrence posture to current American schemes. But, they can claim that an intelligent U.S. offensive strategy, wedded to homeland defenses, should reduce U.S. casualties to approximately 20 million . . . The actual number would depend on several factors. . . .
> Colin Gray and Keith Payne, excerpted from "Victory Is Possible," *Foreign Policy* magazine, no. 39 (summer 1980), p. 25.

And in May 1981 columnist Jack Anderson noted that:

> . . . administration hawks are bringing pressure to exploit the full military potential of the space shuttle. Intelligence analysts say that within three years the Pentagon could ferry enough weapons into space on the shuttle to give the United States an "overwhelming" strategic advantage. What they mean by this, according to a recent Defense Intelligence Agency analysis, is that we could annihilate the Soviet Union while suffering "acceptable" losses of 40 percent of our industry and 20 percent of the population, or 40 million casualties.
> Jack Anderson, *The Washington Post* May 20, 1981, © 1981 United Feature Syndicate, Inc. By permission.

Review Questions

1. What brought about this crisis?
2. What are the key provisions of Plan R? Why was Plan R approved? How was it approved?
3. What are Turgidson's arguments for following up Ripper's attack? How does the president respond?

Discussion Questions

1. General Turgidson, although the object of Kubrick's biting satire, is clearly not a stupid man. On the contrary, he appears to be a highly organized, efficient thinker. What qualities of his are being satirized? Does he represent the military mind? Or something broader?
2. Why does President Muffley seem so ineffectual? Is Kubrick satirizing the ineffectiveness of civilian controls?
3. What is Turgidson's attitude toward nuclear war? To what extent does he seem conscious of, or worried about, the imminent catastrophe?
4. Is this a "funny" scene? If so, what is the source of the humor? When this film was first released, many people thought that it was inappropriate to treat the subject of nuclear war in a comic way. Do you feel the same way? Why or why not?
5. Although *Dr. Strangelove* was a comedy — a black comedy, to be sure — its ironies were frequently so subtle that many people missed them. Indeed, many people listened to characters like General Ripper and General Turgidson in respectful silence. For instance, consider Turgidson's six-point plan for following up Ripper's first strike before the inevitable counterattack, or his presenting the president with the necessity "to make a choice: to choose between two admittedly regrettable, but nevertheless *distinguishable* postwar environments . . ." Are these plans entirely unrealistic? Should these arguments for preventing the deaths of millions of Americans be taken at all seriously, or are they too horrible to even contemplate? What is the source of the humor (if humor exists here)?
6. What is the significance of the funny names (General Jack D. Ripper, General Turgidson, Dr. Strangelove, etc.)?
7. Responding to the president, Turgidson admits that "the human element seems to have failed us here," and that it's not "quite fair to condemn a whole program because of a single slip-up." What is the point of these comic references to human fallibility?
8. Why does Kubrick have Turgidson's girlfriend call him in the middle of this sequence? Is this totally out of place, or is there some significance to the call and Turgidson's response?

9. This film was preceded by a disclaimer to the effect that the U.S. Air Force categorically denied that the events depicted in *Dr. Strangelove* (and particularly the unleashing of a nuclear bomber force and the inability of the command center to recall it) could happen. If this is indeed the case, then how is the validity of this scene affected?

Writing Suggestions

1. Assume that you are a film reviewer and that *Dr. Strangelove* has just been released. Write a review based on this sequence (or on the film as a whole if you have seen it).

2. What is Kubrick *saying* in this sequence? Isolate the main ideas he is concerned with, and write an analysis to show how he illustrates and develops them. Include a thesis sentence in your introduction, and begin each subsequent paragraph with a topic sentence.

WHO SPEAKS FOR EARTH?
Carl Sagan

Carl Sagan (b. 1934) is an astronomer of multiple accomplishments. Educated at the University of Chicago, and now teaching at Cornell, he has been a visiting professor and lecturer at many other colleges and universities. He has served as an advisor to NASA and the National Academy of Sciences, as a lecturer to Apollo flight crews, and as chairman of the U.S. delegation of the U.S. National and Soviet Academies of Science on Communication with Extraterrestrial Intelligence. Among his numerous books are *Intelligent Life in the Universe, The Cosmic Connection,* and the Pulitzer Prize-winning *Dragons of Eden.* This selection is from the final chapter of *Cosmos,* a companion volume to his acclaimed television series.

The Cosmos was discovered only yesterday. For a million years it was clear to everyone that there were no other places than the Earth. Then in the last tenth of a percent of the lifetime of our species, in the instant between Aristarchus and ourselves, we reluctantly noticed that we were not the center and purpose of the Universe, but rather lived on a tiny and fragile world lost in immensity and eternity, drifting in a great cosmic ocean dotted here and there with a hundred billion galaxies and a billion trillion stars. We have bravely tested the waters

1

From *Cosmos* by Carl Sagan. Copyright © 1980 by Carl Sagan. Reprinted by permission of Random House, Inc.

and have found the ocean to our liking, resonant with our nature. Something in us recognizes the Cosmos as home. We are made of stellar ash. Our origin and evolution have been tied to distant cosmic events. The exploration of the Cosmos is a voyage of self-discovery.

As the ancient mythmakers knew, we are the children equally of 2 the sky and the Earth. In our tenure on this planet we have accumulated dangerous evolutionary baggage, hereditary propensities for aggression and ritual, submission to leaders and hostility to outsiders, which place our survival in some question. But we have also acquired compassion for others, love for our children and our children's children, a desire to learn from history, and a great soaring passionate intelligence — the clear tools for our continued survival and prosperity. Which aspects of our nature will prevail is uncertain, particularly when our vision and understanding and prospects are bound exclusively to the Earth — or, worse, to one small part of it. But up there in the immensity of the Cosmos, an inescapable perspective awaits us. There are not yet any obvious signs of extraterrestrial intelligence and this makes us wonder whether civilizations like ours always rush implacably, headlong, toward self-destruction. National boundaries are not evident when we view the Earth from space. Fanatical ethnic or religious or national chauvinisms are a little difficult to maintain when we see our planet as a fragile blue crescent fading to become an inconspicuous point of light against the bastion and citadel of the stars. Travel is broadening.

There are worlds on which life has never arisen. There are worlds 3 that have been charred and ruined by cosmic catastrophes. We are fortunate: we are alive; we are powerful; the welfare of our civilization and our species is in our hands. If we do not speak for Earth, who will? If we are not committed to our own survival, who will be?

The human species is now undertaking a great venture that if 4 successful will be as important as the colonization of the land or the descent from the trees. We are haltingly, tentatively breaking the shackles of Earth — metaphorically, in confronting and taming the admonitions of those more primitive brains within us; physically, in voyaging to the planets and listening for the messages from the stars. These two enterprises are linked indissolubly. Each, I believe, is a necessary condition for the other. But our energies are directed far more toward war. Hypnotized by mutual mistrust, almost never concerned for the species or the planet, the nations prepare for death. And because what we are doing is so horrifying, we tend not to think of it much. But what we do not consider we are unlikely to put right.

Every thinking person fears nuclear war, and every technological 5 state plans for it. Everyone knows it is madness, and every nation has an excuse. There is a dreary chain of causality: The Germans were working on the bomb at the beginning of World War II; so the

Americans had to make one first. If the Americans had one, the Soviets had to have one, and then the British, the French, the Chinese, the Indians, the Pakistanis. . . . By the end of the twentieth century many nations had collected nuclear weapons. They were easy to devise. Fissionable material could be stolen from nuclear reactors. Nuclear weapons became almost a home handicraft industry.

The conventional bombs of World War II were called block-busters. Filled with twenty tons of TNT, they could destroy a city block. All the bombs dropped on all the cities in World War II amounted to some two million tons, two megatons, of TNT — Coventry and Rotterdam, Dresden and Tokyo, all the death that rained from the skies between 1939 and 1945: a hundred thousand block-busters, two megatons. By the late twentieth century, two megatons was the energy released in the explosion of a single more or less humdrum thermonuclear bomb: one bomb with the destructive force of the Second World War. But there are tens of thousands of nuclear weapons. By the ninth decade of the twentieth century the strategic missile and bomber forces of the Soviet Union and the United States were aiming warheads at over 15,000 designated targets. No place on the planet was safe. The energy contained in these weapons, genies of death patiently awaiting the rubbing of the lamps, was far more than 10,000 megatons — but with the destruction concentrated efficiently, not over six years but over a few hours, a blockbuster for every family on the planet, a World War II every second for the length of a lazy afternoon. 6

The immediate causes of death from nuclear attack are the blast wave, which can flatten heavily reinforced buildings many kilometers away, the firestorm, the gamma rays and the neutrons, which effectively fry the insides of passersby. A school girl who survived the American nuclear attack on Hiroshima, the event that ended the Second World War, wrote this first-hand account: 7

> Through a darkness like the bottom of hell, I could hear the voices of the other students calling for their mothers. And at the base of the bridge, inside a big cistern that had been dug out there, was a mother weeping, holding above her head a naked baby that was burned bright red all over its body. And another mother was crying and sobbing as she gave her burned breast to her baby. In the cistern the students stood with only their heads above the water, and their two hands, which they clasped as they imploringly cried and screamed, calling for their parents. But every single person who passed was wounded, all of them, and there was no one, there was no one to turn to for help. And the singed hair on the heads of the people was frizzled and whitish and covered with dust. They did not appear to be human, not creatures of this world.

The Hiroshima explosion, unlike the subsequent Nagasaki explosion, was an air burst high above the surface, so the fallout was 8 insignificant. But on March 1, 1954, a thermonuclear weapons test at Bikini in the Marshall Islands detonated at higher yield than expected. A great radioactive cloud was deposited on the tiny atoll of Rongalap, 150 kilometers away, where the inhabitants likened the explosion to the Sun rising in the West. A few hours later, radioactive ash fell on Rongalap like snow. The average dose received was only about 175 rads, a little less than half the dose needed to kill an average person. Being far from the explosion, not many people died. Of course, the radioactive strontium they ate was concentrated in their bones, and the radioactive iodine was concentrated in their thyroids. Two-thirds of the children and one-third of the adults later developed thyroid abnormalities, growth retardation or malignant tumors. In compensation, the Marshall Islanders received expert medical care.

The yield of the Hiroshima bomb was only thirteen kilotons, the   9
equivalent of thirteen thousand tons of TNT. The Bikini test yield was fifteen megatons. In a full nuclear exchange, in the paroxysm of thermonuclear war, the equivalent of a million Hiroshima bombs would be dropped all over the world. At the Hiroshima death rate of some hundred thousand people killed per equivalent thirteen-kiloton weapon, this would be enough to kill a hundred billion people. But there were less than five billion people on the planet in the late twentieth century. Of course, in such an exchange, not everyone would be killed by the blast and the firestorm, the radiation and the fallout — although fallout does last for a longish time: 90 percent of the strontium 90 will decay in *96 years;* 90 percent of the cesium 137, in *100 years;* 90 percent of the iodine 131 in *only a month.*

The survivors would witness more subtle consequences of the   10
war. A full nuclear exchange would burn the nitrogen in the upper air, converting it to oxides of nitrogen, which would in turn destroy a significant amount of the ozone in the high atmosphere, admitting an intense dose of solar ultraviolet radiation.[1] The increased ultraviolet flux would last for years. It would produce skin cancer preferentially in light-skinned people. Much more important, it would affect the ecology of our planet in an unknown way. Ultraviolet light destroys crops. Many microorganisms would be killed; we do not know which ones or how many, or what the consequences might be. The organisms killed might, for all we know, be at the base of a vast ecological pyramid at the top of which totter we.

----

[1] The process is similar to, but much more dangerous than, the destruction of the ozone layer by the fluorocarbon propellants in aerosol spray cans, which have accordingly been banned by a number of nations; and to that invoked in the explanation of the extinction of the dinosaurs by a supernova explosion a few dozen light-years away.

The dust put into the air in a full nuclear exchange would reflect   11
sunlight and cool the Earth a little. Even a little cooling can have
disastrous agricultural consequences. Birds are more easily killed by
radiation than insects. Plagues of insects and consequent further
agricultural disorders are a likely consequence of nuclear war. There
is also another kind of plague to worry about: the [bubonic] plague
bacillus is endemic all over the Earth. In the late twentieth century
humans did not much die of plague — not because it was absent, but
because resistance was high. However, the radiation produced in a
nuclear war, among its many other effects, debilitates the body's
immunological system, causing a deterioration of our ability to resist
disease. In the longer term, there are mutations, new varieties of
microbes and insects, that might cause still further problems for any
human survivors of a nuclear holocaust; and perhaps after a while,
when there has been enough time for the recessive mutations to
recombine and be expressed, new and horrifying varieties of humans.
Most of these mutations, when expressed, would be lethal. A few
would not. And then there would be other agonies: the loss of loved
ones; the legions of the burned, the blind and the mutilated; disease,
plague, long-lived radioactive poisons in the air and water; the threat
of tumors and stillbirths and malformed children; the absence of
medical care; the hopeless sense of a civilization destroyed for nothing; the knowledge that we could have prevented it and did not. . . .

The global balance of terror, pioneered by the United States and   12
the Soviet Union, holds hostage the citizens of the Earth. Each side
draws limits on the permissible behavior of the other. The potential
enemy is assured that if the limit is transgressed, nuclear war will
follow. However, the definition of the limit changes from time to
time. Each side must be quite confident that the other understands
the new limits. Each side is tempted to increase its military advantage,
but not in so striking a way as seriously to alarm the other. Each side
continually explores the limits of the other's tolerance, as in flights of
nuclear bombers over the Arctic wastes; the Cuban missile crisis; the
testing of anti-satellite weapons; the Vietnam and Afghanistan
wars — a few entries from a long and dolorous list. The global balance of terror is a very delicate balance. It depends on things not
going wrong, on mistakes not being made, on the reptilian passions
not being seriously aroused. . . .

[T]he development of nuclear weapons and their delivery sys-   13
tems will, sooner or later, lead to global disaster. Many of the American and European émigré scientists who developed the first nuclear
weapons were profoundly distressed about the demon they had let
loose on the world. They pleaded for the global abolition of nuclear
weapons. But their pleas went unheeded; the prospect of a national

strategic advantage galvanized both the U.S.S.R. and the United States, and the nuclear arms race began.

In the same period, there was a burgeoning international trade in 14 the devastating non-nuclear weapons coyly called "conventional." In the past twenty-five years, in dollars corrected for inflation, the annual international arms trade has gone from $300 million to much more than $20 billion. In the years between 1950 and 1968, for which good statistics seem to be available, there were, on the average, worldwide several accidents involving nuclear weapons per year, although perhaps no more than one or two accidental nuclear explosions. The weapons establishments in the Soviet Union, the United States and other nations are large and powerful. In the United States they include major corporations famous for their homey domestic manufactures. According to one estimate, the corporate profits in military weapons procurement are 30 to 50 percent higher than in an equally technological but competitive civilian market. Cost overruns in military weapons systems are permitted on a scale that would be considered unacceptable in the civilian sphere. In the Soviet Union the resources, quality, attention and care given to military production is in striking contrast to the little left for consumer goods. According to some estimates, almost half the scientists and high technologists on Earth are employed full- or part-time on military matters. Those engaged in the development and manufacture of weapons of mass destruction are given salaries, perquisites of power and, where possible, public honors at the highest levels available in their respective societies. The secrecy of weapons development, carried to especially extravagant lengths in the Soviet Union, implies that individuals so employed need almost never accept responsibility for their actions. They are protected and anonymous. Military secrecy makes the military the most difficult sector of any society for the citizens to monitor. If we do not know what they do, it is very hard for us to stop them. And with the rewards so substantial, with the hostile military establishments beholden to each other in some ghastly mutual embrace, the world discovers itself drifting toward the ultimate undoing of the human enterprise.

Every major power has some widely publicized justification for its 15 procurement and stockpiling of weapons of mass destruction, often including a reptilian reminder of the presumed character and cultural defects of potential enemies (as opposed to us stout fellows), or of the intentions of others, but never ourselves, to conquer the world. Every nation seems to have its set of forbidden possibilities, which its citizenry and adherents must not at any cost be permitted to think seriously about. In the Soviet Union these include capitalism, God, and the surrender of national sovereignty; in the United States, socialism, atheism, and the surrender of national sovereignty. It is the same all over the world.

How would we explain the global arms race to a dispassionate extraterrestrial observer? How would we justify the most recent destabilizing developments of killer-satellites, particle beam weapons, lasers, neutron bombs, cruise missiles, and the proposed conversion of areas the size of modest countries to the enterprise of hiding each intercontinental ballistic missile among hundreds of decoys? Would we argue that ten thousand targeted nuclear warheads are likely to enhance the prospects for our survival? What account would we give of our stewardship of the planet Earth? We have heard the rationales offered by the nuclear superpowers. We know who speaks for the nations. But who speaks for the human species? Who speaks for Earth?

16

Review Questions

1. What is the "great venture" that the human species is now undertaking — a venture as important as colonizing the land or descending from the trees?

2. Why were some of the conventional bombs used in World War II called "blockbusters"?

3. What are some of the "more subtle consequences" of an atomic war that survivors would undergo?

4. In what ways does Sagan demonstrate that "money is no object" for any nation when it comes to spending for military hardware?

5. How do the U.S. and the Soviet Union justify their stockpiling of weapons of mass destruction, according to Sagan?

Discussion Questions

1. Why does Sagan say that the "exploration of the Cosmos is a voyage of self-discovery"?

2. What does Sagan mean by "fanatical ethnic or religious or national chauvinisms"? Do you agree with him as to the viciousness of these aspects of our humanity? Or are our ethnic differences (for instance) "beautiful"?

3. Sagan writes of "primitive brains" and later, "reptilian passions" within us. What does he mean? Do you recognize a primitive brain, reptilian passions in yourself? When? What kind of controls do you exert over them? What kind of controls can be exerted over a nation's primitive brain and reptilian passions?

4. Does Sagan draw a fair picture of the arms race? Of the justifications for the arms race? Is he being simplistic, even naive? Is he taking a very broad overview? Or both?

5. In what way is Sagan's perspective different from the perspectives of some of the other pieces in this unit — Kubrick's, for instance, or Knoll and Postol's? One of the ways you can detect perspective is to analyze your own feelings while you read the article. What kind of feeling about the subject does the author create in you?

6. Why does Sagan begin and end this discussion of nuclear war with a discussion of the cosmos and our place in it? In particular, what is the purpose of the second paragraph?

7. How does the "But . . ." halfway through the fourth paragraph signal a shift in Sagan's focus, a new direction for his line of thought?

8. Notice the two balanced sentences at the beginning of the fifth paragraph. How does the structure of these sentences reflect Sagan's larger meaning?

9. To what degree does Sagan use irony to point up the absurdities of the arms race and of our reptilian passions? Consider, for example, the final sentence of the second paragraph, "Travel is broadening." Cite other examples and show how the irony functions.

Writing Suggestions

1. Sagan asks rhetorically, "Who speaks for Earth?" Argue that he does — or does not.

2. Sagan writes that during our stay on earth, "we have accumulated dangerous evolutionary baggage, hereditary propensities for aggression and ritual, submission to leaders and hostility to outsiders, which place our survival in some question." If we somehow manage to do away with all of these things, including submission to leaders, then what kind of world would we have? How would we set it up? How would we operate it? Write a description of such a world.

3. Argue that Sagan is a humanist, in the best sense of the term.

4. Put yourself in the position of the "dispassionate extraterrestrial observer." What other kinds of questions would you have for the residents of the third planet from the local sun?

5. Imagine that you are one of the few survivors of a nuclear holocaust. You have the opportunity to write and to preserve a letter to some future race of humans capable of deciphering it, or to an extraterrestrial civilization. What do you write?

SUMMARY, SYNTHESIS, CRITIQUE ACTIVITIES

Summary

Summarize one or more of the passages in this chapter. Follow the suggested six-step process. Take into account the answers to the Review Questions for each passage. (Recommended: "Second Strike")

Synthesis

1. *Describe* the effects of a nuclear war — on people, on cities, on industry, on the social order. Suggested sources: "Second Strike," "The Day the Bomb Went Off," "Who Speaks for Earth?"
2. Discuss some of the ways a nuclear war might start, giving *examples* to support your statements. Suggested sources: "Second Strike," "The First Nuclear War," "The War Room Scene from *Dr. Strangelove*" (be careful handling this one, though).
3. Do assignment 2 above, but place the emphasis on *comparing and contrasting,* rather than on giving examples. For instance: how does the absurdity of *Dr. Strangelove* compare with the more credible scenarios for nuclear war in Boroson and Snyder's article?
4. Almost everyone agrees that a nuclear war would be madness, and many think that the political and military policies that could lead to nuclear war are also madness; but there is less agreement about what should be done to reduce the possibility of nuclear war. Some of the writers represented in this unit deal directly with this question; others deal with it indirectly, by implication. *Compare and contrast* some of the explicit and implicit ideas for reducing the threat of nuclear war.
5. *Argue* that the United States and the Soviet Union cannot afford *not* to come to an agreement to reduce the nuclear threat to humankind. Use as many of the sources as seem relevant, perhaps with special attention to Sagan.
6. *Argue* that there appears to be no way that humankind can escape nuclear devastation — because of the rate of nuclear proliferation and because of the persistence and domination of what Sagan calls our "reptilian passions." *Or* argue the validity of a more optimistic outlook.
7. *Argue* that the "balance of terror" — terrifying though it may be — must be maintained at all costs, for the clear superiority or inferiority of one side would be an irresistible invitation to a preemptive first strike. *Or* argue that humanity cannot afford the risks of a permanent balance of terror.

Critique

Write a critique of either "The War Room Scene from *Dr. Strangelove*" or "Who Speaks for Earth?" In either case, address yourself to the question of how seriously each piece comes to grips with the question of nuclear war, the assumptions each makes about human nature, and the effectiveness of each as a plea for sanity.

RESEARCH TOPICS

1. Write a paper on the reactions of people around the world to the beginning of the atomic age in 1945.
2. Write a research paper on the attempts of the major powers to control nuclear weapons. Focus on (a) the steps leading up to the signing of the Partial Test Ban Treaty of 1963, or (b) the progress of SALT (Strategic Arms Limitations Talks) during the 1970s and early 1980s.
3. Examine and assess some of the nuclear warfare strategies and policies developed by the U.S. government and by nuclear strategists. Then report on the ways that individuals and groups (such as the Committee for a SANE Nuclear Policy) have attempted to counter or influence these nuclear policies.

ADDITIONAL READINGS

Aldridge, Robert C. "First Strike: The Pentagon's Secret Strategy." *Progressive,* 42 (May 1978), pp. 16–19.

Calder, Nigel, *Nuclear Nightmares: An Investigation into Possible Wars.* New York: Viking, 1979.

Gray, Colin S. and Keith Payne. "Victory Is Possible." *Foreign Policy,* no. 39 (Summer 1980), pp. 14–27.

Griffiths, Franklin and John C. Polyani, eds. *The Dangers of Nuclear War: A Pugwash Symposium.* Toronto: University of Toronto Press, 1979.

Grodzins, Morton and Eugene Rabinowitz, eds. *The Atomic Age: Scientists in National and World Affairs* [Articles from the *Bulletin of the Atomic Scientists,* 1945–62]. New York: Basic Books, 1963. See also current issues of the *Bulletin of the Atomic Scientists.*

Kahn, Herman. *On Thermonuclear War.* Princeton: Princeton University Press, 1960.

———. *Thinking about the Unthinkable.* New York: Horizon, 1962.

Kissinger, Henry. *Nuclear Weapons and Foreign Policy.* New York: Harper, 1957.

Lewis, Kevin N. "The Prompt and Delayed Effects of Nuclear War." *Scientific American,* July 1979, pp. 35–47.

Lifton, Robert Jay. *Death in Life: Survivors of Hiroshima.* New York: Random House, 1967.

Morgenthau, Hans. "Fighting the Last War." *New Republic,* 20 October 1979, pp. 15–17.

Russell, Bertrand and Albert Einstein. "The Russell-Einstein Manifesto." In *Pugwash: The First 10 Years.* Ed., J. Rotblat. New York: Humanities Press, 1968.

Shaheen, Jack, ed. *Nuclear War Films.* Carbondale, Ill.: Southern Illinois University Press, 1978.

Weisskopf, Victor F. "On Avoiding Nuclear Holocaust." *Technology Review,* October 1980, pp. 28ff.

"What Hath Man Wrought!" editorial on A-bombing of Hiroshima, *U.S. News and World Report,* 17 August 1945. [reprinted in *Bulletin of the Atomic Scientists,* December 1975, pp. 34–35. For other articles and editorials on the Hiroshima bombing, see *The New York Times,* 7 August 1945, pp. 1, 22; 8 August 1945, p. 1; 13 August 1945, p. 9.]

12

Personality: A Rhetorically Organized Chapter

This chapter, like the others in this book, consists of passages representing the viewpoints of several academic and professional disciplines on a single subject: personality. Discussion and writing suggestions follow groups of passages; and you will find questions on summary, synthesis, and critique at the end of the chapter.

Our main purpose, however, in this particular chapter is to help you recognize patterns of writing, to recognize some of the most common rhetorical strategies, so that you can recognize them in your other reading assignments, understand why and how they are used, and use them when you need to in your own writing. The strategies we will deal with here are: classification, description, narration, definition, example, comparison-contrast, and cause and effect. This sequence (except for classification) parallels the order of presentation of the various types of syntheses in Chapter One.

In the Rhetorical Index (following this chapter) you will find a selective listing of passages from this book under each of these main headings. By reading, for example, two or three passages under the "Classification" heading, you will be able to study the use of this particular rhetorical strategy in various disciplines.

For at least twenty-five centuries, people have been trying to describe and to account for personality. Why do people have such different temperaments? What are the most common types of personality? How should personality best be analyzed? To what ends may these analyses be put? What is the relationship between personality and vocation? Between personality and body type? Between personality and health?

These are some of the questions the authors of the following passages try to answer. Their answers, of course, are largely determined by their distinctive points of view. These, in turn, are largely determined by their professions. A psychoanalyst's approach will be different from that of a political scientist — whose approach will in turn be different from that of a cardiologist.

CLASSIFICATION

The first set of passages have as their main purpose the *classification* of personality. That is, the authors arrange the almost infinite variety of individual temperaments into a limited number of sets or types, on the basis of essential similarities within a type and essential differences between types. Such a procedure carries the obvious risk of oversimplification. (For instance, it clearly oversimplifies world politics to classify nations as either belonging to the free world or to the non-free world.) On the other hand, such a procedure can increase our understanding of a subject by allowing us to organize our knowledge usefully. (Simplification or not, there is a certain amount of truth to the idea that some nations are politically "free," and other nations are not.)

The three passages that follow are examples of attempts to classify personalities. Their differences from one another derive not only from the different *points of view* from which they were written, but also from the different *purposes* for which they were written.

THE FOUR HUMOURS
Edgar F. Borgatta

A classical theory of human types, offered by ancient Greek physicians, focussed on the emotional (temperamental) attributes of human personality and was based on a relatively primitive understanding of human biology (specifically, bodily physiology), which prevailed at that time. According to these early theorists, emotional equilibrium (indeed, general health) depended on an appropriate balance among four fluids (humours) within the body. It was held that physiological imbalance (produced by an excess of one of the humours, for example) would be reflected in bodily illness and in exaggerated personality traits. Thus, if a person had an excess of blood (one of the four humours), he was expected to have a sanguine temperament; that is, to be optimistic, enthusiastic, and excitable. The modern term hot-blooded may be a survival of this Greek theory of human personality; the notion was so influential that for many centuries physicians throughout the Western world continued the practice of bleeding people who suffered from medical and psychiatric disorders. Such people are still said to be in "bad humour." 1

Too much of a humour called black bile (congealed blood from the spleen) was believed to produce a melancholic temperament. The term melancholia literally means black bile, and there are literary allusions to venting one's spleen. When someone was oversupplied with yellow bile (the yellow-green gall secreted by the liver and stored 2

From "Personalities, Theories of" in *Encyclopaedia Britannica*, 15th Edition (1974), 14:115.

in the gall bladder), he was held to become choleric; that is, to be angry, irritable, and to view his world with a jaundiced eye. Jaundice remains in modern medical language as a disease of the liver or gall bladder in which bile is present in the body to such a degree that the eyeballs and body may turn yellow. Finally, with an abundance of the humour called phlegm (as secreted in the throat), people were supposed to become stolid, apathetic, and undemonstrative; that is, to grow phlegmatic.

As biological science has progressed, these primitive concepts of body chemistry have been replaced by more subtle and complex biological theories of personality. Thus, the chemical factors associated with given psychological dispositions are now more likely to be understood in terms of hormones (as from the thyroid gland), nerve impulses, and so-called psychotropic drugs such as tranquilizers. 3

THREE TYPES OF CHARACTER STRUCTURE
David Riesman, Reuel Denny, and Nathan Glazer

One way to see the structural differences between the three types is to see the differences in the emotional sanction or control in each type. 1

(1) The tradition-directed person feels the impact of his culture as a unit, but it is nevertheless mediated through the specific, small number of individuals with whom he is in daily contact. These expect of him not so much that he be a certain type of person but that he behave in the approved way. Consequently the sanction for behavior tends to be the fear of being *shamed*. 2

(2) The inner-directed person has early incorporated a psychic gyroscope which is set going by his parents and can receive signals later on from other authorities who resemble his parents. He goes through life less independent than he seems, obeying this internal piloting. Getting off course, whether in response to inner impulses or to the fluctuating voices of contemporaries, may lead to the feeling of *guilt*. 3

Since the direction to be taken in life has been learned in the privacy of the home from a small number of guides and since princi- 4

Reprinted by permission of Yale University Press from *The Lonely Crowd* by David Riesman, Reuel Denny, and Nathan Glazer. Copyright © 1950 by Yale University Press.

ples, rather than details of behavior, are internalized, the inner-directed person is capable of great stability. Especially so when it turns out that his fellows have gyroscopes too, spinning at the same speed and set in the same direction. But many inner-directed individuals can remain stable even when the reinforcement of social approval is not available — as in the upright life of the stock Englishmen isolated in the tropics.

(3) Contrasted with such a type as this, the other-directed person learns to respond to signals from a far wider circle than is constituted by his parents. The family is no longer a closely knit unit to which he belongs but merely part of a wider social environment to which he early becomes attentive. In these respects the other-directed person resembles the tradition-directed person: both live in a group milieu and lack the inner-directed person's capacity to go it alone. The nature of this group milieu, however, differs radically in the two cases. The other-directed person is cosmopolitan. For him the border between the familiar and the strange — a border clearly marked in the societies depending on tradition-direction — has broken down. As the family continuously absorbs the strange and so reshapes itself, so the strange becomes familiar. While the inner-directed person could be "at home abroad" by virtue of his relative insensitivity to others, the other-directed person is, in a sense, at home everywhere and no-where, capable of a rapid if sometimes superficial intimacy with and response to everyone. 5

The tradition-directed person takes his signals from others, but they come in a cultural monotone; he needs no complex receiving equipment to pick them up. The other-directed person must be able to receive signals from far and near; the sources are many, the changes rapid. What can be internalized, then, is not a code of behavior but the elaborate equipment needed to attend to such mes-sages and occasionally to participate in their circulation. As against guilt-and-shame controls, though of course these survive, one prime psychological level of the other-directed person is a diffuse *anxiety*. This control equipment, instead of being like a gyroscope, is like a radar. . . . 6

If we wanted to cast our social character types into social class molds, we could say that inner-direction is the typical character of the "old" middle class — the banker, the tradesman, the small entrepre-neur, the technically oriented engineer, etc. — while other-direction is becoming the typical character of the "new" middle class — the bureaucrat, the salaried employee in business, etc. Many of the eco-nomic factors associated with the recent growth of the "new" middle class are well known. . . . There is a decline in the numbers and in the proportion of the working population engaged in production and 7 extraction — agriculture, heavy industry, heavy transport — and an increase in the numbers and the proportion engaged in white-collar work and the service trades. People who are literate, educated, and provided with the necessities of life by an ever more efficient machine industry and agriculture, turn increasingly to the "tertiary" economic realm. The service industries prosper among the people as a whole and no longer only in court circles. . . .

These developments lead, for large numbers of people, to 8 changes in paths to success and to the requirement of more "social-ized" behavior both for success and for marital and personal adapta-tion. Connected with such changes are changes in the family and in child-rearing practices. In the smaller families of urban life, and with the spread of "permissive" child care to ever wider strata of the population, there is a relaxation of older patterns of discipline. Under these newer patterns the peer-group (the group of one's associates of the same age and class) becomes much more important to the child, while the parents make him feel guilty not so much about violation of inner standards as about failure to be popular or otherwise to manage his relations with these other children. Moreover, the pressures of the school and the peer-group are reinforced and continued . . . by the mass media: movies, radio, comics, and popular culture media gener-ally. Under these conditions types of character emerge that we shall here term other-directed. . . . *What is common to all the other-directed people is that their contemporaries are the source of direction for the individ-ual — either those known to him or those with whom he is indirectly ac-quainted, through friends and through the mass media. This source is of course "internalized" in the sense that dependence on it for guidance in life is implanted early. The goals toward which the other-directed person strives shift with that guidance: it is only the process of striving itself and the process of paying close attention to the signals from others that remain unaltered through-out life.* This mode of keeping in touch with others permits a close behavioral conformity, not through drill in behavior itself, as in the tradition-directed character, but rather through an exceptional sensi-tivity to the actions and wishes of others.

Of course, it matters very much who these "others" are: whether 9 they are the individual's immediate circle or a "higher" circle or the anonymous voices of the mass media; whether the individual fears the hostility of chance acquaintances or only of those who "count." But his need for approval and direction from others — and contemporary others rather than ancestors — goes beyond the reasons that lead most people in any era to care very much what others think of them. While all people want and need to be liked by some people some of the time, it is only the modern other-directed types who make this their chief source of direction and chief area of sensitivity.

CORPORATE PERSONALITIES
Michael Maccoby

[There are] types who man the technostructure of the advanced-technology corporation. Here are brief introductions to each type. [1]

1. *The craftsman.* The craftsman holds the traditional values of the productive-hoarding character — the work ethic, respect for people, concern for quality and thrift. When he talks about his work, his interest is in the *process* of making something; he enjoys building. He sees others, co-workers as well as superiors, in terms of whether they help or hinder him in doing a craftsmanlike job. Most of the craftsmen whom we interviewed are quiet, sincere, modest, and practical, although there is a difference between those who are more receptive and democratic versus those who are more authoritarian and intolerant. Although his virtues are admired by everyone, his self-containment and perfectionism do not allow him to lead a complex and changing organization. Rather than engaging and trying to master the system with the cooperation of others who share his values, he tends to do his own thing and go along, sometimes reluctantly, toward goals he does not share, enjoying whatever opportunities he finds for interesting work. [2]

Some corporate scientists we interviewed are essentially craftsmen but there is a type of scientist who shares some of the craftsman's interest in knowledge and creating, but who is more of a prima donna, and is found exclusively in research labs. Although these scientists might be more at home in universities than in corporations, among them are some of the most independent contributors who work in corporations. Since so few are successful managers, and do not reach the top levels of the technostructure, the "corporate scientist" type will be sketched only in passing. [3]

Some of the most creative and gifted scientists whom we have seen in the corporate world are included in this type, together with the most unhappy misfits, resentful failures whose gifts do not measure up to their ambition. What most distinguishes the "scientists" from the craftsmen is their narcissism, their idolatry of their own knowledge, talents, and technology and their hunger for admiration. They are the corporate intellectuals and many are fascinated by esoteric issues (e.g., outer space or eternal life) only tangentially related to either corporate goals or social needs. In exaggerating their own importance, some of the scientists we interviewed belittled those [4] who were more down to earth. Yet beneath their narcissism we found a receptive and dependent attachment to those in power, both corporate and state leaders, the "decision makers" who could support them and make their ideas into reality. A grandiose scientist does not trust the public to understand him, and it doesn't occur to him that the reason may be that he does not create things that benefit the public. He invents what is demanded by those who pay him — the corporation and the state. Both at home and at work, the grandiose scientist seeks a protected nest. He wants an admiring mother-wife to meet his needs in return for a chance to share in his glory, and he seeks patrons at work who will agree to similar symbiotic relationships.

2. *The jungle fighter.* The jungle fighter's goal is power. He experiences life and work as a jungle (not a game), where it is eat or be eaten, and the winners destroy the losers. A major part of his psychic resources is budgeted for his internal department of defense. Jungle fighters tend to see their peers in terms of accomplices or enemies and their subordinates as objects to be utilized. There are two subtypes of jungle fighters, lions and foxes. The lions are the conquerors who when successful may build an empire; the foxes make their nests in the corporate hierarchy and move ahead by stealth and politicking.

3. *The company man.* In the company man, we recognize the well-known organization man, or the functionary whose sense of identity is based on being part of the powerful, protective company. His strongest traits are his concern with the human side of the company, his interest in the feelings of the people around him and his commitment to maintain the organization's integrity. At his weakest, he is fearful and submissive, concerned with security even more than with success. The most creative company men sustain an atmosphere in their groups of cooperation, stimulation, and mutuality. The least creative find a little niche and satisfy themselves by feeling that somehow they share in the glory of the corporation.

4. *The gamesman.* The gamesman is the new man, and, really, the leading character in this study. His main interest is in challenge, competitive activity where he can prove himself a winner. Impatient with others who are slower and more cautious, he likes to take risks and to motivate others to push themselves beyond their normal pace. He responds to work and life as a game. The contest hypes him up and he communicates his enthusiasm, thus energizing others. He enjoys new ideas, new techniques, fresh approaches and shortcuts. His talk and his thinking are terse, dynamic, sometimes playful and come in quick flashes. His main goal in life is to be a winner, and talking about himself invariably leads to discussion of his tactics and strategy in the corporate contest.

In the sixties, the gamesman went all out to win. In the seventies, both the country and the corporations are more skeptical about adventurism and glory-seeking. Some of the biggest companies have discovered that symbiosis with the military weakens their ability to compete in other markets. Watergate shamed those who flew the banner "Winning is not everything; it's the only thing," which in the sixties decorated corporate walls and desks. In the seventies, America no longer considers itself the land of unlimited abundance. Rising energy costs and international competition still call for competitive, risk-taking corporate gamesmen as leaders, but they have become more sober and realistic, more concerned with reducing costs than overwhelming the opposition with innovation.

The new corporate top executive combines many gamesman traits with aspects of the company man. He is a team player whose center is the corporation. He feels himself responsible for the functioning of a system, and in his mind, his career goals have merged with those of the corporation. Thus he thinks in terms of what is good for the company, hardly separating that from what is good for himself. He tends to be a worrier, constantly on the lookout for something that might go wrong. He is self-protective and sees people in terms of their use for the larger organization. He even uses himself in this way, fine tuning his sensitivity. He has succeeded in submerging his ego and gaining strength from this exercise in self-control.   9

To function, the corporations need craftsmen, scientists, and company men (many could do without jungle fighters), but their future depends most of all on the gamesmen's capacity for mature development.   10

The early biologists who developed the theory of humours believed that personality differences resulted primarily from differences in body chemistry, specifically from various imbalances among bodily fluids. In contrast, for sociologists David Riesman, Reuel Denny, and Nathan Glazer, the most significant (though not the *only*) way of approaching personality is by means of an individual's psychic and moral relationships with other people. Is people's behavior determined primarily by a small group representing their culture, by an internalized signal representing the moral authority of their parents, or by the other people in whatever environment they find themselves? Riesman, Denny, and Glazer recognize that there are other ways of classifying personality: they recognize, for instance, that a tradition-directed person may be either aggressive or easygoing. Nevertheless, from their *sociological* standpoint, the fact that a person is aggressive or easygoing is less important than the fact that he or she is tradition-directed.

Michael Maccoby has a different viewpoint: he is concerned with the relationship between personality types and *career types.* His purpose is to describe certain types commonly found in corporations — and in particular, one "new" type, the gamesman. Thus, Maccoby's scheme has a considerably narrower scope than the other two, since he makes no attempt to classify *all* types of personality. Of course, certain of the corporate types may have their counterparts in other occupations. For instance, among politicians as well as among professors, there may be craftsmen and jungle fighters. But the reader must draw any such conclusions for himself or herself. Maccoby writes explicitly only about the corporation.

Discussion Questions

1. Even if personality differences can't be traced to differences in body chemistry, how well do you think the "humours" approach classifies distinct and actual personality types (sanguine, etc.)?

2. How does the imagery of "psychic gyroscope" (for the inner-directed person) and "radar" (for the other-directed person) help clarify the essential difference between them?

3. What do you think is the relationship between the rise in the number of other-directed people over the last generation, and the shift from a production-oriented to a service-oriented society? Give examples.

4. Discuss Maccoby's four types in terms of their possible correspondence to other classifications in this chapter.

Writing Suggestions

1. Classify, in an essay, according to the "humours" approach, some characters you have encountered in fiction, plays, or movies.

2. Classify, in an essay, some of the people you know (better change the names) into tradition-directed, inner-directed, and other-directed types. Justify your classifications.

3. Classify, in an essay, in terms of Maccoby's corporate types, some of the characters you have encountered in fiction, plays, or movies. Justify your classifications.

DESCRIPTION

To describe is to present details and qualities. Details are parts or aspects of the subject that can be seen or otherwise sensed (like a person's separate articles of clothing). Qualities are generalized or abstracted from your impression of the subject (the way that person loves another). Along with *example, description* is perhaps the most common strategy of clarifying your subject for the reader. Your success with description depends largely on how skillful and perceptive you are in choosing just those details and qualities that are most telling about your subject. And of course, the more logically related those details and qualities, the more coherent and clearly focused your description.

We present below two examples of the description of personality, one by a psychologist, the other by a novelist.

SELF-ACTUALIZING PEOPLE
A. H. Maslow

I have suggested that self-actualizers can be defined as people who are no longer motivated by the needs for safety, belongingness, love, status, and self-respect because these needs *have already been satisfied.* Why then should a love-gratified person fall in love? Certainly not for the same reasons that motivate the love-deprived person, who falls in love because he needs and craves love, because he lacks it, and is impelled to make up this pathogenic deficiency (D-love). 1

Self-actualizers have no serious deficiencies to make up and must now be looked upon as freed for growth, maturation, development, in a word, for the fulfillment and actualization of their highest individual and species nature. What such people do emanates from growth and expresses it without striving. They love because they are loving persons, in the same way that they are kind, honest, natural, i.e., because it is their nature to be so spontaneously, as a strong man is strong without willing to be, as a rose emits perfume, as a cat is graceful, or as a child is childish. Such epiphenomena are as little motivated as is physical growth or psychological maturation. 2

There is little of the trying, straining, or striving in the loving of the self-actualizer that so dominates the loving of the average person. In philosophical language, it is an aspect of being as well as of becoming and can be called B-love, that is, love for the Being of the other. 3

A paradox seems to be created at first sight by the fact that self-actualizing people maintain a degree of individuality, of detachment, and autonomy that seems at first glance to be incompatible with the kind of identification and love that I have been describing above. But this is only an apparent paradox. As we have seen, the tendencies to detachment and to need identification and to profound interrelationships with another person can coexist in healthy people. The fact is that self-actualizing people are simultaneously the most individualistic 4 and the most altruistic and social and loving of all human beings. The fact that we have in our culture put these qualities at opposite ends of a single continuum is apparently a mistake that must now be corrected. These qualities go together and the dichotomy is resolved in self-actualizing people.

We find in our subjects a healthy selfishness, a great self-respect, 5 a disinclination to make sacrifices without good reason.

What we see in the love relationship is a fusion of great ability to 6 love and at the same time great respect for the other and great respect for oneself. This shows itself in the fact that these people cannot be said in the ordinary sense of the word to *need* each other as do ordinary lovers. They can be extremely close together and yet go apart when necessary without collapsing. They do not cling to each other or have hooks or anchors of any kind. One has the definite feeling that they enjoy each other tremendously but would take philosophically a long separation or death, that is, would remain strong. Throughout the most intense and ecstatic love affairs, these people remain themselves and remain ultimately masters of themselves as well, living by their own standards even though enjoying each other intensely.

Obviously, this finding, if confirmed, will necessitate a revision or at least an extension in the definition of ideal or healthy love in our culture. We have customarily defined it in terms of a complete merging of egos and a loss of separateness, a giving up of individuality rather than a strengthening of it. While this is true, the fact appears to be at this moment that the individuality is strengthened, that the ego is in one sense merged with another, but yet in another sense remains separate and strong as always. The two tendencies, to transcend individuality and to sharpen and strengthen it, must be seen as partners and not as contradictories. Furthermore, it is implied that the best way to transcend the ego is via having a strong identity.

Earlier in his book, *Motivation and Personality,* Maslow has defined the state of self-actualization; and he refers to this definition in the first sentence of the passage. (That is, self-actualizers are people who have already satisfied their basic needs — for "safety, belongingness, love, status, and self-respect"). The remainder of the passage extends the definition *in one particular area* by means of description — description that focuses on a particular *quality* of self-actualizing people, the manner in which they love others.

As a second example of description, consider the type of personal description that we are most familiar with — the descriptions of characters in fiction. In the following passage, *novelist* Charles Dickens describes the tragicomic schoolmaster of *Our Mutual Friend,* Bradley Headstone:

BRADLEY HEADSTONE
Charles Dickens

Bradley Headstone, in his decent black coat and waistcoat, and decent   1
white shirt, and decent formal black tie, and decent pantaloons of
pepper and salt, with his decent silver watch in his pocket and its
decent hair-guard round his neck, looked a thoroughly decent young
man of six-and-twenty. He was never seen in any other dress, and yet
there was a certain stiffness in his manner of wearing this, as if there
were a want of adaptation between him and it, recalling some mechanics in their holiday clothes. He had acquired mechanically a great
store of teacher's knowledge. He could do mental arithmetic mechanically, sing at sight mechanically, blow various wind instruments mechanically, even play the great church organ mechanically. From his
early childhood up, his mind had been a place of mechanical stowage.
The arrangement of his wholesale warehouse, so that it might be
always ready to meet the demands of retail dealers — history here,
geography there, astronomy to the right, political economy to the
left — natural history, the physical sciences, figures, music, the lower
mathematics, and whatnot, all in their several places — this care had
imparted to his countenance a look of care; while the habit of questioning and being questioned had given him a suspicious manner, or a
manner that would be better described as one of lying in wait. There
was a kind of settled trouble in the face. It was the face belonging to a
naturally slow or inattentive intellect that had toiled hard to get what
it had won and that had to hold it now that it was gotten. He always
seemed to be uneasy lest anything should be missing from his mental
warehouse, and taking stock to assure himself.

Suppression of so much to make room for so much had given   2
him a constrained manner, over and above. Yet there was enough of
what was animal, and of what was fiery (though smouldering), still
visible in him to suggest that if young Bradley Headstone, when a
pauper lad, had chanced to be told off for the sea, he would not have
been the last man in a ship's crew. Regarding that origin of his, he was
proud, moody, and sullen, desiring it to be forgotten. And few people
knew of it.

Dickens begins with a purely physical description of the schoolmaster,
although even in the first sentence, the constant repetition of the word
"decent" suggests a man trying too hard to be respectable. As the description continues, Dickens goes beyond the surface to probe Headstone's
character. His knowledge and talents, the author tells us, have been

Charles Dickens, from *Our Mutual Friend*.

mechanically acquired, though with great labor, and with the unceasing fear that he might easily lose everything that he had with so much difficulty gained. Finally, Dickens examines the deep-rooted conflict between Headstone's original "animal" nature and his present civilized one. Thus Dickens's description has progressed from an emphasis on *details* to an emphasis on *qualities*.

Discussion Questions

1. Maslow claims that "the tendencies to detachment and to need identification and to profound interrelationships with other people can coexist in healthy people." And later he says that self-actualized lovers "do not cling to each other or have hooks or anchors of any kind. One has the definite feeling that they enjoy each other tremendously but would take philosophically a long separation or death, that is, would remain strong." Do you know any such people? Can you envisage any such people? Or does this seem a description of the ideal rather than the real?

2. E. M. Forster, the novelist and critic, divided literary characters into two types: round (fully developed, plausibly unpredictable) and flat (types, fully predictable). Does Bradley Headstone seem, in conception, round or flat? Does he seem a recognizable "type" — or does he seem a distinctive, imaginative creation?

Writing Suggestions

1. Explore the implications of the first sentence of paragraph 2 of Maslow's passage ("Self-actualizers have no serious deficiencies to make up. . . ."). Do you see a statement like this (and perhaps also the one about self-actualized lovers not having "hooks or anchors of any kind") as providing a justification for the "me generation," the "new narcissism," or the fad of "growing as a person"? Is this one of the bases of a philosophy of selfishness? If not, what does "growth, maturation, development . . . the fulfillment and actualization of their highest individual and species nature" mean? In an essay, explore some of these questions.

2. Write a description, in the manner of Maslow's description of self-actualizers, of a type of people that you have encountered. Try not to inject your approval or disapproval into the description; focus on their motivations, their qualities, their behavior.

3. Write a personal description, in the manner of Charles Dickens's description of Bradley Headstone, of someone you know. Like Dickens, begin with a description of the physical aspects of this person. Then try to get below the surface, to his or her mental and emotional makeup.

NARRATION

Narration tells what happened. It recounts events and activities. We associate narration with stories and novels, that is, with fiction. But of course real events are narrated all the time, in newspapers, magazines, and nonfiction books. Like the other rhetorical strategies, narration frequently incorporates other modes of writing.

The following narrative passage deals with a famous case of multiple personality and is excerpted from *The Three Faces of Eve* by psychiatrists Corbett H. Thigpen and Hervey Cleckley, who treated Eve. Their book, later made into a film, is an expanded version of a professional article that first appeared in the *Journal of Abnormal and Social Psychology.*

THE THREE FACES OF EVE
Corbett H. Thigpen and Hervey Cleckley

She did not at first appear to be an unusual or a particularly interesting patient. This neat, colorless young woman was, she said quietly, twenty-five years of age. In a level, slightly monotonous voice she described the severe headaches from which she had suffered now for several months and for which she had been unable to obtain relief. Unlike some patients to whom the elastic term *neurotic* is applied, she did not say that the pain was "unbearable," or that it was "as if an ax were splitting her skull." Nor did she otherwise take a histrionic role in telling her troubles. Without emphasis she described the attacks. 1

Demure and poised, she sat with her feet close together, speaking clearly but in soft, low tones. Her dark hair and pale blue eyes were distinctly pretty, though she seemed too retiring and inert to utilize, or even to be very clearly aware of, her good features and her potential attractiveness. 2

Her local physician had sent her from her home in a town approximately a hundred miles away for psychiatric consultation. Ordinary physical examinations, X-ray and laboratory studies, had disclosed no cause of the headaches. This superlatively calm, utterly self-controlled little figure of propriety showed no suggestion of anything that the layman might think of as *nervousness*. Her hands lay still on the arms of her chair as she spoke. Her head and shoulders drooped just a little. So thorough was her quality of gentle formality that it was difficult to believe that her eyes might ever flash in merri- 3 ment, that she could ever have told a joke, or that even as a child, she could have teased anyone in some spontaneous outburst of feeling. . . .

It was almost impossible to imagine this gentle little woman 4 raising her voice in anger or participating aggressively in a personal argument. Her deep and genuine humility seemed to enforce a meekness upon her that one felt might even prove a serious handicap in what lay ahead. Something about her also suggested a few of the admirable qualities implied in the Christian principle of turning the other cheek. This was a woman, it seemed, not lacking in spirit, but who would not be likely to assert herself actively in opposition to another. Surely it must be an unusual man who would lose his temper with this unprovocative unvengeful woman. What were the grounds for his anger?

"He must have his reasons," she granted thoughtfully. "I am not 5 quite sure what it is I do that aggravates him so." She hesitated then sadly admitted, "I've never seemed to make him happy."

So this is how the patient, Eve White, appeared in her first 6 psychiatric interview. She was not undernourished but seemed somehow very delicate, the reticent, meticulous manner suggesting a physical fragility. This manner also tended to make some of the troubles she described seem inevitable. Her clinical symptoms were not unusual. Her personal problems were complicated and serious, but by no means extraordinary. . . .

. . . [T]he physician . . . was able to assure her, despite what she 7 had told him, that he did not consider her to be psychotic. She spoke of her incessant dread that she would lose her little girl. Relations with her husband seemed to be deteriorating dangerously. No matter what she planned, or intended, or tried to do, events so shaped themselves that instead of progress only retrogression occurred. The headaches had been more frequent and more severe. There had been more blackouts. She could not tell how long they lasted.

Eve White was clearly frightened and baffled by something she 8 sought to cope with or to escape. Its dreadful threat was palpable to her, and she braced herself as one who awaits what might prove to be an invisible guillotine. But she spoke softly in her characteristic steady voice. The delicate long-fingered hands remained on the arms of her chair as usual. Their immobility conveyed not relaxation but tensions more acute than she had shown on previous visits.

Hoping to avoid a further mobilization of anxiety, the physician 9 endeavored to direct discussion toward the more encouraging features of her situation. She returned, however, to the episode of the clothes. Clerks at the stores where she tried to return them had insisted it *was* she who had bought them. She spoke again of the voice she had heard, apparently wishing to say more and finding herself at a loss for adequate expression. She hesitated. There was perhaps a minute or more of silence.

The brooding look in her eyes became almost a stare. Eve seemed momentarily dazed. Suddenly her posture began to change. Her body slowly stiffened until she sat rigidly erect. An alien, inexplicable expression then came over her face. This was suddenly erased into utter blankness. The lines of her countenance seemed to shift in a barely visible, slow, rippling transformation. For a moment there was the impression of something arcane. Closing her eyes, she winced as she put her hands to her temples, pressed hard, and twisted them as if to combat sudden pain. A slight shudder passed over her entire body. 10

Then the hands lightly dropped. She relaxed easily into an attitude of comfort the physician had never before seen in this patient. A pair of blue eyes popped open. There was a quick reckless smile. In a bright unfamiliar voice that sparkled, the woman said, "Hi, there, Doc!" 11

With a soft and surprisingly intimate syllable of laughter, she crossed her legs, carelessly swirling her skirt in the process. She unhurriedly smoothed the hem down over her knees in a manner that was playful and somehow just a little provocative. From a corner of his preoccupied awareness the physician had vaguely noted for the first time how attractive those legs were. She settled a little more deeply into the cushions of the chair. The demure and constrained posture of Eve White had melted into buoyant repose. One little foot crossed over the other began a slow, small, rhythmic, rocking motion that seemed to express alert contentment as pervasively as the gentle wagging of a fox terrier's tail. 12

Still busy with his own unassimilated surprise, the doctor heard himself say, "How do you feel now?" 13

"Why just fine — never better! How you doing yourself, Doc?" 14

Eve looked for a moment straight into his eyes. Her expression was that of one who is just barely able to restrain laughter. Her eyes rolled up and to one side for an instant, then the lids flicked softly before opening wide again. She tossed her head lightly with a little gesture that threw the fine dark hair forward onto her shoulder. A five-year-old might have so reacted to some sudden, unforeseen amusement. In the patient's gesture there was something of pert sauciness, something in which the artless play of a child and a scarcely conscious flirtatiousness mingled. The therapist reacted to the new presence with feelings that momentarily recalled some half-remembered quotation about the devil entering the prompter's box. But the patient remained at ease and, apparently, for some reason of her own, quite amused. The silence went unbroken for a minute or more. 15

"She's been having a real rough time. There's no doubt about that," the girl said carelessly. "I feel right sorry for her sometimes. 16

She's such a damn dope though. . . . What she puts up with from that sorry Ralph White — and all her mooning over the little brat . . . ! To hell with it, I say!"

She leaned forward in a little movement that suggested a kitten. 17 With one hand she half-heartedly began to scratch her leg just below the knee. She stretched out the other hand amiably and said, "Would you give me a cigarette, please, Doc?"

He handed her a cigarette, and then lighting it, said, "Who is 18 'she'?"

"Why, Eve White, of course. Your long-suffering, saintly, little 19 patient."

"But aren't you Eve White?" he asked. 20

"That's for laughs," she exclaimed, a ripple of mirth in her tone. 21 She tossed her head slightly again. "Why, you ought to know better than that, Doc!" She paused and looked at him intently. Her face was fresh and marvelously free from the habitual signs of care, serious-ness, and underlying stress so familiar in the face of the girl who had come into the office. Shifting her position in the chair, she raised her hand and rolled a lock of hair slowly between her fingers. Open-eyed, she looked again directly at him. As an impish smile flickered over her childlike face she said softly:

"I know you *real* well, Doc . . . lots better than she knows you. 22 . . . And I kind of like you. I bet you're a good dancer, too."

After he had disclaimed any special talents for the dance, they 23 exchanged several inconsequential remarks. Then the physician said, "Can you tell me anything more about those dresses that upset your husband so much?"

"I ain't got no husband," she replied promptly and emphatically. 24 "Let's get that straight right now." She grinned broadly.

"Well, who *are* you?" he asked incredulously. 25

"Why, I'm Eve Black," she said (giving Mrs. White's maiden 26 name). "I'm me and she's herself," the girl added. "I like to live and she don't. . . . Those dresses — well, I can tell you about them. I got out the other day, and I needed some dresses. I like good clothes. So I just went downtown and bought what I wanted. I charged 'em to her husband, too!" She began to laugh softly. "You ought've seen the look on her silly face when he showed her what was in that closet!"

There is little point in attempting to give in detail here the 27 differences between this novel feminine apparition and the vanished Eve White. Instead of the gentleness and restraint of that conven-tional figure, there sparkled in the newcomer a childishly daredevil air, an erotically mischievous glance, a rippling energy, a greedy appetite for fun. This new and apparently carefree girl spoke casually of Eve White and her problems, always using *she* or *her* in every reference, always respecting the strict bounds of a separate identity.

It was also immediately apparent that this new voice was differ- 28
ent, that the basic idiom of her language was plainly not that of Eve
White. Eve White regularly gave the impression of a taut fragile
slenderness. Perhaps because of the easy laxness of this girl's posture
and her more vigorous movements, the lines of her body seemed
somehow a little more voluptuously rounded. A thousand minute
alterations of manner, gesture, expression, posture, of nuances in
reflex or instinctive reaction, of glance, of eyebrow tilting, and eye
movements — all argued that this could only be another woman. It is
not even possible to say just what all these differences were.

It would not be difficult for a man to distinguish his wife (or 29
perhaps even his secretary) if she were placed among a hundred
other women carefully chosen from millions because of their close
resemblance to her, and all dressed identically. But would one wager,
however articulate he might be, that he could tell a stranger, or even a
person very slightly acquainted with her, how to accomplish this task?
If the husband should try to tell us how he himself recognizes his wife,
he might accurately convey something to us. But what he conveyed,
no matter how hard he tried, would be only an inconsequential
fragment. It would not be enough to help us when we ourselves set
out to find the designated woman. So, too, we are not equal to the
task of telling adequately what so profoundly distinguished from
Eve White the carefree girl who had taken her place in this vivid mutation.

Talking came easy to Eve Black. She not only answered all ques- 30
tions readily but often digressed or went on to reminisce in exuberant
loquacity. This was in sharp contrast with the habits of her predecessor in the chair, who spoke slowly and carefully and sometimes as if
her answers cost considerable effort.

The new Eve spoke at length about the expensive clothes which 31
had caused trouble for Mr. and Mrs. White.

"She tried to take 'em all back," she said with relish, "but some of 32
the stores wouldn't do it. Of course, they thought I was her, and they
told her she'd bought 'em and she'd have to keep 'em! I'm glad, too. I
need something fit to wear when I do get out. She never gets anything
but those prim little jobs that make you feel like an old maid Sunday-
school teacher or somebody's great-aunt. Just look at this, will you?"
she said, with a deprecatory glance down at the neat but inconspicuous skirt she brushed with a lively flourish of her hands.

"What can you tell me about Eve White?" the physician asked. 33

"Well, I really haven't been paying much attention to her re- 34
cently," she said, as if ready to dismiss a subject of minor importance.
Then her eyes brightened. "But I can tell you plenty, Doc," she added
eagerly, with a flash of pride that suggested a child sure she has the
answers. " I know just about everything about her — lots and lots of

things she don't know herself. For one thing, she's a lot more sick of that husband than she'll admit. She and her fine airs about always having to do the right thing — the *right thing* even if it kills her."

"Is it because of little Bonnie?" he asked.   35

"Little Bonnie, little Bonnie, little Bonnie! That's all she can think   36
about. Running herself crazy from morning to night with worry about her brat. Oh, the kid's all right — a nice enough kid most of the time. But why the hell should a girl find nothing to do but fret all the time about a four-year-old child?"

"Don't you *love* your daughter?"   37

"My daughter! I don't *have* no child, Doc. Never will have one   38
either. There's no percentage in it. Not for me. I like to have a good time — like to live. Life don't last forever. Bonnie's *her* child. I got nothing to do with her."

When asked if Eve White's all-absorbing devotion to Bonnie was   39
genuine, she hesitated for a moment. "Yes, Doc, I reckon you'd say that's real. . . . But it's silly. . . . To me it just don't make real good sense."

Eve Black did not deny that the body from which she spoke was   40
also the body of Eve White, or that from it had been born not quite four years ago the little girl under discussion. When pressed for explanations about this, she still insisted that she herself was not a mother, that she was not married to Ralph White "or to anybody else either." For many questions she had no satisfactory answers but on these points she was emphatically positive.

"Where were you when the baby was born?" he inquired.   41

She paused for a moment, flicked the ash off her cigarette. A   42
triumphant flash of mischief lit her face as she replied:

"Now, Doc, that's one for you to answer! There's a lot about it I   43
can't explain," she then admitted, "an awful lot I don't understand. But I do know I'm not her and she's not me. I ain't going to worry myself about it too much, either. I want to have some fun while I can. There's life in me, Doc," she added, with a light little sigh of pleasure. "I've been getting out a lot more recently, too." Her bright eyes snapped with a look of childlike deviltry. "Now, Eve White would worry about all those questions you've been asking, but not me."

"*Does* she worry about them?"   44

"That's one trouble she's got she don't know nothing about!"   45
replied the young woman in amused tones but with conviction. She went on to say that Eve White was completely unaware of Eve Black's existence.

"She don't know anything about me. . . ." She broke off sud-   46
denly and a flash of defiance lit her eyes. "And don't you go and tell her either! When I get out she don't know a thing about it. I go where I please, and do like I please and it's none of her damned business."

She had no explanation to offer for this. She could not tell the   47
doctor where Eve White disappeared to or what happened to her
when she herself "got out" and went on her merry way. She was able
to maintain awareness, she claimed, of everything, or nearly everything, that the cautious housewife and mother did, and had access
most of the time to her thoughts and her memory. She did not,
however, always take advantage of this ability. She found Eve White's
thoughts and activities so boring that she often withdrew her attention for long periods. On the other hand, Eve White had no contact
with Eve Black's consciousness, no suspicion of her existence.

By means of *narration,* Thigpen and Cleckley render interesting and vivid
what could have been a dry, analytical account. Through narration, they also
convey their own sense of wonder and bewilderment at the startling
personality shifts in their patient during the course of her treatment. (Later,
still another personality, "Jane," was to emerge.)

Even so, this passage is not pure narration. For instance, in the first
five paragraphs the emphasis is on a *description* of the drab Eve White.
And throughout the narrative passage that follows, Thigpen and Cleckley
interject their descriptive and analytical comments — for instance, the
paragraph in which they try to explain just how difficult it is to distinguish
between Eve White and Eve Black.

Discussion Questions

1. Thigpen and Cleckley often considered the possibility that they had
   been taken in by a consummate actress, but finally dismissed such
   doubts by asking themselves why on earth anyone would go to the
   trouble (over several years) of putting on such an act. In what other
   ways within this passage do the authors attempt to convince us that
   this change of personality was genuine?
2. Here's your chance to play amateur psychiatrist. How could such a
   thing happen? (For the full story, read the book!)

Writing Suggestions

1. Describe by means of narration how you or someone you know
   sometimes appear to have more than one distinct personality. Of
   course, this "multiple personality" will not be as dramatic or as deep-
   rooted as Eve White's; but it may be noteworthy and surprising, all the
   same. You may choose to tell the narration from the viewpoint of a
   psychiatrist, counselor, or a good friend writing a diary.
2. If you are intrigued with the subject of multiple personality, you may be
   interested in writing a report on Eve or others like her. Corbett H.
   Thigpen and Hervey Cleckley's original report, "A Case of Multiple

Personality," appeared in the *Journal of Abnormal and Social Psychology,* 49 (1954), pp. 135–51. Their book, *The Three Faces of Eve,* was published in 1957 by McGraw-Hill and is also available in paperback. "Eve" is the pseudonym of Chris Costner Sizemore, whose own account of her experiences may be found in *I'm Eve* (Doubleday, 1977), prepared in collaboration with her cousin, Elen Sain Pittillo. According to this book, "Eve" 's personality continued to fragment into at least 22 separate personalities. Other cases of multiple personality are narrated in *Sybil,* by Flora R. Schreiber (Chicago: Henry Regnery Co., 1973), and *The Five of Me* (a male case of multiple personality), by Henry Hawksworth with Ted Schwartz (Regnery, 1977).

DEFINITION

A *definition,* of course, tells what a word or a term means, and is most commonly found in the dictionary. But writers often use *extended definitions* as part of their exposition. They do this when the term on which the discussion hangs is new or unfamiliar, or when it is a term — like "personality" — about whose exact meaning even specialists disagree. Although extended definitions work largely through *description* (see the passage below about Type A behavior), we can broadly distinguish the two strategies by saying that definitions tend to be the more comprehensive, descriptions the more particular. Definition deals with the whole; description deals with parts or aspects of this whole.

Below are examples of definition. The first passage is excerpted from the final section of Thigpen and Cleckley's original article about Eve. In the second passage, cardiologists Meyer Friedman and R. H. Rosenman define at length what they have called the "Type A Behavior Pattern."

WHAT IS PERSONALITY?
Corbett H. Thigpen and Hervey Cleckley

We ask ourselves what we mean by referring to that which we have observed by such a term as *multiple personality?* Immediately we face the more fundamental question: What is the real referent of this familiar word *personality?* In ordinary use we all encounter dozens of unidentical referents, perhaps hundreds of overlapping concepts, all with vague and elusive areas extending indefinitely, vaguely fading out into limitless implications.

Any day we may hear that John Doe has become a *new man* since he quit liquor three years ago. Perhaps we tell ourselves that Harvard actually made a *different person* of that boy across the street who used to aggravate all the neighbors with his mischievous depredations. Many religious people describe the experience of being *converted* or *born again* in terms that to the skeptical often seem chiefly fantastic.

With considerable truth, perhaps, it may be stated that after her marriage Mary Blank *changed*, that she has become *another woman*. So, too, when a man's old friends say that since the war he hasn't been the *same fellow* they used to know, the statement, however inaccurate, may indicate something real. We hear that an acquaintance when drinking the other night was *not himself*. Another man, we are told, *found himself* after his father lost all that money. Every now and then it is said that a certain woman's absorption in her home and children has resulted in her losing her *entire personality*. Though such sayings are never taken literally, there is often good reason for them to be taken seriously.

Are they not exaggerations or distortions used to indicate very imperfectly what is by no means totally untrue but what cannot be put precisely, or fully, into words? The real meaning of such familiar statements, however significant, helps us only a little in explaining what we think we have encountered in the case reported. Some relation seems likely, as one might say there is some relation between ordinary vocal memory or fantasy and true auditory hallucinations.

Though often distinguished from each of the other terms, "personality" is sometimes used more or less as a synonym or approximation for "mind," "character," "disposition," "soul," "spirit," "self," "ego," "integrate of human functioning," "identity," etc. In common speech it may be said that John has a good mind but no personality, or that Jim has a wonderful personality but no character, etc. Often this protean word narrows (or broadens) in use to indicate chiefly the attractiveness, or unattractiveness, of some woman or man. In psychiatry its most specific function today is perhaps that of implying a unified total, of indicating more than "intelligence," or "character," more than any of the several terms referring with various degrees of exactness to various qualities, activities, responses, capacities, or aspects of the human being. In the dictionaries, among other definitions, one finds "individuality," "quality or state of being a person," "personal existence or identity."

There is, apparently, no distinct or whole or commonly understood referent for our word "personality." It is useful to us in psychiatry despite its elasticity, often because of its elasticity. If they are to be helpful all such elastic terms must be used tentatively. Otherwise they may lead us at once into violent and confused disagreement about what are likely to be imaginary questions, mere conflicts of arbitrary definition. Bearing this in mind we feel it proper to speak of Eve Black, Eve White, and of Jane as three "personalities."

WHAT IS TYPE A BEHAVIOR?
Meyer Friedman and R. H. Rosenman

Type A Behavior Pattern is an action-emotion complex that can be observed in any person who is *aggressively* involved in a *chronic, incessant* struggle to achieve more and more in less and less time, and if required to do so, against the opposing efforts of other things or other persons. It is not psychosis or a complex of worries or fears or phobias or obsessions, but a socially acceptable — indeed often praised — form of conflict. Persons possessing this pattern also are quite prone to exhibit a free-floating but extraordinarily well-rationalized hostility. As might be expected, there are degrees in the intensity of this behavior pattern. Moreover, because the pattern represents the reaction that takes place when particular personality traits of an afflicted individual are challenged or aroused by a specific environmental agent, the results of this reaction (that is, the behavior pattern itself) may not be felt or exhibited by him if he happens to be in or confronted by an environment that presents no challenge. For example, a usually hard-driving, competitive, aggressive editor of an urban newspaper, if hospitalized with a trivial illness, may not exhibit a single sign of Type A Behavior Pattern. In short, for Type A Behavior Pattern to explode into being, the *environmental challenge must always serve as the fuse for this explosion.*

The person with Type B Behavior Pattern is the exact opposite of the Type A subject. He, unlike the Type A person, is rarely harried by desires to obtain a wildly increasing number of things or participate in an endlessly growing series of events in an ever decreasing amount of time. His intelligence may be as good as or even better than that of the Type A subject. *Similarly, his ambition may be as great or even greater than that of his Type A counterpart.* He may also have a considerable amount of "drive," but its character is such that it seems to steady him, give confidence and security to him, rather than to goad, irritate, and infuriate, as with the Type A man.

1

2

In our experience, based on extensive practices in typing and 3 then observing many hundreds of individuals, the general run of urban Americans tend to fall into one or the other of these two groups. The Type A's, we have found, predominate; they usually represent somewhat over half of all those in the open samples we have tested. There are somewhat fewer true Type B individuals, perhaps 40 percent of the whole. People in whom Type A and Type B characteristics are mixed account for about 10 percent. If our testing procedures can be further refined — and we are, of course, constantly trying to do this — we believe that the number in this middle group can be reduced. In other words, most Americans are in fact either Type A or Type B, though in varying degrees.

Again we should like to reiterate that, with exceedingly rare 4 exception, the socioeconomic position of a man or woman does not determine whether he or she is a Type A or Type B subject. The presidents of many banks and corporations (perhaps even the majority) may be Type B individuals. Conversely, many janitors, shoe salesmen, truck drivers, architects, and even florists may be Type A subjects. We have not found any clear correlation between occupational position held and the incidence of Type A Behavior Pattern. Why is this so? Because (1) a sense of job or position responsibility is not synonymous with the Type A sense of time urgency; (2) excessive drive or competitive enthusiasm may only too frequently be expended upon economic trivia rather than affairs of importance; and (3) promotion and elevation, particularly in corporate and professional organizations, usually go to those who are wise rather than to those who are merely hasty, to those who are tactful rather than to those who are hostile, and to those who are creative rather than to those who are merely agile in competitive strife. (And if you who are reading this happen to be a wife of a Type A executive, attorney, physician, or florist, this last should not be forgotten, even if your husband insists that it isn't true.)

Before we begin to draw a detailed portrait of the Type A man, 5 we should like to forestall one rather important source of misunderstanding. We are not psychologists. What follows is an honest description of symptoms and signs as *we have observed them.* We are convinced that they form, in themselves, a significant behavior pattern, and we *know,* by virtue of our own professional expertise, that this group of traits is closely linked to the pathology of coronary artery and heart disease. It is possible that our *psychological* analysis may be criticized as superficial, perhaps rightly so. But this by no means invalidates its *medical* significance. The Type A man is prone to heart disease; these characteristic behavioral habits identify the Type A man.

Once again, notice how authors use several rhetorical modes in the same passage. Thigpen and Cleckley, rather than attempting to define "personality" formally ("Personality is . . ."), ask a series of questions and then give a series of examples to show how impractical it is to think of anyone's "personality" as a constant. The authors then discuss some of the common conceptions of personality, including some dictionary definitions. They tentatively conclude that it is better not to pin down the concept of "personality" to a particular meaning, and that in fact the chief value of the term to psychiatrists lies in its "elasticity" of meaning.

Doctors Friedman and Rosenman, on the other hand, are quite prepared to define precisely the more specialized term (which they themselves devised), "Type A Behavior Pattern." They begin almost as a dictionary might: "Type A Behavior Pattern is an action-emotion complex that can be observed in any person who is *aggressively* involved in a *chronic, incessant* struggle to achieve more and more in less and less time. . . ." Thus, they place the term, "Type A Behavior Pattern," into a class ("an action-emotion complex") and then show how that class is different from other classes: ("[It is] present in a person who is *aggressively* involved in a *chronic, incessant* struggle to achieve more and more . . ."). But the extended definition that follows is make up chiefly of *descriptions,* as well as generalized *examples* of Type A people. Toward the end of the passage, the authors turn the definition to the service of the *cause and effect* argument that is central to their book (*Type A Behavior and Your Heart*): the "Type A man is prone to heart disease."

Discussion Questions

1. Thigpen and Cleckley never arrive at a firm definition of personality. Does that mean that they have shed no light on the problem of defining the term? Explain.

2. Friedman and Rosenman note that "the general run of urban Americans tend to fall into one or the other of these two types." Would you expect suburban and rural Americans also to fall into these same types, and if so, in similar proportions (i.e., about 60 percent Type A's)?

3. Based on Friedman and Rosenman's analyses, which of Maccoby's four corporate types would seem to be most prone to Type A behavior, and therefore, heart attacks? Which would be most prone to Type B behavior?

4. Apart from their medical advice, what *values* do Friedman and Rosenman appear to be promoting in their descriptions of typical Type A and Type B behavior?

Writing Suggestions

1. Write an extended definition of one of the following terms:

character	law and order	mature
progress	democracy	sentimental
environment	education	great

   Use *examples* to clarify your definition.

2. Friedman and Rosenman, at one point in their book, refer to the "enslaving and spiritually devastating . . . habits and traits that only yesterday were held in high esteem by all — including Horatio Alger and his prosperous friends." Alger, of course, is the fictional youth whose upwardly mobile drive and ambition appear to classify him as a Type A personality. Write an essay on what you believe to be the relationship between a nation of Type A people and that nation's economic success. Give *examples*.

EXAMPLE

The most common way of making abstract writing specific, of making flat writing vivid, is to illustrate the main ideas with *examples*. For example, read the following passage:

NIXON AS ACTIVE-NEGATIVE
James D. Barber

Strangely, no one seems to have suggested that Watergate (by which I mean the whole wash of woe that flooded forth after that gate was opened in June 1972) gave us a "new Nixon." Through so many even-numbered years in the past, the discovery of new Nixons seemed to have become a national pastime as observers hoped against hope that he was not what he had been. In the event, though, old reliable Nixon came through.

The clearest continuity was Nixon's active-negative character. As 2 he had before 1972, he poured on energy, night and day, at home and away. His Presidential activities came to take up nearly all his waking hours and, more and more frequently as his end approached, he woke and worked at night. "As long as I am physically able," he pledged in November 1973, "I am going to continue to work sixteen to eighteen hours a day. . . ." He was a man in motion, restlessly flying off to Camp David, Key Biscayne, or San Clemente, where he often plagued his Secret Service guards to "drive somewhere, any-

From the book *The Presidential Character*, 2nd Edition by James David Barber; © 1977 by James David Barber. Published by Prentice-Hall, Inc., Englewood Cliffs, N.J. 07632. Reprinted by permission of the publisher.

where." As of the end of November 1973, the President had stayed in the White House only four of the forty-four weekends of his second term; in his last six weeks in office he spent only six days there.

Reliable Nixon continued also in his stance as a suffering martyr 3 in the Presidency. Even the version of the White House tapes he himself released to the public has him in continual complaint: "This damn case!" "I've been working very hard as you can imagine with everything." "I was up so late last night." He told visiting Congressmen he had been through "seven months of pure hell." He refers again and again to his troubled life, in all sorts of circumstances: he wants the truth "even if it hurts me," he says, and he has "broken my ass to try to get the facts of this case." Even after his enormous victory in the 1972 election, Nixon conveyed a "joyless, brooding quality," one of his Cabinet members remembered, and talked of how all Presidents had gone down hill in their second terms. Even when he sat at ease in Washington while his bombers smashed out the lives of Vietnamese peasants, his sense of proportion and comparison deserted him: the Vietnam bombing became "my terrible personal ordeal."

Extensive data about Nixon's character, unavailable in 1972, appeared as the tragedy of his Presidency deepened. His intimates had 4 cause to blacken his name, but the detail and convergence of their stories lent them plausibility. Occasional visitors from Congress and the press gave shocking and similar accounts and the President's own voice — heard on tape by members of the House Judiciary Committee and read in print by the world at large — exhibited with unusual clarity the depth and nature of his struggle. Near the end, as his political defenses crumbled, so did his psychological defenses. Then Nixon revealed the fragility of his self-esteem, the fear and trembling which lay hidden behind his mask of stoic toughness. At the end he was drinking heavily, sleeping sporadically, often enraged and raging, frequently out of touch with the reality gathering around him; by one report, he was a weeping, staggering, irrational man. Theodore White saw the task of the White House staff, as of August 1974, as "the management of an unstable personality," and others, similarly averse to hyperbolic diagnoses, used similarly strong language.

Nixon's own penchant for hyperbole lasted on past 1972, as he 5 dramatized his history, seeing his life as a series of sharp discontinuities. From "the largest dinner ever held at the White House" to "the greatest year of progress since World War II," Nixon zigged and zagged through wide varieties of "toughest" decisions, "most difficult crises," and "deepest valleys." As Watergate deepened, he came to think of it as a "war" — a war in which the stakes were far higher than his personal fate. He told his friend Rabbi Korff that if he resigned, foreign affairs might "suffer irreparable harm." As Jonathan Schell put it, Nixon "invented crises and then he made 'great decisions' to resolve them." Clearly, the Nixon who saw, as we wanted and needed to see, his life as a fascinating and heroic drama was still there after 1972.

He was a insightful as ever about his own character. His speech-writer William Safire, aping Gertrude Stein, noted that "to the real Nixon, the real Nixon is not the real Nixon." "Ego is something we all have," Nixon admitted, "and either you grow out of it or it takes you over. I've grown out of it. It's really a compensation for an inferiority complex. Henry [Kissinger] has that of course. . . ." As he saw himself, "I could always get along with anybody . . . no matter what I thought of them." At the very time when he was refusing to obey subpoenas from the House Judiciary Committee, President Nixon issued his Law Day 1974 proclamation: "The law retains its value and force because every person knows that no man or woman is above the requirement of the law." Discussing the fate of John Mitchell with John Ehrlichman, Nixon, scoutmaster for the whole troop, says, "But what the hell, I am always kind." His attitude toward the press was tolerant and easy, Nixon said: "The critics don't bother me, even though I have had the most unfriendly press in history, it has never bothered me, but it deeply bothers Pat and my daughters. They see it in personal terms whereas I see the press totally in impersonal terms." Again and again, Nixon demonstrated, as Safire put it, "the uncanny ability to step outside of himself and coolly misread the man he observed." As in the years up to 1972, those who looked to Nixon's own statements for guidance to his character would soon be lost. 6

Nixon the manager of himself, "RN" the stage director or pro-ducer of the Nixon project — that is the place, I argued in 1972, to look for Nixon's strongest emotional investment. The typical compul-siveness of the active-negative person, which usually takes the form "I must," with Nixon invariably became "I must do it my way." Into his second term Nixon continued to insist on just that. The Watergate saga — particularly the cover-up — took its shape from Nixon's old sense that nothing would be right unless he controlled the way of it. His fear of being dead though living, of having no feelings, contrib-uted heavily, I think, to his need to feel he had to do what he had to do — and in just the right way. In the Autumn of 1973, Nixon said, "What matters most, in this critical hour, is our ability to act — and to act in a way that enables us to control events, not to be paralyzed and overwhelmed by them." His Watergate vocabulary is full of the lan-guage of compulsion: "We've just got to ride it through." "I've got to get [it] out and I've got to get it out today! . . . The White House has got to move. . . . we have to get out in front in some way." The "way" was infinitely important. Safire pointed out to Nixon that his three favorite words were "in a way." Nixon never seems to have judged the 7 rightness of the "way" by any external criteria of ethics, morality, or even expediency. What mattered most was that things be done in a way that he could feel was *his* way — that is, a way that reflected his own dramatic sense of himself.

In a perceptive passage, Jonathan Schell says that on one occasion, "the President seemed to have thrown himself so wholeheartedly into his false role that in his private conversations he had begun to agonize over moral questions that were appropriate to the false role but wholly inappropriate to his real role. . . . What the President imagined to be true soon was true, as the result of his own actions." The White House became a theater in which "scenarios," "scripts," "players," and "orchestration" were employed to create just the right move at the right time and place. Nixon the self-manager saw to that. In what turned out to be a key comment, Nixon says, "For Christ's sake, get it. In a way that — "

8

In the chapter on the Presidency we included another selection from Barber's book, *The Presidential Character,* a *classification* passage entitled "Four Types of Presidential Character." As a political scientist, Barber is concerned with classifying presidential personalities only, not with human personalities in general. Nevertheless, his method of classification obviously has wider implications. As he notes, the baselines of *activity-passivity* and *positive-negative* "stand for two central features of anyone's orientation toward life" — that is, how much energy a person invests in what he is doing, and how he feels about what he is doing.

Recall that after briefly classifying the four main types, Barber shows how the first four presidents *exemplified,* in their turn, each of the types. The rest of *The Presidential Character* is concerned with showing in considerably more detail how individual presidents exemplified one type or another. Barber exemplifies Richard Nixon as an active-negative president; and in the second half of the passage above, he provides many *examples* of Nixon's behavior and Nixon's own words to support his classification. For instance, he quotes Nixon's desperate words, as he fought to keep Watergate from closing in on him: "As long as I am physically able . . . I am going to continue to work sixteen to eighteen hours a day. . . ."

An important point to keep in mind is that when we speak of "classification" and "example," we are not speaking of hard and fixed categories. Seldom will you come across a passage of writing that is *purely* classification or *purely* example. Rather, most writing represents a mixture of approaches. For example, the first passage by Barber in Chapter Two employs *classification* (of types of presidential personalities), *example* (the first four presidents), *description* (of each type), *comparison-contrast* (among types), and *cause and effect* (certain personality structures will lead, predictably, to certain types of behavior in office). So when we use a particular piece of writing as an example of some particular approach, such as classification, we are doing so only because this is a convenient way of isolating and focusing upon a particular mode of expression or organization. By focusing upon this mode, you will learn to recognize it in the writing of others and to use it purposefully in your own writing.

Discussion Questions

1. Barber provides many examples of Nixon's behavior and of his statements. Do these examples justify Barber's categorizing Nixon as an "active-negative" president, in your view?
2. What separate aspects of Nixon's personality are exemplified in Barber's passage?
3. Barber notes: "Active-negative types pour energy into the political system, but it is an energy distorted from within." What does he mean by this? How does his analysis of Nixon exemplify his proposition?

Writing Suggestion

Explain how people you know, or people in public life or in entertainment can be classified according to Barber's "baselines." Exemplify through their statements and their behavior.

COMPARISON-CONTRAST

To compare is to discuss similarities among two or more articles, stories, objects, ideas, etc.; to contrast is to discuss differences. Comparison-contrast is one of the most useful expository modes, because the first step in understanding almost anything is to measure it against something similar and yet different. To cite an example from the passage that follows: "a neurotic personality is similar to a psychotic personality in that it is disordered; but it is different in that it is able to function — however inefficiently — in the normal world" (Karen Horney, *The Neurotic Personality of Our Time*).

NEUROTIC, NORMAL, PSYCHOTIC
Karen Horney

. . . On the basis of his ambitions [the neurotic] has built up fantastic   1
notions of his own value and importance. He cannot help measuring his realistic accomplishments against his notions of being a genius or a

Reprinted from *The Neurotic Personality of Our Time* by Karen Horney, M.D., with the permission of W. W. Norton & Company, Inc. Copyright 1937 by W. W. Norton & Company, Inc. Copyright renewed 1964 by Renate Mintz, Brigitte Swarzenski, and Marianne von Eckardt.

perfect human being, and in this comparison his real acts or his real possibilities appear inferior.

The total result of all these recoiling tendencies is that the neurotic incurs real failures, or at most does not get on as well as he should, considering his opportunities and his gifts. Others who started with him get ahead of him, have better careers, greater success. This lagging behind does not concern only external success. The older he becomes the more he feels the discrepancy between his potentialities and his achievements. He feels keenly that his gifts, whatever they may be, are going to waste, that he is blocked in the development of his personality, that he does not mature as time goes on. And he reacts to the realization of this discrepancy with a vague discontent, a discontent which is not masochistic but real and proportionate. 2

A discrepancy between potentialities and achievement may be due, as I have already pointed out, to external circumstances. But the discrepancy which develops in a neurotic person, and which is a never-failing characteristic of neuroses, is due to his internal conflicts. His actual failures and the consequent increasing discrepancy between potentialities and achievements inevitably give even greater force to his existing inferiority feelings. Thus he not only believes himself to be, but actually is inferior to what he might be. The impact of this development is all the greater since it puts the inferiority feelings on a realistic basis. 3

Meanwhile the other discrepancy which I have mentioned — that between high-flown ambitions and the comparatively poor reality — becomes so unbearable that it demands a remedy. As such a remedy fantasy offers itself. More and more the neurotic substitutes grandiose ideas for attainable goals. The value they have for him is obvious: they cover up his unendurable feelings of nothingness; they allow him to feel important without entering into any competition and thus without incurring the risk of failure or success; they allow him to build up a fiction of grandeur far beyond any attainable goal. It is this blind-alley value of grandiose fantasies that makes them dangerous, because the blind alley has definite advantages for the neurotic when compared with the straightforward road. 4

These neurotic ideas of grandeur should be distinguished from those of the normal person and those of the psychotic. Even the normal person will at times think himself wonderful, attribute undue importance to what he is doing, or indulge in fantasies of what he might do. But these fantasies and ideas remain decorative arabesques and he does not take them too seriously. The psychotic person with ideas of grandeur is at the other end of the line. He is convinced that he is a genius, the Emperor of Japan, Napoleon, Christ, and will reject all evidence of reality which tends to disprove his conviction; he will 5 be wholly unable to comprehend any reminder that he is actually a poor doorman or a patient in an asylum or the object of disrespect or ridicule. If he becomes aware of the discrepancy at all he will decide in favor of his grandiose ideas, and will believe that the others do not know any better, or that they are deliberately treating him with disrespect in order to hurt him.

The neurotic is somewhere between these two extremes. If he is   6
at all aware of his exaggerated self-valuation his conscious reaction to it is rather like that of a healthy person. If in dreams he appears as royalty in disguise he may find such dreams funny. But his grandiose fantasies, although consciously he discards them as unreal, have for him an emotional reality-value similar to the value they have for a psychotic. In both cases the reason is the same: they have an important function. Although slender and shaky, they are the pillar on which his self-esteem rests, and therefore he has to cling to them.

The danger that lies in this function manifests itself in situations   7
in which some blow is dealt the self-esteem. Then the pillar tumbles, he falls, and cannot recover from his fall. For example, a girl who had good reasons to believe that she was loved realized that the man was hesitating to marry her. In a talk he told her that he felt too young, too inexperienced to marry, and that he thought it wiser to know other girls before he tied himself definitely. She could not recover from this blow, became depressed, began to feel insecure in her work, developed an enormous fear of failure, with a subsequent desire to withdraw from everything, from people as well as from work. This fear was so overwhelming that even encouraging events, such as the man's later decision that he wished to marry her, and the offer of a better job with much flattering appreciation of her abilities, did not reassure her.

The neurotic, in contrast to the psychotic, cannot help registering   8
with painful accuracy all the thousand little incidents of real life which do not fit in with his conscious illusion. Consequently he wavers in his self-valuation between feeling great and feeling worthless. At any minute he may shift from one extreme to the other. At the same time that he feels most convinced of his exceptional value he may be astonished that anyone takes him seriously. Or at the same time that he feels miserable and down-trodden he may feel furious that anyone should think him in need of help. His sensitivity can be compared with that of a person who is sore all over his body and flinches at the slightest touch. He easily feels hurt, despised, neglected, slighted, and reacts with proportionate vindictive resentment.

Horney is primarily concerned with the neurotic (as opposed to the psychotic or the normal) personality. But after describing one particular aspect of neurotic behavior (i.e., recoiling from competition because of inferiority feelings), Horney finds it necessary to clarify her description by comparing the neurotic conceptions that she has described to normal and psychotic conceptions on the same subject: ideas of grandeur. Indeed, this is not simply a matter of clarification; some people, on reading Horney's description must get the uncomfortable feeling that she is describing *them!* But Horney reassures them by her contrast and explains the essential difference: the "fantasies and ideas [of the normal person] remain decorative arabesques and he does not take them seriously." The psychotic, on the other hand, is convinced that his delusions of grandeur are quite true. In the middle is the neurotic, who does take his fantasies seriously, but who knows, at heart, that they are not true. His fantasies, like those of the psychotic, serve "an important function," that is, to ward off harsh reality. In the final section of the contrast, Horney drives home the paradox that the neurotic may be more miserable than the psychotic, for the latter is at least comfortably secure in his delusions, while the neurotic is always aware of the ability of real life to intrude upon his and so destroy them.

This passage, like most of the others in this chapter, employs a combination of rhetorical modes. After a few paragraphs of description of the neurotic personality, Horney includes a paragraph in which she contrasts the ideas of grandeur of the normal person and of the psychotic with those of the neurotic. She then resumes her description of the neurotic personality until, in the final paragraph of this passage, she once more draws a brief contrast between the neurotic and the psychotic.

Discussion Question

In her passage Horney does not account for the psychological origins of the neurotic personality (this is done earlier in the book). Can you, as a layperson, suggest any? Have you seen or read anything to give you some idea of what creates neuroses of the type discussed? Why should one person have realistic notions of his or her abilities to achieve, and another person, equally intelligent, unrealistic notions?

Writing Suggestion

Draw a specific contrast between some normal ways of behavior and (in your view) corresponding neurotic ways of behavior, based on your own observations of real or fictional persons. Explain what it is that makes the behavior normal or neurotic. Use particular examples.

CAUSE AND EFFECT

The cause and effect pattern is a means of explaining *why* something happens, of explaining the relationship between one event or situation and another. You have already seen in this chapter at least one example of cause and effect analysis: Friedman and Rosenman's argument that the Type A behavior pattern is a cause of heart disease. Another pattern of cause and effect, used to account for personality, is revealed in the following passage.

BODY TYPE AND PERSONALITY
Gregory A. Kimble, Norman Garmezy, and Edward Zigler

There have been many classifications of body builds, perhaps begin- 1
ning some 2,500 years ago when Hippocrates divided mankind into
two basic types, the long thins and the short thicks. There has also
been a long history of interest in the question of whether body build
and personality are related. One approach to this issue is the constitutional view, which postulates that an individual's biological constitution gives rise to both physical and psychological attributes, and thus
that these two sets of attributes are inevitably related.

The best known modern work involving body type and personal- 2
ity is that of Sheldon (1949), who suggested that there are three basic
body types or **somatotypes** (see Figure). Sheldon was aware that few
individuals represent a pure type and developed a classification system involving three numerals to denote the dominance of each body
type found in a single individual. The three numerals always refer in
order to endomorphy, mesomorphy, and ectomorphy, and range
from 1 (none of the body type) to 7 (all of the body type). Thus, the
most extreme endomorph is a 7–1–1, the most extreme mesomorph
is a 1–7–1, and the most extreme ectomorph is a 1–1–7. An individual whose body build is less extreme may have a somatotype expressed as, for example, 2–6–1; this would indicate some endomorphy, predominant mesomorphy, and no ectomorphy.

Relationships to Personality

To test the prediction that a particular body type was associated 3
with a particular temperament, Sheldon examined the degree of
relationship between the numerical body type scores and a score
which represented the degree of dominance of one temperament
type over another. These correlations proved suprisingly high:

Endomorphy and viscerotonia   .79
Mesomorphy and somatotonia   .82
Ectomorphy and cerebrotonia   .83

Sheldon's   study   suffered   from   certain   methodological 4
difficulties, and more refined subsequent studies have not resulted in

Somatotype	Physical characteristics	Personality type
Endomorphy	Digestive viscera large and predominant	*Viscerotonia*
		Love of physical comfort, relaxation; sometimes gluttonous
	Body soft and round	Relaxed, tolerant, complacent
	Bones and muscles underdeveloped	Sociable, dependent, needs affection
		Seeks others when troubled
Mesomorphy	Muscle and bone predominate	*Somatotonia*
		Vigorous physical exertion; active, bold, adventurous
	Body hard and rectangular	Assertive, aggressive, energetic
	Strong body resistant to injury	Much self-expression; direct, competitive
		Needs action when troubled
Ectomorphy	Delicate form	*Cerebrotonia*
		Restrained, tight posture and movements
	Body linear and thin	Tense, inhibited, poor sleep habits; more thought than action
	Lightly muscled	Introverted, keeps to self
		Needs solitude when troubled

Sheldon's three body types and the personality characteristics attributed to each.
From *The Varieties of Human Physique,* New York: Harper & Bros., 1940.

such striking findings. Nevertheless, enough positive findings have appeared over the years to make investigators feel that there is some truth to Sheldon's hypotheses. The small relationships that continue to be discovered are still open to various interpretations.

Cause or Effect?

It is important to remember that discovering an empirical relationship between two variables, e.g., body type and psychological temperament, does not clarify the direction of causality. We have already seen that there are a number of environmental factors which can influence the body build itself. (Certainly one would not expect to find many endomorphs in a concentration camp.) Furthermore, there is no question that environmental factors also influence an individual's temperament. Thus, the relationship between body type and temperament may be due to a series of complex interactions between the individual and his environment.

One obvious interpretation is that temperament, rather than inhering in a particular body type, results in part from the fact that individuals of different body types naturally engage in different behavior, and that they are reacted to on the basis of the particular body type they possess. For instance, the mesomorphic boy, who is stronger and more muscular, is much more likely to try hanging by his knees. Other children admire and praise this feat, thus giving the boy a sense of being the center of attraction as well as of being effective. Such a boy is chosen first when athletic games are played and often assumes a leadership role. The reaction of others and his own self-image will soon cause him to be assertive, aggressive, and the model for other children. A lifetime of such psychological conditioning could well explain the relationships sometimes observed between body type and temperament. 6

Social Expectations

Another explanation for the empirical relationship found between body types and temperament is the existence of societal stereotypes concerning ways in which people with particular body types are supposed to behave. How an individual acts is in large measure determined by how others act toward him. By employing a stereotype in our interactions with an individual, we often cause him to behave in exactly the fashion we expect. 7

There is no question that some rather strong stereotypes exist for the various physiques. In several studies people have been asked to describe the psychological characteristics of persons with the body types shown in the figure (p. 545). A clear finding is that the preferred figure and the heroic stereotype is the mesomorph. In a study with adults, Brodsky (1954) found that the mesomorph was viewed as the individual who would make the best athlete, best soldier, and most successful leader. People also expect the mesomorph to be the most aggressive, to endure pain the best, and to be most preferred as a friend. Having nothing more to guide them than the silhouette, people also predicted that the mesomorph would not smoke at all, would drink the least, would be self-sufficient, and would never have a nervous breakdown. 8

The stereotype of the ectomorph that emerged was less favorable 9 than that of the mesomorph. It could be summarized as that of the socially acceptable neurotic. The ectomorph was viewed as most likely to have a nervous breakdown before the age of 30, to smoke three packs of cigarettes a day, to have the greatest need for friends but to have the fewest friends, to hold his liquor poorly, and to make a poor father. As a military leader, he was expected to experience great distress if he had to sacrifice his troops.

The least favorable stereotype was that of the endomorph. He   10
was described as the person who would make the worst soldier, athlete, or leader, would be the least aggressive, and would be least preferred as a personal friend. (Interestingly, he was thought to have the most friends.) It was also thought that the endomorph would make the poorest philosophy professor, university president, or doctor, and would put his own interests before those of others.

Rather similar stereotypes emerged in a study with children,   11
suggesting that not only are these stereotypes strong but they are learned early. Endomorphs were thought to be socially offensive and delinquent; mesomorphs aggressive, outgoing, active, and leaders; and ectomorphs retiring, nervous, and shy. Children overwhelmingly picked the mesomorph as the body build they would like to have. This finding has some dire implications in that the stereotypes that have been developed around body build may result in many children's being unhappy with and rejecting their own body build. If this dissatisfaction becomes great enough, it alone can produce the negative behavior attributed to endomorph and ectomorph physiques.

At first, this passage appears to be a simple classification of personality types, based on body build. And indeed such a classification forms a significant part of the passage. But the authors caution that the relationship between body type and personality is not so clear as W. H. Sheldon would have had it — that is, that body type is the *cause* and personality is the *effect*. They point out that environmental factors — and in particular, the reaction of other people — can influence the development of personality as much as body type. Social stereotypes also have a significant influence. Thus, a person who is summarily rejected by his or her peers because of body build may acquire the negative qualities stereotypically associated with that body build: for instance, lethargy with fatness. These negative qualities are not *caused* by the body build, but rather by the reaction of others, including children, to that build.

Discussion Questions

1. The authors caution that "environmental factors" also influence an individual's temperament. What are some of the most obvious ways that environment influences (if not determines) temperament? Discuss particular examples, if possible.

2. Do you know of individuals who seem to contradict the theory of body types — for instance, a tense, intellectual endomorph? Or does the theory of body types, allowing for the inevitable exceptions, seem reasonably accurate?

Writing Suggestions

1. How do various movie heroes and heroines of different periods represent shifting audience tastes for endomorphs, mesomorphs, and ectomorphs? (Consider heroes like Cary Grant on the one hand and Woody Allen on the other.) How does movie casting and typecasting confirm the stereotypes? How do movies gain effectiveness by casting against (body) type? Write an essay on some of these questions.

2. Select one or two particular qualities or behavioral characteristics and write an account of their causes. You may choose to focus on a particular person, or on people who share the particular qualities you have chosen to discuss. You may not be "right," but try to be systematic and plausible!

   For instance, how do you account for generosity? Aggressiveness? Cruelty? Shyness? Competitiveness?

SUMMARY, SYNTHESIS, CRITIQUE ACTIVITIES

Summary

Summarize one or more of the passages in this chapter. Follow the suggested six-step process. Take into account the answers to the Review Questions for each passage. (Recommended: "Body Type and Personality")

Synthesis

1. *Describe* three different approaches to the classification of personality. Essentially, you will be summarizing material in three of the passages in the chapter and then joining your summaries together with appropriate transitions.

2. *Describe* three types of aggressive personalities *or* three types of healthy personalities. You may want to draw brief comparisons and contrasts among them in a concluding paragraph.

3. By means of *process* analysis, explain how people develop their distinctive personality types.

4. Describe one particular type of personality and then give *examples* of this type as it shows up in three different classifications of personality.

5. *Compare and contrast* two opposite types of personality (for example, aggressive and nonaggressive), explaining how these types fit into three different classifications of personality.

   To do this assignment, you will have to cite and explain the resemblances among corresponding personality types in different classification schemes. Then you will have to explain the significant differences among these types.

6. Is a healthy personality the same as a well-adjusted personality? *Compare and contrast* what you understand to be healthy and well-adjusted personalities, giving examples of both types.

7. *Compare and contrast* types of business personalities. Possible sources are Maccoby, and Friedman and Rosenman. Draw also upon your own observations.

8. The authors of the selections in this chapter write from many different perspectives: sociology, politics, business, psychology, psychiatry, medicine, narrative fiction. *Compare and contrast* some of these passages, showing how the perspective and profession of the writer have influenced both what he or she has to say on personality and how he or she has said it.

9. *Argue* that a formed personality can or cannot be changed by an effort of will power. For this assignment, you will naturally have to consider the origins of personality, as described by the authors you draw upon, and how difficult or possible it is to neutralize or counteract those origins. Use at least three sources.

Critique

Write a critique of *one* of the following passages:

"Three Types of Character Structure," Riesman
"What Is Type A Behavior?" Friedman and Rosenman
"Self-Actualizing People," Maslow

Among the questions to consider:

1. Does this approach to personality strike you as plausible?
2. Is it in harmony with your own observations of human behavior?
3. What assumptions does the writer make about why people act the way they do? What assumptions does he make about the essential causes of variations in personality?
4. Do you find this approach to personality particularly appealing or unappealing? To what extent is your reaction a function of your own personality?

Rhetorical
Index

Following is a selective listing of articles and parts of articles in this book that further demonstrate the use of the rhetorical modes discussed in the Personality chapter.

DEFINITION

EXAMPLE

COMPARISON-CONTRAST

CAUSE AND EFFECT